NEOPLATONISM AND GNOSTICISM

NEOPLATONISM AND GNOSTICISM

Richard T. Wallis, Editor

Jay Bregman, Associate Editor

INTERNATIONAL SOCIETY FOR NEOPLATONIC STUDIES

Volume 6 in *Studies in Neoplatonism: Ancient and Modern*
R. Baine Harris, General Editor

STATE UNIVERSITY OF NEW YORK PRESS

Published by
State University of New York Press, Albany

© 1992 State University of New York

For information, address State University of New York Press,
State University Plaza, Albany, N.Y., 12246

Production by Marilyn P. Semerad
Marketing by Fran Keneston

Library of Congress Cataloging-in-Publication Data
Neoplatonism and gnosticism/Richard T. Wallis, editor, Jay Bregman,
  associate editor.
      p. cm. — (Studies in Neoplatonism; v. 6)
   Papers presented at the International Conference on Neoplatonism
and Gnosticism, University of Oklahoma, Mar. 18-21, 1984.
   Includes bibliographical references and index.
   ISBN 0-7914-1337-3. — ISBN 0-7914-1338-1 (pbk.)
   1. Neoplatonism—Congresses.   2. Gnosticism—Congresses.
I. Wallis, Richard T., d. 1985. II. Bregman, Jay.
III. International Conference on Neoplatonism and Gnosticism (1984:
University of Oklahoma)   IV. Series.
B517.N455 1992
186′.4—dc20   92-11542
                                                          CIP

10 9 8 7 6 5 4 3 2 1

CONTENTS

v

PREFACE

R. Baine Harris

Although some twenty five scholars have been involved in its production, this book is primarily the result of the efforts of one person, the late Richard T. Wallis, of the Classics Department of the University of Oklahoma in Norman, Oklahoma. It was some time in the early spring of 1980 that I first suggested to him the idea of a major conference that would bring together authorities on Gnosticism and Neoplatonism from throughout the world for a serious discussion of the similarities, differences, and historical interrelation of the two. He readily accepted the challenge and spent most of his professional energy for the next four years of his life in making this possibility a reality.

Early along the way, he was able to enlist the support of Professor John Catlin, chairman of the Classics Department and Professor Kenneth Merrill, then chairman of the Department of Philosophy of the University of Oklahoma. Working together they were able to arrange adequate financial support from a number of sources, including a large grant from the University of Oklahoma and a major grant from the National Endowment for the Humanities. Due to their efforts, the Sixth International Conference of the International Society for Neoplatonic Studies was held in the University of Oklahoma, March 18-21, 1984, and the conference was a great success.

What sort of man was Richard T. Wallis, and what would cause him to give so much of his time and energy to what some would regard as an esoteric theme? A transplanted Englishman, he first came to the University of Oklahoma in August, 1970 to teach in the Department of Classics. The site was chosen partly for health reasons, since he had suffered for most of his adult life from a severe case of asthma, an

ix

illness that eventually caused his death in 1985 at the early age of 43. His undergraduate education was in Trinity College, Cambridge, where he obtained his B.A. degree with First Class Honors in both parts of the Classical Tripos and as a result of his performance in Part II of the Tripos was awarded the Craven Research Studentship and Chancellor's Classical Medal.

His graduate training was in Churchill College, Cambridge, where he received both his M.A. and Ph.D. degrees, his dissertation for the latter being entitled "DIANOIA and PRONOIA from Plato to Plotinus." In addition to his regular teaching schedule during his fourteen year tenure at Oklahoma, he published eight articles and nineteen book reviews, mainly in *Classical Review* and *Classical World*, and in 1972 produced a major book entitled *Neoplatonism*. The latter was well received and an Italian translation of it was released in 1974. He was also invited to give special lectures in the University of California at Berkeley and the University of Manchester and was a charter member and served on the Advisory Committee of the International Society for Neoplatonic Studies, participating in its various international congresses.

About his willingness to focus upon the relationship between Neoplatonism and Gnosticism we can only speculate; but we can conjecture that he was quite aware of the fact that the differences between Neoplatonism and Gnosticism are of more than antiquarian interest. The Gnostic notion of salvation through individual special revelation apart from faith is still with us both inside and outside of the main established religious traditions of Christianity, Buddhism, Hinduism, and Islam. Some of the issues debated by the Third and Fourth Century Neoplatonists and Gnostics, namely, whether higher knowledge emerges from a foundation of reason or can occur apart from reason, whether nature and man can be regarded as a lower form of a higher reality and thus essentially good or must be taken to be essentially evil, and whether evil can or cannot be reconciled with divine providence are issues that still must be dealt with in any contemporary religious philosophy. As Wallis himself once wrote, "the debate between Plotinus and the Gnostics . . . involves movements that left a permanent mark on Christian theology, and thus on Western thought as a whole, while, more generally, it raises the perennial problems of reconciling evil with divine providence and of the perspective roles of reason and revelation in religion." (See p. 7 below.)

After his untimely death in April, 1985, the task of editing the conference papers, including arranging for translation of some of them, was assumed by one of the participants of the congress, Professor Jay

Bregman of the Department of History of the University of Maine at Orono, a task that required most of his time for most of a summer as well as additional time throughout the next year. He also continued and elaborated Wallis' unfinished introduction included in this volume.

In addition to those already mentioned, five other persons, John Anton, A.H. Armstrong, John Dillon, Peter Manchester, and Leo Sweeney were especially helpful in giving advice concerning the formation of the congress. Special thanks go to Leo Sweeney, S.J. of Loyola University in Chicago for his considerable contribution. Finally, Elaine Dawson of the Old Dominion University Arts and Letters Office of Research Services, is to be commended for her excellent work and dedication in preparing the camera-ready manuscript, including the text of the Greek passages.

Old Dominion University
September, 1990

INTRODUCTION

Part I - by Richard T. Wallis

Of the two movements whose relations form the subject of the title of this book, "Neoplatonism" denotes the religiously toned synthesis of Plato's thought inaugurated in the third century A.D. by Plotinus and continuing in its pagan form down to the sixth century A.D. The school thus formed the dominant philosophical movement of the later Roman Empire, and was extremely influential on Medieval Christian and Moslem thought and mysticism, on many later European thinkers down to the present day, and on such movements as Renaissance art and Romantic poetry. For our purposes the term will be largely confined to the ancient pagan Neoplatonists, but attention will also be given to their immediate forerunners, the so-called "Middle Platonists," of whom Plutarch and Apuleius are the best known. "Gnosticism," as known until recently, comprised for the most part a number of otherworldly theological systems maintained by early Christian heretics, claiming salvation through "gnosis" (knowledge) rather than faith, and chiefly known through the criticisms of the orthodox. Outside the church, but with many affinities to Gnosticism, was Manichaeism, the dualistic religion founded by Mani in Iran in the third century A.D., while from a slightly earlier date such documents as the *Hermetica* (revelations composed in Greek and attributed to the Egyptian Hermes Trismegistus) and the *Chaldean Oracles*, which some later Neoplatonists regarded as equal to Plato in importance, formed a bridge between Middle Platonism and Gnosticism. Plotinus, however, bitterly attacked the Gnostics, especially in his polemical treatise *Enneads* II. 9, on two fundamental grounds. First, Gnostics despise both the sensible world and its creator, whereas Platonists recognize its relative importance as

1

a divinely-produced imitation of an ideal model. Second, while Gnostics agree with Platonists on many points, owing, Plotinus charges, to borrowings from Plato, they abuse him and the other ancient philosophers and seek knowledge through divine revelation, instead of giving a reasoned account of their beliefs.

The debate between Plotinus and the Gnostics is thus of far more than academic interest; historically, it involves movements that left a permanent mark on Christian theology, and thus on Western thought as a whole, while, more generally, it raises the perennial problems of reconciling evil with divine providence and of the respective roles of reason and revelation in religion. Its study has, however, been hindered until recently by lack of original Gnostic writings, the main exceptions being a few short texts quoted by the Church Fathers and some (mostly late) works translated from Greek into Coptic, the native Egyptian language.[1] Our picture has, however, been revolutionized by the discovery in late 1945 of a Coptic Gnostic library at Nag Hammadi in Upper Egypt. Scholarly and political jealousies unfortunately kept most of the library unavailable to all but a few specialists until the late 1970's, when a complete English translation was published.[2] Editions, with translations and explanatory notes, of all the texts in the library are also in process of publication.[3]

Though collected by Christians, apparently in the late fourth century A.D., the library includes translations of some texts composed at least two centuries earlier and, while containing many Christian works, shows Gnosticism as a phenomenon extending far beyond Christianity. What particularly concerns us is that several texts, both Christian and non-Christian, show strong Platonic influence; most important, the non-Christian works include two, *Zostrianos* (VIII.1) and *Allogenes* (XI.3), which on literary and doctrinal grounds are almost certainly identical with those named by Plotinus's pupil Porphyry in Chapter 16 of his biography of his master as having been used by the latter's opponents.[4] Two further non-Christian texts, the *Three Steles of Seth* (VII.5) and *Marsanes* (X.1), bear strong doctrinal resemblances to these. Despite the regrettable fact that *Zostrianos* and *Marsanes*, originally among the longest works in the library, are now among the most mutilated, their importance for the study of Neoplatonism remains considerable. That the subject has so far received little attention has been due, first, to the rarity of scholars at home in both disciplines and, second, to the concentration by most Nag Hammadi scholars on the light thrown by the new discoveries on the origin of Gnosticism and its relation to Christianity. The most important conference on the texts to date, held at Yale early in 1978, was largely concerned with these questions and with identifying the Gnostic sects who produced the writings.[5] A further conference on Gnosticism and Christianity will be held at Southwest Missouri State University in March 1983; the same topic has been the focus of two recent English-language studies, Elaine Pagels' *The Gnostic Gospels*[6] and Pheme Perkins' *The Gnostic Dialogue*.[7] The papers presented at Yale on the relation of Gnosticism to Platonism, by contrast, dealt mainly with general topics, largely because Neoplatonic scholars as yet lacked access to most of the new materials.

It was, in fact, scholars on the Gnostic side who first began to clarify the picture. Jan Zandee saw strong resemblances between Plotinus and the so-called *"Tripartite Tractate"* from Nag Hammadi, with its relatively favorable view of the cosmos' creator.[8] Of even greater importance was the demonstration by M. Tardieu, J.M. Robinson and others[9] that the Neoplatonic triad Being-Life-Intellect, which P. Hadot had long ago argued to be pre-Plotinian,[10] was fully formulated in the *Zostrianos-Allogenes* group of texts. Birger A. Pearson has similarly shown strong Platonic influence on *Marsanes*, leading to a more optimistic world-view.[11]

That Plotinus was right in seeing strong Platonic tendencies in Gnosticism, despite the latter's basically mythological structure, has long been recognized. The new texts, however, re-open the much more controversial question whether Neoplatonism received substantial Gnostic influence,[12] or whether resemblances like those just noted are merely parallels deriving from a common Platonic tradition. Even if the latter answer is correct, did Plotinus and his successors modify their system to eliminate Gnostic tendencies? And was the opposition between the two systems (both of which admitted considerable internal divergences) really as sharp as Plotinus claimed? Another long-debated point posed anew by the Nag Hammadi texts is whether, as Porphyry seems to state,[13] Plotinus's opponents were Christians and, if so, whether they should be identified with followers of the second-century heretic Valentinus.[14] The *Zostrianos-Allogenes* group of texts is without obvious Christian influence; furthermore, it belongs to an older Gnostic sect (or perhaps two closely related sects), the Sethians (self-proclaimed followers of Adam's son Seth) or Barbelo-Gnostics (devotees of Barbelo, goddess of Wisdom). On the other hand, the Sethian Nag Hammadi texts include both Christian and non-Christian works,[15] while the library itself shows that Christians sympathetic to Gnosticism could use and revere pagan works, and confirms, what we knew already, that Gnostic sects borrowed freely from one another. Hence these questions also must remain open.

Part II - by J. Bregman

In recent decades there has been considerable interest in the study of Gnosticism, in literary as well as scholarly circles. A widespread revival of interest in mysticism, Oriental philosophy and the forms of religious experience occurred in the 1960s. The revival included spiritual options that could be described as "gnostic." For example, the psychologist C.G. Jung and novelist Hermann Hesse have been considered "modern gnostics." Universities offered more courses in Comparative Religion as scholarly work on the Gnostic problem (aided by the Nag-Hammadi discoveries) became a priority among historians of religion.

The reasons for this are perhaps not far to seek. Like Late Antiquity and the later Middle Ages, our own age is one of basic transformation and re-orientation. In such ages groups often emerge that can be generally characterized as "gnostic" in outlook. This has been well known and much discussed for some time. Today "gnosticism" seems to be a viable religious possibility both within and without contemporary Christianity; therefore some contemporary theological discussions will probably follow a pattern analogous (perhaps somewhat distantly analogous) to the ancient debates between Plotinus and the Gnostics and to other Platonic-Gnostic questions raised herein.

Serious scholarly and philosophical interest in Gnosticism has arisen in large part because of philosophers and historians such as Hans Jonas, who did much to determine the agenda and to act as guides for recent generations of students of religion and philosophy. That Jonas' work, the *Gnostic Religion*, has stood the test of time in light of recent discoveries is evidence of the profundity of his thought and insight.

The papers in this volume discuss in detail the similarities, differences and possible mutual influences between two movements of great significance for the development of Christian theology and later Western thought. Of central — but by no means exclusive — importance is the anti-Gnostic polemic composed by Plotinus, and the recently published Gnostic texts discovered, in Coptic translation, at Nag-Hammadi in Egypt. Many of these show strong Platonic influence, and some are almost certainly among the works used by Plotinus's Gnostic opponents. While volumes on the Nag Hammadi discoveries have been published or are being planned, their emphasis has been on the texts' relevance to the origin of Gnosticism and its relation to early Christianity. The present volume, the first to concentrate on Gnosticism's philosophical implications, by contrast brings together Neoplatonic scholars and experts working on the new Gnostic materials and considers both specialized problems of historical scholarship and the relevance of the Neoplatonic-Gnostic debate to important contemporary religious issues. No book or conference so far produced or planned has taken the philosophical implications of the new Gnostic texts or their relation to the dominant philosophy of the time as its theme. Detailed discussion to date has in fact been confined to individual topics, presented in short articles or monographs. This conference volume thus attempts to meet the perceived need to bring together a body of scholars, some more versed in Gnosticism, others in Neoplatonism, to consolidate and advance the valuable discussions so far provided on these and other relevant questions. We hope that the articles herein have to some extent accomplished this important task.

The International Conference on Neoplatonism and Gnosticism, was held at the University of Oklahoma, March 18-21, 1984. At the opening ceremonies, R.T. Wallis welcomed the international group of participants and appropriately quoted John Dillon's literary characterization of Middle Platonism: "It seems fated to remain in the position of those tedious tracts of the Mid-Western United States through which one passes with all possible haste, in order to reach the excitements of one coast or the other. In Platonism likewise, one tends to move all too hastily from Plato to Plotinus . . ." He then briefly spoke about the special significance of the study of Neoplatonism and Gnosticism for our understanding of ancient Christian as well as contemporary religious and philosophical thought. Continuing the welcoming remarks in a similar spirit, Professor R. Baine Harris presented Professor Hans Jonas with a special award from the International Society for Neoplatonic Studies, for his pioneering work on Gnosticism, its relation to the "spätantiker Geist," and its modern spiritual significance. A cordial reception followed in honor of Professor Jonas.

The conference began the next morning and remained consistently excellent for over three days. In addition to those who read papers at plenary sessions several papers not on the theme of the conference were read at sessions on "Neoplatonism and Nature" and "Studies in Neoplatonism." The plenary sessions were well attended and the subsequent discussions were stimulating and interesting. Often Professor Jonas, himself, would be available to discuss questions concerning the relationship of his work to recent studies in Gnosticism and Neoplatonism. Also present were students and scholars residing in Argentina, Canada, England, France, India, Ireland and the United States. Some important thinkers participated vigorously in discussions formal and informal although they did not all present papers, among them John Rist, L.G. Westerink, Kurt Rudolph and many others. Perhaps it is not too strong an assertion to say that this conference's participants actually resolved some controversial scholarly issues. One example immediately comes to mind: late in the morning of the second day, after John D. Turner presented his paper there was a lively discussion about the historicity of the Gnostic authors and "schools" listed by Porphyry in his "Life of Plotinus," ch. 16 (including Zoroaster, Zostrianus, Nicotheus, Allogenes, Messus and others). R.T. Wallis interrupted and asked whether anyone present objected to considering it now an historically established fact that the Gnostic and Valentinian authors mentioned by Porphyry were the same as those whose "signed" works were found at Nag Hammadi. The group agreed: an informal plenary decision was now a "fact."

The late John N. Findlay's beautiful keynote address "My Philosophical Development: Neoplatonic and Otherwise," complemented the proceedings. In the course of his presentation Findlay described his youthful interest in "Theosophical-gnosticism" whose cosmology has many things in common with Neoplatonism, and, with some modifications, to Christian Neoplatonism and to Gnosticism. His involvement with the *Enneads* of Plotinus, at first in Creuzer's Greek text and his conviction that "the descriptions of the intelligible world that are elaborated by Plotinus in his tract on Intelligible Beauty certainly *ought* to be true: they tell us how things ought to be and appear, if the sort of value-determined cosmos, in which we can't help having some rational faith really exists at all." Several of his remarks on the theme of the conference were both humorous and seriously philosophical:

> Since, however, this is a conference devoted to Neoplatonism and Gnosticism, I shall end this discourse by saying something about their influence on my thought. Gnosticism I studied rather superficially in my early twenties in South Africa and in Oxford, chiefly from a book by a man called G.R.S. Mead, and entitled *Fragments of a Faith Forgotten*. It was actually quite a useful book. You will perhaps be amused to hear that I wrote a poem at Oxford in which I was supposedly tackled by the University Police, because I was walking the streets late at night with a lady whom they thought to be a disreputable street-walker. I did not in fact indulge in such street-walking, except in poems. I was asked to give my name and college, answered that in so far as I was anyone definite I was Simon Magus, and that the lady at my side was none other than Sophia, the Divine Wisdom, who had descended from her high estate among the Aeons, having desired to see a reflection of her face in the mirror of Matter and Humanity. Gnosticism and Neoplatonism meant something to me in those days, and

when I had finished with Greats I embarked on a study of Neoplatonism. . . . I may, however, end by saying that I accept the view of Plotinus and Proclus of an absolute Unity at the center of Being, which has, however, to go forth from itself as part of fully reverting to itself in a living and significant manner . . .

Findlay's remarks received a long and warm round of applause at the end of the second day of the conference.

At the close of the convention, there was a general discussion of the scholarly import of questions raised and issues resolved as well as those still open to investigation. Richard T. Wallis made some concluding remarks and thanked all of the participants for their attendance and contribution. He received a sustained standing ovation from all present. His tragic loss is perhaps even more poignant to those of us who had some idea of how much he knew and had not yet even begun to publish.

I would like to thank the following people for their assistance in the difficult task of completing the editing of the volume under less than ideal circumstances. Professor R. Baine Harris for his availability and helpful suggestions. Professor Kenneth Merrill for sending me all the necessary materials and making several helpful suggestions; Professor Peter Manchester whose editorial experience and willingness to help with crucial decisions have been invaluable; Professor Raoul Mortley for facilitating and checking the translations from French during his stay at the CNRS in Paris; Professor John Dillon for some timely editorial help and advice. To all of the contributors whose papers were carefully written and manageable and to Nancy Ogle and Carol Rickards for typing help; finally to Professor C. Stewart Doty, Associate Dean Raymie McKerrow and Dean Michael Gemigniani of the University of Maine for a timely financial subsidy to complete the volume. To James Breece, Jason Thompson, Stuart Marrs and George Markowsky for invaluable help with computers.

Orono, Maine, May Term, 1989

NOTES

1. The best account of Gnosticism as known before the publication of most of the next texts was Hans Jonas' *The Gnostic Religion* (Boston 1958); the second edition, published in 1963, contains a preliminary survey of the new discoveries.
2. *The Nag Hammadi Library in English*, ed. James M. Robinson, New York, 1977.
3. *The Coptic Gnostic Library*, 11 vols. projected, Leiden 1975-.

4.   For *Zostrianos* see J. Sieber, "An Introduction to the Tractate *Zostrianos* from Nag Hammadi," *Novum Testamentum* 15(1973): 223-240.

5.   Proceedings published as *The Rediscovery of Gnosticism*, 2 vols., Leiden 1981.

6.   New York 1979.

7.   New York 1980.

8.   *The Terminology of Plotinus and Some Gnostic Writings, mainly the Fourth Treatise of the Jung Codex* (Istanbul 1961). (The treatise in question has now been renumbered I.5).

9.   M. Tardieu, "*Les Trois Steles de Seth*; un ecrit Gnostique retrouvé a Nag Hammadi," RSPhTh 57 (1973): 545-575; James M. Robinson, "*The Three Steles of Seth* and the Gnostics of Plotinus," *Proc. of the International Conference on Gnosticism*, 1973 (Stockholm 1977): 132-142; John D. Turner, "The Gnostic Threefold Path to Enlightenment," *Novum Testamentum* 22 (1980): 324-351.

10.   *Entretiens Hardt* V, "Les Sources de Plotin," Vandoeuvres-Geneva 1960, pp. 107 ff., with the ensuing discussion.

11.   "The Tractate *Marsanes* and the Platonic Tradition" in B. Aland (ed.) *Gnosis: Festschrift fur Hans Jonas*, Gottingen 1978; a further article, "Gnosticism and Platonism with special reference to *Marsanes*" will appear shortly.

12.   A view most strongly urged in Hans Jonas' *Gnosis and Spatantiker Geist* (2 vols. published out of 3, Gottingen 1939 and 1954).

13.   Cf. H.-Ch. Puech, *Entretiens Hardt* V, "Les Sources de Plotin" (Vandoeuvres-Geneva 1960), pp. 159ff. with the ensuing discussion.

14.   These views have recently been restated by J. Igal, "The Gnostics and the 'Ancient Philosophy' in Porphyry and Plotinus" in *Neoplatonism and Early Christianity; Essays in Honor of A.H. Armstrong* (London 1981) and F.G. Bazán, *Plotino y la Gnosis* (Buenos Aires 1981) and "Tres Decadas de Estudios Plotinianos," *Sapientia* 13 (1980): 292ff.

15.   The best-known Christian Sethian text, the *Apocryphon of John*, is also the best-preserved of all Gnostic works, being preserved in two copies of a longer version at Nag Hammadi (NHL. II.1 and IV.1) and two of a shorter version (ibid. III.1 and in the Berlin papyrus BG 8502.2). The longer version refers to a "book of Zoroaster" (NHL.II.1.18), which may be the work of that name mentioned by Porphyry as used by Plotinus's opponents.

Theourgia - Demiourgia:
A Controversial Issue in Hellenistic
Thought and Religion

John P. Anton

Introduction

The celebrated quarrel between philosophy and poetry Plato dramatized in *Republic*, X. has been the frequent topic of discussion and generated an enormous body of literature, philosophical and otherwise. What has not engaged much attention is the historical side of the quarrel, if this opposition of cultural determinants is taken seriously, to find out which of the two was declared the winner. We may recall at this point that prior to the emergence of classical philosophy in the fifth and fourth centuries in Athens as a serious contender for the position of command, another important art, that of rhetoric, appeared on the scene to make its claim as the proper arbiter of educational values. Thus, the issue of institutional primacy involved three, not two contenders. When Plato juxtaposed philosophy and poetry, he was probably convinced that rhetoric had fallen behind as a negligible opponent second to both poetry and philosophy. His sustained criticisms had done much to discredit the contention formulated in the *Protagoras*, where Protagoras declares: *. . . I acknowledge myself to be a Sophist and instructor of mankind.*[1]

Though Plato defended the rights of philosophy to serve as the educator of man, he did not decide the actual outcome of the confrontation or its development. In retrospect neither opponent carried the day or determined the direction of the political and cultural institutions for the centuries that followed. The arts did their part, but so did rhetoric and philosophy. Each of the arts played its special role in the drama of the cultural destiny of the Hellenic tradition, and so did religion, especially after the demise of the city state and the consolidation of the *Pax Romana*. But in the minds of the cultural elite, it became obvious that without philosophy and a certain sensitivity toward the arts, and poetry in particular, *paideia* could not claim respectable credentials. It is therefore, not an idle question to ask what became of Plato's celebrated theory of the quarrel between poetry and philosophy, each seeking to hold the exclusive rights to state the ideals of the education of man and thus set the parameters for individual and collective well being. Probably the safest answer would be to say that Plato bequeathed a view of art that called for the justification of art in a philosophy of life and a theoretical vision of reality. Part of that vision was the view that the artist is an imitator of the divine demiurge. However, Plato's conception of the divine craftsman as creator had little if any relevance to religious practices outside the spiritual confines of Greece. Centuries after Plato's time, when the idea of the demiurge came up for serious reconsideration and reconstruction, the *Timaeus* took on a significance and seriousness that would have surprised Plato to see how much religious intent was generously supplied to the Platonic account of the making of the world. Evidently the idea of the demiurge was not accepted in its original Platonic setting, and so it was with the conception of the arts which the attendant philosophy of creativity, its scope, functions and ends, meant to support.

The recasting of the idea of Plato's demiurge signaled the emergence of a new opponent to philosophy: religion. The main issues that were destined to shape the new quarrel began to exhibit their delineation when the social and political conditions of the Hellenistic world brought about a shifting of loyalties and the introduction of different styles in personal conduct, especially the increasing dependence for individual security on the appeal for divine aid from a transcendent source. The trend became a widespread movement and it gained unprecedented momentum during the middle and later Hellenistic periods, which by way of contrast with what was obviously a Greco-Roman way of life, signaled the reorientalization of values and attitudes. One of the most important concepts in philosophy that became subject to reorientalization was Plato's conception of the demiurge. The correlative conception of the role of art was not only suitably modified but more importantly, superannuated. In the eyes of the faithful followers of the spreading religions the mission of the arts to adorn the world of man in this sensible reality no longer constituted a function of the highest order. Another art was slowly winning the hearts of the followers of the emerging religious cults, whose function was fundamentally one of providing assistance to attain God's ends by means of performing divine works. The demiurgic artist of the classical era was gradually replaced by the theurgic artist of religion: the priests as masters of the hieratic arts (*hieratikai technai*).

To be sure, the demiurgic artists did not disappear; they simply took a back seat to the emerging rivals and eventually learned to receive their assigned role from a reorganization of the arts on the basis of spiritual service. The reassignment of the place of the classical tradition, including the defense of its relevance when the issues called for the appraisal of a particular art, as in the case of tragedy, was a direct consequence of the triumph of the *hyperkosmia* over the *enkosmia*. As it turned out, there was more to the implications of Plato's expression *epekeina tēs ousias* than Plato ever suspected.

The Setting of the Problem

According to the *Timaeus*, the demiurge's vision of the Forms compelled him to mold a universe, a *kosmos*, out of the available materials. It is reasonable to assume at this point that Plato meant this conception of the activity of the Divine Craftsman to serve as the model for human creativity and artistic work. The human artist, including the poet, performs best when he becomes a conscious imitator of the creativity of this God. But even so, the artist cannot compete with the philosopher in the pursuit and disclosure of truth; the poet relies on inspiration, not dialectic.

Aristotle's system found no place for a demiurge. Neither the Unmoved Mover nor Thought-Thinking-Itself qualifies for this cosmic role. As for the controversy between poetry and philosophy, the issue loses its intensity once the inalienable connection between art and reason is allowed to surface in full. Art, as good art, according to Aristotle, completes the possibilities of the processes of nature, and in its own way exhibits unmistakably the universal in the particular. When poetry — good poetry or art with reason — does this well, it manifests its ability to be more philosophical than history. Admittedly, poetry does not function the same way as philosophy does, since they differ in method and purpose, yet its distinctness does not negate its philosophical aspect. Therefore, the quarrel Plato discussed in *Republic*, Bk. X (595a-608b) need not have been assigned so prominent a place in the quest for educational standards.

Working within the Platonic tradition and extending it to solve new cultural problems, Plotinus struck a strange non-Platonic note when he disallowed the principle of symmetry from serving as a criterion of the beautiful in the sensible world. The irrelevance of the criterion of symmetry to beauty in the suprasensible world presents no special problems, but its denial in the sensible realm is not without difficulties. The ideal of the *epistrophē*, the end of the philosopher's *nostos*, demanded of art the same obedience to the pursuit of the unitary vision as it did of all ethical conduct. As if to make things more cumbersome for the artist, Plotinus regarded the man of the Muses least qualified to master the supreme art of dialectic, especially when compared to the kindred souls of the lover and the philosopher. The artist is condemned never to see his medium receive fully the superior visions of his intellectual imagination, for it is a principle of reality that the effect be inferior to the cause. Thus the artist is caught in the snares of two difficulties: the downward process confronts him with the resistance of the inferior medium, while the upward quest poses such rational demands for the mastery of dialectic that the dominant quality of his soul qua artist prevents him from dwelling in the level of *dianoia*.

There is hardly any evidence to support the view that the artist in the late Hellenistic period, including the poet, occupied the elevated position he did in classical times. Neither the Stoics nor the Epicureans had any interest in arguing in favor of the arts as cultural paragons. It is to Plotinus's credit that he formulated an aesthetic theory by drawing out the consequences of Plato's idealism. However, missing from Plotinus's re-assessment of Plato's approach was the political context of the criticism of the arts. With that gone, and with the demise of the classical polis, there seemed little reason to raise the issue of the relevance of the quarrel between philosophy and poetry. The place of the artist as demiurge, as performer and revealer of cosmic beauty, was gradually taken over by the theurgist, as performer of divine works. In a way, Plotinus correctly saw that the new quarrel was going to be between philosophy and a different opponent, theurgy, mainly understood as the theurgy of the Gnostics. What made the new challenger respectable was the radical changes the idea of the *dēmiourgos* had undergone in the hands of the middle Platonists long after the days Plato had told the story about the Divine Craftsman. With the process of the replacement completed, and to which philosophical speculation contributed rather generously, the rise of *theourgia* followed with inexorable logic. Eventually the new art found in Proclus its most eloquent theoretical defender.

In the development of the complex movement of Neoplatonism we see two traditions, each working out its own relatively independent method to attain union with the One: the theoretic way and the theurgic way. They reflect distinct modes of conceiving the nature of the demiurge, what the demiurgic principle does, how it works and whether it is numerically one or many. What is of importance in this connection is the fact that during the middle and late Hellenistic periods the shift in the conception of the concerns and nature of the demiurgic act contributed largely to a significant rearrangement of the arts in the spectrum of human conduct. As the movement progressed, Plato's views on the rivalry between poetry and philosophy became increasingly obsolescent. The fate of the classical city-state had already been decided by factors that did not include philosophy or poetry. Whatever philosophical appeal Plato's Demiurge retained, its attractiveness as the prototype for creativity in the arts and civic craftsmanship was practically gone. Eventually, it took on the significance of a principle in the ontology of a soteriological conception of reality and was assigned a different value in the pursuit of the spiritual life. This transformation of the role of the demiurge made possible certain evaluations that contributed largely to the eventual elevation of the theurgic man over the theoretical and dialectical thinker. It was a cultural change that brought into prominence the ancient priestly arts to serve the post-classical quest of the life of salvation.

The question should be raised whether in the development of Neoplatonism the dialectical analysis of the nature and place of the demiurge in a theory of hypostases, joined as it was to a salvational end, made inevitable the relegation of the theoretic function to a secondary place and hence whether it inadvertently adumbrated the rise of theurgic performances to a superior position.

The expression *"theourgia-dēmiourgia"* in the title of this paper is not meant to imply that performing theurgic works reduces the significance of the concept of the demiurge. Rather, it is intended to draw attention to the consequences that attended the separation of the concept of the demiurge from its initial classical setting where it was intimately tied to artistic work. It was also meant to suggest why the role of the demiurgic act, once recast to suit the encroaching demands of a new art, it helped to promote an attitude that rendered the speculative function of reason inept for the pursuit of salvation. Therefore, it is not an accident that eventually theurgy was to be preferred over both art and philosophy and also defended as being both a superior art and powerful method. This reversal of roles, in no small measure aided and abetted by concessions which were made by philosophers in certain cases, was quickened to a greater extent by the rise and expansion of the Gnostic movement. It was the Gnostics who had openly given primacy to magic, evocation, purifications, accepted the study of the Chaldaean Oracles, and believed in the saving power of a secret type of hyper-cosmic knowledge and the efficacy of the hieratic arts. The most surprising development in Neoplatonism occurred when certain followers not only came to share the Gnostic concern for theurgy but also advocated its use. Olympiodorus, in his *Commentary on the Phaedo*, stated the issue with admirable succinctness:

> ... Some put philosophy first, as Porphyry, Plotinus, etc., others the priestly art (*hieratikēn*), as Iamblichus, Syrianus, Proclus and all the priestly school.[2]

Olympiodorus appears to have recognized two stages in the development of the Neoplatonic attitude towards theurgy. During the first stage, there was a strong tendency to conceptualize the demiurgic principle in ways that would make it suitable to the dialectical explorations of a hypostatic ontology.[3] This is particularly true of Plotinus. It was during the second stage, starting with Iamblichus, when the idea of the demiurge was remythologized and brought closer to the theological mode of philosophizing that sought to utilize elements from the theurgic tradition of Gnosticism. Proclus, who came at the end of this stage, proved to be the great theoretician of theurgy.[4]

A Note on Gnostic Theurgy

Discussion on the aims and components of the complex movement known as Gnosticism falls outside the scope of this paper. For the purpose of identifying its contribution to the rise of the hieratic art of theurgy, it will be sufficient to refer to the main features of Gnosticism and glance quickly at the diverse views it held as regards the nature of the demiurge. Unlike Stoicism or Neoplatonism, that relied on the power of the intellect, the Gnostic movement exploited the powerful appeal the diverse mystery religions exert especially through the use of ritual and drama. However, this alone does not explain its popularity; much of its attractiveness, particularly at a time when theology had not yet reached its philosophical prime, was due to the promise of salvation and immortality.[5] These were values that could be readily grasped with the aid of initiation rituals and the dramatic use of symbolism. The prospective followers had but one expectation: union with the divine by means of a higher and esoteric knowledge made available only to special persons. Two basic items in Gnosticism gave its doctrines their idiosyncratic slant: the unworthiness of the sensible world and God's dissociation from nature.

As a doctrine of secret knowledge employing religious, mythological and speculative elements, while maintaining in the foreground a crude symbolism with the promise of salvation, Gnosticism was able to effect a blend of itself with two other strong cultural currents, one religious, and one philosophical.

As Christian Gnosis, it remained a doctrine of sacred knowledge, utilizing certain compatible distinctions it found in Greek philosophy, especially Plato and the Stoics, and arranging them in terms of esoteric and exoteric knowledge. The former was considered a continuation of a sacred tradition and claimed Jesus to be a part of it, but it was a *gnosis* made available only to the privileged as a revelation of a totally new religion in which the *logos* is a living person and not a philosophical abstraction. Christianity, it was claimed, offers only the exoteric teaching and discloses the doctrine of the world drama. Within this scheme, given the relationship which the Gnostic believes he has with God and his own spiritual identity as regards the nature of his soul, theurgic acts are performed to complement faith in a Savior of Souls. Such acts also contribute to make possible the deliverance from a sensible world, one that is not the true God's work but that of a creator, who is powerful but prone to blunder. This demiurge, begotten by Sophia, a lower Aeon, made a world totally unfit for the spiritual nature of the soul. It served only as the stage for the drama of salvation but was otherwise dispensable and condemnable.

Gnosticism in its pagan setting and version provided an alternative to the Christian claim to having access to the only true religious mystery. Evidently we are dealing here with a multifaceted movement. Generally, it emerged as a doctrine of secret knowledge through religious mythological speculation. Christian *Gnosticism* also retained the distinction of esoteric and exoteric knowledge, found explicitly in Plato and upheld by the Christian Neoplatonists Clement and Origen.[6] Similarly, working with the Greek intellectual tradition, pagan philosophers like Plotinus stood for a *gnosis* totally opposed to the crude *gnosis* of oriental salvation.

The device of a secret and sacred *gnosis* proved to be highly useful to the proselytizing efforts of the new religion. But by viewing itself above rational criteria, Christian *gnosis* regarded the philosophies of the Hellenistic world as being more than rivals; it considered them obstacles to the spreading of its salvational doctrine. Its inherent inability to proceed with the search of needed intellectual tools to articulate its conceptual framework led to insularity and heresy. Generally speaking, philosophy as the acknowledged way to theoretical truth, had found the new opponent to be far more defiant of reason than poetry was in Plato's times.   As a proselytizing movement, Christianity regarded philosophy to be as much a rival as it did all the persistent lingering strongholds of polytheism. The need therefore to uphold a doctrine of sacred *gnosis* to counterbalance the venerable Greek tradition of the philosophical truth gained in significance as the combatants closed their ranks. Evidently, for a Gnostic sect to speak of its superior knowledge as being due to divine revelation, it had to assume that it was a response to a quest and the fulfillment of an expectation that could only be done in a special kind of universe. Closer inspection shows that the Gnostics did not hold the same conception of reality the Greek theorists held. It should be of no surprise then to see why the demiurge of the Gnostic movement is so unlike the demiurge of Plato's *Timaeus*, and comparably, why the art of theurgy is not to be found among the Platonic *technai*.

Theurgy and Neoplatonism

It appears that the term *"theourgia"* was coined by the younger Julianus,[7] in contrast to *"theologia"* (talking about the gods); the expression refers to "doing divine works" in the sense of helping persons to transform their status into godlike existence with the aid of mystical union. The term was also used by Porphyry to stand for "pious necromancy or magical cult of the gods,"[8] to which he raised objections on the ground that the theurgists' procedures were wanting in logic. Plotinus, his teacher, insisted that only the life of reason is free from magic.   From a different perspective, the Christian theologians, in defense of their practices, argued that only the Christian life of faith is free from magic. The opposition of both parties to magic is clear, but the agreement ends there. Plotinus, however, admits that while the irrational side of human existence can be affected by the influence of magic and drugs, such is not the case with the rational part (IV. 4.44).[9] Thus the true philosopher who pursues wisdom can in no way become the victim of sorcery or any of the arts of magic, should their practitioners seek to harm him.[10]   As for attributing diseases to daemonic forces, Plotinus denies that there is any connection, although his expression "each man's own daemon" suggests other possibilities. But what he means by "daemon" is not magic but the leading power in each soul. While Plotinus stood firm on his rationalist approach to such problems as diseases and magic, it was Porphyry who discussed the connection between the art of theurgy and the way daemons relate to magic.[11]   In so doing, as E. R. Dodds remarks characteristically, Porphyry "made a dangerous concession to the opposing school."[12]

The turning point in the Neoplatonic change of attitude toward theurgy came with Iamblichus.   The ingredients that converged in Iamblichus's outlook can be traced to oriental influences as well as Greek modes of rational justification.   As R.T. Wallis has pointed out, Iamblichus, while trying to prevent "the swamping of philosophy by religion" by distinguishing between philosophizing and the performance of theurgy, still went to considerable lengths in order "to offer a rational justification even of theurgic ritual."[13]   He speaks of *hieratikē theourgia* and justifies it in his *De mysteriis*, 9.6.   Whether the work was written by Iamblichus himself or by one of his faithful disciples, is of minor significance, since the shift of emphasis from *theoria* to *theourgia* as the key to salvation is an essentially Iamblichean faith.

In order to understand how he views *theurgy*, we may pause to see how he approaches the issue of its defense.   First he distinguishes theurgy from magic as well as from science and philosophy.   Magic aims at dealing with the physical powers of the universe, but is unable to effect spiritual communion with the gods, and hence it distorts law and harmony in order to accomplish the perverse use of natural forces. Unlike Plotinus's insistence on the intuitive powers of reason to attain union with the One, Iamblichus sees the theoretical work as being limited and hence unable to succeed in effecting communion with the divine (V. 20).   In II, 11, he states:

> It is not thought that links the theurgist to the gods: else what should hinder the theoretical philosopher from enjoying theurgic union with them? The case is not so. Theurgic union is attained only by the perfective operation of the unspeakable *acts* correctly performed, acts which are beyond all understanding; and by the power of the unutterable symbols which are intelligible only to the gods.[14]

The objectives and the operations of theurgy contain little, if anything, to connect the *De mysteriis* to the experience of communion with the Beautiful itself in Plato's *Symposium*. The ladder of love which the lover must climb unaided, as it were, to reach the beloved ideal, is removed in favor of theurgic acts, and the Socratic initiate into the mysteries of love, along with his self-ascendancy through acts of love, is replaced by a person of *pistis* whose salvation requires assistance from the theurgist. Theurgy, according to Iamblichus, is "the art of divine works," operations that relate man to the divinities by using "signatures" or characters and inexplicable symbols "consecrated from eternity for reasons our reason does not comprehend fully" and higher than our way of understanding and more excellent (I. 11). Iamblichus's belief is that the practitioners of theurgy act properly when they use stones, herbs, perfumes and sacred animals, for physical objects are related to the gods in either of three way: ethereally, aerially, aquatically (V. 23). By using such means, the theurgist attains command over spiritual powers. He can also employ invocations and incantations since certain works, especially names, comprehend "the whole divine essence, power and order," when viewed as belonging to another language which is also higher.

What the individual soul cannot attain on account of its limited powers, it can through theurgy. For instance, the soul can know the *logoi* of the World Soul but not the Forms of The Intellectual Principle.[15] On this point Iamblichus differs sharply from Plotinus, and since he insists on the exclusion of the Forms from the reach of man's cognitive powers, Iamblichus bridges the gap by introducing theurgy, which in consequence he declares superior to philosophy. The philosopher cannot by himself as thinker unite with the divine. Whether the attainment of union with God, as conceived by the Neoplatonists of the Iamblichean School, is also a genuine Platonic tenet, is another question. Actually this type of ultimate objective is an importation and hence non-Platonic. What needs to be stressed as a point of difference is that Iamblichus's view of union with the divine addresses a conception of a universe that no longer represents the one Plato conveys in his dialogues. More importantly, the demiurge Plato spoke about in the *Timaeus* bears no close resemblance to the divinities mentioned in the *De mysteriis*. Iamblichus's God is the Ineffable One, a God even beyond Plotinus's One — a view Proclus found unacceptable. Because of this incomprehensible remoteness, acts that pave the union with this God lie outside the province of theoretical vision;[16] they point to appropriate rites and theurgic actions. The threat that poetry as the rival of philosophy posed in Plato's times hardly compares to the magnitude of the challenge the art of theurgy presented to the theoretical man of wisdom seven centuries later.

Proclus saw theurgy as "a power higher than all human wisdom, embracing the blessings of divination, the purifying powers of initiation, and in a word, all the operations of divine possession."[17] And in agreement with Iamblichus, he states: "It is not by an act of discovery, nor by the activity proper to their being, that individual things are united with the One" (II. vi. 96), but as Dodds comments, to complete Proclus's thesis, "by the mysterious operation of the occult 'symbols' which reside in certain stones, herbs and animals" (ibid., intro., xxii-xxiii).

Marinus in his *Life of Proclus* refers to *theourgikē aretē* and *theourgika energēmata*.[18]   He also mentions that Proclus gave a sympathetic account of the sacred science of the priests and their old tradition. Proclus's approval invokes two important priestly practices: (a) securing the presence of daemons by means of certain rites and substances, and (b) employing the instructions the daemons afford, together with the interpreting of symbols, to inspect the good and attain "communion with the Gods."[19]   His approval of theurgic practices are also reflected in his religious poetry, the seven hexameter hymns on the divinities, prayers to Helios, Aphrodite, the Muses, all the gods, Hecate, Janus and Athene. These hymns ask for enlightenment and assistance to avoid mistakes and reach higher levels of life that are free from errors.[20]

The extant evidence also shows that the religious theurgists depended on theurgy mainly as ritual performance. They were basically responsible for the strong currents of irrationalism which Dodds criticizes. Granted that a case may be made in defense of Proclus, as Sheppard had done,[21] there is still the issue of his radical departure from Plato's views given in the *Timaeus*. The issue points to a serious compromise. Proclus's way of approaching Plato's conception of the Divine Craftsman indicates that certain radical transformations have already taken place as the Hellenistic theoreticians of *dēmiourgia* developed their own speculative views on the subject.   A radical innovation in Neoplatonism that finds no parallel in Plato is the distinction between the demiurge as creator of cosmic order and as Supreme God, a distinction made even more pronounced since the latter is identified with the form of the Good, as the One beyond *ousia*, thus leaving for the demiurge his identification with *Nous*.

Students of Plato have noticed the problems one encounters when trying to offer a consistent interpretation of what Plato says about God in the *Timaeus* and the *Laws* in relationship to *nous*, *psychē* and *physis*. The Neoplatonists were well aware of the alleged discrepancies in Plato's accounts and responded to the challenge by proposing a hierarchy of being, placing *nous* above *psychē* and the One above both as being at once *proaiōnion* and *hyperousion* (pre-eternal and super-essential). Proclus's answer to the nature of the demiurge is based on two basic Platonic premises: (a) *nous* is the demiurge, and (b) *nous* exists in a *psychē*, itself the best soul, and acts as the cause of all orderly motions. Proclus's conclusion is that there are really two Creators, a higher, proceeding from the Good, which is also the One, and lower, which is *psychē aristē*. Whether the justification for this interpretation may be found in the Platonic texts is clearly a question to which we must give a negative answer.[22] The activity of the Platonic God as the divine *dēmiurgos*, together with the kind of universe he created, underwent significant changes in the Hellenistic age as new religions and different cultural elements pressed their demands for revisions and accommodations on the part of those philosophers who claimed Platonism as their heritage.

Demiourgia and *Theourgia*

With the advent of Neoplatonism, the concepts of *dēmiourgia* and *dēmiourgos* were dealt with by means of two types of emerging concerns, both bent on adjusting ontology to theistic cosmogonies. Both had to face the problem of how to determine the meaning of demiurgic activity in (i) cosmological theories and (ii) religious speculation.

The tension between these two concerns and the ensuing types of the uses of the concept of the demiurge is no more evident than in the role these speculations came to play in promoting either theoretical or soteriological ends.

In cosmological speculation the method for defining the nature and function of the demiurge was fundamentally that of dialectic. Given the employment of argument for the crystallization of meaning the eventual demythologizing of the concept at issue, at least to a serious degree, seems to have been inevitable. This much and perhaps more can be gleaned from the summaries of the critiques and debates Proclus, for instance, discusses in his *Commentary on the Timaeus*. On the other hand, the imaginative use of religious speculation, in contrast to the theoretical and dialectical assignations of meanings, extended the concept of the demiurge and multiplied its uses in response to the need for ritual by giving it a soteriological direction that called for the drastic employment of mythic imagination. Religious speculation no doubt succeeded in recasting the concept and more importantly it presented it as an alternative to its theoretical counterpart. More as a competitor than a cooperator, the soteriological use of the concept demanded that the concept be recognized as a truth-bearing myth endowed with ritual significance capable of securing the attainment of salvation.

Depending on which of the two types, the theoretical-dialectic or the religious-soteriological-mythic way of assigning meaning to the concept of *dēmiourgia* one chose to work with, the meaning of the term "theourgia," i.e., "to do the work of god for men," was left open to different significations to accord with practice. It should therefore be of no surprise to find two kinds of *theourgia*, one philosophical and one religious, and with further refinements and variations in each, as we do, for instance, in Porphyrian, Iamblichean or Proclean conceptions of theurgy, and in the case of the religious type, between Gnostic and Orthodox Christian. Once the philosophers started making concessions to the practice of theurgy there was no way to predict how far other parties would go in their effort to make use of the concept. Porphyry, as we know, opened the door to permissiveness, inadvertently no doubt. His pupil Iamblichus laid the foundation for the new trend, and this despite his distinction between two kinds of theurgy. The fact is that as a philosopher he practiced as well as defended a non-dialectic kind of theurgy. On the whole, it was the Athenian school of Neoplatonism that tried to maintain a balanced position by keeping together the theoretical and the religious types, yet making them distinct from each other, convinced as those philosophers were that by so doing the philosophical mode was neither theoretically weakened nor practically compromised. Working with totally different interests, the Gnostics and in their own way the Christians, accepted the magic side of religious theurgy with the aid of soteriological speculation. However, each religious group worked out its own justification as well as understanding of the mysteries that they deemed necessary for the completion of the tasks beyond what theurgy was employed to perform. While each would develop its own related ritual and sense of mystery, both came to differ from the mysteries of the pagans for whose revival the Emperor Julian (332-363) risked the undying hostility of the diverse Christian sects from Constantinople to Antioch.

The Case of the Emperor Julian

Julian himself proved to be a soteriological theurgist, at least an ardent advocate though not a practitioner. He was not a licensed theurgist but had some preparation to appreciate the theoretical demands of the growing institution of theurgy. His education in the school of Athenian Neoplatonism gave him a shock and a start.

The Julian experiment aside, the fact remains that, while we can speak of a tension between demiurgy and theurgy, we can also speak meaningfully about conflicting theurgic practices as being oriented toward different soteriological ideals and in differently constructed speculative universes. These differences help us explain why and what eventually made Julian's predicament so acute and his failure inevitable.

His preference for a non-Christian and non-philosophical theurgy convinced him that it was right to outlaw the practice of the Christian view of theurgy and demand the suppression of the Christian set of mysteries. Julian had no philosophy of education and no political philosophy that heirs to Plato's thought could discern in his Imperial policies. The theurgists Maximus and Priscus used Julian as much as he used them. What they had in common was the preoccupation with the practice of mysteries and the power they expected to derive from it.

Julian was an enthusiastic follower of Iamblichus and praised him in his *Hymn to the Sovereign Helios*. High also was his regard for the "blessed theurgists" for the ability to grasp the hidden meanings of the unspeakable mysteries. In the *Helios* hymn, the universe is eternal and divine, with the planets, signs and decans being visible gods, while the Sun itself is the link between the sensible and the intelligible worlds; praise is due to this king of the intellectual gods. A firm believer in divination and astrology, he accepted the oracles of Apollo as the civilizing power of ancient Greece, whose aid he sought for his own plan to revitalize the pagan rites. When Eusebius of Myndus, who studied under Iamblichus's pupil Aedesius, founder of the Pergamene School, took the position that magic was an affair of "crazed persons," Julian, who was a young prince at that time in search of a sacred wisdom, opposed him and went to the side of the co-disciples of Iamblichus, Maximus and Priscus. While Julian was still at Pergamum, Eusebius is reported to have warned the future Emperor about trusting that "stagy miracle-worker," Maximus. Julian's reply was: "You can stick to your books; I know where to go." He went to Maximus, and later asked Priscus to send him a copy of Iamblichus's commentary on Julianus the Theurgist: "I am greedy for Iamblichus in philosophy and my namesake in theosophy, and think nothing of the rest in comparison."[23] At the age or 23, he went to Athens, where he studied under the Neoplatonists there and was initiated to the Eleusinian Mysteries. After becoming Emperor, he reinforced the priestly arts and supported a quasi-Hellenic version of paganism. His policies toward the Christians make it clear that he became embroiled in a controversy over two rival practices of the hieratic arts rather than the promotion of classical philosophy, poetry and the arts. What consumed him most was not the renaissance of Greek *paideia* and its ideals of excellence, but the desire to establish the superiority of the hieratic arts associated with the pagan mysteries insofar as they promised to assist in personal salvation.[24]

The Christian Solution: A Reconciliation

It is possible to give a positive answer to the original question: "Is there a controversy between *theourgia* and *dēmiourgia*?" but, it would be a reply best suited to a Platonist of the old School, the early Academy, and from one who has read his *Timaeus* without concern for the Gnostic movement or the Christian experience.

The opposition between *dēmiourgia* and *theourgia* is one that the more orthodox Neoplatonists, like Plotinus, would prefer to ignore, and in fact tried to avoid by rejecting or ignoring theurgic practices. In any event, for Plotinus there could be no real opposition between the two because the demiurge made the world in a way that theurgic acts were not needed for the attainment of the flight of the alone to the alone. Nor could the controversy have excited Plato or any of his contemporaries. In classical times, as was said at the beginning of this paper, the controversy was seen as one between philosophy and poetry. The Divine Craftsman, as the *Timaeus* intimates, calls for man to emulate a model of creativity that traditional poetry did not and would not espouse. Plato's conception of the demiurge proclaimed for the artist a model that included the employment of dialectic for creative enlightenment; there was no such provision or interest in the case of the Gnostic demiurge or even Proclus's conception of the demiurge. Rather the emphasis fell not on dialectic but on theurgic acts. This shows that by the time we come to the rise of Neoplatonism and the beginnings of the Gnostic movement, including the time of the first consolidation of the Christian faith, the controversy between poetry and philosophy had lost its political and cultural relevance to whatever was left of the classical polis.

The new trend, the resorting to theurgic practices, Gnostic and otherwise, had eliminated the poet as a potential opponent in matters of spiritual controversy. If the poet had an assignment it was not one that could make serious claims to truth or to serving as the arbiter of educational policies and standards. The poetic domain had become that of the gentle pleasures and lyrical praise; it lacked the authority to address the soul and the spirit of man. In general, all signs indicated that the fate of art had already been sealed by the sweeping force of new cultural currents and that its former adversary, philosophy, needed to face a new and comparably formidable opponent: religious *theourgia*, supported by a no less venerable discipline, *theologia*. As it turned out, the future of spiritual affairs was decided not in the agora and the theatre, but in the consecrated places of the mystery practices and the pulpits that heralded the ideal of salvation.

By the second century A.D. there was for all practical purposes an end put to the production of tragedies and comedies. Pseudo-Lucian reports that "new poetry in honor of Dionysus, comedies and tragedies, has ceased to be composed; so they serve contemporary man by producing those of the past."[25]

Yet there were new uses to which certain types of poetry could be and were in fact put. There is the case of a certain Methodius, Bishop of Olympus (d. 311 A.D.) who wrote dramatic dialogues in opposition to the Gnostics.[26] Such were the signs of the times for the arts. This is not to say that the traditional arts were totally eclipsed by the priestly arts; rather, what we see is the gradually increasing pressure to have the artistic functions serve new religious ends and religious institutions.

It is ironic that the curriculum of the Athenian School of Neoplatonism would have instruction begin with Aristotle as the appropriate introduction to Plato, and then crown the learning process with the writings of the "theologians," namely Orpheus and Chaldaean Oracles.[27] It was in classical Athens that the rational tradition of philosophy found its highest expression and competed with poetry for the leading role in education, only to end centuries later an inferior second to theurgy. With the emergence and establishment of theurgy, the quarrel between philosophy and poetry lost whatever was left of its educational significance.

With the rise and acceptance of the various forms of theurgy came a decline of interest in philosophical ethics as well as non-religious conceptions of theurgy, such as the one Iamblichus and Proclus favored. Justinian put an end to the pagan mysteries. As for the Gnostic version of theurgic mysteries, they went out with the condemnation of the heresies. At least one important effect on culture which the theurgic movement had proved to be of lasting value. Whether Christian or pagan, the consequences of Gnostic theurgic practices were deeply felt in the world of the arts, including poetry. The movement and the mood that generated theurgy made possible the emergence of a new style suitable to the needs of the developing religious culture of Christendom. Thus:

1. It established the pattern of subordination of the artist to other more dignifying types of disclosure of messages from the beyond. With the gods gone, there was no way the artist could any longer claim the experience of the *entheos*. Divine *mania* became discredited.

2. It prepared the grounds for the surrender of the individuality of the classical artist and his personal signature in exchange for the anonymity of the post-classical artist, the servant of God, ikonographer

as well as hymnographer. One is reminded at this point of the paucity of the names of artists who lived during the peak of the religious culture in Byzantium.

3. It introduced new criteria for approval and acceptance of the individual arts and works of art in response to the needs of the new culture. The problem now was what arts and what works serve best the purpose of theurgy and salvation. For instance, sculpture was given a prominent place in the West, while the East opted for painting. Both East and West developed significantly new styles in architecture to celebrate the glory of God. Comparably, each developed different styles of music to suit the liturgical needs.

4. It provided new and canonically controlled thematography. The new themes were so delineated as to cover not only the soteriological view of life but also to respond to a freshly populated universe with new and radically different entities, archons, angels, demons, and elevated or downgraded souls of human beings. The power of human imagination was challenged to meet new tasks mainly to learn how to render visible the mysterious world of theurgy.

5. It called for a style in art that would suit the suprasensible world with the molding of imagery different from the one the classical mind had developed. Imagery, vocabulary, similes and metaphors, as well as color schemes, designs and decor, took on a character that was appropriate to apprehending a world which the symbols of Christianity meant to convey. Poetry, in particular, continued mainly as hymnography and developed its imagery and vocabulary around two basic ideas: the expression of humility of man before God and the glorification of the Creator with the aid of superlatives and hyperboles.

6. The most conspicuous change it brought about was to replace tragedy with the unique enactment of the divine drama in liturgy. In a way, Christianity perfected not art and tragedy, but an old art given a new dress: divine liturgy. Unlike what happened in classical times when Plato could oppose poetry to philosophy to reassess the cultural values and declare the superiority of philosophy over poetry, the art of theurgy, once under the control of religious speculation and ecclesiastical structures, acquired a permanent place in the culture of the Christians. And it came to pass that in the architectonic of institutions and the arts, religion should reign supreme and the priestly arts become both arbiter and consecrating agent. The quarrel between philosophy and poetry had become completely irrelevant. The transformation of the art of theurgy and its integration into the supreme ritual of divine liturgy concluded the telestic work required of men of faith in a universe created by a God absolutely good and powerful and omnipresent, the only creator and

savior of man: God as Holy Trinity, God the Father and the Son and the Holy Spirit.   With the new macrocosmos, the microcosmos of man was reconstructed from top to bottom.   One of the most effective tools for carrying out this assignment was forged in the mysterious laboratory of theurgy.   Faith and its mysteries carried the day for all centuries ever since, sometimes more successfully than others, depending on the respect and confidence the priestly arts could inspire.

NOTES

1.   *Prot.* 317b. B. Jowett's translation.

2.   οἱ μὲν τὴν φιλοσοφίαν προτιμῶσιν, ὡς Πορφύριος καὶ Πλωτῖνος καὶ ἄλλοι πολλοὶ φιλόσοφοι οἱ δὲ τὴν ἱερατικὴν, ὡς Ἰάμβλιχος καὶ Συριανὸς καὶ Πρόκλος καὶ οἱ ἱερατικοὶ πάντες. 123.3, Norvin; tr. E.R. Dodds in *Proclus: Elements of Theology,* p. xxii.   According to Dodds, who bases this remark on the Suda and other sources, "the earliest person to be described as θεουργὸς was one Julianus, who lived under Marcus Aurelius," and either he or his son, Julianus the Younger, wrote the *Oracula Chaldaica.* "By his own account, Julianus received these oracles from the gods; they were θεοπαράδοτα." Ibid., p. 284, esp. p. 300, note 14.

3.   R.T. Wallis aptly remarks that "for the Neoplatonists . . . the universe was a spontaneous production of the intelligible order, with no question of an anthropomorphic creator at all." *Neoplatonism,* p. 102.

4.   See Ann Sheppard, "Proclus's Attitude to Theurgy," *Classical Quarterly* 32 (1982): 212-24. Sheppard argues against Dodds's thesis that by accepting theurgy Neoplatonism abandoned its rational basis of Plotinian mysticism. The point of her article is to show that Proclus developed a theoretical defense of theurgy and that he distinguished between lower and higher levels.   It was to such higher levels that "philosophical" theurgists like Syrianus and Proclus could appeal in order to refer to a higher theurgy in the sense of *theia philosophia* (complemented with a theory of symbols and related signs and rites (esp. pp. 220ff). Sheppard's views throw new light on the members of the Athenian School of Neoplatonism as theorists of theurgy.   However, we need to be reminded of the fact that there were many influential **non-theoretical** theurgists who by depending heavily if not exclusively on the practice of the priestly art of theurgy were part of the movement that aided the rising dominance of irrationalism.

5.   It has been generally recognized that Gnosis utilized aspects of Greek philosophy, Babylonian myths, Persian and Egyptian religious elements as well as Jewish teachings.   Professor R.T. Wallis notes: "In its strict sense, however, the term [Gnosticism] denotes a group of systems, the majority of those known to us maintained by Christian heretics, and all of them opposed to Neoplatonism in that the 'knowledge' they sought was the product, not of philosophical reasoning, but of revelation by a divine savior" (op. cit., p. 12).

6. W. Jaeger notes that "the gnosis that early Christian theology pretended to offer was for its followers the only true mystery in the world that would triumph over the many pseudo-mysteries of the pagan religion." *Early Christianity and Greek Paideia*, p. 56.

7. Julian, *Or*. 7, 219a.

8. See L. Thorndike, *History of Magic and Experimental Science*, Vol. I, p. 308.

9. See also IV. 4. 40, where magic is explained. In IV. 4. 43, Plotinus answers his own question why the wise man is beyond magic, lines 1-7. Comp. A.H. Armstrong, "Was Plotinus a Magician" *Phronesis* I (1955-56): 73-79.

10. Porphyry notes that such a practitioner was Olympius of Alexandria, who acting out of rivalry tried to bring upon Plotinus a star-stroke. *Vita Plot.* Ch. 10.

11. *Letter to Anebo*, 46, p. xliv Parthey: ἐρωτῶ δὲ μήποτε ἄλλη τις λανθάνῃ οὖσα ἡ πρὸς εὐδαιμονίαν ὁδὸς ἀφισταμένη τῶν θεῶν. ἀπορῶ δὲ εἰ πρὸς δόξας ἀνθρωπίνας ἐν τῇ θείᾳ μαντικῇ καὶ θεουργίᾳ βλέπειν δεῖ, καὶ εἰ μὴ ἡ ψυχὴ ἐκ τοῦ τυχόντος ἀναπλάττει μεγάλα.

12. See his *The Greek and the Irrational*, p. 287.

13. R.T. Wallis, *Neoplatonism*, p. 14; also ". . . the philosophical concepts by which theurgy was justified appear to be mainly Greek; Ptolemy and others had similarly justified Chaldaean astrology in terms of scientific theory," p. 15.

14. Translated by E.R. Dodds, in Proclus: *The Elements of Theology*, Intro., p. xx; see also his article "Theurgy" in *The Greeks and the Irrational*, Appendix, pp. 283ff. The text reads: . . . οὐδὲ γὰρ ἡ ἔννοια συνάπτει τοῖς θεοῖς τοὺς θεουργούς. ἐπεὶ τί ἐκώλυε τοὺς θεωρητικῶς φιλοσοφοῦντας ἔχειν τὴν θεουργικὴν ἕνωσιν πρὸς τοὺς θεούς, νῦν δὲ οὐκ ἔχει τό γε ἀληθὲς οὕτως, ἀλλ᾽ ἡ τῶν ἔργων τῶν ἀρρήτων καὶ τῶν ὑπὲρ πᾶσαν νόησιν θεοπρεπῶς ἐνεργουμένων τελεσιουργία ἥ τε τῶν νοουμένων τοῖς θεοῖς μόνοις συμβόλων ἀφθέγκτων δύναμις ἐντίθησι τὴν θεουργικὴν ἕνωσιν.

15. See R.T. Wallis, *Neoplatonism*, p. 119.

16. E.R. Dodds's remark about the Neoplatonists who resorted to theurgy applies mostly to Iamblichus: ". . . theurgy became the refuge of a despairing intelligentsia which already felt *la fascination de l'abîme*. "Theurgy" in *The Greeks and the Irrational*, p. 288. The quotation is given in p. 291, to which Dodds adds his own paraphrase: "It may be described more simply as magic applied to a religious purpose and resting on a supposed revelation of religious character." Ibid.

17. *Platonic Theology* I. xxvi. 53.

18. Marinus, Proclus c. 28f.: ἐκ τῆς παρὰ τὰ τοιαῦτα σχολῆς ἀρετὴν ἔτι μείζονα τελεωτέραν (sc. τῆς θεωρητικῆς) ἐπορίσατο τὴν θεουργικήν, οὐκ ἔτι μέχρι τῆς θεωρητικῆς ἔστατο. Also, c. 29: καὶ πολλὰ ἄν τις ἔχοι λέγειν μηκύνεις ἐθέλων, καὶ τὰ τοῦ εὐδαίμονος ἐκείνου θεουργικὰ ἐνεργήματα ἀφηγούμενος.

19. See also Proclus's περὶ τῆς καθ᾽ Ἕλληνας ἱερατικῆς τέχνης (fragment) in Bidez, *Catalogue des MSS Alchimiques Grecs*, Vol. VI.

20. C. Trypanis writes: "In language and meter they are reminiscent of the school of Nonnus, but their mystic dualistic spirit comes close to that of Christianity. The syncretic theosophy of the period is perhaps best expressed in the hymns of Proclus, with which the long and glorious tradition of pagan hymnography ends." *Greek Poetry from Homer to Seferis*, p. 403.

21. Op. cit., p. 213: "I shall not attempt to deny that Iamblichus, Syrianus and Proclus all gave theurgy an important role to play in the ascent to union with the gods or with the One, but I do deny that a simple substitution of theurgy for mystical experience was all that was involved."

22. I find myself agreeing with A.E. Taylor's extensive analysis of the complex issues surrounding the Neoplatonic views of the demiurge. He is correct in stating that "there is no hint of any part of this theosophy in Plato." *A Commentary on Plato's Timaeus*, esp. "The Concept of Time in the Timaeus*," pp. 678-81.

23. *Ep.* 12 (Bidez = 71 Hertlein = 2 Wright); also Gregory of Nazianzus, *Orat.* 4. 55 (*P.G.* 35, 577C). On Eusebius see Eunapius, *Vit. Soph.* 474f (Boissonade); comp. E.R. Dodds, *The Greeks and The Irrational*, p. 288.

24. W. Jaeger has aptly described the shift in the religious outlook that Julian sought to consolidate: "The sharp polemic of Clement against the pagan mystery religions in his *Protrepticus* is more easily explained when we consider that from the fourth century B.C. on, the forms of Greek religion that appealed to most of the people of higher education was not the religion of the Olympic gods but that of the mysteries, which gave the individual a more personal relationship with the godhead." *Early Christianity and Greek Paideia*, p. 55. The modern Greek Alexandrian poet, Constantine P. Cavafy, (1863-1933) has captured Julian's obsession as well as fascination with the hieratic arts of pagan mysteries in a series of remarkably powerful poems, especially in the one titled "Julian at the Mysteries." For a recent study of these poems, see G.W. Bowersock, "The Julian Poems of C.P. Cavafy," *Byzantine and Modern Greek Studies*, 7 (1982): 89-104.

25. Demosth., enc. 27; quoted in C.P. Trypanis, op. cit., p. 374.

26. Ibid., p. 387.

27. *Vit. Pr.*, 13 and 26.

BIBLIOGRAPHY

Sources

Eunapius. *Lives of the Sophists*, ed. J. Giangrande. Rome, 1956.

Foester, W. *Gnosis: A Selection of Gnostic Texts*. 2 vols., Oxford, 1974.

Iamblichus. *De Mysteriis*, ed. G. Parthey. Berlin, 1857; *De Mysteriis*, ed. with French translation, E. des Places. Paris, 1966.

Marinus. *Vita Procli*, ed. J.F. Boissonade. Leipzig, 1814; repr. Paris, 1864.

Olympiodorus. *In Platonis Phaedonem Commentaria*, ed. W. Norvin, Leipzig, 1913.

_____. *Commentary on the First Alcibiades of Plato*, ed. L.G. Westerink. Amsterdam, 1956.

Oracles Chaldaiques, ed. de Places, E., Bude. Paris, 1971; *De Oraculis Chaldaicis*, ed. W. Kroll. Breslau, 1994; repr. Hildesheim, 1962.

Plotinus. *Enneads*, eds. P. Henry and H.R. Schwyzer. 3 vols., Oxford, 1964-82.

Porphyry. *The Life of Plotinus*, tr., notes by A.H. Armstrong, in Loeb Classical Library, Plotinus's *Enneads*, vol. 1, London, 1966.

_____. *Letter to Anebo*, in A.R. Sodano, ed. and tr. Porfirio, *Lettera ad Anebo*. Naples, 1958.

Proclus. *The Elements of Theology*, text, transl., introd., and comm., by E.R. Dodds. Oxford, 1963.

_____. *Hymni*, ed. E. Vogt. Wiesbaden, 1957.

_____. *On the Hieratic Art*, ed. and tr. J. Bidez, *Catalogue des manuscrits alchimiques grecs*, (appendix). Brussels, 1928.

The Nag Hammadi Library in English, ed. J.M. Robinson. San Francisco, 1981.

General

Aland, B., ed. *Gnosis: Festschrift für Hans Jonas*. Göttingen, 1978.

Armstrong, A.H., ed. *The Cambridge History of Later Greek and Early Medieval Philosophy*. Cambridge, 1967.

Bowersock, G.W. *Julian the Apostate*. London, 1978.

Bowersock, G.W. "The Julian Poems of C.P. Cavafy," *Byzantine and Modern Greek Studies*, 7 (1981), 89-104.

Chadwick, H. *Early Christian Thought and the Classical Tradition*. Oxford, 1966.

Dillon, J. *The Middle Platonists: 80 B.C. to A.D. 220*. Ithaca, 1977.

Dodds, E.R. *The Greeks and the Irrational*. Berkeley and Los Angeles, 1951.

_____. *Pagan and Christian in an Age of Anxiety*. Cambridge, 1965.

Jaeger, W. *Early Christianity and Greek Paideia*. Oxford, 1969.

Jonas, H. *The Gnostic Religion*, 2nd ed. Boston, 1963.

Laistner, M.L.W. *Christianity and Pagan Culture in the Later Roman Empire*. Ithaca, 1951.

Lewy, H. *Chaldaean Oracles and Theurgy*. Cairo, 1956; 2nd edition, Paris, 1978.

Merlan, P. *From Platonism to Neoplatonism*. 2nd edition. The Hague, 1960.

Momigliano, A., ed. *The Conflict Between Paganism and Christianity in the Fourth Century*. Oxford, 1963.

Remus, H. "Plotinus and Gnostic Thaumaturgy," *Laval theologique et philosophique* 39 (1983), 13-20.

Rosan, L.J. *The Philosophy of Proclus*. New York, 1949.

Sheppard, Anne. "Proclus's Attitude to Theurgy," *Classical Quarterly* 32 (1982), 212-24.

Smith, A. *Porphyry's Place in the Neoplatonic Tradition*. The Hague, 1974.

Thorndike, L. *A History of Magic and Experimental Science*, Vol. I. New York, 1923.

Trypanis, C.P. *Greek Poetry from Homer to Seferis*. Chicago, 1981.

Trouillard, J. *La Purification Plotinienne*. Paris, 1955.

Wallis, R.W. *Neoplatonism*. New York, 1972.

Dualism: Platonic, Gnostic, and Christian

A.H. Armstrong

There are a number of terms whose use or abuse in a large, vague, fluctuating way can confuse our understanding of the history of thought and sometimes our own theological and philosophical thinking: this has often been true of "dualism," as also of "pantheism," "Platonism," "Gnosticism," and "Christianity." It seems to me an important part of the task of historians of thought to give such terms the precise and varied contents which they should have in varied contexts and environments. I see our work rather as Cézanne saw his painting when he said that he wanted to "do Poussin over again from nature." In this paper I shall try to give precision and variety to some senses in which "dualism" can legitimately be used when we are discussing the thought of the early centuries of our era, with particular reference to the Pythagorean-Platonic tradition, Gnosticism, and Christianity. I shall consider mainly one of the ways of thinking which can properly be described as dualist: cosmic dualism, which sees the whole nature of things as constituted by the meeting and interaction of two opposite principles: though I shall also briefly discuss two-world dualism, in which there are two cosmoi or levels of reality, that of our normal experience and a higher one (which may itself be conceived as complex and many-levelled).

Cosmic dualism, the dualism of two opposite principles, can take, and in the period which we are considering did take, a number of different forms. We may begin with a suspiciously tidy-looking scheme, which as we shall see, will require some qualification and modification.

33

1. The two principles may be thought of as both unoriginated, independent and everlastingly operative in the nature of things. They may be perceived as (a) intrinsically opposed and in perpetual conflict (or conflict as long as this world lasts). This gives a conflict-dualism of what may be called the Iranian pattern. In this case one principle must be qualified as "good" and the other as "evil," and one is expected to take the good's side.   Or (b) they may be conceived as equally independent, but working together in harmony. This seems to be prevalent in Chinese thought, and is certainly very well expressed by the Yang-Yin symbol. Its most radical and fiercely original expression in the Greek world is in the thought of Heraclitus: here it takes a very dynamic form, and the conflict and tension, which any doctrine of cosmic harmony which is sufficiently attentive to experience must recognize, is powerfully emphasized.

2. Or the second principle may be thought of as derived from and dependent on the first. (I shall refer to this second principle as the "dark other," to avoid prejudging various questions about it which will arise.) This derived and dependent "dark other" may be thought of as either (a) in revolt against, or at least opposed to, the first principle or (b) working in accord and co-operation, at least passive, with it.

This very neat generalized classification of four possible forms of cosmic dualism is a useful starting-point for thinking about the subject. But when we begin to apply it to the dualisms with which we are here concerned, we shall find that it has to be used with a good deal of caution and qualification. This is particularly true when we are considering the various forms which cosmic dualism takes in the Pythagorean-Platonic tradition. The thinkers of this tradition range over all the four varieties of cosmic dualism listed above, but profess them, for the most part, in distinctive ways and with important modifications. When they think of the two principles as independent they do not maintain an absolute and unqualified conflict-dualism: and even when the "dark other" is thought of as dependent for its existence on its opposite, it is not, through most of the history of Platonism, accepted and qualified as "good": though at the very end, in the final and most fully and carefully thought out form of Platonic dualism which we find in Syrianus and Proclus, we do arrive at a dualism of cosmic harmony which can be very well symbolized by the Chinese Yang-Yin circle. As we shall see, a great deal depends on what one means in various contexts of thought by classifying the "dark other" as "evil."

In the earliest form (or forms) of Pythagorean dualism known to us the two principles (or groups of principles) seem to be independent and everlastingly coexistent. This is clearly brought out in the Pythagorean Table of Opposites.[1] And we learn from this that the light, male, limiting, ordering principle is qualified as "good" and the dark, female, indefinite principle as "evil." But we need to consider carefully the sense in which the "dark other" seems to be thought of as principle of evil in early Pythagoreanism. As the principle of indefinite multiplicity it is (or can be) the principle of formlessness, disorder and irrationality, and so opposed to the good principle of light and musical order. But both principles are absolutely necessary if there is to be a cosmos at all. They are the parents of the numbers which are the very stuff of reality: without both, number and the great musical order of the whole cannot exist. And the necessity and goodness of the cosmos is something which early Pythagoreanism may be held to affirm with less qualification than later Platonism and Pythagoreanism, in that for pre-Platonic Pythagoreans there was only one cosmos, not two, a higher and a lower. This very qualified and, from the viewpoint of darker and more passionate dualisms, attenuated understanding of the sense in which the "dark other" is evil persists, with varying feeling-tones and shades of emphasis, throughout the later Platonic-Pythagorean tradition.

In Plato we find two forms of cosmic or two-opposite-principles dualism which were influential later. (I do not believe that in *Laws* X 896E-897D Plato is talking about a cosmic evil soul, though later Platonists interpreted the passage in this way.) These two forms are, first, that contained in our reports of his discussions in the Academy about the generation of the Ideal Numbers from the One and the Indefinite Dyad. I do not propose to say much about this because I do not think we know very much.[2] But I do not think that there is any sufficient evidence to suggest that the Dyad is derived from the One: the two principles seem to be independent. And it seems clear that, if the Dyad is one of the principles from which the Ideas or Forms are generated, Plato can only have thought of it as a principle of evil in some very peculiar sense, even more attenuated than the Pythagorean. Aristotle does say that the principles are respectively πὴν τοῦ εὖ καὶ τοῦ κάκως αἰτίαν[3] of things being in a good state or going well or of being in a bad state or going badly, but this should not be pressed too far.

The dualism of the One and the Dyad influenced later Pythagorean thought and is very important for the Neoplatonists, as we shall see. But much the most influential form of Platonic dualism is that symbolically presented in the great myth of the *Timaeus*. Here the material universe (there is nothing in the *Timaeus* about the genesis of the eternal world of Forms which is its paradigm) comes to be through the encounter of two independent principles or powers: that of the Craftsman looking to his Paradigm, divine Reason active in the formation of the visible cosmos, and that strange, not properly knowable, turbulence of place, which is the receptacle, mother and nurse of becoming and accounts for the element of irrational necessity or brute fact which we find in the world. Of the innumerable questions which have arisen through the centuries about this powerful symbolic presentation of the world-forming activity of the divine, two concern us here. One is, what exactly is there about the other principle which is really "dark," which we (or later Platonists) might want to call "evil" even if Plato does not do so? It is certainly responsible for the fact that, though this is the best of all possible material worlds, everything is not absolutely for the best in it, but only as good as possible: it is responsible for all those faults and failings which make it lower and worse than its paradigm, the World of Forms, and which it would be blasphemous to attribute to the Divine Craftsman: in this sense we can, if we like, call it, in a rather abstract and uninformative sense, a "principle of evil." But of course the *Timaeus* insists most strongly both that there ought to be a material universe, that its existence is an inevitable consequence of the generous goodness of the divine (29E-30A): and that it is itself as divinely good as it is possible to be on its own level, a "visible god" (92 B 7). The element of turbulent, disorderly irrationality in our world, the fact that it is not perfect and absolute cosmos, seems to be a necessary condition for the existence of any material cosmos at all. And it is surely rather inadequate, and may be misleading, to describe this as a "principle of evil."

The other question which we need to ask for our purposes is, how does the good divine power deal with this element the opposition of which it has to overcome? Plato's answer is famous, and deserves continual meditation. Divine intelligence works in the world by persuasion: it persuades necessity to co-operate with it [48A]. To bring out the full force of this and show how central it is to Plato's thought I should like to quote the conclusion of Cornford's *Epilogue* to his running commentary on the *Timaeus, Plato's Cosmology.* Cornford is here comparing the trilogy of dialogues which he supposes Plato intended to write, *Timaeus, Critias,* and *Hermocrates* with the *Oresteia* of Aeschylus. His suppositions about how Plato planned his trilogy are speculative and may be wrong, but this does not affect the force and rightness of the understanding of Plato which he derives from the comparison.

The philosophic poet and the poet philosopher are both consciously concerned with the enthronement of wisdom and justice in human society. For each there lies, beyond and beneath this problem, the antithesis of cosmos and chaos, alike in the constitution of the world and within the confines of the individual soul. On all these planes they see a conflict of powers, whose unreconciled opposition entails disaster. Apollo and the Furies between them can only tear the soul of Orestes in pieces. The city of uncompromised ideals, the prehistoric Athens of Critias's legend, in the death-grapple with the lawless violence of Atlantis, goes down in a general destruction of mankind. The unwritten *Hermocrates*, we conjectured, would have described the rebirth of civilized society and the institution of a State in which the ideal would condescend to compromise with the given facts of man's nature. So humanity might find peace at the last. And the way to peace, for Plato as for Aeschylus, lies through reconcilement of the rational and the irrational, of Zeus and Fate, of Reason and Necessity, not by force but by persuasion.[4]

It makes a great difference, both in theory and practice, which of the privileged images of divine action in the world available to them cosmic dualists adopt. They may, as we shall see, image the divine as a redeemer liberating the children of light from this dark world, or as a general leading the armies of light against the forces of darkness.[5] But Plato in his great cosmic story chose, and by choosing bequeathed to later generations, the image of the craftsman working on his rather awkward and recalcitrant material, humoring it and persuading it to take as well as it can the form of the unchanging goodness and beauty which is his model. It is an image the contemplation of which produces a very different attitude to the world from a passionate longing to escape from its miseries or the partisan pugnacity of the conflict-dualist.

In post-Platonic Pythagoreanism we find that, probably for the first time in the history of the tradition, the "dark other" is generally held to be derived from the One. The most interesting form of the doctrine for our purposes is to be found in a well-known account of the teaching of Moderatus of Gades given by Simplicius on the authority of Porphyry.[6] In spite of recurring doubts as to whether Moderatus has not been somewhat Neoplatonized in transmission, I think his account of the generation and nature of the other principle must be accepted as genuine pre-Neoplatonic Pythagoreanism. It is criticized by Numenius,[7] and there is nothing quite like it in the Neoplatonists. Moderatus says that the Unitary Logos, intending to produce from himself the genesis of beings, by self-privation made room for quantity. This quantity is identified with the disorderly, irrational, formless principle of the *Timaeus*, and probably with the Dyad. It is the principle of evil in the material world in so far as it is the principle of avoidance of and deviation from form. But it is produced by the Unitary Logos as the first stage in its creative activity and it is clear that without it there can be no ordered multiplicity, at least of material beings, no cosmos at all. And at the end of the passage it seems that the "dark other," in spite of its persistent tendency away from form and towards non-being, is pretty thoroughly overcome by the formative power of the divine numbers (231, 20-27). Moderatus remains in this way in the tradition of early Pythagoreanism and the *Timaeus*. His dualism is a qualified and mitigated dualism, compatible with a good deal of cosmic optimism.

The Platonists of the first two centuries A.D. whom we need to consider carefully in the present context are those represented for us by Plutarch and Atticus, who are grouped together by later commentators because of their very emphatic dualism as well as on account of their insistence on taking the *Timaeus* literally as an account of creation in time. Both belong to my first group of dualists, those who hold that the two cosmic principles are both unoriginated, independent, and everlastingly opposed.   At first sight they may appear as rather uncompromising conflict-dualists of the Iranian type. Plutarch in his treatise *On Isis and Osiris* does speak with approval of Iranian dualism;[8] and is led to use a good deal of conflict-dualist language elsewhere in the treatise by his identification of the evil soul which he finds in Plato with the enemy of Osiris, Typhon or Set. But when we come to look at him and Atticus more closely we shall find that their positions are rather interestingly different form straightforward conflict-dualism. Like some Gnostics, they think in terms of three principles, not two. There is the principle of light, form and order, the dark, disorderly evil soul, and between them matter, which is sharply distinguished from the evil soul. In *Isis and Osiris* Plutarch makes clear that matter, which is identified with the goddess Isis, is not just neutral but divinely good, with an innate passionate love for the Good himself, who is Osiris. This is very finely stated in Chapter 53. And the evil soul which is Typhon can disturb and damage, but cannot intrinsically effect, the beauty and goodness of the cosmos which results from the union of these great divine male and female principles. And when we turn to the very interesting accounts of the doctrine of Atticus about the disorderly motion and time which existed before the making of the world which are given by Proclus,[9] we find that Proclus does not distinguish his doctrine on the point which concerns us from that of Plutarch. The evil soul for Atticus is, as throughout the tradition, evil as principle of irrational disorder. But it is clearly distinguished from matter and seems in the process of world-making to be as totally dominated and transformed by the power of the good, intelligent formative principle as matter itself[10] (this seems likely to come from Atticus rather than Plutarch). As Dillon remarks "This [the Maleficent Soul], in terms of Plutarch's *Isis and Osiris* is an Isis-figure rather than a Typhon-figure."[11]

Though the dualism of Numenius sometimes seems to have a darker and more pessimistic color, especially when he is thinking about the nature and embodiment of man, his way of thinking is really not so far removed from that of Plutarch and Atticus. As already mentioned (p. 10), he rejects the Pythagorean view represented by Moderatus of the derivation of the second principle from the One and returns to the two independent and opposed principles which he finds in the earlier Pythagoreans and Plato. He seems to associate the evil soul more closely with matter than Plutarch, and regards its malign influence as extending even to the heavens.[12] But by the end of the passage on Pythagorean teaching which derives from him in Calcidius, the victory of the good principle over the evil of animate matter is strikingly complete; it is not so complete that the evils of this our world are done away with (no Platonist could ever accept this), but it is complete enough for matter reformed by divine providential activity to be spoken of not as the adversary but as the consort of god, the mother of the universe and even mother of "the corporeal and generated gods."[13] And the universe of which matter with its bad soul is the disorderly and irresponsible mother is, as Numenius says elsewhere,[14] "this beautiful cosmos, beautified by participation in the beautiful." For all these philosophers of the Platonic-Pythagorean tradition who were so troubled by the problem of evil and anxious to find a solution to it, the *Timaeus* was naturally of central importance. And in the end it was the spirit of the *Timaeus* which triumphed in them over whatever tendencies they may have had to darker and more passionate forms of cosmic dualism.

In the great final rethinking and development of Hellenic Platonism which begins with Plotinus, which we call Neoplatonism, the view that the "dark other" derives from the Good itself is finally accepted as against the dualism of two independent principles. But this leaves room for some variation, within the Platonic limits which should by now have become clear, in the way in which the second principle is thought of and valued. For Plotinus the matter of this lower world derives from the higher principles, and so ultimately from the Good, and there is a "dyadic" or "hylic" element in the intelligible realm. But in his treatise *On the Two Kinds of Matter* (II 4 [12]) he attempts to separate the two matters more sharply than is done anywhere else in the tradition where there is any question of matter at the higher level; and the relationship of the two matters never seems to be made perfectly clear. In II 4 and I 8 [51], and incidentally elsewhere, he speaks of the matter of this world as principle of evil in very strong terms: and in III 6 [26] gives a most remarkable account of its phantasmal and sterile quality, which makes this our world a kind of ghost-world, incapable of further productivity. Yet there is no Platonist who more passionately insists on and defends the divine goodness and holiness of the material cosmos. And it is intrinsic to his whole way of thinking about the Good that its creative self-diffusion will go on till the ultimate limit is reached and everything that can have any, even the smallest, measure of being and goodness has been called into existence. And this means going on down to the material cosmos, where its matter operates, in a very strange way, as the principle of evil. The creative process, in proceeding to the ultimate limit in the generation of positive goodness, evokes the utter negativity which is that limit. For it is as total negativity that matter in Plotinus's universe is the principle of evil. It is perfectly true, in a sense, to say that for Plotinus the dark *hylē* which is absolute and principal evil does not exist. But it is the inevitable cosmogonic approach, which is necessarily a movement away from being and form, to its absolute non-existence which makes *hylē* the principle of cosmic evil, and the approach, closer than is needed, by weaker individual lower souls not perfectly under the command of their higher souls, which enables it to become the principle of moral evil. Its effects in the universe of Plotinus are very limited. They do not extend to the Upper Cosmos, the region of the heavenly bodies, where matter is perfectly obedient and subdued to form.[15] The great embodied gods, including the earth-goddess,[16] are in no way affected for the worse by the "dark other." Even in individuals their higher souls are in no way affected by evil and even their lower souls are not intrinsically affected: there can be no substantial change for the worse in them, only a change of direction due to a failure to attend to the higher. In Plotinus's great theodicy, the work *On Providence*, matter is certainly included as a cause of the evils in this world of ours.[17] But the part which it plays in the justification of divine providence is modest, and a great deal of the work gives an account of cosmic harmony in conflict and tension which is not only in the spirit of Plato but not far removed form the cosmic optimism of the Stoics.

Plotinus has clearly moved a considerable distance from that much more substantial and lively evil principle, the evil soul of the Middle Platonists: and he is moving in a direction which leads towards the final rehabilitation of the "dark other" by the Athenian Neoplatonists. But I now think that it may be a mistake to dismiss his account of matter as principle of evil by its very negativity as a rather unsatisfactory transition stage in the evolution of Platonic dualism. Plotinus, like the Middle Platonists we considered earlier, does take the evils we experience here below very seriously, and this may be to his credit. The "classical" solution worked out by his successors is most coherent and impressive and has much to recommend it. But can it not sometimes become a little too smoothly complacent in its cosmic optimism? There is perhaps a way of looking at the doctrine of Plotinus (I am not suggesting that Plotinus always looks at it in this way) which is not in the end incompatible with the later Neoplatonist position but which gives a more vivid sense of the reality and seriousness of evil. We are often inclined, I think, to solidify and reify rather too much what the ancients are talking about: the language which they use, of course, encourages this distortion: in the present case the words *hylē*, *silva* or *materia* do rather strongly suggest lumps of stuff, and as long as there is even the faintest trace of unconscious tendency to look at *hylē* in this way it is very difficult to understand how what is being talked about can be a principle of evil precisely as absolute non-existence. But if we suppose that Plotinus is trying to speak of a kind of necessary condition of what must be there if the Good is to diffuse itself freely, a world of bodies in space and time, is to exist at all, it may become easier to make sense of his position. We can see that if the productivity, the generative power, of divine goodness, is to go on to its furthest limit, as, since it is absolute goodness, it is inevitable that is should; if it is to produce not only the complete and self-contained beauty of the archetype but the imperfect but real beauty of the image which is all that is left to produce, since the archetypal world contains all that can exist on its level of real being and perfect beauty and goodness; then a world must come into being which has a built-in element of negativity, sterility and unreality simply by not being the World of Forms, just as its harmony must be a harmony of separate beings in clash and conflict because it is a world of space and time (this last characteristic is not for Plotinus, any more than for Heraclitus and the Stoics, necessarily evil).[18] In the end Plotinus remains close to the spirit of the *Timaeus*, on which he meditated so continually.

In the Athenian Neoplatonists the "dark other" at last attains full equality of esteem with its opposite principle of light, form and order. The mother of all reality is honored equally with the father. This first becomes clear in Syrianus, for whom the primal Monad and Dyad which proceed immediately from the One are prior even to the world of real being. They are the co-equal and equally necessary principles of all multiple, that is to say of all derived, reality, of all that comes from and diffuses the Good from the highest gods to the lowest bodies.[19] And they are not only equally necessary but equally valued. Syrianus strongly denies that the Dyad is the principle of evil.[20] He seems to be the originator of the "classical" account of evil in which it is a παρυπόστασις, a by-product, with no existence or principle of its own. As Anne Sheppard puts it "The dyad is only indirectly responsible for evil in so far as it is responsible for otherness and plurality, and it is because of these that evil (παρυφίσταται) in the world. Another way of putting this would be to say that evil is unavoidable because the world is as it is, that it is inevitably involved in the partial and divided condition of the lower realms of the universe."[21] When the Athenian doctrine is stated like this, it is easy to see that it is not too far removed from that of Plotinus, or, for that matter, of the Pythagoreans and Plato whose teachings Syrianus thought he was expounding. Proclus develops the teaching of his master very powerfully. He shows[22] how the two principles operate at every level of his vast and complex universe, and both in a positive way, and how the "dark other," the Infinite, is the principle of life, fecundity and creative expansion without which the great diffusion of the Good through all the levels of multiplicity cannot occur. Jean Trouillard sums up this final development of Platonic dualism very well when he says

> Chaque être est fait de mesure et d'infinité, d'un et de multiple, de clarté et de ténébres. L'ordre a toujours besoin de s'opposer le désordre et de le maitriser, parce qu'il est une mise en ordre active et parce qu'il est soutenu par une puissance de dépassement. Et du moment que l'origine est ineffable, elle s'exprime aussi bien par la dyade multiplicatrice que par la monade unifiante. . . . Puisque il [le dualisme] traverse tous les niveaux et exprime une origine unique, il est pour ainsi dire exorcisé. L'abîme symbolise le sanctuaire. Ni le Chaos ni la Nuit ne sont le mal. Ils figurent l'Ineffable au même titre que l'ordre et la clarté.[23]

One can see very well, if one reads the passages in Proclus on which Trouillard's account is so solidly based, how this doctrine, though it corrects and clarifies earlier language and thought, remains faithful to the essentials of that thought, and even perhaps leaves room for understanding how the "dark other," though of the very highest status in the universe after the Good, and herself wholly good, can be the necessary condition for the existence of evils here below and in this way a "principle of evil" in the restricted and peculiar Platonic sense: so that this intense cosmic optimism need not be too fancifully and inhumanely roseate.

    We must now turn to the Gnostics more or less contemporary with the later Platonists whom we have been discussing. I shall confine myself here to those represented in the Nag Hammadi Library, and I must apologize for the superficiality of my treatment. I do not know this literature really well: I must read it in translation because of my ignorance of Coptic: and I am not at all sure whether my mental limitations as a Hellenist do not preclude me from any deep understanding of it. However, I will offer such tentative observations as I can. The first, and the most important from my point of view, is that it seems to me a mistake to read the Gnostics as if they were bad philosophers. Whatever elements in their stories may seem to derive in some way from their acquaintance with Greek philosophy, they are not doing the same thing as philosophers. They are not giving explanations of why things are as they are and accounts of the nature of the divine powers in terms of concept and system. They are telling exciting stories about the often vividly imagined doings and sufferings of spiritual beings, and it is the stories as told which give their explanation of the universe. To reduce them to abstract terms of principles and concepts will do them a greater injustice than will be done if we do the same thing to those greatest of Greek philosophers, Plato and Plotinus, who frequently use the language of poetry and religion. To try to turn their stories into abstract schemes, as it is so convenient for the comparative historian to do, is likely to be as unsatisfactory as the attempts which have been made to give an account of Beethoven's symphonies, especially the Fifth, in similar terms. I shall not therefore make any systematic effort to place the Gnostic stories precisely in my original scheme of cosmic dualisms.

Another reason for not attempting to do this is that I find it difficult to discover in the Nag Hammadi literature anyone or anything which corresponds closely to the "dark other" as a major force in the development of things to their present state. In other forms of Gnosticism, of course, we do meet with a darkness and powers of darkness which seem to be in ultimate opposition to the powers of light in the Iranian manner, though they are generally rather inert and passive by Iranian standards. But in the Nag Hammadi treatises which I have read, the part played by any ultimate darkness seems decidedly modest. We meet with the important Gnostic idea of darkness as a mirror, the reflection in which of a higher power is a stage in the genesis of the lower world.[24] In *Zostrianos* the darkness is considerably more important, but it seems to denote not a cosmic principle but the whole lower cosmos from which the Gnostic is being shown the way and passionately exhorted to escape.[25] It is notable in our present context that the darkness here is feminine: the message of the whole treatise is summed up in the exhortation "Flee from the madness and the bondage of femininity and choose for yourself the salvation of masculinity."[26] (In other treatises, of course, the feminine is viewed with a good deal more favor: a great deal seems to depend on how the Genesis story of the fall of man is interpreted and on how the ambiguous and androgynous figure of Barbelo is understood.) In the *Tripartite Tractate* the "Outer Darkness," "Chaos," "Hades" or the "Abyss" seems to be just the place which rightly belongs to the turbulent "beings of the likeness," and to which they fall down.[27] In the *Apocryphon of John* the basic darkness which causes all other evil and darkness seems to be identified with the ignorant Archon and Demiurge Yaltabaoth, who of course like all Gnostic Demiurges appears late in the story: he *is* "ignorant darkness."[28] The position seems to be much the same in the *Trimorphic Protennoia*, but here the demonic, aggressive evil of Yaltabaoth is more strongly stressed.

My next observation is, I hope, fairly uncontroversial, but important in our present context. It is that the form in which the Gnostics apprehend the action of the divine power of good and light in this world is predominantly that of a Redeemer, Enlightener and Liberator. The down-grading of the favored image of the Platonists, the Demiurge, by the Gnostics is of course well-known (I shall say something soon about how it continues to operate even in Gnostics who insist that the creation of the lower world is part of a great divine salvific plan.) But it is worth remarking that even though in the end this bad and unhappy world will be done away and the power of light will then finally defeat and triumph over the forces of darkness, the image of champion and war-leader for the great divine power who will bring this about is not generally favored. It is the liberation of the Gnostic children of light from the darkness through the saving enlightenment brought by the Redeemer which is in the center of the picture, not the cosmic defeat of the armies of the darkness. This marks a difference, as we shall see, between Gnostics and non-Gnostic Christians, which is important in practice as well as in thought. During the centuries of the Christian domination of Europe those who can in some extended sense be called Gnostics have been decidedly more crusaded against than crusading.

The stories told by Gnostics of this kind have a common feature which seems to me useful in determining their position in relation both to the Platonist tradition and to non-Gnostic Christianity. This is the importance given to a fall or failure in the spiritual world, a break in the middle of the great process of outgoing which determines the character of the subsequent process and leads in the end to the creation of this lower world. It is of course a very good kind of plot for a story which sets out to explain why things are so unsatisfactory here below in terms of the adventures of higher beings. This picture of some kind of fall or failure occurs even in stories which stress that the whole outgoing, including the creation of the lower world, is part of the great divine plan and which give a comparatively favorable account of the creator. This is particularly noticeable in the *Tripartite Tractate*. Here the Logos, the creative power, acts throughout in accordance with the will of the Father. It is stressed that his aspiration to ascend to the Father and desire to create on his own is intended by the Father.

> Therefore it is not right to criticize the movement which is the Logos, but it is fitting that we should say about the movement of the Logos that it is cause of a system which has been destined to come about.[29]

There is certainly something here which is comparable (with due caution) with Plotinus's idea of *tolma*.[30] But as we read on we find that the Logos "was not able to bear the sight of the light, but he looked into the depth and he doubted. Therefore it was an extremely painful division, a turning away because of his self-doubt and division, forgetfulness and ignorance of himself and of that which is."[31] This goes beyond the most Gnostic-like idea in any Platonist, Numenius's concept of the "splitting" of the Demiurge.[32] And in what follows in the *Tripartite Tractate* we discover that all the unreality, disturbance, and trouble of this lower world, the defects and dissensions of the cosmic powers, the Archons, and the conflict between the powers of light and darkness which dominates the present state of things, are due to the weakness and sickness of the Logos which comes from his attempt to attain to the Father. Here we have a real "break in the middle," a real fault and failing in the spiritual world accounting for the origin of an on the whole bad and transitory material cosmos, which is not compatible with the thought of Plotinus or with any kind of genuine Platonism.

It is not easy to fit the Gnostic stories which we have just been considering into any tidy scheme of cosmic or two-principle dualism. But of course the Gnostics, like the Platonists and the non-Gnostic Christians, are dualists in another perfectly legitimate sense of "dualism," that of belief in a duality of worlds, a higher and a lower cosmos. Something must be said here about some possible variations of this. We need to look rather carefully at the variants of two-world dualism which we encounter in the first centuries of our era in order to determine the degree of "other-worldliness," that is of hostility to, alienation from, and desire to escape from this lower cosmos which appears in them. This seems to depend to a great extent on the way in which the relationship between the two worlds is conceived or imagined. It is perfectly correct to say that the Nag Hammadi literature has shown that not all Gnostics were totally alienated from this world and committed to a darkly pessimistic view of the cosmos and its maker. But it must be admitted that a rather dark pessimism does predominate: and even in those treatises where a comparatively favorable view is taken of the creator and his creation, the estimate of the material cosmos does not seem to be high. There is not very much to be said for it as it appears in the latter part of the *Tripartite Tractate*. The sentence in *Marsanes* "<I have come to know> when <I> was deliberating that in every respect the sense-perceptible world is [worthy] of being saved entirely" certainly deserves to be quoted to show that not all Gnostics were utterly alienated and anti-cosmic. But if we also quote what remains of what comes immediately before, "Finally the entire defilement was saved, together with the immortality of that one [feminine] . . .," it does not look as if the material world, presumably identical with or part of the "entire defilement," is very much esteemed after all.[33]   The most deeply and strongly world-affirming of the treatises which I have read is the *Writing Without Title*,[34] with its loving descriptions of the paradises of the cosmic *Erōs* and the symbolic animals of the land of Egypt.[35] Tardieu describes the spirit and mood of the treatise (and of the closely related *Hypostasis of the Archons*) beautifully and accurately.

> Tous les trois [the myths of Adam and Eve, Erōs, and the animals of Egypt] expriment la même nostalgie d'une intimité chaleureuse, d'une fusion originaire et vital entre l'homme et la femme (cycle d'Adam) l'homme et les plantes (jardins d'Erōs) entre l'homme et l'animal (cycle des animaux d'Egypte) nostalgie analogue à celle qui préside à la genèse des mythes de la bisexualité, de l'age d'or et de la régeneration.[36]

It is important to remark that here the female (and the androgynous — Erōs is androgynous) are very highly regarded: in the telling of the story of Genesis the values are reversed and Eve and the serpent are good saving powers. This is certainly not a spirit of mere cosmic pessimism and alienation from this world. But it is a spirit of nostalgia, and nostalgia is generally understood as a passionate longing for something far away and long ago, and generally implies that one is fairly miserable about the state in which one finds oneself. Here we can see an important reason why it is very easy for Gnostics to be very hostile to and alienated from this present world. In the Gnostic stories the higher cosmos is remote and we cannot return to it, except in vision and revelation, till after bodily death: and the material cosmos is not only remote from the world of light but itself a transitory phenomenon: there is no reason to care about it very much.

For Platonists the relationship of the two worlds is very different. From the *Timaeus* onwards the essential truth about the material cosmos is that it is an image, divinely made, of the eternal world of Forms. (The idea that things in this world are in some sense images of things in a higher world does of course occur in some Gnostic writings,[37] as Plotinus notes with hostility.[38] But the archetypes of the images do not usually seem to be on a very high level or to come into existence very early in the story and the stress seems to be very much, as a rule, on the shadowy, phantasmal, and generally unsatisfactory character of the material image. In some Gnostics the valuation of body and the material world may not be very far from the *Phaedo* or from the nostalgia for the higher world of *Phaedrus* 250C, but it never seems to come very near to the *Timaeus*. The idea of the world as image does not seem to be really central for the Gnostics and, at their most cosmically optimistic, they are very far from regarding it as the everlasting icon of the eternal glory.) I have for some time found it useful, in considering the attitudes of Platonists to body and the material universe, to observe that the concept of *image* allows, and indeed demands, a sliding scale of valuation. At the lower end of the scale one says *How poor, trivial and inadequate a thing the image is compared with the original*; at the higher end *How beautiful and venerable is this icon of the eternal glory not made by human hands.* And many intermediate stages are possible, according to mood, temperament and context. We have seen how even in the more dualistic and pessimistically inclined Middle Platonists, the influence of the *Timaeus* prevented the higher valuation of the cosmos as image from ever being forgotten. And it is particularly clearly and strongly evident in Plotinus, in spite of a considerable number of pessimistically other-worldly utterances. We can see very well in him how the beauty of the everlasting image depends on the continual presence in it of the invisible and eternal archetype; indeed, not only its beauty but its very existence, for it is a *natural* image, like a shadow or reflection, which cannot exist without the archetype's presence.[39] The two worlds are very close to each other in Plotinus; so close that many good modern interpreters of the *Enneads* find it better and less misleading to understand his thought in terms of one world, one set of entities, apprehended in different ways at different levels, rather than two.[40] In terms of comparison with Gnostics, and non-Gnostic Christians, this means that for Plotinus heaven, or the Pleroma, or the World of Light, is not remote and our sojourn there is not something which belongs to the past or the future. The eternal is here and now present in its everlasting image. The only Parousia there will ever be is here and now. And those who are capable and prepared to make the great moral and intellectual efforts to do so can live in heaven and rise beyond it to God here and now. Porphyry was, it seems, more inclined than his master to follow Numenius in regarding this world as a place to escape from. But the Athenian Neoplatonists incline even more strongly than Plotinus to the highest evaluation of the image: and for them too the One and the Henads and the Forms are intimately and immediately present at every level of their vast hierarchy of being, the highest more intimately and immediately present in this lower cosmos of ours than those of lower rank. And through the sacred rites their presence may be experienced by at least some of those who cannot rise to the austere contemplation of the sage.

I have left myself little room to discuss the formidably complex subject of the forms of cosmic dualism which are to be found in the thought of non-Gnostic Christians. But it will already be apparent that a good deal which has been said in the earlier parts of this paper about both Platonists and Gnostics can be applied to mainstream Christians: and the best thing I can do here is to suggest at least a partial explanation for the remarkable variations in Christian theory and practice in terms of the different solutions adopted by Christians to the problems of the evils and imperfections apparent in the world and human beings. Non-Gnostic Christians have generally rejected with great passion and emphasis interpretations of the Jewish and Christian stories which made the creator of the world other than and inferior to the one God and Father of Jesus Christ. They have rejected the kind of "break in the middle" which figures so prominently in the Gnostic stories. As a result they affirm very strongly the goodness of the creation as well as of the creator: and eventually classical Christian theology came to accept the later Neoplatonist view of evil as having no real existence, as a *parhypostasis*. On this side of Christian thinking Platonic influence has been strong and deep. In the West as well as in the East Christians have often arrived at a theophanic view of the material creation in which it appears as the God-made icon of the eternal glory. I was myself brought up in an English Christian tradition which saw no fundamental difference between Platonism and Christianity, and instinctively and unselfconsciously accepted God's self-revelation in nature as equal in honor to his self-revelation in scripture and church: a way of faith admirably summed up in St. Maximus

Confessor's discussion of the proper interpretation of the white garments of the Transfiguration in which he concludes ". . . the two laws, of nature and of scripture, are equal in honor and teach the same as each other, and neither is greater or less than the other . . ."[41] But there are of course important differences between the normal Christian creationist position and that of the later Platonists. The Christians lay much greater stress on God's will and have a more unbridled and absolute conception of divine creative power than Plato and his followers: as a result they not only reject the independent principle of evil of the Middle Platonists but have little room in their thought for the "dark other," still so important in the last Neoplatonists, and in general, at least till quite recently, reject any limitation on God's omnipotence which would mean that he works by persuasion rather than force. This can result in leading those Christians, like Augustine in his later years, who incline to a gloomy view of the present state of affairs, not only to a pessimism about the world as great as that of the Manichees but to a way of thinking about God darker and more terrifying than that of any thorough-going cosmic dualists.[42]

The darker view of this world is strongly assisted by the older and more popular Christian way of explaining its evils. This is a story-explanation, in terms of persons rather than principles, about the fall of angels and men, and in this way resembles the Gnostic stories. In patristic thought, and sometimes in later Christian thought, the fall of the angels plays an important part in the explanation of cosmic or physical evil: though no other Christian thinker goes as far as Origen in making the whole creation depend on the fall of the spirits who, according to the depth of their fall, became angels, men or devils: a doctrine which he is enabled to reconcile with his firm anti-Gnostic faith that the creation is essentially good, because it is the work of the perfectly good and wise Father working through the Logos in whom there is no fault or failing, by his vision of the whole creative process as one of redemption, education and purification which will bring all the spirits back to that original state form which they, freely and of their own motion, in no way impelled by God, chose to fall. The vital difference between the way of thinking of the *Peri Archon* and the at first sight not entirely dissimilar one of the *Tripartite Tractate* is that for Origen there is no element of fault and failing, no falling below the best, in the divine creative act itself. Origen's view was of course generally rejected by non-Gnostic Christians: but in less wholesale forms the explanation of cosmic evils by the fall of the angels has not, perhaps, been uncommon. My father, who was an Anglican clergyman, reconciled his passionate belief in the goodness of the creation with the undoubted existence of evils in it by an interesting Christian adaptation of what is said in the *Timaeus* about the part taken by the "younger gods" in the formation of the world, which he regarded as perfectly orthodox and traditional. He held that the angels had had bestowed on them by God limited powers of creation which the devils were not deprived of, and continued to exercise after their fall by creating all the things in the world of which my father disapproved, notably slugs and snails, to which, being an enthusiastic gardener, he had the strongest objection.

But it is when the doctrine of the fall of the angels is combined with that of the fall of mankind to provide an explanation of the evils which beset humanity here below that we may find the foundations in Christian thought for a world-view as dark as that of the Manichaeans or a conflict-dualism fiercer than that of the Mazdaeans. J.H.W.G. Liebeschütz, in his excellent book on Roman religion, has shown very well how the passionate early Christian belief in devils and the identification of the pagan gods with devils darkened the later antique world-view, by strengthening the tendency which had already appeared in it to believe in supernatural personifications of evil. He says,

> The transformation of the gods into demons had a significant psychological consequence. The gods had sometimes been cruel or arbitrary, but they could be placated by offerings in quite the same way as arbitrary or tyrannous humans. They were not essentially hostile or spiteful. Christianity offered man enormously powerful assistance, but it also proclaimed the existence of powerful and totally evil adversaries. Life became a battle in which men must fight for God against "the enemy."

and he adds in a footnote

> There had been a tendency to believe in supernatural personifications of absolute evil, especially in connection with magic, in later Greek or Roman paganism. . . But it was left to Christianity to fill the world with evil spirits.[43]

Peter Brown has unforgettably described the consequences in Augustine's latest thought of combining this devil-dualism with the anti-dualist insistence on the omnipotence and sovereign will of God.

> God had plainly allowed the human race to be swept by his wrath: and this human race, as Augustine presents it in his works against Julian, is very like the invaded universe of Mani. Augustine had always believed in the vast power of the Devil: . . . Now this Devil will cast his shadow over mankind:

the human race is "the Devil's fruit-tree, his own property, from which he may pick his fruit," it is "the plaything of demons." This is evil, thought of much as the Manichees had done, as a persecutory force. The demons may now have been enrolled as the unwitting agents of a superior justice: but it is they who are seen as active and man as merely passive.[44]

Here, as Brown shows, we are very close to the Gnostic view of the world at its darkest, and, though the figure of God is invested with a transcendent and absolute horror exceeding that of any Gnostic demiurge or even the Manichaean evil principle, his most eminent activity in the world in its present state is seen as the redemption and deliverance of the small number of the elect from its darkness. For the rest of humanity, of course, there is no hope at all, as God simultaneously with his work of redemption pursues his "awesome blood-feud against the family of Adam."[45]

But those Christians who have not the tormented genius of Augustine for drawing out the full horror of the consequences implicit in some traditional Christian doctrines, and who do not see the world as so totally devil-ridden as Augustine did in his later years (and many of his Christian contemporaries did not) have often come to attach much importance to the third image which I mentioned (p. 9) as available to cosmic dualists, that of the war-leader, commanding the armies of light against the forces of darkness. They have found that the qualified conflict-dualism of the belief that all the evils of this world are due to the sins of the fallen angels and the men and women whom they have seduced into following them provides admirable support for the ferocious, though sometimes quite cheerful, pugnacity, exceeding that of mainstream Iranian conflict-dualists, which has been a distinguishing characteristic of historic Christianity. The belief that those whom one regards, at any place or time, as enemies of authentic Christian faith, civilization, or interests are of the Devil's party is a powerful stimulus to crusading: that is, of course, if one does not pay too much attention, as Christians in this sort of context have generally quite successfully avoided doing, to where and how Christ chose to overcome evil, and so is not inhibited by the reflection that the Cross is a singularly inappropriate symbol for a Crusader. Those, of course, who do attend to the meaning of the Cross, as the best of those who have used the language of "spiritual combat" have done, will come to use that language in a very different way, and understand the overcoming of evil in very different terms from the polemists and crusaders. In their thought and practice this strange triumph will be achieved by accepting and carrying evil and requiting it with good and with love. Most of us have not got nearly as far as this. But, as we contemplate the overcoming of evil by the way of the Cross, we may be permitted to observe that the language of conflict-dualism is not really appropriate to it, except in a most violently paradoxical sense: so that we may come to prefer other images, including the great Platonic image of the Craftsman, for our struggle in this imperfect, but good and lovable world.

NOTES

1. Aristotle *Metaphysics* A. 5. 986a 22-26. I accept the view that Aristotle is much our best and most reliable source of evidence for pre-Platonic Pythagoreanism.

2. I agree on the whole with the skeptical assessment of the evidence for Plato's oral teachings given by Gregory Vlastos in his review of H.J. Krämer *Arete bei Platon und Aristoteles, Gnomon* 41 (1963): 641-655, reprinted in *Platonic Studies* (Princeton University Press 1973) as no. 17, pp. 379-403.

3. Aristotle *Metaphysics* A. 6. 988a 14.

4. F.M. Cornford's *Plato's Cosmology* (London, Kegan Paul, 1937), pp. 363-364.

5. In the third part of the great theodicy of *Laws* X, in 906, the gods are compared to generals, as they are to skippers, charioteers, doctors, farmers — and sheepdogs, and the everlasting war against evil in which gods and spirits are our allies is mentioned (906A 5-7): but this is very incidental, and the main point of the comparisons is to show how unlikely it is that the gods are corruptible.

6. Simplicius *In Phys.* 230, 34-231, 27 Diels. See P. Merlan in the *Cambridge History of Later Greek and Early Medieval Philosophy* I.5, pp. 90-94.

7. Numenius Fr. 52 des Places (Test. 30 Leemans), 15-24.

8. Chapters 46 and 47, 369D-370C.

9. *In Tim.* I 276-277 and 382-382 Diehl.

10. 382, 7-12 Diehl.

11. J. Dillon, *The Middle Platonists* (Duckworth, London, 1977), p. 254.

12. Calcidius *In Timaeus* 296-297. (Fr. 52 65-70, 82-87 des Places).

13. Calcidius 298 (Fr. 52, 101-102 des Places).

14. Fr. 16 des Places (25 Leemans), 16-17.

15. II 1 [40] 4, 12-13; II 9 [33] 35-36; IV 4 [28] 42, 25-6.

16. For the Earth as a goddess see IV 4 [28] 22, 26-27.

17. III 2 [47] 2.

18. Pierre Hadot's exposition of Plotinus's allegorical interpretation of the myth of Ouranos, Kronos and Zeus in his great anti-Gnostic work brings out very well how and why Plotinus thinks it necessary that the diffusion of the Good should go on beyond the self-contained, inward looking perfection of the world of Noûs. (Pierre Madot "Ouranos, Kronos and Zeus in Plotinus's treatise against the Gnostics," in *Neoplatonism and Early Christian Thought*

[Variorum, London 1981], pp. 124-137).

19. The doctrine of Syrianus is very well expounded by Anne Sheppard in her contribution (pp. 1-17), "Monad and Dyad as Cosmic Principles in Syrianus," in *Soul and the Structure of Being in Late Neoplatonism* (University Press, Liverpool, 1982). Very difficult problems arise, in Syrianus and still more in Proclus, about the place of the primal pair (Monad and Dyad in Syrianus, Limit and Infinity in Proclus) in relation to the Divine Henads, as Sheppard indicates (pp. 11-12).

20. In Metaph. 184. 1. ff; 185. 15 ff. Kroll.

21. Art. cit. p. 10.

22. *In Tim.* I 54 D-E, 176 Diehl; *In Parm.* VI 1119, 4-1123, 21; El. Th. propositions 89-92; *Platonic Theology* III 7-9.

23. Jean Trouillard, *La Mystagogie de Proclos* (Les Belles Lettres, Paris 1982), p. 247.

24. *Hypostasis of the Archons* (II 4) 11-14; cp. *Poimandres* (*Hermetica* I) 14, p. 11 Nock-Festugière.

25. *Zostrianos* (VIII 1) 1.

26. 131.

27. *Tripartite Tractate*, 78.

28. *Apocryphon of John* 11.

29. *Tripartite Tractate* 77, (translation by Harold Attridge and Dieter Mueller in *The Nag Hammadi Library in English* [Brill Leiden, 1977]).

30. On this see Naguib Baladi *La Pensée de Plotin* (Presses Universitaires de France, Paris, 1970) and my own treatment in "Gnosis and Greek Philosophy," pp. 116ff. (*Gnosis*, Vandenhoek and Ruprecht, Göttingen, 1978, pp. 87-124, reprinted as no. XXI in A.H. Armstrong, *Plotinian and Christian Studies*, Variorum, London, 1979).

31. *Tripartite Tractate* 77.

32. Numenius Fr. 11 des Places (20 Leemans).

33. *Marsanes* (X.1.) 5.

34. II 5.

35. As M. Tardieu observes, this praise of Egypt brings the treatise close to the Hermetic *Asclepius* (M. Tardieu, *Trois Mythes Gnostiques, Études Augustiniennes*, Paris, 1974; ch. 5, 67, pp. 269-272).

36. Tardieu, p. 269.

37. E.g. *Zostrianos* 48, 55, 113 (a treatise which Plotinus may have known).

38. II 9 [33] 26-27. "Why do they feel the need to be there in the archetype of the universe which they hate?" A great deal of II 9 is devoted to severe criticism of the Gnostics' perverse use of the concept of image and the false other-worldliness which springs from it.

39. On the distinction between "natural" and "artificial" images see VI 4 [22] 9-10. A text which well brings out the closeness of the two worlds is V 8 [31] 7.

40. Cp. two recent articles in *Dionysius* (Halifax, Nova Scotia, Canada, Dalhousie University Press). K. Corrigan, "The Internal Dimensions of the Sensible Object in the Thought of Plotinus and Aristotle," V (December 1981): 98-126 and Michael F. Wagner, "Plotinus's World," VI (December 1982): 13-42.

41. Maximus *Ambigua* VI PG91, 1128C-D.

42. Peter Brown brings this out very well in his *Augustine of Hippo* (London, Faber, 1967) in c. 32 on the controversy with Julian of Eclanum.

43. J.H.W.G. Liebeschütz, *Continuity and Change in Roman Religions* (Clarendon Press, Oxford, 1979), p. 269 and note 2.

44. Peter Brown, l.c. (n. 42), p. 395. The quotations are from Augustine *De Nuptiis et Concupiscentia* I xxiii 26 and *Contra Julianum VI* xxi 67.

45. Brown l. c., p. 393. I have referred to this chapter because in it Brown has said, with great precision and sympathy for Augustine, whatever can decently be said in defense of his later doctrine. Cp. Th.G. Sinnige, "Gnostic Influences in the Early Works of Plotinus and in Augustine," in *Plotinus amid Gnostics and Christians*, ed D.T. Runia (Amsterdam, Free University Press, 1984), pp. 94-97.

The "Second God" in Gnosticism and Plotinus's Anti-Gnostic Polemic

Francisco García Bazán
translated from Spanish by Winifred T. Slater

Nous as a "Second God" According to Plotinus

In *Enneads* V, 1 (10), 8, a writing belong to the first literary period of Plotinus's teachings,[1] the following ideas are set forth:

> 8. This is the reason why Plato says that all things are threefold "about the king of all" — he means the primary realities — and "the second about the second and the third about the third." But he also says that there is a "father of the cause," meaning Intellect by "the cause": for Intellect is his craftsman; and he says that it makes Soul in that "mixing-bowl" he speaks of. And the father of Intellect which is the cause he calls the Good and that which is beyond Intellect and "beyond being." And he also often calls Being and Intellect Idea: so Plato knew that Intellect comes from the Good and Soul from Intellect. And [it follows] that these statements of ours are not new; they do not belong to the present time, but were made long ago, not explicitly, and what we have said in this discussion has been an interpretation of them, relying on Plato's own writings for evidence that these views are ancient. And Parmenides also, before Plato, touched on a view like this, in that he identified Being and Intellect and that it was not among things perceived by the senses that he placed Being, when he said "Thinking and Being are the same." And he says that this Being is unmoved — though he does attach thinking to it — taking all bodily movement from it that it may remain always in the same state, and likening it to "the mass of a sphere," because it holds all things in its circumference and because its thinking is not external, but in itself. But when he said it

55

was one, in his own works, he was open to criticism because this one of his was discovered to be many. But Parmenides in Plato speaks more accurately, and distinguishes from each other the first One, which is more properly called One, and the second which he calls "One-Many" and the third, "One and Many." In this way he too agrees with the doctrine of the three natures.[2] (tr. A.H. Armstrong)

This passage is rich not only in personal doctrine, but also in that it indicates some of the sources of thought which nourished that doctrine. Specifically, they are the three ontological categories of Plato's *Epistle II* which serve as the basis for outlining the theory of the hypostases and their hierarchy;[3] the reflection of the first three hypotheses of the *Parmenides* upon "The One"[4] so as to be able to distinguish amongst the three hypostases as units of diverse content and complexity. Lastly, Intellect, the second hypostasis in hierarchy, is not a single or isolated One, ultimately ineffable, but a Unity-Totality, The One as an undivided whole which contains all and which thereby claims particular requirements.

This, observes our philosopher, Parmenides had already perceived and maintained, albeit in imprecise language. But the core of the nature of the second hypostasis was already firmly grasped by the Presocratic under the following conceptual scheme:[5]

1. Parmenides had already comprehended clearly and as a lucid rational necessity that what is (*to on*) is absolutely opposed to what is not. In this respect, being can neither begin to be nor stop being nor be transformed, for that would imply passing from not being to being, form being to not being, or identification through coexistence of being and not being. In any one of these cases the logically absurd may apply.[6]

2. From this central conviction derive the signs or attributes which characterize being as motionless, complete, eternal, etc.[7]

3. Furthermore, this logical intuition of the reality of being cannot derive from what is not, whether in an absolute or a relative sense. With careful scrutiny, it is seen to be the consciousness which being has of itself and which asserts itself as a constant awareness, as does the reality which is known. So being and thinking are actually one and the same thing. It is not a question of being coming from thinking — far from it; but neither does thinking come from being. They have always been and shall forever be the same, a connaturally indivisible reality. What does happen, historically, is that at a given moment the philosopher, by his thinking, discovers that identity; but the reality was already there, immutable, waiting to be awakened.[8]

4. None the less, although Parmenides has seen and written about the inseparable unity of being and thinking and has called it "One," he has not expressed exactly of what that not-one, wherefore multiple, unity consists. It was Plato who, in the expository development of the second hypothesis of his dialogue about unity, *Parmenides*, expressed it with sufficient clarity.[9]

Therefore, (a) based on an essential intellectual position regarding Parmenides and the interpretation which Parmenides's central ontological intuition had elicited in Plato; and (b) according to a Pythagorizing-Platonic exegesis well assimilated by Plotinus and which favors a *Plato pythagoricus*, the different perspectives and problems Nous holds for Plotinus are as follows:

A. Internal configuration of Intellect or Spirit.
B. Derivation and self-constitution of Intellect as a second hypostasis.
C. Function of Intellect as producer as an intermediary hypostasis between the Good/One and the Soul or third hypostasis.

Of what does Nous consist or what is Nous?

The first thorough presentation setting forth of the subject topic appears in *Enneads* V, 9 (5) under the title: "On Intellect, Ideas and Being."[10] The subject matter is introduced with a reference to the three types of men or categories, varieties, kinds of philosophers: the Epicurean, the Stoic, and the Platonic (the latter really knows and seeks the basis of his knowledge and "takes pleasure in that real place").[11]

It is explained, first of all, that what is referred to here is the *nous alethinos*, the real nous. This means an Intellect which constantly is Intellect, since an Intellect which is partial or which at times is and at other times is not Intellect will not be Intellect in an absolute sense. True Intellect is, therefore, total knowledge and always knowledge.[12]

Moreover, this Intellect, perceived as being always the same and all-inclusive, corroborates the same reasoning (*logos*); that is, "real being and real essence" (τὸ ὂν ὄντως καὶ τὴν ἀληθῆ οὐσίαν). Undoubtedly, Being, by not being mingled with the changeable entities, is separate (*chorismos*) and by being the totality, carries within its bosom the ideas.[13] Intellect in the real sense is always Intellect in actuality, as it cannot go from potentiality to actuality and be always existent (καὶ ἀεὶ νοῦν ὄντα).[14]

> But if its thinking is not as acquired, if it thinks something, it thinks it from itself and if it possesses something, it possesses it from itself. And if it thinks from itself and starting from itself, it itself is what it thinks. Because if it were an essence, and what it thinks were different from itself, its very essence would be unknown to it and so would be potential and not actual. Consequently, it is necessary not to separate these realities from each other (we are in the habit of separating them also analytically — *tais epinoiais* — according to our conditions depending on what may be current among us). What is it, then, that acts and thinks, that it should be recognized that that which is acting and thinking is the same as what it is thinking? It is obvious that it is *nous* which, really being, thinks beings and is; so then it itself is those beings, because it will think of them as being externally, or as being contained within itself as something identical. Now then, externally it is impossible, for where would they be? Therefore it thinks itself and in itself.[15]

Then some exact formulas stated by Parmenides, Aristotle, and Heraclitus, as well as the Platonic doctrine of reminiscence (*anamnesis*), become present and meaningful. Here beings dwell — not one is left outside; here where there is no birth nor corruption is what really is. Inferior beings have only a borrowed or shared reality.[16]

Intellect, then, is total unity;[17] that is, nothing eludes Intellect, since it is one-all. Then all things must be in it and at the same time and, therefore, together and separate, as a whole, but several.[18] How is this possible? Because in the unity of the Spirit, lacking in sensible matter, but living in itself, it is possible for complete beings, forms or ideas to coexist as intellectual realities.[19] Knowing themselves constantly and completely, these realities do not lock themselves into their selfsameness, but admit into their identical intellection with its reality all the remaining forms which comprise the intelligible organism or place. There is, therefore, in each idea or archetype identity of being and of thinking in a particular sense,[20] but at the same time awareness of a reality which is what it is in itself. Furthermore, this is true to the extent to which it communicates freely and unhindered with the total Intellect. In the same way, the full Spiritual Order is reflected or concentrated in each being — each self-transparent individuality, and it could not be what it is were it not for that presence of all else in its own constitution.[21] "There it is the all in the one."[22]

One who refers to the fundamental duality of thought as being intelligible and intelligent in itself, is at the same time affirming intellection. Indeed, true Intellect, which, as such, is necessarily Intellect in actuality, is, primarily and totally, triple unity. It is a one which, as thought, thinks itself as a known object, as a knowing subject, and as a cognitive activity. Or, if you will, a thinking foundation (intellect) which, conceptually determining itself (what it is), is a full noetic activity (intellectual life as noesis).[23] So it is multiple unity which is eternity and life in the whole totality and in the particular beings under the limitation of what each one of them is — their sameness, their difference, their repose and movement, their quality, etc., affording in advance a brief outline of the internal framework of the spiritual.[24]

The actuality of intellect is life (*zōē-bios*), intelligible activity in its fullness, which stands (*en hesycho*) in the presence of the One and engenders the intelligible gods. This activity of implicit triple content and with the Good as its source and root that will be the source also of life, of intellect, and of being.[25] It is this triad, fully and loftily defining the second hypostasis, which Plotinus will continue using in his classes throughout the years.

But in the uni-trinity of being-life-thought Plotinus finds not only the doctrine of essential number, but also the anticipation of the great genera [*megiste gené*] of Plato's *Sophist*.[26] It is these genera [*gene*] which justify the delimitation of ideas as such in the intelligible world and reciprocal communication among them. With these concepts in mind he is able to write the following:

But Nous is all beings. It contains, therefore, all things firm in itself, it only and always is thus and never in the future shall be thus, because every then is a now. Neither is it in the past, because here nothing is preterit; rather all beings are always present; remaining so because, in a manner of speaking, they love one another in that state. Each of them is intellect and being and the whole is total Intellect and total being; intellect by means of thinking causing being to exist, but being by means of being thought giving to intellect thought and existence. The cause of thinking, none the less, which is the same as the cause of being, is different; therefore they both at the same time have a different cause. Undoubtedly they both exist together and do not separate, but this unity which is simultaneously intellect and being, that which thinks and that which is thought, is a duality, intellect as it thinks and being as it is thought. This must be so because thinking could not arise without the existence of difference and identity. And so the basic genera emerge: Intellect, Being, Difference, and Identity. Motion and Rest should also be added; for if there is thinking there must be motion and being the same requires rest. . . Once this multiplicity is brought into being, Number and Quantity arise and Quality as well, for it is the characteristic proper to each one of these Ideas which are the principles from which all else derives.[27]

The foregoing evinces implicit distinction of the great genres looking toward ideas and numerical constitution in addition to total intelligible reality and essential realities, unities in either case, but also multiples.

We interpret as follows: Each form, each individual intellect, being a particular reflection of Intellect, is a being in actuality; but each being, each *ousia*, is elementally constituted by or has in common with the others entity, difference, mobility, and stability. By means of this amalgamation of elemental principles it settles itself or is inserted into the spiritual whole. That is, each idea is what it is in the intelligible world to the degree to which, being in eternal and intransferable actuality a permanent "this" or "that" in itself; that is, a determined or clear form (being) in full activity (life) of self-transparency (knowledge), it contemplates or lives in itself, the totality of the order of Intellect, opening itself up without restraints or barriers to that whole and possessing it in itself according to its own particularity. Therefore, each such form is a distinct being comprised of entity, identity, and stability, of the difference by virtue of which the remaining ideas make room for it and flow back to themselves, and the mobility through which it aspires to be all ideas and all other ideas conspire towards it.[28] Each idea communicates supragenerically with the intelligible living whole by means of its triune internal dynamism of being-life-knowledge, but communicates with the eternal beings by means of its generic constitution. It is life and interrelation, since each *ousia* is simultaneously organ within an organism and organ of an organism along with other organs.[29]

But in the dynamic or organic reality of the "living in itself," in its whole and in its parts, is concealed the essential number rendering possible this same multiple order in both the broad and the restricted sense. This hold true in the architectural dimension because, by its constitution, the intelligible living presupposes trinity; its earlier moment (intellect) presupposes duality; and the object which claims it (being), presupposes unity. Furthermore, ideal beings add to their entitive unity the remaining four genres so as to subsist in order.[30] However, in a strictly ideal characterization, order is maintained because each form contains a number which assures its cohesion[31] with the whole. In any idea, therefore, the essential number participates in a complex fashion to allow the idea its spiritual place and to give it internal unity. The decad, then, harboring in its bosom the hidden power of number, is the ultimate and first shaping element of Nous and of its ideal contents. Consequently, Plotinus says:

> The essential number is that which is one aspect of ideas and co-generates them, but primally it is in being and with being and before all beings. In it beings have their basis and fount, root and first principle. For the One is the principle for being and being is in the One (because it would be diversified), but the One does not rest upon being, because then it would be one before possessing Unity, and that which is part of the decad would be decad before possessing decadhood.[32]

In brief, Nous, the second hypostasis, sphere of intelligible being or multiple unity, consists of the following elements, going from the center to the periphery:

Inclusive characteristics of the container: (a) Elemental principles (Form/Matter); (b) Principles of order (essential number); (c) Suprageneric nature (Being-Life-Intellect).

Characteristics of the contents: (a) General (megiste gene) major categories; (b) Special (specific or individual conditions).

The philosopher's characteristic activity consists precisely in serenely knowing and traversing without difficulties the "plain of truth."[33]

But how can Intellect be constituted in this manner if plurality comes from Unity? This is the question Plotinus asks himself early in his teachings.[34]

Derivation and self-constitution of Intellect as the second hypostasis.

The answer to this problem is related to the formation of the second hypostasis as an image of the One, for:

> The One remains as the object of thinking, that which arises as the object of thought; but being thought and thinking from whence it derives (because it has no other) is Intellect, which has, so to speak, another object of thought, like the former, and is the reflection and image of It.[35]

The Spirit likewise is represented as an irradiation or luminous projection (*perilampsis*) which comes from the One.[36] Later on it is asserted that:

> This is certainly what occurs with the Good as spiritual power encircles it, being in its turn like the model of its image in the One-multiple, which also

> is on the way to multiplicity and because of that has become Nous. . . . It is like a light which comes from one single center, keeping its transparency in itself. The scattering light is an image, but the light from which it radiates is the real One.[37]

How is this derivation or generation of the second hypostasis ontologically possible? Because the One/Good remains in itself and, to the extent that it rests established in its own plenitude it generates the different, as a product which is its immediate image or glow and the effect of its overabundance.

> It is not Being, but rather its generator. Being is, so to speak, its first generation. Because it neither seeks nor possesses nor needs anything, It overflows and this overabundance produces something different from It.[38]

How is Intellect formed as a Multiple-Unity? It is formed as a reflection, but a reflection which is the result of its own self-constitution. So Good remains in itself, absolutely in its own nature, but it gives off its nature upon another, its imprint (*ichnos*) which attracts and is able to captivate Intellect and which is its intelligible content. It is the same as the heat which is in fire and the heat in a warm body. Thus it is the essence of cause and effect.[39] For this reason, this production, as seen from the One, or in general from the producing level, is an emanation and spontaneous productive capability; whereas, observed from the perspective of Intellect, it is a complex operation which brings into play all its components and possibilities of internal organization.

Plotinus says that the second hypostasis had the audacity (*tolma*) to separate itself from the One.[40] In fact, that which as regards the One is overabundance (*hyperpleres*), from the point of view of *Nous* is boldness. Within this concept the multiple potentialities of matter begin to function. The substratum or spiritual receptacle, swollen with separating tension, is the indefinite or the other-than-the-One, which, ever in potentiality and yearning for its origin, seeks Unity.

Plotinus corroborates this doctrine on several occasions:

> But why is Intellect not the generator? Because thinking is the actuality of Intellect; on the other hand, that thinking seeing the intelligible turned towards it and receiving from it its consummation, is in itself indefinite, like sight, and is defined by the intelligible. This is why it has been said that "ideas and numbers arise from the indefinite dyad and the One."[41]

Consequently he can point out a little further on:

Who, then, has generated this multiple god? It is generated by simple Being, which is prior to this multiplicity, the cause of its multiple existence, and that which produces number. Certainly number is not primal. And because Unity is prior to the dyad and the dyad is in turn second and springs from Unity, the latter defines it but it is in itself indefinite. Once it has been defined, it is already number, number as substance. . . . Therefore, what is called number and duality in the spiritual world, are informing principles and Spirit. Even so, the indefinite dyad exists, so long as it be taken, so to speak, as the substratum. Each number which proceeds from it and from the One, is an Idea, having been formed by the ideas generated in It (= spiritual substratum). On the one hand, Nous is formed from the One, but on the other, from Itself, the same as sight in actuality, because thinking is vision which sees, both of them being one.[42]

With that same mentality, Plotinus maintains likewise that the Good or the One "lacks thinking so as not to have otherness"[43] and that there is a relation of "similarity and identity" between the subject which knows and the Intelligible which allows the being that knows through self-denial an exaltation and even identification with the known, once the obstacles have disappeared:

For bodies hinder bodies in communicating, but incorporeal bodies are not hindered by bodies; therefore they are not apart from each other spatially, but rather because of otherness and difference. Thus when otherness disappears, the several beings are present to one another. So that which has not otherness is always present and we are present with it when we put away otherness. Neither does That aspire to us, as if it were round about us, but rather we aspire to It, being round about It.[44]

Now the passage to which we alluded earlier[45] becomes fully meaningful. Its most interesting lines, pointing out the self-generated character of Intellect, read as follows:

But Nous is all beings. . . . But in order that there be that which thinks and that which is thought, otherness is required. Otherwise, if you remove otherness, the emerging unity will remain silent. It is likewise necessary that the things which are thought be both different from and somewhat like each other, since it is a unit in itself and as a unit all have something in common. Difference is also an otherness. This multiplicity which comes into being produces number and quantity. Quality, moreover, as the characteristic proper to each of them and to all else, derives from these in the sense that they are principles.[46]

We consider the above to be Plotinus's central notion. Nous a knowledge implies duality: that which thinks and that which is thought. Since in the behavior of Nous that which allows this act is exterior to that which thinks as well as to what is represented, it will follow that their generator is also the generator of Being and of knowledge of Being. Being is the object represented in Intellect, the awareness of that which is represented, Intellect. In the fulfilled action of thinking Being remains identical to and different from Intellect, and Intellect remains inchoately *other* than Being, on the point of becoming identical to itself and different from Being, that which it should know; therefore it thinks that. Going to the essence of the matter, then, we summarize as follows: The cognitive action of Nous, potentially knowing, brought Being to determination or existence and the constant awareness of Being sustains the intellect of Nous. First place in logical analysis goes to Intellect, because, in order to constitute itself as the transparent self-representation, in which Being and Being's thinking are identified the same, identical in the double unity of the actuality of knowing, Nous, sensing itself to be another, aspired, as to something not attained, to intuit the constantly One. Therefore, in the epinoetic analysis examination the broadest fullest functions and the great genres appear as self-constituting stages of cognitive activity, which is then reflected from Being upon beings, self-constituting them and arranging them in intelligible life as its principles. The internal components of the cognitive act are the subject which knows (Intellect) and the object known (Being). Both of them, in active knowing, are different and alike in that they perform a function which distinguishes and defines them in a unity and in motion and at rest; for that which knows, when it is knowing involves both genres, as does that which is known, once it is being known. But, embracing all these principles is found otherness, that ultimate element of Nous which, being somewhat different from the One, aspires to be not undefined Intellect, but rather, with its own content of thinking and Being, the representation or image of the One. This capability of undefined understanding, this real spiritual substratum in which knowledge and Being as projections of Good will be possible, is true *otherness*. By means of otherness arise the great genera of Nous or its internal properties; it allows the cognitive duality of thinking and Being; and from it is generated difference as the first note of division, since it has to do with what is different in itself. Moreover, upon it, with Being already formed, is constructed the plurality of the being of Nous, identical and different. From this foundation the entire architecture of the intelligible world will be arranged, duly emphasizing that the basic component with regard to procession and that which permits an orderly development of everything beneath the One, is this reality of otherness. It is a deep aspiration, forever unsatisfied, which attains in Nous all it desires. That otherness in no way differs from the above-mentioned "indefinite dyad," which together with Unity forms the ideal numbers and which is here referred to as the multiplicity which produces number.[47]

The Neoplatonist was right, then, to conclude his reflections concerning intelligible matter with these words so well worth remembering:

> In effect, spiritual otherness exists always, which produces matter; for this is the principle of matter and the primary movement. For this reason Movement, too, was called Otherness, because Movement and Otherness sprang forth together. The Movement and Otherness which came from the First are undefined and need the First to define them; and they are defined when they turn to it. But before the turning, matter, too, was undefined and the Other and not yet good, but unilluminated from the First. For if light comes from the First, then that which receives the light, before it receives it has everlastingly no light; but it has light as other than itself, since the light comes to it from something else. And now we have disclosed about the intelligible matter more than the occasion demanded.[48]

In fact, it is that *Other* which, risen from the One and turning towards It in undefined Movement, impregnates the eager substratum to become self-constituted thereupon as knowledge and order in the presence of the unattainable vision of the Good.[49]

For all this, in *Enneads* III, 8 (30), 11 we read that: (1) Nous is considered to be a kind of sight which is seeing and therefore a potentiality which has come to be an actuality and thus composed of form and matter. Intelligible matter, and Nous forms a double unity. (2) So, while the One needs nothing, Intellect does need the One, for in Intellect there subsists something *other* than the First, which is It Itself and nothing else, and which makes it be something different. (3) But still, in spite of the duality ingrained in matter, its desire for Good and its tendency towards It is complete; it attains what it desires, wholeness. Thus in Nous there persists a flawless adaptation between matter and form, induced by a firm and constant aspiration. This adaptation manifests itself as intellectual activity which is powerful, whole, and effective life and thereby beauty in itself, but a beauty which, although it be the height of movement, harmonious vigor, or unlimited activity, or complete joyous life, is not the Good; it is but its antechamber.[50] In the Good has its Principle, as the source of life, being, and knowledge. Therefore there is in Intellect, which is totally saturated with light, a double faculty, a double *dynamis*: one part is its total tendency toward itself in cautious intellectual moderation; the other, enraptured, seeks to break all limits, to be Silence and Nothingness,[51] no longer philosophy but rather the mysticism which makes whole again.[52]

It is that Intellect, so organized and self-constituted as a complete organism dependent upon the First, to which Plotinus refers, only once, as a "second god." The reference occurs in *Enneads* V, 5, 3 in the lessons preparatory to his treatise "Against the Gnostics"; the designation becomes fully meaningful only in so far as we also analyze the third point of our discussion on the third hypostasis.

Nous as a generating hypostasis.

But how does Intellect produce the Soul and by means of it the sensible world? Simply by contemplating itself, secure in itself, and by an excess of its own fullness, in imitation of the One.[53] On this point Plotinus is once again clear and coherent. The basis upon which he structures his teaching is the interpretation of the Platonic *Timaeus*.

An early statement of the difficulty is found in *Enneads* V, 9 (5), 3:

> It will be inquired . . . whether Nous is in itself at the same time both as the form in the bronze and as the one who creates (*poiesas*, maker) the form in the bronze. Transferring the same principles to the soul of the universe, at this point one will rise to Intellect, affirming that it is the true maker (*poieten*) and craftsman (*demiourgon*).[54]

In the same way there is an apparent contradiction reflected in *Enneads* III, 9 (13), 1:

> "Intellect," says Plato, "sees the Ideas which are in that which is the Living." Later he says: "the demiurge thought that what Intellect sees in that which is the Living, this universe may also have." Is he not saying, then, that ideas already exist prior to Intellect and that Intellect thinks them as they are existing? Therefore, one should first inquire whether the Living may be not Intellect, but something other than Intellect. That which contemplates is Intellect; thus the Living itself is not Intellect but the intelligible, and Intellect has outside itself that which it sees. In that case, it also has images and not the real things, if real things are there. For, as Plato says, the truth is there, in that which is, where each thing is "in itself." Therefore, even though one and the other are different, they are

not so separately, but only in that one is distinct from the other. Besides, so far as we are able to observe from the preceding statement, there is nothing to preclude that both be a unity and that they be distinguished by thought, because only in this way do the intelligible and that which understands exist. For the term "sees" by no means says in another, but in itself, since Intellect has the intelligible in it. But neither does anything prevent the intelligible from being an intellect in repose, unity, and silence; and nothing hinders the nature of the intellect which sees that intellect which is in itself from being a certain action of that intelligible which is intellect in repose, unity, and silence. This latter seeing the former, while it is seeing it, may be, so to speak, intellect of the former, because it thinks it. On the other hand, that which is thinking these things is also simultaneously intellect and intelligible, in order to produce in this world the four classes of the Living.[55]

Finally, in opposition to a Gnostic thesis, *Ennead* II, 9 (33), 1 refutes such a subdivision in the second hypostasis:

It is not even possible to do this in the things which come after these. One cannot conceive one intellect of some sort in a sort of repose and another in a kind of way in motion. What would the repose of Intellect be, and what its motion and "going forth," or what would be its inactivity, and what the work of the other intellect? Intellect is as it is, always the same, resting in static activity.[56]

Is it possible, then, having in mind the productive capacity of Nous, to imagine in it an inactive content, in itself an archetype and apart from the copy, and that same archetype as an active form? The same thing is true for a thorough analysis of any kind of craftsmanship. It appears upon examination to be a complicated activity which includes the universal model in the mind of the creator, fused with his own thought, and that same model when it is thought about in order to be molded into a specific piece of work for which it serves as a model. In the first case we would have an intellective action at rest and inoperative; in the second case, an intellective action in motion.

Thus approached, the difficulty is ultimately more Judaic and Christian than Greek in its origin, for in it is involved the decisive or volitional act (the act of decision or volition) which creates the world.[57]

According to *Timaeus* 39E, Plotinus, bearing in mind one aspect of the cosmogonic myth, recognizes the logical moments of content, thought and operation (*Enneads* V, 9, 3), but without accepting a literal anthropomorphic interpretation.

If the intelligible paradigms are outside intellect, Intellect, as Plato maintains, will not be true Intellect; for, with the immediacy of the known object-knowing subject broken, not the realities in themselves, but their intellectual reflections, will be in Intellect.[58] This topic, here presented in a very condensed form, is fully examined and considered proven[59] in the anti-Gnostic "Great Tetralogy." Besides, the separation of aspects in Intellect — in repose (*stasei*), unity, and silence (*henotati kai hesychia*), and in itself (*en auto*) and in self-contemplation — will be only an epinoetic distinction, but not real. As the philosopher expressed it at around that same time, "When we are thinking ourselves we are looking at a thinking nature."[60] Thinking itself is the restricted and secondary activity of a being which is thinking and which therefore can think itself. The character of intellect at rest (*hesychos*) is that which is underlying and proper to a being which can reflect upon itself, such as man; therefore, in the former, which is eternal and simultaneous or entirely being-life-knowledge, such a separation will never be possible.[61]

Consequently, when the Gnostics, specifically the Valentinians, distinguish really an Intellect in the bosom of God in silence and repose; that is to say, unuttered and inactive, as origin in itself of the Pleroma, and another which is uttered and in motion; that is, fixed as a total concept or sum of everlasting attributes and projected toward the real future world (the one which is to be saved) and the false one (the product of Sophia's fall), they are surreptitiously introducing into Plato's exegesis materials which have nothing to do with the Greek tradition.[62]

With the above-cited assertions in mind we shall enter into a full discussion of our second topic.

The "second god" among Platonists, Pythagorean-Platonists, and Gnostics. Plotinus's tradition.

The question is treated in the important chapter on "ideas as the thoughts of God" in Ancient Philosophy in which an essential role is played by Aristotle's proclamation on the unsurpassable sublimeness of Nous as the most excellent living god.[63] The chapter further treats of the different ways of dividing the interpretation of the demiurgic god of the *Timaeus* which gazes upon ideas,[64] in some cases possibly influenced by oriental religious thought.

The positions can be synthesized in three groups:

a. Those which consider ideas as forming a unity with the divine intellect.

b. Those which consider ideas to be external to divine thinking, coming from outside.

c. Those which consider ideas to be internal to the divine mind, but in the form of an internal process.

a. Behind this interpretation can be discovered a doctrine which may go back to the Ancient Academy,[65] but which in its most representative example may have adopted stipulations of Aristotelian philosophy. Such is the case with Albinus. He considers ideas as the thoughts or specific intellective actions of his first God or first Intellect. It is Intellect in actuality of itself and of those contents which are the paradigms of the world and of that world as a complete universe. The first god is first intellect and in actuality with respect to its own intellection, since it is the intellective basis of its eminently intellectual activity. In this sense it is light in itself, because it provides form itself the clarity of the cognitive action and its contents or intellectual objects and, in a second moment, is that cognitive and intellectual clarity for the celestial intellect. Ideas, then, are internal to God and are constantly generated by Him as his proper intellectual activity. God thinks himself and thinks ideas producing the cosmos according to such paradigms. To such a transcendent God the rational methods of negative theology may reasonably be applied, but with a meaning profoundly different from their application to Plotinus's One or to the "God who is not" of the Gnostic Basilides, for example. For while the One, by virtue of being Universal Possibility or productive Nothingness, is beyond all attribution, neither can the one-everything logically be named, because it would require all the names or attributes.[66]

b. In the second group are Atticus and Numenius. It is possible that Atticus may have reacted against an already Aristotelian Plato on this point, considering that the demiurge thinks the models, which as "first and fundamental natures" or ideas, are outside his thinking. The models thought are the archetypes which lead to things,[67] but as "realities in themselves" they are independent of the demiurgic thoughts.[68]

Numenius, however, considers a First Principle, first Nous, and first God, which is the Good in itself, Nous previous and superior to the intelligibles (ousia and idea), the One, etc. A second Nous is subordinate to it, a second god which contemplates the ideas, essences, or the beautiful and, applying them to sensible matter, creates the world.[69]

There is in Numenius, then, (1) a first god, in itself and also in life, which owes much of its characterization to Aristotle, and (2) a second intellect, called second god, which manifests a double function: at rest, contemplative and in motion, creative. The influence here may have been Gnostic.[70] His conception of the world, none the less, is Greek: third god and *poiema*.[71]

c. The third group, the one in which we are most interested at the moment, is that of the Gnostics.

In book II of his *Adversus Haereses*, Irenaeus of Lyon, pointing out the false doctrine taught by the Valentinians when they refer to the inexplicable fact of the divine generation of the Son by the Father, tries on several occasions to demonstrate the logical absurdities into which his adversaries fall. Among them is the glaring contradiction by which they proclaim two principal stages, moments, or levels in the constitution of the Pleroma (= second Neoplatonic hypostasis).

The following arguments demonstrate the logical absurdities which Irenaeus sought to expose:

1. It is impossible that the *Ennoia* (interpreted as notion) can generate Nous (= Intellect). Both it and Enthymesis (intention), thinking, reasoning, judgment, concept, etc. are activities of Intellect of a different cognitive nature. But these are all fixed in intellect and therefore cannot be its source. All the foregoing, obviously ill used by the Gnostics and imitating intellectual activities, breaks the unity of that which acts in a different way:

> But those who assert that Ennoia was produced by God, that Nous arose from Ennoia and afterwards in succession, Logos from both of these, ought, in the first place, to be censured for having made an improper use of these products.[72]

2. Since in God his Intellect (*Nous*) is identified with its ideal contents (*Logos*), then the prolation (*prolatio*) Bythos, Nous, Logos is false.[73]

3. If they maintain that the Father produced Intellect within Himself, recourse to production is superfluous.[74]

4. On the basis of this same mentality and wishing to find absurdities in the enumeration of the elements of the *triakontada* by excess and by defect, it is maintained with respect to the superior Ogdoad that it is impossible that Sige and Logos form part of the Pleroma, because they are conceptually opposed. And even though it be held that this Logos is not a perceptibly pronounced word but is rather internal, neither is there offered a coherent solution, for Logos in Sige eliminates Sige by being identified with it.[75]

Saint Irenaeus betrays in his objections the personal exegetic interests implicit in them, but at the same time stresses the technicalism of his adversaries, just as when Plotinus opposes them with other doctrinal concerns.

Behind the criticism of both opponents is the Valentinian teaching on the first pleromatic emission as transmitted by Ptolomeus:

> There is, so they say, a certain perfect Aeon previous to what is, in invisible and nameless heights. They call it Pre-Principle, Pre-Father, and Abyss. Incomprehensible, invisible, constant, and unbegotten, it was for endless centuries in peace and great solitude. Thinking (Ennoia), also called Grace and Silence, existed together with it. Once the Abyss thought of emitting from itself a Principle of all and this emission which he thought of emitting he placed like a seed within the womb of Silence who lived with him. Having received this seed and being pregnant she gave birth to an Intellect (Nous), similar and identical to the one who had emitted it and the only one which encompasses the grandeur of the Father. This Intellect they also call Only Begotten, Father, and Principle of all. Truth also was emitted along with it. This is the first and principal Pythagorean tetrad, also called root of all; for there are Abyss and Silence, and then Intellect and Truth. The Only Begotten, perceiving the purpose for which it was emitted, in like manner emits Reason and Life, as father of all who are to come after it and as principle and formation of the whole Pleroma. After Logos and Life, Man and Church are emitted as spouses. This likewise is the principal Ogdoad, origin and subsistence of the universe, which severally are called by four names: Abyss, Intellect, Logos, and Man.[76]

Summarizing the general conceptual line of discourse, then, we have: Ineffable Father and Only Begotten in its double aspect: (a) in potentiality, in the paternal apperception, once the mysteries of divine thought and will develop in the bosom of Silence into necessary external projection;[77] and (b) consolidation of thinking outward as Intellect or utterance of the Father, which analyzed, will constitute Plenitude, place, manifestation or glory of the Unutterable with all its eternal aeons or attributes. This is the image consisting of the unimaginable Simplicity, which is kept solidly united as total plenitude by a necessary maternal link, unspoken, pre-intellectual, and in the process of being formed; that is, the Ennoia as the unspokenness of the Father giving shelter to Thinking and Will.

Plotinus cannot accept this composition of the tetrad, because in it are combined elements of Greek and Semitic-Christian thinking which essentially subdivide Intellect into one internal and one external moment, so as to explain the generated as being not so much a product of the divine's spontaneity as of its thinking and will.[78]

In the first part of the Apocryphon of John, a Barbelo-Gnostic document from before 180 A.D., is found a remarkable attempt to describe the divine, expanding upon the incommunicable, intimate, or in itself fundament of the divinity. Given that constant and unchanging disposition which characterizes God in His very nature and which therefore is maintained uninterruptedly concealed and inexpressible by virtue of its natural propensity, any manifestation whatsoever is a betrayal of His being.[79] It is about the deepest plane or dimension of the divine, of the divine transcendence, in a proper sense. Consequently, to attempt to suggest the consistency of the divine reality in itself, several means of exposition are employed simultaneously.[80] He begins by describing how and what it is that may be revealed or manifested immediately about God by God's own self-experience, which already is a first or potential delimitation:

> What shall I be able to tell you about Him, the Inconceivable? He is the image of light. To the degree to which I may be able to know Him — for who will ever know Him? — and to the extent to which I may be able to tell you, [I shall speak to you of Him]. His aeon is indestructible, it is at rest, it rests in silence, it is the one that is before the All. He is therefore the head of all the Aeons, if there be something else with Him. He who perceives Himself in His own light which surrounds Him is the fountain of the water of life, light filled with purity. The fountain of the Spirit flowed from the living water of the light and arranged all the aeons and every kind of world. He recognized His own image when He saw it in the water of pure light which surrounds Him. His intellection accomplished a work; this was manifested and remained firm in His presence, in the radiance of the light. He is the Potency which is before the All, which was being revealed; the perfect Pre-Intellect of the All, the light, the likeness of the light, the image of the Invisible. He is the perfect Potency, Barbelus.[81]

This is the description of God's self-consciousness or direct experience of Himself while being naturally at the same time concealed or unknowable. As a first delimiting experience, it is the possibility of manifestation of the Pleroma. As a phase in emanation it is equal to the previous presentation of the Pleroma or spiritual plenitude which remains internally in potentiality of production, and therefore in the divine abyss or bosom, virginal Spirit, female cavern ready to open out fit to be displayed in pleromatic manifestation. It is, then, the unspoken Aeon which precedes the Aeons. It is the Aeon which exists "at rest and rests in silence"; that is, in peace with the divinity as its constant self-experience and as knowledge or secret word, unuttered, since it dwells mentally or internally in God. It is that level of the divine alone within itself, although self-conscious, which neither extends itself outward, nor projects itself architecturally in relation to history as the active attributes of divinity. Here we are in the Pre-Intellect or the Power of generating the Word, which becomes the uttered Word, Knowledge or the active Nous poured out away from the divine depth, once the supreme will thus determines it shall be.

In this way, the first divine irradiation or emission, its necessary doubling as perception of itself, rests upon its awesome unknowableness, foreshadowing in unspoken or internal synthesis the possibility of the totality of the articulated and distinct forms of the Pleroma, the plan of God. It is the divine mind, which looks simultaneously toward God and toward the world, that world which has the ability to be saved and so to be a part of the divine crown or glory. Thus, Pre-Intellect and Barbelus is also Triple Potentiality; that is, germinal possibility which contains within itself the subsequent crystallization of the Pleroma as androgynous divine pentad: the Only Begotten and the four luminaries which proceed from him.[82]

The *Epistle of Eugnostus* in its characterization of the Pre-Father, the Auto-Pater or Antopos, and his Antopoi, exhibits the same mental discipline. It includes the *Allogenes* and the *Zostrianus* known by Plotinus, further adding the analysis of the transcendental triad: Life, Intellect, and Being, in potentiality in the Father's rest and in actuality in the Pleroma. In the first instance, number would also be found as the generating power of order.[83] All of this must have led Plotinus to a series of philosophical elucidations subsequent to the "great treatise."[84] Also of utmost interest for the present study is Bruce's *Anonymus*, which we would identify with the *Apocalypse of Nicotheus* to which Porphyry alludes in *V.P.* XVI.[85]

From the first chapter, the above-mentioned writing points out that the first Father of All is the first eternity (*aei*), the Self-Generated and Self-Begotten Place, the Depth of the All (*bathos*), the unutterable and unknowable (*atnoi*) and the first sound until it is perceived and comprehended by the All. In this sense it is also said of him that he is the great Abyss and first Fountain.[86] The second Place, however, is rightly demiurge, father, logos, source, nous, man, eternal (*aidios*) and infinite (*aperantos*) and Father of the all. Reasonably, he is "the fountain (*pegē*) which flows out from Silence (*karof*)," whose head is crowned by the aeons.[87] We will not linger to explain the implications of a doctrine which gives so much importance to the Gnostic interpretation of John I:1.[88] None the less, it is worth noting that the "silent fount,"[89] also Pre-Father, Protophanes and Self-Begotten,[90] as a monad which is connaturally *anousios* and through which that state of definitive rest is attained,[91] proceeds from the One *stricto sensu* and that the said monad is the embryonic Totality.[92] Similarly, Setheus or the hidden or potential Only Begotten (*Ennoia*) which includes the three powers that are in each power[93] becomes Nous and the demiurgic or creative Word.[94] It is likewise immeasurable depth and as Father-Mother, like the aforementioned first Father, Mother of the All.[95] Thus it is spoken of the Father/Mother/Son trinity:

> And they praised the One and the internal Thought (Ennoia) and the intelligible Word (*logos noeron*). And thus did they glorify the three which are one, for because of him they became of no substance (*anousios*).[96]

The internal Thought referred to is the Mother, monad in stillness (*eremos*) and repose (*hesychia*) which begets the Only Begotten. It is appropriate to recall that herein lies the Gnostic's goal of ascent or liberation and that this is represented by the body of light (*soma nouein*) or immortal body (*athanatos*). This body is obtained once the grace of the Only Begotten, Father of the particles of light, the unction or eternal crown, is received.[97] The resurrection of bodies is attained through him. The topic and the expression were in circulation at the same time among the Valentinians and Plotinus also tried to correct such great confusion on the part of his adversaries.[98]

Conclusion

In the last analysis, it seems to us that in *Enneads* II, 9, 1 and 6, Plotinus has in mind the Valentinian Gnostics with whom he disputes in the *Adversus Gnosticos* and in other parts of the Enneads.[99] It appears that with respect to the notion of the "second god," there is a clash of two doctrines of analogous structure, both nourished by the same philosophical literature, but different in their essential fundamental intuitions. On the one hand we would distinguish the Gnostic tradition of Jewish and Christian esoteric origin, whose speculations regarding the Name of God, internal, invisible, or in peace and uttered, comprehensible, or in motion,[100] may have, under the philosophical form of Gnosis, influenced the *Chaldaean Oracles*, Numenius, and the *Corpus Hermeticum*.[101] This tradition subdivides the Second Hypostasis regarding the divinity into its intrinsic nature and its action in creation and history. On the other hand, we would emphasize the tradition which Plotinus follows which in framing its Second

Hypostasis views it as the Living in itself or ideal world, having Plato essentially in mind but without underestimating the Aristotelian conception of nous.[102] It further enriches its internal structure with elements drawn from Pythagorean-Platonism which date back to the Ancient Academy, specifically to Speussipus, concerning the exegesis of the ideal numbers, in particular that of the *tetraktys*:

> . . . the remaining other half of the book is entirely about the decad, demonstrating it to be the most natural and perfect of beings, like an artifice form with respect to cosmic effects (but not existing because we may happen to have believed or established it) and pre-existent as a totally perfect model for the god maker of the universe.[103]

This unitary and hierarchical manner [way] of interpreting Intellect must have been transmitted through authors whose entire works and testimonies escape [are lost to] us: Neo-Pythagoreans,[104] Eudorus of Alexandria,[105] and Moderatus of Gades.[106] Nicomachus of Gerasa shines as a glowing link in this series.[107]

The terminology of the tetrad as *fountain and root*[108] was assimilated by Plotinus with arithmological and ontological rigor. The Valentinians, for their part, identified them with their own ideas and hermeneutical concerns.[109] Nicomachus of Gerasa combined sounds, letters, and numbers,[110] as did also the Gnostics and soon thereafter the Valentinians, such as Mark the Magus.[111] It was also Nicomachus who allowed writings of Zoroaster and Ostanes as sources of his information.[112] At this juncture it is possible to surmise how the lines could become confused and to explain why the Valentinian Gnostics of Plotinus's school represented themselves as coming from the *traditional philosophy,* that of Pythagoras and Plato, though believing that in the conceptual development of the intelligible world/Pleroma their elaborations were more profound.[113] It is likewise understandable that Plotinus should have rejected their claims to traditionalism and sagacity.[114] At the same time it can also be shown how some recently discovered Gnostic text, such as the *Tractatus Tripartitus*, could owe its composition to Plotinus's anti-Gnostic polemic and contact with doctrinal aspects touching on these same topics.[115]

NOTES

1. See Porphyry, *V.P.* IV, 66-68, years 259-260, according to J. Igal, *Le cronologia de la vida de Plotino de Porfirio* (Bilbao, 1972), p. 98.

2. The last textual citations are of Parmenides fr. 28 B3; B8, 26, 43, 6, and Plato, *Parmenides* 137 c- 142 a, 144 e 5 and 155 e 5.

3.   Cf. J. Souilhé, Platon, *Lettres* (Paris, 1960), pp. lxxvii-xxxii and H.D. Saffrey-
       L.G. Westerink, Proclus, *Théologie Platonicienne* II (Paris, 1974), pp. xx-lix.
       Plotinus quotes the passage thirteen times. See P. Henry-H.R. Schwyzer,
       Plotini Opera III (Oxford, 1982), p. 349 and below footnote no. 99.

4.   Cf. E.R. Dodds, "The Parmenides of Plato and the Origin of the
       Neoplatonic One," *CQ* 22 (1928): 129-142; J.M. Rist, "The Neoplatonic
       One and Plato's Parmenides," *TAPA* 93 (1962): 389-401; Ph. Merlan, in
       A.H. Armstrong (ed.), *The Cambridge History of Later Greek and Early
       Medieval Philosophy* (Cambridge, 1967), pp. 91-94; H.R. Schwyzer,
       "Plotinos," in P.W., Band XXI, 552-554, and H.D. Saffrey-L.G. Westerink,
       Proclus, *Théologie Platonicienne* I (Paris, 1968), pp. lxxvii-lxxix.

5.   On the base of fr. 28B 3 (seven times) and B 8 (thirteen times). About
       Parmenides in Plotinus cf. V. Cilento, *Saggi su Plotino* (Milano, 1973), pp.
       123-134; G. Calogero, "Plotino, Parmenide e il 'Parmenide,'" in *Plotino e
       il Neoplatonismo in Oriente e in Occidente* (Roma, 1974), pp. 49-59, and at
       present the full reference in Henry-Schwyzer, op. cit., p. 347.

6.   Cf. *Enn.* IV, 7 (2), 9, i ff., 10-19, teaching that Plotinus here put on the
       Soul as immortal being and beginning of all life, but that with more reason
       it concerns the being in itself. For the reference to the Soul see R. Harder,
       Plotinus Schriften Bd. Ib, Anm. p. 386.

7.   Cf. *Enn.* VI, 4 (22), 4, 25 (πᾶν ὁμοῦ); IV, 3, (27), 5, 5-8 (οἱ νόες οὐκ
       ἀπολοῦνται); VI, 6 (34), 18, 7-8 (ἀλλ' ὅς ἔστι, πᾶς ἔστιν ἐν ὃν καὶ ὁμοῦ καὶ
       ὅλος); III, 7 (45), 5, 19-21 (τὸ εἶναι ὡς ἀτρεμές); ibid. 11, 3-4 (τὴν ἀτρεμῆ
       ἐκείνην καὶ ὁμοῦ πᾶσαν) and 53-54 (τὸ ἐν συνεχείᾳ ἔν).

8.   Cf. *Enn.* V, 9 (5), 26-30 and see farther on. III, 8 (30), 8, 6-8; VI, 7 (38),
       41, 18 ff.; I, 4 (46), 10, 6; III, 5 (50), 7, 50-52.

9.   Cf. likewise *Enn.* V, 6 (24), 6, 22-24 and VI, 6 (34), 18, 42-46.

10.   Although there are references in *Enn.* I, 6 (1), 5, 17-18, and 6, 18-20; IV,
       7 (2), 10,34 ff. and 13 *in initio*, and IV, 2 (4), 1.

11.   Cf. *Enn.* V, 9, 1, 1-2, 10, with Bréhier's *Ennéades* V, p. 153.

12.   Cf. 2, 20-27. With more technical development *Enn.* V, 5 (32) 1-2 and V,
       3 (49), 5.

13.   Cf. 3, 1 ff.; 4, 2-3, and see below.

14.   Cf. 5, 1-4.

15.   Cf. 5, 4-16. For the conception "*tais epinoiais*" see F. García Bazán,
       "Sobre la nocion de 'epinoiai' en *Eneada* II, 9 (33), 2, 1," in *Cuadernos de
       Filosofia* 26-27 (1977): 83-94.

16.   Cf. 5, 24-38.

17.   According to the developments of the chapter 6, 7, 8, and 9. See likewise
       Enn. IV, 8 (6), 3, 5-10.

18.   Cf. *Enn.* VI, 9 (9). 5, 7ff. as well.

19.   Cf. *Enn.* V, 9, 9, 8 with *Tim.* 39 E. In 6, 10, ff. it is remarked the relation
       genus/ideas; all/parts; seed/capacities.

20.   Cf. 8 *in initio*. Likewise 6, 9.

21.   See 6, 33 ff.; 7, 11 ff.

22.   Cf. 9, 15.

23. Cf. 8, 16-19.
24. Cf. 10, 9-15.
25. Cf. also *Enn.* V, 1 (10), 4, 9-10; 17-18 and VI, 9, 9 *in initio*.
26. Cf. *Sophist* 254 d-e. See P. Hadot, *Porphyre et Victorinus* I (Paris, 1968), pp. 216-222; J.M. Charrue, *Plotin lecteur de Platon* (Paris, 1978), pp. 206-229.
27. Cf. *Enn.* V, 1 (10), 4, 21-36 and 41-43.
28. Cf. *Enn.* VI, 2 (43), 8.
29. Cf. *Enn.* VI, 2, 18, 12-15; 20, 10-29; 21, 47-59 and VI, 6 (34), 15, 1 ff.
30. Cf. *Enn.* VI, 6, 8 *in fine* and 9.
31. Cf. *Enn.* VI, 6, 16, 20-30.
32. Cf. *Enn.* VI, 6, 9 *in fine* (for the full exegesis of the treatise see J. Bertier, L. Brisson, A. Charles, J. Pépin, H.D. Saffrey, A. Ph. Segonds, Plotin, *Traité sur les nombres (Enneade VI, 6 [34])*, Paris (1980), cf. likewise H.J. Krämer, *Der Ursprung der Geistmetaphysik*, Amsterdam (1967), pp. 298-311. Cf. also *Enn.* V, 5 (32), 4.
33. Cf. *Enn.* I, 3 (20), 3-5.
34. Cf. *Enn.* V, 9 (5), 14 *in initio*.
35. Cf. *Enn.* V, 4 (7), 2, 22-26.
36. Cf. *Enn.* V, 1 (10), 6, 28-30 and F. García Bazán, *Neoplatonismo y Vedanta. La doctrina de la materia en Plotino y Shankara* (Buenos Aires, 1982), p. 75.
37. Cf. *Enn.* VI, 8 (39), 18, 25 ff.
38. Cf. *Enn.* V, 2 (11), 1, 6-9.
39. Cf. *Enn.* V, 4 (7), 1, 23-34 and see F. García Bazán, op. cit., p. 79.
40. Cf. *Enn.* VI, 9, (9), 5, 27-29 and III, 8 (30), 35-36 with our commentary in op. cit., pp. 15 and 45.
41. Cf. *Enn.* V, 4 (7), 2, 38.
42. Cf. *Enn.* V, 1 (10), 5, 3-19 and see F. García Bazán, op. cit., p. 14.
43. Cf. *Enn.* VI, 9 (9), 6, 42.
44. Cf. *Enn.* VI, 9, 8, 29-36.
45. Cf. pp. 59-60.
46. Cf. *Enn.* V, 1 (10), 4, 31-43.
47. Cf. F. García Bazán, *Neoplatonismo y Vedanta*, pp. 17-19.
48. Cf. *Enn.* II, 4 (12), 5 *in fine*.
49. Cf. García Bazán, op. cit., pp. 27ff. and likewise J. Igal, *Porfirio, Vida de Plotino. Plotino, Enéadas I-II* (Madrid, 1982), pp. 418-419 with the footnotes.
50. Cf. *Enn.* VI, 9 (9), 4, 10 ff.; V, 8 (31), ch. 8 to 11; V, 5 (32), 12; VI, 7 (38), 32, etc.
51. Cf. *Enn.* VI, 7 (38), 35-36 and see likewise V, 8 (31), 10, 32-35.
52. Cf. our paper: "Filosofia, religion y teurgia," in *Primeras Jornadas de la Sociedad Argentina de Historia de las Religiones* (Buenos Aires), August, 1983.
53. Cf. *Enn.* V, 2 (11), 1, 9-18. See *Neoplatonismo y Vedanta*, p. 81.
54. See lines 19-24.

55.   See formerly our *Plotino y la Gnosis* (Buenos Aires, 1981), p. 277, n. 9.
56.   Cf. *Enn.* II, 9 (33), 25-30.
57.   Cf. Proverbs 8, 22 ff.; Aristobulos Judaeus, *Wisdom* 7, 22-8, 1, Philo (see the docket of Eusebius in *Praeparatio Evangelica* VII, 12, 2-15, 2) and G. Kittel, ThWzNT, *sub voc. lego*, IV, 139-140. For the two *Logoi* in the primitive patristic that also have relations with this theme cf. F. García Bazán in *Revista Biblica* (1981/4), p. 237, n. 9.
58.   Cf. *Enn.* V, 5 (32), 1-2.
59.   Cf. *Enn.* II, 9 (33), 1, 33-57.
60.   Cf. *Enn.* III, 9 (13), 6.
61.   Cf. *Enn.* V, 8 (31), chapters 3 to 6 with an implicit gnostic terminology and the repulse of the artisan image in Ch. 7. Cf. *Plotino y la Gnosis ad loc.*
62.   Cf. *Enn.* II, 9 (33), 6, 14 y ss. Can be seen the remarks of D.J. O'Meara in *The Rediscovery of Gnosticism* I (Leiden, 1980), pp. 374-378.
63.   Cf. Aristotle, *Met.* 1072 b 19 ff. and 1074 b ff. and R. Bultmann *sub voc. Zoe* in ThWzNT, II, 834 ff. See T.A. Szlezak, *Platon und Aristoteles in der Nuslehre Plotins* (Basel/Stuttgart, 1979), pp. 139ff. and G. Verbeke, in D.J. O'Meara (ed.), *Studies in Aristotle* (Washington, 1981), pp. 116ff.
64.   Cf. A.N.M. Rich, "The Platonic Ideas as the Thoughts of God," in *Mnemosyne*, Ser. IV, 7 (1954): 123-133; A.H. Armstrong, in *Les Sourcês de Plotin*, Entretienns sur l'Antiquité Classique V (Génève, 1960), pp. 391-425; J. Pépin, *Théologie cosmique et théologie chrètienne* (Paris, 1964), pp. 17-71; D.J. O'Meara, *Structures hierarchiques dans la pensèe de Plotin* (Leiden, 1975), pp. 19-31; E. Zeller/R. Mondolfo, *La filosofia dei Greci*, II, III/2, pp. 958-962.
65.   Cf. Xenocrates Frs. 15, 69, 16, 68 y 36 (Heinze, pp. 164-165; 187; 165; 187 and 172); can be seen Krämer, op. cit. pp. 40-46 and in *Theologie und Philosophie*, XLIV (1969): 481-505; Speussipos, Fr. 38 (Lang, p. 71) and Aristotle, *Peri euches* Fr. 1 (Ross, p. 57), see J. Pépin, *Idées greques sur l'homme et sur Dieu* (Paris, 1971), pp. 249ff. On the testimony of Alcimus (Diogenes Laertius III, 13), see R.E. Witt, *Albinus*, 1937 (reprint Amsterdam, 1971), p. 71 and the critique of H. Cherniss, *Aristotle's Criticism of Plato and the Academy* I (New York, 1944), pp. 498-499.

    I believe that at this ancient tradition are linked the scattered rests testified by Varro *apud* Augustine, *De civitate Dei* VII, 28; Seneca, *Epist.* 65, 7, into of the Stoic line which has done of the Logos/Pneuma/*pyr technykon* the form of all the forms of the things (*logoi spermatikoi*) (cf. M. Pohlenz, *La Stoa*, Firenze 1967, I pp. 125ff.), and for the transition of the transcendent *Nous* to the immanent *logos* see J. Moreau, *L'Âme du Monde de Platon aux Stoiciens* (Paris, 1939), pp. 94ff., A.J. Festugière, *La RHT* II (Paris, 1949), pp. 153ff., H.J. Krämer, *Platonismus und Hellenistische Philosophie* (Berlin-New York, 1971), pp. 117ff. I should like to connect the teaching of Antiochus of Ascalon (see formerly W. Theiler, *Die Vorbereitung des Neuplatonismus* [Berlin/Zurich, 1934], pp. 34-48) — strongly eclectic and wishing to be linked with Polemon, to this mentality (cf. J. Dillon, *The Middle Platonists* [London, 1977], pp. 93-95 mainly). Philo

Judaeos undoubtedly support the notion of "kosmos noëtos" (the "one day") as the thoughts of God, but to interpret the *Timaeus* according to a determinate Jewish scheme and against the spiritual interpretation (platonic-pythagorean) (cf. *De opific. mundi* 15-35; 36 *in initio*, 55 initio; 76, 129, 134 and 139; *De Prov.* I, 7; *De Poster.* 91; *De confus. ling.* 81 and 146-147 with footnotes of pp. 176-182 (J.G. Kahn's edition, Paris, 1963). Cf. also A.F. Segal, *Two Powers in Heaven* (Leiden, 1977), pp. 159-181.

Other independent or platonizing evidences: Aetius, *Placita* I, 3, 21; Diog. Laertius III, 69 ("he calls God mind and cause"); Apuleius speaks of the "primus deus" (cf. *De Platone* I, VI, 193), but not of the ideas as "thoughts of God." See, however, I, IX, 199: *"sed illam . . . subservire etiam fabricatori deo et praesto esse ad omnia inventa ejus pronuntiat"* and also II, I, 220: *"Prima bona esse deum summun mentemque illam, quam noun idem vocat,"* also *Apol.* 64, 5-7: *"ratio . . . opifex . . . sine operatione opifex."* Maximus of Tyre in *Dissertationes* XVII (Dübner), 5 *in initio*: θεὸς εἷς πάντων βασιλεύς, καὶ πατήρ, καὶ θεοὶ πολλοί, θεοῦ παῖδες, συνάρχοντες θεοῦ; 8 *in fine*: ὁ νοῶν ἀεὲ, καὶ πάντα, καὶ ἅμα, and 9, 30-31: πατέρα καὶ γεννητὴν τοῦ σύμπαντος. Can be seen Festugière, *La RHT IV*, pp. 111-115; Galen in *Compendium Timaei Platonis* II, 15-26, says: *"Deinde propositum considerare instituit secundum quod (creator) opus suum exstruxerit; atque dixit eum id ita exstruxisse ut semper permaneret. . . . Quam duabus illis quas commemoraverat -creatori scilicet et effigiei ad quam (mundum) creavit. . .",* R. Walzer (ed.), *Plato Arabus* I-III, London (rep. 1973), pp. 39-40. Cf. A.J. Festugière, in *Études de Philosophie Grecque*, Paris (1971), pp. 494-495. Hippolytus, *Elenchos* I, 19, 1-4: . . .Τὸ δὲ παράδειγμα τὴν διάνοιαν τοῦ θεοῦ εἶναι, ὁ καὶ ἰδέαν καλεῖ . . .

66. Cf. *Epitome* IX, 1, 2, *in fine*, 3 *in initio*; X, 2, 3, 4, 5 *in fine* and XII, 1, 2, 3. Cf. roughly G. Invernizzi, *Il Didaskalikos di Albino e il medioplatonismo* I-II (Roma, 1976). For the last assertion see already S. Lilla, *Clement of Alexandria* (Oxford, 1971), pp. 223-226, with other references concerning Clement, (*nous de chora ideon*), Ammonius Saccas and Origen the Neoplatonist.

67. Cf. *Fr. 9, Apud*, Eusebius, *Praep. Ev.* XV, 13, 1-6 (E. des Places, pp. 67-69). See also frs. 12 and 13 (des Places, pp. 70-71).

68. For our interpretation cf. E. des Places, Atticus. *Fragments* (Paris, 1977), p. 86, Fr. 9.

69. Cf. fr. 11, (des Places) (L.20), 15 (L.24), 16 (L.25).

70. Cf. fr. 12 (L.21), 19 (L.28), 18 (L.27), 17 (L.26), 5 (L.14), 6 (L.15), 20 (L.29).

71. Cf. F. García Bazán, *Plotino y la Gnosis*, pp. 279-281. For Amelius, who interprets the three gods or kings of the *Second Letter* in relation to *Tim.* 39 e, cf. ibid., pp. 281-282. On Longinus see Porphyry V.P. XX and *Plotino y la Gnosis*, p. 189, note 1.

72. Cf. *Adversus Haereses* II, XV, 2-3 (Harvey I, pp. 281-282). For the trivial use of *ennoia* as conception with Stoic meaning between the Christian writers cf. M. Spanneut, *Le stoicisme des pères de l'Église* (Paris, 1957), pp. 204ff.

73. Cf. *Adv. Haer.* II, XLII, 2-3 (Harvey I, pp. 354-355).

74. Cf. *Adv. Haer.* II, XVI, 2 (Harvey I, pp. 283-284).

75. Cf. *Adv. Haer.* II, XIV, 1 (Harvey I, p. 278).

76. Cf. *Adv. Haer.* I, I, 1 (Harvey I, pp. 8-10; A. Rousseau-L. Doutreleau, S. Ch. no. 264, pp. 29-31).

77. That is to say the *"dynamei kai energeia"* of *Enn.* II, 9, 1, 24-25 implicated in *"ennoethenai pote"* of S. Irenaeus. Cf. *Adv. Haer.* I, 12, 1 (Harvey I, pp. 109-110). Ennoia is the necessary female element of the bisexual God (cf. Irenaeus's and Hippolytus's doubts in F.M. Sagnard, *La Gnose Valentinienne* [Paris, 1947], pp. 349-350) for the phenomenon of the autogenesis, the only that produces permanent beings without necessity of an external partner to generate.

78. Nous in repose, Nous which contemplates and Nous which plans (Ennoia, Monogenes or Nous and Logos), but often is considered as maker the Soul (i.e. the external Sophia) or him, because he inspires the Sophia by means of the Second Logos — *Enn.* II, 9, 1, 57 ff. — Cf. *Enn.* II, 9, 6, 19-23. The *Evangelium Veritatis* (*NHC* I, 3) relates the theme of the Word and the stable generation which are implicated in the Irenaeus exposition (cf. E.V. 16, 31-17, 1; 19, 34-20, 2; 21, 18-22, 15; 24, 6-20; 26, 34-27, 31; 36, 35-41, 3).

79. Cf. our *Gnosis* 2 (Buenos Aires, 1978), pp. 104-111 and likewise Y. Janssens in *Le Muséon* 83 (1970): 157-165, and 84 (1971): 403-432.

80. Cf. F. García Bazán in *Revista Biblica* 4 (1981): 234-235.

81. Cf. *Ap. Johannis* 26.1-27.14.

82. Cf. F. García Bazán, l.c., pp. 236-238. For one extensive discussion concerning the Pleromas' formation see A. Orbe, *Estudios Valentinianos* IV (Roma, 1966), pp. 39-174.

83. Cf. García Bazán, l.c., pp. 239-244.

84. Cf. *Allogenes* (*NHC* XI, 3), 48.20 ff. and 63.5-10 with the footnote no. 32 in F. García Bazán, l.c., p. 247.

85. Cf. F. García Bazán, *"Plotino y los textos gnosticos de Nag-Hammadi,"* in *Oriente-Occidente* II/2 (1981): 196-202.

86. Cf. *The Books of Jeu and the Untitled Text in the Bruce Codex*, text edited by Carl Schmidt. Translation and notes by Violet MacDermot (Leiden, 1978), p. 226.

87. Cf. Chapter 2, pp. 226-227.

88. Cf. Ch. 7, pp. 237-238 and our observations on Tatian (*Adv. Graecos* 5, 1) in l.c., p. 237, note 9.

89. Cf. Ch. 14, p. 254.

90. Cf. Ch. 13, pp. 252-253.

91. Cf. Ch. 10, p. 245.

92. Cf. Ch. 7, p. 236.

93. Cf. Ch. 11, p. 246 and also Ch. 10, p. 243.
94. Cf. Ch. 11, p. 247 and Ch. 12, p. 248.
95. Cf. Ch. 11, p. 246.
96. Cf. Ch. 21, p. 266.
97. Cf. Ch. 23, pp. 242-243.
98. Cf. Epiphanius, *Panarion* 31, 7, 6 and F. García Bazán, in *Oriente-Occidente* 3 (1981/1): 36 and n. 70.
99. Concerning the phrase of *Enn.* V, 5 (32), 3, confront also with *Enn.* II, 9, 6, 34 and 39, where the First Hypostasis (*to proton*, 1. 32) is called *he prota physis* and *protos theos* (see also *Enn.* III, 9 [13], 7). The fundament of the reasoning is always the interpretation of the *Second Letter* 312e traditional already to Plotinus as three levels of reality, three kings, three gods (cf. *Enn.* IV, 7 [2], 13 *in fine*; V, 4 [7], 1, 3-5; V, 1 [10], 8, 1-4; VI, 4 [22], 11, 9; VI, 5 [23], 4, 21 and 24 *in fine*; III, 5 [50] 8, 8). Therefore the *Second God* cannot be divided and it is capricious the exegesis of the Valentinians on this text (cf. Hippolytus, *Elenchus* VI, 37, 6-8). The Psalm of the Valentinus is not sound, but the explanation of *Enn.* VI, 7 (38), 42, 3-25 (ratified by *Enn.* I, 8 [51], 2). According to Plotinus the exegetic twistings of the Gnostics are manifest as well as in *Enn.* II, 9, 9, 26 ff. that it is linked to the theme of *Great King* (cf. *Plotino y la Gnosis*, p. 191, n. 13; 194, n. 47 and 260 n. f.). The same triadic scheme is applied to Ouranos, Kronos and Zeus in the *great tetralogy* (cf. P. Hadot, in H.J. Blumenthal and R.A. Markus (eds.), *Neoplatonism and Early Christian Thought, Essays in honor of A.H. Armstrong* [London, 1981], pp. 124-137). *Enn.* VI, 8 (39), 9, 18-23, nevertheless, could go against the Neoplatonist Origen for these reasons: 1) the title of his book: *That the King is the Only Maker,* that identifies the first Principle with god as Nous (king and maker); 2) the Nous is justified by itself, therefore the One is by chance and king of chance (cf. the information and vocabulary about the first Principle of Origin according to Proclus, *Theol. Plat.* II, 4); there are not strong reasons to assert the gnostic nature of *Enn.* VI, 8, 7, 11-15 or 11, 13-22, cf. *Plotino y la Gnosis*, pp. 306-308.
100. Cf. *Ev. Ver.* 36, 35-40, 33 and *Extracts of Theodotus* 22, 4-5; 26, 1-27, 1; 31, 3; 80, 3; 82, 1. Cf. H. Bietenhard, art. *Onoma,* in ThWzNT, V, 265 ff.; G. Scholem, in *Conoscenza Religiosa* 4 (1973): 375-412; I. Gruenwald, *Apocalyptic and Merkavah Mysticism* (Leiden, 1980), pp. 10ff.; J. Danielou, *Théologie du Judéo-Christianism* (Paris, 1957), pp. 199-216; G. Quispel, in *The Jung Codex* (London, 1953), pp. 66-76; A. Orbe, *Estudios Valentinianos* I: 69-97; F. García Bazán, in *Filosofar Cristiano* 9-12 (1981-1982): 230-237. Perhaps this transcendent concentration be analogous to the mystic trance: *"loquente vero eo in spiritu sancto in audito omnium statim tacuit. Et exinde videbant stantem quemdam ante eum. Oculi autem eius erant aperti, os vero clausum, sed inspiratio sancti spiritus erat cum illo"* (*Ascensio Isaiae*, VI, 10-12). Can be seen also Gruenwald, op. cit., p. 58, n. 102.

101. Cf. *Oracles* 18 (πατρικὸν βυθόν); 28 (ἐκ τριάδος κόλπος); 4 (δύναμις σὺν ἐκείνῳ, νοῦς ἀπ' ἐκείνου); 20 (ἄνευ νοὸς νοητοῦ, καὶ τὸ νοητὸν οὐ νοῦ); 7 (νῷ δευτέρῳ); 8 (δυάς... ἀμφότερον... νῷ, αἴσθεσιν); 31 and 22 about the triad. Cf. also the interpretation of Michael Psellus, *Ekthesis* 1149: 1-10; *Hypotyposis in initio* and *Neoplatonismo y Vedanta*, p. 116 and *Revista Biblica* (1981/4): 238, n. 9 *in fine*. For C.H. see *Poimandres* 8, 9, 11; C. H. 2, 13 and 14; C.H. XII, 1, 14. In C.H. VIII, 1, 2, 5 and X, 10, the "second god" is the world, image of the First. Cf. C.H. Dodd, *The Bible and the Greeks* (London, 1935), pp. 115, 128ff., 132ff., 194ff. For parallels with the *Hermetica* of Nag Hammadi see J.P. Mahé, *Hermes en Haute-Egypte* (Québec, 1978).

102. Cf. A.H. Armstrong, *The Architecture of the Intelligible Universe in the Philosophy of Plotinus* (Cambridge, 1940) (reimp. 1967), pp. 76-81 and Th. A. Szlezak, op. cit., pp. 160-166.

103. Cf. Fr. 4 (Lang, p. 54).

104. Cf. Aetius, *Placita*, I, 3, 8 and A. Delatte, *Études sur la littérature pythagoricienne* (Paris, 1915), p. 249ff. Likewise Archytas, *Peri Archon*, p. 280, 11-14 and *Peri tes dekados*, 1-5 (H. Thesleff, *The Pyth. Textes*, pp. 20-21).

105. Cf. J. Dillon, op. cit., pp. 128-129.

106. Cf. Simplicius *In Phys.* 230, 37-231, 1: "while the Second One — which is the 'truly existent' and the object of intellection — he says is the Forms." C.H. fr. 28 is an isolated evidence of this kind of trend of ideas. Cf. A.J. Festugière, *Hermétisme et mystique paienne* (Paris, 1967), pp. 131-137.

107. Cf. *Int. to Arithm.* I, VI, 1 (transl. H.L. D'Ooge) and I, IV 2. Besides for the expression "*pegē kai rixa*," "into which everything is resolved and out of which everything is made," see I, XI, 3. Cf. the commentary of J. Bertier, Nicomaque de Gérase, *Introduction of Arithmétique* (Paris, 1978), pp. 148, 3; 150, n. 2; 151, 3; but the metaphor of principle/fountain/mother/ and root is dynamic, one twofold reality in gestation, the female with her offspring. With the same expressive force it is used by Plotinus in *Enn.* VI, 6, 9, 38 (see already note 32) for the essential number, because it is not first, but double. In *Enn.* III, 8, (30), 10, however, he uses the images of the fountain and the root to mean the One, separately, as every symbol can mean the absolute origin and end.

108. Cf. the former note.

109. Cf. the textes gathered by Sagnard, op. cit., pp. 335ff. assimilable to the "fountain and root" (see Irenaeus, *Adv. Haer.* I. XV, *in fine* — Harvey I, p. 189 — and Hippolytus, *Elenchos* V, 26, 2).

110. Cf. *Int. to Arith.* II, 1, 1 and Flora R. Levin, *The Harmonics of Nicomachus and the Pythagorean Tradition*, The American Philological Association (1975), pp. 33, 52 and 55-56.

111. Cf. Irenaeus, *Adv. Haer.* I, 21, 5 and I, 14, 1-9 and 15, 1-3.

112. Cf. *Theol. Ar.* 56, 15 and see Bidez-Cumont, *Les Mages Hellénisés* (Paris, 1938), II, p. 283. Here is fundamental the notion of Plotinus about the *"palaioi"* strictly Greek and transcendentalist against Gnostics, Eclectics, and so on.

113. Cf. *Enn.* ii, 9, 6 and Porphyry V.P. XVI.

114. That which limits their interest to Pleroma and its procession, the rupture of the spiritual world and the liberation of Pneumatics, therefore they repulse all the rest. In this manner they make fun of all the Greek cosmology. Cf. *Enn.* II, 9, 6, etc.

115. Cf. our discussion in *Revista Biblica* (1981/4): 245-250.

Synesius, the Hermetica and Gnosis

Jay Bregman

Synesius of Cyrene,[1] 365-414? C.E., studied Neoplatonism in the 390s with Hypatia at Alexandria. His early works already demonstrate familiarity with all of the pagan syncretistic religious currents of the age: Neoplatonic-Pythagorean, Chaldaean, and Hermetic. A distinguished member of the *Boule* of Cyrene, he made Christian friends at home, as well as in Constantinople and Alexandria. Theophilus, the patriarch of Alexandria, presided at his wedding to a Christian. In the works of his middle and later years he used Christian imagery in an attempt to reconcile his pagan views with the new religion to which he was building bridges. At times his ideas are reminiscent of Gnostic and Hermetic notions. By 410, when he became Bishop of Ptolemais, he still maintained a Platonic position[2] on the eternity of the Cosmos and the pre-existence of the soul, and he considered the resurrection to be an allegorical presentation of an ineffable mystery. He promised that as bishop he would "mythicize in public, but philosophize in private." (Garzya, 105) So his expressed intention was to tell a Christian story to the congregation and to reserve the right to understand the nature of things according to Platonic dogma.

During his sojourn at Constantinople Synesius visited churches and temples as places that contained divinity; demonstrating the tolerance of his religious position. Hypatia's "school" probably included Christians, and was "confessional neutral." It is also likely that she was familiar with the *Hermetica*.[3] She principally followed Porphyry's teaching, which enabled Synesius to "telescope" the hypostases and read the First Intelligible Triad of the Chaldaean Oracles as the horizontal *on-zoe-nous* — being-life-intelligence; ironically an old

85

"Gnostic-Platonist" doctrine easy to harmonize with an Orthodox view of the Trinity. In this interpretation his ideas resembled those of Marius Victorinus.[4] In line with Porphyry's critique of the Incarnation, Synesius remained vague on the issue. Perhaps he saw it as similar to the "divine-man" epiphanies from the *Lives* of Apollonius of Tyana and Pythagoras: a man-god incarnation on one of the lower rungs of the *seira* (of being and existence).[5] The Hermetic myth (of the Anthropos) should also be taken into account, since it is a pagan myth in which *nous* itself, or a close relative of *nous*, is *both* cosmological and soteriological;[6] whereas even the *noetic* or intellectual Helios-Mithras of the later Hellenes does not descend himself, but sends down Asclepius "with his saving right hand."[7]

It is necessary to make certain assumptions about Synesius with respect to Gnostic influences on his thought. He was a conservative Hellenic gentleman who expressed himself in Greek philosophical language. At times his ideas appear to be Sethian or Valentinian, but the terminology he uses can always be found in the Chaldaean Oracles;[8] for example, *sphragis, synthema, symbola.*[9] The basic thrust of this thought is "anti-Gnostic"; e.g., in the *Dion* he recommends careful preparation for the ascent of the soul: first one must read literature, including Homer, then one can begin to climb the ladder of dialectic in order "to look upon the Sun." As on the way up, so on the way down, one proceeds with caution. Synesius is wary of the "spiritual athletes" of his day, the ascetic monks and the false philosophers. The latter are perhaps the neo-Cynics (despised by Julian) or certain Hermeticists; but he allows immediate grasp of the divine to spiritual proficients, among whom he includes Hermes Trismegistus.[10]

Julian[11] had achieved a fairly definite "religious horizon" by his early twenties; Synesius's task and response was complicated by the fact that he was a Hellene of the generation of "declining paganism," who also by inclination and training followed the Porphyrian (*not* the Iamblichean) path which ultimately led him, because of his historical circumstances, in the direction of "official" Christianity; these "paths" really represent spiritual options available to Neoplatonists from the third to sixth centuries, who agreed on most essentials, not distinct "earlier or later schools" which drew rigid party lines.[12]   A.H. Armstrong has well summed up this position:

> When we think about the mentality of these fourth century pagan pluralists we should also take into account another aspect of the Neoplatonism of Plotinus and Porphyry, in which it differs most sharply from that of Iamblichus and his successors. This is the conviction that the only true

religion is philosophical religion, and that the stories and practices of non-philosophical religion are, at the best, no more than helpful popular expressions of philosophic truth for non-philosophers. This sort of Neoplatonism is of course compatible with the hostility shown by Porphyry himself to the alien barbarian Christian attack on the whole of Hellenic thought and culture: but it can also issue in a tolerant pluralism or in considerably more positive attitudes towards Christianity. The kind of probably more or less Porphyrian Neoplatonism which he learnt from Hypatia at Alexandria certainly helped Synesius in his decision to accept episcopal office when that seemed to him the best way of serving the community (A.H. Armstrong, *VC*, 38, pt 1 (1984) 10-11).

The probably availability to Synesius of the Nag Hammadi texts is not very significant, even if their ideas did influence earlier forms of Platonism. What is significant is the imposed limits (at times ambiguous) of his "religious horizon." He is not likely, while accepting Hermetic ideas, to have openly identified himself with, e.g., avowedly Valentinian notions, any more than most modern American politicians would openly profess "socialist" ideas.

Synesius the Hellene, then, would accept the *Hermetica* (and the *Chaldaean Oracles*) as canonized Hellenic "scriptures," but he would either overlook, ignore or be unaware of most Gnostic influences. (Let us not forget that the bishop was not above persecuting heretics.) He was probably anti-Gnostic, but certainly not anti-Christian. Thus he would not object to "receiving" Hermetic texts from Orthodox friends who read them, any more than from Neoplatonists.[13] Synesius, of course, would read the same texts from a completely different perspective: at this point his approach was necessarily somewhat idiosyncratic, if not unique. The importance and the meanings of texts in a given culture is not simply a question of who read what, what books were circulating, what was in vogue, and so on. But why, how, to what end, with what aim, scope and purpose (with relation to one's world view) one was reading those books.[14] Thus, any mutual influences or connections between the *Hermetica* and Gnosticism or any contacts of adherents would probably be beside the point for Synesius.

Synesius wrote after *Ennead* II-9. In line with those third century and later Platonists who appreciated the beauty of the cosmos, he had a high regard for the proportion and number of a unified, congruent, confluent, conspirant and complete (*sympleromenon*) cosmos, with sympathies, consummate beauty, and every kind of embellishment.[15] Where he presents "gnosticizing" middle Platonic ideas his reasons are often rhetorical; e.g., to display his Hellenic cultural links to Dion and

Plutarch; or to explain on the level of political allegory, the "evil soul" of one leader, and the "good soul" of another.[16]

In *On Providence or the Egyptian Tale*, Synesius presents notions of providence and demons, and of the nature, origin and destiny of souls. The world is filled with *hylic* demons, intent on attacking human beings. The gods are of little help, arriving only reluctantly on missions of salvation when the divine impetus, given to human souls before incarnation, runs down and can only be renewed by divine intervention. The father of Osiris admonishes his son:

> Try to ascend yourself, but do not cause the gods to descend, employ every form of prudence on your own behalf, as if you lived in an army camp in enemy territory, a divine soul among demons, who being earth born, it is reasonable to suppose will attack you, since they become angry if anyone maintains foreign laws and customs within their borders.[17]

The doctrine on souls that Synesius outlines in the *On Providence* is also dualistic in conception:

> The kinships of souls and of bodies are not the same; for it is not fitting for souls to be born on earth from the same two parents, but to flow from a single source. And the natural process of the cosmos furnishes two types: the luminous and the indistinct. The latter gushes up from the ground, since it has its roots somewhere below, and leaps out of the earth's cavities, if somehow it compels the divine law by force. But the former is suspended form the back of the heavens.[18]

This conception of souls having their ultimate sources in different places, both higher and lower, implies a type of dualism not typical of Neoplatonism. Is it from Numenius of Apamea or a Gnostic or Hermetic treatise? Porphyry reports that certain philosophers, among them Numenius, do *not* think (that e.g.) we have a single soul with three parts rather than two, but that we actually have two souls, and, it follows, one is rational, the other irrational. Moreover, some (of them) think *both* (souls) are immortal, while others, etc. (Leemans, *Numenius*, Text 36; Des Places, Fr. 44). In *fr*. 24 (*Kore Kosmou*) of the *Hermetica* (Nock-Festugière, ed.), Isis instructs her son, Horus, on the origin and destiny of different souls, the royal, the noble, and so on,

> Just as on earth, my son Horus, there are different types of streets, so it is with souls. For they also have places from which they arise, and one which originates from a finer place is nobler than one which does not.[19]

Jonas points out[20] that there was a two-soul theory current among Alexandrian Gnostics (Basilides and Isidorus) and Hermeticists, and that Iamblichus in *De Myst.*, VIII-8, presents the Hermetic theory: one soul is from the First Mind and the other from the spheres. The former leads us beyond *Heimarmene*[21] to the Intelligible gods. (Iamblichus adds that Theurgy lifts us to the unengendered realm, according to the purified life of such a soul.)

The passage on souls from *Kore Kosmou* seems especially close to that of Synesius. It is possible, then, to speak of "gnostic elements" in his thought. The doctrine taken at its face value admits a rationally irreconcilable dualism. The earlier passage from *On Providence*, on souls and demons, also appears to be Gnostic in spirit. Many Gnostics believed that man is not at home in this world, that he is in alien territory and must always be on guard. Similar doctrines can be traced to Middle Platonism. The idea of two world-souls is important in Plutarch's work on *Isis and Osiris*, one of the sources of *On Providence*. Numenius also thought that evil was present in the celestial spheres, and the *Chaldaean Oracles* present doctrines reminiscent of Zoroastrian dualism. Some scholars think that the source of the two-souls doctrine, Plato's Laws 10, 896E, reflects Zoroastrian influence;[22] others[23] that it is a false interpretation of Plato which arose as a result of anti-Stoic polemic: evil could not be in matter, thus it must somehow be in soul. Thus, John Dillon asserts that Plutarch's evil world-soul "seems not to imply just the rather negative unruly principle of the *Timaeus*, but a positive force, a maleficent soul, which has at some stage itself broken away from the intelligible realm."[24] Synesius's dualistic tendency, then, is within the Platonic tradition.

Synesius also affirms the cosmos in a non-dualistic spirit: the spirit of *Enneads* II-9. The world is not literally enemy territory, but this doctrine provides moral armament for the soul so that it can maintain its purity in connection with higher realities. The *Hermetica* shares much spiritual territory with Middle Platonism and Neoplatonism; at times it also displays a pro-cosmic "pantheism" far removed from the mainstream of Gnosticism. Souls incarnate, on the one hand, to make this world better;[25] on the other, as the result of a fall, as punishment. This attitude is in line with the tension brought about between the dualism and other worldliness of (e.g.) the Phaedo and Phaedrus and the optimism of the *Timaeus*, common in the Platonic, Orphic and Pythagorean traditions.

Many other passages in the works of Synesius either have a Gnostic tone or are more or less closely connected with the *Corpus Hermeticum*. The "paternal depth" (*ho bythos patroas*) of "Hymn II" engenders the son (*kydimos huios*) and the Holy Spirit (*hagia pnoia*). But the *Bythos* here probably refers not to Valentinian Gnosis, but to "the primal source and root" of the *Chaldaean Oracles*, which contains within itself (potentially) the entire noetic being.[26] In "Hymn VI" he calls upon the Son to "dry up the destructive billows of matter" (1-26-27).[27] A Christ who breaks through matter suggests associations with a Gnostic or docetic Christ, who carries the message of the "alien God." In "Hymn V," Synesius speaks of Christ incarnate: "the ineffable counsels of the Father caused the generation of Christ, the sacred labor of the Bride manifested the *form of man*, who arrived among mortals the conveyor of light from the source" (1. 4-9). He himself is the "light from the source." In 1-12, like the light of the Logos which is the life of men in the Fourth Gospel, and the life and light of the *Hermetica*; e.g., *nous* as *zoe kai phos*, *C.H.* I-9.[28] Hymn V: portrays the Logos as both cosmological and soteriological: founder (*ktistas*) of the cosmos, fashioner of the spheres, root of the centers of earth and savior of man (*autos d'anthropon soter*, 1. 16-20).[29]

Synesius conceives of the incarnation along Platonic lines as a soul taking on a body: *broteion pheron demas*.[30] He is often vague, but does not appear to be docetic: "the sacred labor of the bride, manifested the form of man";[31] *morphe anthropou* indicates a real human figure rather than a phantasm. It is perhaps wishful thinking to consider his *morphe anthropou* as a manifestation of the *Hermetic Anthropos*, the Archetypal Man who falls into matter because he is enamored of his own reflection in the "hylic realm" of nature.[32] *Morphe anthropou* does indeed seem to be little more than a periphrasis for the god-man, while the *eidos anthropon* of the *Corpus Hermeticum* clearly refers to the Platonic *eidos* of man. However, a late Neoplatonic definition of the word *morphe*[33] indicates a close relationship with intelligible form (as it manifests itself in particulars in the spatio-temporal realm).

In one passage, though, Synesius represents Christ as an analogue of the *Anthropos*, something like a second Adam who, "has driven the treacherous source," the "chthonic serpent" from the gardens of the Father; the serpent who gave the forbidden fruit to the primal man (*Archegonus*).[34] He depicts the "sin" of *Archegonus* as if it were a determined fact of cosmic history. The chthonic serpent symbolizes the material defilements from which the Savior came to free us. The phrase "nourisher of painful destiny" (*trophon argaleou morou* 1. 8-9) might be a reference to the *Heimarmene*, by which the *Archegonus* was subjected to conditions of the material world. Hence the fall of

Archegonus resembles that of the *Hermetic Anthropos*.

Other passages of Synesius have been singled out by scholars of the *Hermetica*:   W. Scott[35] pointed out the strong similarity of his description of *manteia* through dreams, augury, inspiration and oracles (*De Ins*. 1284A, *P G* 66) to the same description in *C.H.* XII-19.   He believed they came from a common Stoic source.   Synesius compares the cosmos as a sphere like a human head (*C.H.* X (106)) with *Calv. Enc.* 1181B (*P G* 66), for his part, believing that spheres are like heads and (bald) heads microcosms of spheres.   The cosmic sympathy of *C.H.* VIII-5 compares with that of *De Prov*. 7, 1277a and *De Ins*. 2, 1285a, (*P G* 66), along standard Stoic Platonic lines.   In *C.H.* IV-10 *theos* is *monas*, *arche* and *riza panton*, as he is, in Synesius's *Hymns*, the monad of monads, the principle of principles, the root, the source (*paga*), the unity of unities (*henas henadon*), and so on.

Festugière employs the *Hymns*[36] as parallels to demonstrate the liturgical nature of *C.H.* V-10 and ff., itself a mystical hymn.   He points out that god, according to the doctrine, can be named in terms of opposites, can be known, is unknowable, is both anonymous and polynomous, is everywhere and nowhere, and can ultimately only be reached by the *via negationis*.   The passages cited from the *Hymns* speak of him as one and three, sound and silence, male and female.   Of importance here is the notion of pagan liturgical works, which show some connection with the writings of Synesius.   We find this even in the case of the "literary mysteries" (very much a part of later Hellenism) such as the so-called Mithras liturgy and the Hermetic prayers to the *arche*, *pneuma*, *aion* and *Helios*:   (1) the *Hymns* are themselves prayers to such principles.   (2) Synesius rejected (for the most part) the theurgic ritual aspect of the *Chaldaean Oracles*, while accepting much of their intellectual content.[37]   (3) A pagan religious tradition, less controversial in the early 5th century, involving ritual and liturgical patterns along with compatible ideas would make the transition to Christian ritual smoother for Synesius.   (4) The rhythm of the *Hymns* (pagan and/or "Christian") often suggests ritual prayer.   Thus the Hermetic tradition, with its ideas of rebirth and salvation, its basically Platonic outlook and its suggestions of religious liturgy and ritual, offers the basic materials for a syncretistic bridge between paganism and Christianity.

Synesius the bishop accepted revelation as a kind of *gnosis*.   In one of the few explications of a Christian text to be found in his extant works, he writes of the divine inspiration of scripture:

For one spirit inspired the prophet and the apostle, and after the fine ancient painters, he drew in outline and then subsequently portrayed in exact detail the features of the *gnosis*.[38]

I have excerpted this, a fragment of an allegorical exegesis of a portion of a Psalm, because it reads like an exercise from the catechetical schools of Alexandria:

There is a cup of unmixed wine in the hand of the Lord.[39]

The cup is the word of God, says Synesius, freely offered to men in the Old and New Testaments, "for the soul is watered by this drink." Inasmuch as it is a word, each (Cup-Testament-Word) is unmixed. Yet it is mixed as a double word. For the unity which is formed from the two is a perfection of *gnosis (teleiosis gnoseos)*.[40]

In short, the unity of the Logos in both Testaments is the perfection of Christian *gnosis*. Although there is no evidence that Synesius ever read Clement or Origen, he follows the Alexandrian tradition here. His *gnosis* is not the special saving, purifying and liberating knowledge of the Gnostics; but *gnosis* as philosophical understanding of a divinely inspired text — like that which (e.g.) Clement claimed as the true *gnosis* in opposition to the heretics.

Yet Synesius, true to his heterodox outlook, sermonizes and interprets passages in accordance with his Neoplatonic preferences. Speaking of the cup in the hand of the Lord: "that cup is *aristopoion*, filled with wine, and having been sought after is able to raise us up to Intellect" — *eis noun*.[41]

Although he knows the meaning and importance of the Christian *Logos*, the bishop uses the term *Nous*. If he is following a *Gnostic* tradition here — as well as a Neoplatonic one — it is very likely that of the *Hermetica* rather than any form of Christian *Gnosis*.

In *Corpus Hermeticum* XIII, the secret discourse on rebirth between Hermes Trismegistus and his son Tat, there is a hymn-prayer after which the lord is called *nous*

god, you are the father, — *theos . . . . pater*

the lord, the intellect — *sy o kyrios, sy o nous*[42]

Synesius considered Hermes to be one of the great spiritual autodidacts, along with Ammon, Antony, and Zoroaster. Thus the *Hermetica* and its soteriological mystery language could be most useful to the newly ordained bishop, who complains in a letter to Peter the Elder (Garzya, *Ep.* 13) of his inability (due to lack of scriptural knowledge) to preach a proper Easter sermon.

Fortunately, that Easter Eve sermon to the newly baptized members of the congregation in the Pentapolis has been preserved. The language of Homily II reflects an outlook that virtually transforms the Easter ceremony into a Neoplatonically or Hermetically interpreted mystery initiation: it is a holy night in which the light (*phos*) manifests itself to the purified (*tois katheramenois*). It is a light far surpassing that of the sun, for even the fairest thing on earth cannot be compared to the Demiurge. This light, which illuminates souls and the visible (*aistheton*) sun, is not a created thing.[43] He warns the newly baptized concerning the danger of incurring a pollution (*molysma*) after purification (*katharsis*).[44] The language, metaphor and sense here are closer to the Orphic, Platonic and Hermetic than to the Christian. Several chapters before the Hymn of praise in *C.H.* XIII, after which the lord is called *nous*, Hermes warns Tat to purify himself from the irrational torments of matter (*hyle*)[45] — caused by ignorance of the nature of the passions in relation to the body. *Gnosis* is the holy source of the illumination of our minds and the light is incorporeal and intelligible[46] — *to noeton phos*.[47]

The idea of purification and pollution, the juxtaposition of spiritual to visible light, the Demiurge, the created world as *demiourgema*, all are evocative of late pagan spirituality. Synesius facing a Christian congregation in fifth century Libya, a province notorious for Arianism, is not likely to have made use of mystery language in order to bridge the gap between the Church and Hellenism for a pagan audience. His language reflects his own religious stance.

There are basically two important scholarly interpretations of the Hermetic religion.[48] Reitzenstein and Geffcken think that a "religious brotherhood" used the *C.H.* as a sacred "book" on which to base its dogmas, rites and liturgy. On the other hand, Bossuet, E. Kroll and Cumont point out that the *Corpus* contains irreconcilable doctrines and the fact that there is no trace of specific ceremonies in *C.H.* precludes a religious community. Festugière accepts the latter notion as a working hypothesis: "there is nothing that resembles the sacraments of the Gnostic sects. No confession, communion, consecration, hierarchy of degrees of initiation. The only two classes are those that hear and those that refuse the word."[49] M. Eliade,[50] however, asserts that despite this the great treatises of Hermetic philosophy "presuppose closed groups practicing an initiation" — there is a *religio mentis* in the Hermetic *Asclepius*, and "god receives pure spiritual sacrifices" (*C.H.*

1-3). There are also ritual patterns of behavior: disciples gather in a sanctuary, they keep the revelations secret, there is a ceremonial catachesis, and a mystery ritual of baptism in a *krater*.

C.H. IV 3-6, tells us that in the beginning *theos* filled a *krater* with *nous*, and those who submerge themselves become "perfect men." Festugière has shown that this has parallels to the mysteries: 1) ingestion of a sacred drink from a *krater*; 2) a purifying and initiatory bath.[51] Synesius's cup (of the *Logos*) is alternately called *poterion* and *krater*; a cup which disturbs thought and disrupts rationality does not befit reason (*logoi*).[52] This is a typically Hellenic statement.

Eliade maintains that the *Hermetica* also indicate ecstatic practices: Hermes tells Tat of an ecstatic experience after which he entered an "immortal body" and Tat imitates him (*C.H.* XIII-3, 13).[53] These ideas (literary or otherwise), especially baptism, purification, perfection and ecstasy, would fit well in a syncretistic Easter ritual.

The pattern of parallels, then, between the works of Synesius and the *Hermetica* is not without significance. The Platonic "philosopher-bishop" led his congregation on an ascent of the soul to *nous*; this was probably not the result of purely Neoplatonic or even Chaldaean influences: it was also inspired by the Hermetic mysteries. Surely the *C.H.*, with its creative *and* salvific noetic beings (*nous-demiurge*; *logos*; *anthropos*) provides the clearest analogue to the Christian myth. The *theios aner*, Heracles, Asclepius and the other *late* Hellenic savior figures do not "create," and they exist on a much lower level of the *seira* of procession and cannot be said to be at the level of the *logos* or *nous*. They are lower reflections, although still divine. Although the notion of a specifically Hermetic ritual remains problematic, the idea that Synesius echoes the *C.H.* in both his Easter sermon and his metaphysical thought, is attractive. This orientation could help students of late antiquity better to understand the syncretism of Hellenism and Christianity attempted by those serious pagans who had put aside the standards of the emperor Julian, at least in part because they thought that the victory of the new religion was already a *fait accompli*.

NOTES
1.   For a full account of Synesius's development (here briefly outlined) see J. Bregman (1982), passim.
2.   For this and ff. see Bregman, pp. 155-163. This section deals with the famous *Ep.* 105. On this and other questions concerning the *Ep.* it is necessary to consult the fine edition of the letters brought out by A. Garzya (Rome, 1979). My work on Synesius was ready for the press shortly before

the publication of Garzya's work.

3. Bregman, p. 20: the Byzantine Chronographer John Malalas says that: her father Theon was a commentator on the works of Hermes Trismegistus and Orpheus. Thus it is most likely that Synesius was already familiar with the *Hermetica* when he was a student at Alexandria.

4. For a clear and cogent presentation of triads in the thought of Marius Victorinus (and others) see Peter Manchester, "The Noetic Triad in Plotinus, Marius Victorinus and Augustine," in this volume, pp. 207-222.

5. Bregman, pp. 103-108.

6. As the *nous-theos*, *nous-demiurge*, and *anthropos* of *Poimandres*.

7. Bregman, p. 108.

8. Bregman, pp. 34-35 and n. 57.

9. Bregman, pp. 91-92.

10. Bregman, p. 114; on the rejection of spiritual extremes see Bregman, p. 130 and Garzya, *Ep.* 154.

11. See Athanassiadi-Fowden (1981), pp. 24-25. My own view of Julian is in large part similar to that of this author.

12. On this see A.H. Armstrong (1984), p. 6. My view of Synesius has been challenged recently in a review by G. Fowden (*CP* 80 [July 1985]: 281-285), who thinks my notion that Synesius adhered to a "Plotinian-Porphyrian" position distinct from Iamblichean theurgy, cannot be proved and contradicts itself, since with regard to theurgy Porphyry marks an intermediate stage between Plotinus and Iamblichus. Perhaps the phrase *Plotinian*-Porphyrian (a *generalizing* label) confused Fowden. I am well aware of the distinction. GF also thinks I assume that Synesius, a gentleman, could not be influenced by theurgy and other "superstitions." His statements and parade of erudition cannot hide the fact that he has not *read carefully* important sections of my monograph. On pages 145-154, I discuss in detail Synesius's complex and problematic position vis-a-vis Porphyry, theurgy and the *ochema-Pneuma*; I even entertain the idea that he might have accepted some form of intellectual "higher theurgy," but certainly could not have accepted Iamblichean sacerdotalism. I also believe Synesius liked both the *Chaldaean Oracles* and the *Hermetica*; I admire Julian and Iamblichus and I do not consider theurgy a symptom of the "decline" of Neoplatonism. This is evident from even a superficial perusal of my work.

13. Fowden cites Alan Cameron, who in turn thinks pagan philosophical influences do not "necessarily conflict with the possibility that Synesius was a Christian (of sorts) all his life," (*YCS* 27 [1982]). It seems to me that the evidence points in the opposite direction, whatever one means by a Christian of sorts. GF then states that neither Cameron nor my view quite catches the subtlety of the process. Neither does GF, who does not really explain what he means. He might have a better grasp of the issues involved had he understood the beginning of the Introduction, p. ii to my *Synesius*: "The traditional view of the relationship between Hellenic thought and Christian doctrine does not provide an appropriate framework for an interpretation

of Synesius's religious position . . ." (pp. 9 and ff.)   In fact it must be
reversed. Synesius (although he might have known of the religion) did not
have Christianity in his background like Augustine; nor, for similar reasons,
can he be compared to the Alexandrian or Cappadocian Fathers. Whatever
the importance of "social structures" and "context," only a naive
reductionist would vastly undervalue the significance of these notions.

14.   Fowden (p. 285), seems to think I should have been more aware of possible
Gnostic influences in the work of Synesius. His remarks are beside the
point. In rather arbitrary fashion he asserts that my *Synesius* "is not a good
omen for the ongoing study . . . of the religious attitudes . . . of late
antiquity" (p. 285). On the other hand one need not be an augur or a
theurgist to see that GF does not understand the intellectual issues, has
difficulty apprehending modes of religious perception and has a tendency to
distort what he reads. But, in fairness, of *this* he appears to have some
awareness: "of his extensive and exceedingly speculative discussions of how
and under what influence Synesius *may* have proceeded in his attempt to
build 'hermeneutical bridges' between paganism and Christianity, those of
more experience in such matters will judge" (p. 385). Very well, then: "I
accept the account of Synesius given by Jay Bregman in the latest book on
him." (Armstrong, p. 16, n. 18)

In addition, Averil Cameron (*Phoenix* 38, 3 [1984]) says I show too little
caution in "assuming that we can take what (S.) wrote purely at face value.
. . . Too much of a gap still exists for us in understanding late antiquity
between the literary text and its reception . . . the central interpretation . . .
rests on the questionable assumption that Synesius invariably says what he
means, and what he does not say he cannot therefore be allowed to
mean."(!) These statements seem to me to be essentially vacuous and to
have the quality of rhetorical "mystique." Not everything written in late
antiquity must be "decoded" as if it were part of some Procopian "secret
history." The works of Synesius are, if sometimes ambiguous, hardly
unintelligible (on this Av. Cameron might consult well known works of
Lacombrade, Marrou, Terzaghi, Theiler and others). We *do* know the main
lines of Platonic thought in late antiquity. (See, e.g., the works of A.H.
Armstrong, R.T. Wallis, R. Hadot, L.G. Westerink, the contents of this
volume, and many others.) For example, on how much we know about the
doctrine of the soul and related matters see John Dillon, *Later Platonist
Psychology, C.R.* V, XXXV, no. 1 (1985): 80-82. For more cogent opinions,
among others, J.A.S. Evans, *Catholic Historical Review* (Oct 1985);
J.H.W.G. Liebeschütz, *JHS*, vol. CIV (1984).

15.   Synesius, *De Prov* II-7 127B-128A (Terzaghi, ed.); see Bregman, p. 70.

16.   The seminal work on the *De Prov* as a moral political allegory is O. Seeck
(1894). Synesius started this work around the turn of the 5th century, but
could not have been completed until 414, thus Seeck's identifications and
other ideas must be modified; on this see, e.g., J.H.W.G. Liebeschütz (*JHS*
CIV [1984]).

17. *De Prov* X 99C (Terzaghi ed.): cf. Festugière, *Hermetisme* (1967), p. 37, describing the character of the Hermeticist: "one must behave here below like a stranger."

18. *De Prov* 89B-C.

19. *C.H. Fr.* XXIV, 7, Nock-Festugière, vol. IV, p. 54.

20. H. Jonas (1963), pp. 159-160.

21. Cf. Jonas, pp. 43-44.

22. *E.g.* M. Anastos, *DOP* 4-283; cf. Bregman, p. 69, n. 27.

23. See especially Pheme Perkins, "Beauty, Number and the Loss of Order in the Gnostic Cosmos," in this volume, pp. 277-296.

24. *The Middle Platonists* as quoted by Bregman, p. 69, n. 27.

25. *E.g.* Asclepius VIII, "to admire and worship celestial to govern terrestrial things." *C.H.* IV-2 the cosmos as the "mortal living being, ornament of the immortal living being." *C.H.* XI is basically optimistic. On the issue of optimistic vs. dualistic gnosis in the *Hermetica* see F. Yates (1964), pp. 22-38. On the importance of "the worldly" and the immanent see S. Gersh, "Theological Doctrines of the Latin Asclepius" in this volume, pp. 129-166.

26. Bregman, pp. 88-89 and n. 36.

27. Cf. also *Hymn* III, 1. 539-540; 548-550; *Hymn* V, 1. 14-15.

28. For some further references to light imagery in the *Hermetica* and the *Oracles* see Bregman, p. 99, n. 22.

29. Bregman, p. 100.

30. For a discussion of this phrase see Bregman, p. 102 and n. 39.

31. *Hymn*, V, 1. 4-9.

32. On the *Anthropos* myth see Jonas, pp. 161-162; Yates, pp. 23-25; Rudolph (1982), pp. 92-94.

33. *Hymn* IX, 1. 4-9; Proclus *In. Tim* X, 1-3.

34. See Bregman, pp. 116-117.

35. The passages cited here are to be found with Hermetic and other comparisons in W. Scott (repr. 1968): *Calv. Enc.* II, 249, 364, 423; *De Ins* II, 200, 342; *De prov* II, 200, IV, 393. *Hymn* II, 152. Nicephoras Gregoras *Comm De Ins* (on *Hermetica*), IV, 247-248.

36. Festugière, *La Révèlation*, vol. IV, p. 68 and n. 1, p. 70, n. 1; cf. e.g., Julian's *Hymn to King Helios*, *Proclus's Hymns*, *the Orphic Hymns*.

37. See Bregman, pp. 2, 39, 92.

38. *Homily* I 296A-296D.

39. *Homily* I 295C.

40. *Homily* I 296A; Bregman, p. 165.

41. *Homily* 295C.

42. *C.H.* XIII, 21.7-8; Nock-Festugière, vol. II, p. 208.

43. *Homily* II, 297A-B.

44. *Homily* 297C.

45. *C.H.* XIII, 7.6-7.

46. *C.H.* 7.10 and ff; 8, 9.

47. *C.H.* 18.5. Light imagery is of course common in the Orthodox Church, and to this day the service includes elements that remind one of the mysteries. This is the legacy of late antiquity and never a proof of "paganism" (then or now). But even a superficial reading of the so-called *Catechetical Discourse of S. John Chrysostom* or the sermons of the Fathers will reveal the differences with Synesius; the *orientation* is Biblical, emphasis is on the central elements of the Christian myth, especially the risen Christ. The terminology *per se* to some extent shared by *all* the late antique religious traditions is less important. Nevertheless, one is hard pressed to find Easter sermons in which *nous* is where one would expect *logos*.

48. In this section I follow closely the summary and argument of M. Eliade (1982), pp. 298-301 and nn. 521-522. G. Fowden's attempt to place the *Hermetica* in a "social context" has added little to our knowledge. Furthermore, the "context" gives the impression of being manufactured, the artificial construction of a social historian. G. Fowden, *The Egyptian Hermes: A Historical Approach to the Late Pagan Mind* (Cambridge, 1986).

49. Quoted by M. Eliade (1982), p. 299 and n. 49; tr. Festugière.

50. Eliade (1982), p. 299.

51. Eliade (1982), p. 299, n. 50; for possible connections between the Hermetic *krater* and the Grail legends cf. Eliade (1985), pp. 106-107 and notes.

52. *Homily* I, 295B.

53. Eliade (1982), pp. 299-300. On the implications for Renaissance Humanism of a "Synesian approach" (in reverse mirror image) to "para-Christian" Neoplatonism and Hermeticism, see also Eliade (1985), pp. 251-255 and notes.

Pleroma and Noetic Cosmos : A Comparative Study

John M. Dillon

The process of identifying philosophical concepts in the various documents of the Nag Hammadi Corpus is a delicate one. One must avoid overhastiness in discerning parallels, while also taking due account of the degree of mythologizing and personification of philosophical themes that may in fact be taking place.

A case in point is the general concept of a non-material, spiritual or intelligible world parallel to our physical one, and serving as an ideal paradigm of it. It is safe to say, I think, that such a concept forms no part of traditional Jewish thought,[1] nor is it a feature of primitive Christianity. Certainly, God is in his heaven, and he is the creator of our world, but he did not create it according to a pattern laid up in his mind, which is co-extensive with his heaven. If we find such a concept in a Jewish thinker such as Philo, or a later Christian theorist such as Clement or Origen, we reckon that it has been imported from somewhere else; and the same is the case if we come upon it in a document of Gnosticism, Christian or otherwise.

There is, of course, no great mystery as to the source of such a concept. In the form in which we find it in Philo or the Alexandrian Fathers, it stems from Plato, and in particular from his *Timaeus*, though to a lesser extent from the *Phaedo*, *Republic* and *Phaedrus* also.

Let us begin by considering the structure of the ideal realm as it is presented in the *Timaeus*, or at least, what is more important, as it was thought to be presented by later Platonists (what Plato himself precisely had in mind is often obscure).

We meet, first of all, in 28Aff. a sharp distinction between the realms of Being (*to aei on*) and Becoming (*genesis*), and a Demiurge figure who uses as a model (*paradeigma*) "the eternal" (*to aidion*, 29a 3) and unchanging, in order that what he creates may be good. "This cosmos," the physical world, is declared to be "a copy of something" (*eikōn tinos*, 29b2), although a continually moving and coming-to-be copy of a paradigm which is neither of these things. As Plato presents the scenario, the Paradigm is independent of the Demiurge, being an ultimate reality, external to him, which he contemplates and copies, but most later Platonists (with whom I agree) took the description of the craftsman and his model as figurative, even as the creation of the world in time was figurative. If we are thinking in terms of metaphysics rather than poetry, it makes no sense to have an ultimate reality ontologically independent of the supreme god — and there is no suggestion in the *Timaeus* that the Demiurge is not the supreme god, though some later Platonists, such as Numenius, tried to solve the metaphysical puzzle by taking the Demiurge as a secondary god, with the Good of the *Republic* enthroned above him. The Paradigm must therefore be subordinate to the Demiurge, and in fact nothing else but the contents of his mind.

Let us look more closely at the contents of his mind. In 30B, we learn that the physical cosmos as a whole is a body containing a soul which contains a mind. In this it is an image of its model. The model, we learn further in 30CD, is a living thing (*zoon*), which comprises all the intelligible living things (*noēta zōa*), even as this cosmos contains all visible ones. This picture of a living thing containing within it a vast multiplicity of non-material entities, which are themselves living, but are also identified (later, at 39E) with the Forms or Ideas must, it seems to me, have given much food for thought to later generations of Platonists. Indeed, it is clear from later developments that it did so. Necessarily, from what has been said in 30B, this Essential Living Being (*autozōon*) is an Intellect, and all the living Forms within it are also "intellects." All this is certainly less than explicit in the *Timaeus* itself, but by the time of Plotinus, as we shall see, it is regarded as obvious, and it must have become obvious long before his time.

In 39E, as I say, we learn that the Essential Living Creature contains within it Ideas of all the living creatures that are manifest on earth, and in addition, it would seem, archetypes of the four elements of fire, air, water and earth. More and more, the *Autozōon* begins to appear like a completely coherent and comprehensive matrix, timeless, ungenerated, immaterial and perfect, of the physical cosmos. And, itself a "well-rounded whole," it is composed of a vast number of individual minds, arranged, necessarily, in hierarchies of genera and species, and of Forms of greater and lesser generality, each of which has its own "point of view" — almost its own personality. In Plotinus's striking image, it may be likened to "a globe of faces radiant with faces all living" (*Enn.* VI, 7, 15). The image of a face made up of faces is particularly apt as a description of the noetic world, reminding us that the individual forms are not just objects of intellection, but themselves intellects, each looking out on the rest.

Easy as it may be to see how the conception of the Ideas as thoughts of God arose, it is remarkably difficult to pin down exactly where it originated in any explicit form. I am on record[2] as suggesting that, since Xenocrates declared the supreme principle to be an intellect, and an intellect is necessarily engaged in thinking, it is very tempting to see the Ideas, which Xenocrates identified with numbers (Fr. 34 Heinze), as the contents of its mind, but I have been chided for that assumption, and I must admit that there is no explicit evidence for it. All we know is that by the time of Philo of Alexandria the doctrine is accepted as obvious. In the *De Opificio Mundi* (16-20) Philo describes God as first creating the *noētos kosmos* (a phrase which he is, by the way, the first extant author to use), and then using it as a model on which to create the *aisthētos kosmos*. That Philo himself did not originate the idea of subordinating the noetic cosmos to the Supreme Being is indicated by the fact that Varro[3] is reported as allegorizing Minerva springing from the head of Jupiter as the Ideas springing from the mind of God. Varro was in philosophy a follower of the Stoicized Platonism of Antiochus of Ascalon, for whom an equation of the Ideas with the Stoic *logoi spermatikoi*, and thus of the Paradigm of the *Timaeus* with the Logos, would be no trouble at all. Philo, of course, while maintaining the transcendence of God, does adopt the Stoic concept of the Logos, which he identifies with the noetic cosmos in its dynamic aspect.

Having reached this far in the Platonic tradition, let us turn to consider the Pleroma, as we find it represented in various tractates of the Nag Hammadi corpus. I would like to begin with an eloquent passage from the *Tripartite Tractate*, a work generally agreed to be of Valentinian inspiration,[4] which presents the Aeons as "thoughts of the Father" (60):

> . . . all of the aeons were forever in the thought of the Father, who was like a thinking of them and a place [for them]. When the generations had been established, the one who controls everything wished to take, to lay hold of, and to bring forth those who were deficient in the . . . [and he brought] forth those who [are] in him. But since he is [as] he is, [he is like] a spring

> which is not diminished by the water which abundantly flows from it. At the time that they were in the Father's thought, that is, in the hidden depth, the depth knew them, but they were unable to know the depth in which they were, nor could they know themselves; nor could they know anything else. In other words, they were with the Father; they did not exist by themselves. Rather, they only had existence in the manner of a seed. Thus it has been discovered that they existed like a fetus. Like the word, he begot them, and they subsisted spermatically.

This is a most interesting passage, containing, as it does, in only slightly mythological form, all the features of that Stoicized Platonism which we find also in Philo.[5] The aeons are thoughts of God; he is their "place" (cf. Philo, *Opif.* 20), he is compared to an undiminished spring, an image beloved both of Philo[6] and of Plotinus;[7] and they reside in him like a *logos*, and *spermatikōs*.

But this is not all. Two stages in the life of the aeons are distinguished. In this passage they still do not have knowledge nor separate existence. But the text continues (61):

> Therefore the Father who first thought them — not only so that they might exist for him, but also that they might exist for themselves as well, that they might then exist in his thought with the mode of existence proper to thought, and that they might exist in themselves too — he sowed a thought like a seed of [knowledge] so that [they] might know [what it is that has come into being for them].

A second stage in the generation of the aeons is here envisaged, where the Father endows them with intellect, so that they become self-subsisting entities. At this stage, the Aeons are fully equatable to the Ideas of Platonism. How seriously we need take this sequence of two stages in the life of the Aeons is not clear to me. If the Father's activity is in fact timeless,[8] then the distinction of two stages could be taken as mythological elaboration. For our purposes, at any rate, it is not of great importance. It is the final state of the Aeons that is significant, and that finds them as self-subsistent intellects within the thought of the Father.

Having established this, let us consider what is the nature of an Aeon[9] and how it differs from a Platonic Form. Plainly, Aeons have rank and title, in a way in which Forms do not. For example, in *The Gospel of the Egyptians* (III, 40, 12-55, 16; IV, 50, 1-67, 1), the Aeons are arranged in ogdoads (a system owing something, surely, to Egyptian religion). Each member of the trinity of Father, Mother and Son, themselves Aeons, is made up of an ogdoad of Aeons, mostly with abstract titles, such as Will, Thought or Imperishability. Five further entities are then revealed, each consisting of an ogdoad, and following on them two others, the Logos and Adamas, the latter of whom, Adamas, begets Seth. All of these are in fact ogdoads, producing a total of eleven so far. This total, though large, is still manageable, but it becomes clear further on (54) that the Pleroma is filled with myriads of "thrones, powers and glories" which do not merit individual characterization.

All this personification brings the Pleroma closer to a Neoplatonic version of the noetic world, and even to the later Neoplatonic conception (which I must say I would still see as going back to Iamblichus, and therefore to the beginning of the fourth century C.E.) of the world of henads around the One, than to the less developed Middle Platonic doctrine. The important development that occurs in later Platonism is that the traditional gods, Olympian and otherwise, are identified with metaphysical entities, for Plotinus and Porphyry the individual *noes* of the noetic world (whom Plotinus refers to repeatedly as *theoi*),[10] for Iamblichus and later Platonists as henads in the realm of the One. The coexistence of figures as Apollo or Athena with such entities as the Ideal Horse or the Ideal Triangle might seem an uneasy one, but these matters are beyond our comprehension, and speculation would be impertinent. Certainly, for the Neoplatonists all noetic entities, and later, all henadic entities, are *theoi*, and some of them are certainly arranged in families or other groupings, with varying levels of generality or specificity.

But the Pleroma is not only replete with personalities, it also contains, in an intelligible mode, all things that are manifest in this world: "Everything which is manifest is a copy of that which is hidden," as we learn from *The Teaching of Silvanus* (99, 5). In *G Egypt* III, 50, 10 (=IV, 62, 8), we find mention of "the ethereal earth" (*aerōdēs gē*, presumably);[11] where the holy men of the great light receive shape. In *Zostrianos*, 48, we find an elaborate description of a noetic world corresponding to ours, apparently present in each of the Aeons:

> Corresponding to each of the Aeons I saw a living earth and a living water and (air) made of light, and fire that cannot burn (. . .), all being simple and immutable with trees that do not perish in many ways, and tares (. . .) this way, and all these and imperishable fruit and living men and every form, and immortal souls and every shape and form of mind, and gods of truth, and messengers who exist in great glory, and indissoluble bodies and an unborn begetting and an immovable perception.

It is a pity that this passage is somewhat fragmentary, since it is of great interest. What we seem to have portrayed here is a comprehensive archetype of the physical world, right down the tares among the wheat (a detail that I find particularly interesting — if the very fragmentary text can be trusted). We may note also noetic archetypes of body, begetting (presumably *genesis*), and perception (presumably *aisthēsis*).[12] The description occurs again at 55, 15-25, with more or less the same list, though this time including "animals." In both passages it seems that each Aeon is deemed to contain such a world, like a Leibnizian (or Anaxagorean) monad, but in any case, it is all present in the Pleroma.[13]

A third relevant passage occurs at 113-117, where once again a whole world is being presented within an Aeon, but, here it is further specified that on the one hand there are hierarchies of being, genera and species, within the world, and on the other hand that "they do not crowd one another, but they also dwell within them, existing and agreeing with one another as if they exist from a simple origin" (115, 1-5), and "in that world are all living beings existing individually, yet joined together" (117, 1-5). All this is again most interesting, since it describes excellently the conception of the noetic world which we find in Plotinus, especially in *Ennead* VI, 7, to which I will now turn. (The fact that *Zostrianos* was one of the Gnostic treatises known in Plotinus's circle makes the question of influence somewhat more of a live one than it might otherwise be.) The problem from which Plotinus starts in VI, 7 (one arising in his mind from *Timaeus* 45B), is whether or not the individual soul had capacities for sense-perception before it descended into the body. This particular question leads him, in ever-increasing circles, to the general one of whether there are pre-existent in the noetic world all things which are present in the sense-world, even such a thing as an archetype, or noetic correlate, of sense-perception, as well as irrational animals, trees, earth and stones.

A particular problem arises for him by reason of the fact that he accepts that souls may transmigrate from humans to animals, and this is plainly a declination. How then can there be noetic archetypes of things that are (at least comparatively) evil? His answer (VI, 7, 8, 1ff.) is most interesting:

> But if it is by becoming evil and inferior that the Soul produces the nature of beasts, the making of ox or horse was not at the outset in its character; the *logos* of the horse, for example, and the horse itself, must be contrary to nature (*para physin*).
>
> Inferior, yes; but contrary to nature, no. What is There (sc. Soul) was in

some sense horse and dog from the beginning; given the condition it produces the higher kind; let the condition fail, then, since produce it must, it produces what it may; it is like a skilful craftsman competent to create all kinds of works of art, but reduced to making what is ordered and what the aptitude of his material indicates. (trans. MacKenna, adapted).

This may or may not commend itself as an entirely satisfactory solution to Plotinus's problem, but that does not matter for our purpose. What we find is that the noetic realm contains in itself a comprehensive articulated pattern of all the phenomena of the physical world, down to its most lowly aspects. Plotinus is even prepared to speak of *aisthēsis* and *aisthēta* in the noetic realm (6, 1-2 and 7, 24-31), producing at the end of ch. 7 the striking formula: "perceptions here are dim intellections and intellections there are vivid perceptions."[14]

The Forms even of irrational and inanimate things are necessarily intellects (ch. 9). This line of thought comes to its completion in ch. 11, where Plotinus envisages a noetic archetype of the earth and all its contents, fire, water, trees, stones, and so on:

But earth; how is there earth There? What is the being of earth, and how are we to represent to ourselves the living earth of that realm?

First, what is earth in the physical realm, what is the mode of its being? Earth, here and There alike, must possess shape and a *logos*. Now in the case of plants, the *logos* of the plant here was found to be living in the higher realm: is there such a *logos* in our earth? (tr. MacKenna).

His answer is that there is. What he calls "the creative formal principle of earth" (τὸ εἶδος τῆς γῆς τὸ ποιοῦν) forms the mountains and valleys, forests and plains, down to the individual rocks, and the whole is alive, through its dependence on its living intelligent archetype, the Essential Earth (*autogē*, Ch. 11, 35).

This seems to me to come very near to the conception we find adumbrated in *Zostrianos*, though here, as one would expect from Plotinus, it is exhaustively argued for instead of being baldly stated. The notion of a noetic archetype of earth is certainly implicit in the account of the *Timaeus*, but only in Plotinus do we find the full implications of the doctrine worked out. It is not, I think, necessary to suppose that Plotinus was in any way influenced by the *Zostrianos* text, though the analogies are interesting. What is more probable is that the author of *Zostrianos* was himself influenced by trends in second century Platonism, and more particularly, perhaps, by contact with what has been termed the "Platonic Underworld." In the Hermetic *Poemandres*, for instance, we find the concept of a noetic archetype of the physical world, a *kalos kosmos* (sect. 8), by contemplation of which the Will of God (*boulē theoû*), having received into itself the *Logos*, creates this cosmos. The relations between Hermetics and Gnostics, though obscure, were close, to judge by the inclusion of a section of the *Asclepius* in the Nag Hammadi corpus, but it is not necessary to suppose mutual influence in the matter of the concept of an intelligible world. They can have derived it from Platonism independently.

An objection which might be made to too close a comparison between Pleroma and noetic cosmos is that the Pleroma is not really a model upon which the physical world is based. The physical world is an error and an abortion for the Gnostics, and the Demiurge receives little or no guidance from above in creating it, nor has he access to the Pleroma as a model to work with.[15] Most of the Aeons are not conceived of as models or paradigms for anything, and the Christ or Saviour figure, when he/she emerges, makes no particular use of them.

However, there are elements in the Pleroma, in both Valentinian and Sethian systems (if we can still use such terms), which do seem to serve as paradigms. First of all, in some systems at least, there is the god "Man" (*Anthropos*), presented as the archetype of which earthly man is the copy.[16] In the *Second Treatise of the Great Seth* (*NHC* VII, 53-4), for example, we find Adam presented as an image of "the Father of Truth, the Man of the Greatness," who is an Aeon, if not the supreme God himself.[17] In the *Apocryphon of John* (*NHC* II, 1, 2; 5; 14), we find mention of "the perfect Man" or "first Man," serving as an epithet of Barbelo, of whom, again, Adam is an image. In other treatises, such as the *Hypostasis of the Archons* (II, 4, 91) and *On the Origin of the World* (II, 5, 103; 107; 115) we find also an intermediate figure, the Light-Adam, who enters into the physical body prepared by the Demiurge and his agents, and thus fulfills the role of an immanent Form in Platonism.[18]

This distinguishing of three levels of man finds, I think, a curious echo in Plotinus, *Enn.* VI, 7, 6 where we have a hierarchy of grades of man, consisting of (1) a noetic or archetypal Man, (2) a Man who is a copy (*mimēma*) of the first, containing the *logoi* in copy form (*en mimesei*), but which is still distinct from (3) the embodied man, which it illuminates (*ellampei*), even as the first illuminates it. This sequence strikes me as being rather closer in spirit to the Gnostic doctrine than to the traditional Platonist system of Form and particular.

Besides Man himself, the Sethians at least believed that archetypes of all the pneumatics existed in the Pleroma, or perhaps just that the pneumatics existed in the Pleroma as aeons or *logoi* before becoming embodied. It is possible that the Sethians did not distinguish very clearly between these two possibilities, only the former of which is truly Platonist. A Platonist concept may indeed by mingling here with notions originally Iranian, of divine "sparks" of light inserted into the darkness of Matter.[19]

A key term in this connection is *typos*, which is used in Gnostic texts as a virtual synonym for the more Platonic *eikōn*. In *Eugnostos*, for example, much use is made of the term, both to describe entities within the Pleroma being *typoi* of other entities (e.g., III, 3, 82, where the Saviour "reveals six androgynous beings whose *typos* is that of those who preceded them"), or to describe phenomena of this world as *typoi* of entities in the Pleroma. At 83-4 for example, we find the following:

> Now our aeon came to be as a *typos* in relation to Immortal Man. Time came to be as a *typos* of the First Begetter, his son. [The year] came to be as a *typos* of the [Saviour. The] twelve months came to be as a *typos* of the twelve powers. The three hundred and sixty days of the year came to be as a *typos* of the three hundred and sixty persons who were revealed by the Saviour.[20]

This envisages quite an extensive parallelism between the noetic and physical worlds, and goes some way towards establishing a relation of archetype and image between them. In general, however, it is not clear to me how coherent a theory of archetypes the Gnostic writers had. Is the Aeon Ecclesia, for instance, the quasi-Platonic form of the Church on earth (and if so, of what church?), or is "Ecclesia" simply an evocative label for an aeon? Do the aeons which become the sons of Seth remain above, while sending "sparks" down into the physical world? And if so, do we have here, in effect, Ideas of Individuals?

I will leave this question in the air, and end with a question of terminology. The actual term (*Pleroma*) for the noetic world is not Platonic,[21] though Philo uses it on occasion in a non-technical sense)[22] but the adjective (*pleres*) and the verb (*pleroō*) are frequently used in Platonism to describe the realm of Forms. Philo repeatedly describes God or the *Logos* as "full";[23] Seneca, in *Ep.* 65, 4, reporting Platonic doctrine, describes God as "full" (*plenus*) of these geometrical shapes, which Plato calls "ideas." Plotinus describes the intelligible Totality (*to alethinon pan*) as "filling itself" (*peplerokos heauto, Enn.* VI, 4, 2, 15), and of Nous as being "filled" by contemplation of the One at *Enn.* VI, 8, 16, 19ff. Only the substantive (*plērōma*) is never used. It spreads as far as the Hermetic Corpus, but even there is something less than a technical term.[24]

We may accept, then, that the term *Pleroma* is derived from the language of the New Testament, even as is the term *aiōn* in the plural, and the mythological details are distinctive of Gnosticism, but the concept which it represents is, I would maintain, an implantation from the Platonist tradition into Gnosticism. Nowhere in the purely Jewish tradition do we find the idea of a whole, articulated archetypal world, by reference to which, as a pattern, God makes this one. That is a distinctively Hellenic contribution.

NOTES

1. This is not to disregard such interesting Rabbinic traditions as that there pre-existed an archetype of the Torah, or of the Ark of the Covenant. Such traditions cannot be traced back further than the 2nd Century C.E. and thus are almost certainly dependent on Greek conceptions, or even specifically on Philo. The "heavenly Jerusalem" of Heb. 12:22, similarly, is interesting, but it is not quite clear whether it is intended to serve as an archetype of the Platonic sort. One may note, though, that the Valentinians, as reported by Hippolytus (*Ref.* VI, 32, 9) took it to refer, not to the Pleroma, but to the Ogdoad below it — which does, however, serve as a sort of paradigm for Sophia (ibid. 34, 3-4).

2. *The Middle Platonists*, p. 29.

3. *Ap.* Aug. *CD* VII, 28.

4. The fact that the Father in *Trip. Trac.* is presented "alone, without any companion" puts it at variance with the teaching of Valentinus himself, as Attridge and Pagels note in their introduction, and of Ptolemaeus, as represented in Irenaeus, but agrees with the variety of Valentinianism presented by Hippolytus in *Ref.* VI, 29, 5ff.

5. Direct influence from Philo cannot be ruled out, of course, but is not necessary to assume. See on this passage the excellent discussion of G.C. Stead, "In Search of Valentinus," in *The Rediscovery of Gnosticism*, Vol. I (Leiden, 1980), pp. 90-92.

6. E.g. *Opif.* 21; *Leg. All.* II, 87; *Cher.* 86; *Post.* 136 (ἀπὸ σοφίας θεοῦ, τῆς ἀνελλιποῦς πηγῆς).

7. E.g. *Enn.* III, 8, 10, 5 (the One compared to an undiminished spring); VI, 7, 12, 24. Fountain imagery is also characteristic of the Chaldaean Oracles, e.g., Fr. 30 DP: *pēgē tōn pēgōn*; 37, 49, 52.

8. Cf., however, 62, 20ff., just below, where a reason is given for the Father not granting their full status to the Aeons from the beginning, "that they might not exalt themselves to the Father in glory, and might not think that from themselves alone they have this." There is no comparable problem of insubordination within the Platonist noetic cosmos!

9. The term *aeōn* presumably originates from such NT locutions (e.g., Eph. 3:21) as εἰς τοὺς αἰῶνας τῶν αἰώνων, where the literal-minded could see a reference to a plurality, and even a hierarchy, of aeons. (Cf. Iren. *Adv. Haer.* I, 3, 1). In the singular, the term appears, of course, in the *Timaeus*, as the noetic archetype of Chronos. It may be noted that such a group as the Ophites, according to Irenaeus's account (*Adv. Haer.* I, 30, 2), termed the realm presided over by the Father "Aeon" rather than "Pleroma," in this according more closely with the *Timaeus*; as also does the Valentinian Heracleon (e.g., *Comm. in Joh.* Fr. 1; Fr. 22). *Aion* is also the Chaldaean term for the entity which presides over the intelligible realm.

10. E.g., I, 8, 2; III, 5, 6; V, 8, 3 and 5.

11. The concept of an "etherial" or "heavenly" earth turns up in 2nd-century Platonism, in Plutarch's *De Facie*, 935C, and *Def. Or.* 416E, where the epithet *olympia gē* is said to be applied by "some people" to the Moon, but this is not the same as the concept of an archetypal earth here.

12. Philo postulates a noetic archetype of *aisthēsis*, *Leg. All.* I, 21-26, as does Plotinus later, in *Enn.* VI (see below).

13. This concords with the doctrine of the Valentinian Theodotus (*Exc. ex Theod.* 32, 1) that "each of the aeons has its own pleroma."

14. ὥστε εἶναι τὰς αἰσθήσεις ταύτας ἀμυδρὰς νοήσεις, τὰς δὲ ἐκεῖ νοήσεις ἐναργεῖς αἰσθήσεις.

15. While generally true, this is not the case with the Demiurge as presented by the Valentinian Marcus (*ap.* Iren. *Adv. Haer.* I, 17, 2). Marcus satirizes the Demiurge for wishing to imitate "the eternity, the limitlessness and the timeliness" of the Ogdoad, in the Pleroma, but being unable to do so, and therefore producing Time as an image of Eternity — a clear reference to the Demiurge of the *Timaeus*.

16. See the discussion of this concept in H.M. Schenke, *Der Gott "Mensch" in der Gnosis* (Berlin, 1962).

17. "The Father of Truth" in *Gr. Seth.* sounds as if he is supreme (e.g., 50, 10-15) and the expression "Son of Man" as used in the tractate for Jesus/Seth is interpreted as if "Man" meant the supreme God.

18. In *Eugnostos* III, 3, 85, (= *Sophia Jes Christ* III, 4, 108), we find the sequence Immortal Man, Son of Man, and the Saviour, all as aeons in the Pleroma, Immortal Man being the offspring of the First Father, so things can become quite complicated.

19. In the *Gospel of the Egyptians* (III, 60, 9-18 = VI, 71, 18-30) Seth "sows his seed in the aeons" (in IV "the earth-born aeons"), but this seems to refer to his sowing the pneumatics in the world (specifically in Sodom and Gomorrah). It is not clear whether anything remains above.

20. A similar system of imaging is presented by Irenaeus, *Adv. Haer.* I, 17, 1, 1 as the doctrine of the Valentinian Marcus, but there "brought about through the Mother, by the Demiurge, without his being aware of it."

21. In the technical sense of "full and perfect nature" (LSJ) it seems to go back to the writings of St. Paul (e.g., *Rom.* 11:12; *Eph.* 3-9; *Col.* 2:9).

22. *V. Mos.* II, 62, *Spec. Leg.* I, 272, *Prob.* 128.

23.   E.g., *Leg. All* I, 44; *Quod Det.* 54; *Somn.* I, 75 (*logos*); *Spec. Leg.* II, 53
      (θεὸς . . .πλήρης ἀγαθῶν τελείων).
24.   E.g., God the (*plērōma tou agathou*), VI, 4, 3; or (*plērōma tōn pantōn*),
      XVI, 3, 4.

Plotinus's Anti-Gnostic Polemic and Porphyry's *Against the Christians*

Christos Evangeliou

I

Porphyry divides the work of Plotinus chronologically into three parts on the basis of his own association with the great philosopher. The three parts are: (1) The twenty-one treatises written before the year A.D. 263, when Porphyry came to Rome from Athens and joined Plotinus's circle; (2) the twenty-four treatises written during the six-year period of his residence in Rome; (3) the nine treatises which Plotinus wrote after Porphyry's departure and before his own death in A.D. 270. According to Porphyry's evaluation, the treatises vary in power depending on the time of writing, but the twenty-four produced in the mid-period display, he thinks, "the utmost reach of the powers and, except for the short treatises among them, attain the highest perfection."[1]

I think that no one who has read the *Enneads* carefully can disagree with Porphyry's expert judgment on this matter. What should be emphasized is the fact that about one-third of the treatises produced in the mid-period have a distinctly polemical tone, and they include some of the longest treatises that Plotinus ever wrote. Specifically, to this group belong the treatises numbered in chronological order 42, 43 and 44, which bear the common title *On the Genera of Being* and which were written to defend Plato's ontology against Aristotelian and Stoic criticism.[2] The treatise *Against the Gnostics*, which is numbered 33 and comes as an epilogue to the series of treatises numbered 30, 31, and 32,

111

belongs to the same polemical group.[3]   In writing these treatises,
Plotinus's purpose was to defend both Plato against the attacks of some
apostates from the ancient philosophy, and Hellenism, that is, the
Hellenic κόσμος, the Hellenic λόγος, and the Hellenic ἀρετή, against
metaphysical fancies and fearful cries coming from certain alienated
men, the so-called Gnostics.[4]   In this respect, Plotinus definitely has a
place in that illustrious series of distinguished men who took it upon
themselves to defend their Hellenic heritage when they felt that it was
seriously threatened.   This great effort, which started with Celsus[5] in the
second century A.D. and ended with Julian in the fourth century A.D.,
found in Porphyry its greatest spokesman.[6]

My main purpose in this study is to compare critically Plotinus's
treatise *Against the Gnostics* with Porphyry's work *Against the Christians*
in order to determine the common elements in these movements which
the two philosophers found objectionable.   It is to be understood that
such an investigation cannot give us a complete list of points shared by
Gnosticism and Christianity, as the philosophers perceived them, due to
the fate of Porphyry's burned book, from which only a number of
fragments remain.[7]   In spite of this and their differences in style, the
two authors share certain basic ideas and ideals about the Cosmos and
man's place in it which are distinctly Hellenic and, therefore, anti-
Gnostic and anti-Christian.   But, before I come to that, I should like to
briefly address a question which is important for the correct
understanding of the relationship of Gnosticism to the Greek
philosophy of the third century A.D.   This question relates to the
identity of the men against whom Plotinus wrote his diatribe.

II

In his long treatise against the strange Gnostic teachings, Plotinus
never mentions his opponents by name.[8]   He does not even refer to
them as Gnostics.   At one point only (II.9.10.3), he calls them his
friends who had been so badly contaminated by the new teaching before
they met him that they could not get over it even after they had been
taught the true doctrine by him.   However, we do have Porphyry's
reliable testimony (*Vita Plot.* 16) that Plotinus's target was the circle
around Adelphius and Aquilinus who had abandoned the ancient Greek
philosophy and declared in favor of the revelations of such masters as
Zoroaster, Zostrianus, Allogenes, Nicotheus and others.   Since these
apostates believed and openly taught that Plato did not penetrate "the
depth of Intelligible Being" (βάθος τῆς νοητῆς οὐσίας), they became

the subject of frequent discussions in Plotinus's classroom. At the end, the master was compelled to write against them and urged Amelius and Porphyry to do the same in more detail, which they did.[9] These, then, are the men whom Porphyry, but not Plotinus, refers to as "Gnostics."

Porphyry's information is valuable, but it helps us little to solve the enigma regarding the identity of those "Gnostics." For, given the fact that in Rome at that time there were many Gnostic sects, such as Sethians, Barbelognostics, Ophites, Archontics, Valentinians and others,[10] the question arises: To which of these sects did Plotinus's Gnostic friends belong? Furthermore, since some of the Gnostic sects were Christian and others were pagan, we would like to know whether Plotinus addressed Christian or pagan Gnostics here. Unfortunately, the experts who have looked into this problem hold different opinions depending on the interpretation of an ambiguous passage in *Vita Plotini* 16. This passage reads as follows in Greek:

Γεγόνασι δὲ κατ' αὐτὸν τῶν Χριστιανῶν πολλοὶ μὲν καὶ ἄλλοι, αἱρετικοὶ δὲ ἐκ τῆς παλαιᾶς φιλοσοφίας ἀνηγμένοι οἱ περὶ Ἀδέλφιον καὶ Ἀκυλῖνον οἵ. . .

The following three varying translations of this passage seem possible depending on what one takes to be the syntactical connections and references of the two ambiguous words, ἄλλοι and οἱ.

(a) "There were at that time many Christians and other sectaries, like the followers of Adelphius and Aquilinus who had abandoned the ancient philosophy, who . . ."

(b) "There were at that time many other Christians and among them were the sectarian followers of Adelphius and Aquilinus who had abandoned the ancient philosophy and who . . ."

(c) "There were at that time many Christians — among them the sectarian followers of Adelphius and Aquilinus who had abandoned the ancient philosophy — who . . ."

According to (a) there were two distinct groups, the Christians and the sectarian pagans, who made use of the Gnostic books and revelations. Reitzenstein, Bossuet, Festugière, and other scholars who, according to H.C. Puech,[11] identified Plotinus's opponents with the pagan Gnostics, presumably adopted this rendering of the passage. Puech himself opts for (b) because he believes that Porphyry here distinguishes from the mass of Christian Gnostics that special group which had certain connections with the "philosophie antique."[12] Unless one is prepared to take the liberty of amending the text by deleting the words μέν and the second δέ, it would seem that (b) is definitely preferable to (a). However, (b) seems to go too far in the direction of making the αἱρετικοὶ in Porphyry's text look like Christian heretics. They certainly were not.[13] Moreover, this rendering implies that the followers of Adelphius and Aquilinus were the only Christians who made use of the Gnostic revelations specified by Porphyry in the lines which have been left out of the above quotation. But the text, as we have it, makes such a restriction unwarrantable. Therefore, I think that (c), which is basically the same as MacKenna's rendering of this admittedly difficult passage,[14] avoids the pitfalls of (b) while it saves the important point of identifying Plotinus's opponents as Christians. Another merit of (c) is that it also agrees with (a) in that it allows for the case that other Christian groups, besides the followers of Adelphius and Aquilinus, made use of the Gnostic books and revelations, which is quite possible.[15]

Be this as it may, the important point, for an accurate understanding of Plotinus's anti-Gnostic polemic, is that he was interested neither in Christian Gnosticism nor in pagan Gnosticism in general, but only in Adelphius, Aquilinus and their followers. The reason for this, I think, was the fact that these fellows were, as Porphyry put it, apostates in the sense that they had abandoned the honorable tradition of Platonic philosophy and tried to set up a new school.[16] Unlike Plotinus, these people were unable to find in the *Dialogues* the whole truth regarding the realm of Intelligible Being (νοητὴ οὐσία) and, in their search for a higher knowledge and wisdom (γνῶσις, σοφία), they had embraced certain forgeries which passes as revelations of Zoroaster, Zostrianus and the other great prophets from the East.[17] This apostasy embarrassed Plotinus and scandalized many in his school.

In writing against these Gnostics and in urging Porphyry and Amelius to do the same, Plotinus did not aim at, nor did he hope to, bring the apostates back to the right road (II.9.10). Rather he desired to enlighten the rest of his pupils about the truth and inform them that (a) whatever is worthy in the apostates' teaching had been taken from Plato, and (b) what had been added to it is far from being true. "For, in sum, a part of their doctrine comes from Plato; all the novelties through which they seek to establish a philosophy of their own have been picked up outside of the truth" (II.9.6.10-12). In another passage, echoing St. Irenaeus's apt characterization of the Gnostics as poor translators of what has been well said, Plotinus remarks: "All this terminology is piled up to conceal their debt to the ancient Greek philosophy which taught, clearly and without bombast, the ascent from the cave and the gradual advance of the souls to a truer and truer vision" (II.9.6.6-9).

In view of this direct and important evidence regarding the relationship of Greek philosophy to Gnosticism (or, more precisely, a certain Gnostic sect), I find it necessary to make a parenthetical comment. I must say from the outset that I am fully aware of the complexity of this problem and the variety of the proposed solutions, ranging from Harnack's oft-quoted aphorism that "Gnosticism was the acute Hellenization of Christianity,"[18] to A.H. Armstrong's sweeping generalization as follows: "I think, then, in general, that any kind of influence of Greek philosophy on Gnosticism was not genuine but extraneous and, for the most part superficial."[19] It is true that Professor Armstrong makes this strong statement after he has drawn two important distinctions between the wider and the narrower senses of "Gnosticism," and between genuine and extraneous "influence." In his opinion, one should speak of "genuine influence" only in the case

> . . . when someone's mind has been formed to an important extent by a tradition: when, that is, he has been taught by great thinkers of that tradition and/or has read the writings considered authoritative in that tradition in their languages (which may or may not be his own) under the guidance of competent inheritors of that tradition. (p. 100)

Evidently, the two basic criteria of determining "genuine influence" are, according to Armstrong, (1) instruction of the recipient by the great thinkers of a given tradition, and/or (2) ability to read in the original the authoritative writings of that tradition. So far, so good.

With due respect for Professor Armstrong, I must say that his two criteria seem to apply well in the case of those Gnostics about whom Porphyry speaks in *Vita Plot.* 16, and against whom Plotinus wrote the diatribe of II.9. But if they do meet his criteria, then how is it possible for Professor Armstrong to deny "genuine influence" of Greek philosophy on Gnosticism and be consistent? Let me try to be more specific and less critical. There is no doubt that Plotinus and Porphyry considered the followers of Adelphius and Aquilinus as apostates from Greek philosophy who were led astray by Gnostic teaching. It is also clear that the apostates had read Plato in the original and had adopted many Platonic doctrines. Furthermore, Plotinus calls them his "friends," as we have seen, and Eunapius reports that Origen, Amelius and Aquilinus were Porphyry's συμφοιτηταί (fellow disciples).[20] So, at least in the case of Aquilinus, we have a Gnostic who was very well-read in the Greek philosophical tradition and taught by no less a great teacher than Plotinus. From this clearly follows that one cannot, on Professor Armstrong's criteria, reach his negative general conclusion. Either the criteria should be changed or the conclusion must be revised.[21]

These remarks should not be misunderstood. I do not say that Greek philosophy influenced all spiritual movements of the first three centuries of our era, especially Gnosticism and Christianity, in the same way or to the same degree; nor do I assert that the Christian preaching was less or more absurd than the Gnostic teaching to the philosophically minded people of that time. I simply wish to point out the fact that Plotinus's Gnostic opponents, by being trained in the Greek philosophical tradition, refute Professor Armstrong's statement regarding the relationship of Gnosticism to Greek philosophy, since they easily pass his test of determining "genuine influence."[22] This being the case, I think that any student of this period of intellectual history should keep in mind the following cautious observation of Professor Jonas:

> Modern scholars have advanced in turn Hellenic, Babylonian, Egyptian, and Iranian origins and every possible combination of these with one another and with Jewish and Christian elements. Since in the material of its representation Gnosticism actually is a product of syncretism, each of these theories can be supported from the sources and none of them is satisfactory alone . . .[23]

To close this lengthy parenthesis, the important point for our purposes here is that Gnosticism and Christianity were perceived by Plotinus and Porphyry in the same light, that is, as alien and un-Hellenic voices or, rather, cries.[24] The case of Aquilinus, a "classmate" of Porphyry in the school of Plotinus in Rome and the case of, say, St. Gregory, a fellow student with Julian in the philosophical schools of Athens may or may not seem parallel to a modern scholar, depending on his feelings or biases. But to a pagan like Plotinus, Porphyry or Julian, the fact that Aquilinus used his training in Greek philosophy to serve Gnosticism, while St. Gregory used the same to serve the Christian cause, could make no difference at all. The philosophers considered Gnosticism and Christianity as forms of barbarism and fought both of them as enemies of Hellenism. That Plotinus's opposition to Gnosticism and Porphyry's anti-Christian polemic share a common philosophical ground will become clear from the analysis of their arguments which follows.

III

Porphyry, the editor of the *Enneads*, has given to the last tractate of the second *Ennead* (II.9.), two titles: "Against the Gnostics" and "Against Those Who Declare the Maker of the World and the World to be Evil." The reader of this treatise may notice the following peculiarities. First, the author not only does not mention his opponents by name anywhere, but also he never quotes from their writings the doctrines and the theses which he criticizes. Second, the role of an able attorney, who is determined to defend both the beauty of the Cosmos and the worth of a life led by reason and lived in virtue on this Earth, would hardly seem to fit the traditional image of Plotinus as an austere, ascetic, mystical and otherworldly philosopher who was ashamed to have a body (*Vita Plot.* 1). Third, the first three chapters seem rather loosely connected with the rest of the treatise. The reason for this is that Plotinus here seems to sum up the arguments which he had expounded in three other treatises.[25] It is possible that all this material constituted a large treatise which the editor broke up for pedagogical or other reasons.[26] The point is that in the opening chapters of his anti-Gnostic treatise Plotinus tries to defend the thesis of the Three Hypostases which is important for his philosophy and which is summarized as follows:

> We need not, then, go seeking any other Principles; this — the One and the Good — is our First, next to it follows the Intellectual Principle, the Primal Thinker, and upon this follows Soul. Such is the order of nature. The Intellectual Realm allows no more than these and no less. (II.9.1.12-16)

We will be in a position to better understand Plotinus's concern about the number, the order and the function of the Hypostases if we keep in mind that he sincerely believed that he had found in Plato's writings the doctrine of the Three Hypostases (ἕν, νοῦς, ψυχή),[27] and that one of the Gnostic novelties was the multiplication of the entities of their Intelligible Realm (Πλήρωμα), occasionally to fantastic numbers.[28] Thus the arguments of the first three chapters of II.9. are so designed as to reject all proposals for either reducing or increasing the number of the Three Hypostases by either adding new ones or dividing the old, especially Nous and Psyche, which are naturally multifunctional. Plotinus particularly concentrates on the Gnostic Ἐπίνοια (Thought) and rejects it as a candidate for entering the Plotinian Hypostatic Triad as separate from Νοῦς (II.9.2.1). Having adopted the Aristotelian conception of νοῦς as a "Self-Thinking

Thought," Plotinus was able to combine in one Divine Νοῦς the Thinker, the Thought and the Awareness of it, by arguing as follows:

> No: The Divine Mind in its mentation thinks itself; the object of the thought is nothing external: Thinker and Thought are one; therefore in its thinking and knowing it possesses itself, observes itself, sees itself not as something unconscious but as knowing: in this Primal Knowing it must include, as one and the same Act, the knowledge of the knowing.[29]

Beginning with chapter four, Plotinus devotes the greatest part of this tractate to defending the goodness of the Demiurge, the beauty of the Cosmos, and man's dignified place in it. There are many Gnostic doctrines at which he hints and rejects as being either ridiculous (γελοῖον) or absurd (ἄτοπον).[30] For instance, to justify their claim that the world is the product of ignorance, error, and vainglory on the part of the Maker, the Gnostics had tried to utilize the myth of Phaedrus (246C) which speaks figuratively of the soul as "failing of its wings." Plotinus's view is that this does not apply to the Cosmic Soul but to the individual souls and their follies (II.9.4.1). He also finds ridiculous the Gnostic explanation as to the motives of the Creator in creating the world. They speak anthropomorphically and assert that "glory" (ἵνα τιμῶτο) was His motive, as if He was no better than a sculptor (II.9.4.14). In addition, Plotinus, who had accepted the standard Greek position that this Cosmos is the necessary, timeless, and wonderful outcome of the divine wisdom, goodness, and power, found offensive the dogmatic Gnostic assertion that the Cosmos was created in time and that it will be destroyed when the cosmic drama comes to an end. Scornfully, Plotinus observes:

> And when will it destroy the work? If it repents of its work, what is it waiting for? If it has not yet repented, then it will never repent: it must be already accustomed to the world, must be growing tender towards it with the passing of time. (II.9.4.17-19)

Plotinus also thinks that the Gnostics contradict themselves in that they express their hatred of this Earth and, at the same time, they preach about a "new Earth" (καινὴ γῆ) which has been created for them somewhere in the heavens (II.9.5.24).[31] Besides, in Plotinus's view, the Gnostics prove themselves not very intelligent by expecting this world, which is just an image (albeit the best possible image) of the intelligible archetype, to be as perfect as its model (παράδειγμα). Above all, the Gnostics must surely be very arrogant to believe that of all the immense creation only they and those like them possess an immortal soul which thus enables them to be exclusively in contact with the Supreme God (II.9.5.6-15). But for Plotinus, a human being, no matter how valuable or knowable, cannot be the best creature in the world and, when compared with the greatness of the heavenly bodies or the Cosmos as a whole, a man appears to be rather insignificant. On this Plotinus is in agreement with Aristotle.[32]

From their hubristic and blasphemous attitude towards the world, Plotinus passes next to the Gnostic irreverence for the ancient philosophy, especially Plato, from whom they took whatever is valuable in their teaching, e.g., immortality of the Soul, Intelligible Realm, the Supreme God, the Creator, the rivers and punishments of the underworld and so forth (II.9). Plotinus does not blame them for doing so. What he finds objectionable in the Gnostic behavior is their attempt to set up a new school, "their own philosophy" (ἰδίαν φιλοσοφίαν).[33] Thus, they misinterpret Plato or, worse, as Plotinus put it, "They hunt fame by insult, reviling and seeking in their own persons to replace men honored by the fine intelligences of ages past" (II.9.6.52-54). A short list of Gnostic innovations, of which Plotinus disapproves, includes the complete destruction of the Cosmos, blame of the World-Soul for attaching itself to body and of the Cosmos as a whole and contempt for the Maker and Ruler of this All, to whom they ascribe passions inappropriate to Divine nature (II.9.6.).

The Gnostic cosmology should be rejected, according to Plotinus, not only because it is fanciful and strange but also for the reason that its hubristic and blasphemous doctrines would have deleterious effects on the morals of the people. He was well aware of the vulnerability of human beings to the Gnostic revolutionary and immoral teaching, especially when that sort of teaching is followed by talk like this: "You yourself are to be nobler than all else, nobler than men, nobler than even gods." Or "You, yourself are the child of God; those men whom you used to venerate, those beings whose worship they inherit from antiquity, none of these are His children; you without lifting hand are nobler than the very heavens; others take up the cry." (II.9.9.53-58).

It is, therefore, understandable that the remainder of Plotinus's criticism concentrates on the Gnostic ethics and immoral practices, although chapters 10-13 contain many references to such important Gnostic terms and figures as σοφία (Wisdom), μήτηρ (Mother), δημιουργὸς (Demiurge), τόλμα (audacity), νεῦσις (decline), ἔλλαμψις (illumination), ἐνθύμησις (remembrance), ὕλη (matter), πῦρ (fire), etc.[34] Particularly, commenting on the Gnostic irrational fear of the spheres, Plotinus asks: "And what, after all, is there so terrible in these spheres with which it is sought to frighten people unaccustomed to thinking, never trained in an instructive and coherent gnosis?" (II.9.13.9-10). It is precisely this morbid fear which, the philosopher thinks, provides a basis for the magical practices of the Gnostic sects. Their "sacred formulas," their "spells" and "evocations" were all designed and sold to the faithful with the assurance that they will secure a safe passage of the soul through the hostile Cosmic powers and even protect the body from disease, which Plotinus finds laughable indeed.[35]

With regard to morality, Plotinus thinks that the Gnostics are worse than the Epicureans, who denied Providence and made pleasure the highest end of life. For the Gnostic doctrine not only carps at Providence but also

> . . . it scorns every law known to us; immemorial virtue and all restraint it makes into a laughing stock, lest any loveliness be seen on earth; it cuts at the root of all orderly living, and of the righteousness which, innate in the moral sense, is made perfect by thought and self-discipline: all that would give us a noble human being is gone. (II.9.15.10-17)

There is something very humane and moving in Plotinus's defense of traditional values, virtue, decency, and a common-sense moral attitude in this passage. The ancient Hellenic ideal of the good life considered as restrained activity of the soul led by reason and capable of bringing out what is best in a man through self-discipline and thought, all this has now become dispensable. Those who claim possession of the supreme knowledge, that is, Gnosis, do not think they need the old virtues, nor do they care for them any more. Not only do they not practice virtue, "they do not even talk about the subject," Plotinus observes and his sad observation sounds so modern and familiar to us.[36] To the Gnostic cry "Look to God" and everything will be fine, Plotinus retorts that "'God' on the lips without a good conduct of life, is a word" (II.9.15.40).

Like a reasonable man, Plotinus considers absurd the arrogant claim that a Gnostic can be "good" while despising every human virtue and decency as well as the whole world and its many gods. He finds it difficult to believe that in a human heart, filled with so much hatred for the Cosmos and everything else in it, there could be any room left for the love of the Supreme Gnostic God. If this is not hubris, it is certainly hypocrisy because, as Plotinus put it, "where we love, our hearts are warm also to the kin of the beloved; we are not indifferent to the children of our friend" (II.9.16.7-8). Comments like this may indicate the true gentleness and humanity of Plotinus's character, but they also tell us that the philosopher did not recognize an all-important aspect of the Gnostic mentality, that is, the abyss which separates mundane things and celestial Archons alike from the God whom they call their Father. For the true God, like the true Gnostic, is not kin but alien to this Cosmos in which he finds himself imprisoned. Their revolutionary spirit is absolutely uncompromising towards everything within this Cosmos. In this sense, the Gnostic spiritual revolt is truly of Cosmic dimensions and has its parallel in certain extreme movements in the twentieth century, such as existentialism and nihilism, as has been observed.[37]

It is true that the Gnostics used Platonic texts, such as *Phaedo* and *Timaeus*, to justify their asceticism and negative attitude towards the body and the material world in general.[38] For this reason, Plotinus found it necessary to close his treatise against the Gnostics by defending Plato and his own interpretation of the Platonic philosophy. Thus he tries to explain that in the divinely ordered system, which is called Cosmos, everything has its proper place, body and soul, men and Gods, the higher and the lower orders, or as he likes to put it, the first, the second, and the third. There are no gaps in this system. The hierarchy is complete and eternally arranged for eternity. The Cosmos as a whole is very beautiful and, in fact, the best possible copy of its supreme archetype, the Κόσμος Νοητός. Even the existing partial imperfections and shortcomings add to the marvelous beauty of the whole. For Plotinus, even man's life on earth can become beautiful if it is guided by reason and crowned with virtue and true wisdom. For him, as for Socrates, the first and highest duty of man is to fulfill Apollo's command: "Know thyself." The true Platonists, no less than the Gnostics, are convinced that their real abode is elsewhere. The basic difference between the two is their attitude towards this life. While the Gnostic constantly complains, blames everything, hates everybody, blasphemes and, nevertheless, goes on living unwisely believing that at the end he will be saved by means of secret revelations and magical spells, the Platonic philosopher tries to live in peace with other people and in harmony with the world, to keep his soul as pure as possible, and to calmly prepare for the great journey when the time comes. In conclusion, Plotinus can say to his disciples:

> I leave it to yourselves to read the books and examine the rest of the doctrine: you will note all through how our form of philosophy inculcates simplicity of character and honest thinking in addition to all other good qualities, how it inculcates reverence and not arrogant self-assertion, how its boldness is balanced with reason, by careful proof, by cautious progression,

by the utmost circumspection — and you will compare those other systems to one proceeding by this method. (II.9.14.37-43)

Recapitulating Plotinus's criticism against the apostate Gnostics, it may be observed that his main objections turn around the following points: (1) inconsistencies in their doctrines as well as between their theory and practice; (2) their irrational assertions about the Cosmos, e.g., that it was created in time by an ignorant Demiurge, that it will come to an end, that it is evil and serves as a prison for the spiritual Gnostics who are alien to it; (3) their arrogant and hubristic attitude towards the visible divinities within the Cosmos and to the Cosmos as a whole; (4) their irreverence for old traditions and great men of the past, especially Plato; (5) their secret revelations and immodest claim that of all the creation only they themselves qualify to be called "sons of God"; (6) their immoral teaching that salvation cannot come from complete virtue and human excellence, but from God's inscrutable will and magic formulae; (7) their libertinism and demagogic capacity to deceive the simple-minded by calling them children of God and promising them a paradise in heaven.

IV

Turning from Plotinus to Porphyry, and comparing the anti-Gnostic polemic as found in *Ennead* II.9. to the anti-Christian polemic as expressed in the few remaining fragments of the fifteen-book long treatise *Against the Christians*,[39] it does not take long to notice that, despite their differences in style, the two works share many of the essential arguments.

Regarding the style, it may be noted that Porphyry, unlike Plotinus, names and frequently quotes the prophets of the Old Testament, the Evangelists of the New Testament, and the Apostles of Jesus, especially Peter and Paul. Also, unlike Plotinus's criticism which is doctrinal and general, Porphyry's sharp remarks are always specific and to the point, betraying a literary critic who is well-read in the literature of his opponents.[40] Furthermore, Porphyry took from Plotinus the technique of capitalizing on the ridiculous and absurd aspects of his opponents tenets, and he developed it to such a degree that it reminds us of such spirited writers as Renan and Voltaire.[41] No wonder, then, that Porphyry was considered a most formidable foe of Christianity. It is not an accident that of all anti-Christian books of that time only Porphyry's treatise was committed to flames. Finally, while Plotinus often gives the impression that he is more interested in defending Hellenism that in attacking Gnosticism, Porphyry only attacks, and is shrewd enough to make his target the very foundations of the new faith. Since the basis of the Christian claim to uniqueness and to monopoly of truth and salvation is the belief that their sacred books are God-inspired, Porphyry's strategy is to prove to an educated person beyond doubt that those writings are, in fact, full of inconsistencies, exaggerations, impossibilities, fabrications and falsehoods. And if so, they cannot be inspired by the true God as the Christians claim, nor can they provide a road to salvation, let alone *the only* road available to men. Porphyry hoped that his fellow-pagans would get the message and stay away from the basilicas and the strange God. If we judge from the reaction to the treatise, his message was getting across quite well.[42]

Regarding the doctrinal argumentation, it may be observed that Porphyry's criticism parallels Plotinus's objections in the essential points.   Specifically, Porphyry objects to Christian Cosmology, eschatology, morality and religious practices in a way which is reminiscent of Plotinus's anti-Gnostic polemic. The question, What are Porphyry's grounds of criticism in each of these areas?, cannot be fully answered, due to the fragmentary state of his extant work. However, the available evidence allows us to get a glimpse of the direction and the general tone of his arguments against Christianity. Take, for instance, the Christian doctrine that the world as a whole will perish one day. To Porphyry's mind, this doctrine is illogical and unacceptable, because it entails that the Cosmos as a whole, which is God's work, is not as perfect as it could be. But deficiency in the product would reflect, in the final analysis, an imperfection in the Maker himself, who is perfect by definition. Therefore, the Cosmos as a whole cannot change, let alone perish. Like Plotinus and other Greek philosophers, Porphyry was convinced that there is no sufficient reason for entertaining the idea that this Cosmos either came into being in time or it will pass away in time. Either hypothesis would allow for an unreasonable change in the immutable nature of God, which is logically impossible. In a Plotinian manner, Porphyry concludes that the Christian doctrines of creation and Cosmic destruction are irrational and blasphemous and, therefore, should be rejected.[43]

But there is something else about the Christian eschatology which, to Porphyry's eyes, is more ridiculous than absurd. He knew very well that Christians believe not only in Jesus's resurrection but in their own. They go so far as to assert that the believer's body no less than his soul is immortal. Now Porphyry, like all genuine Platonists, was himself convinced about the immortality or, rather, eternity of the soul. Yet he found the Christian belief in the immortality of the flesh materialistic, base, and absurd. He asks the reader to think for a moment of the simple fact of life that fishermen have been eating fish for thousands of years, and, when drowned, they are eaten up by the fish. Then, let one try to tell, if he can, to whom of all these men the resurrected body will belong on the day of the Christian Last Judgment. Logically and humanly it is not possible to tell, and to say that God will take care of it, when the time comes, makes no sense for the rational philosopher, because even God cannot do the logically impossible. For example, no God can undo the horrible deeds done by the Achaeans when they sacked Troy.[44] At any rate, Porphyry thinks it a sign of ignorance and vulgarity for anyone to assert both contradictory propositions that the beautiful and great Cosmos will perish, and that his own little and dirty body will be preserved by God for eternity.[45]

Porphyry is also very skeptical about the value of the Christian morality, which makes the criterion of goodness to be, not virtue and excellence, but faith and poverty. Having some respect for Jesus, he seriously doubts whether the Christian God ever uttered the famous aphorism "It is easier for a camel to go through the eye of a needle than for a rich man to enter into the kingdom of Heaven."[46] For the philosopher, a doctrine which identifies, as a matter of course, the morally good with the poor, and the morally bad with the well-to-do, can come only from poverty-stricken men having an eye on the possessions of other men. No doubt, such a motto can serve the designs of a political demagogue but it becomes questionable when it comes from a moral reformer, like Jesus. The same can be said about such important Christian practices such as Eucharist and Baptism, which seem to make the way to salvation not only open to everyone but also too easy even for the most mean man. Besides, to promise to any criminal that no matter what he does in his life he will be absolved and enter paradise if only baptized before he dies, is equivalent to putting dynamite at the foundations of an organized society of decent human beings.[47] For Porphyry, there is no greater and more dangerous folly than that which has the audacity to preach this kind of gospel. In this respect, Porphyry's Christian enemies come so close to Plotinus's Gnostic opponents that, for all practical purposes, they are indistinguishable. Because of their irrational revelations, their immoral practices, and their questionable promises, both movements were perceived by the two philosophers as extremely dangerous for the established order, be it moral, social, political or metaphysical.[48]

V

In conclusion, the findings of this study can be summarized as follows. First, the available evidence seems to support the thesis that the Gnostics, whom Plotinus criticized, were in some way related to his circle, that they were trained in Greek philosophy, especially Plato, and that in all probability they belonged to a Christian Gnostic sect. Second, it follows from this thesis that the view, which absolutely denies any influence of Greek philosophy on any Gnostic sect anywhere at any time during the first three centuries of our era, cannot be correct. In the light of this research, it is beyond any doubt that some sort of relationship existed between the two traditions in the middle of the third century A.D. in Rome, especially in or around Plotinus's school, due possibly to the influence of Numenius's teaching.[49] Third, a simple comparison of Plotinus's anti-Gnostic polemic and Porphyry's criticism of Christianity clearly indicates that the two authors, in spite of their stylistic differences, criticized their opponents for essentially the same ethical and metaphysical reasons.

For philosophers, like Plotinus and Porphyry, who felt that they were the heirs of Hellenic culture in terms of language, philosophy, art, morality, and religious traditions, both Gnosticism and Christianity were perceived as alien, barbaric and un-Hellenic movements. In their irrational, excessive and hubristic claims about God, Cosmos, and man's virtue and place in the entire scheme of things, both movements were equally offensive to Hellenic sensibilities and unacceptable to the philosophic ethos of that time. What happened later is another story.

It is also clear that Plotinus, with his anti-Gnostic polemic which is actually an apology and defense of Hellenism, has given a definite answer to those scholars who still wonder about the possible sources of his philosophy.[50] In II.9. as well as throughout the *Enneads*, where there is scarcely one page without at least one quotation or reference to Plato, Plotinus proves himself, I think, as Hellenic a philosopher as any one could be in the third century A.D. or in the subsequent centuries.

NOTES

1. *Vita Plotini*, 6. 32-34. MacKenna's translation, which will be followed throughout, unless stated otherwise.
2. I have pointed this out in "The Ontological Basis of Plotinus's Criticism of Aristotle's Theory of Categories," *Studies in Neoplatonism: Ancient and Modern*, Vol. IV, R. Baine Harris, gen. ed. (New York: SUNY Press, 1982), pp. 73-83.

3.   R.T. Wallis, *Neoplatonism* (New York: Charles Scribner's Sons, 1972), p. 45; R. Harder, "Eine neue Schrift Plotins," *Hermes* LXXI (1936): 5-8; A.H. Armstrong, "Gnosis and Greek Philosophy," *Gnosis, Festschrift für Hans Jonas*, Barbara Aland, ed. (Göttingen: Vandenhoeck and Ruprecht, 1978), pp. 87-124. All of these scholars agree that the four treatises are parts of a larger treatise.

4.   The name derives from the Greek word for knowledge, γνῶσις. However, the meaning of this term as used by Gnostics is far from clear. On this, see H. Jonas, *The Gnostic Religion*, second edition, revised (Boston: Beacon Press, 1963), pp. 34-37.

5.   Lucian, Fronto, Hierocles, and the anonymous philosopher to whom Macarius addressed his *Apocriticus* are included in this series.

6.   That many Christian dignitaries, like Methodius of Tyre, Apollinaris of Laodicea, Eusebius of Caesarea, and the historian Philostorgius, wrote many volumes in response to Porphyry, clearly indicates the alarm which his book created in Christian circles. The book was finally burned in 448 A.D. under the Emperor Theodosius II. A.B. Hulen, *Porphyry's Work Against the Christians: An Interpretation* (Scottdale, PA: Mennonite Press, 1933), p. 6.

7.   The fragments were first collected and published with a German translation by Adolf von Harnack, *Kritik des Neuen Testaments: von einem griechischen Philosophen des 3. Jahrhunderts*, TU 37, 4 (Leipzig: J.C. Hinrich, 1911). The controversy as to whether the philosopher in Macarius's *Apocriticus* is someone who quotes Porphyry, or Hierocles who follows him, is only of philological interest. I refer the interested reader to T.W. Crafer, "The Work of Porphyry Against the Christians and Its Reconstruction," *The Journal of Theological Studies*, Vol. 15 (1913-1914): 360-395, 481-512.

8.   In this Plotinus follows an old Greek tradition.

9.   *Vita Plotini*, 16.

10. H.C. Puech, "Plotin et les Gnostiques," *Entretiens Hardt*, Vol. V (Vandoeuvres-Geneva, 1960), pp. 161-190.

11. Ibid., p. 163.

12. Ibid.

13. Dr. Puech himself makes this clear in his answer to Dodds's question. Ibid., pp. 175-176.

14. MacKenna's translation of this passage reads as follows: "Many Christians of this period — amongst them sectaries who had abandoned the old philosophy, men of the schools of Adelphius and Aquilinus — had . . ."

15. The Gnostic terminology to which Plotinus refers in chapters 9-13 suggests that he had Valentinian Gnostics in mind.

16. In II.9.6, Plotinus accuses the apostates of innovations with the intention to start a new movement, ἰδία φιλοσοφία, ἰδία αἵρεσις. Did Diophanes, whom Porphyry mentions in *Vita* 15, also belong to this Gnostic group? J. Rist thinks so, *Eros and Psyche* (Toronto: University of Toronto Press, 1962), p. 185. I think that Professor Rist is right, but the question needs further investigation.

17. *Vita Plotini*, 16.

18. H. Jonas, ibid., p. 36.

19. A.H. Armstrong, ibid., p. 101.

20. *The Lives of the Sophists*, ed. W.C. Wright (London: William Heinemann, 1922), p. 358.

21. At the end of his long article, Armstrong himself seems to have come a long way from his initial generalization. On p. 123 he writes: "I think that the whole question of the relation of Gnosis to Greek philosophy should be approached very cautiously with a clear definition of what is meant by Gnosis and a precise and detailed study of individual systems and thinkers on both sides in their historical context." With this view I fully agree.

22. For reasons which are not clear to this reader, Professor Armstrong asserts about Christianity what he denies about Gnosticism, that is, influence of Greek philosophy. See *Introduction to Ancient Philosophy* (London: Metheuen and Co., 1947), p. 159. To the eyes of the philosophers of that time, who perceived the two movements in the same light, this would have seemed inconsistent.

23. Ibid., p. 33.

24. "The other feature is the cryptic remark that a mournful or lamenting cry rises up from the agitated darkness," as Professor Jonas put it in a comment on the *Poimandres*. Ibid., p. 170.

25. The other treatises are: III.8., V.5., V.8.

26. The editor's desire to reach the number 54 (i.e. 6x9) may be included in his reasons for breaking up this and other treatises.

27. On this, see *Ennead* V.1.8., and the comments of Professor J.N. Findlay, "The Neoplatonism of Plato," in *The Significance of Neoplatonism*, R. Baine Harris, gen. ed. (New York: SUNY Press, 1976), pp. 23-40.

28. According to Irenaeus, *Adversus Haereses*, I.1., the Valentinian Pleroma had no less than thirty Aeons.

29. *Enneads*, II.9.1.46-51. In this context, Plotinus argues that even λόγος, the Reason Principle, which proceeds from νοῦς to ψυχὴ and makes it νοεράν, should not be viewed as an intermediate and separate principle.

30. The use of these derogatory words in this treatise is surprisingly frequent for the usually cool-headed Plotinus.

31. The location of the Gnostic paradise was "above the third heaven," according to Irenaeus, ibid., I.5.2.

32. *Nicomachean Ethics*, 1145a 7-12, and 1177b 24-1178a 1.

33. This explains, I think, Plotinus's interest in this Gnostic sect.

34. The terminology here is that of Christian Gnostics, in all probability Valentinians. Compare Irenaeus, ibid., I chapters 1-8 and Book II, chapter 1. Also, Jonas, ibid., pp. 174-205, and Puech, ibid., p. 162.

35. γελοῖον is the word used here again.

36. About this see A. MacIntyre, *After Virtue* (Notre Dame: NDU Press, 1981) and my review of this book in *The Review of Metaphysics*, Vol. XXXVII, no. 1 (September, 1983): 132-134.

37. Jonas, ibid., especially the epilogue, pp. 320-340.

38.   It is Plotinus's view that "Perhaps the hate of this school for the corporeal is due to their reading of Plato. . .," II.9.17.1-2.

39.   In Greek the title is Κατὰ Χριστιανῶν. . . . If compared with the title of Plotinus's treatise Πρὸς Τοὺς Γνωστικούς, we notice that a different preposition is used in each case. Κατὰ is much stronger than πρός, but this is lost in English when both words are rendered "against." A more accurate translation would be "To Gnostics," meaning a treatise addressed to Gnostics, and "Against the Christians," meaning a treatise directed against the Christians.

40.   Of Porphyry's ability as a literary critic there are two celebrated cases, (1) his *Commentary on Daniel*, where he proves that the "prophecies" are, in fact, "a chronicle of events that had already taken place," and (2) his claim that the so-called "writing of Moses" was actually written by Ezra, that is "1,180 years later," in M. Anastos's estimation in "Porphyry's Attack on the Bible," *The Classical Tradition* (Ithaca, NY: Cornell University Press, 1966), pp. 421-450.

41.   The similarities are noticed also by J. Moffatt, "The Great Attacks on Christianity: II. Porphyry, 'Against Christians.'" *The Expository Times*, Vol. 43 (October, 1931-September, 1932): 72-78.

42.   See n. 6, above.

43.   *Fragment* IV.1, and 6.

44.   *Fragment* IV.24.

45.   *Fragment* IV.2.

46.   Matthew 19:24; Mark 10:25 and Luke 18:25.

47.   *Fragment* III.5, and *Fragment* IV.19.

48.   I think that Dodds is right in his judgment that "What makes him (Plotinus) exceptional in the third century is his resolute objection to every short cut to wisdom proffered by Gnostics or Theurgists, Mithraists or Christians." "The Parmenides of Plato and the Origins of the Neoplatonic One," *Classical Quarterly*, Vol. 22 (1928): 129-143.

49.   *Vita Plotini*, 17, and E.R. Dodds, "Numenius and Ammonius," in the above cited *Entretiens Hardt*, Vol. V, pp. 3-32.

50.   On this issue, my study confirms T. Whittaker's view that ". . . the system of Plotinus was through and through Hellenic." *The Neoplatonists*, second edition, reprinted (Freeport, NY: Books for Libraries Press, 1970), p. xiv.

Theological Doctrines of the
Latin *Asclepius*

Stephen Gersh

The *Asclepius* is undoubtedly among the most interesting of the Hermetic writings, not only because it contains an extensive survey of doctrine but because — being a translation into Latin — it alone exercised some influence over medieval western thought. Its connection with the Greek *Corpus Hermeticum* has been fully established by A.D. Nock who noted striking parallels both of literary expression and of doctrinal content between the two texts, although it is unclear whether the author of the *Asclepius*'s original can be identified with that of one or more of the extant Greek treatises or whether he was simply acquainted with these other writings and influenced by them. At all events, this Latin dialogue provides a convenient summary of the main teachings of the Greek *Corpus Hermeticum* for those later western writers who will interest themselves in such matters.

The Latin *Asclepius* is a translation or rather adaptation, written by an unknown author active before A.D. 413, of a Greek treatise entitled "the Perfect Discourse" (Λόγος Τέλειος).[1] The fact that the work is a translation rather than an original composition is perhaps made obvious by the numerous Grecisms which it contains,[2] although the existence of a certain amount of direct evidence regarding the Greek original allows us to understand the genesis of the Latin version more precisely. This evidence consists in the first place of certain fragments of the Greek preserved in a magical papyrus, Lactantius, Cyril of Alexandria, Stobaeus, and Iohannes Lydus which allow us to establish parallels with the Latin in brief and isolated passages.[3] It consists in the second place of two excerpts in the Coptic translation of *Nag Hammadi Codex* VI which permit us, especially when these are used in conjunction with the Latin, to conjecture the Greek original of more extended passages with some confidence.[4] The identity of the Latin translator is unknown to us since all attempts to equate him with figures like Apuleius, Calcidius, and Marius Victorinus have failed to carry conviction on stylistic grounds.[5] However, his activity can be placed before A.D. 413 since Augustine cites lengthy passages from this work in the section of his *De Civitate Dei* written around that date.[6]

The *Asclepius* takes the form of a continuous address by Hermes Trismegistus to his disciple Asclepius, punctuated occasionally with questions raised by the latter. Hermes speaks first of the continuity of life throughout the cosmos, and of the hierarchical order in which the creator God rules the heaven, the heaven the changeable bodies; and in which the astral gods communicate with the demons, the demons with mankind.[7] Man plays a special role in the cosmic system since he has two functions: to worship God and to cultivate the earth, in accordance with his dual nature of soul and body.[8] Those who discharge their functions correctly will return after death to the purely divine state, but those who fail in this will endure transmigration into animal form.[9] Hermes next describes the basic principles of the cosmos which are three in number: God, spirit, and matter. Each of these is unproduced and eternal, and corresponds to a different aspect of the various living creatures: God to intellect, spirit to soul, and matter to sensible form.[10] Since the highest of these living creatures — endowed with intellect alone — are the superior gods, a brief digression is inserted on their hierarchical arrangement, one in which a group of five intelligible gods or "rulers of substance" (*ousiarchai*) — Zeus, Phos, Pantomorphos, Heimarmene, Deuteros — presides over a group of five sensible ones — the heaven, the sun, the thirty-six decans, the seven spheres, the air.[11] For Hermes, the primal God is bisexual in the sense that he produces all things without the cooperation of a second principle. Human beings have only one sex, although they can participate in a divinely ordained mystery by copulation.[12] The kinship between the primal God and man is further emphasized in two arguments: first, since man has been endowed with reason in order to control the hostile impulses of matter whereas the astral gods have no need of reason, he is in a sense closer to the creator.[13] Second, since man is a maker of gods by placing statues prepared to receive the higher influences in his temples, while the primal God has produced the superior gods by placing astral bodies in the temple of the cosmos, there is an affinity of function.[14] In fact Egypt is the analogue of heaven in the sense that it serves as a temple for the whole world, a statement which leads to a digression foretelling the decline of religious observances in that land, then the natural disasters — flood, conflagration, or pestilence — to be wrought as instruments of divine retribution, and then the restoration of the ancient beliefs.[15] At this point Hermes returns to his earlier argument that man should correctly discharge the functions enjoined by his dual nature. Thus, he will suffer one kind of death represented by the separation of soul from body but not the other kind of death manifested in the soul's punishment by relegation to the region of turbulence. It is easy to see that these deaths are more apparent than real, a necessary consequence of the fact that the cosmos itself is eternally living.[16] The cosmos is eternally living since eternity contains it and vivifies it from the outside, just as the cosmos contains and vivifies the temporal things within.[17] Furthermore the cosmos is both full — since there is no void surrounding or extending through it, the sensible world being enveloped by the intelligible world — and varied — since there is a diversity of individual forms within a single species, these forms themselves being subject to continual transformations.[18] Hermes once again returns to his argument that man should discharge the functions associated with his dual nature, this time focusing on man's role as a creator of terrestrial gods which are subject to a similar duality. Just as the astral gods exercise a kind of general providence, so the terrestrial gods preside over the individual details of human affairs.[19] This last point gives rise to a question about the role of Heimarmene in this system but, although one can define this as the necessity linking all events, one cannot say whether it is equivalent to the primal God, the world, or the order of celestial and terrestrial things.[20] Finally, Hermes and his disciple terminate their discussion with a prayer.

It will be immediately apparent from this summary that the *Asclepius* is a text which is loose and discursive in its structure. This fact has led certain modern scholars to conclude that the work, as we now have it, is not a literary unity but a composite product. Thus, T. Zielinski argued on the basis of certain inconsistencies in the dialogue structure that the treatise consists of four shorter texts joined end to end,[21] A.S. Ferguson suggested that the final prayer is an addition to the original version,[22] and W. Scott maintained that the work comprises three smaller treatises joined end to end on the grounds that there are unnecessary repetitions of material and radical inconsistencies in philosophical doctrine which cannot be explained on the hypothesis of a single author.[23] The questions raised by these scholars are of considerable importance for, if their conclusions are correct, it will be impossible to reconstruct a single philosophical system for this treatise. However, other scholars have countered these arguments by asserting that the work is mostly a literary unity, as the manuscript tradition indicates, even if its author is revealed to have the mentality of a compiler rather than that of an original thinker. This is the position of A.D. Nock who supports his thesis by pointing out first, that there are certain philosophical themes which run through the entire text and second, that there are numerous verbal parallels between the different sections of the work.[24] If anything can be said in response to this controversy, it is perhaps that we should study the treatise in the form in which it has been transmitted by the manuscript tradition, assuming that there are no really convincing arguments against doing so. That this is the case seems to have been demonstrated sufficiently by Nock's discussion.

The *Asclepius* is an important document concerning the state of Platonism in the third and fourth centuries A.D.[25] That the work does indeed belong to the Platonic current in the history of philosophy is indicated by the author's emphasis upon the radical transcendence of the divine.[26] In this respect his position is similar to that held by Apuleius and other Platonists approximately a century earlier. However, that the work must also be associated with the Stoic tradition in the history of thought emerges from the writer's insistence upon the thorough immanence of the divine.[27] On this point he diverges from the standpoint held by the most influential Platonists of that era. Finally, that the work is a notable example of syncretism between the Platonic and Stoic doctrines in the history of philosophy is demonstrated by the author's interest in the relation of macrocosm to microcosm.[28] On this question again he deviates from the position of Apuleius and his contemporaries. It is obviously necessary to take account of these various influences in interpreting the structure of the *Asclepius*'s philosophical system.[29]

1 i The Positive Approach to God

Since the doctrines of Hermeticism are essentially religious ones, the statements in this treatise regarding the nature of God have the principal claim on our attention. According to the viewpoint of earlier Platonism, descriptions of God can be in the first instance subjective — his nature is explained in terms of our manner of perceiving him; such subjective descriptions being either positive — God can be perceived by a human being, positive and negative — he can be perceived but only in a certain manner, or negative — God cannot be perceived by a human being.[30] The Hermetic text provides us with further examples of all these descriptions of God, among which the following should be especially noted. When the writer states that the first principle is "intelligible by the mind alone,"[31] he is emphasizing the possibility of a cognitive approach along the traditional Platonic lines. When he describes God as the principle "which illuminates man with the intelligence of mind alone,"[32] he is extending the same idea in terms of that epistemology of illumination which can be traced all the way back to Plato's dialogues, although the suggestion that this illumination is a personal act of the divinity is more typical of the later religiosity. One other text encapsulates the Hermeticist's entire theory of our cognitive approach to God: "We thank you, O Highest and Supreme One. It is through your favor that we have obtained this great light of knowing you. You endow us with intellect, reason, knowledge; with intellect[33] that we may know you; with reason that we may pursue you in our thoughts; and with knowledge that we may rejoice in knowledge of you . . . this knowledge of your greatness is alone the reward of humanity."[34] Here, the writer reveals three aspects of the human being's knowledge of God: first, the association between knowledge and illumination; second, the fact that illumination — as indicated by the occurrence of words like "favor," "endow," and "reward" in the text — is dependent upon divine grace; and third, the division of knowledge and illumination into definite stages.[35]

1 ii The Positive and Negative Approaches to God

Elsewhere the Hermeticist argues that, although the doctrine regarding God can be grasped by an application of intellect given by the divine, it descends from above with such headlong rapacity that it outstrips that application in its swiftness.[36] This passage, which connects the simile of a descending stream with the notion that God can be perceived but only in a certain manner, should be compared with another. Here, the Hermeticist states that, since the doctrine regarding God is beyond the application of human minds, it will flow past or back to its source without the attentive acquiescence of its hearers.[37] This text is of great importance in showing that the difficulty of perceiving God necessitates a revealed rather than a demonstrated philosophy.

1 iii The Negative Approach to God

Finally, the Hermetic treatise stresses the impossibility of a cognitive approach to God once more along the lines of earlier Platonism:

> We shall not definitely describe God with any of these names. For if a word is this — a sound arising from our breath striking the air, declaring all the wishes or thoughts which a man has conceived in his mind according to sensible impressions, something whose entire substance is composed of a few syllables, defined and circumscribed to permit the essential communication between speaker and hearer[38] — then the whole name of God includes simultaneously the thought, breath, and air together with everything which is in these, through these, or from these. One cannot hope to describe the creator of all greatness, the father or lord of all things with a single name however so many syllables it may contain, for God is without name or rather has every name on the grounds that — being himself one and all — one must either call all things by his name or him by the names of all things.[39]

Here, the writer makes a complex argument about human being's knowledge of God consisting of three stages: first, since a name comprises conceptual and physical elements which are distinct from one another, while God has cognitive and physical manifestations which are inseparable, then the divine nature cannot be comprehended in a name.[40] Second, since God is identical with all things created by him, his essence can be comprehended by all their names. Third, since a name comprises a limited number of syllables, while God is infinite in his modes of existence,[41] then the divine nature cannot be comprehended in a name. When the Hermeticist elsewhere invokes the deity's "single name by which God alone is blessed according to our ancestral religion" without informing us what the name being invoked is,[42] it is likely that this omission is a deliberate one inspired by his elaborate theory of naming. Such passages as these are clearly examples of descriptions of God which are subjective — his nature is explained in terms of our manner of perceiving him — and negative — God cannot be perceived by a human being — according to the criteria suggested earlier.

2 A i Transcendence

According to the viewpoint of earlier Platonism, descriptions of God can also be objective — his nature is explained without reference to our manner of perceiving it.[43] The Hermetic treatise provides us with numerous further examples of this, among which references to the first cause as "good" (*bonus*)[44] are naturally prominent. The same category would also include the frequent expressions of his transcendence: he is characterized as "one" (*unus*,[45] *unum*)[46] as "complete" (*plenus atque perfectus*),[47] as "highest" (*summus*,[48] *exsuperantissimus*),[49] as "infinite" (*indefinitum*),[50] as "incorporeal" (*ab omnibus rebus corpulentis alienus*),[51] as "lacking quantity" (*nec quantus sit quantitate*),[52] as "lacking quality" (*nec qualis sit qualitate*,[53] *quomodo aut quale sit incertum*),[54] as "non-spatial" (*ubi et quo et unde incertum est*),[55] as "beyond the heaven" (*ultra caelum*),[56] as "everlasting" (*aeternus*,[57] *sempiternus*),[58] and as "unchanging" (*stabile, fixum, inmobile*).[59] Perhaps the most striking feature of these different expressions of God's transcendence is their almost exact equivalence to similar ones which occur in Apuleius.[60] This clearly indicates the extent to which philosophical doctrine has become standardized in the second and third centuries A.D.

2 A ii Immanence

The objective descriptions of God also include various expressions of his causality in relation to other things. Into this category must be placed an important argument which recurs in several passages of the *Asclepius* where the creator is said to be identical with the things created by him. Thus, in the opening section of the dialogue Hermes Trismegistus declares that, if the disciple understands the teaching about to be revealed to him his mind will be filled with all goods. However, it may be more correct to say that his mind will be filled with the one good which contains all, there being a reciprocal relation between the notions of unity and totality: "All things are of one and the one is all things since these are so connected with one another that it is impossible to separate them."[61] It is important to note that, when the Hermeticist speaks of the reciprocal implication of unity and totality, he is referring not simply to a relation between two concepts — "one" and "all" — but to the association of cause and effect — God and his creation. This is indicated clearly in the later passage where Hermes argues that God can be described with the names of all the things which he creates — either by applying his name to all of them or all their names to him — "because he is himself both one and all."[62] Here we learn two facts: first, that unity represents God and totality his creation and second, that God can be described as unity or totality because he is identical with his creation.

2 A iii   Transcendence and Immanence

The presence of such an ontological doctrine in our treatise suggests on initial impression that its writer has retreated from the Platonic doctrine of a God who transcends his creation towards the Stoic position that he is immanent in it (and in a sense identifiable with it).[63] However, some further texts which expand upon the notions of unity and totality show precisely what the Hermeticist's viewpoint is. In one argument, it is stressed that God is identical with his creation in the sense that creation is derived from God: "For God is all things, and all things come from him and depend upon his will."[64] The nature of this derivation is explained in another passage which seems to distinguish a state before and a state after God's creation as two temporal phases: "Have I not said that all things are one and the one all things, since all things existed in God before he created all things?"[65] Such statements would indicate that God is identical in a primary sense with created things as they pre-exist in him before their temporal process of creation, and only in a secondary sense with created things as they exist outside him after their temporal act of creation.[66] If so, there is obviously no compromise in the transcendent nature of God's existence occasioned by the theory. On the other hand, further passages in the treatise show that we cannot rest content with this simple reformulation of the problem, since they reveal that the process of creation itself is not simply temporal. These texts contain the following clear line of argumentation: (i) Creation is the operation of the divine will,[67] (ii) God's will is unchanging,[68] (iii) the divine will operates in time,[69] and (iv) creation is both unchanging and in time.[70] The conclusion to this argument is not self-contradictory but merely a statement that the creative process is neither simply temporal, nor simply atemporal, but of the atemporal in relation to the temporal. On this basis, God is certainly identical in a primary sense with created things as they pre-exist in him before their temporal process of creation, and in a secondary sense with created things as they exist outside him after their temporal act of creation. Yet these two identifications are not completely distinct from one another since the relation of God to created things is not that of the temporal to the temporal but of the atemporal to the temporal.[71] Thus, the divine nature turns out to be both transcendent and immanent from different viewpoints. Some further texts which expand upon the notions of unity and totality are only explicable on the assumption that this is precisely the Hermeticist's viewpoint. In one argument, it is stressed that God is identical with his creation in the sense that creation is part of the divine: "not without reason is God said to be all things, for all things are his limbs."[72] The presence of such an ontological doctrine in this treatise indicates that its author has in actual fact combined the Platonic doctrine of a God who transcends his creation with the Stoic theory that he is immanent in it (and in a sense identifiable with it).[73]

2 A iv   God's Causality

God's causality in relation to other things is exemplified not only by the doctrine of unity and totality but also by the teaching concerning the three principles. Along the lines of the traditional Platonic doxographies, the *Asclepius* maintains that creation takes place through the interaction of God, Form, and Matter, although there are divergences from the tradition in certain details.[74] Unfortunately, since the Latin translator seems not to have fully understood the metaphysical theory involved, we must elicit this doctrine from references which are somewhat oblique.

2 A v   The Divine Intellect

The following passage is of primary importance:

The whole intellect, which is similar to the divinity, is immobile but self-moving in its stability. It is holy, incorruptible, eternal, and whatever higher attribute is applicable, since it is the eternity of the supreme God which exists in truth itself, filled with all sensible things and the whole of knowledge, co-existing so to speak with God.[75]

Here, an obvious difficulty is occasioned by the Hermeticist's reference not to God's intellect but to the whole intellect.[76] However, the context of the passage suggests that these two can be identified, since the next few sentences refer to a descending hierarchy of intellects consisting of (i) the whole intellect, (ii) the intellect of the world, and

(iii) the human intellect; while the sentences following these speak of an ascending hierarchy of intellects comprising: (a) the human intellect, (b) the intellect of the world, (c) the intellect of eternity, and (d) the divine intellect, the first term of the descending hierarchy presumably being equivalent to the last term of the ascending one.[77]   This interpretation might be challenged on the grounds that, since the Hermeticist refers to the whole intellect as co-existing with rather than as identical with God, the main passage must be concerned with a secondary intellect.[78] However, since God's intellect is here treated as consubstantial with that intellect described as secondary in the fuller account of the hierarchy in the sentences which follow — (c) the intellect of eternity — the apparent reference to the former as coexisting with God is merely an indication that it can to a certain extent be viewed as secondary to itself.[79] The upshot is that the main passage can be taken as a statement of the traditional Platonic doctrine that there is a divine intellect which transcends space and time,[80] contemplates its own contents in a manner according with its transcendence,[81] and has as its contents the Forms of sensible objects.[82]

2 A vi   The Theory of Forms

Several passages deal with the Forms in such a way as to indicate that the Greek original of the *Asclepius* entered into an especially high degree of elaboration at this point.[83] It is therefore a pity that the Latin translator has apparently obscured much of the meaning with terminological inexactitude.[84] The following represents a summary of this doctrine of Forms drawn simultaneously from the most important texts which deal with it.[85]

(i) *The range of Forms.* The Hermeticist seems to visualize Forms of two classes of object: first, the physical elements of earth, water, air, and fire,[86] and second, the living species of gods, demons, men, animals, and plants.[87]

(ii) *The distinction of higher and lower Forms.* In several passages we find a distinction of higher and lower Forms, although no single text defines what the precise difference between these is. The terminology for the two kinds of Form varies: (a) *genus* is contrasted with *species*,[88] (b) *genus* is contrasted with *imago*,[89] (c) *species* is contrasted with *imago*.[90] Furthermore, both *forma*[91] and *species*[92] occur in the two senses. The relation between the two kinds of Form is described as follows: (a) species to individual,[93] (b) whole to part,[94] (c) same to different,[95] (d) intelligible to sensible,[96] (e) incorporeal to corporeal,[97] (f) immortal to mortal.[98] A comparison of these passages indicates that, whichever pair of terms is employed, the contrast is between both species and individual and transcendent and immanent Form.

(iii) *Association of God and the higher Forms.* The agent through which Forms combine with matter to produce sensible objects is stated to be God.[99] Some passages associate the latter with the Forms in a general sense,[100] although others connect him specifically with the higher Forms.[101] It is not explicitly stated whether God actually gives existence to these Forms or merely presides over their instantiation.[102]

(iv) *Association of the god* Παντόμορφος *and the lower Forms.* Just as the God whose operation is localized in the world as a whole presides over the instantiation of the higher Forms, so the god whose operation is localized in the zodiac circle presides over the instantiation of the lower Forms.[103] The reason for this is that the relation of higher to lower Form is equivalent to that of species to individual.[104] Since the world as a whole is unchanging, each Form which its God instantiates will be unique in its omnipresence; whereas since the zodiac circle changes in rotation, each Form which its God instantiates will be multiplied according to spatial and temporal position.[105] It is certainly peculiar to speak of the instantiation of the higher Forms, since their transcendence would apparently preclude any combination with matter. But the reason once again is that the relation of higher to lower Form is equivalent to that of species to individual. Thus, the instantiation of the higher Forms signifies their presence as specific characters in individuals while their transcendence indicates their logical priority to the latter.

(v) *The emanation of Forms.* The Hermeticist clearly views the Forms as dynamic in character, since terms such as *influere,*[106] *defluere,*[107] and cognates often appear in conjunction with them.

2 A vii   The Theory of Matter

One further passage is important for our analysis. Here, the writer turns to the consideration of matter which is described as ungenerated "yet having the power and natural ability to engender and produce in itself"; as equivalent to space — "that in which all things are, since they could not exist without it" — having identical characteristics and as ungenerated "yet containing all things by providing a most fertile womb for their generation" including evil things.[108] This text presents considerable difficulties to the interpreter on account of the ambivalence of its terminology. In the first place, the statement that matter is ungenerated could mean either that it has no beginning in time or that it has no beginning at all (it is not causally dependent upon another principle). However, another passage which states that all things can ultimately be reduced to two principles — God and matter — clearly demonstrates that the second meaning is intended.[109]   Furthermore, the assertion that matter has the power to generate all things could be taken in several ways, although presumably the way in which God has the power to generate all things would have to be excluded. Fortunately, other parts of the text delineate matter's role: its identification with space shows that it is the cause of all things in that the latter could not exist without space,[110] while its equation with disorderly motion indicates that it causes all things by underlying the stability of form as a dynamic substratum.[111]   In addition, the statement that matter is the source of evil things could mean either that it produces both good and evil effects or that it produces only evil effects (it is therefore inherently evil). However, another passage which states that matter is the vehicle of chance occurrences — obviously involving good and evil — demonstrates that the first interpretation is correct.[112]   Moreover, it might be argued that the identification of matter and space is not really intended by the writer. This is the most difficult point on which to feel certain, although one parallel text seems to reinforce the interpretation here proposed.[113] In conclusion, then, the writer repeats the traditional doctrine that matter is the ungenerated substratum, spatial and dynamic,[114] of good and evil occurrences, despite the obscurities of his principal discussion.

2 B God and Creation

There now seems little room for doubt that the traditional doctrine of the three principles is a fundamental philosophical motif of the *Asclepius*. It is also clearly established that two of these principles are ultimate in the sense that neither can be reduced to the other, even if some modern interpreters have attempted to find a monistic position expressed.[115] However, the doctrine of the three principles represents only one strand in the more complete fabric of this dialogue, and we must also investigate the role of various further principles such as Eternity, Spirit, and the Second God. Only some of these principles will prove to be independent in the sense that they are not simply aspects of one another, and so it will be necessary to consider them in at least two distinct categories.[116]

2 C i   Eternity as God

According to the Hermeticist, God and Eternity are the "principles" (*primordia*) of all things.[117] However, that these two are not completely distinct from one another is indicated by passages stating that with Eternity, God contains the Forms of all things,[118] that "whether as God or as Eternity or as both or as one in the other or as both in each" (*sive deus sive aeternitas sive uterque sive alter in altero sive uterque in utroque*) he moves in immobility,[119] and that through Eternity, God controls all processes in the cosmos.[120] These remarks clearly show that Eternity is not fully independent of God — like the principle Αἰών in some other Hermetic treatises[121] — although the nature of this quasi-independence is somewhat obscure. Fortunately, there are other passages which illuminate this question by describing Eternity's relation either to the world or else to time, since not only do the relations of God to the world and to time and of Eternity to the world and to time coincide but the relation of God to Eternity is analogous to that of the world to time. The relation of Eternity to the world is described as follows: Eternity "contains" (*intra se habens*) the world,[122] while the world "is vivified by Eternity which is outside it and vivifies those things which are inside it" (*ipse extrinsecus vivificatur ab aeternitate vivificatque ea, quae intra se sunt*).[123] Furthermore, the world "has been made in the image of the highest God since it imitates Eternity" (*huius dei imago hic effectus est mundus, aeternitatis imitator*)[124] — a statement indicating that the relations of God to the world and of Eternity to the world are not separate from one another. The relation of Eternity to time is described as follows: Eternity is "beyond the limits of" (*sine definitione*) time,[125] and is also "stable, immobile, and fixed while the course of time, which is mobile, always returns to eternity" (*stabilis, inmobilis atque fixa . . . temporis, quod mobile est, in aeternitatem semper revocatur agitatio*).[126] Further, "just as Eternity, immobile on its own, seems to move through the time in which it is, thus even God can be held to move himself in himself while immobile" (*ipsa aeternitas inmobilis quidem sola per tempus, in quo ipsa est . . . videatur agitari . . . sic et deum agitari credibile est in se ipsum aedem inmobilitate*)[127] — a statement revealing that the relations of God to time and of Eternity to time are in some way equivalent. Finally, the relation of the world to time is described by saying that "the world is the receptacle of time, through whose course and motion it is sustained" (*mundus est receptaculum temporis, cuius cursu et agitatione vegetatur*).[128] This apparently suggests that the relation of God to Eternity is paralleled by that of the world to time.

These passages have clearly revealed that Eternity does not exist independently of God: indeed, they suggest rather that it is a certain manifestation of his own highest nature. But what precisely is this manifestation? In the first place, God as Eternity transcends the world. This is indicated by his containment of the latter, since a container must be greater than that which it contains; it is indicated by the statement that he vivifies the world *from outside*; and it is indicated by the aspiration of the latter towards him, since the object of desire must lie beyond the subject. On the other hand, God as Eternity is immanent in the world. This is also shown by his containment of the latter, since a container must surround that which it contains; it is also shown by the statement that he *vivifies* the world from outside: and it is also shown by the aspiration of the latter towards him, since the subject of desire becomes progressively like its object. Thus, God as Eternity is simultaneously transcendent and immanent in relation to the world.[129]

2 C ii   Spirit as God

The precise status of Spirit is more difficult to determine since the passages referring to it are extremely brief. At first sight, these leave uncertainty on two fundamental points: first, the relation of Spirit to God and second, the metaphysical or physical nature of Spirit.

In connection with the earlier question, the Hermeticist does not express himself as unambiguously as we might like. Thus, some passages refer to Spirit as that by which all things are "produced" (*ministrantur*), "vivified" (*vegetantur*),[130] "moved" (*agitantur*), or "controlled" (*gubernantur*)[131] according to God's design. This leaves it an open question whether we are dealing with an aspect of God's nature or an instrument employed by him. Furthermore, the allusion to Spirit as ungenerated yet having the power to produce[132] can be understood in two contrasting ways: either it means that Spirit is an independent principle distinct from God, or that it is an independent principle because it is identical with God. However, some passages suggest that the term discussed signifies not an instrument employed by God but an aspect of his nature. Thus, it emerges that Spirit is "inherent in God" (*inesse deo*),[133] or that God has filled all things with Spirit "having breathed" (*inhalata*) upon each thing according to its nature.[134]

The course of discussion so far seems to have provided an answer also to the second question, for a principle which is identified with God would need to be metaphysical rather than physical.[135] However, the matter cannot be disposed of quite so easily since certain passages describe Spirit in a way recalling the physical pneuma of Stoicism. Thus, it is said to be "blended in all things" (*permixtus cunctis*)[136] or "inherent in matter" (*inesse mundo*),[137] its role being the determination of "all Forms in the world" (*omnes in mundo species*)[138] or "each thing's special character" (*cuiusque naturae qualitas*).[139] One may recall that the Stoic pneuma possessed precisely these characteristics of mixture with the passive principle and production of the hierarchy of being through degrees of its tension.[140] On this basis it will be necessary to conclude that the notion of Spirit here represents a transposition of physical into metaphysical theory.[141]

The answers to these two questions provide a reasonable delineation of Spirit. The first answer indicates that it constitutes an aspect of God, while the second reveals that it signifies God in an immanent mode.

2 C iii   Love as God

Love is discussed in one passage which is relatively brief but sufficiently detailed to explain both its relation to God and its special character.[142]

The earlier question is illuminated by the Hermeticist's reference to Love as something "created and bestowed by that God who is ruler of all nature" (*ex domino illo totius naturae deo . . . inventum tributumque*).[143] However with this statement that Love is created by God must be compared further assertions that it is an aspect of God's nature. Thus, the Hermeticist speaks of the union of male and female as an incomprehensible mystery[144] — implying that Love is divine in character; of "the divinity of both natures in the commingling of the sexes" (*utriusque naturae divinitas ex commixtione sexus*)[145] — stating explicitly that it is divine; and of God as embracing the fertility of both male and female[146] — indicating that Love is an aspect of the first principle.

The second question is illuminated in the following ways: first, Love is described as the means of reproducing to eternity;[147] second, it is explained in terms of the coming together of the two sexes — it is their "connection or, more properly speaking, their unity" (*conexio aut, quod est verius, unitas*),[148] it is the moment at which each sex passes over into the other's nature when the climax makes the male weak and the female vigorous,[149] it is their "commingling" (*commixtio*);[150] and third, Love is characterized as an activity of all animal and plant life.[151]

The implication of these texts is that Love represents an aspect of God, although it is difficult to draw any conclusions beyond this. Clearly it does not signify the first principle in its transcendent mode, since it implies the relation of cause and effect. However, whether it signifies God in his immanent mode or in a transcendent and immanent mode must be left an open question.[152]

2 C iv   The Status of Fate

Despite the significant differences outlined, the principles of Eternity, Spirit, and Love are similar in possessing a status not independent of God. With these should be contrasted another group of principles which are alike in possessing a status which is independent in this way. However, before examining the latter we should consider one principle whose nature is seemingly of a type transitional between these two categories.

The following passage instantly reveals the ambivalent status of this principle: "That which we call 'Fate,' O Asclepius, is the necessity in all things which occur, each joined to the others in connective bonds. Fate, therefore, is either the cause of things, or the highest God, or the god produced as second by the highest God, or the order of all celestial and earthly things fixed by divine law" (*Quam* εἱμαρμένην *nuncupamus, o Asclepi, ea est necessitas omnium quae geruntur, semper sibi catenatis nexibus vincta; haec itaque est aut effectrix rerum aut deus summus aut ab ipso deo qui secundus effectus est deus aut omnium caelestium terrenarumque rerum firmata divinis legibus disciplina*).[153] Two questions must be answered in order to interpret this rather difficult passage correctly: first, how many definitions of Fate does it contain and second, what are the historical sources of these definitions? An approach to the first question is suggested by the apparent contrast in the text between (i) definitions of Fate in terms of the nature of the process, and (ii) definitions in terms of association with a specific principle.[154] That this contrast is actually envisaged by the Hermeticist is indicated by studying parallels to this discussion in certain other writers of late antiquity: pseudo-Plutarch, Calcidius, and Nemesius, where an important distinction is made between consideration of Fate in terms of its "activity" (*energeia*) and consideration in terms of its "substance" (*ousia*).[155] If such a contrast does underlie the structure of our text, the (i) the definitions of Fate in terms of the nature of the process can be treated as a single explanation, while (ii) the definitions in terms of association with a specific principle must represent separate explanations.[156] On this assumption the second question can be approached by noting that (i) the definition of Fate in terms of the nature of its process consists entirely of elements derived from Stoic theory, since the concepts of necessity,[157] eternity,[158] connection,[159] and order[160] are habitually associated with that of Fate according to Stoicism. On the other hand (ii) the definitions in terms of association with a specific principle seem to involve a combination of Stoic and Platonic elements, (ii a) the definition of Fate as the highest God being perfectly intelligible according to Stoic theory where it is simply another manifestation of the Logos or Pneuma,[161] while (ii b) the definition as the second god agrees more with the Platonic tradition where Fate is sometimes identified with the world soul.[162]

The text setting out the various definitions of Fate serves to underline the ambiguity of the notion although it does not provide a firm delineation. Certain other passages must be taken into account in order to achieve the latter, and among these is one which establishes a relation between Fate and the planetary motions. According to the Hermeticist, for each celestial motion there must be postulated a higher cause or "ousiarch" (*ousiarches*): for the motion of the cosmos as a whole he posits Jupiter as ousiarch, for that complex motion of the seven planets he posits "Fortune or Fate" (*fortuna aut* εἱμαρμένη), and so on.[163] It is difficult to be sure what the Hermeticist's doctrine at this point is, but it is undeniable that Fate is intended to be a principle independent of the highest God.[164]

Another passage to be taken into account in order to delineate the notion of Fate is one where the natures of Fate, Necessity, and Order are examined. Here, the Hermeticist argues that these three principles by relating to one another as inseparable components of the cosmic process "obey the necessity of eternal reason" (*serviunt necessitati rationis aeternae*).[165] Although this statement seems initially to reinforce the view that Fate is a principle independent of the highest God, the later development of the argument clearly moves in the opposite direction.[166] Thus, the Hermeticist continues by suggesting that the three principles are "equivalent to Eternity" (*haec est aeternitas*) because of the continuous circularity of the cosmic process which they combine in producing.[167] Once again it is difficult to be certain what the doctrine is, but it seems certain that Fate is treated ambivalently as a principle independent of and not independent of the highest God.

At this point, it is perhaps reasonable to suggest that a fairly coherent doctrine of Fate has emerged, since its two manifestations can be identified at least provisionally with parts of the composite definition furnished by the earlier text. In particular, the following identifications between these two manifestations and (ii) the definitions of Fate in terms of association with a specific principle seem to be required. Where Fate is described in connection with Necessity and Order and shown by reason of its relation to Eternity to be both independent and not independent of the highest God, it can be understood as satisfying the requirements of (ii a) the definition of Fate as the highest God. However, where it is described in relation to the planetary motions and shown because of its contrast with Jupiter's relation to the motion of the whole cosmos to be independent of the highest God, it can be held to satisfy the requirements of (ii b) the definition of Fate as the second god.[168] Of these identifications the former is self-evident on account of the equivalence of terminology, whereas the latter will be upheld if the source of planetary motions is equivalent to the second god. Furthermore, that the description of Fate in connection with Necessity and Order can be understood as fulfilling the requirements of (ii a) the definition of Fate as the highest God emerges from the presence of significant Stoic elements in both cases. That the description of Fate in relation to the planetary motions can be held to fulfil the requirements of (ii b) the definition of Fate as the second God would follow from the presence of a mixture of Stoic and Platonic elements in each case.[169] This last point, however, must be left for a later demonstration.

The principle of Fate seems therefore to have an especially ambivalent status within the metaphysical system of this treatise, since it is described in different passages both as possessing a status not independent of God and also as possessing a status which is thus independent. Our next task is to examine those principles which conform entirely to the latter mode of existence.

2 C v   The Second God

In one important passage, the Hermeticist refers to "the God of highest power who is ruler of one god" (*deus primipotens et unius gubernator dei*).[170] Although this text presents certain difficulties of interpretation owing to the survival of a Greek version which contains a significant variation of meaning,[171] since the Latin wording provides a sense consistent with doctrines explicitly taught elsewhere in the treatise we may at least attempt to explain the latter.

The doctrines taught elsewhere are the following. First, the supreme God is said to have "created a second god after himself" (*a se secundum fecerit*) or to have "produced a first god from himself as second to himself" (*hunc fecit ex se primum et a se secundum*).[172] The descriptive epithets attached to this principle — that it is the object of sensation, that it is filled with the goodness of all things, and that God loved it on account of its beauty — suggest that it represents the physical world.[173] Furthermore, that this is the case is demonstrated by two passages elsewhere, one listing three terms: "God is the first, the world second, and man third" (*deus primus est, secundus est mundus, homo est tertius*),[174] the other stating that the world is a sensible god.[175] However, this relatively straightforward doctrine is complicated by a second factor, for in one passage the writer states that "the sun itself must be held to be this second god" (*ipse enim sol . . . secundum etenim deum hunc crede*).[176] What are we to make of this discrepancy?

The answer to this question lies in the association of the world and the sun according to the Hermetic philosophy. Thus, that these are not really independent of one another is indicated (i) by the world's government of all physical processes utilizing the instrumentality of the sun,[177] (ii) by the identity of function between the two: just as the world is "dispenser of life" (*vitae dispensator*)[178] so is the sun "ruler of vital processes" (*gubenator vitalium*),[179] and (iii) by the analogy of the sun's illumination of the world and intellect's illumination of man.[180] Of these points the last is especially revealing about the Hermeticist's philosophical beliefs.

In particular, it is clear that he subscribes to the common teaching that the world is a "living being" (*animal*),[181] and this implies in its turn that the world consists of a body and a soul. The latter doctrine is explicitly stated in at least one passage where God is described as the ruler of the world, its soul, and the world's contents.[182] Furthermore he assents to the traditional notion that this soul is "the container of all sensible Forms" (*receptaculum . . . sensibilium omnium specierum*),[183] thereby indicating that the principle represents a source of knowledge as well as one of life. This epistemological implication is effectively drawn out in a text where the human cognitive faculty ascends to that of the world, the world's to that of eternity.[184]

The last passage, indeed, has yet another significance for our investigation of the creative activity of the highest God, since the writer also states that the world can ascend "to knowledge of the gods who rank above it" (*et deos noscendos, qui supra se sunt*).[185] How do these gods fit into the ontological scheme so far described?

2 C vi   The Hierarchy of Gods

The doctrine of the gods is expounded in a passage couched in all the terminology of religious revelation. It begins: "There are many kinds of gods, and among these some are intelligible and some sensible[186] . . . there are gods who rule all Forms, and these are followed by those whose substance has a ruler. The latter are sensible gods whose nature reflects their double origin"[187] (*deorum genera multa sunt eorumque omnium pars intellegibilis, alia vero sensibilis . . . sunt ergo omnium specierum principes dii. hos consecuntur dii, quorum est princeps* οὐσίας. *hi sensibiles, utriusque originis consimiles suae*).[188] Various interpretations of this highly compressed statement have been proposed, but according to the most plausible reading it provides the following facts: (i) there are two orders of gods: (a) intelligible and (b) sensible,[189] (ii) The nature of (a) is further characterized by their association with the distribution of Forms;[190] (iii) The gods of group (a) have a relation of priority to those of group (b) in that they govern their substance;[191] and (iv) The nature of (b) is further defined by a combination of intelligible and sensible elements.[192]   The passage continues: "The ousiarch of the world is Jupiter . . . the ousiarch of the sun is Light . . . the ousiarch or ruler of those thirty-six known as the Horoscopes is the god called Pantomorphos or 'All-Form' . . . the seven planets have as their ousiarchs or rulers that which is called Fortune and Heimarmene . . . the ousiarch of air is the Second . . ."[193] (*caeli . . .* οὐσιάρχης *est Iuppiter . . . solis* οὐσιάρχης *lumen est . . . XXXVI quorum vocabulum est Horoscopi . . . horum* οὐσιάρχης *vel princeps est, quem* Παντόμορφον *vel omniformem vocant . . . septem sphaerae . . . habent* οὐσιάρχης *id est sui principes, quam fortunam dicunt aut* εἱμαρμένην *. . . aër vero . . . est autem* οὐσιάρχης *huius secundus . . .*)[194] From these remarks the following additional information is obtained: (i) Various specific examples of (a) intelligible and (b) sensible gods are given; and (ii) the gods of group (b) are shown to be astronomical in character.

Modern scholarship has rightly compared the Hermeticist's theological schema with similar systems expounded by late Platonic writers — Porphyry, Iamblichus, and Sallustius.[195] Although the latter often differ in detail, they frequently contain the two fundamental aspects of the Hermetic hierarchy of gods: first, they contrast groups of intelligible and sensible gods and second, they establish correspondences between particular intelligible and sensible gods.[196]   That the Hermeticist's theological doctrine agrees with the teachings of such

Neoplatonic writers is probably the result of a single influence over all concerned — the so-called *Chaldaean Oracles*.

The validity of these parallels is strengthened by the investigation of such items of further theological doctrine as are scattered elsewhere in the treatise. Thus, one passage seems to make another allusion to the gods of group (a) when it suggests that the highest gods have "intellect" (*sensus*) as their soul.[197] This would be consistent with an intelligible status. Other texts provide further information about the gods of group (b): that the supreme God has created them,[198] that they are constituted of the purest physical substance,[199] and that they inhabit the celestial regions.[200] A further passage refers to the dwelling of the god Pantomorphos in the zodiac according to whose rotation each "Form" (*species*) generates "individual instances" (*imagines*).[201] This implies the relation of an intelligible to a sensible principle. Finally, there is another item of theological doctrine which does not strengthen the earlier parallels so much as it extends the system itself. Thus, one passage refers to Jupiter who occupies a station between heaven and earth from which he dispenses life to the various kinds of animate being.[202] This god may perhaps be the ousiarch of the air whose name was omitted by the mutilated text of the theological summary.[203]

2 C vii   The Second God and the Hierarchy of Gods

So far we have examined the accounts of the second god and of the hierarchy of gods as though they were totally independent Hermetic theologies. This is justified inasmuch as the respective descriptions occur in separate sections of the text, while the account of the second god makes no reference to any other gods and that of the hierarchy speaks of no god as second. However, it is impossible for the modern interpreter of this philosophy to avoid asking the question: how do the two theological accounts relate to one another?[204]

The careful re-examination of passages previously noted leads to interesting results. In particular we must conclude that, since both the world and the sun are described as the second god in one account, while they represent the first and second members of the series of sensible gods in the other, then the world and the sun are *second* either (i) because the (intelligible) Jupiter is the first and the (sensible) world the second god,[205] or (ii) because the (sensible) world is the first and the (sensible) sun the second god.[206] However, there are obvious drawbacks since with (i) the (intelligible) Jupiter considered as the first god, the sensible sun cannot be described as second but only as third; and with (ii) the (sensible) world considered as the first god, the (sensible) world cannot also be described a second but only as first. Perhaps the only solution, then, is to consider the series of intelligible gods as a whole as the first god so that either the (sensible) world or the (sensible) sun can be described as second.

This brings us to the further conclusion that, since both the world and the sun are described as the second god in one account, while representing the first and second members of the series of sensible gods in the other, then the world and the sun are *both* second either (i) because the (sensible) world and the (sensible) sun are not completely distinct from one another, or (ii) because the members of the series of sensible gods as a whole are not distinct from one another. Of these solutions it is (ii) which seems to be the most compelling since it not only treats the relations between all members of the series of sensible gods identically but it considers those relations as analogous with those obtaining within the series of intelligible gods.

That the series of intelligible gods as a whole can be considered as the first god and the series of sensible gods as a whole as the second god is an interpretation which is further supported by certain minor features of the account. Thus, regarding the intelligible gods, the fact that Jupiter occurs more than once suggests that the members of the series are not completely distinct from one another,[207] while the identification of one member of the series as Heimarmene indicates that they really constitute elements of the first God.[208] Regarding the sensible gods, the fact that the sun must occur twice suggests that the members of this series are not totally separable from one another,[209] while the interpretation of each member of the series as a celestial motion indicates that they actually represent elements of the world soul.[210]

If this doctrine has been correctly construed, an interesting metaphysical position emerges: that there is a supreme God or intellect consisting of a unity in multiplicity which gives rise to a second god or soul similarly constituted. The most striking element in this system is the notion that these first and second principles are unities in multiplicity. Clearly such a viewpoint is heavily influenced by both Platonism and Stoicism: by the former in the contrast of the highest God or intellect and the second god or soul, and by the latter in the notion of a unitary force underlying the perceived differentiation.

NOTES

1. Lactantius, *Inst. Div.* IV.6.4 (*C.S.E.L.* 19.287.1).
2. A list of these stylistic features can be found in Nock and Festugière: op. cit., pp. 278-279.
3. See Scott, op. cit., pp. 77-78 and Nock and Festugière, op. cit., pp. 275-277.
4. See J.P. Mahé, *Hermès en Haut-Egypte. Les textes hermétiques de Nag Hammadi et leurs parallèles grecs et latins* I-II (Quebec, 1978); and D.M. Parrott, et al., *Nag Hammadi Codices V.2-5 and VI with Papyrus Berolinensis 8502.1 and 4* (*Nag Hammadi Studies* XI) (Leiden, 1979).
5. For a demonstration that Apuleius could not have been the translator see Scott, op. cit., p. 78. For arguments that neither Marius Victorinus nor Calcidius was the translator see Nock and Festugière, op. cit., pp. 277-278.
6. Augustine, *Civ. Dei* VIII. 23 ff. (*C.C.S.L.* 47. 239ff.)
7. *Asclep.* 2-7.
8. Ibid., 8-9.
9. Ibid., 10-14.
10. Ibid., 14-18.
11. Ibid., 19.
12. Ibid., 20-21. The parallel Coptic version begins in the middle of chapter 21.
13. Ibid., 22.
14. Ibid., 23.
15. Ibid., 24-6.
16. Ibid., 27-29. The parallel Coptic version ends early in chapter 29. However, there is a separate extract covering part of chapter 41.
17. Ibid., 30-32.
18. Ibid., 33-36.
19. Ibid., 37-38.
20. Ibid., 39-40. In the foregoing summary I have included only the main arguments of the *Asclepius* so that its underlying logical structure might become apparent. For a more detailed analysis see Festugière, *La révélation d'Hermès Trismégiste II: Le dieu cosmique*, pp. 18-27.
21. T. Zielinski, "Hermes und die Hermetik," *Archiv fur Religions-Wissenschaft* 8, 1905: 321-372. The shorter texts would be (i) *Asclep.* 1-14, (ii) ibid., 14-27, (iii) ibid., 27-37, and (iv) ibid., 37-41.
22. A.S. Ferguson, "Introduction" to Scott, op. cit., vol. IV, p. xxxii. This view is confirmed by the separate preservation of a Greek version among the *Papyri Magicae* and of a Coptic version in *Nag Hammadi Codex* VI. See Mahé, op. cit., vol. I, pp. 137ff.; Parrott, op. cit., p. 376.
23. Scott, op. cit., vol. I., pp. 51ff. and op. cit., vol. III, pp. 1, 68, 92, etc. The shorter texts are (i) *Asclep.* 1-14, (ii) ibid., 14-16, and (iii) ibid., 16-41. In addition to dividing the work into three parts, Scott makes numerous transpositions of the text in (iii). His whole procedure is rightly criticized by A.S. Ferguson in Scott, op. cit., vol. IV, pp. 394-395 and 408ff.
24. Nock and Festugière, op. cit., pp. 292-295.

25. If we think in terms of the Greek original, the *Asclepius* documents Platonism of the third century; if we think in terms of the Latin version, it documents that of the fourth.

26. Both Platonism and Stoicism speak of God's transcendence, but only with the former is this transcendence radical (or metaphysical).

27. Both Stoicism and Platonism refer to God's immanence, but only with the former is this immanence thorough (or materialistic).

28. This theme derives ultimately from Plato (especially from his interpretation of the relation between world soul and individual souls in the *Timaeus*) yet it is more usually associated with the Stoa.

29. The discussion which follows will be arranged partly along the lines appropriate to a Stoic system, and partly along those appropriate to a Platonic one.

30. All these aspects are equally prominent, for example, in the philosophy of Apuleius.

31. *Asclep.* 16.315.17 *mente sola intellegibilis.*

32. Ibid., 29.336.6-7, *hominem sola intelligentia mentis inluminans.* Cf. ibid., 32.341.20-21 and 41.353.2. For the theme of illumination in the Greek corpus, cf. *Corp. Herm.* I.32.19.5, IX.3.97.10-11, XIII.18.208.5, and XIII.19.208.17 together with F.J. Klein, *Die Lichtterminologie bei Philon von Alexandrien und in den hermetischen Schriften. Untersuchungen zur Struktur der religiösen Sprache der hellenistischen Mystik* (Leiden, 1962).

33. *Sensus* = 'intellect.' Comparisons with the Greek version in the *Papyrus Mimaut* and with the Coptic version of *Nag Hammadi Codex* VI indicate the *sensus* represents the Latin translator's habitual rendering of the original νοῦς. See Scott, op. cit., vol. III, p. 290; Nock and Festugière, op. cit., p. 363; Mahé, op. cit., vol. I, pp. 148-9 and 162-3; and Parrott, op. cit., p. 380.

34. *Asclep.* 41.353.1-355.4, *gratias tibi summe, exsuperantissime; tua enim gratia tantum sumus cognitionis tuae lumen consecuti . . . condonans nos sensu, ratione, intellegentia: sensu, ut te cognoverimus; ratione, ut te suspicionibus indagemus; cognitione, ut te cognoscentes gaudeamus . . . haec est enim humana sola gratulatio, cognitio maiestatis tuae.* This passage comes from the final prayer of the *Asclepius* and can be compared with the Greek and Coptic versions. For discussion of the religious sentiments expressed see R. Reitzenstein, *Die hellenistischen Mysterienreligionen nach ihren Grundgedanken und Wirkungen,* 3 (Auflage, Leipzig, 1927), pp. 285ff.; and P.A. Carozzi, "*Hoc lumine salvati tuo (Asclepius* 41)," *Perennitas: Studi in onore di A. Brelich* (Roma, 1980), pp. 115-38 in addition to the works cited in n. 33 above.

35. There has been considerable discussion concerning the precise epistemological values of these three stages although the *Asclepius,* the *Papyrus Mimaut,* and *Nag Hammadi Codex* VI.7 all explain them quite adequately in the respective texts. See Scott, op. cit., p. 291; Nock and Festugière, op. cit., p. 399; Klein, op. cit., pp. 177-180; and Mahé, op. cit., pp. 148ff.

36. *Asclep.* 3.298,21-299.2, *divinitatis etenim ratio divina sensus intentione noscenda torrenti simillima est fluvio e summo in pronum praecipiti rapacitate currenti: quo efficitur, ut intentionem nostram non solum audientium verum tractantium ipsorum celeri velocitate praetereat.*

37. Ibid., 19.318.12-17, *sublimis etenim ratio eoque divinior ultra hominum mentes intentionesque consistens, si non attentiore aurium obsequio verba loquentis acceperis, transvolabit et transfluet aut magis refluet suique se fontis liquoribus miscet.*

38. All the elements contained in this definition are traditional (Platonic and Stoic). See Plato, *Tim.* 67b; Aetius, *Plac.* IV.19.1 (*D.G.* 407.22a and b ff.); Seneca, *Nat. Quaest.* II.6.5, etc. For more parallels see Scott, op. cit., vol. III, pp. 133-134; and Nock and Festugière, op. cit., pp. 375-376.

39. *Asclep.* 20.320.15-321.9, *nullo ex his nominibus eum definite nuncupabimus. si enim vox hoc est — ex aere spiritu percusso sonus declarans omnem hominis voluntatem vel sensum, quem forte ex sensibus mente perceperit. cuius nominis tota substantia paucis conposita syllabis definita atque circumscripta est, ut esset in homine necessarium vocis auriumque commercium — simul etiam et sensus et spiritus et aeris et omnium in his aut per haec aut de his nomen est totum dei; non enim spero totius maiestatis effectorem omniumque rerum patrem vel dominum uno posse quamvis e multis conposito nuncupari nomine, hunc vero innominem vel potius omninominem siquidem is sit unus et omnia, ut sit necesse auto omnia esse eius nomine aut ipsum omnium nominibus nuncupari.*

40. For God as nameless in the Greek corpus see *Corp. Herm.* V.1.60.4, Lactantius, *Div. Inst.* I.6.4 (*C.S.E.L.* 19.19.18) and IV.7.3 (*C.S.E.L.* 19.293.1).

41. For God as many-named in the Greek corpus see *Corp. Herm.* V.10.64.3-10.

42. *Asclep.* 41.353.3-354.2, *nomen unum, quo solus deus est benedicendus religione paterna.* This passage also comes from the final prayer of the *Asclepius*, and so a comparison with the Greek text of the *Papyrus Mimaut* is possible. In the latter we read that god has an "unspeakable name" (ἄφραστον ὄνομα). On the notion of ineffability in the *Hermetica* see A.D. Nock, "The Exegesis of *Timaeus* 28 c," *Vigiliae Christianae* 16 (1962): 79-86.

43. This aspect can be paralleled in Apuleius.

44. *Asclep.* 8.305.10, 20.321.12, and 26.331.20. Cf. *Corp. Herm.* II.15.38.11, VI.1.72.4-5, and X.3.114.7-8.

45. *Asclep.* 2.298.4 and 20.321.7. Cf. *Corp. Herm.* XVI.3.233.1.

46. *Asclep.* 1.296.10 and 2.297.23-4.

47. Ibid., 30.338.19.

48. Ibid., 16.315.17 and 41.353.1. Cf. *Corp. Herm.* I.31.18.9.

49. *Asclep.* 41.353.1. The attribute "highest" is absent from the text of the corresponding Coptic version.

50. Ibid., 31.339.23. Cf. *Corp. Herm.* IV.8.52.12 and XI.20.155.13.

51. *Asclep* 27.332.11-12. Cf. *Corp. Herm.* II.4.33.1-2, V.10.64.5-6, and XI.16.154.1-2.

52. *Asclep.* 29.336.5. Cf. *Corp. Herm.* XII.23.183.12-13.
53. *Asclep.* 29.336.5. Cf. *Corp. Herm.* XII.23.183.13.
54. *Asclep.* 31.339.26.
55. Ibid., 31.339.25-6. Cf. *Corp. Herm.* V.10.64.13.
56. *Asclep.* 27.332.10.
57. Ibid., 14.313.17. Cf. *Corp. Herm.* VIII.2.88.2 and XVIII.9.252.3.
58. *Asclep.* 14.313.16-17 and 26.331.11.
59. Ibid., 30.338.16. Cf. *Corp. Herm.* II.12.37.4 and X.14.120.2.
60. See pp. 6-7 and n. 43.
61. *Asclep.* 1.296.11-13, *omnia unius esse aut unum esse omnia; ita enim sibi est utrumque conexum, ut separari alterum ab utro non possit.* Cf. *Corp. Herm.* XII.8.177.5, XIII.17.207.18, XIII.18.208.3, and XVI.3.232.18-233.3.
62. *Asclep.* 20.321.7, *siquidem is sit unus et omnia.*
63. For the Stoic (or syncretistic Stoic and Platonic) position see the discussion of *spiritus* on pp. 142-143. Of course, the Stoic doctrine holds that God is both transcendent and immanent. However, the transcendence is not metaphysical in this case. On the importance of the Stoic elements see p. 132.
64. *Asclep.* 34.344.22-3, *omnia enim deus et ab eo omnia et eius omnia voluntatis.* Cf. ibid. 2.298.3-4.
65. Ibid., 2.297.23-298.1, *non enim hoc dixi, omnia unum esse et unum omnia, utpote quae in creatore fuerint omnia, antequam creasset omnia?* Cf. ibid., 14.313.7-9.
66. This pre-existence of created things in God is presumably — along traditional Platonic lines — as Forms in the divine mind. For the appearance of this latter notion in the *Asclepius* see pp. 138-139.
67. See n. 64 above.
68. Ibid., 26.331.12-14 "For the will of God has no beginning. It is the same and as it is eternally. Indeed, the plan of God's will is equivalent to his nature" (*voluntas etenim dei caret initio, quae eadem est et, sicuti est, sempiterna. dei enim natura consilium est voluntatis*). Cf. *Corp. Herm.* X.2.113.11-12.
69. *Asclep* 8.305.12-15, "For the will of God itself is the highest completion, since he realises his willing and completion at the same instant of time" (*voluntas etenim dei ipsa est summa perfectio, utpote cum voluisse et perfecisse uno eodemque temporis puncto conpleat*). Cf. *Corp. Herm.* XIII.19.208.14-15.
70. *Asclep.* 20.321.9-11, "He is absolutely filled with the fertility of both sexes: always pregnant with his will and always giving birth" (*utraque sexus fecunditate plenissimus, semper voluntatis praegnans suae parit semper*). That creation is both unchanging and temporal was clearly grasped by Scott, op. cit., vol. III, pp. 184 and 192-193.
71. That God transcends time (as opposed to being eternal in time) is not explicitly stated in the *Asclepius*, although this notion is undoubtedly implied by the essentially Platonic theology expounded there. Cf. *Corp. Herm.* XII.23.183.13-14, "there is no time in relation to God" (οὔτε χρόνος περὶ

τὸν θεόν ἐστι).

72. *Asclep* 2.298.1-2, *nec inmerito ipse dictus est omnia, cuius membra sunt omnia.*

73. This combination of Platonic and Stoic notions would not really be novel, but simply a reflection of tendencies in second-century (and also earlier) thought.

74. See pp. 140-150. The Hermeticist uses the terminology: *deus, genera (species, formae), mundus.* That *mundus* = ὕλη is indicated at ibid., 14.313.4-5, 14.313.20, and 17.315.24.

75. Ibid., 32.340.16-21, *omnis ergo sensus divinitatis similis inmobilis ipse in stabilitate se commovet sua: sanctus et incorruptus et sempiternus est et si quid potest melius nuncupari dei summi in ipsa veritate consistens aeternitas, plenissimus omnium sensibilium et totius disciplinae, consistens, ut ita dixerim, cum deo.*

76. According to Nock and Festugière, op. cit., p. 389, *omnis sensus* = *totus sensus* (an inversion of terms found elsewhere in this text). The Greek original will therefore have been ὁ πᾶς νοῦς signifying the divine intellect of which the intellect of the world and the human intellect are simply participations. One might add that the expression *omnis sensus* fits well with the consubstantiality between the divine intellect and the intellect of eternity mentioned later in the passage.

77. *Asclep* 32.340.21-341.20. The "divine intellect" (*sensus . . . dei*) mentioned at the end of this text is clearly equivalent to the "divine mind . . . reason" (*mens . . . ratio divina*) discussed at ibid., 13.312.7-16.

78. A.S. Ferguson in Scott, op. cit., vol. IV, p. 423 explained the statement in another way. He argued that the Latin translator had confused the original by running together descriptions of two different intellects: that of God in the first half of the main passage and that of eternity in the second half. His conjecture of the Greek original therefore reads: πᾶς μὲν οὖν νοῦς τῷ θείῳ [sc. νῷ] ὅμοιός ἐστιν. αὐτὸς μὲν ἀκίνητος ὢν ἐν τῇ ἰδίᾳ στάσει ἑαυτὸν κινεῖ, σεμνὸς καὶ ἄφθαρτος καὶ ἀΐδιος ὤν, καὶ εἴ τινι ἄλλῳ κρείττονι ὀνόματι κεκλῆσθαι δύναται. τοῦ δὲ ὑψίστου θεοῦ ἐν αὐτῇ τῇ Ἀληθείᾳ ὢν ὁ Αἰών, πληρέστατος πάντων τῶν αἰσθητῶν καὶ πάσης τάξεως, καὶ ὥσπερ συνυφεστὼς μετὰ τοῦ θεοῦ. This interpretation has the advantage of making the ascending and descending hierarchies agree with one another — both having the intellects of God and of eternity as the higher terms; it has the disadvantage of postulating an extraordinary grammatical incompetence on the translator's part — for example he applies the masculine adjective *plenissimus* to the feminine noun *aeternitas*. Fortunately, this speculative explanation is unnecessary if one bears in mind the consubstantial relation of the two higher intellects.

79. The nature of the relation between the divine intellect and the intellect of eternity will be explored in terms of several further texts. See pp. 140-142.

80. Compare the reference to the eternal character of the whole intellect. The Hermeticist does not explicitly interpret this eternity as atemporality here, although a later passage seems to indicate what his meaning is. Thus,

referring to the divine intellect he writes at *Asclep* 32.341.15-17: "One cannot recognize the slightest image of it in this world, for where everything is measured by time there arises deception" (*cuius veritatis in mundo nequidem extrema linea umbra dinoscitur. ubi enim quid temporum dimensione dinoscitur, ibi sunt mendacia*). That the whole intellect is also non-spatial would follow from its identity with God. See pp. 134-135.

81.   Compare the references to immobility and self-motion in stability. As in Neoplatonism, the atemporal and non-spatial character of the divine intellect necessitates that its motion (of thinking or causation) is of a transcendent variety.

82.   Compare the reference to the whole intellect as being filled with all sensible things and the totality of knowledge. That its content is the Forms is implied not only by the terminology itself but by the details of the Hermetic theory of Forms to be studied below.

83.   To the theory of Forms presented in the Latin work it is *Corpus Hermeticum* XVI which furnishes the most striking parallels. See the following passages in relation to each of the categories listed below: (i) *Corp. Herm.* XVI.8.234.20-235.2, (ii) ibid., XVI.9.235.3, (iii) ibid., XVI.17.237.11-12, (iv) ibid., XVI.15.236.18-26, and (v) ibid., XVI.17.237.12-14.

84.   See Nock and Festugière, op. cit., p. 360 (commenting on *Asclep.* 4.300.7-10), "Au surplus, tout le passage est très embrouillé, et je doute que l'auteur se soit compris lui-même."

85.   The main passages are: *Asclep.* 3.299.3-4.300.18 (text I), ibid., 17.316.5-18.318.2 (text II), and ibid., 34.344.13-36.347.3 (text III).

86.   Ibid., 3.299.13-15 (text I), "Nature imprints Forms upon matter through the four elements" (*natura autem per species imaginans mundum per quattour elementa*). Cf. ibid., 36.346.10-347.3 (text III).

87.   Ibid., 4.299.19-300.7 (text I), "The species of gods produces from itself individual gods, the species of demons and similarly that of men produces individuals like itself" (*genus ergo deorum ex se deorum faciet species. daemonum genus, aeque hominum . . . sui similes species generat*). The use of these two types of Form follows the tradition of Platonic doxography.

88.   Ibid., 4.299.17-19 (text I) and ibid., 4.300.10-12 (text I).

89.   Ibid., 35.345.10-11 (text III).

90.   Ibid., 17.316.11-13 (text II) and ibid., 35.345.24-346.2 (text III).

91.   Cf. ibid., 35.345.13-15 (text III) and ibid., 35.345.24-346.2 (text III) — higher Form; ibid., 35.345.19 (text III) and ibid., 35.346.4-6 (text III) — lower Form; ibid., 17.316.11 (text II) — uncertain status.

92.   Cf. ibid., 34.344.20 (text III) and passages mentioned in nn. 87 and 89 above.

93.   Ibid., 4.299.19-300.2 (text I) and ibid., 4.300.8-18 (text I).

94.   Ibid., 4.299.18-19 (text I) and ibid., 4.300.10 (text I).

95.   Ibid., 35.345.11-346.6 (text III).

96.   Ibid., 17.316.12 (text II), ibid., 17.316.17-317.1 (text II), and ibid., 35.345.18 (text III).

97. Ibid., 35.345.17-20 (text III).
98. Ibid., 4.300.8-18 (text I). For the distinction of transcendent and immanent Forms in earlier Platonism see pp. 203ff. and 312ff. The Hermeticist's use of *idea* for the immanent Form at ibid., 17.316.17 deviates somewhat from this traditional theory.
99. Ibid., 34.344.19-22 (text III), "This so-called sensible world is the receptacle of all the qualities or substances of sensible Forms. None of these things can have life without God" (*hic ergo sensibilis qui dicitur mundus receptaculum est omnium sensibilium specierum qualitatum vel corporum, quae omnia sine deo vegetari non possunt*). If the ambiguous *quae* of the last clause refers to *species* rather than *corpora*, then the argument is that God does not merely preside over the instantiation of the Forms but actually gives them existence. See n. 101 below.
100. Ibid., 3.299.11-13 (text I), "Matter has been prepared by God as the receptacle of all kinds of Forms" (*mundus autem praeparatus est a deo receptaculum omniformium specierum*).
101. Ibid., 33.343.2-8 (text III), "Just as this so-called place outside the world (if there is such a thing — which I do not believe) would have to be filled, I think, with intelligible things similar to the divinity of that place, thus the so-called sensible world is filled with bodies and living creatures similar to its nature and quality" (*sicuti enim quod dicitur extra mundum, si tamen est aliquid (nec istud enim credo), sic habeo, plenum esse intelligibilium rerum, id est divinitati suae similium, ut hic etiam sensibilis mundus qui dicitur sit plenissimus corporum et animalium naturae suae et qualitati convenientium*). It is quite clear from the context that the author postulates two levels of reality: the "intelligible world" (*intelligibilis mundus* [ibid., 34.344.14]) comprising God and the higher Forms and the "sensible world" (*sensibilis mundus* [ibid., 34.344.19]) comprising matter and the lower Forms. The implication of the main passage is therefore that the higher level of reality can only be a realm filled with metaphysical principles, and not a realm of empty physical space as visualized in the traditional Stoic doctrine of the surrounding void.
102. See n. 98 above.
103. Ibid., 19.319.1-5.
104. As argued in section (ii).
105. Ibid., 35.345.18-346.6 (text III). Cf. ibid., 3.299.7-11 (text I). Astrological notions gain prominence among Platonists during the second century A.D. The Hermeticist's use of these ideas within a theory of individuation is, however, quite unparalleled in earlier sources.
106. Ibid., 3.299.7-11 (text I), "From all the aforesaid causes which are alike ruled by God, a continuous emanation takes place through the world and through the soul of all species and individuals, throughout nature" (*a supradictis enim omnibus, quorum idem gubernator deus omnium, frequentatio fertur influens per mundum et per animam omnium generum et omnium specierum per rerum naturam*).

107. Ibid., 19.320.3-4, "All things are dependent upon the one and emanate from it" (*ex uno etenim cuncta pendentia ex eoque defluentia*). Cf. ibid., 3.298.7-9, 5.301.2-4, and 19.318.15-17. The emphasis upon dynamism is very characteristic of the later Platonic tradition.

108. Ibid., 14.313.20-314.22 *tamen in se nascendi procreandique vim . . . locum autem dico in quo sint omnia: neque enim haec omnia esse potuissent, si locus deesset . . . in se tamen omnium naturas habet, utpote qui his omnibus ad concipiendum fecundissimos sinus praestet.*

109. Ibid., 19.320.3-8. The writer argues that one can consider all things as a plurality or — in the sense that they depend upon a single cause — as a unity. In the latter case one can consider all things "as one or rather as two" (*unum vel potius duo*): in other words as a unity which is however more correctly a duality.

110. See n. 115 below.

111. Ibid., 17.315.24-316.1. Matter is "the receptacle, source of motion, and origin of multiplicity for all things ruled by God" (*omnium est receptaculum omniumque agitatio atque frequentatio quorum deus gubernator*). The whole passage is extremely difficult to construe, although Nock and Festugière, op. cit., p. 373 suggest the following as the original: πάντων ὑποδοχὴ πάντων τεν κινήσι πυκνότης. The term *frequentatio* is particularly obscure but probably involves the notions of motion and multiplicity. See L. Delatte, S. Govaerts, et J. Denooz, *Index du Corpus Hermeticum* (Rome, 1977), *s.v.*

112. *Asclep* 40.351.22-3. The writer states that "accident and chance are present in all things, blended in their materiality" (*eventus autem vel fors insunt omnibus permixta mundanis*).

113. Ibid., 17.316.9-13. Space is invisible in itself "but is held to have a sort of visibility through the Forms alone with whose images it seems to be impressed" (*per enim formas solas specierum, quarum imaginibus videtur insculpta, quasi visibilis creditur*).

114. As stated above, the attribution of these characteristics to matter is not completely certain. However, it seems reasonable to resolve ambiguities by appealing to Plato's *Timaeus* as a parallel, since the doctrine stemming from that text is a clear ancestor of the Hermeticist's own teaching.

115. Thus, Scott maintained that of the components into which he divides the treatise *Asclepius* I (1-14) and *Asclepius* III (16-41) are monistic while *Asclepius* II (14-16) is dualistic in character. Furthermore, he argued that even *Asclepius* II (14-16) holds its dualism in a restricted form. See Scott, op. cit., vol. III, pp. 82, 87, 123. In accordance with this thesis, Scott suggested that *Asclep* 3.299.11-13 (see n. 100) meant not that God simply ordered matter but that he actually created it (Scott, op. cit., p. 22); that *Asclep.* 14.314.3-4, "Matter is therefore able to produce alone, without joining with another principle" (*haec itaque sine alieno conceptu est sola generabilis*) does not imply really independent causality on matter's part (Scott, op. cit., p. 87); and that *Asclep.* 19.320.5 (see n. 109) was inserted into the argument by an interpolator who misunderstood its real significance (Scott, op. cit., p. 123). Of course, the interpretation of these texts along

such lines is only possible in conjunction with the thesis that the *Asclepius* is composed of several smaller treatises. However, the notion that they expound a monism is held by Scott to be supported (i) by the presence of the one-all doctrine (*Asclep.* 1.296.11-12 and 20.321.7) which seems to contradict dualism; and (ii) by clearly monistic statements in the Greek treatises (*Corp. Herm.* III.44.2-3 and XII.22.183.7-8) and testimonia (Iamblichus, *De Myst.* 8.3.265.6-7; cf. Proclus, *In Tim.* I.386.10-11). See Scott, op. cit., pp. 10, 22, and 138. In reply to this interpretation one must say that the thesis of the *Asclepius*'s composite structure is if not untenable certainly not demonstrated. Furthermore, the presence of the word *receptaculum* in *Asclep.* 3.299.11-13 indicates that the author may be thinking of Plato's ὑποδοχή which has not previously been interpreted as caused by God. In addition, the statement of ibid., 14.314.3-4 that matter is an independent source of causality must be taken at face value in the absence of definite evidence to the contrary. Finally, the notion of an interpolation at ibid., 19.320.5 cannot be maintained without the highly speculative thesis of the work's multiple authorship. We must therefore conclude that, despite the undeniable existence of monistic tendencies in the Greek treatises, the *Asclepius* remains in the tradition of Platonic dualism.

116. The remainder of our discussion of God will be divided up as follows:
Category (i) Principles having a status not independent of God
> a. Eternity 2 C i
> b. Spirit 2 C ii
> c. Love 2 C iii

Categories (i) = (ii) Principles having a status which is both not independent and independent of God. Their position is ambivalent.
> Fate 2 C iv

Category (ii) Principles having a status independent of God
> a. The second god 2 C v
> b. The hierarchy of gods 2 C vi
> c. The second god and the hierarchy of gods 2 C vii

It should be noted that "independent of God" does not mean "not caused by God" — which applies only to matter — but rather "existing apart from God."

117. *Asclep* 32.340.11-12.
118. Ibid., 32.340.17-21. See p. 138.
119. Ibid., 31.339.26-340.3.
120. Ibid., 30.338.22-3.
121. The fullest account of Ἀιων is in *Corp. Herm.* XI.2 where we have a series of distinct principles — God, Eternity, the World, Time, and Becoming — each of which "generates" (ποιεῖν) the next. Among features which parallel the *Asclepius* are the notions (i) that Eternity is "in God" (ἐν τῷ Θεῷ), the World "in Eternity" (ἐν τῶ αἰῶνι) Time "in the World" (ἐν τῷ κόσμῳ); and (ii) that Eternity "is stable around God" (ἔστηκε περὶ τὸν Θεὸν) (*Corp. Herm.* XI.2.147.7-148.6).

122. *Asclep.* 31.339.5-7. At ibid., 30.337.20 Eternity is said to be the "place" (*locus*) of the world.
123. Ibid., 30.338.3-4. Cf. ibid., 30.337.19-20.
124. Ibid., 31.339.7-8.
125. Ibid., 31.340.3-4.
126. Ibid., 31.339.11-13. At ibid., 30.339.1-3 the mobility of time is said to begin and end in Eternity's immobility.
127. Ibid., 31.339.14-20. The whole argument regarding the relation of Eternity and time is of great subtlety (ibid., 31.339.8-18). In brief it runs as follows: (i a) time is moving, (i b) Eternity is immobile, (i c) since time's motion is circular it is also immobile in a sense; (ii a) time has a circular motion from and towards Eternity (held to be a restatement of [i c]); (ii b) Eternity is immanent in time; (ii c) Eternity has a circular motion from and towards itself (resulting from the combination of [ii a] and [ii b]). This argument shows that the relation between Eternity and time is one containing moments of both transcendence and immanence: transcendence in (i a) and (i b), immanence in (ii b), and transcendence and immanence in (i c), (ii a), and (ii c). Historically speaking, it represents a combination of the Platonic notion of a transcendent relation between eternity and time (see Plato, *Tim.* 37 d where the eternity of the Living Creature is the paradigm of the heavenly bodies' temporal motion) and the Aristotelian notion of their immanent relation (see Aristotle, *De Caelo* I.9.279 a 25-8 where eternity is the sum of all time constituted by the heavenly bodies' rotation). There is no definite literary evidence of the combination of these two texts by the Hermeticist, although either he or his source has subconsciously made the doctrinal synthesis.
128. *Asclep.* 30.338.11-12.
129. The relation of God as Eternity to time is of a similar kind. See n. 127.
130. *Asclep.* 16.315.13-15.
131. Ibid., 17.315.22-4.
132. Ibid., 14.313.21-2. Here, Spirit is declared to have characteristics analogous to those possessed by matter.
133. Ibid., 14.313.5-7.
134. Ibid., 17.316.3-4.
135. This metaphysical status is apparently confirmed by ibid., 14.313.5-6, "Spirit was inherent in matter, although not in the way that it was inherent in God" (*inerat mundo spiritus, sed non similiter ut deo*).
136. Ibid., 6.303.5-6.
137. Ibid., 14.313.5-6. *Mundus* here clearly signifies matter. See n. 74 above.
138. Ibid., 17.315.22-3. *Mundus* here seems rather to signify the world. See n. 136 above.
139. Ibid., 17.316.3-4.
140. On the Stoicism of the *Asclepius* see p. 132.

141. I suspect that the sparing use of Spirit in the philosophical system of the *Asclepius* is a sign that its author is aware that many elements in the purely physical doctrine of pneuma cannot be used. In this respect the treatment differs from that in *Corp. Herm.* I.4.7.15ff. where a cosmological process is described using an elaborate blend of metaphysical and physical ideas. Here, on the one hand there are concepts like "intellect" (νοῦς) and "word" (λόγος) and on the other transformations of elemental qualities, while Spirit is manifested alternately as "spiritual word" (πνευματικὸς λόγος) and as the element of fire. But Scott, op. cit., vol. III, pp. 36-38, holds that there is a similar combination in the *Asclepius* where he locates traces of the physical interpretation of Spirit as fire and air. On this doctrine see also *Corp. Herm.* III.1.44.2-9.44.

142. *Asclep.* 21.321.18-323.7. At this point the parallel Coptic version is also available, enabling us to see the increased philosophical technicality of the Latin *Asclepius*.

143. Ibid., 21.322.11-13.

144. Ibid., 21.322.7, 21.322.13, 21.322.15, and 21.323.3-4.

145. Ibid., 21.323.3-6.

146. Ibid., 20.321.9-11 and 21.321.18-19.

147. Ibid., 21.322.11-13.

148. Ibid., 21.322.5-9. The writer adds that it is for this reason that one can call the coming together "Cupid, Venus, or both" (*sive Cupidinem sive Venerem sive utrumque*).

149. Ibid., 21.322.17-323.2.

150. Ibid., 21.323.5-6.

151. Ibid., 21.321.20-21.

152. To a great extent this depends upon the interpretation given to God's bisexuality. On the notion of the "male-female" (ἀρρενόθηλυς) see J. Kroll, *Die Lehren des Hermes Trismegistos (Beiträge zur Geschichte der Philosophie des Mittelalters* 12: 2-4) (Münster, 1913), pp. 51-4; Scott, op. cit., vol. III, pp. 135-138; Nock and Festugière, op. cit., vol. I, p. 20; Festugière, *La révélation d'Hermès Tresmégiste IV: Le dieu inconnu et la gnose*, pp. 43-51; and Festugière, *Hermétisme et mystique païenne*, pp. 257-60. From the evidence assembled by these modern scholars, it seems that the notion appears in at least three contexts: (i) Ancient religions of Egypt and Greece. See the texts assembled by Scott, op. cit., vol. III, pp. 135-137; (ii) Stoicism. See Diogenes of Babylon in Philodemus, *De Piet.* 15-17 (*D.G.* 548b 14-550b 8 = *S.V.F.* III. Diog. 33); Varro, *Logist. Curio* fr. 2 (Augustine, *Civ. Dei* VII. 9 [*C.C.S.L.* 47.193-4]); and Firmicus Maternus, *Math.* V, pr. 3; (iii) Pythagoreanism or Neopythagoreanism. See ps.-Iambl., *Theol. Arithm.* 53.21.4.1. Leaving aside category (i) whose position was later interpreted according to the philosophical views implied by categories (ii) or (iii), it should be noted that the notion of a bisexual God means something different in category (ii) and category (iii) respectively. In the former it signifies the God immanent in the world, that immanence being interpreted as the union of active (male) and passive (female) principles. In the latter

it signifies that God who transcends and is immanent in the world, the transcendence being represented by the priority of the monad (male) to the dyad (female) and the immanence by the production by the monad of the dyad. Since the *Asclepius* is a synthesis of both Stoic and Platonic or Pythagorean notion, it is difficult to say which of these approaches dominates in the Hermeticist's mind. The same can be said of other references to the "male-female" in later eclectic sources like Ps.-Aristotle, Περὶ Κόσμου 7.401 b 2 (= Apuleius, *De Mundo* 37.372) and *Corp. Herm.* I.9.9.16.

153. *Asclep.* 39.349.19-350.6. Part of this text is preserved in the Greek by Lydus, *De Mens.* IV.7.71.1-4, ἡ δὲ εἱμαρμένη ἐστὶ καὶ ἡ εἱμαρτὴ ἐνέργεια ἢ αὐτὸς ὁ θεὸς ἢ μετ᾽ ἐκείνην τεταγμένη κατὰ πάντων οὐρανίων τε καὶ ἐπιγείων μετὰ τῆς ἀνάγκης τάξις.

154. In order to simplify the argument I shall label the various "definitions" as follows: (i a) *quam* εἱρμαρμένην . . . *vincta*, (i b) *effectrix rerum*, (ii a) *deus summus*, (ii b) *ab ipso . . . deus*, and (i c) *omnium caelestium . . . discplina*. The reason for my division into types (i) and (ii) is explained below.

155. See Ps.-Plutarch, *De Fato* 1.158 c-d; Nemesius, *De Nat. Hom.* 38.753B ff.; and Calcidius, *In Tim.* 143.182.5-7. The doctrinal parallels between these texts indicate a common source.

156. That definitions (i a) and (i c) are not really distinct follows from the fact that both refer to Fate abstractly. That (ii a) and (ii b) are distinct follows from the identification of Fate with separate principles. The case of (i b) is problematic, although the original terminology εἱμαρτὴ ἐνέργεια suggests that we are dealing with Fate as a process rather than as a principle.

157. See Aetius, *Plac.* I.27.2 (*S.V.F.* II.916 = *D.G.* 322 b 6-7); ibid., I.27.4 (*S.V.F.* II.976 = *D.G.* 322 a 10-14); and Servius, *In Aeneid.* II.689 (*S.V.F.* II.923).

158. See Cicero, *De Divin.* I.125-6 (*S.V.F.* II.921); Gellius, *Noct. Attic.* VII.2.1-3 (*S.V.F.* II.1000); and Servius, *In Aeneid.* III.376 (*S.V.F.* II.919).

159. See Cicero, *De Divin.* I.125-6 (*S.V.F.* II.921); Servius, *In Aeneid.* III.376 (*S.V.F.* II.919); and Eusebius, *Praep. Evang.* 15.816d (*S.V.F.* I.98).

160. See Aetius, *Plac.* I.28.4 (*S.V.F.* II.917 = *D.G.* 324 a 1-3); Cicero, *De Divin.* I.125-6 (*S.V.F.* II.921); and Nemesius, *De Nat. Hom.* 37.752B (*S.V.F.* II.918).

161. See Arius Didymus, *Epit. Phys.* fr. 29 (*S.V.F.* II.528 = *D.G.* 465.1-2); Seneca, *De Benef.* IV.7.1-2 (*S.V.F.* II.1024); Diogenes Laertius, *Vit. Philos.* VII.135-6 (*S.V.F.* I.102 and II.580); and Alexander of Aphrodisias, *De Fato* 22.191.30 (*S.V.F.* II.945).

162. See Ps.-Plutarch, *De Fato* 2.568 e; Nemesius, *De Nat. Hom.* 38, 753Bff.; and Calcidius, *In Tim.* 144.182.16-183.1. On these doctrinal parallels see n. 155 above.

163. *Asclep.* 19.318.22-319.11. The section dealing with the ousiarch Fate is preserved in Greek at Lydus, *De Mens.* IV.7.70.23-4.

164. In this astronomical passage it is clearly Jupiter alone who could signify the highest God. Fate is contrasted with this Jupiter.

165. *Asclep.* 40.351.3-14.
166. In this account of the three principles their relation to Eternity corresponds to their relation to god. God and Eternity are co-extensive.
167. Ibid., 40.351.14-22.
168. See pp. 144-145.
169. See pp. 144-145.
170. Ibid., 26.330.2-3.
171. The Greek text is quoted by Lactantius, *Div. Inst.* VII.18.3 (*C.S.E.L.* 19.641.2-3) καὶ θεὸς καὶ τοῦ πρώτου καὶ ἑνὸς θεοῦ δημιουργός. This author holds that the words τοῦ πρώτου (not contained in the Latin version) indicate that the second principle is also "first": in other words that the Hermeticist is postulating a consubstantial relation between the first and second principles. On such an interpretation the second god is clearly a transcendent spiritual principle. Lactantius's interpretation is perhaps supported by certain passages in the Greek corpus where the derivation of such a secondary principle is apparently envisaged. See *Corp. Herm.* V.2.60.17-18 where God is described as "not one but the source of one" οὐχ εἷς ἀλλ' ἀφ' οὗ ὁ εἷς. (Comparison with ibid., II.5.33.4 and II.12.37.7-9 indicates that the doctrine here is of a first principle transcending intellect and substance giving rise to a second principle which is intellect and substance). His interpretation is perhaps also supported by the phraseology of the Coptic version which here as elsewhere is closer than the Latin version to the Greek original. However, the wider context of the Latin *Asclepius* itself suggests that the second god is the sensible cosmos. Thus, the words τοῦ πρώτου (occurring only in the Greek version) indicate that the second principle is the "first" in the sense of being the first product of the first principle. On this question see P. Siniscalco, *"Ermete Trismegisto, profeta pagano della rivelazione cristiana. La fortuna di un passo ermetico (Asclepius 8) nell' interpretazione di scrittori cristiani,"* pp. 90-93.
172. *Asclep.* 8.305.1ff.
173. Ibid., 8.305.2-8.
174. Ibid., 10.308.8-9. Cf. *Corp. Herm.* VIII.2.87.14-18, IX.8.99.15-18, X.10.118.7-10, X.12.119.1-3, etc.
175. *Asclep.* 3.299.3. Two Latin terms are used to signify "world": (i) *caelum* (see ibid., 3.299.3, 3.299.5, and 4.300.7), and (ii) *mundus* (see ibid., 10.308.9, 10.308.21, 25.328.20, 27.332.4, and 30.337.23). On another sense of *mundus* (as "matter") see n. 74 above.
176. Ibid., 29.336.16-337.3. Cf. *Corp. Herm.* XVI.6.234.4-6, XVI.12.235.25-236.3, XVI.17.237.11-14, etc.
177. *Asclep.* 3.299.4-5 and 30.337.23-338.2.
178. Ibid., 30.337.23-338.1. Cf. ibid., 3.299.3-4 and 27.332.4-5.
179. Ibid., 29.337.12-14.
180. Ibid., 18.317.14-15.
181. Ibid., 29.337.5.

182. Ibid., 3.299.5-7. The phrase *caeli vero et ipsius animae here* could mean either "of the world and its soul" or "of the world and the soul itself." However, in both cases the reference is to a universal and not an individual soul. See also ibid., 2.298.12-13 and 3.298.17-19.

183. Ibid., 32.340.21-3.

184. Ibid., 32.341.9-13. The world soul is described with varying terminology: (i) *anima* (sc. *caeli* or *mundi*) (see ibid., 2.298.12, 3.298.19, and 3.299.5-6), (ii) *sensus mundi/sensus mundanus* (see ibid., 32.340.21-2, 32.341.10, and 32.342.2), and (iii) *intellectus mundi* (see ibid., 32.342.4). Regarding (ii) two observations are required: first, that *sensus* is the translation of the Greek *nous* (see nn. 42 and 85-86 above) and second, that references to the world soul as ψυχή/*anima* and νοῦς/*intellectus* are equally common in syncretistic literature. This is indicated in the writings of Cicero, Varro, Seneca, and others.

185. Ibid., 32.342.1-5.

186. The author adds a note saying that "we perceive the intelligible gods more clearly than the sensible ones" (*magis enim ipsos sentimus quam eos*).

187. A note is added that the sensible gods "accomplish all things in sensible nature, acting one through another" (*per sensibilem naturam conficiunt omnia, alter per alterum*).

188. Ibid., 19.318.5-21.

189. Festugière, *Hermétisme et mystique païenne*, p. 125 suggests the possibility that the intelligible gods are distinct from the ousiarchs to be mentioned below. This would follow from understanding *specierum principes dii* as "gods who rule (are prior to) substances (transcendent substances)," these latter being interpreted as equivalent to the ousiarchs. However, Festugière, op. cit., pp. 125, n. 19 and 128, n. 30 rightly rejects this complicating factor not supported elsewhere by the text. In short, it seems clear that (i) *specierum principes dii*, (ii) *princeps* οὐσίας (accepting the likely conjecture οὐσία<ς> of Ferguson), and (iii) οὐσιάρχης all refer to the same thing or things.

190. These will be immanent and not transcendent Forms.

191. This substance will correspond to their immanent Form.

192. That the phrase *utriusque originis consimiles suae* indicates that the sensible gods are constituted (i) by their dependence upon the intelligible and (ii) by their association with a material body is convincingly suggested by Nock and Festugière, op. cit., vol. II, p. 375.

193. On the meaning of "ousiarch" (οὐσιάρχης) see Festugière, *Hermétisme et mystique païenne*, pp. 127-130. The writer instances some important texts of Iamblichus's *De Mysteriis* which speak of the relation between intelligible "causes" (ἀρχαί) and the sensible "substances" (οὐσίαι) which they govern. See *De Myst.* VIII.1.260.14-16 and VIII.5.268.6-8. These parallels are validated by the fact that Iamblichus is throughout this discussion referring to the Egyptian or "Hermetic" philosophy. The only difference between Iamblichus and the Latin writer is that the latter interprets οὐσία + ἀρχή as "substance . . . ruler" rather than as "substance . . . cause."

See Festugière, op. cit., p. 121, n. 2.

194. *Asclep.* 19.318.22-319.11.
195. See Festugière, op. cit., pp. 123-125 where parallel texts are listed and summarized. For our purposes the most interesting among these are perhaps Porphyry, *De Regr. Anim.* fr. 6.33*.7-34*.26, fr. 8.36*5-37*6, and Sallustius, *De Diis et Mundo* 5.10.5-6.12.23. For the Iamblichean parallel see n. 193 above.
196. Festugière, op. cit., p. 126.
197. *Asclep.* 18.317.21-318.2.
198. Ibid., 23.325.7-8.
199. Ibid., 22.324.6-7 and 23.325.18-19. This presumably refers to their predominantly fiery composition.
200. Ibid., 38.349.9-10.
201. Ibid., 35.345.22-4. See pp. 138-139.
202. Ibid., 27.332.12-13. The text goes on to speak of a further "Plutonian Jupiter" (*iuppiter Plutonius*) who presides over earth and sea.
203. Festugière, op. cit., p. 125, n. 20; and Nock and Festugière, op. cit., p. 384 both observe that the Jupiter(s) mentioned in this passage are sensible gods contrasting with the Jupiter of *Asclep.* 19.318.22-3 who is an intelligible one. However, Scott, op. cit., vol. III, pp. 107-110 argues with equal plausibility that the Jupiter(s) of the later passage are intelligible gods equivalent to the missing ousiarchs of the earlier one.
204. The following diagram will assist the discussion here:

DEUS =	*DEUS SECUNDUS =*
1. *Iuppiter*	*Caelum*
2. *Lumen*	*Sol*
3. *Pantomorphos*	*Horoscopi*
4. *Heimarmene*	*VII Sphaerae*
5. *<Iuppiter> Secundus*	*Aer*

On the question of *Iuppiter* see above. If *Iuppiter Plutonius* is also to be included in the scheme, then a sixth pair of intelligible and sensible gods must be added.

205. Following the horizontal sequence in the diagram.
206. Following the vertical sequence in the diagram.
207. See pp. 148-149. This might also be suggested by the author's apparent hesitation on the question whether the seven spheres have one or two ousiarchs. See pp. 147-148.
208. See p. 145.

209. See pp. 147-148. The sun appears as a separate sensible god although it must inevitably figure also among the seven spheres.
210. See p. 147.

Negative Theology in Gnosticism and Neoplatonism

Curtis L. Hancock

From ancient times to the present philosophers have commonly maintained that there exist one or more divine realities which are too perfect for human intelligence to apprehend and which therefore can only be the objects of a negative theology — that is, a theology expressing not what a divine nature is but what it is not.[1] Obviously, the degree to which philosophers require negative theology depends on their views regarding the knowability (or should I say unknowability?) of the divine existents. On the one hand, some philosophers, holding that of all divine existents the nature of the supreme God is alone indiscernible, insist that only the supreme God is the object of negative theology. Philosophers accepting this view may themselves disagree depending on whether they take God's nature to be wholly or only partly unknowable.[2] On the other hand, some philosophers, holding that not only God, but also other divine natures are indiscernible, insist that multiple divine existents are fit objects of negative theology. These philosophers may also differ depending on the degree they permit positive theology (that is, a theology expressing what a divine nature is) in their systems, with most excluding it from the higher regions of divine reality, but permitting it on lower levels.[3]

With these helpful distinctions in mind, we are now prepared to take up the task of this paper, which is essentially twofold: first, to generally outline negative theology as it appears in two religio-philosophical Hellenistic schools, Gnosticism and Neoplatonism; second, to show certain fundamental similarities and dissimilarities between the two schools on negative theology, stressing in the end their similarities. To accomplish these aims my discussion will consist of three parts. The first part will simply outline the main features of Neoplatonic negative theology; the second will delineate Gnostic negative theology, showing especially its parallels with Neoplatonism; the third will furnish a brief summary and some conclusions. For the sake of brevity, I will offer only a representative sampling of sources from these two schools. Specifically, my comments on Neoplatonism will focus on Plotinus, while my reflections on Gnosticism will center on the Nag Hammadi tractates.[4]

I

Since the main outline of Plotinus's negative theology remains largely unaltered in the writings of his successors, his development of the subject is representative of Neoplatonism as a whole. The *Enneads* are especially representative because they supply a wealth of passages expressing negative theology, the doctrine appearing in some form in almost every treatise, from the first, I, 6, 7-9, to the last, I, 7, 1, 19-21.[5]

For reasons that will become apparent shortly, the *Enneads* restrict negative theology to the One, the supreme reality of Plotinus's metaphysics, permitting positive theology of the remaining divine hypostases, Intelligence and Soul. Since the One is obviously the most important object of Plotinus's monistic and mystical philosophy, negative theology is not for Plotinus a casual practice but is something fundamental to his entire philosophical endeavor. Moreover, regarding the One, Plotinus makes it clear that his commitment to negative theology is *absolute*; in other words, he subscribes to what we might call an *exclusive* negative theology, which forbids the very possibility of predication of the First Reality.

What exactly accounts for Plotinus's strong commitment to negative theology? It ultimately derives from the basic principle of his entire philosophy: namely, that reality is equivalent to unity; in other words, that to be real is to be one.[6] This principle is common to almost all Neoplatonism, and, therefore, we may assume that the negative theology it inspires will hold not only for Plotinus but for his successors as well.[7]

Now, according to this principle — that to be real is to be one — the supreme or perfect reality must be sheer unity (hence Plotinus names it "the One," and "the Good," since unity is perfection and the *telos* of all reality)[8] and as such must be more real than Intelligence, because even perfect Intelligence, Aristotle's *noēsis noēseōs* admits some multiplicity, at least the logical duality of subject-object, knower-known. But that the One is superior to Intelligence entails a negative theology, for, according to Plotinus, the divine *noēta*, the true objects and the ultimate conditions of all knowledge and predication, constitute a single nature. *Nous* and *eidē* are really identical.[9] Indeed, *Nous* as an active power (*hē dynamis*) is the direct or proximate cause of the Forms (and thereby of its own nature).[10] Since it is only as Form that something is knowable and predicable, the One, by transcending Intelligence and Form, is altogether unknowable and beyond predication.[11] Hence, while the other divine natures, namely, *Nous* and Soul, may be known through a positive theology, since they occupy the universe of forms or *noēta*, the One can only be known through not-knowing, a negative theology which is necessary to prevent the philosopher from describing the superior (the One/Good) in terms of the inferior (Form).

Granted that Plotinus is profoundly committed to negative theology, how does he mainly develop it? To answer this question, let us enumerate and briefly comment on those specific formulations of what God is not which occur most frequently or emphatically in the *Enneads*.

The One is unlimited (apeiron).

Plotinus follows Plato, who in turn follows Parmenides, by identifying form (*eidos*) with determinacy (*horos*) and limit (*peras*). But unlike his predecessors, Plotinus concludes that such predicates cannot apply to the highest reality. Since the One is formless (*aneideon*; *amorphon*),[12] it must be indeterminate (*aoriston*) and unlimited (*apeiron*).[13] Obviously, such a conclusion further supports negative theology: if the One is infinite, it manifestly cannot be the object of finite intelligence; nor can it be the subject of predicates, which, of their very nature, presuppose form and therefore limitation.

The One is absolutely without need.

The transcendence of the One over Form and Intelligence explains its infinity. This same transcendence accounts also for the One's independence. VI, 9 (9), 6, 12-26 explains:

> When you think of Him as Mind or God, He is still more: and when you
> unify Him in your thought, the degree of unity by which He transcends your
> thought is still greater than you imagine it to be. For He exists in and by
> Himself without any attributes. One might conceive His unity in terms of
> His self-sufficiency. For He must be the most sufficient of all things, the
> most independent, and the most without wants. Everything which is
> multiple and not one is defective, since it is composed of many parts. Entity
> needs Him in order to be one: but He does not need Himself; for He is
> Himself. An existent which is multiple needs its full number of parts and
> each of its parts, since it exists with the others and not independently, is in
> need of the others; so an existent of this kind shows itself defective, as a
> whole and in each individual part. If then, as is in fact true, there must be
> something supremely self-sufficing, it must be the One, which is the only
> reality of such a kind as not to be defective either in relation to Itself or to
> anything else.[14]

Pure unity, then, requires no explanation but itself; and yet the One is
required by all else, because where there is multiplicity there is
dependence.

The One is undiminished in production.[15]

The One is the source of all realities and yet it is inexhaustible.
Its productive power is infinite and never depleted. "The First remains
the same even when other existents come out of it."[16] Plotinus mainly
relies on analogies to convey, however inadequately, the inexhaustibility
of the One. In III, 8, (30), 10, 3-7 he states his best-known metaphor
on the subject, likening the One to a great spring:

> But what is above life [=the One] is cause of life; for the act of life, which
> is all beings, is not first, but itself flows out, so to speak, as if from a spring.
> For think of a spring which has no other origin, but gives the whole of itself
> to rivers, and is not used up by the rivers but remains itself at rest . . . .[17]

In the later treatise, V, 5 (32), 5, 2-7, his analogy is less poetic but
conveys the same philosophical point. There Plotinus compares
production of beings out of the One with production of numbers out of
the unit.

> In the case of numbers, number comes about according to the same
> principle [i.e., undiminished giving], with the unit remaining the same, while
> something else produces. In the case of that which is before beings, much
> more for this same reason does the One remain intact. If beings exist by

this principle, it is not something else which produces them, while the One remains the same, but rather the One is sufficient to generate these beings.[18]

The One is not eternal (aiōn).

It clearly follows from the One's infinity that it is not bound by succession or time. Does this not imply that the One is eternal? Plotinus, perhaps surprisingly, answers negatively. The One cannot be eternal because, for Plotinus (and here he again follows Plato), eternity is linked with immutability (stasis), the objects of intellection, the eternal world of Forms.[19] The One is neither mutable nor immutable because it transcends the whole order of reality where such predicates apply. Hence, eternity befits the second hypostasis but not the First.

The One is not Life (zōē).

Just as Plotinus must deny eternity of the One, so he must deny life of it, for life, like eternity, presupposes intellection. In fact, for Plotinus, the best life is eternity, a life which realizes itself by apprehending simultaneously all noēta. This, of course, is the life of Nous. Inferior life, however, is time, a life which realizes itself by apprehending successively all noēta. This is the life of Soul. Life, then, whether perfect or imperfect, whether Nous or Soul, belongs to the order of noēsis and noēta and therefore cannot belong to the One.[20]

The One is not entity (ousia), nor any other megiston genos.

Plotinus interprets the megista genē (ousia, kinēsis, stasis, tauton and heteron) of Plato's Sophist as the logically distinct components of Nous itself.[21] Each of these genera represents from a certain point of view either one or both of the two logically distinct aspects of the intelligible world: noēsis and noēta. As such the megista genē cannot be predicates of the One. That the One is none of the supreme genera is highly significant for Plotinus's negative theology, for it emphasizes the One's radical transcendence over the traditional Platonic conception of highest reality.[22]

Why precisely must the One transcend ousia? The answer derives from the fact that Plotinus, following Plato and Aristotle, equates entity (*ousia*) with form (*eidos*); that is to say, for Plotinus whatever is form is also entity.[23] Thus, the intelligible world, which is the same as the second hypostasis, is not only the world of Forms but also of entities. But if *ousia* describes the intelligible world, it cannot describe the First Reality, for the intelligible world is a unity-in-multiplicity, whereas God is pure unity. For this reason Plotinus, again and again, often ironically invoking the authority of Plato (*Republic* 509 b),[24] declares that the Good is beyond entity (*epekeina tēs ousias*), even beyond the very being of entity (*epekeina einai tēs ousias*).[25]

Similarly, Plotinus holds that the One is neither motion (*kinēsis*) nor rest (*stasis*). The One cannot be motion because for Plotinus, as for Plato, *kinēsis* signifies *noēsis*.[26] *Kinēsis* as a *megiston genos* refers to the intellection of *Nous* actuating the plurality of *eidē* or *ousiai*. However, it does not follow, Plotinus argues, that, because the One is not motion, it must be rest (*stasis*), which denotes the eternal Forms. The One is neither motion nor rest because it is formless, more perfect than the entire order of beings to which motion and rest belong.

> Since the nature of the One produces all beings, It is none of them. It is not a being or quality or quantity or intellect or soul; It is not in motion or at rest, in place or in time, but exists in Itself, a unique Form; or rather It is formless, existing before all form, before motion, before rest; for these belong to being and make it multiple. Why then, if It is not in motion, is It not at rest? Because in being one or both must be present and it is at rest by participation in the Absolute Rest and is not identical with that Rest; so Rest is present to it as an attribute and it no longer remains simple.[27]

In other words, to call the One "rest" or "motion" renders it multiple through predication.

Likewise, the One is neither sameness (*tauton*) nor difference (*heteron*). Sameness denotes the intellection of the second hypostasis which is eternally present to the Forms. Difference denotes the Forms which are the plurality known and unified by intellection. Together these two principles define that which is not one but one-in-many. Therefore, they cannot describe the First Reality.

In sum, the *megista genē* as the supreme principles of Dialectics are the true *noēta*, the true objects of *epistēmē* and the perfect beings. The One, however, by transcending being or entity (*ousia*), is trans-dialectical and beyond *epistēmē*. Consequently, Plotinus's conception of the *megista genē* discloses the truly radical character of his negative theology. By refusing these predicates of the One, Plotinus demonstrates that the One simply can never be a *noēton*.

The One is not energeia.

The *megista genē* together define that which Plotinus conceives as pure *energeia*. For Plotinus, as for Aristotle, *energeia* means *eidos* or *ousia* and therefore describes perfectly the supreme entity, the Separate Intelligence.[28]   Unlike Aristotle, however, Plotinus must deny that *energeia* describes the First Reality. Only in an ontology, such as Aristotle's, where to be real is to be (or to be a being), can *energeia* signify the reality of every existent and thereby most truly signify the First Reality, which for Aristotle is the Separate Intelligence.

However, in an "henology,"[29] such as Plotinus's, where to be real is to be one, *energeia* cannot signify the reality of every existent but only that which partly fails of reality (=unity), that which is not one but one-in-many. Hence, for Plotinus *energeia* describes the second reality but not the First.

As a corollary to this refusal to ascribe *energeia* to the One, Plotinus is willing to describe the One as sheer active power (*dynamis tōn pantōn*).[30]   This ascription also, at least in principle, offends negative theology, but Plotinus tolerates it since *dynamis*, unlike *energeia*, is more compatible with the absolute boundlessness and indeterminacy of the One.[31]   This respect for *dynamis* suggests the general anti-Aristotelian character of Plotinus's negative theology, according to which he rejects the Aristotelian principle that *energeia* is prior to *dynamis* in reality.[32]

Collectively, these several statements of what God is not comprise the heart of Plotinus's negative theology and, if we are justified in taking Plotinus as the school's chief representative, of Neoplatonist negative theology in general. Commenting on these statements, however, is not all we need say about Plotinian negative theology. We must pose a final question: if Plotinus is committed to a profound negative theology, why does he occasionally ascribe positive terms to the One? Does this not render his philosophy seriously inconsistent?

A complex answer to this question is possible,[33] but I shall opt for a simpler one.   Plotinus is sometimes willing to suffer some inconsistency on grounds that the very task of philosophical discourse entails some corruption of negative theology.   Such corruption is necessary unless the philosopher willfully ignores the First Reality. To ignore the One, however, would be to make philosophical discourse pointless, because for Plotinus (and apparently for most Neoplatonists) the chief objective of philosophical discourse is to help those who have never attained mystical union to glimpse, however imperfectly, the transcendent One. For this, the true end of life and philosophy, the philosopher must strain the limits of language and violate the restrictions of negative theology.

Given this important reason, an occasional departure must not obscure the significance Plotinus and his followers assign to negative theology. The doctrine is essential because positive theology in principle is incompatible with the view that reality is unity. The One simply cannot be an object of knowledge or a subject of predication, for, as such, it would be one-in-many rather than purely one. God is not the object of knowledge but of mysticism, an experience transcending knowledge. In a word, Neoplatonic negative theology exists to support a mystical philosophy which holds that to experience God one must strip himself of being, form and cognition as one would strip himself of contaminated linen before initiation into the mysteries.[34]

II

While Gnosticism and Neoplatonism diverge in significant ways, as *Enneads* II, 9 (33) and VI, 8 (39) testify,[35] the Nag Hammadi library shows that the two schools are largely compatible regarding negative theology. Thus, in order to outline Gnostic negative theology, I will simply identify those important features it shares with Neoplatonism.

Before doing this, however, I should comment on what appears as the most noteworthy difference between the two schools concerning negative theology: namely, that Gnosticism applies the doctrine more broadly than Neoplatonism. Whereas Plotinus centers negative theology exclusively on the One, the very highest reality, the Gnostics extend negative theology to intermediaries, which are the manifestations and *logoi* of the highest reality.

If we may step momentarily outside the Nag Hammadi literature, we discover this tendency to broaden negative theology especially in Basilides, whose thought is outlined by the heresiologist Hippolytus. According to Basilides God is too perfect to be the object of knowledge or discourse. Indeed, it is better to define Him as "non-being" than to diminish Him by any positive description. But we must also rely mainly on negations in describing the cosmos of archons which God produces. Some of these intermediaries are more hidden than others, with the highest archon being "more ineffable than the ineffable," a statement which may simply aim to encourage the Gnostic to resign himself altogether to revelation or mysticism in his quest for God.[36]

When we return to the Nag Hammadi library, we find this extension of negative theology apparent in such Christian Gnostic texts as *The Tripartite Tractate*, which depicts the Son, who is the *Logos* and name of the Father, as sharing in divine ineffability. He subsists in God and therefore may be called "the ineffable one in the ineffable one, the invisible one, the incomprehensible one, the inconceivable one in the inconceivable one."[37]

Certain Barbeloite tractates, e.g., *Allogenes, Zostrianos, The Three Steles of Seth* and *The Trimorphic Protennoia*, use similar language when characterizing the "Hidden One," the Aeon Barbelo. In *The Trimorphic Protennoia*, a Barbeloite tractate with some Christian encrustations, Barbelo, also named "Protennoia," the first thought of the Unknown God, shares in divine unknowability, existing as "ineffable silence,"[38] as the Word of the supreme God, "ineffable, incorruptible, immeasurable, inconceivable."[39]

Even more important than the Aeon Barbelo is another intermediate appearing in the Barbeloite tractates, namely, the divine Triple Power, which *Allogenes* describes as standing above the Aeon Barbelo, who (we may note) compares with Plotinus's *Nous*, and below the Invisible Spirit or Unknown God, who resembles Plotinus's first hypostasis.[40] This intermediate derives its name from its threefold nature consisting of Vitality, Mentality and That Which Is — a triad which also belong to Plotinus's *Nous*,[41] suggesting some kind of interchange between Barbeloite Gnosticism and Plotinus's school.[42] *Allogenes* makes it clear that as far as negative theology is concerned the Triple Power is more like the Invisible Spirit, who is completely unknowable, than Barbelo, who (by virtue of his/her status as intellect and form) is only partly unknowable. Indeed, the kinship of the Triple Power with the Invisible Spirit is so striking that in other tractates, such as *Zostrianos* and *The Three Steles of Seth*, the two divine natures become identical. Regardless, Allogenes demonstrates that, even if conceived as an intermediate, the Triple Power is an object of negative theology.

> But concerning the invisible Triple Power, hear! He exists as an Invisible One who is incomprehensible to them all [=the pleroma]. He possesses them all within himself, for they all exist because of him. He is perfect, and he is greater than perfect, and he is blessed. He is always One and he exists in them all, being ineffable, unnameable, being One who exists through them all — he whom should one discern him, one would not desire anything that exists before him among those that possess existence.[43]

We can sum up these remarks by saying that the Gnostics apparently agree with Plotinus in excluding all predication from the supreme God, an *exclusive* negative theology which would seem to follow upon His radical transcendence over the ineffable intermediaries, but disagree with him in extending divine ineffability farther down the scale of realities, especially to the divine Triple Power of Barbeloite Gnosticism.

In spite of this basic difference — that the Gnostics more broadly apply negative theology than the Neoplatonists — the two schools mainly agree in the ways they justify and develop negative theology, at least as applied to the very highest level of reality. Let us now isolate many of these similarities basic to both Gnostic and Neoplatonic negative theology.

To begin, the Gnostics, like Plotinus, indicate that exclusive negative theology — a theology excluding all positive ascriptions of the First Reality — alone is compatible with the transcendent unity of God. This is implied in *The Tripartite Tractate* where the remark that "the Father is a unity, like a number, for he is the first and is that which he alone is"[44] is followed later by a passage stating that He is

> inscrutable greatness . . . incomprehensible depth . . . immeasurable height and illimitable will . . . without . . . things which are understood through perceptions, which the incomprehensible one transcends.   If he is incomprehensible, then it follows that he is unknowable, that he is the one who is inconceivable by any thought, invisible in any thing, ineffable by any word, untouchable by any hand.[45]

That unity belongs on the highest level of reality is expressed in certain Barbeloite tractates as well.   According to *The Three Steles of Seth*, which as we noted above regards the Triple Power as the supreme God, the Triple Power is a pure unity in which the Aeon Barbelo, itself having a tripartite nature divisible into what *Zostrianos* names "Kalyptos," "Protophanes," and "Autogenes," participates.

> Great is the first aeon, male virginal Barbelo, the first glory of the invisible Father, she who is called 'perfect.' Thou hast seen first him who really preexists, that he is non-being. And from him and through him thou has preexisted eternally, non-being from one indivisible, triple power, thou a triple power, thou a great monad from a pure monad, thou an elect monad, the first shadow of the holy Father, light from light.[46]

Finally, *The Apocryphon of John*, a tractate expressing Christian mythological Gnosticism, but which is not without the effects of Barbeloite influence, states that the supreme God is sheer unity, "the Monad . . . a monarchy with nothing above it,"[47] existing "as God and

Father of everything, the invisible one who is above everything, who is imperishability, existing as pure light which no eye can behold."[48] As pure unity He is first reality and indescribable: "he is ineffable because no one could comprehend him to speak about him. He is unnameable because there is no one prior to him to name him."[49]

Not surprisingly, this stress on pure unity leads to another parallel with Neoplatonic negative theology: namely, that the One is not Form. According to *The Tripartite Tractate* form belongs to the intermediaries which utter God. God is revealed through the Son, "the form of the formless."[50] The formlessness of the Gnostic God is particularly evident in the Barbeloite tractates. *Allogenes* implies that both the Triple Power and the Invisible Spirit are formless, given that they transcend the Aeon Barbelo, which like Plotinus's *Nous* constitutes the realm of the true *noēta*. As John Turner has observed,[51] there is a threefold nature to the Aeon Barbelo which makes it comparable to the levels of cognition and intelligibility in the Plotinian *Nous*. Complementing *Allogenes* with other tractates, especially *Zostrianos*, Turner notes that the highest level of Barbelo, the level called "Kalyptos" (*nous noētos*), contains all "those who truly exist," just as Plotinus's second reality contains all *noēta*. Continuing the analogy, Turner notes that the next level of Barbelo, the level of "Protophanes" (*nous nooun*), compares with the Plotinian *Nous* when conceived as the real unity of all Forms (cf. *Enn.* IV, 1 [21], 1). Lastly, the lowest level of Barbelo, "Autogenes" (*nous dianöoumenos*), is similar to the *nous merisas* of Plotinus (cf. *Enn.* III, 9 [13], 1), i.e., *Nous* as the domain of the Forms of individual souls.[52] According to *Allogenes*, then, while the Invisible Spirit and the Triple Power may be the source of Form, they must not be confused with anything having a form or shape that is knowable. When speaking at one point of the Triple Power, *Allogenes* becomes explicit: "he is One who subsists as a sort of being and a source and an immaterial material and an innumerable number and a formless form and a shapeless shape . . . ."[53] Later the tractate supports this same point of view by explaining that mystical ascent to the Triple Power reveals an "undivided motion that pertains to all the formless powers [=Vitality, Mentality, That Which Is], (one which is) unlimited by limitation."[54]

Given these fundamental parallels, it is not surprising to find the Gnostics denying of God, whether the Invisible Spirit or the Triple Power or even a non-Barbeloite conception of highest deity, several other predicates Plotinus denies of Him. First, the Gnostics deny that God is finite. *The Apocryphon of John* is typical in the way it implicitly links divine infinity with ineffability:

But at all times he is completely perfect in light. He is illimitable because there is no one prior to him to limit him. He is unsearchable because there exists no one prior to him to examine him. He is immeasurable because there was no one prior to him to measure him.[55]

This conviction, that God is infinite, appears again and again in the Nag Hammadi tractates, as He is variously described as "infinite light," "unfathomably unfathomable," "immeasurable," "boundless" and as occupying "an airless place of the limitlessness."

Second, God must be without desire or need, since infinity implies independence. Again, according to *The Apocryphon of John*, "he is completely perfect; he did not lack anything that he might be completed by it."[56] For this reason *Allogenes* may declare that "the One . . . is neither concerned for anything nor has any desire;"[57] that "he is not diminished in some way, whether by his own desire or . . . through another. Neither does he have any desire of himself nor from another — it does not affect him."[58]

Third, as the above remarks perhaps imply, the Gnostic Father, like the Neoplatonist One, is undiminished in production. *The Tripartite Tractate* states the matter explicitly: "in order that it may be discovered that he has everything that he has, he gives it away, being unsurpassed and not wearied by that which he gives, but wealthy (precisely) in the gifts which he bestows and at rest in the favors which he grants."[59] At times the Gnostics are even more extreme than Plotinus, refusing to define God even by the negation "undiminished," on grounds that such a term still limits Him. Thus, *Allogenes* cautions that "He does not receive anything from anything else. He is not diminished, nor does he diminish anything, nor is he undiminished."[60]

Fourth, the Gnostic tractates generally imply that God is not eternity. This implication results from the Father's transcendence over the "pleroma," the universe of the aeons or eternal natures. *Allogenes* in particular seems intent on denying eternity of the highest level of reality, stating that the Triple Power is free of time and eternity (*aiōn*): "when he [=the Triple Power] appeared he did not need time or anything from an aeon. Rather of himself he is unfathomably unfathomable."[61] Elsewhere the same tractate states that the Invisible Spirit is neither any perfection nor its opposite, "but like his attributes and non-attributes, he participates in neither aeon nor time. He does not receive anything from anything else."[62]

Fifth, the Gnostics deny that God is life. Of course, *Allogenes* implies this when characterizing the Triple Power, which the Unknown God transcends, as Vitality. The tractate at one point is explicit: "Now he [=the Invisible Spirit] is reified insofar as he exists in that he either exists and becomes, or acts or knows, although he lives without Mind or Life . . . ."[63] And shortly after this remark, *Allogenes* adds, "neither does he give anything by himself lest he become diminished in another way, nor for this reason does he need Mind or Life, or indeed anything at all."[64]

Sixth, the supreme God of Gnosticism is beyond being. This is clear from *Allogenes*, where even the Triple Power, since the source of Being and Barbelo, "the Hidden One of existence," is defined as "a non-substantial substance" and as "non-substantiality and non-being existence."[65] If one transcends the Triple Power, he will approach "the God who truly preexists."[66] This supreme God "is not an existence lest he be in want."[67] Rather, "He has non-being existence."[68]

Finally, we may speculate that the Gnostics place the supreme God and the Triple Power above act (*energeia*) or activity. *Allogenes* seems to suggest this when stating that the Triple Power is "an inactive activity."[69] As for the Invisible Spirit *Allogenes* says that "he does not activate himself so as to become still . . ."[70] and that "nothing activates im in accordance with the Unity that is at rest."[71] Accordingly, the Gnostics often define God as sheer power. But sometimes they even transcend Plotinus in declaring God to be beyond power: "he is limitless and powerless and non-existent."[72]

Faced with these several parallels, one should not be surprised to find the Gnostics charting a mystical ascent much like that presented in the *Enneads*. Like Plotinus the Gnostics characterize mystical union as the consequence of a preparatory stage consisting of knowledge and purgation. Knowledge in the correct sense occurs on the level of the aeons, which roughly approximates the Plotinian level of Soul and *Nous*. Experience of the highest level requires a purgation of all association from being, form and duality, properties of the aeons. The mystic must transcend being so as to know "the non-being Existence." This is a union that is more perfect than the union of *noēsis/noēton*. This union is free of duality. Thus, it is a union about which there can be no description or predication. As with Plotinus, then, the object of the mystic's quest demands a negative theology.

III

Employing the distinctions with which we opened this article, we can briefly summarize our findings. On the one hand, we have found that Plotinus limits negative theology to the highest reality, the One, permitting positive theology of the *Nous* and the Soul. Moreover, Plotinus's negative theology we have called "exclusive," since it follows from the conviction that the One is in principle unknowable and indescribable. On the other hand, we have found that the Gnostics extend negative theology to multiple divine existents, with some Gnostics, such as Basilides, holding that even the archons are altogether unknowable. More commonly, however, the Gnostics limit "exclusive" negative theology to the highest God, permitting some positive theology of the intermediaries, with the possible exception of the Triple Power of the Barbeloite Gnostics, who sometimes is identified with the highest God.

Furthermore, we have found that, except for this Gnostic tendency to extend negative theology farther down the hierarchy of realities, the Gnostics and the Neoplatonists develop negative theology along similar lines. First, both schools accept that the highest God, who is altogether beyond knowledge and predication, is a Monad, pure unity; additionally, that God is beyond Form, since He is indeterminate and free of duality; that He is infinite or boundless; that He is without need or desire; that He is undiminished in production; that He transcends the intelligible world in such a way as to be neither eternity nor life nor intellection nor being (and for Plotinus neither motion nor rest, sameness nor difference); and, finally, that God transcends act but is indeterminate power.

As we have seen these parallels are woven into religious philosophies that aspire after a mystical experience of God, an experience that is not knowledge in the ordinary sense. Both Gnosticism and Neoplatonism develop negative theology as a way of respecting the transcendent goal of moral life, the object of personal salvation. Clearly, in this respect these two schools are compatible with orthodox Christianity; and it is for this reason that they are the chief influences on medieval Christian negative theology.

NOTES

1.   This is the type of theology which Pseudo-Dionysius terms "apophatic," in contrast to "kataphatic" theology, which ascribes predicates to God. See Pseudo-Dionysius's *Mystical Theology*, pp. 2-3, and *The Divine Names*, especially pp. 2, 4-5. Both works appear in Migne, *Patrologia Graeca* (Paris), Vols. 3-4. See also C.E. Rolt's translation of these two works (London: The Macmillan Co., 1966).

2. Pseudo-Dionysius and Aquinas are representatives of a theism which holds that both negative and positive theologies apply to God. See *Summa Theologiae* I, QQ. 12-13. Philo represents the view that God is wholly unknowable. On Philo's negative theology see John Dillon, *Middle Platonists* (Ithaca, N.Y.: 1977), pp. 155-158; and David Winston, *Philo of Alexandria* (New York: 1981), pp. 22-24.

3. As we shall see the Gnostics apply negative theology to existents other than the highest divinity, with most allowing positive theology on lower levels.

4. I will not, of course, altogether neglect other Neoplatonic and Gnostic sources, but I will largely subordinate my remarks on them to the notes.

5. The following intervening treatises contain important passages expressing negative theology: V, 4 (7), 1, 10; 2, 38-40; VI, 9 (9), 11, 42; V, 1 (10), 8, 7-8; III, 9 (13), 9, 8-12; I, 2 (19), 3, 31; I, 3 (20) 5, 7; IV, 4 (28), 16, 27; III, 8 (30), 9, 2; VI, 6 (34), 5, 37; VI, 2 (43), 3, 7-10; 17, 18-22; III, 7 945), 2, 8; V, 3 (49), 10, 5; 11, 2-28; 12, 47-48; 17, 13-14.

6. The following texts state the primacy of unity for Plotinus's metaphysics: VI, 9 (9), 1, 1; V, 5 (32), 5, 11; VI, 6 (34), 1, 1; VI, 2 (43), 11, 17. My discussion here about the primacy of unity in Plotinus is indebted to Leo Sweeney's article, "Basic Principles in Plotinus's Philosophy," *Gregorianum* 42 (1961): 506-516. In this article Sweeney concludes that there are three principles basic to a Neoplatonic metaphysics: (1) that whatever is real is one; (2) that whatever is one is good; and (3) that whatever is prior is of greater reality than that which is subsequent.

7. Neoplatonists generally accept Plotinus's negative theology; however, some differences emerge in his successors. Iamblichus and Damascius later identify the supreme, unknowable reality as a principle standing above Plotinus's One. This higher principle is alone truly ineffable (*pantelos arrhēton*). For a helpful discussion of this feature of later Neoplatonism see John Dillon, *Iamblichi Chalcidensis* (Leiden: E.J. Brill, 1973), especially pp. 29-33.

8. Plotinus notes that these names, "the One" and "the Good," are compatible with negative theology since they do not signify predicates (II, 9 [33], 1, 1-8; VI, 7 [38], 38, 4-9; VI, 9 [9], 5, 29-34). "The One" is implicitly a negative expression, meaning "not multiple" (V, 5 [32], 6, 26-28). "The Good," rather than denoting something about God's essence, actually states only that God is the object of the love of all beings (I, 8 [51], 2, 1-8). The One has no needs and thus is good only for others, not for itself (VI, 7 [38], 24, 13-16; 41, 28-31; VI, 9 [9], 6, 39-42). See Richard Wallis, *Neoplatonism* (New York: Charles Scribner's Sons, 1972), p. 59.

9. See V, 9 (5), 5; IV, 8 (6), 3, 14-16; VI, 5 (23), 7; IV, 4 (28), 2, 3-14; III, 8 (30), 8, 40-45; V, 8 (31), 4, 4-11; VI, 7 (38), 9, 31-38; VI, 2 (43), 20.

10. See V, 4 (7), 2, 4-8; VI, 7 (38), 16, 10-22; 17, 32-34; V, 3 (49), 5, 21-48; 11, 1-16.

11. This argument in essence appears at V, 3 (49), 12-13.

12. See VI, 9 (9), 3-39; V, 5 (32), 6, 4-5; VI, 7 (38), 17, 18, 36-40; 28, 28; 32, 9; 33, 13-21.

13. VI, 9 (9), 3, 4, 39; V, 5 (32), 11, 1-5; VI, 7 (38), 17, 15, 16. The precise nature of the One's infinity has been a subject of some controversy, with most scholars agreeing now that the One is infinite not only in power but also in reality. For a treatment of infinity in Plotinus see Sweeney, "Infinity in Plotinus," *Gregorianum* 38 (1957): 521-535, 713-732. For a contrary view, see W. Norris Clark, "Infinity in Plotinus: A Reply," *Gregorianum* 40 (1959): 75-98. For Sweeney's reply and reassessment, see "Plotinus Revisited," ibid., 40 (1959): 327-331; and "Another Interpretation of *Enneads* VI, 7, 32," *The Modern Schoolman* 38 (1961): 289-303. For a helpful summation of this debate see John Rist, *Plotinus: The Road to Reality* (Cambridge: University Press, 1967), pp. 21-37.

14. ὅταν γὰρ ἄν αὐτὸν νοήσῃς οἷον ἢ νοῦν ἢ θεόν, πλέον ἐστὶ καὶ αὖ ὅταν αὐτὸν ἐνίσῃς/τῇ δάνοᾳ, καὶ ἐνταῦθα πλέον ἐστὶν ἢ ὅσον ἄν αὐτὸν ἐφαντάσθης εἰς τὸ ἑνικώτερον τῆς σῆς νοήσεως εἶναι ἐφ᾽ ἑαυτοῦ γὰρ ἔστιν οὐδενὸς αὐτῷ συμβεβηκότος. τῷ αὐτάρκει δ᾽ ἄν τις καὶ τὸ ἕν αὐτοῦ ἐνθυμηθείη. δεῖ μὲν γὰρ ἱκανώτατον <ον> ἁπάντων καὶ αὐταρκέστατον, καὶ ἀνενδεέστατον εἶναι πᾶν δὲ πολὺ καὶ [μὴ ἕν] ἐνδεὲς μὴ ἕν ἐκ πολλῶν γενόμενον. δεῖται οὖν αὐτοῦ ἡ οὐσία ἕν εἶναι. τὸ δὲ οὐ δεῖται ἑαυτοῦ αὐτὸ γὰρ ἔστι. καὶ μὴν πολλὰ ὄν τοσούτων δεῖται, ὅσα ἔστι, καὶ ἕκαστον τῶν ἐν αὐτῷ μετὰ τῶν ἄλλων ὄν καὶ οὐκ ἐφ᾽ ἑαυτοῦ, ἐνδεὲς τῶν ἄλλων ὑπάρχων, καὶ καθ᾽ ἕν καὶ κατὰ τὸ ὅλον τὸ τοιοῦτον ἐνδεὲς παρέχεται. εἴπερ οὖν δεῖ τι αὐταρκέστατον εἶναι, τὸ ἕν εἶναι δεῖ τοιοῦτον ὄν μόνον, οἷον μήτε πρὸς αὐτὸ μήτε πρὸς ἄλλο ἐνδεὲς εἶναι.

The translation, except for a couple of adjustments, is from Armstrong, *Plotinus* (London: Allen and Unwin, 1953), pp. 60-61. Cf. V, 4 (7), 1, 1-15.

15. This negation the other hypostases share with the One. This common negation, however, does not mean that Plotinus, after all, regards Intelligence and Soul as objects of negative theology. *Nous* and Soul are not ineffable. It just so happens that this particular negation, since it denies a deficiency that should not exist on any higher level of reality, is also compatible with a general positive theology.

16. V, 5 (32), 5, 1-2.

17. Τὸ δὲ ὑπὲρ τὴν ζωὴν αἴτιον ζωῆς. οὐ γὰρ ἡ τῆς ζωῆς ἐνέργεια τὰ πάντα οὖσα πρώτη, ἀλλ᾽ ὥσπερ προχυθεῖσα αὐτὴ οἷον ἐκ πηγῆς. Νόησον γὰρ πηγὴν ἀρχὴν ἄλλην οὐκ ἔχουσαν, δοῦσαν δὲ ποταμοῖς πᾶσαν αὐτήν, οὐκ ἀναλωθεῖσαν τοῖς ποταμοῖς, ἀλλὰ μένουσαν αὐτὴν ἡσύχως.

Translation Armstrong, *Plotinus*, "Loeb Classical Library" (Cambridge, Mass.: Harvard University Press, 1967), Vol. III, p. 395.

18. ἐν μὲν οὖν τοῖς ἀριθμοῖς μένοντος μὲν τοῦ ἕν, ποιοῦντος δὲ ἄλλου, ὁ ἀριθμὸς γίνεται κατ᾽ αὐτὸ ἐν δὲ τῷ ὅ ἐστι πρὸ τῶν ὄντων μένει μὲν πολὺ μᾶλλον ἐνταῦθα τὸ ἕν μένοντος δὲ αὐτοῦ οὐκ ἄλλο ποιεῖ, εἰ κατ᾽ αὐτὸ τὰ ὄντα, ἀλλ᾽ ἀρκεῖ αὐτὸ γενῆσαι τὰ ὄντα.

I wish to thank Dr. John Barrett of the Classics Department of Cardinal Newman College, St. Louis, Missouri, for his advice on translating this brief but difficult Greek passage.

19. See VI, 2 (43), 8; III, 7 (45), 1-12. In Plato see *Sophist*, 248 a-249 d.

20. See especially VI, 7 (38), 17, 9-14; III, 8 (30), 10, 1-5.

21. Plotinus's interpretation of the *megista genē* appears mainly in VI, 2 (43), 7-8. Cf. V, 1 (10), 4, 30-44; VI, 7 (38), 13.

22. Except for the single provocative remark at *Republic* 509 b, where he declares "the Good" to be above being, Plato consistently argues that the highest level of reality belongs to Form and Intelligence.

23. See V, 1 (10), 7, 23-24; II, 6 (17), 1, 8-9; 2, 14; IV, 1 (21), 1; III, 6 (26), 6, 1-3; V, 8 (31), 5, 24-25; V, 5 (32), 6, 2; III, 2 (47), 13, 30-34; V, 3 (49), 5, 35; I, 8 (51), 2, 22.

24. The irony, of course, consists in the fact that Plotinus appeals to the *Republic* to discount the *Sophist*, which maintains that the supreme realities include the highest Forms, the most general principles of Dialectics, and *Nous*.

25. V, 4 (7), 2 42.

26. See VI, 7 (38), 13 and VI, 2 (43), 7-8.

27. VI, 9 (9), 3, 39-49.

γεννητικὴ γὰρ ἡ τοῦ ἑνὸς φύσις οὖσα τῶν πάντων οὐδέν ἐστιν αὐτῶν. οὔτε οὖν τι οὔτε ποιὸν οὔτε ποσὸν οὔτε νοῦν οὔτε ψυχὴν οὐδὲ κινούμενον οὐδ' αὖ ἑστώς, οὐκ ἐν τόπῳ, οὐκ ἐν χρόνῳ, ἀλλ' αὐτὸ καθ' αὑτὸ μονοειδές, μᾶλλον δὲ ἀνείδεον πρὸ εἴδους ὂν παντός, πρὸ κινήσεως, πρὸ στάσεως ταῦτα γὰρ περὶ τὸ ὄν, ἃ πολλὰ αὐτὸ ποιεῖ. διὰ τί οὖν, εἰ μὴ κινούμενον, οὐχ ἑστώς; ὅτι περὶ μὲν τὸ ὂν τούτων θάτερον ἢ ἀμφότερα ἀνάγκη, τό τε ἑστὼς στάσει ἑστὼς καὶ οὐ ταὐτὸν τῇ στάσει ὥστε συμβήσεται αὐτῷ καὶ οὐκέτι ἁπλοῦν μενεῖ.

Again, I follow basically Armstrong's translation, *Plotinus*, pp. 58-59.

28. V, 9 (5), 5; III, 6 (26), 4, 41-44; VI, 7 (38), 13, 28-33; 37, 17; 40, 14-15. In Aristotle see *Metaphysics*, Theta 8, 1050 b 2-3; Eta 3 1043 b 1.

29. This characterization of Plotinus's philosophy as an "henology" (as opposed to an "ontology") occurs in Leo Sweeney, "Basic Principles of Plotinus's Philosophy," p. 510 (see above, n. 6). Also see E. Gilson, *Being and Some Philosophers* (Toronto: Pontifical Institute of Medieval Studies, 1952), pp. 21-22; Cleto Carbonera, *La Philosophia di Plotino* (Napoli: Libreria Scientifica Editrice, 1954), pp. 400-409; E. Bréhier, *Philosophy of Plotinus*, translated by Joseph Thomas (Chicago: University of Chicago Press, 1958), p. 132; Jean Trouillard, *Un et Etre*, in *Les Etudes Philosophiques* 2 (1960): 185-196.

30. III, 8 (30), 10, 1; cf. V, 4 (7), 1, 25.

31. Plotinus is also willing to say that the *Nous* is unlimited (see III, 8 8, 46) but not in the same way as the One. The One is infinite because of His indeterminate nature; and for this reason only *dynamis*, never *energeia* (which implies determination, limit and form), can apply to Him. The *Nous*, however, is determinate, *energeia* and thus cannot be infinite in its very nature. Nonetheless, *Nous* is in one respect unlimited like the One: in that *Nous* is the productive source of potentially innumerable *logoi*.

32. Because *energeia* is *ousia* or *eidos*, Plotinus is willing to accept Aristotle's principle that act is prior to potency for the order of beings. But the principle cannot apply to all reality. *Dynamis* must be first in reality, because the One transcends limitation and duality which *energeia*

presupposes. In fact, it is correct to say that potency is both first and last in the universe, in that both the One and prime matter are purely indeterminate potencies. However, it would be a serious mistake to assume that the One and prime matter are potencies in the same way. The One is potential and indeterminate by virtue of its supreme perfection, whereas prime matter is potential and indeterminate by virtue of its sheer imperfection. Plotinus employs two rather technical expressions — namely, *hē dynamis* vs. *to dynamei on* — so as to distinguish the potency of the One (and of all the hypostases for that matter) from the potency of prime matter. The One is pure potency in the sense of active power, *hē dynamis*. Prime matter, however, is potency in the sense of passive potency, *to dynamei on*. The One is the eternal power to produce Forms; matter is the eternal potency to receive Forms. (These two kinds of potency are carefully separated in II, 5 [25] but appear commonly throughout the *Enneads*. Compare Plotinus's remarks about matter in II, 5, 4-5 with remarks about the One at V, 4 [7], 1, 36; 2, 38; III, 8 [30], 10, 1; 27.)

33.   A more complicated answer might appeal to *extrinsic denomination* to explain away Plotinus's ascriptions to the One. Such an explanation would allow predicates of the One not because they belong to its essence but because they belong to its effects. Accordingly, the One is *noēsis, energeia* and *ousia* because it is the source of such perfections. Additionally, one might attempt to discount these ascriptions because they occur under exceptional conditions. For instance, VI, 8 ascribes *ousia* and *energeia* repeatedly to the One. But, as chapter 13 (lines 1-5) indicates, Plotinus employs these ascriptions for persuasive and pedagogical reasons and does not intend them to be representative of his general position on the One. See below, n. 35.

34.   See VI, 9 (9), 11.

35.   Both these treatises belong to Plotinus's polemical middle period. That II, 9 is aimed at the Gnostics is shown by Porphyry's two titles for the treatise: "Against the Gnostics" and "Against Those Who Declare the Maker of the World and the World to be Evil." VI, 8 appears to be a criticism of the Gnostic position (which Plotinus labels a *tolmeros logos*, ch. 7, line 11) that the One is either being (a determinate nature) or the product of chance. For a helpful discussion of Plotinus's criticism of the Gnostics in VI, 8 see Bréhier's "Notice" in Vol. VI, Part 2 of the Budé edition (Paris, 1938), especially, pp. 119-122. For an alternative interpretation see A.H. Armstrong's forthcoming "Two Views of Freedom: A Christian Objection in VI, 8 (39), 7, 11-15?"

36.   Hippolytus's account of Basilides's negative theology appears in W. Foerster, *Gnosis: A Selection of Gnostic Texts* (Oxford, 1974), Vol. I, pp. 64-74; see also R.M. Grant, *Gnosticism: An Anthology* (London, 1961), pp. 125-134.

37.   *The Tripartite Tractate* I, 56, 25-30. My references to the Nag Hammadi tractates are found in *The Nag Hammadi Library in English*, ed., James M. Robinson (San Francisco: Harper & Row and E.J. Brill, 1977). In my quotations from these writings I have omitted brackets, ellipses and other

grammatical adjustments supplied by translators and editors.

38. *The Trimorphic Protennoia* XIII, 46, 5.
39. Ibid., XIII, 46, 14-15.
40. These comparisons have been noted by John Turner in his article "The Gnostic Threefold Path to Enlightenment," *Novum Testamentum* 22 (1980): 324-351.
41. See V, 1, (10), 4; V, 5 (32), 1; VI, 7 (38), 17-18.
42. There is good reason to think that the schools had some contact with one another since Porphyry in his *Life of Plotinus* 16 refers to the Gnostic revelations of "Allogenes" and "Zostrianos," names which appear as titles in the Nag Hammadi library.
43. *Allogenes* XI, 47, 7-25.
44. *The Tripartite Tractate* I, 51, 8-11.
45. Ibid., I, 54, 20-39.
46. *The Three Steles of Seth* VII, 121, 20-122, 4.
47. *The Apocryphon of John* 2, 26-27.
48. Ibid., II, 2, 28-32.
49. Ibid., II, 3, 14-17.
50. *The Tripartite Tractate* I, 66, 13.
51. John Turner, "The Gnostic Threefold Path to Enlightenment," pp. 328-331, 334-338.
52. Scholars have debated whether there are in fact Forms of individuals in Plotinus. For an affirmative view consult J.M. Rist, "Forms of Individuals in Plotinus," *Classical Quarterly* 13 (1963): 223-231. For a different position see H.J. Blumenthal, "Did Plotinus believe in Ideas of Individuals?," *Phronesis* 11 (1966): 61-80. Blumenthal holds that Plotinus is undecided on the question.
53. *Allogenes* XI, 48, 19-25.
54. Ibid., XI, 60, 25-28.
55. *The Apocryphon of John* II, 3, 6-13.
56. Ibid., II, 3, 4-6.
57. *Allogenes* XI, 64, 25-27.
58. Ibid., XI, 62, 6-13.
59. *The Tripartite Tractate* 53, 13-20.
60. *Allogenes* XI, 63, 24-27.
61. Ibid., XI, 65, 20-21.
62. Ibid., XI, 63, 20-23.
63. Ibid., XI, 61, 32-37.
64. Ibid., XI, 62, 14-20.
65. Ibid., XI, 55, 29-30.
66. Ibid., XI, 56, 20.
67. Ibid., XI, 28-30.
68. Ibid., XI, 65, 32-33.
69. Ibid., XI, 48, 28-29.
70. Ibid., XI, 65, 26-28.
71. Ibid., XI, 66, 21-23.

72.   Ibid., XI, 66, 26-27.

The Platonism of the *Tripartite Tractate* (NH I, 5)

John Peter Kenney

No less an authority than A.D. Nock once remarked[1] that Gnosticism might be viewed as "Platonism run wild," and some observers of at least the Valentinian Pleroma may still be inclined to agree. In this brief paper I should like to continue this line of analysis and to consider the metaphysical structure of the *Tripartite Tractate* from the standpoint of Second and early Third Century Platonism. My focus will be upon the document's ontology, in particular the degrees of reality and divinity outlined therein, with the details of its cosmological myth treated only in relation to this principal concern. I should note that as a student of philosophical theology I am an unqualified amateur in this now very specialized field, so that this paper represents only a tentative inquiry on my part, ventured because of the importance of extending our understanding of the relationship between Late Antique philosophy and Gnosticism.

A few qualifications seem necessary before proceeding. By considering the *Tripartite Tractate* in this fashion, I do not mean to suggest that my purpose is discovering any neat and exact connection between this treatise and some particular Middle Platonist (or Neopythagorean). It seems to me that this is beyond the persuasive force of our current evidence, at least as I can interpret it. Furthermore, it is not my intention here to maintain that this theology belongs fundamentally to the Platonic tradition, and hence to the Hellenic trajectory in Ancient religious thought.[2] Instead it would be more accurate to see the *Tripartite Tractate* as representing a version of

Valentinian theology[3] which has undergone important alterations that in part involved the recasting of this theology into a more philosophical form. In cannot myself assess in any detail the resultant modifications within Valentinianism itself, or comment on the reason for this philosophical restatement, although Professor Perkins's suggestion that it involved an appeal by Gnostics to pagan Hellenes seems quite plausible.[4] In any case it seems clear that the document is concerned to develop its ontology in philosophical terms, and it is this system which I should like now to examine. I shall begin with an investigation of the initial part of the document (51:1-104:5), concentrating upon: (1) the nature of the Father, (2) the constitution of the Aeons, (3) the Logos. I shall conclude with a philosophical assessment, using Middle Platonism as a foundation for analysis.

1. The nature and status of the highest level of reality are articulated by the *Tripartite Tractate* in terms which are fairly abstract and which indicate an intention to locate this entity philosophically. While there is some suggestion of an ontological characterization of the Father, e.g., in the essentialism of 51:10 ff. ("he . . . is that which he alone is")[5] or 52:10 ff. ("he is also invariable in his eternal existence, in his identity, in that by which he is established, and in that by which he is great"), the burden of the portrayal is carried by cosmological concepts. As might be expected, these include his pre-existence (51:5 ff.; 10), and his unbegotten nature (51:25 ff.; 52:5 ff.; 52:35 ff.), the latter being taken as compatible with the assertion of his own self-generation (56:1-15).[6] The primary status of the Father is also secured by appeal to his unique perfection and his unique inclusiveness (52:5 ff.; 53:40-54:5).

One indication that the author of the *Tripartite Tractate* is concerned to delineate the Father in precise cosmological terms is the summary presented at 53:20-40:

> He is of such kind and such form and such great magnitude
> that no one else has been with him from the beginning;
> nor is there a place in which he is, or from which he has come forth, or into which he will go;
> nor is there a primordial form which he uses as model in his work;
> nor is there any difficulty which accompanies him in what he does;
> nor is there any material set out for him, from which he creates what he creates;
> nor any substance within him from which he begets what he begets;
> nor a co-worker who, along with him, does what he does.

This passage seems to reflect in part a break with the dyadic tradition of first principles, proximately to be found in some extant versions of Valentinianism,[7] and more remotely in a variety of Platonic and Pythagorean systems.[8] In addition there can be seen here a critique of the constitutive features of Middle Platonic theology which had their foundations in the *Timaeus* cosmology: the cosmic paradigm and a pre-existent, recalcitrant substrate.[9] The specific presentation of this latter point may perhaps suggest some acquaintance with those ancient scholastic formulations of cosmological principles which Theiler aptly termed the "metaphysics of prepositions."[10] In any case, the principal theme underscored throughout is the status of the Father as a single, unique first principle.

The most striking feature of the *Tripartite Tractate*'s strict monotheism is its rigorous negative theology, and its reflective account of the inevitable qualification of such thought by the use of at least some divine predications. No names (and one assumes also predicates) can apply to the Father, however honorific, since his existence, being, and form exceed limitation and specification (54-55). The use of such names is, however, possible in a non-referential way, to give the Father glory and honor, in accordance with the spiritual capacity of the user (54:5-15). This position indicates a clear disposition in this theology both to proscribe direct claims to discursive knowledge of the Father and to permit some protreptical terminology in the interest of proper spiritual orientation. Two points should be noted about this apophatic theme in the document. In addition to clarifying the residual terminology which continues to be used in relation to the Father, there is also an effort to forestall any suggestion that impossibility of description entails deficiency. It is by virtue of his perfection and greatness that the Father surpasses description (54-56); the *via negativa* is thereby linked to the *via eminentiae*. There is, furthermore, a prominent assertion within this discussion of negative theology of the unique self-knowledge of the Father, as can be seen clearly at 54:40-55:15:

> He alone is the one who knows himself as he is, along with his form and his greatness and his magnitude, and who has the ability to conceive of himself, to see himself, to name himself, to comprehend himself, since he alone is the one who is his own mind, his own eye, his own mouth, his own form, and the one who conceives of himself, who sees himself, who speaks of himself, who comprehends himself, namely, the inconceivable, ineffable, the incomprehensible, unchanging one.

Both the status of the Father as a unique first principle and his sharp separation from all other realities is effected by the conjunction of these themes. It is important to note that as a result the *Tripartite Tractate* is assuming that the primordial deity is a *nous* of a specialized sort, one which is engaged in self-contemplation, and is thus deserving of his preeminence in the divine hierarchy.[11]

The theology of Father in the *Tripartite Tractate* might be said therefore to be philosophically interesting primarily for its thoroughgoing monotheism, to the exclusion of the standard catalogue of common cosmological principles, for its extreme, though reflective, apophatic theology, and finally for its acceptance of a qualified version of *nous* theology. Given such a construal of the Father, this system's next problem is addressing the question of the motive and method of that deity's production, and the related issue of the access which lower entities have to him. It is in this regard that the overall cosmology of the *Tripartite Tractate* becomes especially intriguing, since the document does not construe the Father's production as clearly a devolution. The prominence of what might be called "apophaticism," the necessary epistemic distance of lower entities from the Father, helps to exhibit the deeper necessity of ontological separation between the Father and all else. The production of secondary and tertiary powers appears, therefore, less as a failure than as the result of a metaphysical law. This theme is conjoined with a version of the principle of plenitude,[12] that the perfection of the Father entails his production of necessarily distinct consequent beings.

The notion of plenitude is clearly to be seen in the description of the generation of the Son, the first and most special of the Aeons. Production is treated both as the result of the Father's fecundity and as a means of self-revelation (55:25-35):

> If this one, who is unknowable in his nature, to whom pertain all the greatnesses which I already mentioned, if in the abundance of his sweetness he wishes to grant knowledge so that he might be known, he has the ability to do so.

While the Father is formally ineffable, nevertheless his production is his revelation of himself to the extent to which this is possible. A further reflexive character is assigned to this process of self-projection by the Father, as the following lines from 56:30-57:5 indicate:

> Thus, the Father exists forever . . . in an unbegotten way, the one who knows himself, who begot himself, who has a thought, which is the thought

of himself, that is, the perception of himself, which is the [foundation] of his constitution forever.

The Father, "the one who projects himself in this manner of generation" (56:15-20), knows himself through production, and this is the Aeonic constitution. As the whole of 56-57 makes clear, the Father's perfect, self-begotten, self-thinking nature is the foundation of his projective act; hence the derivative products are the expressions of the nature of the primordial deity and the process itself is a positive act of divine expression.

As the texts already cited indicate, this is an eternal generation, which the thesis of reflexive and connatural self-projection tends to support. It is also not construed primarily in volitional terms; whenever the divine will is introduced, it is not central and is frequently interpreted as another expression for divine productive power.[13] What is crucial to the process is the self-reflective, noetic character of the Father: this is the basis for production and the key to any evaluation of his products (56:5-10).

2. Beneath the Father is found the Pleroma of Aeons; it is in the development of this level of reality that some of the most interesting features of the *Tripartite Tractate* are to be found. Consistent with the description of the Father, the Aeonic constitution is generally viewed as a natural result of his primordial fecundity, and hence as a positive and indeed necessary cosmological fact. A number of themes are introduced in order to maintain this conception of production, and to explain how this generation of distinct, individual existence outside the Father is not a fundamentally negative process.

The *Tripartite Tractate* considers the Son as the first and most important of the Father's offspring. Although uniquely related to the Father, the Son seems nonetheless to belong to the pleromic level. As has been noted, the idea of the Father's generation of a Son for the purpose of self-knowledge inevitably links the two very intimately, although the image also requires that there be a sense of projective separation. We find then that the Son is described with language such as "the ineffable one in the ineffable one" (56, 25 ff.), and his function in relation to the other Aeons set out at length, although the details are difficult to specify exactly. It is clear that his distinctness from the Father is tied to his self-contemplative activity:

He wonders at himself [along with the] Father and he gives [him(self)] glory and honor and [love]. Furthermore, he too is the one who conceives of himself as Son, in accordance with the conditions "without beginning" and "without end."

There is also a sketchy depiction of the Church as an aeonic power along lines similar to the Son; this is, as Professor Stead has remarked, a somewhat intrusive feature,[14] one which is not especially relevant to our particular line of analysis.

The production of the remaining Aeons in the Pleroma is viewed most interestingly as a process which results from the Father through or along with the Son, with the latter as the proximate *telos* for the self-contemplative generation of each Aeon.   Once again production of lower level entities is treated as a form of self-generation based upon the exercise of a capacity for self-conception; in this case this theme is applied to an innumerable realm of Aeonic powers:

> The matter [of the Son] exists just as something which is fixed.   His offspring, the things which exist, being innumerable, illimitable, and inseparable, have, like kisses, come forth from the Son and the Father . . . (58:15-25)

> These [comprise the] constitution which [they form] with one another and [with those] who have come forth from them toward the Son, for whose glory they exist.   Therefore it is not possible for mind to conceive them. They were the perfection of that place, and no word designates them, for they are ineffable and unnameable and inconceivable. They alone have the ability to name themselves in order to conceive of themselves.   For they have not been planted in these places.

Separate existence within the Pleroma is, therefore, a function of self-conception, of self-naming, of self-constitution; it is not the result of the superimposition of properties by a demiurgic first principle.

It is to a version of the Divine Thoughts doctrine that the *Tripartite Tractate* appeals in order to elucidate this model of contemplative production further.   The Aeons are treated as having a pre-existent phase within the Father's mind as his thoughts:

> [. . .] all of the aeons were forever in the thought of the Father, who was like a thinking of them and a place [for them]. (60:1-10)

This doctrine helps to establish, as it were, a chain of contemplative levels, with the Father's self-contemplation being primary, something which seems to involve primordial Divine Thoughts, which are the

Aeons in their initial phase.   The next stage in this contemplative descent is the separate self-contemplation of each Aeon, and this explains the nature of individual existence.   According to the *Tripartite Tractate*, separate Aeons are distinct contemplative powers which are the manifestation or unfolding of the Father's inner mental life.   This ties the pleromic level closely to Father, and reinforces the evaluative significance of individual existence.   All this can be discerned at 60-62:

> At the time that they were in the Father's thought, that is in the hidden depth, the depth knew them, but they were unable to know the depth in which they were; nor could they know themselves; nor could they know anything else. In other words, they were with the Father; they did not exist by themselves. Rather, they only had existence in the manner of a seed. (60:15-25)

> Therefore the Father who first thought of them — not only so that they might exist for him, but also that they might exist for themselves as well, that they might then exist in [his] thought with the mode of existence proper to thought, and that they might exist for themselves too — he sowed a thought like a seed of [knowledge], so that [they] might know [what it is that has come into being] for them. He graciously [granted the] initial form that they might [think about] who is the Father who exists [. . .]. (61:1-15)

I have cited this material at some length in order to indicate that these explanations of divine production in terms of divine contemplative activity and of Aeonic existence in terms of self-contemplation are central and sustained themes in this treatise. The value of such separate Aeonic existence is also clearly vindicated in this way, both as a productive expression of the Father, and as having a fundamentally self-reflexive character, related to the Father's own self-knowing at the level of finite existence. It is evident that a primary function of the Aeons is to contemplate the Father to the extent that this is possible: "they had the sole task of searching for him, realizing that he exists, ever wishing to find out what it is that exists" (61:20-30).[15]   Despite the "apophaticism" of this theology, the Aeons are viewed as powers of the Father, produced in the way they are in order that the Father might be fully expressed in the form of finite beings, who become his extensions through their own contemplative activity:

> Each of the aeons is a name, each of which is a virtue and power of the Father. (73:5-15)

> . . . their begetting is like a process of extension, as the Father extends himself to those whom he desires, so that those who come forth from him might become him as well. (73:20-30).

We have here a theological model which considers Aeons as having two distinct phases: an immanent stage within the thought of the primordial deity and a manifest phase of distinct existence, in which each Aeon is a separate contemplate power. As such an Aeon is an expression or name of the Father, although the fundamental ineffability of the Father precludes any true analogy. In the same way the Son seems to have immanent and manifest aspects, since he is treated as being the Father in so far as he can be known and can be said to have distinct existence. He is called "the form of the formless" and is the unity of the divine names, i.e., the Aeons (66:5-10). It is the Son who represents the Father at the level of knowledge, "whose identity is known," who clothes himself with the divine names, who "first exists" (65:25-35).

The relationship of Son to the Aeons appears to have a whole-part character, although the exact nature of this conjunction is not entirely clear. Nonetheless the Aeons are clearly intended to have a collective existence as a unity, and this unity in diversity is capable of varying aspectual appraisals depending upon one's focus. It is, I think, especially important to notice that the *Tripartite Tractate* represents the relation of Father to Son, and of both to the Aeons, in a way which suggests that integral connections are involved throughout, making any significant separation impossible. Out of the Father's thought there emerge the separate Aeons, but even so they have a collective unity, forming a "pleromatic congregation which is a single image although many" (68:30-35). This single unity seems often to be identified with the Son, but never to the exclusion of the Father, and it is clear that the omnipresence of the Father is meant to be underscored through the collective unity of the Aeons. These themes emerge succinctly at 66:30-67:20:

> All of these are in the single one. . . . And in this unique way they are equally a single individual and the Totalities. He is neither divided as a body, nor is split up into the names which he has. . . . He is now this, now something else, with each item being different. Yet he is entirely and completely himself. [He] is each and every one of the Totalities forever at the same time. He is what all of them are. He, as the Father of the Totalities, also is the Totalities, for he is the one who is knowledge for himself and he is each one of the qualities. He has the powers and he is

beyond all that which he knows, while seeing himself completely and having a Son and a form.

In their latent stage the Aeons are intradeical divine thoughts, and are unified by their presence within the scope of his self-knowledge ("He knows them — which things he himself is . . .," 67:25-30). In their manifestation as his individual powers this unity is preserved (" . . . he brings them forth, in order that it might be discovered that they exist according to their individual properties in a unified way" (67:30-35), so that the Aeonic constitution is an approximation of the Father's perfection, rather than a radical devolution (70:35).

Further production of lower levels of reality by the Aeons is also treated as being the result of their collective interaction (67:20-30), and this corporate process, which is eternal, is not envied by the Father, since it is his own act of self-revelation (70:20-40). It would seem, therefore, that the Aeonic realm is a societal representation of the Father, which contemplates him to the extent possible and is both unified and capable of further production. This "upward" contemplation by the Aeons is explicitly seen as the foundation of their collective as well as their separate existence, and the notion of an innate longing for knowledge of the Father is introduced as a constituative aspect of their nature (71:5-15):

> The entire system of the aeons has a love and a longing for the perfect, complete discovery of the Father, and this is their unimpeded union.

This recursive contemplation is the basis for each Aeonic mind's[16] activity of production, thereby continuing the chain of ontological revelation of primordial divine perfection.

3.   The Logos theology of the *Tripartite Tractate* is complex, standing in a long tradition of such speculation and developing it in ways which are beyond my scope in this paper. It is, however, important that we consider the notion of the Logos in at least a limited way, so that our sketch of the *Tripartite Tractate*'s theology may be complete in its outline. Now, it should not be thought that the Logos has merely been substituted for Sophia in this version of the Valentinian myth, perhaps to give the story a more philosophic air. It seems instead that the Logos theology is very much a natural part of the metaphysics of this document,[17] providing an account of the further manifestation of the Father at the sub-pleromic level of reality. The myth of an errant Aeon is absorbed into this philosophical model; as a result the Sophia myth is altered in its implications. While this mutation of the Sophia

myth cannot be examined in any detail, it is possible to link up the Logos doctrine with the philosophical theology we have examined thus far and examine how it functions in that context.

All Aeons have a desire for contemplative recursion, and as we have seen, this allows both for their integration within the Pleroma and for their capacity for further production. It is therefore an established metaphysical doctrine within the *Tripartite Tractate* that Aeons are engaged in generation of lower powers based upon their knowledge of the Father, admittedly a qualified and paradoxical sort of knowledge, given the major apophatic thesis. In any case the desire of the last Aeon, the Logos, to know the Father is not wholly inappropriate, nor is his generation of lower beings an anomalous act. It is the type, manner, and intent of such activities which are problematical. The principal mistake of the Logos was his attempt to grasp the incomprehensible Father (75:20-25) by an act of his own will (75:35). Despite this act of immoderation in his desire to know the Father, the *Tripartite Tractate* does not dwell upon this failure. In fact, the Logos's purpose is treated as something good ("The intent of the Logos was something good" (76:1-5), and beyond criticism. Although the Logos is said to have been forgetful of the nature of things and ignorant of himself and "of that which is" (77:20-25), his action is also construed as a pre-destined event (77:5-15):[18]

> . . . it is not fitting to criticize the movement which is the Logos, but it is fitting that we should say about the movement of the Logos, that it is a cause of a system, which has been destined to come about.

The myth of the mistake of the Logos has been mitigated by this notion of predestination, with this core Valentinian theme hemmed in, as it were, by the claim that even this errant act of causation fits into the broader pattern of the Father's self-revelation.

The action of the Logos is responsible for the production of a class of beings which are ambiguous in nature. They are the products of an Aeonic power and seem to be viewed as reflections of the natures of the various Aeons, while at the same time lacking a proper self-contemplative character and a recognition of their origin. Hence they amount to a break in the chain of production until they are restored to their proper place. Lack of proper self-recognition is repeatedly stressed:

> They thought of themselves, that they are beings existing by themselves and are without a source, since they do not see anything else existing before them. (79:10-20)

> The things which had come into being unaware of themselves both did not know the Pleroma from which they came forth, and did not now the one who was the cause of their existence. (80:20-35).

Even though the offspring of the Logos are misguided and thus severed from proper line of generation, they remain as the "likenesses of the things which are exalted" (79:25-30), and so of some minimal worth. Each lower being takes its nature from an Aeon, of which it is a "name," or shadow, or likeness. On this basis each being can be said to have beauty, although they are themselves ignorant of this nature and its source. The *Tripartite Tractate* is, therefore, attempting to assert the continued significance even of these miscreant products of the Logos, based upon the idea of the resemblance of lower beings to higher ones. The following excerpt indicates this conjunction of themes:

> Like the Pleromas are things which came into being from the arrogant thought, which are their [the Pleroma's] likenesses, models, shadows, and phantasms, lacking reason and the light. . . . The ones, however, who by themselves are great [the Pleromas], are more powerful and beautiful than the names which are given to them, which are [their] shadows. In the manner of a likeness are they [the names] beautiful. For the [face] of the image normally takes its beauty from that of which it is an image. (78:25-79:15).

It is this very concept of resemblance which is used to explain the motivation for massive confusion and conflict which ensues among these lower beings. In their ignorance they base their desire to subordinate one another upon the worth of their individual natures, which they have as images of the Aeons. "They were brought to a lust for power over one another according to the glory of the name of which each is a shadow, . . ." (79:25-35). While the Logos has set awry the revelation of the Father, nonetheless there is still some residual connection between this lower, conflicted plane and the Pleroma, conferring a limited value on these lost divarications of the Aeonic world.

With the restoration of order by the Son, we find this theory of resemblance used again to explain the relationship between the Aeonic and lower worlds, and to clarify the proper status both of the Logos and his products. In this case the reformed Logos is illumined and takes up an active role in governing the world below the Pleroma:

> . . . the Logos received the vision of all things, those which preexist and those which are now and those which will be, since he has been entrusted with the administration of all that which exists. (95:15-20)

Functioning now as "a basic principle and cause and ruler of things which come to be" (95:15-25), the Logos creates images, using the Pleroma as a paradigm. Appeal is thereby made to the notion of a Demiurge figure,[19] and to the logic of paradigmatism ("of every goodness which exists in the Pleroma: . . . the Logos established each one in his order, both the images and the representations and the likenesses, . . ." (98:20-25). Underscored is the fact that this relation of resemblance between levels is now recognized by the lower beings, which share in the nature and beauty of Aeons:

> Things which belong to the thought which is transcendent are humble, they preserve the representations of the pleromatic, especially because of the sharing in the names by which they are beautiful.

There remains one final point which bears consideration and that is the form of production which prevails with the Logos and his consequents. In describing the method of generation employed by the Logos, the language becomes more that of agency than of contemplative emanation. We find notions such as "administration" (95:20) or "establishment" (98:20) being used. This is extended by the introduction of a ruling Archon which the Logos produces, and "uses" (100:30) to structure lower level entities. Demiurgic imagery comes to the fore here: the Logos employs this instrument, which is a representation of the Father, to order and beautify. Similar language of direct production is then applied to this Archon (101ff.). This suggests that the mode of production within the Pleroma is non-demiurgic and based upon contemplation, while below the Logos (the last Aeon) this changes to a more direct form of active agency.

This cursory review of some aspects of the Logos theology in the *Tripartite Tractate* is intended only as an indication that notion of the Logos itself is not disjoint from the metaphysical structure of this system. It is clearly integral to that metaphysics, although I must admit both that the burden of the Sophia myth does strain the structure of the thought and that many of the details of these grave cosmogonic events are lost on this reader. I would, however, maintain that a basic philosophic model can be discerned within this document, one which coherently includes the concept of the Logos. On this foundation, the *Tripartite Tractate* has revised the Sophia myth, making this tale of tragic declension over into a pre-destined instance of a broader pattern of contemplative production of levels of being. As such the evaluative force of the theology shifts, and the depreciation of lower worlds outside the Pleroma is significantly qualified, especially in view of the pervasive importance of its theology of resemblance and divine names.

4. Our knowledge both of Platonism and Gnosticism in the Second and Third centuries has certainly improved in the last few decades, but I do not think it possible at present to determine with precision the lines of influence, or to build a very full picture of the context of theological debate. We know enough, however, to get a grasp on the key points of this discussion and to be appraised of the salient elements of systematic development in a work such as the *Tripartite Tractate*. It is in this light that I should like now to review this theological system, setting it against contemporary forms of Platonic theology. In doing so, I must admit to having a rough general hypothesis about the document for which I cannot argue: that it reflects an effort by Valentinians to produce a more "philosophical" version of their tradition. While we do not have a genuine philosophical theology here, if one means by that a rational theology articulated in terms of discursive argumentation, we do at least have a theological structure which seems to make an effort to describe certain of its features in terms of current philosophical views. I suspect that this process was the result of interscholastic discussion among Valentinians, proto-orthodox Christian philosophers, and various sorts of Hellenic Platonists (or Neopythagoreans), and that this theology bears the stamp of that debate. Professor Perkins has suggested[20] a Second century Alexandrian locus; my guess would be late Second or early Third century, with either Alexandria or Rome being plausible.[21] My reasons for this particular estimate will emerge presently.

If one assays the formal structure of the *Tripartite Tractate*'s ontology, the basic model which emerges is one which fits into the pattern of late Middle Platonic speculation. In order to locate it philosophically, it is important to consider some features which have emerged from our analysis. In its general character, it is a type of *nous* theology with a first principle which exercises an intellective capacity. As we have seen this first mind is self-directed; its mode of production of a Son or of the Aeons as a group is intellective. Despite its strong apophatic character, this system has not thought through the implications of such a position in relation to a primordial Divine Mind, as we find in Plotinus. It is also important to notice the location of the Aeons as divine thoughts within the Father's mind before their emergence as separate beings in the Pleroma. Both of these positions indicate that the philosophical theology underlying the *Tripartite Tractate* reflects that of Middle Platonists such as Numenius or Albinus. To refine this judgment further, we need to consider the divergence of the major Middle Platonists on the question of the Divine mind, its thoughts, and their use in production.

Early Middle Platonists such as Philo Judaeus or Plutarch considered the Platonic Forms to be intradeical thoughts[22] and the upshot of this position was the treatment of the Divine Mind as a demiurgic power, exercising a direct form of causality in cosmic generation. The Forms became internal paradigms of sorts which were used by the Divine Mind in constructing the lower world. Now it seems that the *Tripartite Tractate* is not following this type of philosophical theology, since the divine thoughts doctrine is not used to articulate this sort of intradeical paradigmatism at the level of the Father. In addition, the Father is not construed according to a demiurgic model: he does not fashion his products directly.

We can also exclude another major type of Middle Platonic theology, that of Atticus and the Athenian school. This version of Middle Platonism made an effort at separating the Divine Intellect from the Forms along the lines of the *Timaeus* theology, although some of the language of the divine thoughts doctrine was employed.[23] It is this position which was debated in the Plotinian school according to Porphyry,[24] further evidence of which may be found in *Ennead* V.5. According to this theology, the Divine Intellect is the first principle, while the Forms exist at a separate but lower level.[25] Forms are thus extradeical, in the sense that they are outside the supreme deity and distinct from it; indeed Porphyry criticized Atticus for this very sense of pronounced separation.[26] This is not the type of theology which our document endorses.

The theology of the *Tripartite Tractate* is closest in its philosophical design to the sort of Middle Platonism represented by Albinus (Alkinoos) or Numenius.[27] This type of Platonism viewed the Ideas as thoughts within a primordial *nous*, but it revised the method of production, denying in particular the notion of direct demiurgic activity of the first god. The demiurgic function is shunted to lower divine powers, requiring a new explanation for the first principle's causation. The divine hierarchy in Numenius includes: (1) a first god who is a stable, unified, and self-directed mind,[28] (2) a second god, initially unified, which exercises a demiurgic function[29] and (3) a third god, equivalent to the rational world soul. The demiurge has been demoted here to at least a secondary position, with the first god being self-contemplative. The second looks to the first god in order to work upon matter, so that a contemplative relationship between divine minds is thereby established as central to production. There is also little doubt that Numenian theology located the intelligible powers at the level of the intellective first god; the evidence from Proclus indicates that Numenius treated the "Living Creature" of the *Timaeus* as being at this level,[30] hence the entire intelligible world seems to be within the primary deity's mind. While Numenius does use demiurgic language of the first god, the production of the second divinity is considered primarily to be the result of its self-production through contemplation;[31] this explains the generation of the active second god from the self-directed first. The second god makes his own formal nature[32] through his contemplation and imitation of the first. Finally, it should be mentioned, with respect to this connection between divine levels, that Numenius appears to have held that the first divine principle makes use of the second in relation to his own contemplation, such that his own nature connects him with the next level of divinity.[33] This obscure logic of *proschrēsis* is applied to all levels, so that each level's contemplative activity would seem to entail the characteristic function of the next. The implication of this concept is a theology in which each level of divinity is bound up with the next. The highest god is self-contemplative and the primordial locus of the Ideas, and yet it also expresses its contemplation at the level of the active *nous*. The second mind is distinct from the first by virtue of its contemplative self-generation, yet it imitates the first, and exercises a demiurgic function towards the third god, the world soul.

A similar theology can be found in Albinus, whose theological hierarchy included a non-demiurgic first mind, a demiurgic or active mind, and it seems, a passive mind which is the world soul.[34] Once again the first god's self-contemplation entails the thinking of the Ideas.[35] Because of the pronounced characterization of the first god as a final cause, the vectorial quality of Albinus's theology tends to emphasize the ordering of lower principles by higher ones.[36] This is particularly interesting because Albinus treats the world soul as a pre-existent principle which is awakened and reordered by its contemplation of the Forms within the primary *nous*, and having received these Forms, it orders the lower world on this basis.

While I do not think we can be certain, I suspect that it is this general type of Middle Platonism which lies at the foundation of the

Tripartite Tractate, providing a tacit architectonic for its sometimes bewildering complexity, and informing its efforts to revise the Sophia myth.   In particular I would argue that the treatment of Aeons as intradeical thoughts of the Father, the emphasis upon non-demiurgic forms of production, the consequent resort to a model of contemplative self-generation at the Aeonic level (in this case that of the restored Logos and its subordinate ruling Archon), and the restoration of the Logos through contemplation of the Pleroma, are all indicative of the late Middle Platonic theology of the Numenius-Albinus sort.   In addition, one central means of differentiation of levels outside the Pleroma is the shift to a demiurgic mode of production, as is the case for entities outside the intelligible world in the type of Middle Platonism in question. Because of the state of our present evidence, I cannot claim anything more than this suspicion, nor can I be more specific than I have been about particular versions of Middle Platonism. Even if we cannot be as precise as we would like, we are nevertheless in a position to recognize the basic philosophical background against which the more abstract Valentinianism of the *Tripartite Tractate* developed.

Given this general philosophical locus, the *Tripartite Tractate*'s theology emerges as a form of *nous* theology which differentiates its self-contemplative first principle from all consequents by a reliance upon apophatic theology. It is certainly distinct from Middle Platonism in its strong assertion of monotheism and its consequent denial of the elements of the *Timaeus* model of production. It is, however, a theology which places divine fecundity and plenitude at the center of its understanding of divinity, and so it develops its account of non-demiurgic production based upon the notion of the projection of the Father's intellection at the Aeonic level. Aeons are the result of the Father's self-expression: they proceed by contemplative self-generation through reference back to the Father, out of whose thought they emerge. We should note again the fundamental logic of resemblance, the reliance upon complex lines of contemplative dependence between levels of reality, and the presence of the Father which results from his use of lower levels as his contemplative extensions. All these themes, which are central to the *Tripartite Tractate*, are resonant of late Middle Platonism, and establish the formal, philosophical structure of this Gnostic system of theology.

I should like in closing to append a brief speculative coda to what is probably an already too venturesome essay. It is tempting to consider the *Tripartite Tractate* in the light of Plotinus's attack on Gnosticism in the "Gross-Schrift": III.8[30], V.8[31], V.5[32], II.9[33]; while I cannot do so properly, a few cursory points might still be apposite. One of the chief themes of this entire work is non-demiurgic, contemplative production, and its differing forms at many levels of reality. III.8 and V.8 are concerned to articulate the continuous contemplative progression, with each level being an imitation of its prior, while V.5 argues for, among other things, a proper recognition of the integral relationship of the intelligibles as distinct living powers at the level of *nous*, and therefore "within" the Intellect in this special sense. The anti-Gnostic arguments of II.9 rest upon an understanding of these Plotinian positions.[37]

It is interesting to note how the *Tripartite Tractate* integrates many of these same themes, not always in the same way in which Plotinus would have developed them, and certainly not at the same philosophical level of articulation. Nevertheless some of the positions singled out for attack in II.9 have been modified in the *Tripartite Tractate*, especially the radical theory of the declension of Sophia and the pronounced separation of lower levels from the Pleroma.[38] The modifications involved often reflect the type of positions which Plotinus develops elsewhere in this major work, e.g., contemplative generation and continuity between levels, or non-demiurgic causality at the intelligible (i.e., pleromic) level. At the very least, the *Tripartite Tractate* seems to be a system of theology not highly vulnerable to some of these Plotinian metaphysical criticisms.

It would be too much to claim that the *Tripartite Tractate* was the product of Plotinus's Gnostic associates, or that it was a systematic answer to his criticisms. The case would be at best circumstantial, and there are philosophical points which remain unanswered. Chief among these is the initial attack, in II.9.1, against any *nous* theology with multiple intellects, and any theology lacking the three Plotinian hypostasis. While the proximate target for Plotinus is usually viewed as being Numenius,[39] a system such as the *Tripartite Tractate*, with a Father-Intellect which brings forth a Son-Intellect as the product of its thought, may also have been the actual Gnostic target for Plotinus. Without significant changes in its theology of the Divine Intellect, the *Tripartite Tractate* would remain vulnerable to this Neoplatonic assault. I would suggest, then, that the *Tripartite Tractate* is likely to have been the result of general scholastic discussions among philosophical theologians from various camps, which continued through the late Second and early Third centuries at Alexandria and perhaps Rome, and which Plotinus drew upon in his anti-Gnostic critique. While the philosophical form of Plotinus's arguments is certainly his own, there is no reason to assume that he was original in his conceptual criticisms of the Sophia myth, the method of demiurgic production, etc. The

Tripartite Tractate probably emerged from this interscholastic discussion, resulting in the philosophical character I have been analyzing; Plotinus is likely to have drawn from this same tradition of debate. This would have been standard for the rather agonistic world of ancient philosophy,[40] and there seems no reason to assume an exception. Although it does not answer some specifically Neoplatonic arguments, the *Tripartite Tractate* does seem to have generated a Valentinian system with a philosophical character which would have made it resilient to many Platonic criticisms.

I would conclude then with the judgment that the *Tripartite Tractate* represents a philosophically informed Gnosticism, and is part of what has been called the "Platonic Underworld,"[41] the diffusion of Platonic metaphysics into the religious thought of Late Antiquity. A cursory reading of its admittedly rather rococo ontology might suggest to an austere student of philosophical theology that there has been a riot in Plato's cave. These sentiments notwithstanding, I hope to have indicated that the metaphysical foundations of this system are quite intelligible in terms of later Middle Platonism, and that the theology of the *Tripartite Tractate* was not the product of persons wholly freed from the reins of philosophical probity.

NOTES

1. Arthur Darby Nock, "Gnosticism," in *Essays on Religion and the Ancient World*, Vol. II, ed. by Zeph Stewart (Cambridge, Mass., 1972), p. 949.

2. Cf. A.H. Armstrong's discussion of this issue: "Gnosis and Greek Philosophy," *Plotinian and Christian Studies* (London, 1979), xxi.

3. Pheme Perkins, "Logos Christologies in The Nag Hammadi Codices," *Vigiliae Christianae* 35 (1981): 379ff.

4. Ibid.

5. Quotations are taken from the translation of Harold W. Attridge and Dieter Mueller, *The Nag Hammadi Library in English*, ed. by James M. Robinson (New York, 1977).

6. John Whittaker, "Self Generating Principles in Second-Century Gnostic Systems," *The Rediscovery of Gnosticism*, Vol. I, ed. by Bentley Layton, (Leiden, 1980), pp. 176-193, and "The Historical Background of Proclus's Doctrine of the ἀυθυπόστατα," De Jamblique à Proclus, Fondation Hardt, *Entretiens* 21 (Vandoeuvres-Geneva, 1975), pp. 193 ff.

7. E.g., the dyadic system recounted by Irenaeus, *Adversus Haereses*, Bk. I. This so-called "type A" Valentinianism tends to have an initial pair of figures, e.g., Bythos-Sige. Cf. G.C. Stead's excellent discussion: "The Valentinian Myth of Sophia," *Journal of Theological Studies*, N.S.-Vol. XX, Pt. 1 (April, 1969): 75ff. In this respect our document is closer to the monadic tradition, "type B," found for example in Hippolytus.

8. Cf. E.R. Dodds, "The *Parmenides* of Plato and the Origin of the Neoplatonic One," *Classical Quarterly* 22: 129ff.; John Whittaker, "Neopythagoreanism and the Transcendent Absolute," *Symbolae Osloenses* XLVII: 77ff.; Philip Merlan, "Greek Philosophy from Plato to Plotinus," *The Cambridge History of Later Greek and Early Medieval Philosophy*, ed. by A.H. Armstrong (Cambridge, 1967).

9. Cf. John Dillon, *The Middle Platonists* (Ithaca, NY, 1977).

10. W. Theiler, *Die Vorbereitung des Neuplatonismus* (Berlin, 1930), pp. 16ff.; John Dillon, op. cit., pp. 136-137. We should note the use of "the one by whom" at 65:10 as a name. Seneca's scheme in *Epistula* 65 includes among others a material cause, "*id ex quo*," a demiurgic cause, "*id a quo*," and a formal cause, "*id ad quod*." Philo's version, found at *Prov.* I, 23ff., and *Cher.* 125ff., has a material cause, τὸ ἐξ οὗ, a demiurge, το ὑφ' οὗ, an instrument (the Logos), τὸ δι οὗ, and a final cause, τὸ δι ὅ. It is this shorthand tradition of prepositional descriptions for cosmological causes which is behind these passages in the *Tripartite Tractate*, indicating familiarity with this mode of theological reflection from late Stoic and Middle Platonic thought.

11. Cf. 55:20 ff.: "above all intellect."

12. Cf. A. Lovejoy, *The Great Chain of Being* (Cambridge, Mass., 1936).

13. E.g., 55:30-35: "He has his Power, which is his will." Cf. 55:35.

14. G.C. Stead, "In Search of Valentinus," *The Rediscovery of Gnosticism*, Vol. I, p. 91.

15. Another important theme which emerges at this point and cannot be examined here is the Father's withholding of knowledge. Cf. 62:10 ff. and 64:30 ff. The Aeons are too fragile for a sudden revelation of the Father, so that this is only gradually available. The Logos seems to have been too impatient for this process.

16. On aeons as distinct minds cf. 64:1-10 and 70:5-10. A similar doctrine of intellects can be found in fragment 37 of the *Chaldaean Oracles*. The notion of immanent and manifest Divine Thoughts is discussed by R.P. Casey, "Clement and the Two Divine Logoi," *Journal of Theological Studies* 25: 43-56, and by H.A. Wolfson, *The Philosophy of The Church Fathers* (Cambridge, Mass., 1956).

17. Cf. Perkins, op. cit.

18. Cf. 76:20-35:
    for it was not without the will of the Father that the Logos was produced, which is to say, not without him [the Father] does he [the Logos] go forth. But the Father himself had brought him forth for those of whom he knew that it was fitting that they should come into being.

19. This idea is later extended with the Logos producing an Archon which he uses in the control of nature. Cf. 100, 15ff.

20. Perkins, op. cit.

21. Let me reiterate that this is only an estimate.

22. E.g., Plutarch, *De Plac. Philos.* 882d

    Σωκράτης καὶ Πλάτων χωριστὰς τῆς ὕλης οὐσίας τὰς ἰδέας ὑπολαμβάνουσιν, ἐν τοῖς νοήμασι καὶ φαντασίαις τοῦ θεοῦ, τουτέστι τοῦ νοῦ, ὑφεστώσας.

    (adopting S. Lilla's reading, *Clement of Alexandria* (Oxford, 1971), pp. 202-203). Cf. R.M. Jones, "The Ideas as the Thoughts of God," *Classical Philology* XXI: 317 ff.; A.N.M. Rich, "The Platonic Ideas as the Thoughts of God," *Mnemosyne*, Series IV, 7, pp. 123ff.

23. Atticus, according to Porphyry in Proclus, *In Tim.* I, 394, 6 (Baudry):

    οἱ δὲ ἀνδρανεῖς τὰς ἰδέας τύποις κοροπλαθικοῖς ἐοικυίας ἐφ᾽ ἑαυτῶν οὔσας καὶ ἔξω τοῦ νοῦ κειμένας εἰσάγουσιν.

24. Cf. *Vita Plotini* 18; John Dillon, op. cit., p. 256, remarks: "This distinction of Ideas from the essence of God seems, on Porphyry's evidence, to have been the doctrine of Athenian Platonism up to Longinus."

25. Cf. Dillon, ibid., pp. 253-256.

26. *Vita Plotini*, Chs. 18, 8-19, and 20, 89-95.

27. I have used "Albinus" since it remains the conventional name, e.g., in Dillon, op. cit.. On the problem see John Whittaker, "Parisinus gr. 1962 and the Writings of Albinus," *Phoenix* 28: 320ff., and 450ff.

28. Numenius fragments will be listed according to the numbering of E. des Places, *Numenius* (Paris, 1973). Cf. Fragment 11.

29. Fragment 12, 1-3 and 12-14.

30. Fragment 22.

31. Fragment 16.

32. Fragment 16, 7-8.

33. Fragment 15.

34. Albinus, Hermann 164, 16-37.

35. 164, 26-27.

36. 164, 35ff.

37. Cf. D.J. O'Meara, "Gnosticism and The Making of the World in Plotinus," *The Rediscovery of Gnosticism*, Vol. I, pp. 365ff.

38. II.9, 10, 11, 12.

39. The two intellects doctrine is found in *Numenius*, fragment 25. A similar system is examined by Plotinus in III.9. Cf. Dodds's discussion, *Proclus: The Elements of Theology*, Commentary to Props. 167 and 168.

40. Although the Longinus-Plotinus debate on the location of the intelligibles, mentioned in note 24, seems to have been uncommonly amicable, at least in Porphyry's version.

41. John Dillon, op. cit., Chapter 8, 384ff.

The Noetic Triad in Plotinus, Marius Victorinus, and Augustine

Peter Manchester

Students of the history of the Christian doctrine of divine trinity, among whom I count myself, have long recognized a degree of complicity between the progressive "metaphysicalizing" of the doctrine in the Third and Fourth Centuries and the emergence of triadic conceptual schemes in the new Platonism of Plotinus and his successors. At one time it was commonplace to gesture toward the arrangement of the Plotinian system into three "hypostases" as the speculative counterpart of the Christian triad. Today the naive clarity of this older purported parallel has given way to a vast confusion of triads, differing among themselves, sometimes intersecting with one another, and in general introducing into Christian discussion such complexity of speculative motivation that the older kinds of history of the doctrine have been completely undone. It is not just the historian's reconstruction that has come apart; the whole grand vision of a consolidating universal orthodoxy must be abandoned.

The notion that the Plotinian hypostases were an exemplar for Christian trinitarian metaphysics was often based on crude verbalism: the emerging technical terms for the Greek doctrine were *mia ousia*, *treis hypostaseis*. The term hypostasis however is a very weak basis for comparison, first because in Plotinus it is an editor's convention and not a technical term Plotinus uses for what the One, Nous, and Soul are each "one" of, and second because among the Greek Christian writers it was prized initially for its vagueness and openness to various interpretations. Beyond this misleading verbal echo, excessive weight was given to the case of Origen's account of the triad in *Peri Archŏn*, and that entirely on its subordinationist side that led into Arianism. But even if, in Origen, the Father and the Son can be placed in hierarchical series, in parallel to the One and the Nous in Plotinus (which is not at all clear in *Peri Archŏn* or the *Commentary on John*, which seem much more Middle- than Neo-platonist), there is no systematic parallel between the Holy Spirit and the Plotinian Soul, since the former acts in this world only within the circle of the elect, whereas the latter is universal and world-constituting.

The Plotinian hypostatic series never made a plausible model for the Christian trinity even when it held the field more or less alone. But current scholarship in the Second and Third Centuries has shown that a very different type of triad abounded in the philosophical and gnostical religions of the period. Perhaps of Orphic or Pythagorean derivation, it is attested in the Nag Hammadi materials,[1] and became especially influential through the *Chaldaean Oracles*, in the famous proposition that "in every world shines a triad ruled by a monad."[2] If we call the Plotinian hypostasis series "vertical" and derivational, then this new triad is "horizontal" and structural. It gave rise to a late Platonic speculative development which was not essentially Plotinian and indeed was integrated into the Plotinian series only with difficulty, requiring supplementary complications that were developed in conflicting ways in various schools.

The critical and historical effort to track the evolution of this horizontal triad, from its Second Century invocation, through Porphyry and Iamblichus, into Proclus and Damascius, is well underway. There begins to be careful study of early Christian participation in that development, centering especially on the Fourth Century writers Synesius and Marius Victorinus. But it seems to me that the complications of this scholastic history, which begin to take on near-fabulous dimensions by the time we get to the Athenians, have created a classic forest-and-trees problem. What, after all, is "the Triad" really *about*? Is it a numerological device? Symbolical in some other way? Is it a dialectical schema? Is it an analytical artifice or in some sense empirical? And finally, is the accommodation of the New Testament themes of Father, Son, and Holy Spirit to this philosophical speculation a capitulation or an insight? Does the Christian trinity genuinely belong in this discussion, or is all of that a gigantic kind of category mistake?

My goal in the provisional discussions which follow is to contribute to the clarification of these substantive questions. I am only indirectly concerned with the transmission of ideas through channels of influence and literary dependency, as experts will already have discerned from the figures juxtaposed in my title.

Marius Victorinus was the translator of what treatises of Plotinus Augustine knew, and in that sense knew Plotinus himself, but Pierre Hadot has shown conclusively that he took his instigation from Porphyry to a much larger degree.[3] Some of the differences this makes will figure in our discussion below (section 2). The movement I propose to track from Plotinus to Marius Victorinus is therefore not in the dimension of literary derivation. Similarly, it seems clear to me (for reasons indicated in section 3 below) that Augustine may not even know, and in any case does not understand Marius Victorinus's trinitarian metaphysics. If he has dabbled in it, as some indications suggest, his conscious attitude is wariness. Where he can be shown to continue and even more to radicalize certain themes from Marius, the relationship is at most unconscious and the material is experienced by Augustine as his own discovery. Once again, the movement of thought is controlled by the substance, the matter itself, and not the paper track.

Or better: it is the thesis of this paper that there *is* a matter of thought underlying speculations about the noetic triad. And the working assumption is that the adaptation of this triad to the Christian trinity by Augustine is natural and appropriate, and therefore instructive about its meaning.

1. Three Triads Distinguished

I have already indicated the difference between the triad we are considering, most properly called the "noetic triad," and the three hypostases of the Plotinian hierarchical scheme. The latter is founded in what we perceive to be Plotinus's innovation, but that he takes to be essential to Platonism, the projection of One "beyond Mind and Being" from which all else originates in a fashion differing from all causation or exemplarity. In this perspective the true and eternal world of familiar Platonism, the Being One which is also Nous, is a Second One, and the All One of its sensible effigy, the world of Soul, is a Third. The directionality of this "one, two, three" is strongly vertical, each succeeding level dependent on its prior for a perfection and a unity which, taken by itself, it lacks or has devolved into powerlessness. I take pains not to speak of "emanation" or of the "chain of being" to give the sense of this verticality. Being, in the first place, is properly ascribed to the second level alone, the Nous. But more than that, the image of emanation suggests that it is outflow or declination alone which makes each derived hypostasis, whereas it is Plotinus's distinctive claim that it is each level's halt, self-collection, and turning back to its source which is constitutive.[4] Another way to make the same point is to note that derivation in Plotinus has two phases, *proödos* and *epistrophē*, and that it is the second phase above all which completes the communication of power.

In the Plotinian scheme, the notorious problem of participation becomes the problem of the derivation of Soul from Nous. At this point there emerged in later Neoplatonism a second triadic schema, again vertical in sense but concerned with relations between hypostases in the overall systematic series. First given explicit formulation in Iamblichus, I call this triad the *schema of participation.* According to this formalism, one discriminates among three states of any given element in the hypostasis series:

i. that factor unparticipated (*amethektos*), *in itself,* absolute;

ii. that factor participated (*metechomenos*), which involves a self-disposition and action by the factor, not a reaction to what participates in it; and

iii. that factor as *participant* (*kata methexin, en tois metechousi, en schesei*), that is, as enacted in the derived hypostasis and now *its* action, no longer that of the higher hypostasis.[5]

In the end this schema reacted back upon the hypostatic series itself, causing the introduction of additional layers and, in Iamblichus himself, generating the eccentric postulation of an Unparticipated One higher than the Plotinian One, which, because it was the participated One (the noetic One its participant), was now a second. Though in this sense the effect of the schema of participation is to introduce new levels in the overall hierarchy which seem to be of the same kind as the original threesome of Plotinus, I would argue that the two triadic schemas ought to be kept distinct.

The third kind of triad, and the one with which we are concerned in this discussion, emerges from reflection on the relative self-constitutedness of each hypostasis, that inner economy of power which belongs to its own proper truth and unity. Again I emphasize that a derived level in the Plotinian system is not an organized defectiveness or a pure dependency, but a self-gathered life and power, and in precisely *that* way an epiphenomenon of its source. The canonical example of such a triad is the noetic triad, Being, Life, Nous (*on, zōē, nous; esse, vivere, intelligere*). This triad is horizontal in the sense that, in each of its variant developments, it interprets the interior integrity of the Second Hypostasis itself. Even when relations of priority and consequence are seen among them, when Porphyry for example makes the first moment the "father" or Iamblichus construes them in the dialectical sequence *hyparxis, dynamis, nous*, they remain moments within the Second Hypostasis and components of its integrity.[6] It remains a great question in the history of later Neoplatonism whether the noetic triad intrinsically envisions the derived status of Nous in relation to the hypernoetic One, but what it articulates is not external reference but self-constitution and completion.[7]

It was in this role that the noetic triad was touched on by Plotinus, in this role that a Porphyrian version attracted Marius Victorinus, and in this role that an analogue worked out in considerable independence by Augustine proved permanently suitable for the trinitarian theology of the Latin kataphatic tradition.

2. Plotinus and Marius Victorinus

When a threefold is a form of completeness, and its counting-out a return to unity, it proves invariably to be some kind of dialectic. In particular, if two terms comprise a difference, the remaining term will work a mediation. It is therefore a natural question about Being, Living, and Knowing (I would like to use "knowing" for *noein/intelligere* as a matter of pure convenience and euphony, asking it to bear the sense of "intellectually apprehending" or "understanding"), which of the three is the middle or mediating factor.

The juxtaposition of Plotinus and Marius Victorinus immediately makes this a puzzlement. In the first place, Plotinus very rarely cites this threesome, either nominally (*on, zōē, nous*) or verbally (*to einei, to noein, to zōein*), in any kind of tightly schematic way, and in discussions where the three can be recognized by implication it is not necessarily clear whether they should be listed in that order. But if we ask about a two-against-one pattern in his thought, it is very clear that Being and Nous make an important twosome, and that Life is the third between them. But in Marius Victorinus the principal dialectical movement is the development between *esse* and *vivere* which is resolved through the final term, *intelligere*.

Though it would have its own fascination to map out the role of Porphyry as the intermediary of this dialectical shift, there is more to be learned from directly comparing the patterns as though they were competing interpretations of a single phenomenon. A certain peculiarity of Christian theology is immediately thrown into relief, concerning the way in which the "father" is first principle.

To begin with Plotinus, let us first recall why any sort of structural complication in the Second Hypostasis would become thematic in the first place. Because the hypernoetic One is such a dramatic innovation in the history of Platonism from a modern point of view, our expositions of Plotinus allow themselves to begin with the One much more freely than Plotinus does, and therefore to give the production of the Second and the Third a much more deductive and "causal" account than is justified. Plotinus himself is much more sparing in taking the point of view of the One, seeking reasons for its "overflow," or characterizing what results in that direction. Much more central to his own "logic of discovery" is intuiting, on the level of Nous itself, the evidence of its derivative and secondary nature. Nous after all is eternal, true, and essential being. In it all diversity is embraced by unity, all partiality made whole through interior communion and concentricity. As the domain of ideal being, unity is in a certain sense its very nature; as Aristotle puts it, "the idea explains what it means to be a thing and unity explains what it means to be an idea."[8] As the domain of perfect transparency and reflective immediacy, Nous is flawlessly "present to itself," *synōn hautōi*, moving always and only within itself as it plays over the intelligible field that it unifies.[9] Above all, Nous is the primal life and hence *autozōon*, self-living, composed in perfect self-equality, self-mastery, and self-sufficiency. In what possible way is Nous marked within itself as derivative? What distinguishes Plotinus is that he senses and responds to this question in a new and radical way, precisely within his experience of Nous.

It is said too quickly that Nous is manifestly derivative because it is a unity-in-multiplicity, the multiplicity namely of the numbered intelligibles. Many Middle Platonists had felt this problem and resolved it with invocation of Nous as the "divine Mind." In the radical intuition of Plotinus, nous is not just contaminated by numbersomeness but is itself the *origin* of number, which is to say that it is the aboriginal *twofold*. In that very compactness of unity signaled in the two terms cited above, *synōn hautōi*, present to itself, and *autozōon*, self-living, a certain intrinsic *doubleness* is signalled. Nous is both knowing and known, i.e. it is both Mind and Being. The very structure of selfhood is bipolar. The reflexivity of the reflexive pronoun, the self-reference involved in self-identity, requires that what is so addressed be taken twice, in itself and for itself. In the language of contemporary "intentional analysis," which has not just lexical but substantive proximity to Neoplatonic discourse, Nous is both noesis and noema. The unity of Nous is complete, but it is not simple. And so, Plotinus judges, it is not just given, but has arisen, and therefore has a source.

Perhaps the most graphic and dramatic portrayal of the noetic double as arising from its source, the simplex One, is as follows:

> The One, perfect because It seeks nothing, has nothing, and needs nothing overflows, as it were, and Its superabundance makes something other than Itself. This, when it has come into being, turns back upon the One and is filled, and so becomes its contemplator, Nous. Its halt and turning toward the One constitutes being, its gaze upon the One, Nous. Since it halts and turns toward the One that it may see, it becomes at once Nous and being.[10]

If, as Plotinus sometimes does, we take the image here of overflow another step and ask about the "stuff" or substrate, the "intelligible matter" which pours forth from the One, we could not do better than to call it, with A.H. Armstrong, an "indeterminate vitality."[11] It is this "life" which becomes determinate in the noetic twofold, functioning therein both as medium of its derivation and as mediator of its unity. And so Plotinus can refer to

> that world There where there is no poverty or impotence, but everything is filled full of life, boiling with life. Things there flow in a way from a single source, not like one particular breath or warmth, but as if there were a single quality containing in itself and preserving all qualities.[12]

This background helps us understand the one passage where Plotinus seems consciously to advert to the noetic triad of *on, zōē, nous*, chapter 8 of VI 6 [34] "On Numbers." The derivation just reviewed is embedded in the opening propositions:

> There is a living being (*zōon*) which is primal and by consequence self-living (*autozōon*); there is both Nous and there is Essence, actually being (*ousia hē ontōs*).[13]

It becomes clear this primal *zōon* is the Nous, and that precisely because it is self-*living* in the noetic dipole it can be addressed correctly by the noetic triad:

> Now first all sensation is to be put away; by Nous is Nous contemplated. And it is to be taken to heart that in us is Life and Nous, not in mass but in massless power, and that true essence has given away mass and is power founded upon, itself, not some feeble thing, but altogether most living and most intelligent — nothing more living, nothing more intelligent, nothing more essentially real. . . .

If being (*to einai*) is sought, it is to be sought especially in what is most being; and if wholly knowing (*to noein holōs*), then in what is most Nous; and so too of Life itself.

So if one needs to take primal Being as being first, and then Nous, and then the living being (for this already seems to contain all things), then Nous is second (for it is an activity of essence).[14]

Plotinus here strongly registers the fact that considerations of *order* attach to discussions of the noetic triad, but insists on a revisionist arrangement. Being is first, second Nous, third Life. The third term is the mediating and unifying factor, and in this respect Plotinus gives the triad its canonical dialectical form. But he has reversed the second and the third moments with regard to the "content."

It is worth pointing out that because Plotinus is here so plainly commenting on the horizontal *on, zōē, nous* triad, it is clear that the "Nous" which is accounted second is not the Second Hypostasis in distinction to the First, but that hypostasis taken in relation to itself, as *autozōon*, and hence at first Being, and then Nous. Neither is there any exceptional designation of the First One as "primal Being." The series *on, nous, zōē* seems to be a conscious and deliberate adaptation of the more celebrated Chaldaean order.

Like Plotinus, Marius Victorinus has reasons of his own for considering the noetic triad, and does not merely take it up because it is a famous topic. His context is the effort of Christian theology to lay out some horizontal dialectic for Father, Son, and Holy Spirit in the wake of the catastrophic wrong-headedness exposed by the Arian controversy. Arianism is simply a vertical dialectic rigorously imposed. The error of Arianism is not subordinationism, if that means that the Son is second after and dependent upon the Father, because an asymmetry of this kind is built into doctrine by the New Testament. The error of Arianism is to think that the systematic question of the distinction between First and Second in the Neoplatonic hypostatic series has anything to do with the "three hypostases" of the Christian trinity.   There *is* a deep question in trinitarian theology that is structured according to the ontological difference between the First One and the Being One — the question namely whether beyond the divine life which is Father, Son, and Spirit there is an absolute Godhead — but this is *not* the question that led Latin trinitarianism to adapt Neoplatonism.   That question, which arises in the dialectic we have called "horizontal," asks about *mediation* within the structure of *self-constitution.*

Whether the structure of self-constitution is itself "derived" is not, in the Christian theological sense, a trinitarian question.

Marius Victorinus expounds the Father, Son, and Holy Spirit of the Christian scriptures as respectively *esse, vivere, intelligere*, and therefore as the unitary and creative principle that biblical faith calls God. There is no doubt that, following Porphyry, he has "telescoped" the Plotinian distinction between the One and Nous and, further, that he routinely confuses talk of the Father and the Son with talk about the First and the Second One. But what is interesting is the content of his triad, not its schema. He thinks *esse* and *vivere* make a pair, and that *intelligere* is the medium. What can we make of this?

Being for Marius is a moment of potentiality, not actuality. Of course it is potency, active power, not mere possibility incapable of its own act. But it is not "alone," so to speak, the divine creative principle. Creation is seen above all as a "doing," *agere*, and this requires not just agency but agitation. Being must become doing, and only living being can "do" anything. In the Gospel According to John, God in action is the Logos, and this Logos is "life" and the "light of men." God must "be," therefore, in such a way that life in action is already implicated in that being, and implicated not just in anticipation but in enactment.

From this it follows that the aboriginal divine "substance" (that is, *ousia*, the authentic being) is, as a matter of constitution and structure, eternally in action. In that action, being-as-potency, pure *esse*, is constantly coming into concretion or existence as *vivere*. As the pre-actual "to be" which harbors life as power, the divine substance is Father; as the living actuality which eternally declares and manifests the divine potency, God is Logos and Son. Along with the other "names of God" that Victorinus finds in scripture — Spirit, Wisdom, Nous — Logos designates the same as substance.[15] And yet because that substance is the dyad of *esse* and *vivere*, the Logos "in whom was life" (*John* 1: 4) is the Son of the Father, the image or revelation of the invisible God.

In the Fourth Century the controlling context in Christianity for this kind of analysis was in part the interpretation of the *homoousion* in the creed of Nicaea. The term is notably ambiguous, quite apart from its contrast with the rejected term *homoiousion*, "like in substance." It can be taken to say that Father and Son are one single substance; but it can also imply, as the Latin translation that eventually became current, consubstantial, does imply, that each of Father and Son are equally substantial. Victorinus affirms both:

> We hold therefore according to order, with the permission of God, that
> Father and Son are *homoousion* and *homoousia* according to identity in
> substance.[16]

Substance itself is the ground of this difference in God, because divine
einai is both *on* and *zōē*, is internally dynamic in the form of this dyad.

But being and life express only the outgoing procession of divine
power, its self-constitution as creative and salvific activity. Within the
divine substance this difference is not just action but also contemplation.
The very same Logos that is declarative in the Son is also recursive in
the Spirit. What proceeds from divine Being as Life also returns upon
divine Being as Mind, contemplative knowing or intelligence. Under
this aspect, the very same substance that is Logos is also Wisdom, Nous,
and Spirit. *Intelligere*, contemplative self-knowledge, is not super-added
to the Father and Son as Being and Life, but is the medium of that very
distinction. Being and Life are brought back to what they were from the
start by the Nous, so that the third moment is again the first, and the
gospel denomination "God is Spirit" (*John* 4: 24) identifies the one
divine substance.[17]

It can be shown that Victorinus has achieved a dialectical analogue
for the later Latin orthodox distinction between proper predication of
such terms as "principle," "logos," "wisdom," "nous," and "spirit,"
which all denote substance, and the "appropriation" of such terms to
one or another of the relational threesome. It is even possible to show
that his handling of the reciprocities among the moments of the noetic
triad amount to a functional precursor of the Augustinian doctrine of
predication by relation. Our interest however does not attach to the
question of his doctrinal orthodoxy, as though the Christian doctrine of
the trinity were a formalism stabilized independent of philosophical
reflection. The post-Augustinian orthodoxy of substance, relation, and
appropriation is itself shaped by philosophical reflection on the noetic
triad.

What springs to attention for us is the portrayal of Being and Life
as the primary dyad, and of Nous as the mediating moment. For
Plotinus, Being and Nous were the dyad, and the medium was Life. Is
this difference empty schematism, or is there a corresponding
phenomenology? We must turn to Augustine for this question, since it
is he who first arrives at the noetic triad by means of an explicit and
recognizable phenomenology.

3. Marius Victorinus and Augustine

A particularly sensitive calibration of the degree to which *The Trinity* of Augustine is in conscious conversation with Marius Victorinus can be derived from the question whether the Spirit is the "mother of the Son" and more generally a female principle in the divine. Marius embraces this view with enthusiasm,[18] whereas Augustine, seeming to have Marius's very argument in view but citing it without attribution, reproves the thesis with barely concealed impatience.[19] I judge that Augustine is aware of Victorinus as a theologian in his own right and not just as translator of Plotinus and Porphyry, but that he does not adopt or even consciously respond to the Porphyrian-Victorine analysis of the noetic triad itself. Where he does respond, and even dramatically build upon an opening in Victorinus, is in the thesis that human noetic life is an *image* of the divine noetic triad, and therefore offers a *via interior* for the argument to God as trinity.

That Augustine does not even understand the *esse, vivere, intelligere* triad is evident from his remarks about Porphyry in *The City of God*.[20] We know in general how clearly he found a doctrine of the Father and the Son in the "Platonic books,"[21] and it appears that the theme he so interpreted was the derivation of the Second Hypostasis, Nous, from the First One. When he considered the Porphyrian discussion of the noetic triad, which apparently included the designation of *on, zōē, nous* as "three gods," he immediately assumed that the third term, *nous*, meant the Son, and was then perplexed by how *zōē* signified the Holy Spirit. But from our glance at Victorinus we see that this reading is entirely off the track, since there *vivere* is the Son and *intelligere* the Spirit. It is barely possible that Plotinus, who did make *zōē* the third and mediating term, is part of Augustine's confusion, but the noetic triad is so weakly thematized in Plotinus, compared to the elaborate and explicit application in Victorinus, that this seems to me unlikely.

As I will argue, Augustine comes to a dialectical pattern in the "trinity which is God" analogous to the Neoplatonic noetic triad not at all through a scholarly engagement of "the Platonists," but from a direct intentional analysis of his own noetic experience. The schema of his triad, *memoria, intelligentia, voluntas*, is too eccentric to be an adaptation of any of Plotinus, Victorinus, or Porphyry: *intelligentia* is Nous, and one can think of ways to make the *voluntas* be Life, but Augustinian *memoria* is simply *sui generis*, an expression of his own introspective genius, and even Thomas Aquinas could not understand how it could be the first hypostasis or *esse* of the human mind.

It was not the content of his noetic analysis that Augustine took from Victorinus, but instead the sheer invitation to explore such an analysis as an image of the divine trinity. As Victorinus wrote,

> our soul is "according to the image" [*Gen*. 1: 26] of God and of the Lord Jesus Christ. If indeed Christ is life and Logos, he is image of God, image in which God the Father is seen, that is, in life one sees "to be." For this is the image, as was said. And if Christ is life, but "to live" is the Logos, and if life itself is "to be," and "to be" is the Father, if again life itself is "to understand," and this is the Holy Spirit, all these are three, in each one are the three, and the three are one and absolutely *homoousia*. If then the soul as soul is at once "to be" of soul, "to live" and "to understand," if it is therefore three, the soul is the image of the image of the Triad on high.[22]

In order to appreciate the innovation involved in this proposal, it is worthwhile to situate Augustine within the history of specifically Christian dogmatic trinitarianism.

It is a remarkable fact, demonstrated at length by John Edward Sullivan,[23] that no major theologian before Augustine had argued that the image of God in man included an image of the divine trinity. To the contrary, since "image of God" meant preeminently the Son, man's being "in the image" meant being "in the Son," called to participate in the Logos. Insofar as an avenue for argument to God was seen to be opened by Genesis 1:26, it concluded to the Son specifically, and then to the Father only "in the Son."

Augustine by contrast argues to the entire trinity, Father, Son, and Spirit, first "in an image in an enigma" (I *Cor.* 13: 12), and then by transformation into the image of glory (II *Cor.* 3: 18). In the pre-Augustinian Greek theology, the "vision of God" in the consummation would be a human participation in the Son's vision of the Father; in Augustine the vision is of the entire trinity.[24]

Coordinate with this innovation in Augustine is his shift in the identification of God the creator. In the New Testament and even still in the Cappadocians, God the creator is the Father. Though he creates through his Logos, which by the Nicene creed is said to be not just equal to God but "God from God," it remains true prior to Augustine that the doctrine of creation is part of the article on the Father, who is strictly identified as the Lord God of the Old Testament. But in four long exegetical books at the beginning of *The Trinity*, Augustine argues in detail that the Lord God and creator is the trinity itself, no longer the Father.

Compared therefore to the Greek Christian tradition, both the doctrine of God and of man the image of God have been trinitized with a new radicality in Augustine. One of the familiar sticking points in Augustinian interpretation, however, is the question of which of these innovations is the substantive discovery and which is epiphenomenal. The treatise *On The Trinity* itself is divided in two, with the exegetical prelude and the exposition of the logic of substance and relation occupying the first half (Books I-VII), and the argument via the unveiling of the trinity in the mind the second half (Books VIII-XV). Especially as the distinction between Reason and Revelation took on its medieval exclusivity and the trinity became a paradigm "datum of revelation," it was the first half that was regarded as authoritative doctrine, with the second relegated to the position of mere illustration, eventually no more privileged than images like spring, stream, water. In the spiritual theology that ran through Bonaventure the ascent through the interior triad was kept intact, but precisely as a spiritual itinerary, and not the foundation for the truth of doctrine itself.

My own conviction is that the logic of relation in Augustine is *consequent* upon his breakthrough with the noetic triad, or better, that the two halves of his work in *The Trinity* comprise a single intuition. It is important first of all to note that the phenomenology of *memoria*, *intelligentia*, and *voluntas* which he drives to ever greater interiority, transparency, and self-sufficiency is a *noetic* analysis and not, as so often expressed, a "psychology." The three moments, especially when purged of all dependency on external being so as to be pure self-memory, self-understanding, and self-love, are the self-constituted life of the *mens animi*, the *mind* of the soul. They are not, in the medieval or modern sense, "faculties" of the soul, but instead the internal structure of pure spiritual self-disclosedness. The dialectical pattern Augustine finds in them makes the third term, the *voluntas*, the mediating or unifying moment. Mind for Augustine is always retention begetting attention in the unity of an intention. In the way this triad unfolds "in the image," the uniting intentionality on any given level of "conversion to the inner man" is already alive on the next higher level, and as the ascending meditation proceeds we reach at last the level where the freedom of the mind is the Spirit of God itself, as *donum dei* in the subjective genitive,[25] and therefore the ground of participation in the trinitarian life. Within the divine life on the other hand, the unification of Father and Son in the one Spirit constitutes the "giveability" of that life, its communicability as life. The noetic triad is mind given and mind received, alike the structure of creative exemplarity and of created imaging.

It follows on my account that God the trinity in Augustine subsists on the level of the Plotinian *second* hypostasis and is an *on, nous, zōē* structure. This is confirmed in the classic Latin metaphysics for which God is *summum ens*, the highest being, spiritual substance in the sense of mind-like being. It is equally confirmed by the criticism of the metaphysical God in the apophatic tradition as it comes to a head, through Dionysius, in the Godhead beyond the trinity of Meister Eckhart and the author of the "Cloud of Unknowing."

The effect of Augustine's original application of the noetic triad to the doctrine of the trinity was to claim the trinity for an emphatically kataphatic theology, a theology of "horizontal" self-constitution on the level of Nous. This theology not only broke with the old efforts to model the trinity in the vertical hypostatic series of Plotinus, but dissolved the hypernoetic and hyperontic One entirely into the mystery of noetic or spiritual freedom. To the Plotinian intuition that even in the perfection of its unity the freedom was derived, not aboriginal, metaphysical trinitarianism would counterpose the "*causa sui*." If the apophatic mystic could not stop with this, he could no longer use the trinity against it.

4. Concluding Observation

What then is the noetic triad about? I would argue that it is about that kind of being which *is* as it is *revealed*, whose very "to be" is disclosedness. In the New Testament Father, Son, and Spirit are the economy of revelation, and in no way speculation about the nature of the divine principle "in itself." No one knows the Father but the Son and anyone to whom the Son reveals him; but no one can confess that Jesus is Lord, or in union with him pray as Son to the Father, except by the Spirit; and yet the Spirit does not speak for itself, but what it hears it speaks, and its presence brings the Father and the Son. This dialectic of revelation, given classic form in the Synoptic Icon (the baptismal scene) and in the Last Supper discourse in the Fourth Gospel (*John* 14-17), does not purport to unfold a divine substance, but only a divine life. If the Father in this scheme is invisible, if exposure to the Father opens an abyss, the abyss is here the revealed abyss, not the hidden one, the abyss experienced in finite and historical memory, not in the search for an ever more transcendently "first" First Principle.

Because it developed in dialogue with the Neoplatonic form of the search for the transcendent First, the doctrine of the trinity has come to seem the most intemperate fruit of metaphysical positivism in theology.

But if, like the noetic triad which contributed so much to its historical development, the trinity is simply being, light, and life having dawned on itself, then trinitarian theology can be quite agnostic about Principles and still be faithful to the divine which approaches and withdraws.

NOTES

1. *Allogenes*, CG xi 3, 47, 8-37.
2. Ed. Kroll, p. 18, as cited by R.T. Wallis, *Neoplatonism* (London: Duckworth, 1972), p. 106.
3. *Porphyre et Victorinus* (Paris, 1968).   For discussion of Hadot's "maximalism" about Porphyry's role between Plotinus and Augustine, see the "Introduction" to *Marius Victorinus: Theological Treatises on the Trinity* (The Fathers of the Church, 1978), translated by Mary T. Clark, R.S.C.J., pp. 1-10; and also John J. O'Meara, "The Neoplatonism of Augustine," in *Neoplatonism and Christian Thought*, ed. Dominic J. O'Meara (I.S.N.S. at SUNY Press, 1982), pp. 34-35.   A "minimalist" position is taken by Robert J. O'Connell, S.J., in *St. Augustine's Early Theory of Man* (Harvard, 1962), pp. 286-291, and *St. Augustine's Confessions* (Harvard, 1969), passim.
4. See, for Nous, V 2 [11], 1.
5. Cf. Wallis, pp. 126-127; also A.C. Lloyd, "The Later Neoplatonists," in *The Cambridge History of Later Greek and Early Medieval Philosophy*, ed. A.H. Armstrong (1970), pp. 298-301.   My account does not follow Lloyd completely but is taken from Iamblichus's analysis of time in the materials assembled by S. Sambursky and S. Pines, *The Concept of Time in Later Neoplatonism* (Jerusalem, 1972).
6. Wallis, p. 106, is therefore mistaken, I believe, when he sets these two forms of the noetic triad — being, life, nous and subsistence, power, nous — in parallel to abiding, procession, and reversion.   There is interaction, but not parallel, as I suggest in section 2 below.
7. An exceptionally lucid and instructive presentation by Jay Bregman, "Trinity versus Quaternity in Later Neoplatonism," was presented in the working group on Platonism and Neoplatonism, annual meeting of the American Academy of Religion, December 22, 1983.
8. *Metaphysics* A7, 988b5.
9. That the *energeia* of Nous involves motion, but pure motion (*kinēsis kathara*), was first pointed out by A.H. Armstrong in his 1969 Royaumont paper, "Eternity, Life, and Movement in Plotinus's Accounts of *Nous*," in *Le Néoplatonisme* (Paris, 1971), pp. 67-76. Perhaps the most dramatic text is VI 7 [38], 13, with its assertion of a noetic *planē*, "*nous en hautōi planēthentos*."
10. V 2 [11], 1, translated A.H. Armstrong, *Plotinus* (New York, 1962), p. 51.
11. "Plotinus," in the *Cambridge History*, p. 241.
12. VI 7 [38], 12, 22-26, as cited by Armstrong, ibid., pp. 245-246.

13.   VI 6 [34], 8, 1-2, my translation.
14.   Ibid., lines 7-13, 15-22.
15.   *Adv. Ar.* IB, 55, ed. M.T. Clark.
16.   *Adv. Ar.* IB, 60.
17.   Cf. M.T. Clark's discussion, "Introduction," pp. 13-16, especially paragraph (18).
18.   *Adv. Ar.* IB, 56.
19.   *The Trinity (De trinitate)*, XII 5, 5-6, 8.
20.   *Civ. Dei* X 23 and 29.
21.   *Conf.* VII 9, 13.
22.   *Adv. Ar.* IB, 63. Compare the lines following this citation with Augustine, *Trin.* IX 4, 4-5, 8.
23.   John Edward Sullivan, O.P., *The Image of God: The Doctrine of St. Augustine and Its Influence* (Dubuque, Iowa: Priory Press, 1963).
24.   Cf. esp. XIV, 10-19.
25.   XV 19, 36.

"Plenty Sleeps There": The Myth of Eros and Psyche in Plotinus and Gnosticism

Patricia Cox Miller

> It is proper, then, that I should begin with the first and most important head, that is, God the Creator, who made the heaven and the earth, and all things that are therein (whom these men blasphemously style the fruit of a defect), and to demonstrate that there is nothing either above him or after him.[1]

So Irenaeus begins his devastating critique of Gnostic theology, with special emphasis on its attribution of creation to a secondary God. As Rowan Greer has argued, I think persuasively, Irenaeus's theological critique is founded in the doctrine that the one God is to be defined by his creative act; he is the Maker, and all else that one might say about God flows from that primal characterization.[2] From Irenaeus's perspective, his opponents had deprived the One God of the very name that various Biblical texts uphold.[3] It is a perversion of Scripture not to realize that to say "God" is to say "Creator."[4]

My interest, however, is not to discuss Irenaeus's perspective, but rather to engage what I see as a — perhaps the — fundamental theological disagreement between Irenaeus and his opponents: how is God to be named, and what is at stake in that naming?

That "fox," as Irenaeus so scathingly describes the Gnostic creator of the world, is variously imagined by Gnostic texts to be an "arrogant ruler," a "blind chief," foolish Saclas, the erring Samael.[5] This God is the "sinister Ialdabaoth" (to use a phrase of Hans Jonas's)[6]; he not only creates the world but makes the "vain claim" that he is the only God who exists, thus revealing his ignorance of the greater divine powers within whose context he actually works.[7]

From Irenaeus's day to the present, readers of Gnostic texts have understood these derogatory names for the Creator-God to indicate a Gnostic revulsion either against the world that was created by this God or against that God himself. On the one hand, the Gnostics are pictured as a group of people nauseated by the miseries of life in this world; their derisive characterization of the Creator of the world is really an attack on the world itself.[8] On the other hand, the Gnostic revulsion is imagined to be not so much against the created world as against the Biblical monotheistic view of God and in favor of two (or more) divine "powers"; the demotion of the Creator is really an attempt to save the upper echelons of divinity from blasphemous attributes like anger and jealousy which suggest that the Godhead is the source of evil as well as good.[9] These explanations of the Gnostic portrait of the Creator agree that the portrait is evidence of some sort of alienation, whether existential or theological. Further, both place that alienation in a moral context: the Gnostic depreciation of the Creator and/or his creation is most basically an attempt to draw the line between good and evil more decisively.

While I agree that the Gnostic picture of the Creator-God is evidence of a real revolt, I do not agree that the basis of the Gnostic critique is a moral one, nor do I agree with the conclusion usually drawn from that argument, namely, that Gnostic thinking is dualistic. Such explanations confine the Gnostic view of the Creator — and the creation — within the very set of assumptions that they were criticizing. The Gnostic thinkers with whom this essay is concerned, the authors of the *Apocryphon of John*, the *Hypostasis of the Archons*, and especially *On the Origin of the World*, have not simply turned Genesis on its head. Rather, they have placed it in an ontological framework whose vision of reality has forced a radical reimagining of this revered picture of God and the world.

My thesis is as follows: when Gnostic texts picture the Creator as blind, arrogant, and foolish, they are not objecting to the world that this God created, nor are they objecting to God as creator; rather, the target of their critique is the reduction of God to a single name, "Creator," and thus to a particular understanding of his creative function. From the Gnostic perspective, the name "Creator" does not exhaust divine being; indeed, to insist upon such a name as the dominant metaphor of one's theology constricts God, binding divinity to a particular model of making. Using the issue of the name "Creator" as a mode of entrée,

I propose to explore the Gnostic attitude toward the naming of God and to place that fundamental theological activity within a Plotinian context, which provides a perspective on naming more akin to Gnostic thinking than Irenaeus's perspective does.

*

"Be sure that your theory of God does not lessen God."[10] Precisely in the context of a discussion about how to name God in relation to all else, Plotinus utters this cautionary statement. Strictly speaking, no name is appropriate to this profound reality, although, since "name it we must," Plotinus uses a variety of names, from the numerical "One" through the topological "There" to the familial "Father."[11] More important than any particular name, however, is one's attitude toward naming: unless one realizes that such names are radical metaphors that "sting" one into awareness of overwhelming presence, one will always be cut off from what Plotinus describes as an "erotic passion of vision known to the lover come to rest where he loves."[12] Names, while they are signposts on the path and thus aid one's understanding, do not constitute or in any way circumscribe that Presence: "our teaching is of the road and the travelling."[13]

In the group of texts under consideration here, one of the most notable features of the Creator is his "vain claim," a statement that does indeed "lessen God." After this God makes heaven, earth, and various angelic beings, he "boasts": "I do not need anything. I am god and no other one exists except me."[14] Precisely in the context of creation, the claim that the name "Creator" provides the only access to God's existence is shown to be an arrogant boast, a blind assertion. That assertion has immediate consequences. As the *Apocryphon of John* tells it, the Creator's jealous guarding of his exclusivity provokes, not belief, but disbelief: "But by announcing this he indicated to the angels who attended to him that there exists another God, for if there were no other one, of whom would he be jealous?" The angels are not the only figures to be disturbed. For after the boast, the mother begins to "move to and fro," repenting of the monster she has produced. As recognition of her repentance, the pleroma or fullness of heavenly powers pours holy spirit upon her and she is taken up "above her son." Finally, a voice "from the exalted aeon-heaven" announces the existence of man, who has been given "perfect, complete foreknowledge" by the "holy Mother-Father." This revelation causes the Creator and his minions to tremble and shake, for the man has intelligence "greater than that of the chief archon."[15]

The structure of the consequences of the Creator's arrogant claim is much the same in the *Hypostasis of the Archons* and *On the Origin of the World*: the claim is described as a sin "against the Entirety" or "against all of the immortal ones"[16]; a feminine figure (Sophia or Pistis) denounces the claim as a mistake[17] and the existence of the true man is revealed: "An enlightened, immortal man exists before you. This will appear within your molded bodies. He will trample upon you like potter's clay."[18] This latter statement is striking: turning the "potter" metaphor of creation in Genesis back upon itself, it suggests that enlightened human understanding rejects "Creator" as the presiding metaphor of theological reality and shatters the accompanying artistic or plastic model of creating. What the true man sees when he sees through the repressive dominance of "Creator" is a theological reality that is pleromatic — and organic.

The "vain claim" is a sin against "the entirety" of the immortal ones, and that claim is immediately countered by a feminine dimension of deity that is doubled (Pistis-Sophia), tripled (Pistis-Sophia-Zōē), almost endlessly multiplied.[19] The feminine dimension of reality not only appears, but is intensified, underscored, by its multiplied form, setting the masculine world of Ialdabaoth atremble. Accompanied by metaphors of desire, erotic ecstasy, flowing and pouring, and watery reflection, these figures carry a vision of reality that is organic rather than plastic, sexual rather than technological.

This view of theological reality, characterized as authentic human understanding, is offered in the context of the creation story. To be enlightened, in other words, involves coming to terms with metaphors of divine making. Our texts do not deny the pivotal importance of "making" as a theological metaphor; on the contrary, meditation on "making" provides the occasion for reflections on the nature of divine reality as well as on the nature of human speech about that reality. Just as, under the aegis of an explosive name, "Nous," Plotinus sees human language to be a metaphoric fullness and reality to be an assembly of "real beings,"[20] so these Gnostic authors, by "exploding" the name "Creator," express a pleromatic vision. The figures who compose the pleroma, like the "real beings" of Plotinus's realm of "Nous," are the metaphors of divine reality; they are the collection of signposts that dot the "road and the travelling" of human attempts to express in language the profound mystery at the heart of things.

Like Plotinus and like Irenaeus, the Gnostic texts under discussion here do arrive at names for this mystery. For the author of *On the Origin of the World*, the name of names is "the boundless one," who is "unbegotten" and dwells in a "kingless realm."[21] For the *Hypostasis of the Archons*, it is the "Father of Truth," also characterized as "Incorruptibility," "Root."[22] Finally, there is the God of the *Apocryphon of John* who, being "illimitable," "unsearchable," "immeasurable," "invisible," and "ineffable," is not surprisingly "unnameable."[23] "Not one of the existing ones," this God who has no name is like Plotinus's God who plays or broods over all that is,[24] not incarnating meaning but presiding silently over a flow of meaning, a pleroma of names. The realm of names — the mobile world of language — is plenteous and bountiful, and when one's understanding of reality is "structured" in this way, the ineffable One is a loving and instantaneous presence everywhere.[25] This One is "all things and no one of them"; "seeking nothing, possessing nothing, lacking nothing," it "overflows," and what we know is what its "exuberance" has produced.[26]

The Gnostic pleroma is such an exuberance, and it is revealed to human understanding when exclusive focus on the plastic model of making signified by "Creator" is shown to be a restrictive view of divine making. Gnostic language about God attempts to be faithful to the Gnostic vision of reality, and this dynamic is nowhere more forcefully shown than in the erotic, profusely productive qualities of both its conception of divine making and its language about that process. It is to Eros that we now turn.

*

Gnostic texts about making, which are also about the inner dynamics of the divine world, speak a poetry of the body that has few rivals in late antiquity. Expressed primarily in metaphors of desiring, love-making, and giving birth, Gnostic theological language has sensuous qualities that are striking. This did not escape Irenaeus, who at one point chooses to ridicule Valentinus's sexual vision of making with an equally organic and sensuous language, not from the human but from the vegetative world, envisioning fruit "visible, eatable, and delicious."[27] Valentinus's "melons" might be "delirious," but Irenaeus's choice of metaphor is revealing; he seems to have realized that Gnostic thinking about making had placed "the intercourse of Eros" at center stage.[28] Of course along with Eros come Psyche and Aphrodite; indeed, as Tardieu has shown, the mythic constellation of Eros and his feminine companions provided a language with which to describe cosmology and anthropology that many Hellenistic and late

antique authors used.[29] One of the most stunning appropriations of
the sensuous imagery of the myth of Eros can be found in the Gnostic
text *On the Origin of the World*, which will serve as the focal point of the
present investigation of the Gnostic revision of "making."

Although *On the Origin of the World* had "companions" in the
work of reimagining the creative process in terms of sexualized,
feminized, and organic language, it was in this text that such language
was intensified.[30] Pleromatic making is here carried by a group of
feminine figures: Pistis, Sophia, Zōē, Pronoia, Psyche, Eve. It is
tempting to view the successive appearance of these figures as a
progressively articulate and ever more differentiated picture of woman,
beginning with the cosmic Pistis and moving to the human Eve.
However, the relationships among these figures cannot be plotted along
such linear lines. Linear order is confounded in the first place by the
fact that the names of these figures tend to flow together; thus in
addition to Pistis, Sophia, Zōē, Pronoia, Psyche, and Eve, there are also
Pistis Sophia, Sophia Zōē, and Zōē "who is called Eve."[31] The
biological or generational notion of successive pairs of mothers and
daughters does not work either, since Pistis is the source of both Sophia
and Zōē, Sophia is responsible for the "patterning" of Eve, and Psyche
is given no mother at all. As we will see, the "order" of making that
is set in motion by these feminine figures is a pattern of repetitions, a
flow of likenesses, and not a hierarchical structure of fixed entities.

It is significant that the apparently discreet figures of this feminine
pleroma tend to flow together, for their stories are variations on a single
motif. As Plotinus remarked, myths "must separate in time" things
that fundamentally belong together because of the constraints of the
narrative form of myths.[32] In the mythic narrative under consideration
here, the diverse feminine figures belong together because they express
a shared vision of the erotic foundations of creating. Impelled by desire,
they are figures in travail, and their making, which is their very being,
is described in terms of movement. The "first reality" is a flow,[33] not
the work of a potter.

When making is seen from the perspective of the metaphor of the
potter, it is an action of forging. The maker shapes a reality other than
himself and is related to the objects that he has forged from nothing by
power rather than by nature.[34] By contrast, our text envisions making
under the banner of desire. It is the kind of desire that is set in motion
when God is dead — that is, when God cannot be personified or finally
characterized in understandable terms but is rather called "boundless,"
an unfathomable something that constantly eludes human categories and
defies "objective" language that would distance the maker from what

is made. The "boundless" cannot be captured, as Plotinus remarks about the "One"; but it can be imagined. Indeed, it imagines itself as it "breaks into speech," unleashing a flow of likenesses, a dynamic "middle" where maker and thing made, knower and known, come together in a bond of love.[35]

It is this erotic "middle" in which the vision of *On the Origin of the World* is situated:

> After the nature of the immortals was completed out of the boundless one, then a likeness called "Sophia" flowed out of Pistis. (She) wished (that) a work (should) come into being which is like the light which first existed, and immediately her wish appeared as a heavenly likeness, which possessed an incomprehensible greatness, which is in the middle between the immortals and those who came into being after them, like what is above, which is a veil which separates men and those belonging to the (sphere) above.[36]

In this text, the "middle" is a realm of likeness that has flowed from the desire of Pistis (or Sophia; the "she" is ambiguous).[37] It is a "veil" that marks the paradoxical nature of the boundless one (the "aeon of truth") whose inside is light and whose outside is darkness.[38] Pistis, Sophia, and the other feminine figures in the text are creatures of this middle realm; neither pure light nor pure darkness, they preside over the watery flowing and pouring that mark the middle. Liquid metaphors are prominent: thus Pistis "pours" light and is herself visible as a watery reflection, a floating image, and Sophia casts a "drop" of light that both floats on and patterns water.[39] Impelled by desire, these figures show making to be a fecund process of watery reflection in which light is poured into receptive darkness.

The "middle" is erotic. The desirous flowing of Pistis is repeated and intensified by a later feminine figure, Pronoia, and it is in the context of her flowing that Eros, who is himself an intensification of the desire of the middle, appears. In one of the many watery appearances of Pistis, a human likeness is reflected.[40] Pronoia falls in love with this reflection and, in her ardor, desires to embrace it but is not able to do so.[41] Like Pistis, whose desire for the boundless one ended, not in a captivating grasp or an embrace but rather in a flow, Pronoia who was "unable to cease her love" "poured out her light upon the earth." At this point the text itself becomes a swirl of liquid metaphors. From the moment of this pouring of light, the human likeness is called "'Light-Adam,' which is interpreted 'the enlightened bloody (one).'" Also

> at that time, all of the authorities began to honor the blood of the virgin. And the earth was purified because of the blood of the virgin. But especially the water was purified by the likeness of Pistis Sophia. . . . Moreover, with reason have they said, through the waters. Since the holy water gives life to everything, it purifies too.[42]

The watery flow that is the medium of reflection is now imagined as feminine blood. It is out of this blood that Eros appears.

The dynamic character of the "middle" is at this point revealed. It is Eros, love, who "appeared out of the mid-point between light and darkness" where his "intercourse" is "consummated."[43]   The desirous making of Pistis and the other figures in the "middle" is founded in love, which, as Eros, is described as "Himeros," a "yearning" which is the "fire" of the light, and as psychic blood ("blood-Soul"). The blood of intercourse, or the flowing of organic connectedness, is what characterizes the erotic making "out of the mid-point between light and darkness."[44] Eros, as the ambiguous uniter of two realms, the fire and the blood, dry and humid, male and female,[45] is a fitting embodiment of the middle. There is, however, another figure or name for this realm, and it is revealed in the course of yet another repetition of feminine flowing.

Following the appearance of Eros there is a description of his gardens, whose plants reinforce the view of erotic movement as a "desire for intercourse" (*epithymia tēs synousias*).[46] This most basic desire for "being-with" is then pictured again with yet another trope on the liquid movement so characteristic of this text:

> But the first Psyche loved Eros who was with her, and poured her blood upon him and upon the earth. Then from that blood the rose first sprouted upon the earth out of the thorn bush, for a joy in the light which was to appear in the bramble. After this the beautiful flowers sprouted up on the earth according to (their) kind from (the blood of) each of the virgins of the daughters of Pronoia. When they had become enamored of Eros, they poured out their blood upon him and upon the earth.[47]

This picture bears striking resemblances to the myth of Psyche and Eros written, in a more detailed form, by Apuleius.[48]   The Psyche of Apuleius's tale, who desires to pour light on her unseen lover, loses him (is unable to grasp or capture him), but that moment marks the beginning of her initiation into the realm of Aphrodite, the mother of love and primal mistress of flowing waters.[49]

So also here, Psyche, in love with love itself, pours, and from her flow of blood comes the rose, the Aphroditic dimension of herself.

Named after the flood of perfume that pours from it (*rhodos: rheuma tēs odōdes*),[50] the rose was Aphrodite's favorite flower and was said to have been born from the drops of blood that fell from her foot when she pricked it on bramble thorns.[51] An unspoken presence who comes forth in this text in the "likeness" of a rose, Aphrodite is a crucial figure for the erotic "middle" where making is a flow of desire for *synousia*, connection, being-with. From the Aphroditic perspective, the picture of the "middle" is not a veil or a mid-point, but a garden full of flowers where the rose presides as a compact image of the bleeding that flows and creates.

The flowing that characterizes this text's view of making might seem to indicate that creating is an irenic process were it not for the fact that flowing is characterized as bleeding as the narrative moves on. That the flowing of Pistis becomes the pouring blood of Pronoia and Psyche is surely an indication that the image is being intensely feminized, but it also suggests that the "desire for intercourse" involves a painful giving of life's very substance. Love is a "sting," as Plotinus remarked,[52] and this sentiment was given graphic — even gruesome — shape in the Great Paris Magical Papyrus, where instructions for engraving an amulet (appropriately, on a magnet!) picture Aphrodite astride Psyche as on a horse, holding her hair as reins in her hands, with Eros underneath burning Psyche with a flaring brand.[53] Aphrodite "rides" on the erotic yearnings of the soul, just as love "stands under" or gives the foundation for the Aphroditic dimension of psychic reality.

*

That there is a flow at the heart of things, rather than a creator set over against a thing created, seems to be the guiding insight of *On the Origin of the World*. The love of "being-with," the desire to connect — the dynamic which *is* the "middle" — provides the basis for all distinction. The essence of making, in other words, is loving. This text, as its modern title aptly says, is concerned with origins. Where do things come from? However, as I have tried to show, by attacking the model of making signified by the name "Creator," this text implies that the question of origins is not to be phrased as above, "where do things come from?" The question of origin is rather a question of the dynamic that empowers the coming-to-be of all things. By rejecting the dichotomy of creator and creation, *On the Origin of the World* has revisioned the question of origins. The insight that underlines this revision is, it seems to me, a Plotinian one; or, better, it is a perspective on the issue of origins that informs both the Gnostic text and Plotinus, and I would like to move now to a brief consideration of Plotinus's thoughts on this topic.

Generally more discursive than his poetic Gnostic counterpart, Plotinus poses the problem directly: "But this Unoriginating, what is it?"[54] What is this principle, best defined as "undefinable,"[55] which we imagine as father and source of all?

> The difficulty this Principle presents to our mind in so far as we can approach to conception of it may be exhibited thus: We begin by posing space, a place, a Chaos; into this container, whether conceived in our imagination as created or pre-existent, we introduce God and proceed to inquire: we ask, for example, whence and how He comes to be there; we investigate the presence and quality of this newcomer projected into the midst of things here from some height or depth. But the difficulty disappears if we eliminate all space before we attempt to conceive God.[56]

As Plotinus continues his discussion in this passage, he develops a whole catalogue of terms that may not be used in conceiving of this Principle: space, environment, limit, extension, quality, shape, all these lead to erroneous ways of imagining the source. God is not a Being among other beings, nor the Thing of things, but rather their wellspring.[57] Our problem seems to be that we place God within an objective category or frame and then posit God as the "subject" of that object; such a procedure is dualistic from the start and opposes maker to thing made.[58] We should rather conceive of this principle "sheerly as maker; the making must be taken as absolved from all else; *no new existence is established*; the Act here is not directed to an achievement but is God Himself unalloyed: here is no duality but pure unity."[59] This is an outright rejection of the view of origin that understands the maker in terms of a making of things. From Plotinus's perspective, making "is not directed to an achievement"; making is the very being of God, but it is not to be understood in terms of objects.[60]

What, then, is this "origin"? It is, says Plotinus, "the productive power of all things" (*dynamis tōn pantōn*)[61]; it is the active force present to all things that enables them to witness the spectacle of their own unity, their own self-gathered center.[62] The principle in which "all centers coincide," the "Supreme" contains no otherness; indeed, it might be described as absolute connectedness: "Thus the Supreme as containing no otherness is ever present with us; we with it when we put otherness away."[63] Experienced by the soul as a drunken revel of love, this dynamic "origin" is what makes of desirer and desired, seer and object seen, one: "Here is no duality but a two in one; for, so long as the presence holds, all distinction fades; it is as lover and beloved here, in a copy of that union, long to blend."[64] The One is an "allurer,"[65] and its magic is manifested in the experience of the "two in one," the relatedness that allows things to be what they are.

The One is love,[66] and the soul that experiences the relatedness described above becomes love itself.[67] John Rist has argued convincingly the possibility that "Plotinus regarded *Erōs* as an all-embracing term" and has noted what he calls Plotinus's deliberate use of sexual metaphors to describe the relationship between God and the soul.[68]

There are indeed many erotic metaphors in Plotinus's discussions of the dynamic of the One, but what is specially striking in our context is the feminized character of Plotinus's erotic language. In the course of one of his discussions of "the making principle," Plotinus stops to question what he has been doing as an interpreter. As though reading over what he has just written, he asks:

> May we stop, content with that? No: the soul is yet, and even more, in pain. Is she ripe, perhaps, to bring forth, now that in her pangs she has come so close to what she seeks? No: we must call upon yet another spell if anywhere the assuagement is to be found. Perhaps in what has already been uttered, there lies the charm if only we tell it over often? No: we need a new, a further incantation.[69]

Here is a picture of the interpreter himself as a woman in travail, laboring to find a language appropriate to that "love-passion of vision"[70] that he is trying to express. The problem is that the experience of the One as love takes the interpreter beyond discursive knowing and writing: "The vision baffles telling; we cannot detach the Supreme to state it."[71] The interpreter must remember that his teaching is "peregrination"; it is "of the road and the travelling," and to forget that is to make of Love itself a "common story."[72]

Given this perspective on the travailing nature of language,[73] it seems fitting that, when Plotinus names what the soul always is, he turns to a feminine image. That the soul's "good" is with the One

> is shown by the very love inborn with the soul; hence the constant linking of the Love-God with the Psyches in story and picture; the soul, other than God but sprung of Him, must needs love. So long as it is There, it holds the heavenly love; here its love is the baser; There the soul is Aphrodite of the heavens; here, turned harlot, Aphrodite of the public ways; yet the soul

is always an Aphrodite. This is the intention of the myth which tells of Aphrodite's birth and Eros born with her.[74]

As in *On the Origin of the World*, Aphrodite appears as image of the soul in love with love, and it is again an agonized picture.

When Plotinus discusses love directly in a treatise devoted exclusively to that topic, he does so in terms of the myth of Eros, Psyche, and Aphrodite. What is significant here for the purpose of the present discussion is that the doubled Aphrodite gives birth to, and presides over, a view of loving that is remarkably similar to the perspective that guides the feminine flowing of *On the Origin of the World*. The first Aphrodite that Plotinus presents is shown as a figure directing her energy toward and feeling affinity with her source. "Filled with passionate love for him," she brings forth love. "Her activity has made a real substance," says Plotinus, and he goes on to describe that love as "a kind of intermediary between desiring and desired."[75] The second Aphrodite is she whose birthday party provides the occasion for another story about the birth of love. The scene is a garden in which Poverty and Plenty make love and give birth to an Eros marked by a simultaneous fullness and emptiness.[76]

In both of these pictures of the loving of the Aphroditic soul, Plotinus emphasizes the dynamic and productive qualities of loving. To be in love is to make, and the making is founded in achieving an experience of connectedness, of the "two in one" that is the flow between desiring and desired. There is, of course, an agony here. The "sting" of love is that "he is a mixed thing, having a part of need, in that he wishes to be filled, but not without a share of plenitude, in that he seeks what is wanting to that which he already has."[77] The loving soul is like the interpreter who cannot rest content with a single telling lest he profane the mystery by pretending to have "grasped" what is not "graspable." Like the feminine figures of *On the Origin of the World*, he is condemned to repetition; he must be alive to the Poverty of his Plenty. Yet that awareness makes of his vision a continuous flow which is both source and substance of all making.

That making is a loving that sees through dichotomous structures is the perspective that links the work of Plotinus and our Gnostic author. Creation is not, in this view, a single event that establishes distance between maker and thing made but rather a continuous process of the birth of the boundless One in the soul, and the erotic, sexual imagery of both texts serves, I think, to underscore this point. There is an Aphroditic rose blooming in these gardens.

NOTES

1.   Irenaeus, *Haer.* 2.1.1.
2.   Rowan Greer, "The Dog and the Mushrooms: Irenaeus's View of the Valentinians Assessed," in *The Rediscovery of Gnosticism*, Vol. I: *Valentinian Gnosticism*, ed. by Bentley Layton (Leiden: E.J. Brill, 1980), pp. 140, 155-160, 167.
3.   See especially *Haer.* 2.2.5.
4.   Irenaeus, *Haer.* 2.8.10.
5.   A catalogue of these names collected from the *Hypostasis of the Archons*, *On the Origin of the World*, the *Apocryphon of John*, and the *Gospel of the Egyptians* can be found in a convenient collection in Nils A. Dahl, "The Arrogant Archon and the Lewd Sophia: Jewish Traditions in Gnostic Revolt," in *The Rediscovery of Gnosticism*, Vol. II: *Sethian Gnosticism*, ed. by Bentley Layton (Leiden: E.J. Brill, 1980), pp. 693-694.
6.   Hans Jonas, *The Gnostic Religion*, 2nd ed. rev. (Boston: Beacon Press, 1963), p. 193.
7.   For a detailed discussion of the "vain claim," see Dahl, "The Arrogant Archon," pp. 692-701.
8.   This is the thesis that guides the interpretation of Hans Jonas in *The Gnostic Religion*; see, more recently, Jonas's article, "Delimitation of the Gnostic Phenomenon — Typological and Historical," in *Le Origini dello Gnosticismo*, ed. by Ugo Bianchi (Leiden: E.J. Brill, 1967), p. 96: "This figure of an imperfect, blind, or evil creator is a gnostic symbol of the first order. In his general conception he reflects the gnostic contempt for the world. . . ." See also Kurt Rudolph, *Gnosis*, ed. by Robert McLachlan Wilson (New York: Harper and Row, 1983), pp. 67-84.
9.   See Dahl, "The Arrogant Archon," and Alan Segal, *Two Powers in Heaven: Early Rabbinic Reports about Christianity and Gnosticism* (Leiden: E.J. Brill, 1977).
10. Plotinus, *Enn.* 6.8(39).21. For *Enneads* 4 through 6, I have used the translation of Stephen MacKenna, *Plotinus: The Enneads*, 4th ed. rev. by B.S. Page (London: Faber and Faber, 1962). For the passage cited here, however, I have used MacKenna's original translation of 6.8.21, 28 rather than Page's revised translation, since I think it captures the sense of the whole passage more faithfully.
11. On the issue of the inappropriateness of names, see *Enn.* 6.9(9).5 and *Enn.* 5.3(49).14.
12. *Enn.* 6.9(9).4; true expression is, as Plotinus says in 5.5(32).6, an "agony," and "we name, only to indicate for our own use as best we may." Strictly speaking, "we should put neither a This nor a That to it; we hover, as it were, about it, seeking the statement of an experience of our own, sometimes nearing this Reality, sometimes baffled by the enigma in which it dwells" (6.9(9).3). Yet at the same time, the soul "breaking into speech" carries "sounds which labor to express the essential nature of the being produced by the travail of the utterer and so to represent, as far as sounds may, the origin of reality" (5.5(32).5). The point is that we must

be "in collusion with" language, "everywhere reading 'so to speak,'" that is, reading all words as metaphors (see 6.8(39).13: *sũnchõreõ*, which MacKenna translates as "have patience with," has a range of meanings including to "defer," "concede," "be in collusion with," "connive at").

13.   *Enn.* 6.9(9).4.

14.   *NHC* II, 5, 103 (*On the Origin of the World*). I have used *The Nag Hammadi Library in English*, dir. by James M. Robinson (Leiden: E.J. Brill, 1977), for all quotations from Gnostic texts.

15.   *NHC* II, 1, 13-15 (*Apocryphon of John*).

16.   *NHC* II, 4, 86 (*Hypostasis of the Archons*); *NHC* II, 5, 103 (*OrgWrld*).

17.   *NHC* II, 4, 87 (*HypArc*); *NHC* II, 5, 103 (*OrgWrld*).

18.   *NHC* II, 5, 103 (*OrgWrld*).

19.   See especially the multiple feminine figures in *NHC* II, 5 (*OrgWrld*).

20.   See Plotinus's comments on dialectic, which is the language and mode of thinking appropriate to *nous*: "It is not just bare theories and rules; it deals with things and has real beings as a kind of material for its activity" (*Enn.* 1.3[20].5). For descriptions of the realm of *nous* see, among others, *Enn.* 5.8(31) and the helpful discussions by Richard T. Walls, "*NOUS* as Experience," in *The Significance of Neoplatonism*, ed. by R. Baine Harris (Norfolk, Virginia: Old Dominion University Research Foundation, 1976), pp. 121-153, and by A.H. Armstrong, "Form, Individual, and Person in Plotinus," *Dionysius* I (Dec., 1977): 49-68.

21.   *NHC* II, 5, 98 and 127 (*OrgWrld*).

22.   *NHC* II, 4, 86, 87, and 93 (*HypArc*).

23.   *NHC* II, 1, 3 (*ApocryJn*).

24.   *Enn.* 1.1(53).8, where the verb *epocheomai* carries the meanings "ride upon," "float upon," "brood," "hover," "play upon." For *Enneads* 1 through 3, I have used the translation of A.H. Armstrong, *Plotinus* (Cambridge, Massachusetts: Harvard University Press, 1966-1967), 3 vols.

25.   *Enn.* 5.5(32).11.

26.   *Enn.* 5.3(49).1.

27.   Irenaeus, *Haer.* I.11.4.

28.   *NHC* II, 5, 109 (*OrgWrld*).

29.   Michel Tardieu, *Trois Mythes Gnostiques: Adam, Éros et les animaux d'Égypte dans un écrit de Nag Hammadi (II, 5)* (Paris: Études Augustiennes, 1974), pp. 141-214, especially pp. 146-148.

30.   On Gnostic use of "biological" metaphors, see Pheme Perkins, "On The Origin of the World (CG II, 5): A Gnostic Physics," *Vigiliae Christianae* 34 (March 1980): 36-46, especially 37-38.

31.   *NHC* II, 5, 100, 113, and 115 (*OrgWrld*).

32.   *Enn.* 3.5(50).9.

33.   *NHC* II, 5, 98 (*OrgWrld*). For an understanding of "first work" as first "reality," see Tardieu, *Trois Mythes Gnostiques*, p. 56.

34. In "The Dog and the Mushrooms," Greer has shown that Irenaeus, arguing on behalf of the Creator, insists that the relationship between God and creation is based on knowledge, not on a community of nature between the two. "The gnostic understanding that God and the universe (at least the spiritual seeds in it) are related by nature but not by knowledge is contrasted with the orthodox view that the relation is one not of nature but of knowledge" (p. 161).

35. On the One breaking into speech, see *Enn.* 5.5(32).5; on the One and love, see *Enn.* 6.8(39).

36. *NHC* II, 5, 98 (*OrgWrld*).

37. See the comments by Tardieu, *Trois Mythes Gnostiques*, pp. 57-58, on the ambiguity of Sophia.

38. *NHC* II, 5, 98 (*OrgWrld*).

39. *NHC* II, 5, 100, 104, 111 (*OrgWrld*).

40. *NHC* II, 5, 107-108 (*OrgWrld*).

41. *NHC* II, 5, 108 (*OrgWrld*).

42. *NHC* II, 5, 108 (*OrgWrld*).

43. *NHC* II, 5, 109 (*OrgWrld*).

44. *NHC* II, 5, 109 (*OrgWrld*).

45. See the comments of Tardieu, *Trois Mythes Gnostiques*, pp. 163-174, on Eros and his ambiguous, doubled functions and powers. From Tardieu's perspective, Eros is marked by *"sa duplicité fondamentale"* (p. 174).

46. See Tardieu, *Trois Mythes Gnostiques*, pp. 207-208.

47. *NHC* II, 5, 111 (*OrgWrld*).

48. See Tardieu, *Trois Mythes Gnostiques*, pp. 146-148.

49. For valuable discussions of Aphrodite, see Geoffrey Grigson, *The Goddess of Love* (London: Constable, 1976), and Paul Friedrich, *The Meaning of Aphrodite* (Chicago: University of Chicago Press, 1978).

50. See Marcel Detienne, *Dionysus Slain*, trans. by Mireille Muellner and Leonard Muellner (Baltimore: The Johns Hopkins University Press, 1979), p. 50.

51. See Charles Joret, *La Rose dans l'Antiquité et au Moyen Age* (Paris: Émile Bouillon, 1892), pp. 47-50.

52. *Enn.* 3.5(50).7.

53. *Papyri Graecae Magicae*, ed. by Karl Preisendanz, 2nd ed. rev. by Albert Henrichs (Stuttgart: B.G. Teubner, 1973), Vol. I, P IV, lines 1718-1745 (p. 126).

54. *Enn.* 6.8(39).11.

55. *Enn.* 5.5(32).6.

56. *Enn.* 6.8(39).11.

57. *Enn.* 6.9(9).9 and 5.3(49).11.

58. See *Enn.* 6.8(39).13 and 6.8(39).20.

59. *Enn.* 6.8(39).20; italics added.

60. See the very astute discussion of this issue in Plotinus by Dominic J. O'Meara, "Gnosticism and the Making of the World in Plotinus," in *The Rediscovery of Gnosticism*, ed. by Bentley Layton (Leiden: E.J. Brill, 1980), Vol. I: *Valentinian Gnosticism*, pp. 365-378.

61. *Enn.* 3.8(30).10.

62. *Enn.* 3.8(30).10: oneness; 6.9(9).8: centering.

63. *Enn.* 6.9(9).8.

64. *Enn.* 6.7(38).34-35.

65. *Enn.* 6.6(34).18.

66. *Enn.* 6.8(39).15.

67. *Enn.* 6.7(38).22.

68. John Rist, *Eros and Psyche: Studies in Plato, Plotinus, and Origen* (Toronto: University of Toronto Press, 1964), pp. 78-79, 99.

69. *Enn.* 5.3(49).17.

70. *Enn.* 6.9(9).4.

71. *Enn.* 6.9(9).10.

72. *Enn.* 5.3(49).17: peregrination; 6.9(9).4: the travelling; 6.9(9).11: the common story.

73. See *Enn.* 5.5(32).5.

74. *Enn.* 6.9(9).9.

75. *Enn.* 3.5(50).2.

76. *Enn.* 3.5(50).6-8.

77. *Enn.* 3.5(50).9.

"The Name of the Father is the Son"
(Gospel of Truth 38)

Raoul Mortley

These striking words have aroused the interest of many, and there has been much effort expended on providing a background or context for them.* It is the intention of this paper to press for Philo as a probably stimulus for much of what is said in the Gospel of Truth, and to offer a reconstruction of the philosophy underlying the words "The name of the Father is the Son." There seems to be no doubt about the translation of these words from the Coptic: all translators agree, though their commentaries may differ.[1] The Coptic text at this point makes use of the word *ren*, which is generally agreed to be the equivalent of the Greek *onoma*.

Attempts to explain the statement have varied. On the other hand the literary critics offer views formed by the application of a particular hermeneutic: Standaert seeks to lay bare the structure of the text, by pointing out the use of repetitions, and by analyzing the rhetorical forms deployed by the author.[2] Fineman uses a Lacanian hermeneutic to disclose the dynamics of the metaphors used, in response to the Freudian picture of father/son relations.[3] On the other side, the methods traditional to scholars of antiquity have been pursued, through the finding of parallels and verbal reminiscences. The general tendency has been to situate The Gospel of Truth in the Valentinian tradition,

---

* I owe particular thanks for her highly valued work in the preparation of this paper to my research assistant, Anne Stark.

and it has even been supposed that Valentinus himself was the author.[4] There are undoubted affinities between the philosophical concerns of the Valentinian School and those of The Gospel of Truth: the emphasis on the incomprehensibility of the Father, on error and ignorance in the constitution of reality, on the dependence of all reality on the Father, on the relation between knowing and being, on the Pleroma, and on self-knowledge as the route to knowledge of the All. But the central theme of the Gospel of Truth is not particularly associated with Valentinianism: its philosophy of names is of crucial importance in the development of the Gospel, which is not so much about truth as its title would appear to indicate. Its theme is really the relationship between naming and being, and here it strikes an original note in the history of Christian philosophy. Apart from the novelty of this theme, other concerns may cause us to doubt the alignment with the Valentinian school. First, the Gospel has no mythical content: the saga of Sophia, or of the aeons, or of Jesus himself,[5] is absent. The Gospel is entirely conceptual. Second, the role of Jesus Christ is closer to center stage: God the Father and God the Son are the key figures in the Gospel, whereas in Valentinian thought Jesus Christ tends to become one of a whole series of performers. To this extent the Gospel is somewhat closer to orthodoxy than is Valentinian Gnosticism. A further remark which can be made is that it is unlike other Gnostic gospels, in that it does not feature the *teachings* of Jesus. It resembles them in that it does not focus on the deeds and the general historical enactment of the incarnation — the Gnostic gospels are more interested in teachings than the acts carried out on the stage of history — but it differs in that it offers a theological exposition of God and the Son, rather than attributing certain teachings to Jesus himself. However, it should be noted that Tardieu's addendum differs on this, in that he allows for the possibility of a Valentinianism, which developed markedly different perspectives from those of its founder.

The problem of how to affiliate the Gospel of Truth is, in the view of the present author, completely open. Clearly what we do with Irenaeus's evidence is crucial here: Irenaeus says that the Gospel of Truth was Valentinian, and that it was produced "not long ago."[6] I take this as meaning not long before the time of writing, and therefore the Gospel could be dated to some time in the 170s.[7] It seems pretty hard to resist the conclusion that Irenaeus is referring to the Nag Hammadi Gospel of Truth: if there were several Gospels of Truth, somebody would surely have said so. However one cannot help sensing that there is more to it than a simple identification of the Irenaeus reference with the fortuitous discovery of that part of the Nag Hammadi corpus. Perhaps there was an original Gospel of Truth, as known and referred to by Irenaeus, but subject to evolution, perhaps through repeated redactions. That Gnostic documents should evolve would seem to be consistent with the Gnostic taste for innovation, and with the Gnostic depreciation of authority and historical authentication. Orthodoxy, on the other hand, very quickly acquired a belief that the exact texts should be preserved for posterity. We should therefore allow for the shifting character of Gnostic texts, and this is probably a neglected principle, particularly by those who seek information about the very early form of Christianity from the Gnostic Gospels. In my view, the Nag Hammadi corpus should be taken as a collage of documents, with pieces dating from the second to the sixth century. We should suspect a variety of interpolations, and the study of late Platonism and later Arian philosophy will help pinpoint some of these.

It is the suspicion of the present writer that part of the Gospel of Truth, at least in the form as given in the Nag Hammadi corpus, might be quite late. It could belong to the Arian period: the statement *The name of the Father is the Son* looks like a sophisticated entry into the Trinitarian debate, an attempt to say the ultimately paradoxical thing, that God is both identical with, and different from, the Son. In other words, the Gospel of Truth is reacting to the philosophical problems generated by the Trinitarian debate. Now these problems were not clearly perceived until the impact of Arius was felt, and he lived from 250-336 approximately. Though Clement of Alexandria and Justin had a hand in creating the problems of subordinationism,[8] neither of them perceived them in the manner of people who lived after Arius. The author of the Gospel of Truth, or at least of the version we have now, seems to perceive the problem, and to offer a harmonizing solution, since the Son is seen to share in the identity of the Father by being his name (not *having* his name, but *being* it). The Arian Eunomius, bête noire of Basil and Gregory of Nyssa, discusses names over and over again in his Apology.[9] He lived roughly from 340-396, and opposed the idea of likeness between the Father and Son: he saw the question of naming and being as crucial, and chose to give the Father a negative name, *the ingenerate* (*agennētos*). Eunomius bases his whole case for dissimilitude on the separateness of names:

> For similarity of being compels those, who hold this opinion about them, to name them with the same nouns.[10]

Different names imply difference in being: this is Eunomius's principle, repeatedly advanced in his Apology.[11] Now we are closer to the milieu of the Gospel of Truth; the philosophy of names occupies the same prominence, and the same concern to handle the problem of the Trinity through this approach is present. Perhaps the author of the Gospel even agrees with Eunomius's principle, whether he knew it from him or someone else, since with a bold stroke he solves the problem. There is no difference in names, but one *is* the name of the other. Christ is an *onoma*, a noun: his being is not material, or historical, but semantic.

Let us now, having attempted to situate the problematic of the Gospel more exactly, return to the substance of the philosophy involved. Many scholars have attempted to find a context for the Gospel by exploring the name terminology. The commentary by Malinine et al.[12] refers to Clement of Alexandria's *Excerpta ex Theodoto* 26.1, and 31.4: the first of these identifies the name with the Son, and adds that this name is invisible. (The invisibility of the name is found in the Gospel of Truth 38.17.) The second passage identifies the name and the Son, but adds that He is the "shape of the aeons."[13] These parallels are two of the closest to have been adduced so far, despite the years of research which have passed since 1956, the date of the Malinine/Puech/ Quispel commentary. Other attempts at parallels have been looser: those of the Puech/Quispel/Van Unnik work are limited to the New Testament. The expression *onoma kainon* is adduced,[14] and in relation to Gospel 38.10 (. . . he begot him as a son. He gave him his name which belonged to him . . .), they cite Luke 3.22 (υἱός μου εἶ ον, ἐγὼ σήμερον γεγέννηκά σε). Giversen[15] takes up a hint of Van Unnik to explore the Epistle to the Hebrews as a possible background, but the identification of Father and Son is one case which cannot be shown to have a precedent in the Epistle to the Hebrews:[16] Giversen however cites some Jewish sources which bear on the name as an independent hypostasis of God,[17] and believes that the name theory of the Gospel must derive from an interpretation of Hebrews 1, 1-5. Giversen also describes what appears to be a rejection by the Gospel of certain claims made in the Epistle to the Hebrews, and indeed the phenomenon of negative parallels, or parallels which correct or revise existing tradition, would seem to be characteristic of Gnosticism. Ménard's commentary[18] claims that the theology of the name is based on Judaeo-Christian sources, as well as on Talmudic Judaism, referring to Daniélou,[19] and sees some expression of this Judaeo-Christian tradition in the Shepherd of Hermas. These passages, however, simply refer to the "name of the Lord" in a common-or-garden way.[20] Arai[21] refers to the view of Quispel, enunciated in "The Jung Codex,"[22] that there may be here a play on words involving the meaning of Jahweh, but also to the texts of Clement mentioned above,[23] to the Pistis Sophia CA 12, 11 and to various Jewish apocryphal sources. Lastly, J.D. Dubois[24] has carried out detailed study of the background through a review of Ménard's work, and in particular of the differences between his 1962 and 1972 editions of the Gospel of Truth.[25] Dubois emphasizes the early date of the Gospel, aligning it with Justin, or the Shepherd of Hermas, and this of course runs counter to the suggestion of the present article, at least in some respects. His inquiry into the background of the name theology is exhaustive, and covers virtually every lead possible.

One difficulty with tracing the pedigree of the name theology is that almost every religious culture of the day attached some mysterious significance to names. Even Rome had a secret name, which could not be divulged except at secret ceremonies.[26] Virtually every superstition or religion which graced the Roman Empire probably had some interest in the power of names, and in discovering the real precedents for the Gospel of Truth, we must try to limit the field somehow. It is useless to repeat here the list of possibilities compiled so thoroughly by Dubois, but it should be noted that the works of Quispel[27] and Daniélou,[28] discussed by him, gave the study of the issue a great deal of impetus in their day. But one thing is crucial here, against which the validity of all parallels must be tested: it is the principle of the identification of the being of the Son with the name of the Father. That the name of Jesus should have some significance is scarcely surprising. That it should have come to acquire some magical properties is in no way astounding; indeed it would have been more surprising if it had not. The Judaeo-Christian background shows how this developed, but this is not important. What is important is the identification, Name of Father = Son, and the thought that a being can be a name for someone else. There is here a real conceptual leap, which is not explained by any of the parallels which limit the name to the sphere of the Son, and to Christological explorations. Quispel is probably on the right track when he develops the theme of the unpronounceable name, Shem Hammephorash, of Jewish mysticism.[29] But we really need here is an unspeakable God, unknowable except through the Son, and the unpronounceable name of Judaism does not only refer to the highest principle. The problem being dealt with by the Gospel of Truth is much more akin to the Arian problem of the remote transcendent Father, coupled with the visible and knowable Son. And the Gospel uses the seemingly unusual idea of the name as existent, as having an ontic status of its own.

On this basis, we should pursue the issue not through the Christological development of Jewish name theology, but rather through the study of Father/Name connections. A passage of Philo[30] provides a real precedent: in the Confusion of Tongues 145ff., Philo is discussing God in a Middle-Platonist vein, with much use of Platonic vocabulary.[31] Philo then refers to the intermediary principle, the Logos, who is an agent of meaning and reason in the world:

> And many names belong to [the Logos]:   for he is called . . . the Name of God . . . and the Man after his image.[32]

Substitute "the Son" for "the Logos" and the precedent for the Gospel of Truth is clear.   It is clearer still when we reflect on Philo's understanding of the Logos: it is the "most senior" image of God,[33] and gives meaning to things, much like the Stoic *logos spermatikos*.[34] That the principle of reason and meaning should be called a "name" for someone else is at least comprehensible.   Plato's intermediary is not a person but an hypostasis, and so it can more easily embrace abstract ideas.   The logos/name identification can be readily understood, and it is the addition of Jesus Christ to the logos theme which leads to the Gospel of Truth name theology.

This is not a chance reference.   There is as strong a philosophy of names in Philo as there is in the Gospel of Truth.   In Philo there is an aetiology of names: Adam is said to provide them for all creatures, as one of his tasks.   Philo is aware of the Cratylus discussion of the value of names, but seems to believe that names are natural, or that they necessarily belong to the things of which they are labels.   One passage suggests that if one knows the nature of things, one will be able to give them the right names.[35]   Philo also practices the science (or the art) of etymology,[36] in the hope of finding truths about nature from the dissection of words into pseudo-derivations: he is not alone in this, since many of the late Greek thinkers toy with words in this manner, despite the elaborate jokes played on etymology in Plato's Cratylus.

The initial names were given by God himself,[37] but after the creation of day and night comes the creation of life.   With the creation of Adam, the task of assigning names is given over to him.[38]   He carries out this task as far as he is able, but when he comes to himself, he falls silent.   Why is Adam unable to name himself?   Philo gives the following answer:

> And it must be asked why, when assigning names to all other creatures Adam did not assign one to himself.   What can be said?   The mind (*nous*) which is in each of us is capable of apprehending other objects, but is incapable of knowing itself. . . . It is likely, then, that Adam, that is the Mind

(*nous*), though he names and apprehends other things, gives no name to himself, since he is ignorant of himself and his own nature.[39]

Naming and knowledge are thus intimately related. Philo does not believe in the self-thought of Thought (*noēsis noēseōs*) at least on the human level. Such reflexiveness is impossible, and so self-naming is impossible. There is no doubt a reflection here on the ordinary human experience of name-giving: a child receives a name from its parents, and does not name itself. One receives one's name from that which is ontologically prior. Adam is the antecedent for the whole human race, but he must be named by his own antecedent, God himself. God only knows himself, and so he only can offer a name for himself. All this gives meaning to Philo's claim that the Logos is the name of God: it is his self-expression. It is an entity, an hypostasis, a thing, but also a semantic entity. It is a thing which signifies.

This line of thought is quite close to the Gospel of Truth. There is an intimate relationship between knowledge and naming in the Gospel: The Father knows, gives form, and names in that order (27). But in the Gospel there is the variation that by receiving a name from God, one ceases to be ignorant: that is, by being known, one knows (21). If one receives a name (from above), one knows whence one comes, and whither one is going (22). But again, as in Philo, names reveal nature, and they have a real rather than conventional meaning.

The culmination of this development comes with section 38. In 39 the Philonic principle seems to be reiterated: "He gave a name to himself since he sees himself, he alone having the power to give himself a name."[40] The relationship of knowledge, being, and naming is preserved throughout this passage, aided and abetted by the Philonic identification of the *logos* as God's *onoma*.

> Now the name of the Father is the Son. It is he who first gave a name to the one who came forth from him, who was himself, and he begot him as a son. He gave him his name which belonged to him; he is the one to whom belongs all that exists around him, the Father. His is the name; his is the Son. It is possible for him to be seen. But the name is invisible because it alone is the mystery of the invisible which comes to ears that are completely filled with it. For indeed the Father's name is not spoken, but it is apparent through a Son.[41]

One comparison with the last sentence is irresistible: that with Wittgenstein, who also believes in the category of that which is shown, but which is inexpressible:

> There are, indeed, things which cannot be put into words. They *make themselves manifest (Dies zeigt sich)*. They are what is mystical.[42]

But the oddity of the Gospel of Truth position is that this manifestation of the inexpressible is also a name, which is, on the face of it, an expressible entity. Nevertheless the author grasps the contradictions necessary to the maintenance of this view: God has a name, which is not spoken; this name is visible, but it is not seen. (We may compare the Gospel's "sons of the name" to Philo's "sons of the most holy logos."[43]) The contradictions here seem to be deliberate, and this technique is not foreign to the Gnostic writings in general. The Gnostics are not great devotees of the law of the excluded middle, since they deliberately use contradictions.

The closest Gnostic parallel to this theorizing may well be the passage of the *Tripartite Tractate* which refers to the aeons as names: they are said to "be" names, rather than have them.[44] The aeons are all emanations of the Father, as well as names, and their existence makes speech possible. This passage also shows a tendency to reify the semantic, to make being itself significant.

Thus the background in Philo seems to provide some elements of the philosophical substance of the Gospel passage. This must be said. But we need not conclude that this is the only proximate text, nor that the Gospel passage is early by virtue of the link with Philo.

Philo's influence was not limited to his century, nor to the second century. His thought was one of the major ingredients in the development of Christian philosophy, and cannot be contained in the early sphere of Christian development (see note 46). Indeed Gregory of Nyssa asserts that Eunomius borrowed from Philo (*contra Eun.* III, 8 Jaeger), and so the apparent link with Philo need not detain us in the second century.

For the fact is that the Arian controversy of Eunomius's time (i.e. the fourth and fifth centuries) provides an even more closely related context for this passage of the Gospel of Truth. We have already quoted from Eunomius on the importance of names. But further, Eunomius makes the crucial step of assimilating names with being: that is, he regards certain specific names as existents. Names and being are identified, and the tendency to objectify language is the crucial part of our search, since this is what enables the Gospel of Truth to say that the Son is the "name-entity" of the Father. Scholars often find this part of Eunomius baffling, and the Gospel of Truth causes the same puzzlement, for the same reason: language is given ontic status.

Gregory of Nyssa, in attacking Eunomius, could almost be attacking the Gospel of Truth:

"For being is not the same thing as being uttered. (οὐ γὰρ ταυτόν ἐστι τῷ εἶναι τὸ λέγεσθαι) (*Contra Eun.* II, 161 Jaeger.)

Or alternatively:

God is not an utterance, nor does his existence consist in being voiced or uttered. (οὐ γὰρ ῥῆμα ὁ θεὸς οὐδε φωνῇ καὶ φθόγγῳ ἔχει τὸ εἶναι) (*Contra Eun.* II, 148 Jaeger)

Gregory is of course attacking Eunomius, but his point is that language and being have been confused, and that there is a tendency to assimilate the linguistic with the ontological. His attack could equally well apply to this passage of the Gospel of Truth. Names do not have existence (*hypostasin echei*), says Gregory (*Contra Eun.* II, 589).

My claim is then, that our passage of the Gospel of Truth belongs to this particular context of debate, and that it has drawn its inspiration from the same source which influenced Eunomius, and against which Gregory reacted at such length. Without this background, in which names can be said to "be," it is almost impossible to understand the Gospel of Truth, at least in this passage.

Where does all this come from? We may consider the "divine names" of the Pseudo-Dionysius, those names which are statues (*agalmata*) before the contemplating mind (PG 3, 909B), and work back from here. The tradition that certain specific names have a privileged status, and that they exist as beings to the contemplative mind, can be traced back to Proclus.[45] For Proclus certain names are products of the divine procession: they are strewn across the real as *ichnē* (traces) of the divine (*On the Cratylus*, ed. Pasquali, pp. 29-35). In these pages Proclus provides an archaeology of names of all types (p. 34), and claims that conceiving and naming the gods is the same thing (p. 33). But the essential is the passage which suggests that names are part of transcendent being (τον . . . ἰδρυμένων ὀνομάτων, p. 29; names are ἴχνη and συνθήματα, p. 30). For Proclus, names exist like forms: they fix the mind, and guarantee language. Proclus's word may not be made flesh, but it is at least reified.

Thus Proclus, though later, provides evidence of an interest in name-beings. It is probably that the Neoplatonist sources of Aetius and Eunomius already contained material of this kind, and that they also had some influence on Gnostic speculation. This interest in the ontology of names is probably associated with a revival of interest in both Plato's Cratylus, and in some circles with a recovery of certain of Philo's ideas.

It is suggested therefore, that Aetius and Eunomius were receptive of Neoplatonic influences, or Philonic influences, or both, on the subject of the ontological basis of certain privileged names. It is further suggested that the Gospel of Truth passage about the name of the Father can only be explained in terms of such a context as this: it is probably that it represents an interpolation intended to address this new phase of the Trinitarian debate.

On grounds provided by intellectual history, therefore, the "name of the Father" passage appears to be a late addition to an early text. The onus is on those who believe this passage to be early to offer an "*explication de texte*" in philosophical terms, which allows us to understand its meaning. The adducing of loose parallels simply leaves it in limbo, an enigma to the reader. The philosophical substance needs to be drawn out of this text, in order for it to articulate clearly.

It is not, of course, the first time that Trinitarian philosophy has been perceived in a Gnostic text. In relation to *The Three Steles of Seth*, Tardieu comments on the triadic structure of the divinity in that writing:

> . . . it can be said that the modalism of the monad-triad notion in the three steles of Seth contains in raw form some of the conceptual matter of the Arian crisis, which found its birth in Egypt, the land of the Gnostics, and which was in full cry when Codex VII was being written and bound . . .[46]

In conclusion. The philosophy of names in the Gospel of Truth begins with a familiar model: the family experience. Fathers give sons their names: in this way they create them, and give them something of their own identity. Names do create dynasties, traditions and realities, where there was previously nothing. They bring about being. The Gospel now proceeds, in a manoeuvre typical of the *Via negativa*, to cancel parts of the model. This family, or more exactly Father/Son relationship, differs in that normally two beings use the one family name. In this case, however, the Son becomes the name of the Father. He is nothing other than this name.

The Gospel of Truth also shows a tendency to reify the semantic, and this is not entirely unfamiliar in earlier Gnosticism. Marcus's system of thought has all reality generated from a word, and reality in its successive stages is composed of discourse. Whereas the Pythagorean view emphasizes number as the essential structure of reality, and the Neoplatonist emphasizes being, Marcus emphasizes language. For him the texture of the real is linguistic: the beginning is the word "beginning" (*archē*), and each letter of this word generates another word (*alpha, rho* and so on). These words generate other words in a proliferating series, and the most material or most mundane sounds are the vowel sounds. These are more "sounded" than the consonants, and so they are lower and more matter-like. The emanation and procession of Marcus is entirely linguistic: it is a self development of language.[47]

This tendency to objectify the semantic, to make a place for it within ontology, is therefore already present. We have it here in the Gospel of Truth, but deployed in a unique way, and in a unique context. The text seems to bespeak a sophistication in Trinitarian matters which is not characteristic of second century Christianity. The Gospel of Truth responds to a problem which has arisen, and belongs to a period in which the problem has been clearly identified. It offers a solution as Augustine's *De Trinitate* offers a solution, to the yawning gap between Father and Son that had been opened up by the Christian Platonists. It maintains the unity of the Father and the Son and at the same time safeguards both the incommunicability of the Father and the communicability of the Son. What closer relationship can there be, than being someone's name? As indicated earlier, the philosophy of Eunomius has a great preoccupation with names and their use in respect of the Trinity, and it seems that Eunomius is responding to the same set of problems.

It is possible that the Gospel of Truth was first written in about 170, subjected to revision and development in later periods, and that the Nag Hammadi text constitutes a version which includes a response to the Arian debate, coming from the period 320-360 A.D. The author may have used the ideas of Philo[48] for the purpose of responding to the Arian problem, or he may have used contemporary thinking about the Cratylus, or both; but in any case he was able to build on the existing Gnostic tendency to reify the semantic.

Addendum by Michel Tardieu

The thesis put forward by Mortley appears to me to be sound, on condition that two further arguments, which are fundamental and closely associated with each other, are brought forward. The first is a *textual* argument.

The formula: *pren de mpiōt pe psēre* (I.38, 6-7) is absent from the Sahidic version of the *Ev. Ver.* (Codex XII). The Akhmim version, Codex I 30, 27-37, 21 corresponds to XII 53, 19-60, 29; the two missing pages in XII (= 55-56) correspond to I.32, 1-34, 4. Thus the beginning and the end of the Codex I text of the Gospel of Truth do not figure in Codex XII; strictly speaking, this does not allow us to say that the above-mentioned formula is an interpolation belonging to the Akhmim version. However it *is* odd that Codex XII stops exactly where the passage on the name of the Father begins in Codex I, so that the middle of Codex I 38, line 6 gives the impression of being the logical conclusion of the end of the early text (Codex XII), and it must have appeared at the beginning of the last page 61.

A careful comparison of the two extant versions shows that the Sahidic version (Codex XII) is based on a short text, on which the Akhmim version (Codex I) appears to be a commentary. Moreover, in a thesis presented to the Ecole Pratique des Hautes Etudes (5th section) in 1980 (page 31), M. Pezin has drawn this conclusion, on the basis of elements common to both versions: this view is still valid.

Consequently, the Sahidic text (Codex XII) provides evidence of a non-glossed *Ev. Her.*, that is, the writing of Valentinus himself; that of (Codex I) belongs to a later stage of development of a school which calls itself Valentinian, but whose theological interests were very different from those of its founder. Thus, not only the formula but the whole discussion on the name of the Father, which concludes the Akhmim version, involve additional material which reflects a contemporary debate, and I agree with Mortley that this is the Arian debate.

At this point one may refer to a second argument of an historical kind, raised by me in another connection in the Bulletin de la Société Française d'Egyptologie 94 (1982) 14-15.

The first and foremost adversaries of Arius, Aetius and Eunomius were the Gnostics. The evidence of Arius himself, and that of the pro-Arian historian Philostorgius, is clear on this point. Further, I have found an unpublished fragment of a Nag Hammadi text, which is quoted and attacked in debate, and this is a fragment of Eunomius himself.

Mortley's discovery must be upheld, in my view. It brings a new element to the Arian controversies, and gives an historical context to the recasting of the *Ev. Ver.* given in Codex I. I further consider that careful comparison of the whole passage on the name of the Father in *Ev. Ver.* I with Eunomius's Apology, confirms Mortley's view: a Gnostic response to the Arian debate.

M.T. 12.03.1984.

NOTES

1. See W.W. Isenberg, "The Gospel of Truth," in *Gnosticism*, ed. R.M. Grant (N.Y., 1978), p. 158; W. Foerster/R. McL. Wilson, *Gnosis II* (Oxford, 1974), p. 78; K. Grobel, *The Gospel of Truth* (Abingdon, 1960), p. 180; R. Haardt, *Gnosis* (Brill, 1971), p. 234; J.E. Ménard, "L'Évangile de Vérité," *Nag Hammadi Studies*, Vol. II (Brill, 1972), p. 66; S. Arai *Die Christologie des Evangelius Veritatis* (Brill, 1964), p. 62; M. Malinine, H.-Ch. Puech, G. Quispel, *Evangelium Veritatis* (Zurich, 1956), p. 106.

2. B. Standaert, "L'évangile de Vérité; critique et lecture," *New Testament Studies* 22 (1976): 243-275.

3. J. Fineman, "Gnosis and the Piety of Metaphor: The Gospel of Truth," in *The Rediscovery of Gnosticism*, Vol. I, ed. Bentley Layton (Brill, 1980), pp. 289-312.

4. By van Unnik, in *The Jung Codex* (London, 1955), pp. 81ff, followed by Grobel, op. cit., p. 26.

5. But see the questions raised by Wilson, in *Rediscovery of Gnosticism*, pp. 133-145.

6. *Adv. Haer*. III. XI.9.

7. But see Grobel, op. cit., p. 27, who thinks that Irenaeus means "not long ago" by contrast with the canonical Gospels, and that a date between 140 and 170 would fit this description. He reasons that Irenaeus would have said "very recently" if he had meant after 170. There is a lot of supposition here: we do not *know* that Irenaeus was thinking primarily of a comparison with the date of the canonical Gospels, nor do we *know* that he would have thought of five years before, say, as "very recent." He might well have written in, say, 180, of a work written in, say, 172, that it was composed "not long ago."

8. Clement, for example, assimilates God the Father to the One pure, and God the Son to the One-of-parts. He thus creates a relation of superiority to inferiority (Strom. IV.25.156.1-2; Strom. V.12.81.6).

9. See, for example, Migne PG 30, col. 852D, but also throughout.

10. Loc. cit., col. 961A: ἡ γὰρ τῆς οὐσίας ὁμοιότης ταῖς αὐταῖς ὀνομάξειν τροσηγορίαις ἀναγκάξει τοὺς ταύτην περὶ αὐτῶν ἔχοντας τὴν δόξαν.

11. Loc. cit., cols. 848-861.

12. Op. cit., p. 58.

13. *Morphē tōn Aiōnōn* . . .

14. On p. 118; see Revelation 2.17, 3.12.

15. "Evangelium Veritatis and the Epistle to the Hebrews," *Studia Theologica* 13 (1959): 87-96.

16. Op. cit., 89.

17. *Isaiah* 30. 27ff; *Exodus* 23.20. See also *Exodus* 33.18-19. Giversen believes that the author of the Gospel speculated on the first words of the *Epistle to the Hebrews* (1, 1-5) in the light of this material.

18. Op. cit., p. 182.

19. *Théologie du judéo-christianisme*, pp. 199-226.

20. *The Shepherd* VIII.1.1, VIII.6.4. for example.

21. "Die Christologie . . .," op. cit., p. 64.
22. P. 74.
23. P. 71.
24. "Le contexte judaïque du 'nom' dans l'évangile de vérité," *Revue de Théologie et de Philosophie* 24 (1974): 198-216.
25. See Dubois, nn. 1 and 2.
26. Pliny, *Natural History*, 3.65. I owe this information to Dr. T.W. Hillard.
27. "Qumran, John and Jewish Christianity," in *John and Qumran*, ed. J.H. Charlesworth (London, 1972).
28. *Théologie du Judéo-Christianisme* (Paris, 1958), pp. 199-226.
29. "Christliche Gnosis und jüdische Heterodoxie," *Evangelische Theologie* 14 (1954): 474-484.
30. Dubois lists this without comment (p. 211).
31. God is the "maker and father of all," + the "One."
32. The Confusion of Tongues 146: . . . ὄνομα Θεοῦ . . . ὁ κατ᾽ εἰκόνα ἄνθροπος.
33. Op. cit., p. 148.
34. *The Migration of Abraham* 3; The Special Laws III.207.
35. On Husbandry 1.
36. For example, *On the Creation* 127.
37. *On the Creation* 15.
38. Op. cit., p. 148, and *Allegorical Interpretations* I. 91ff.
39. *Allegorical Interpretations* I. 91-92.
40. Trans. MacRae, in *The Nag Hammadi Library*, ed. J.M. Robinson.
41. *Gospel* 38 (trans. MacRae).
42. *Tractatus* 6.522.
43. *Gospel* 38; Philo, *On the Confusion of Tongues*, 147.
44. *Tri. Trac.*, 73.
45. See H.D. Saffrey, "Nouveaux liens objectifs entre le Pseudo-Denys et Proclus," *Revue des sciences philosophiques et theologiques* 63 (1979): 3-16.
46. *Revue des sciences philosophiques et théologiques* 57 (1973): 562-563.
47. Irenaeus, *Adv. Haer.* I.14.1. One notes the ambiguity of the word *stoicheion*: Plato started with four elements (*stoicheia*) in the *Timaeus* (air, earth, fire and water); Marcus also starts with four *stoicheia* (letters) which happen to be the letters of the word "beginning." We should further note that Plato himself treated the logos as a living creature (*logon . . . zōnta empsychon Phaedrus* 276A), a passage interestingly analyzed by J. Derrida, "La Pharmacie de Platon," in *La Dissémination* (Paris, 1972), p. 89: "The logos, an animate living being, is therefore also a begotten being. An *organism*: a body proper, differentiated, with a center and extremities, connections, a head and feet." Derrida compares verbal discourse with the "cadaverous rigidity" of writing (in Plato).
48. Wolfson's *Philo* (Cambridge, Mass., 1948) together with his *The Philosophy of the Church Fathers* (Cambridge, Mass., 1970) provides ample testimony to the way in which Philo was repeatedly used by Christian thinkers.

Theurgic Tendencies in Gnosticism and Iamblichus's Conception of Theurgy

Birger A. Pearson

1. Introduction

The theme of this volume, and the conference out of which it has emerged, focuses upon one of the most intriguing problems in the philosophical and religious history of late antiquity, that of the relationship between Platonism and Gnosticism in the early centuries of our era. It is therefore very significant that scholars from both sides have come together for discussion of this issue — specialists in Platonism on the one hand, and specialists in the "wild underworld" of the Gnostics on the other[1] — and I do not doubt that much new light has been shed on it as a result.[2]

While much of the discussion has focused on setting up comparisons between various platonic systems of thought and language and the metaphysical-mythological systems of the Gnostic texts,[3] relatively little attention has been given in this comparative enterprise to the problem of religious ritual. In this paper, therefore, I have taken up some aspects of ritual in Gnosticism and Neoplatonism. This is admittedly a difficult task, and I hasten to state at the outset that this paper represents an experimental and highly tentative enterprise. Not least of the difficulties involved in this comparative project is that Platonists and Gnostics alike had various and sundry attitudes toward ritual.[4] Not all Platonists appreciated religious ritual (to understate the case!), but then, neither did all Gnostics. If Plotinus (*Enn.* II.9.14) could criticize the Gnostics he knew for their ritual activities — he dismissed their recourse to strange chants and charms and other practices as *goēteia*[5] — some Gnostics could also adopt a critical attitude toward ritual of any sort, claiming that *gnosis* alone is what saves:

> One must not perform the mystery of the ineffable and invisible power through visible and corruptible things of creation, nor that of the unthinkable and immaterial beings through sensible and corporeal things. Perfect salvation is the cognition itself of the ineffable greatness: for since through "Ignorance" came about "Defect" and "Passion," the whole system springing from Ignorance is dissolved by knowledge.[6]

As is well known, ritual came to occupy an increasingly important role in Neoplatonic circles from the time of Porphyry on, especially as a result of the appropriation and study of the *Chaldaean Oracles*.[7] The most extensive and consistent defense of religious ritual by a Neoplatonist author is Iamblichus's treatise *On the Mysteries of Egypt*.[8] On the Gnostic side, we have a number of primary texts which reveal a concern for ritual, containing references to baptism and other rites, as well as ineffable names and *nomina barbara* which doubtless had ritual significance. One of the problems in dealing with the ritual aspects of Gnosticism and Neoplatonism, and especially of considering them together under a common rubric, is that, on the one hand, the Gnostic material lacks a theoretical framework with which to understand the ritual elements; and, on the other hand, the Neoplatonist material, including Iamblichus's famous treatise itself, provides rather scanty information on the actual ceremonies utilized by the Platonist "theurgists." Another obstacle, of course, is the difference in world-view between the Gnostics and the Platonists, high-lighted especially in Plotinus's tract *Against the Gnostics* (*Enn.* II.9). However, it must also be pointed out that some later forms of Gnosticism reflect a temporizing of the original Gnostic anti-cosmism. Moreover there is a discernable development in Neoplatonism which eventually brings it closer to Gnosticism in certain respects.[9] The question can, therefore, be entertained whether the Gnostic and the Neoplatonic rituals are in any way comparable, and whether they might have had some theoretical presuppositions in common. This is what I propose to consider in what follows, knowing full well that many pitfalls lie in the way; knowing, too, that the entire enterprise might turn out to be a blind alley.

Specifically, what I propose to do is to apply Iamblichus's theories concerning ritual to some Gnostic ritual texts, on the hypothesis that some of our Gnostics might have shared something of Iamblichus's theoretical assumptions. If, in addition, some of the Gnostics' ritual activity sheds some light on actual Neoplatonic practice, so much the better.

2. Iamblichus's Defense of Theurgy

Iamblichus's defense of religious ritual in his *DM* is, more specifically, a defense of "theurgy," written in reply to some critical questions on the practice raised by Porphyry.[10] As is well known, "theurgy" still has a "bad press" among scholars of late antiquity. E.R. Dodds, for example, refers to Iamblichus's philosophical defense of theurgy as "a manifesto of irrationalism."[11] Now I do not wish to enter the debate for or against the practice of theurgy, nor do I wish to comment on theurgy at all as it was practiced by the *Juliani*, as reflected in the *Chaldaean Oracles*.[12] What I do want to do is look at Iamblichus's theories in his *DM* as possibly of use in understanding Gnostic ritual. (In any case, Iamblichus's theories do not necessarily coincide with those of the *Juliani*.) In doing so, I also here cheerfully acknowledge the work done on Iamblichus and theurgy by my former student, Gregory Shaw.[13]

The first and most important point to make is that, at least for Iamblichus, "theurgy" does *not* mean "acting upon," or "creating" the gods.[14] Theurgy involves, rather, the works (*erga*) of the gods (*theoi*); the emphasis is on *divine*, not human, activity. This is a central theme in Iamblichus's *DM*.[15] The "work" done in theurgic ritual is the work of the gods, even though it is performed by human beings. Thus, for example, ritual invocations and prayers, and chanting of sacred words, ostensibly directed to the gods, really involves the gods "calling upward" (*anakaloumenoi*) the souls of the theurgists (*DM* I.12).

The *locus classicus* for Iamblichus's position on theurgy, indeed his preference for theurgy (*theia erga*) over intellectual activity, is found in Book II of the *DM*:

> For it is not thought which joins the theurgists to the gods, since (if that were the case) what would prevent those who philosophize theoretically from having theurgic union with the gods? . . . For when we are not engaged in intellection, the *synthēmata* themselves perform by themselves the proper work, and the ineffable power of the gods, to whom these (*synthēmata*) belong, knows by itself its own images. . . .[16]

In other words, the divine rituals are effective *ex opere operato*. A comparison with Christian sacramentalism naturally suggests itself.[17]

The *synthēmata* which are here considered so powerful can be regarded as sacramental elements, consisting of such things as *voces mysticae* and *nomina barbara*, presumably chanted by the theurgists.[18] It is also important to note that Iamblichus considers theurgy to be superior to philosophical contemplation, and not a mere concession to the popular mind.

Iamblichus's view of theurgy is closely connected with his solution to a basic philosophical problem left unresolved by Plato himself, i.e. the problem of the soul's embodiment, and how this embodiment is to be understood. As Shaw puts it,

> This theme of embodiment, and of the descent of the soul, lie at the heart of understanding theurgy; depending on one's solution to this problem, the world and matter, all one's embodied existence, could be seen either as a punishment and burden or as an opportunity to cooperate in manifesting the divine. Theurgy θεουργία, as its etymology suggests, exemplifies the latter solution, for in theurgic rites man became the instrument and beneficiary of the gods.[19]

From what has been said, it is clear that Iamblichus's understanding and practice of theurgy was not simply an aberrant aspect of his life existing alongside his philosophical work, but an integral part of his Platonic philosophy, based essentially on his interpretation of Plato's dialogues. This will be developed further in what follows, as we take up for discussion some examples of Gnostic ritual as reflected in three Coptic Gnostic texts.

3. Three Gnostic Texts

The three Gnostic texts I have chosen to treat here are all found in the Coptic Gnostic "library" discovered near the upper-Egyptian town of Nag Hammadi in 1945: *The Gospel of the Egyptians* (*NHC* III, 2; IV, 2); *The Three Steles of Seth* (*NHC* VII, 5); and *Marsanes* (*NHC* X, 1).[20] These documents are part of a group of Gnostic texts which are considered to belong to the "Sethian" system,[21] a type of Gnosticism which was known to Plotinus and his school in Rome.[22] *Gos. Eg.* and *Steles Seth* have been identified as of special significance for the study of Sethian ritual praxis.[23]   *Marsanes* is, in my view, the most "Platonic" of the Nag Hammadi texts,[24] and contains some features which appear to reflect a kind of Platonism very close to that of Iamblichus.[25]

a. *The Gospel of the Egyptians.*[26]

The title by which this document is usually cited occurs in a secondary colophon (III 69, 6), to which is added yet another title: "the holy book of the great, invisible Spirit" (III 69, 18-20). In the body of the text, at the end, it is stated that the book was written by "the great Seth" (III 68, 2.10-11).[27] The document is referred to by its editors as "a typical work of mythological Gnosticism,"[28] consisting of the following sections:

I.   The origin of the heavenly world (III 40, 12 - 55, 16 = IV 50, 1 - 67, 1)

II.   The origin and salvation-history of the race of Seth (III 55, 16 - 68, 8 = IV 67, 2 - 78, 10)

III.   Concluding invocations of a liturgical character (III 66, 8 - 67, 26 = IV 78, 10 - 80, 15)

IV.   Conclusions, dealing with the writing and transmission of the book (III 68, 1 - 69, 17 = IV 80, 15 - 81, 2+)[29]

It would appear from this outline that the material in this document oriented to ritual is concentrated in the third section, containing the liturgical invocations. The first section presents a highly complicated heavenly world, beginning with the supreme God dwelling in light and silence, and featuring successive emanations from him down to the "seed of the Great Seth." But H.M. Schenke has pointed out that *Gos. Eg.* is not simply a treatise developing a mythological system. Its main subject is not emanation, but *prayer.* As Schenke puts it, "the writing aims to demonstrate and teach how to invoke the super-celestial powers correctly and efficaciously, and which powers to invoke." *Gos. Eg.* is therefore to be understood as "the mythological justification of a well-defined ritual of baptism including the invocations that must be performed therein."[30]

Consider the following passage (unfortunately broken up by lacunae in the MSS.), dealing with a manifestation of God called "Domedon Doxomedon":[31]

[The] Father of the great light [who came] forth from the silence, he is [the great] Doxomedon-aeon in which [the thrice-]male child rests. And the throne of his [glory] was established [in it, this one] on which his unrevealable name [is inscribed], on the tablet, . . . whose name [is] an [invisible] symbol. [A] hidden, [invisible] mystery came forth: IIIIIIIIIIIIIIIII[III] HHHHHHHHHHHHHHHHHHHHH[HH O] OOOOOOOOOOOOOOOOOOOOO YY[YYY] YYYYYYYYYYYYY-YYYY EEEEEEEEEEEEEEEEEEEEE AAAAAAA [AAAA]-

AAAAAAAAAA   ΩΩΩΩΩΩΩ[ΩΩΩ]ΩΩΩΩΩΩΩΩΩ   (III   43,
13 - 44, 9)

Note that the ineffable name given to the Doxomedon aeon is
made up of the seven Greek vowels written 22 times each (the number
of the letters in the Hebrew/Aramaic alphabet, which, of course, has no
vowels). The vowels are not given in order. The order presented here
may conceal another divine name: *Iēou e(stin) A (kai) Ō.* That is,
Doxomedon may be identified with the being called "Yeou" in some
other gnostic texts, such as the "Books of Jeu."[32]
However one construes the ineffable name hidden in the vowels,
it is most probable that this name was meant to be chanted in a ritual
context, in a language thought to be appropriate to the divine beings
invoked, as revealed to the Gnostics. Iamblichus, too, knows of the use
of ineffable names, including "unintelligible" (*asēma*) names, and
argues that they are not, in fact, without sense to the gods:

> But to us let them be unknowable, or known only to some (of us), the
> interpretations of which we have received from the gods. To the gods,
> indeed, all are significant (although) not in an effable manner, nor in such
> a way as that which is significant and indicative to men through their
> imaginations, but either intellectually, according to the human mind, itself
> divine, or ineffably, both better and more simply, and according to the mind
> which is united with the gods.[33]

Iamblichus goes on to discuss the use of "barbarian" language in
invocations of the gods. With special reference to the sacred nations of
the Egyptians and the Assyrians, he says,

> We think it is necessary to offer our communication to the gods in a
> language related to them. . . . Those who first learned the names of the
> gods, connecting them with their own proper tongue, handed them down to
> us, that we might always preserve inviolate, (in a language) peculiar and
> proper to these (names), the sacred law of tradition.[34]

Iamblichus's rationale for the use of unintelligible (*asēma*) and
foreign (*barbara*) names would surely strike a responsive chord with the
Gnostics. The Gnostics undoubtedly had similar notions concerning the
"appropriateness" of certain names or vowel-combinations to the
various heavenly beings invoked in their ritual. Such ritual not only
included chanting, but also the use of ritual devices. The text cited
above is a case in point: Reference is made to the name inscribed "on
the tablet (*pyxos*)." This tablet, as the Greek "loan-word" used for it

suggests,[35] was a piece of boxwood on which the name was inscribed. It is at least possible that the Gnostics would have considered a boxwood tablet to be an appropriate receptacle for the divine name, along the theoretical lines set forth by Iamblichus in his discussion of various "stones, plants, animals, aromatics," etc. deemed in some way to be "sacred" and "divine-like" (*DM* V.23). Iamblichus also refers, in his discussion of divination, to the use of "sacred inscriptions of characters" (*DM* III.14; 134, 5-6). The ritual chanting of the divine names by the Gnostics, in any case, can easily be understood, along the lines suggested by Iamblichus, as vehicles by which man is "called up" to the gods (*DM* I.12).

The second section of *Gos. Eg.* (as delineated above) tells of the origin and salvation-history of the seed of Seth (=the Gnostics). In this document Seth is the gnostic Savior who passes through three "advents" (flood, fire, and final judgment) "in order to save (the race) who went astray" (III 63, 4-9). In his work of salvation Seth undergoes a "baptism through a Logos-begotten body which the great Seth prepared for himself, secretly through the virgin in order that the saints may be begotten by the holy Spirit, through invisible secret symbols" (III 63, 10-15). This section of the text culminates in a reference to the baptism which the Gnostics are to undergo, a ritual which involves "invocations," "renunciations" (of the world), "five seals" of baptism (presumably in water), and sacred instructions (III 66, 2-6). The whole process entails immortalization: "These will by no means taste death" (III 66, 7-8).

It is, of course, clear that the kinds of rituals approved by Iamblichus in his *DM* do not specifically include baptism,[36] but his general defense of ritual would surely cover such a rite. In any case, it is the invocations associated with baptismal ritual which receive prominence in *Gos. Eg.* Indeed, the climax of the book is the passage which consists entirely of prayer-invocations (III 66, 8 - 67, 27 = IV 78, 10 - 80, 15). In this set of invocations the Gnostic ritually experiences the divine light, and feels himself purified and drawn upward to God, as the following excerpts surely imply:

> I have become light. . . . Thou art my place of rest . . . the formless one who exists in the formless ones, who exists, raising up the man in whom thou wilt purify me into thy life, according to thine imperishable name . . . (III 67, 4.16-22)

This experience could equally well be that described by Iamblichus, who speaks of invocations of the gods as really involving the benevolent act of the gods in illuminating the theurgists and drawing their souls up to themselves (*DM* I.12). In this experience the soul,

> leaving behind her own life, has exchanged it for the most blessed energy of the gods. If, therefore, the ascent through invocations bestows on the priests purification from passions, deliverance from generation, and unity with the divine principle, how then could anyone connect it with passions? For such (an invocation) does not draw the impassible and pure (gods) down to passibility and impurity, but, on the contrary, it makes us, who had become passible through generation, pure and immoveable.[37]

Even more to the point are Iamblichus's remarks on the power of prayer (*DM* V.26).[38]   Iamblichus discusses three types of prayer: *Synagōgon*, leading to union with, and knowledge (*gnōrisis*) of, the divine; *syndetikon*, eliciting the gifts of the gods even prior to the uttered prayer; and *hē arrētos henōsis*, establishing ineffable union with the gods and causing the soul's perfect repose in the gods.   He goes on to say that

> the first pertains to illumination; the second to a common effectiveness; and the third to the perfect plenitude of the (divine) fire . . .

Prayer, for Iamblichus,

> offers us habitual contact with the splendid stream of light, and quickly perfects our inner being for contact with the gods until it raises us to the very summit. . . .[39]

Such observations, indeed, could be taken as a veritable commentary on the Gnostic passage cited.

b. *The Three Steles of Seth (NHC VII, 5).*[40]

The *incipit* of this document identifies it as a "revelation of Dositheos[41] about the three steles of Seth, the Father of the living and unshakable race." The document consists essentially of three sets of prayer-invocations corresponding to three "steles"[42] of Seth, addressed, in ascending order, to the three divine beings of the Sethian Gnostic Triad: (Ger-)Adamas (the Son, 118, 24 - 121, 17); Barbelo (the Mother, 121, 18 - 124, 15); and the transcendent Father (124, 16 - 126, 31). The concluding section of the text (126, 32 - 127, 21) provides the key to understanding the function of the three "steles," consisting, as it does, of liturgical references and directions. Despite the similarities with other "Sethian" Gnostic texts in which the theme of mystic "ascent" occurs, especially *Allogenes*,[43] *Steles Seth* stands apart as a liturgical text. H.M. Schenke has drawn special attention to this feature, referring to the concluding material as liturgical "rubrics," directing how the prayer formulae are to be used and what is to be achieved in the ritual. Schenke concludes that "the *Three Steles of Seth* is the etiology of a mystery of ascension of the Sethian community."[44]

The main thread running through the three sets of invocations is that of praise or "blessing." The first stele begins, "I bless thee Father, Geradama(s)" (118, 25-26). The third concludes, "We have blessed thee, for we are empowered. We have been saved, for thou hast willed always that we all do this" (126, 29-31). In the course of these blessings and invocations, the three-fold nature of God is underscored with reference to the Neoplatonic triad of "Existence-Life-Mind," and language derived from Middle Platonism is found throughout. These details have been commented on before,[45] and need not occupy us here. What we are especially interested in is the ritual use made of this text, and such light as might be shed on it with reference to Iamblichus.

We have seen that *Gos. Eg.* is to be understood in relation to the Gnostic rite of baptism. In the case of *Steles Seth*, we presumably have to do with another rite, that of "cultic ascension."[46] The following passage from the concluding material in *Steles Seth* is crucial:

> He who will remember these and give glory always will become perfect among those who are perfect and unattainable from any quarter. For they all bless these individually and together. And afterwards they shall be silent. And just as they were ordained, they ascend. After the silence, they descend. From the third they bless the second; after these the first. The way of ascent is the way of descent (127, 6-21).

From these rubrics one can see that the prayers in Seth's three steles are recited in ascending and descending order: 1-2-3-3-2-1, with an observance of ritual silence between the first and second recitations of the third stele, the invocation of the Primal Father. The efficacy of these prayers can easily be understood on the same terms as the invocations in *Gos. Eg.*, discussed above, with reference to Iamblichus's theories. These prayers can, in fact, be called "theurgic" prayers, and were probably chanted as hymns.[47] In this case, we have a special ritual of "ascent," arguably comparable to the theurgic ritual of *anagōgē* reflected in the *Chaldaean Oracles*.[48] Though the rituals of the "Sethians" and the "Chaldaeans" are not the same, their meaning and efficacy can presumably be understood on the same terms.

Of special interest is this rubric: "The way of ascent is the way of descent" (127, 20). This enigmatic statement, with its allusion to a famous fragment of Heraclitus,[49] has parallels in other Gnostic and mystical texts. For example, the (Valentinian) Marcosians are said to have claimed that their "Redemption" mystery "leads them *down* into the profundities of Bythos."[50] The Jewish Merkabah mystics enigmatically referred to their mystical journeys as a *descent* to the Merkabah, i.e. the Throne of God.[51] Perhaps phenomenologically closer to the ritual use of the invocations in ascending and descending order in *Steles Seth* is Epiphanius's description of ritual intercourse practiced by the Phibionites, a "libertine" Gnostic sect (*Haer.* 26.9.6-9). At each act of intercourse the "barbarian name" of one of the 365 archons is invoked. After 365 acts of intercourse, the acts and invocations are repeated in descending order. Completing the sum total of 730 acts, Epiphanius tells us, the adept boldly says, "I am the Christ, for I have descended downward through the names of the 365 archons."[52]

The Gnostic understanding of ritual "ascent" as "descent" can be illuminated with reference to Iamblichus's understanding of the ascent and descent of the soul, and the place of ritual in effecting the soul's ascent. Iamblichus asserts that ascents and descents of souls are essentially two sides of the same coin, as the following passage in *DM* indicates:

> The works of sacred ritual have been determined from of old by pure and intellectual laws. Lower (states) are liberated by means of a greater order and power, and when we change from (the inferior) to a better lot, we abandon the inferior (states). And this is not effected contrary to the divine law (laid down) from the beginning, as though the gods were changed according to the sacred rite subsequently performed. But from the first descent God sent souls down here that they might return again above to him. Therefore there is no change (in the divine plan)[53] arising from such an ascent, nor are descents and ascents of souls opposed to each other.[54]

Of course Iamblichus does not mean that "ascent" and "descent" are merely a mechanical process. Ascent can only be realized as the soul fulfills its responsibilities as a descended soul, specifically with recourse to the proper ritual, including, perhaps, even ritual re-enactments of the descent.[55] For Iamblichus, every divine or demonic power[56] governing the various levels of the cosmos, even the most base, must be appropriately honored. In this respect, the Gnostic ritual

ascent reflected in *Steles Seth* differs from Iamblichus's theurgy, in that
the prayers are addressed, not to lower, cosmic beings, but to the primal
heavenly Triad of Father, Mother, and Son. The power of these prayers
are nevertheless to be understood, with Iamblichus, in his discussion of
prayer and sacrifice, as "anagogic, effective, and fulfilling."[57]

Perhaps more clarity can be achieved on what is meant by "ascent
as descent" in *Steles Seth* by turning to the last text to be taken up in
this paper: *Marsanes*.

c. *Marsanes (NHC X, 1)*.[58]

This tractate is unfortunately very badly preserved. It occupies the
entirety of the extant material in Codex X, at least 68 discrete pages, of
which many consist of only small fragments.[59] The first ten pages are
relatively intact; here we encounter material relating to a Gnostic ascent
experience, including discussion of the various levels of reality,
symbolically referred to as "seals." The middle portion of the tractate
contains materials on the mystical meaning of the letters of the
alphabet, and their relation both to the human soul and to the names
of gods and angels. The rest is hopelessly fragmentary; the bulk of this
tractate, therefore, is totally lost. This is unfortunate, for it must have
been an important text in Gnostic circles, if one can judge from what is
said of the prophet Marsanes in the Untitled Text from the Bruce
Codex.[60]

I have already indicated (above) my view that this text contains
some features which reflect a kind of Platonism close to that of
Iamblichus. The starting point for this observation is the surprising
statement, very surprising for a Gnostic text, that "in every respect the
sense-perceptible world is [worthy] of being saved entirely" (X 5, 24-
26).

Such a statement coheres very well with Iamblichus's understanding
of the Platonic tradition, both with respect to his view of matter and his
understanding of the descended soul.[61] For Iamblichus, matter is not
evil *per se*, and the descent of the soul into matter is not regarded as a
"fall," but as a demiurgic function. In this, Iamblichus is following
Plato himself, particularly Plato's discussion of the *psychogonia* in his
Timaeus (41a-42a).[62] Indeed, such a view can even be brought into
conformity with other passages in Plato, including the famous passages
in which the body (*sōma*) is referred to as a "tomb" (*sēma*). In the
Cratylus (400c), for example, it is said that the soul has the body as a

"tomb," i.e. an "enclosure" (*peribolos*), "in order that it might be saved" (*hina sōzētai*).[63]

In *Marsanes*, in the very next passage after the statement just now discussed, a figure called "The Self-Begotten One" or *Autogenés* is referred to. This figure, I think, represents symbolically the descending soul in its demiurgic function.[64] Unfortunately the text is corrupt and riddled with lacunae, but his descent progressively ("part by part") into the world of multiplicity is clearly reflected; the result of this descent is that "he saved a multitude" (X 5, 27 - 6, 16). Autogenes here plays the same role as "the demiurgic intellect" in Iamblichus's discussion of Egyptian theology (*DM* VIII.3). There Iamblichus describes the progressive unfolding of the divine from the Ineffable God prior even to the First God, down to the demiurgic intellect, and then down to the world of generation. In a summary statement he says,

> And thus the doctrines of the Egyptians concerning first principles, from above (down) to the last things, begins from One and proceeds into multiplicity, the many being governed by the One. And everywhere the indefinite nature is controlled by a certain definite measure and by the sole supreme Cause of all things. God produced matter by dividing materiality from essentiality. This matter, being living, the Demiurge took and fashioned from it the simple and impassable spheres. The last of it (matter) he ordered into generated and corruptible bodies.[65]

For Iamblichus, the soul, in order to ascend, must properly learn to descend. Ascent to the One is mediated through the Many,[66] specifically with recourse, in ritual, to the various levels of the cosmos ordained by God. The rituals themselves are appointed in conformity with sacred law:

> (Each ritual) imitates the order of the gods, intelligible and heavenly. (Each ritual) contains the eternal measures of beings and the wonderful deposits such as are sent down here from the Demiurge and Father of All. By means of them, the unutterable things are given expression through ineffable symbols. The formless things are mastered in forms; the things which are superior to any image are reproduced through images, and all things are accomplished solely through a divine cause.[67]

In a very important passage in *Marsanes* (X 2, 12 - 4, 23) dealing with the various levels of reality, from the material level to the level beyond being, each is symbolically related to a "seal" (*sphragis*). There are thirteen of these "seals," presented in ascending order. The first three seals are "cosmic" and "material" (2, 16-19); the thirteenth expresses the unknown, "silent" God. The writer periodically reminds his readers (unfortunately!) that he has already taught them about these seals (2, 19-21; 3, 4-9). The question now arises as to the function of these "seals." Though this passage is not a liturgical text, it is probable that our Gnostic author is enigmatically referring to a ritual praxis when he discusses the thirteen "seals." Indeed, what may be reflected here is a theurgic ascent-praxis in which the various "seals" are to be understood as equivalent to what Iamblichus calls the *synthēmata*.[68] The reference to "cosmic" and "material" "seals," indeed, reminds us of Iamblichus's use of material *synthēmata* and his recourse to material objects in theurgic ritual, such as stones, plants, etc. (*DM* V.23). It is in such a context that we can understand another passage in *Marsanes* (unfortunately fragmentary), in which "wax images" and "emerald likenesses" are mentioned (35, 1-3).[69]

It is also in this general theurgic context that we should understand the extended passage in *Marsanes* treating the various letters of the alphabet (pp. 19-39). This passage (unfortunately riddled with lacunae and textual corruptions) is not a model of clarity, to be sure. But in it there is a quasi-learned discussion of the nature of the letters of the alphabet, based, in fact, on the technical discussions of the grammarians.[70] But the discussion clearly has religious purposes, and resembles somewhat the speculations of the Valentinian Gnostic Marcus (Iren. *Haer.* I.13-21). In *Marsanes*, however, the entire discussion is tied to the nature of the soul and its ascent through the spheres. The ascent of the soul presupposes knowledge of the "nomenclature" of the gods and the angels. The letters of the alphabet and their syllabic combinations are understood to have their counterparts in the angelic world of the Zodiac and the planetary spheres. The Gnostic adept, in order to ascend beyond these spheres, must know their natures and be able to chant the proper names.

All of this is intelligible in terms of Iamblichus's theurgic theories, as discussed above. Just as God has "expressed" (*ekphōnein*) the ineffable through mysterious symbols,[71] so must the Gnostic/theurgist give utterance to the sounds consecrated to the various gods and angels. Iamblichus specifically mentions the motive power of music (*DM* III.9), and goes on to say,

> Sounds and melodies are consecrated appropriately to each of the gods, and a kinship with them has been assigned appropriately according to the proper ranks and powers of each, and (according to) the motions in the universe

itself and the harmonious sounds whirring[72] as a result of these motions.[73]

The soul must adapt itself to these various sounds and thus be enabled to ascend, being drawn upward through the spheres to its divine root. In this connection we also recall what was said above concerning the efficacy of the divine names (*DM* VII.5).

Before bringing this discussion to a close it is necessary to comment on the following passage in *Marsanes*, wherein the use and efficacy of the various vowel-consonant combinations is stressed:

> And [the] consonants exist with the vowels, and individually they are commanded and they submit (*hypotassein*). They constitute the nomenclature (*onomasia*) [of] the angels. And [the] consonants are self-existent, [and] as they are changed <they> submit to (*hypotassein*) the hidden gods by means of beat and pitch and silence and impulse. (30, 3-18)

One of the problems here has to do with how the Greek "loanword," *hypotassein*, should be translated. In terms of Coptic grammar, it could be rendered either "subject" (v.t.) or "submit."[74] What appears to be said here, though, is that certain combinations of vowels and consonants, properly intoned, bring various gods and angels into subjection (even if the vowels, etc., are "subject to" the gods and angels). On the face of it, this would be more "magical" than "theurgical," given what was said of theurgy at the beginning of this essay. Yet even this passage can be understood in Iamblichian terms. At *DM* IV.1 Iamblichus takes up the problem, posed by Porphyry, how superior beings, when invoked, can be commanded by inferior beings.[75] Iamblichus, of course, cannot grant such a thing, even though he does stress the *ex opere operato* character of the invocations. He solves this problem by arguing that the theurgic practitioner acts both as a man and as a god. By means of the *synthēmata* he is elevated to, and conjoined with, superior natures (*DM* IV.2). The theurgist

> invokes, as superior natures, the powers from the universe, inasmuch as the one invoking is a man, and again he commands them, since somehow, through the ineffable symbols, he is invested with the hieratic form of the gods.[76]

It is in this way, I think, that our passage in *Marsanes* can be understood.

4. Concluding Remarks

I have tried to show in the preceding discussion that Gnostic ritual can be understood in terms of Iamblichus's ritual theories. To be sure, I have considered a very limited amount of evidence, both in terms of the Gnostic material and in terms of Iamblichus's total presentation in his *DM*. Indeed, I think much more can be done along these lines.[77] But I should clearly state what I have *not* attempted to argue: I have not tried to show that the actual rituals performed by the Gnostics, on the one hand, and by Iamblichus on the other, are the same in terms of content, though the "ascension" rituals in both cases are quite comparable. Nor have I tried to show that the mythological background is the same; on the contrary, the gods, demons, angels, etc. are different. As for world-view and ontology, Iamblichus's Platonism would not allow him to describe the Demiurge and the material world in the terms used by *The Gospel of the Egyptians*.[78] It is nevertheless to be noticed that such typically "Gnostic" details are absent both from *Steles Seth* and from *Marsanes*. In fact, it is the latter document which comes closest to Iamblichus in its view of the world and matter.

While I do not wish to refer to Iamblichus as a Gnostic, or even a "crypto-Gnostic," I think it is worthwhile to point out, in the present connection, that Iamblichus's attitude to the Gnostics was undoubtedly different from that of Plotinus. This is indicated in what he says (and does not say!) about them. He refers to "the Gnostics" once in his *De anima*, in a doxographical discussion of various beliefs that have been advanced concerning the activities of the soul, and sandwiches them in between Heraclitus and Albinus![79] While he would probably take issue with the views he attributes to the Gnostics concerning the soul's "derangement" and "deviation,"[80] it is interesting that he even considers them worth mentioning. And, of course, he could not possibly have joined in Plotinus's criticisms of their ritual activity.[81]

It has been the burden of this paper to show that, despite the differences that must be assumed between Iamblichus and the Gnostics, they can be understood in similar terms when it comes to their use and understanding of religious ritual. Whether this implies, in the case of "divine Iamblichus," a degeneration of Neoplatonism, I must leave to others to decide.

NOTES

1.   Cf. A.D. Nock's reference to Gnosticism as "Platonism run wild" ("Gnosticism," in *Essays on Religion in the Ancient World*, ed. Z. Stewart [Cambridge: Harvard University Press, 1972] 2.949); and J. Dillon's use of the term, "the underworld" of Platonism (*The Middle Platonists* [London: Duckworth, 1977], pp. 384-396).

2.   I would like to take this opportunity to express my thanks to Professor R.T. Wallis and his colleagues for conceiving and organizing this event, and for affording me the opportunity to contribute to it.

3.   For my own modest contributions to this discussion see "The Tractate *Marsanes* (*NHC* X) and the Platonic Tradition," in *Gnosis: Festschrift für Hans Jonas*, ed. B. Aland (Göttingen: Vandenhoeck & Ruprecht, 1978), pp. 373-384; and "Gnosticism as Platonism: With Special Reference to *Marsanes* (*NHC* X, 1)," *HTR* 77 (1984, Appeared 1986): 55-72.

4.   On the varieties of Gnostic ritual and Gnostic attitudes to religious ritual see e.g., K. Rudolph, *Gnosis: The Nature and History of Gnosticism*, English translation ed. by R. McL. Wilson (New York: Harper & Row, 1983), pp. 218-252.

5.   See now H. Remus, "Plotinus and Gnostic Thaumaturgy," *Laval théologique et philosophique* 39 (1983): 13-20. Plotinus himself has not escaped criticism as a practitioner of magic. See esp. P. Merlan, "Plotinus and Magic," *Isis* 44 (1953): 341-48; and A.H. Armstrong's reply, "Was Plotinus a Magician?" *Phronēsis* 1 (1955): 73-79. On the difference between Plotinus's and Iamblichus's attitudes to the Gnostics see below.

6.   Iren., *Haer.* I.21.4, as rendered by H. Jonas, *The Gnostic Religion* (Boston: Beacon, 1963), p. 176, in his discussion of Valentinian Gnosticism. He refers to the *Gospel of Truth* and parallel passages therein (*NHC* I, 3: 18, 7-11; 24, 28-32); see *Gnostic Religion*, pp. 311-312. This anti-sacramentalism is clearly a minority viewpoint within Valentinian gnosis.

7.   See e.g., R.T. Wallis, *Neoplatonism* (London: Duckworth, 1962), pp. 105-10. On the *Chaldaean Oracles* see esp. H. Lewy, *Chaldaean Oracles and Theurgy*, ed. (with compléments and indices) by M. Tardieu (Paris: Études Augustiniennes, 1978). For a new edition of the fragments, with English translation and commentary, see Ruth Majercik, *The Chaldaean Oracles: Text, Translation, Commentary* (SGGR 5; Leiden: E.J. Brill, 1989).

8.   *De Mysteriis Aegyptiorum*, hereafter cited *DM*. The standard edition is now E. des Places, *Jamblique: Les Mystères d'Égypte* (Paris: "Les Belles Lettres," 1966). Still useful is Thomas Taylor's English translation: *Iamblichus on the Mysteries of the Egyptians*, 2nd ed. (London: Bertram Dobell, 1895).

9.   See my articles cited above, n. 3.

10.   In his "Letter to Anebo." The text of this letter has been edited by A.R. Sodano, *Porfirio, Lettera ad Anebo* (Naples: L'arte tipografica, 1958). A translation is included in Taylor's English translation of Iamblichus (pp. 1-16).

11. E.R. Dodds, *The Greeks and the Irrational* (Berkeley/L.A.: University of California Press, 1951), Appendix II: "Theurgy," pp. 283-311, esp. p. 287.

12. Cf. Lewy-Tardieu and Majercik, op. cit., n. 7.

13. A paper by him entitled, "Putting Theurgy into Perspective," was presented to the section on "Platonism and Neoplatonism" of the American Academy of Religion at its annual meeting in Dallas, December, 1983. A revised version of that paper was subsequently published: "Theurgy: Rituals of Unification in the Neoplatonism of Iamblichus," *Traditio* 41 (1985): 1-28. Shaw was very helpful to me in the preparation of my article, and I gratefully acknowledge his assistance. See now his doctoral dissertation: "Theurgy: The Language of the Embodied Soul — A Study of the Work of Iamblichus of Chalcis," University of California, Santa Barbara, 1987.

14. See Dodds, *Irrational*, pp. 283-284; cf. Lewy-Tardieu, pp. 461-466.

15. See F.W. Cremer, *Die Chaldäischen Orakel und Iamblich de Mysteriis* (Meisenheim: Anton Hein, 1969), pp. 21-22.

16. *DM* II.11; 96, 13 - 97, 8. Text: οὐδὲ γὰρ ἡ ἔννοια συνάπτει τοῖς θεοῖς τοὺς θεουργοὺς ἐπεὶ τί ἐκώλυε τοὺς θεωρητικῶς φιλοσοφοῦντας ἔχειν τὴν θεουργικὴν ἕνωσιν πρὸς τοὺς θεούς; ... Καὶ γὰρ μὴ νοούντων ἡμῶν αὐτὰ τὰ συνθήματα ἀφ᾽ ἑαυτῶν δρᾷ τὸ οἰκεῖον ἔργον, καὶ ἡ τῶν θεῶν, πρὸς οὓς ἀνήκει ταῦτα, ἄρρητος δύναμις αὐτὴ ἀφ᾽ ἑαυτῆς ἐπιγιγνώσκει τὰς οἰκείας εἰκόνας. English translations of passages from the *DM* in this paper are my own, though I have found Taylor's translation helpful.

17. Indeed, J. Trouillard thinks that theurgy and Christian sacramentalism are essentially the same ("Sacrements: La Théurgie païenne," in *Encyclopedia Universalis* vol. 15, p. 582; cf. *L'Un et l'Âme selon Proclos* [Paris: "Les Belles Lettres," 1972], pp. 171-89). For criticism of this view see Majercik, *Chaldaean Oracles*, pp. 23-24. Cf. Shaw's discussion in "Theurgy: Rituals of Unification," op. cit., n. 13, p. 11.

18. Cf. Lewy-Tardieu, pp. 437-39.

19. Shaw, "Theurgy: Rituals of Unification," op. cit., n. 13, pp. 12-13. The phrase "instrument and beneficiary" is derived from Trouillard's article, "Sacrements," op. cit., n. 17, p. 582. Shaw goes on to discuss Iamblichus's doctrine of the soul in the *De anima*, specifically Iamblichus's rejection of the views of Numenius, Porphyry, and Plotinus that the descending soul leaves a portion of itself in the divine world. Cf. also J. Dillon, "Iamblichi Chalcidensis in Platonis Dialogos Commentariorum Fragmenta," *Philosophia Antiqua*, Vol. 23 (Leiden: Brill, 1973), pp. 41-47 and 382-383.

20. For a convenient one-volume translation of all of the Nag Hammadi texts (including also those from the Berlin Gnostic Codex) see *The Nag Hammadi Library in English*, ed. J.M. Robinson, (Leiden: E.J. Brill/San Francisco: Harper & Row, 1977, 1981, 1988). For bibliography on Gnosticism and the Nag Hammadi Codices, see D.M. Scholer, *Nag Hammadi Bibliography 1948-1969* (NHS 1; Leiden: E.J. Brill, 1971), updated annually in *NovT*.

21.   See H.M. Schenke, "Das Sethianische System nach Nag-Hammadi-Schriften," in *Studia Coptica*, ed. P. Nagel, (Berlin: Akademie-Verlag, 1974), pp. 165-172; and esp. Schenke, "The Phenomenon and Significance of Gnostic Sethianism," in *The Rediscovery of Gnosticism: Proceedings of the Conference At Yale March 1978*, Vol. 2: *Sethian Gnosticism*, ed. B. Layton, (Leiden: E.J. Brill, 1981), pp. 588-616. The Gnostic texts which belong to the Sethian system, according to Schenke, are as follows:

The Apocryphon of John (NHC II, 1; III, 1; IV, 1; BG, 2)
The Hypostasis of the Archons (NHC II ,4)
The Gospel of the Egyptians (NHC III, 2; IV, 2)
The Apocalypse of Adam (NHC V, 5)
The Three Steles of Seth (NHC VII, 5)
Zostrianos (NHC VIII, 1)
Melchizedek (NHC IX, 1)
The Thought of Norea (NHC IX, 2)
Marsanes (NHC X, 1)
The Trimorphic Protennoia (NHC XIII, 1)
Bruce Codex, Untitled Text

For the last-named text, see C. Schmidt and V. MacDermot, *The Books of Jeu and the Untitled Text in the Bruce Codex* (NHS 13; Leiden: E.J. Brill, 1978).

22.   See Carl Schmidt, *Plotins Stellung zum Gnosticismus und kirchlichen Christentum* (TU 20; Leipzig: H.C. Hinrichs, 1901), p. 63. Of course, Schmidt did not know the Nag Hammadi texts, though he did know *Ap. John* (in the Berlin Codex version). Porphyry (*Vit. Plot.* 16) refers to "apocalypses," used by the Gnostic opponents of Plotinus, attributed to "Zoroaster and Zostrianos and Nikotheos and Allogenes and Messos and others." We now have, in the Nag Hammadi collection, *Zostrianos* (VIII, 1) and *Allogenes* (XI, 3). The name "Messos" is given in the last-named tractate to the "son" of Allogenes. "Allogenes" is another name for Seth; see B. Pearson, "The Figure of Seth in Gnostic Literature," in *Rediscovery*, vol. 2, pp. 472-504, esp. p. 486. Nikotheos appears in the Bruce Codex as an important Gnostic authority, associated in that capacity with another prophet, Marsanes. We now have a revelation of the latter: *Marsanes* (X, 1). Perhaps *Marsanes* should be considered as included in the "others" left unnamed by Porphyry. On *Marsanes*, see below.

For an alternative identification of the Gnostic opponents of Plotinus as Valentinians, rather than Sethians, see F. García Bazán, *Plotino y la gnosis* (Buenos Aires: Fundación para la Educación, la Ciencia y la Cultura, 1981); "Plotino y los textos gnosticos de Nag-Hammadi," *Oriente-Occidente* 2 (1981): 185-202; and his contribution to this volume.

23.   Schenke, *Gnostic Sethianism*, pp. 600-607.

24.   See my article, "Gnosticism as Platonism," cited n. 3 above.

25.   Cf. the contributions to this volume by J. Turner and R.T. Wallis, pp. 427-483.

26. The standard edition of the two extant versions of this text is that of A. Böhlig and F. Wisse, *Nag Hammadi Codices III*, 2 and *IV*, 2: *The Gospel of the Egyptians* (NHS 4; Leiden: E.J. Brill, 1975). Their translation is the one used in *NHLE*, 3rd ed., pp. 209-219; the version in Codex III is presented there, except for missing sections where the Codex IV version is used instead.

27. "Of the Egyptians" is restored in lacunae in the *incipit* (III 40, 12; IV 50, 1-2), but Schenke prefers to read the *incipit* as "The Book of the H[ol]y [Invocation]" and "[The Ho]ly [Book] of the [Invocation]s" in the respective versions. This is relevant to the question of the genre of the document, on which see below. Cf. Schenke, *Gnostic Sethianism*, p. 601.

28. See their introduction, p. 24.

29. This outline is basically that of Böhlig-Wisse, p. 26.

30. Schenke, *Gnostic Sethianism*, p. 600.

31. Possible (mixed) etymologies for these names are "Lord of the House" and "Lord of Glory"; see Böhlig-Wisse, p. 41. The full name, "Domedon Doxomedon," occurs in the preceding context (III 43, 8-9) of the passage quoted here, where, however, only "Doxomedon" occurs. In the quotation here, some material is omitted from III 44, 21-24. The translation is that of Böhlig-Wisse. There are many examples of the Gnostics' use of, and probably chanting of, the seven vowels, which are probably understood as associated with the seven planetary spheres. See e.g., E. Poirée, "Le chant gnostico-magique des sept voyelles grecques," in *Congrés International d'Histoire de la Musique* (Paris, 1900); *Documents, Memoires et Voeux* (Solesnes: Saint-Pierre, 1901), pp. 15-38; F. Dornseiff, *Das Alphabet in Mystik und Magie* (Leipzig/Berlin: B.G. Teubner, 1922), esp. 126-133 (on Marcus: Iren., *Haer.* I.13-22). Iamblichus does not deal specifically with this in his *DM*.

32. Böhlig-Wisse, pp. 43, 173. For the *Books of Jêu* see n. 21.

33. *DM* VII.4; 254, 17 - 255, 6. Text: ἀλλ' ἡμῖν μὲν ἄγνωστα ἔστω ἢ καὶ γνωστὰ ἔνια, περὶ ὧν παραδεξάμεθα τὰς ἀναλύσεις παρὰ θεῶν, τοῖς μέντοι θεοῖς πάντα σημαντικά ἐστιν οὐ κατὰ ῥητὸν τρόπον, οὐδ' οἷός ἐστιν ὁ διὰ τῶν φαντασιῶν παρ' ἀνθρώποις σημαντικὸς τε καὶ μηνυτικός, ἀλλ' ἤτοι νοερῶς [κατὰ τὸν θεῖον αὐτὸν ἀνθρώπειον νοῦν] ἢ καὶ ἀφθέγκτως καὶ κρειττόνως καὶ ἁπλουστέρως [καὶ] κατὰ νοῦν τοῖς θεοῖς συνηνωμένος.

34. *DM* VII.4; 256, 8-15. Text: τὰς κοινολογίας οἰόμεθα δεῖν τῇ συγγενεῖ πρὸς τοὺς θεοὺς λέξει προσφέρειν, ... οἱ μαθόντες τὰ πρῶτα ὀνόματα περὶ τῶν θεῶν μετὰ τῆς οἰκείας γλώττης αὐτὰ συμμίξαντες παραδεδώκασιν ἡμῖν, ὡς οἰκείας καὶ προσφόρου πρὸς αὐτὰ ὑπαρχούσης, ἀκίνητον διατηροῦμεν δεῦρο ἀεὶ τὸν θεσμὸν τῆς παραδόσεως.

35. Böhlig-Wisse, p. 173; cf. *Zostrianos* (*NHC* VIII, 1) 130, 2.

36. On "Sethian" Gnostic baptism see Schenke, *Gnostic Sethianism*, esp. pp. 602-607; and Rudolph, *Gnosis*, pp. 226-28.

37. *DM* I.12; 41, 16 - 42, 5. Text: τὴν ἑαυτῆς ἀφεῖσα ζωὴν τὴν μακαριωτάτην τῶν θεῶν ἐνέργειαν ἀντηλλάξατο. Εἰ δὴ κάθαρσιν παθῶν καὶ ἀπαλλαγὴν γενέσεως ἕνωσίν τε πρὸς τὴν θείαν ἀρχὴν ἡ διὰ τῶν κλήσεων ἄνοδος παρέχει τοῖς ἱερεῦσι, τί δήποτε πάθη τις αὐτῇ προσάπτει; οὐ γὰρ τοὺς ἀπαθεῖς καὶ

καθαροὺς εἰς τὸ παθητὸν καὶ ἀκάθαρτον ἡ τοιαύτη κατασπᾷ, τοὐναντίον δὲ τοὺς ἐμπαθεῖς γενομένους ἡμᾶς διὰ τὴν γένεσιν καθαροὺς καὶ ἀτρέπτους ἀπεργάζεται.

38. Cf. Dillon, *Iamblichi Fragmenta*, Appendix A, "Iamblichus's Theory of Prayer," pp. 407-411.

39. *DM* V.26; 238, 10-12 and 239, 2-4. Text: τὸ μὲν εἰς ἐπίλαμψιν τεῖνον, τὸ δὲ εἰς κοινὴν ἀπεργασίαν, τὸ δὲ εἰς τὴν τελείαν ἀποπλήρωσιν ἀπὸ τοῦ πυρός... συνήθειαν δὲ παρέχει πρὸς τὰς τοῦ φωτὸς μαρμαρυγάς, κατὰ βραχὺ δὲ τελειοῖ τὰ ἐν ἡμῖν πρὸς τὰς τῶν θεῶν συναφάς, ἕως ἂν ἐπὶ τὸ ἀκρότατον ἡμᾶς ἐπαναγάγῃ.

40. See *NHLE*, 3rd ed., pp. 397-401. There is as yet no critical edition of this text. For an excellent discussion, with French translation, see M. Tardieu, "Les trois stèles de Seth: Un écrit gnostique retrouvé à Nag Hammadi," *RSPhTh* 57 (1973): 545-75. Cf. also K. Wekel (for the Berliner Arbeitskreis für koptisch-gnostische Schriften), "'Die drei Stelen des Seth': Die fünfte Schrift aus Nag-Hammadi-Codex VII," *ThLZ* 100 (1975): 571-80 (introduction and German translation). I have not seen Wekel's dissertation, "Die drei Stelen des Seth (*NHC* VII, 5): Text-Übersetzung-Kommentar" (Th.D. diss., Humboldt Universitat, Berlin, 1977).

41. 118, 10-13. It is debatable whether this "Dositheos" is to be identified with one or more figures of the same name mentioned in some traditions related to Samaritanism and Simonian Gnosticism. On this see esp. Tardieu, *Trois stèles*, p. 551.

42. Cf. the "tablets" mentioned in *Gos. Eg.*, above. For the motif of revelatory steles associated with Seth see e.g., Tardieu, *Trois Stèles*, pp. 553-555; cf. also my article, "The Figure of Seth," op. cit., n. 22, esp. pp. 491-496.

43. See e.g., J.M. Robinson, "The Three Steles of Seth and the Gnostics of Plotinus," in *Proceedings of the International Colloquium on Gnosticism, Stockholm August 20-25, 1973*, ed. G. Widengren, (Stockholm: Almqvist & Wiksell, 1977), pp. 132-142, esp. pp. 133-136. Cf. J. Turner, "The Gnostic Threefold Path to Enlightenment: The Ascent of Mind and the Descent of Wisdom," *NovT* 22 (1980): 324-51, esp. 341-51.

44. Schenke, *Gnostic Sethianism*, pp. 601-602.

45. Cf. the articles by Robinson and Turner (above n. 43) and esp. Tardieu, *Trois stèles*, pp. 558-567; see also Turner's contribution to this volume.

46. See Schenke, *Gnostic Sethianism*, p. 602; also Wekel, "drei Stelen," in *ThLZ*, op. cit., n. 40, col. 571.

47. C. Colpe uses the term "theurgisch" in his brief reference to the prayers of *Steles Seth*. See Colpe, "Heidnische, jüdische, und christliche Überlieferung in den Schriften aus Nag Hammadi," II, *JAC* 16 (1973): 106-26, esp. 124.

48. On the Chaldaean *anagōgē* see Lewy-Tardieu, *Chaldaean Oracles*, pp. 177-227; cf. also Majercik, *Chaldaean Oracles*, pp. 30-45.

49. Fragment B 60 (Diels): ὁδὸς ἄνω κάτω μία καὶ ὡυτή. Cf. Rudolph, *Gnosis*, p. 172 (but the reference to B 90 is a misprint). This fragment is also (partially) quoted by Plotinus, *Enn.* IV.8.1 (ὁδὸν ἄνω καὶ κάτω).

50. Iren., *Haer.* I.21.2, as translated in *Gnosis: A Selection of Gnostic Texts*, ed. W. Foerster, English translation ed. by R. McL. Wilson, vol. 1 (Oxford: Clarendon, 1972), p. 218. Cf. A.J. Welburn, "Reconstructing the Ophite Diagram," *NovT* 23 (1981): 261-87, esp. 264, where he entertains and then rejects the suggestion that the reverse order of the Ophite invocations of the planetary archons given by Origen (*Cels.* VI.31) refers to a mystic "descent." He cites the Marcosian and Jewish parallels at n. 12 of his article.

51. See G. Scholem, *Major Trends in Jewish Mysticism* (New York: Schocken, 1961), pp. 46-47. Cf. I. Gruenwald, *Apocalyptic and Merkavah Mysticism* (Leiden: E.J. Brill, 1980), esp. his chapter on the Hekhalot literature (pp. 98-123), wherein he describes the "theurgic" elements in the ascent rituals reflected in these mystical texts. The use of the verb *yarād* ("descend") in an ascent context is reflected in the Valentinian etymology of the river "Jordan," in the *Valentinian Exposition, On Baptism A* (*NHC* XI,2): "The interpretation of that which [is] the Jord[an] is the descent which is [the upward progression], that [is, our exodus] from the world [into] the Aeon" (XI 41, 32-38). G. Stroumsa, in his review of Gruenwald's book (*Numen* 28 [1981]: 107-109, esp. 108ff.) plausibly suggests that the "descent" language in the Jewish mystical texts reflects influence from the Hellenistic mystery initiations, in which a symbolic *katabasis* into Hades and mystic visions are featured. There may be something of this influence in the Gnostic examples as well.

52. ἐγώ εἰμι ὁ Χριστός, ἐπειδὴ ἄνωθεν καταβέβηκα διὰ τῶν ὀνομάτων τῶν τ̅ξ̅ε̅ ἀρχόντων, *Haer.* 26.9.9. Cf. Rudolph, *Gnosis*, pp. 247-250. Rudolph expresses some skepticism as to the accuracy of Epiphanius's descriptions of such libertinist cults. Cf. n. 77, below.

53. Cf. des Places's ed., p. 201, n. 3.

54. *DM* VIII.8; 272, 2-12. Text: Νόμοις γὰρ ἀχράντοις καὶ νοεροῖς ὥρισται πάλαι τὰ ἔργα τῆς ἱερᾶς ἁγιστείας, τάξει τε μείζονι καὶ δυνάμει λύεται τὰ καταδεέστερα, εἰς βελτίονά τε μεθισταμένων ἡμῶν λῆξιν ἀπόστασις γίγνεται τῶν καταδεεστέρων. καὶ οὐ παρὰ τὸν ἐξ ἀρχῆς τι θεσμὸν ἐπιτελεῖται ἐν τῷ τοιῷδε, ἵνα μεταστραφῶσιν οἱ θεοὶ κατὰ τὴν εἰς ὕστερον γιγνομένην ἱερουργίαν, ἀλλ᾽ ἀπὸ τῆς πρώτης καθόδου ἐπὶ τούτῳ κατέτεμψεν ὁ θεὸς τὰς ψυχάς, ἵνα πάλιν εἰς αὐτὸν ἐπανέλθωσιν. Οὔτε οὖν μεταβολή τις γίγνεται διὰ τῆς τοιαύτης ἀναγωγῆς οὔτε μάχονται αἱ κάθοδοι τῶν ψυχῶν καὶ αἱ ἄνοδοι. There may be a possible allusion to Heraclitus's fragment here (cf. n. 44). Plotinus quotes Heraclitus frg. B 60, together with frg. 84ab, in his discussion of the descent of the soul, *Enn.* IV.8.1. Iamblichus quotes from the same fragments in his *De anima*, apud Stob. I.49 (I.378, 21-23, Wachsmuth); cf. A.-J. Festugière, *La révélation d'Hermès Trismégiste*, Vol. 3 (Paris: Gabalda, 1953), p. 219.

55. G. Shaw refers to the "upside-down" state of the embodied soul taught by Plato (*Tim.* 43e), and argues that theurgy, for Iamblichus, achieves the rectification of the soul, its "turning around" (*periagōgē*; cf. *Resp.* 521c). See "Theurgy: Rituals of Unification," op. cit., n. 13, 14-15.

56. He treats the various gods, demons, heroes, and souls in Book I of *DM*.

57. ἀναγωγὸν καὶ τελεσιουργὸν καὶ ἀποπληρωτικόν, *DM* V.26; 240, 4. Cf. the previous references to *DM* V.26, above.

58. The only critical edition of this text is that found in B. Pearson, *Nag Hammadi Codices IX* and *X* (NHS 15; Leiden: E.J. Brill, 1981), pp. 211-352; cf. *NHLE*, 3rd ed., pp. 460-71. Cf. also my articles cited above, n. 3.

59. On these problems see my introduction to Codex X in *Nag Hammadi Codices IX* and *X*.

60. Ch. 7, in Schmidt-MacDermot, *Books of Jeu*, op. cit., n. 21, p. 235. Cf. n. 22.

61. Cf. my discussion above.

62. Cf. my discussion, with reference to the *Marsanes* passage, in "Gnosticism as Platonism," op. cit., n. 3.

63. See the penetrating study by C.J. de Vogel, "The Sōma-Sēma Formula: Its Function in Plato and Plotinus Compared to Christian Writers," in *Neoplatonism and Early Christian Thought*, ed. H.J. Blumenthal and R.A. Markus, (London: Variorum, 1981), pp. 79-99.

64. Cf. the "Naasene" Gnostic system, in which "Autogenēs-Adamas" is interchangeable with "soul." Cf. e.g., Hipp., *Ref.* V.6.3-9 (the "commentary") and V.10.1 (the "Naasene Psalm").

65. *DM* VIII.3; 264, 14 - 265, 10. Text: Καὶ οὕτως ἄνωθεν ἄχρι τῶν τελευταίων ἡ περὶ τῶν ἀρχῶν Αἰγυπτίοις πραγματεία ἀφ' ἑνὸς ἄρχεται, καὶ πρόεισιν εἰς πλῆθος, τῶν πολλῶν αὖθις ὑφ' ἑνὸς διακυβερνωμένων καὶ πανταχοῦ τῆς ἀορίστου φύσεως ἐπικρατουμένης ὑπό τινος ὡρισμένου μέτρου καὶ τῆς ἀνωτάτω ἑνιαίας πάντων αἰτίας. Ὕλην δὲ παρήγαγεν ὁ θεὸς ἀπὸ τῆς οὐσιότητος ὑποσχισθείσης ὑλότητος, ἣν παραλαβὼν ὁ δημιουργὸς ζωτικὴν οὖσαν τὰς ἁπλᾶς καὶ ἀπαθεῖς σφαίρας ἀπ' αὐτῆς ἐδημιούργησε, τὸ δὲ ἔσχατον αὐτῆς εἰς τὰ γεννητὰ καὶ φθαρτὰ σώματα διεκόσμησεν.

66. See Shaw's excellent discussion in "Theurgy: Rituals of Unification," pp. 14-16.

67. *DM* I.21; 65, 4-12. Text: μιμεῖται δὲ τὴν τῶν θεῶν τάξιν, τήν τε νοητὴν καὶ τὴν ἐν οὐρανῷ. Ἔχει δὲ μέτρα τῶν ὄντων ἀίδια καὶ ἐνθήματα θαυμαστά, οἷα ἀπὸ τοῦ δημιουργοῦ καὶ πατρὸς τῶν ὅλων δεῦρο καταπεμφθέντα, οἷς καὶ τὰ μὲν ἄφθεγκτα διὰ συμβόλων ἀπορρήτων ἐκφωνεῖται, τὰ δὲ ἀνειδέα κρατεῖται ἐν εἴδεσι, τὰ δὲ πάσης εἰκόνος κρείττονα δι' εἰκόνων ἀποτυποῦται, πάντα δὲ διὰ θείας αἰτίας μόνης ἐπιτελεῖται.

68. Cf. Majercik, *Chaldaean Oracles*, pp. 44-45. She points out that Synesius (*hymn*. 1 [3], 539.620) uses the terms *synthēma* and *sphragis* interchangeably in an anagogic context. Cf. her notes to fragment 2 of the *Oracles* (p. 141). Cf. also my notes to *Marsanes*, in *Nag Hammadi Codices IX* and *X*, pp. 253-61.

69. Cf. my notes in *Nag Hammadi Codices IX* and *X*, p. 315, where references to magical texts are also given.

70. In my notes to the text (*Nag Hammadi Codices IX* and *X*, ad loc.) I refer to the theories of Dionysius Thrax and his later commentators. Cf. also the classic monograph on the use of the alphabet in magic and mysticism: F. Dornseiff, *Das Alphabet*, op. cit., n. 31.

71. Cf. the passage from *DM* 1.21, quoted above.

72. See p. 109, n. 2, in des Places's edition, on *rhoizoumenas*.

73. *DM* III.9; 118, 16 - 119, 4. Text: ἠχοί τε καὶ μέλη καθιέρωνται τοῖς θεοῖς οἰκείως ἑκάστοις, συγγένειά τε αὐτοῖς ἀποδέδοται προσφόρως κατὰ τὰς οἰκείας ἑκάστων τάξεις καὶ δυνάμεις καὶ τὰς ἐν αὐτῷ <τῷ> παντὶ κινήσεις καὶ τὰς ἀπὸ τῶν κινήσεων ῥοιζουμένας ἐναρμονίους φωνάς.

74. See my notes to the text.

75. This question is already implicit in Plotinus's polemic against the Gnostics (*Enn.* II.9.14).

76. *DM* IV.2; 184, 9-14. Text: ὡς κρείττονας καλεῖ τὰς ἀπὸ τοῦ παντὸς δυνάμεις, καθόσον ἐστίν ὁ καλῶν ἄνθρωπος καὶ ἐπιτάττει αὐταῖς αὖθις, ἐπειδὴ περιβάλλεταί πως διὰ τῶν ἀπορρήτων συμβόλων τὸ ἱερατικὸν τῶν θεῶν πρόσχημα.
    Iamblichus makes a similar point in *DM* VI.6.

77. It would be especially interesting, I think, to look at the ritual activities of the so-called "libertine" groups, e.g., those Gnostics described by Epiphanius in his *Panarion*, chs. 25-26 (including the "Phibionites" mentioned above), in terms of what Iamblichus says about the ritual use of obscene objects, gestures, and words (*DM* I.11).

78. Esp. III 56, 22 - 60, 2. Cf. Plotinus's criticisms, *Enn.* II.9.10-11.

79. *De anima*, apud Stob. I.49 (I.375, 9); cf. Festugière, *révélation* 3, p. 210. I owe this reference to Michel Tardieu.

80. *Paranoia* and *parekbasis*. While I have not found these specific terms used in any Gnostic sources, they might be applied in general to what is said of the fallen soul in such Gnostic treatises on the soul as *NHC* II, 6: *The Exegesis on the Soul* and *NHC* VI, 3: *Authoritative Teaching*. The latter treatise has been referred to, however, as more of a "Platonist" writing than a "Gnostic" one! See R. van den Broeck, "The Authentikos Logos: A New Document of Christian Platonism," *VigChr* 33 (1979): 260-86. Plotinus ascribes to the Gnostics a doctrine of the soul's "declination" (*neusis*, *Enn.* II.9.11), but this is a term he uses himself of certain souls (*Enn.* I.6.5)!

81. *Enn.* II.9.14, referred to above.

Beauty, Number, and Loss of Order in the Gnostic Cosmos

Pheme Perkins

The Nag Hammadi codices have provoked as many questions about the relationship between Gnosticism and the philosophical speculation of the first three centuries of our era as they have answered. Some of these tractates appear to be those read in Plotinus's circles or those referred to in Christian authors. Others appear to reflect adaptation of Gnostic speculation to meet philosophical objections.[1] However, it has been much more difficult to argue that Gnostic speculation, itself, had a major influence on the development of Neoplatonic thought.[2] Dominic O'Meara has suggested that the turn away from demiurgic production of the lower world toward a contemplative process in Plotinus's middle period may have been partially provoked by his polemic against the Gnostics.[3] However, O'Meara also points out that Plotinus's polemic is not dictated by the Gnostic agenda. He develops themes from his own thought which might lead those inclined toward Gnostic views to reject them. The explicit condemnation of Gnostic teachings in the reduction to absurdities of *Enn.* II.9 is predicated upon the independent metaphysical arguments of the earlier treatises.[4]

Prof. Armstrong's survey of possible contacts between Gnosis and Greek philosophy reaches the same conclusion. He points out that it is necessary to distinguish between occasional ideas taken from a particular tradition and the shaping of a person by a tradition in such a way that one would never think otherwise.[5] Not only are the Platonists of the second century consistently "anti-Gnostic" in the structure of their thought; the Gnostics are only marginally influenced by Platonism. Some of the monistic Gnostic writings have adapted elements of Platonic cosmology to their systems, but their structure remains that of a foreign faith and feeling.[6] Even for the most negative of the second century Platonists, this world reflects the intelligible world and remains "well-ordered." That order is based upon the conviction that matter, space and time are limited.

The consistency of the Platonic reading of the cosmos makes the intellectual attractiveness of Gnostic "disorder" all the more puzzling. Armstrong points out that one must beware of presuming that the myth of the Gnostic generates a particular mystical experience. Myth may be used to describe such experiences but it is not their source. The Gnostic treatment of its own mythology suggests a secondary, literary exercise quite unlike primary expressions of the human psyche.[7] Anti-Gnostic polemic of the second and third centuries provides some indication of how their contemporaries viewed Gnostic thinkers. Both Irenaeus and Plotinus address a monistic Gnosticism, which claimed to provide its adherents with a "philosophical" reading of the world. They both ridicule the gnostic "melodrama of terrors" (*Enn.* II.9, 13) — particularly, the myth of Sophia and her passions.[8] They both attribute arrogance to the Gnostics, a desire to be superior to the "heavenly world," to step above their place in the hierarchy of beings.[9] They both presume that this arrogance is correlated with a lack of moral purpose, an unwillingness to undergo the harder discipline of "becoming good oneself."[10]

The principles on which Plotinus and Irenaeus proceed to reject the Gnostic cosmology are quite different. Irenaeus argues from the Biblical account of God as creator, an account which he has apparently also read in an anti-Platonist vein.[11] Plotinus, on the other hand, speaks from the Platonist position. Both thinkers reject the multiplicity of beings in the Gnostic cosmogony. Irenaeus insists that multiplication of creators can only lead to an infinite (unlimited) series. Consequently, the unity of the single Creator is the only reasonable account of the origin of the sensible world.[12] In the process, he rejects the view that creation is patterned after "forms" in the intelligible world. Such a pattern, he insists, would require infinite forms and would introduce into the intelligible world the disharmony and tension evident in the material world.[13] Plotinus, on the other hand, even with some inconsistency in his own thought, finds the living diversity of this world expressed in the intelligible realm.[14] However, the Gnostics have failed to recognize that a tendency toward unity governs the intelligible realm. They have thought that they would gain understanding by giving names to a whole multitude of intelligible realities. All they have done is to reduce the intelligible world to the level of the sensible.[15] However, as Irenaeus recognizes, this irrational positing of beings has its roots in a tendency that was fostered in Platonic circles, number speculation.[16]

Both Irenaeus and Plotinus reject such Neopythagorean speculation in principle as well as the association of numbers and sounds with certain magical elements in Gnosticism. Plotinus was generally not interested in mathematical speculation.[17] Gnostic magic is predicated on the absurd premise that incorporeal beings could be affected by sounds.[18] Irenaeus's argument against number speculation proceeds from two principles: God as creator and the presumption of "disharmony" in the lower world. Both were part of his argument against the Forms. Number systems, he points out, are purely arbitrary. They can be arranged to suit any speculation. The truth is that numbers spring from a system (*regula*), which has God as its origin. Further, one should not be deceived by looking at the intervals between notes. The melody as a whole is the work of an artist and arises from opposition as much as harmony. Listening to music is not based on ratios but upon the tension between some notes; the sound of some, and the loudness or softness of others.[19]

Irenaeus and Plotinus thus differ on a fundamental principle. Irenaeus presumes against theories of Forms and of mathematical ratio that the material world contains within it elements of disharmony, discord, irrationality, which are overcome in the larger perspective of God as the creator of all. Perhaps it is not surprising, then, that he does not reflect Plotinus's final case against the Gnostics, their failure to perceive the true nature of Beauty. Armstrong suggests that third century Platonists, especially Plotinus, recovered in Beauty an element in perceiving the world that had been neglected in the second century.[20] The "disharmony" presumed by Irenaeus may represent a view of the cosmos that was held widely enough to provide some plausibility for Gnostic arguments. On the other side, we find a few references to the beauty of the intelligible world in the Nag Hammadi writings. These references suggest that Gnostic thinkers would have been influenced by objections such as those raised by Plotinus.

The Beautiful and Order in Middle Platonism

Before investigating the Nag Hammadi material, a brief survey of the treatment of "the Beautiful" as an ordering principle in the first and second century Platonic tradition is appropriate. To what extent is Beauty lost as an ordering principle? To what extent is Irenaeus's presupposition of discord in the sensible world shared by the philosophical tradition? That the second principle is common in some circles may already be obvious from surveys like Armstrong's. Second century accounts of necessity, multiplicity and irrationality in the lower world tend to exegete Plato in such a way that an "evil" soul is operative in the material world. This interpretation is based upon a combination of *Tim.* 52-53 and *Laws* 896E-897D. Plutarch, Atticus and Numenius provide examples of such interpretation.[21]

Emphasis on the "disorder" to be found in the lower world and the consequent decline in use of the argument from its "beauty" appears to originate in anti-Stoic argument. The Stoic argument for an immanent divine Providence turned on three points: (1) the cosmos is the structure best suited for survival; (2) the cosmos is complete in itself; (3) the cosmos is one of consummate beauty and contains every kind of embellishment.[22] The order, perfection and beauty of nature prove that it is produced by a divine reason, which guides all things for the benefit of humanity.[23] The Platonic tradition insists on God's transcending the "ordering principle of the lower world." This transcendence is often expressed in the conviction that the highest God transcends the Good and the Beautiful.[24]

Philo's treatise on the creation of the world demonstrates the eclectic tendencies of first century Platonism. Its speculation about the numbers involved in the creation account is indebted to Pythagorean traditions.[25] God, the active cause of all that is, transcends virtue, knowledge, the Good and the Beautiful (*Opif.* 8). Philo agrees with the Stoic of Cicero's *De Natura Deorum* that Providence is the most beneficial and necessary incentive to piety.[26] The Beautiful applies most properly to the *paradeigma* of the sensible world. Philo concludes that a god-like, incorporeal pattern was created prior to the production of the sensible world. He concludes that the number of types of object in the two worlds must coincide and that the "ideas" are in the divine Logos, since nothing else could contain God's power.[27] The substance which receives the Forms has nothing but the capacity to change, to become all things. It contains inconsistency and disharmony because it is without any qualities. It has no soul, beauty or order. However, its capacity to receive the Good is limited. Consequently, the beauty, harmony and order of the material world is not equivalent to that in the intelligible world.[28]

However, Philo's account of the elements suggests a further source of discord in the lower world. "Light" the noetic *paradeigma*, the surpassingly beautiful, is not only dimmed in the material world, it meets the void and darkness. God puts "air" between the two, which are naturally in conflict, so as to keep discord and perpetual warfare from arising. Evening and dawn function as boundaries in the heavenly spheres. (*Opif.* 30-33). Not only is there a natural enmity between primordial elements, but God is not entirely responsible for creation. Those things which are Good of themselves or those which are neither Good nor Bad are attributed to God. Deeds of a contrary sort are attributed to subordinates (*Opif.* 74-75).

According to Philo, the human soul is particularly suited to perceive true beauty. It was not constructed according to a pattern such as those for the visible world but in the likeness of God's Word. What has been copied from a beautiful pattern will be itself beautiful. The Word of God surpasses any beauty to be found in nature. Consequently the first human surpassed any human who now exists. The descendants of that first human, like successive copies of work of sculpture or painting, have grown weaker and inferior to the original, (*Opif.* 139-45). Such decline helps explain the acknowledged difference in the return of individuals to the vision of God. *Fug.* 97-99 distinguishes three types of piety. The noblest reaches to the divine Word, the image of God. The next grasps God's creative power and comes to love the one to whom the person owes his or her being. Finally, the last form grasps God's ruling power and gains life through obedience to divine decrees. Only the person who is free from even unintentional offense possesses God himself. Others must take refuge in the three cities, the Word of God, his creative power and his kingly power. Humans need these three refuges because they are by nature prone to intentional and unintentional sin. (*Fug.* 102-105).[29] Philo's description of the fall equates Eve with the senses through which reason becomes ensnared (*Opif.* 165).[30] While hardly the beginnings of a Gnostic system, Philo's account does presume that the sensible world contains certain elements that are not harmonious and not reducible to reason or order. Philo's monotheism and his doctrine of divine powers holds these elements within the bounds of a "good" creation. However, one also finds in the doctrine of God's double act of creation, first the intelligible world, then the sensible one, a way of removing the creator from the ills of this world. The perfection of divine power and beauty can only be expressed in the intelligible realm.

Plutarch is less tentative than Philo in attributing discord in the sensible world to a principle other than God. Against the Epicureans, he argues that matter alone will never produce life, since matter is inanimate. Against the Stoic identification of God, Providence, the Logos and the creative Demiurge, he argues that nothing bad could ever be engendered.[31] But, and here we find the image exploited by

Irenaeus, the harmony of the universe is like a lyre. It rebounds from being disturbed. Good and bad are not kept apart in the universe. This fact is evident in the dualistic myths of both barbarians and Greeks. It is also evident in our own experience of life. We find that Nature constantly mingles good and bad, success and failure. The most logical conclusion from both ancient wisdom and our experience of the world is that there are two "souls" at work. Nature as we know it requires both, intelligence and reason and the irrational and destructive soul.[32] However, the struggle between the two is not equal. Fundamentally, Nature inclines toward the good and has an innate tendency to reject evil. The divine Word cripples the destructive force in the universe and creates concord out of discord.[33]

Plutarch's rather idiosyncratic exegesis of the World Soul in the *Timaeus* attaches this doctrine of two principles to Plato.[34] It would be absurd to suppose that the universe could come into being merely out of the incorporeal, since God would not turn what is incorporeal to body. Nor could he turn the inanimate into soul. Both are fitted together in a living being which is as beautiful and perfect as possible. Plutarch rejects the view that matter could be the source of evil and disharmony, since it is a substrate without any qualities. It cannot be spoken of as "ugly," maleficent, subject to excess and deficiency. Therefore, the principle of what is disorderly and maleficent must be the soul itself. The material principle needed beauty, shape and the regular geometric figures in order to give birth to creation (*De An. Proc.* 1014B-1015E). This disorderly soul only becomes the soul of the cosmos when it partakes of intelligence, reason and harmony. Plutarch claims that this principle is evident in the dual motion in the heavens, that of the fixed stars (the same) and the contrary motion of the planets (the other), (1015A). The discord inherent in this principle is removed by harmony, proportion and number. They become inerrant (*aplanē*) and stable (*stasima*) in a way that is similar to those things which are invariably the same (1015F). Plutarch finds other examples of the unity of same and other. Within the soul, for example, one encounters both what belongs to the intelligible world, the objects of knowledge, and what belongs to the perceptible one, the objects of opinion. They are combined in mental images and memories.[35] Plutarch combines psychological and cosmological examples of the same/other antithesis. (*De Proc. An.* 1026DE). The divine and impassive soul longs for what is best, while the mortal and passible part has an "innate desire" (*epithumia emphuton*) for pleasure. He suggests a periodic alteration in the heavens between the period in which the "same" dominates and that in which "discernment" has fallen asleep and forgotten what is proper to it. The soul's association with body puts a drag on the "right hand" motion and pulls it back without being able to disrupt it entirely. The period of the "other" ends when the better part recovers, looks up to the intelligible *paradeigma* and is aided by God's turning and guidance, (*De An. Proc.* 1026EF).

The cosmos as we experience it provides evidence for both principles. However, Plutarch insists that the portion of evil in the soul has been arranged by God. The commingling of same and other shows order and change, difference and similarity, so that as far as possible everything has come into being in friendship (*philia*) and fellowship (*koinōnia*).[36] The basis of this concord in harmony and number is demonstrated by extensive numerological speculation that Plutarch has apparently taken over from earlier sources.[37] This emphasis on number, harmony and concord contains the establishment of disharmony and evil as cosmological principles. Plutarch's lost treatise on Beauty appears to have included a defense of the bodily as part of the definition of a human being.[38] "Desire" is attached to the irrational soul and not to matter in any case. But one cannot escape the insistence upon an account of the world which includes disharmony and evil among its principles. For Plutarch, this account demonstrates the superiority of Plato to the Epicurean or Stoic accounts. It also demonstrates that the true source of order lies in the intelligible realm.

The myth of the sleeping World Soul also appears in Albinus. It cannot be found directly in Plato but may represent a tradition that is earlier than both thinkers. It suggests a view that the interweaving of the irrational and rational souls is responsible for maintaining a constant cosmic tension.[39] Atticus, according to Proclus, agreed with Plutarch's view that prior to the divine ordering of the cosmos, the disorderly soul was responsible for its chaotic motion.[40] Thus, one may presume that much of Plutarch's account would have found a ready hearing among second century Platonists.

Numenius can be read as standing in this tradition of Platonism. Yet, where Plutarch and Atticus see harmony, he finds constant struggle.[41] Numenius also appears to have associated evil more closely with matter, the unorganized, infinite Dyad than did Plutarch. As a result, the material character of the heavenly bodies suggests that they, too, fall under the influence of evil.[42] Numenius also appears to have divided the Demiurgic figure into two. The Demiurge forgets itself and is distracted out of concern for matter. However, the Demiurgic figure remains "good" and contemplative. The world which comes into being as a result of the action of the demiurge is one which participates in beauty.[43]

Even at its most negative, second century Platonists presumed that the sensible world reflected the beauty and order of the intelligible one. If they emphasized the elements of discord and evil, it served a polemic on behalf of transcendent divine order against the Stoic version of an immanent providence to be identified with the divine Logos. It appears likely that the few references to intelligible beauty in Gnostic writings reflect the influence of such Platonic *topoi*.

Intelligible Beauty in the Nag Hammadi Codices

The rupture between the Pleroma and the material world in Gnostic mythology permits an antitype of numerical order in the heavens created by the Demiurge, but not continuous reflections of the Beautiful. Plotinus concludes his work against the Gnostics with the charge that they are impervious to the beauty in the world. A person who cannot be moved by beauty is incapable of contemplation, he argues. Therefore, such a person cannot claim to attain to God, (*Enn.* II.9, 17). This charge strikes at the foundation of Gnostic piety.

Plotinus preceded the charge with the argument that the Gnostics have abandoned the providential ordering of the lower world. Disputes over providence were common in the second century. Several Gnostic writings construct their own accounts of providence.[44] The Gnostic response to Plotinus's charge that they have abandoned the providential ordering of the world and fail to see its beauty can be exemplified in *Eugnostos*.[45] The lower heavens are constructed according to an ordered sequence of powers of ten in androgynous pairs.[46] However, *Eug.* argues, the perfect and good aeons created in the heavens also reveal the defect of the female.[47] The aeons which come to be from the Immortal Man and his consort Sophia provide the types for what appears in the sensible world.[48] This region of ineffable joy, rest and glory is apparently the realm which the Gnostic reader of the tractate is summoned to contemplate. The cosmological speculation in *Eug.* apparently formed the basis for the writing which follows it in the collection, *Sophia of Jesus Christ*. The Christian Gnostic revelation dialogue combines the cosmology with a myth of the fall of Sophia's "drop" into the material world and the rescue of her offspring from the "powers" by the Gnostic revealer.[49] Although it repeats much of *Eug.* word for word, *SJC* lacks the speculation on numerological order and the origin of time. It retains the reference to the defect of the female in the heavens, which is clearly interpreted to refer to the Sophia myth. It presumes that the Gnostic is to "shine more than" the glorious heavenly powers with which *Eug.* concludes.[50] SJC has a different image of heavenly resting place of the soul derived from the Sophia myth. Those who know the Father in pure knowledge depart to be with the Unbegotten. Those who know him defectively are in the Eighth. Others become a light in the spirit of silence or attain the Eighth through their knowledge of the Son of Man.[51] *Eug.* apparently proposes some form of contemplation of heavenly order as a key to the knowledge of the divine received by the Gnostics. They apparently become participants in the joyous, immortality of the heavenly aeons. Perhaps the defect of the female evident in the heavens motivates this turn toward knowledge. However, SJC reflects quite a different pattern of redemption. It depends upon a salvation gained through the revealer, who is finally identified with Christ. Such Gnosis has no interest in contemplating the order of the heavens. It is possible that the present version of *Eug.* is as much a redaction of an earlier cosmological treatise as is SJC. The two writings reflect a diverging path in Gnostic piety.

The path of spiritual ascent and contemplation is clearly evident in those tractates which are also reputed to have circulated in Plotinus's circles. *Allogenes* assures its readers that the Invisible One, God, transcends all things. He is even spoken of as "non-being." The One is a triad, Life, Mind and Existence, of unsurpassable greatness and beauty. It is the source of all things.[52] Ascent takes the form of a heavenly journey through the spheres to the One. The author concludes that the transcendence of the One, which includes its perfection and beauty, implies that He is "unknown" to the lower powers. There is no activity in the One; no concern with what is below. Yet, the One contains all things. The paradoxes of "non-being existence" and unknowability, suggest that the One cannot be known directly. *Allog.* rejects the claims of those who might say they have done so. Only Gnostic revelation provides access to the One.[53] Against Plotinus, then, *Allog.* holds that beauty, goodness and the other attributes attached to God have nothing in common with their use in this world. Claims to a contemplative ascent without revelation are mere self-deception.

Marsanes also contains a vision of the ascent of the soul through the various grades of being. It includes correspondences between the sounds of vowels, diphthongs and the shapes of the soul, which might address Plotinus's argument against the influence of sounds on incorporeal entities.[54] Speculation about the monad, dyad and subsequent numbers attaches beauty to the number seven.[55] The fragmentary nature of the work makes interpretation of its cosmological structure difficult. The visionary claims to seek the Three-powered One and to understand "what really exists." This claim is attached to a sketch of the levels of being, which suggests that knowledge of the intelligible world leads to the conclusion that the sensible world is to be saved completely.[56] What survives of *Mar.* does not permit us to reconstruct the argument for that conclusion. Unlike *Allog.*, *Mar.* does not appear to emphasize the radical transcendence of the three-powered One or its relationship to the Good and the Beautiful. It would appear that the numerological correspondences and the correlation between sounds and shapes of the soul are the foundation of its understanding of ascent. The soul has to be summoned out of its infatuation with the sense-perceptible world that is the result of embodiment. *Mar.* suggests that contemplation of the celestial order of the seven planets, the twelve signs of the zodiac and the thirty-six decans are the beginning of the turn away from the sensible world toward the intelligible.[57] The affirmation of the sensible world in *Mar.* represents one of the strongest in any Gnostic text. This affirmation appears to have been attached to an equally strong conviction that the heavenly spheres reflect the order of the intelligible world.

The *Gospel of Truth* stems from a monistic form of gnosis, which appears to be closely related to that opposed by Irenaeus in *Adv. Haer.* II.[58] It presumes a close identification between the story of ignorance among the aeons and the situation of the Gnostic.[59] We have already seen hints of such coordination in Plutarch's parallels between cosmic and psychic reflections of the "same and other." Irenaeus's reading presumes that Gnostic statements are to be read on the cosmological level simply. *Gos. Truth* presupposes that ignorance of the Father occurs within the divine pleroma. For *Allog.* such "ignorance" was an expression of the transcendence of the Father. *Gos. Truth* on the other hand, ties the incomprehensibility of the Father to the story of the emergence of the sensible world. The drama of salvation unfolded around the figure of Jesus leads to the overcoming of that condition of ignorance.[60] Since the Father contains all things, this entire drama takes place "within" the pleroma.[61]

The coordination between a story of the "fall" as the origin of a world that is ignorant of the Father and the pleroma as the place in which the story is enacted, appears in the peculiar role played by beauty in *Gos. Truth*. Ignorance of the Father leads to anguish and error which set about making a creature, "preparing in beauty a substitute for truth."[62] This assertion is immediately followed by an affirmation that error and ignorance are no humiliation to the Father. The Father is established, immutable truth, which is perfect in beauty.[63] Therefore, the Gnostic should despise error. This argument follows the image of transcendence set out in *Allog*. Nothing which happens in the lower world can be of concern to the transcendent, self-sufficient One. Therefore, those, like Irenaeus, who might argue that the Gnostic account of the lower world is somehow unworthy of God, simply fail to understand that God's perfect Truth is beyond such concerns.

The correlation between the beauty in the material world and the true beauty of the Father is unclear. Since the Gnostic requires revelation to turn away from error, *Gos. Truth* does not appear to hold that the former can direct the soul to the latter. Ménard observes that Philo has a similar contrast in *Opif*. 139. The true beauty of the divine Logos is contrasted with that found in the cosmos.[64] According to *Gos. Truth*, the lower world is characterized by a "deficiency" which will come to an end with the revelation of the Father. Both matter and the "form of the world" will be consumed by the knowledge of God and all will exist in unity. Thus, nothing remains outside the Father.[65] The exhortation to the Gnostic is to see to it that "the house" is purified and silent for the Unity. Awakening to gnosis means that the Gnostic recognizes that he or she is "in the Father" and is thus able to come forth from error and ignorance and ascend to the Father.[66] It would appear that material beauty could only be a deficient substitute for the true beauty of the Father, since it is characterized by a deficiency, which is to be overcome. Unlike Irenaeus, who must also agree that the material world comes to an end, Plotinus insists upon the permanence of the sensible world. (*Enn*. II.9, 3). He insists that one who thinks that the universe will end would have to argue that matter itself is dissolved, which *Gos. Truth* does appear to hold. Such a doctrine is philosophically incoherent, he argues, because whatever comes into being as the result of the operation of a spiritual principle must always remain so. Indeed, *Allog*. appears more consistent than *Gos. Truth* in its account of the "necessary" ignorance of the Father without revelation.

The alternation between cosmic and psychic metaphors continues in the dream sequence. Existence in the world prior to the awakening granted by revelation is like persons suffering a series of nightmares. When one awakens, all the terrors of the dream vanish.[67] Plutarch used the image of the "slumbering World Soul" to describe the cosmic alteration of principles of the "same and other." Plotinus comments that the Gnostics create their own terrors through ignorance. If they understood the true nature of the cosmic spheres, they would not fear them. They cannot be treated as tyrannical rulers but are set over the universe as givers of beauty and order.[68]

Gos. Truth would appear to reject any claim that the ultimate truth can be known through philosophical reflection. The work consistently returns to revelation through the activity of the Son as the way in which one comes to know the Father and so attain stability and rest. For one who has awakened to the Truth, the drama of salvation has been played out. That person is no longer living in the nightmares of the ignorant. However much *Gos. Truth* owes to philosophic speculation, the author never supposes it to be a substitute for revelation.[69] In the end, as *Allog.* and *Mar.* also contend, philosophy must give way to revelation of the Father.

The *Tripartite Tractate* presents an even more elaborate systematization of Gnostic traditions. Instead of an errant Sophia, we find the logos as the aeon responsible for the creation of the lower worlds.[70] *Trip. Trac.* opens with an elaborate exposition of the transcendence of the Father in categories drawn from the Platonic traditions of negative theology.[71] The demiurgic mode of creation had been seen to be inappropriate for the highest God. Plotinus rejects the idea that the World Soul could have engaged in any activity that might require deliberation to create the universe. *Trip. Trac.* shows a similar concern in its insistence that the Father does not create on the basis of a Form or have to overcome any obstacle. Indeed, the Father does not create from any external matter or generate the lower aeons from any internal substance.[72]

Like the other Gnostic writings in this group, *Trip. Trac.* finds an "ignorance of the Father" to be characteristic of the lower aeons. Several explanations are offered to make that view more acceptable. The unity of the entire system is one of love and longing for the Father, which stems from the fact that he is not perfectly known. Instead, the names provided for the Father by the Spirit provide knowledge through a "divided unity." The Father will graciously grant knowledge of himself, but withholds it so that the aeons will be perfected through the process of searching. Had they not gone through that process, they would think that such knowledge came through their own powers and would be arrogant. Had the Father revealed himself all at once, the aeons would have perished.[73]

Ignorance of the Father also guards his incomprehensibility. The devolution of the lower world results from the attempt of the Logos to grasp the incomprehensibility of the Father. Quite unlike many Gnostic myths, *Trip. Trac.* insists that this attempt was good. It was the result of great love for the Father and according to the will of the Father.[74] The world which the Logos begets is the realm of shadows and likenesses, of division, doubt, deliberation and the two opposing movements of the "same and other," of ascent back to the pleroma and descent into deficiency. As in Philo, the lowest world is the one in which the desire for power and command represents the fundamental principle of order. Association with this world of division means that the Logos must be awakened and turned toward the pleroma and its likenesses.[75] *Trip. Trac.* uses the dream image in a cosmological sense to describe the two types of powers: some are like forgetfulness in a heavy, troubled sleep; others like creatures of light looking for the rising sun who dream pleasant dreams.[76]

Even the hostile powers in the lower order are ultimately subject to the administration of the Logos. The Logos creates and administers the world through the intelligible world of Forms, which is an image of the Pleroma and is superior to the strife in the material world.[77] Throughout its account of the devolution of the lower world, *Trip. Trac.* emphasizes the elements of beauty which belong to the various realms. Things in the lower realm are divided between those due to discordant powers, which are shadows and will ultimately vanish, and those which are images of the Pleroma. The latter have beauty derived from the things of which they are images.[78] When the repentant Logos turns toward the higher world, he gives honor and praise to the Pleroma and is able to generate images of "the living Forms, beautiful in that which is good, resembling them in beauty, but unequal to them in truth."[79] The administrative function of the Logos is reflected in a process of beautification. This process does not extend to all of the lower world, but to the creation of "spiritual places" in which those who belong to the aeon "church" belong.[80]

However, *Trip. Trac.* also operates on a threefold division of humanity, pneumatics, psychics and hylics. It appears to claim that both the pneumatics and psychics attain salvation. Like *Gos. Truth*, the story of the aeons becomes that of the Gnostic soul. Consequently, a further division is introduced into the same/other, right/left, dualism of the account. The distinction between beauty and thought provides the vehicle for this development. The realm of thought, the pleroma, the world of the things which pre-exist, is separate from the world of images which have come into being from the Logos. We find a triple division in the cosmos. The truly beautiful are the things which belong to thought and represent the pleroma. The middle realm, generated by the repentant Logos, is the realm of conversion. Finally, the lowest realm is that administered by law, the region of condemnation and wrath. Even the things which come to be there are images, those images are phantasies. No knowledge is associated with what comes into being through phantasies of arrogance and power.[81] However, the sensible world and its images are ruled by an Archon established by the Logos after the pattern of the Father of the pleroma. The Logos uses the Archon as a "hand" to beautify the lower regions, as well as to prophesy and to administer that world.[82]

Trip. Trac. suggests that the action of the Logos differs with regard to each of the three types of person. Those who belong to thought are drawn into a material union with the lower Logos, so that they cease to be attracted by evil or by the glories of the world. Instead, they love and search for the one who can heal them from deficiency. Those who belong to the "likeness" are set under the "word of beauty" so that the Logos can bring them into a Form. The final group falls under judgment. Their lust for power is used by the Logos to administer the world.[83] The distinction between the process for those belonging to thought and those belonging to beauty is not clear. Later in *Trip. Trac.*, we find that the "spiritual" receive salvation immediately in the revelation of the Logos. The "psychics," apparently a category which includes Gnostics, require instruction. They are said to receive forms resembling the images and archetypes until the whole church can be assembled. *Trip. Trac.* appears to associate this process with the Gnostic sacraments, though it also presumes that Christians are rewarded for their faith, good deeds and good dispositions.[84]

Trip. Trac. introduces this section on salvation with the cosmological image of the cyclic alteration between the powers on the right and on the left. When those on the left dominate, the "wise" powers on the right appear like them in using force. When those on the "right" dominate, the powers of the left seek to copy them in doing good. This shifting alteration of powers provides an explanation for the diverse philosophical accounts of the origins of the cosmos that have been offered by the philosophers. However, *Trip. Trac.* argues, none of the philosophers have been able to advance a true explanation of the cosmos. Their arrogance and confusion reflects the "fighting" that takes place among the powers of the lower world. Philosophical systems depend upon imagination and speculation. Consequently, they mistake the realm of images for reality.[85] Much of this attack on the philosophers could be paralleled in Plotinus's polemic against the Gnostics. It clearly reflects conventional inter-school polemic. However, it also shows that *Trip. Trac.*'s debts to philosophic speculation are not aimed at philosophical analysis for its own sake. Its revelation entails a conversion away from philosophy. Similarly, *Trip. Trac.* speaks of a conversion away from the gods sparked by the coming of the Son of the unknown God.[86] *Trip. Trac.*, at least, would agree with Armstrong's conclusion. Gnosis is fundamentally a different mode of faith from Platonism, however much it may have learned to express the transcendence of God and the ordering principles of the world in Platonic terms.

Plotinus and Gnostic Christianity

Much of the cosmological speculation in *Trip. Trac.* can be paralleled in Plotinus. Even the introduction of division and multiplicity into the Logos as part of the generation of the lower world can be given a good Platonic reading.[87] But the contemplative structure of the world by which even "unconscious nature" can be said to engage in a sleeping movement toward the good is impossible in the Gnostic cosmos.[88] The Gnostic thinkers have appropriated a second century Platonism, which had already pointed to the disharmony and evil in the sensible world to counter Stoic cosmological speculation. *Trip. Trac.* points out that while some philosophers are impressed with the harmony and unity of all things, others are equally influenced by evils and discord. The conventional Platonist argument insists that the imperfections of the sensible world merely serve to turn the soul toward the reality of the intelligible. However, Irenaeus uses an anti-Platonist argument that the theory of sensible things as the images of "Forms" requires that disharmony and discord characterize the intelligible world as well as the sensible one. In a milder vein, the second century Platonists like Plutarch who exegeted Plato to provide a "disorderly World Soul" as a cosmic principle answered that objection while granting it in principle. *Trip. Trac.* has used that theme to provide a monistic reading of early Gnostic myths of the devolution of the lower world.

But for all of the Gnostic systems the transcendence of God and the disorder in the sensible world combine to indicate the necessity of revealed knowledge of the Father. Plotinus lays hold of another fundamental difference between his vision and that of the Gnostics when he objects to the "temporality" of the Gnostic stories, (*Enn.* II 9, 3-4). Principles of generation in the intelligible realm must always be operative. The Gnostics, on the other hand, constantly speak of things coming to be in a way that implies change in that realm just as much as they presume that the material world will ultimately be dissolved. For the Platonist, beauty and order in the sensible world are images of eternity. For the Gnostic, disorder bespeaks the illusory character of a world that is not eternal. Unlike the philosophical image of an eternal alteration of the two opposing powers, the Gnostic view is incoherent. Plotinus protests that if this world is destined for destruction, its creator should have done so. If the Gnostic protests that not all the souls have been liberated, one should respond that there has been more than enough time for them to reject this world in favor of their true home (*Enn.* II.9, 4-5). Fundamentally, the Gnostic is trapped by categories of time and space that belong to the sensible world. These categories are mediated in stories which depend upon their applicability. Thus, Plotinus concludes his refutation of the Gnostics by contrasting the contemplation of the philosopher who knows what it means for the soul to be "outside" this world with the claims of the Gnostics that they will ascend beyond the stars. Whatever happens in this world, the philosopher can withdraw into the untroubled contemplation of the intelligible realm. The Gnostics, on the other hand, must finally dissolve this world, its order and beauty, in order to transcend it (*Enn.* II.9, 18).

NOTES

1. See the comment on *Tripartite Tractate* in Dominic J. O'Meara, "Gnosticism and the Making of the World in Plotinus," *The Rediscovery of Gnosticism*, Vol. 1: *The School of Valentinus*, ed. B. Layton (Leiden: Brill, 1980), p. 371, n. 26.

2. See Luise Abramowski, "Marius Victorinus, Porphyrius und die römischen Gnostiker," *ZNW* 74 (1983): 108-128.

3. O'Meara, "Making," pp. 368-375.

4. O'Meara, "Making," pp. 375-378. Plotinus's style of reflection sought to respond to individual philosophical questions rather than to create a systematic exposition of doctrine (see R.T. Wallis, *Neoplatonism*, [New York: Scribner's, 1972], pp. 41-42, 47). Plotinus protests that he hopes to persuade those who are "friends" to engage in courteous, philosophical inquiry into the logic of the Gnostic beliefs (*Enn.* II.9, 10).

5. Arthur Hilary Armstrong, "Gnosis and Greek Philosophy," *Gnosis. Festschrift für Hans Jonas*, ed. B. Aland (Göttingen: Vandenhoeck & Ruprecht, 1978), pp. 100-102.

6. Armstrong, "Philosophy," p. 101. Armstrong consistently rejects explanations of the Gnostic phenomenon which appeal to a pessimistic "spirit of late antiquity." He insists that ancient views of the world were quite diverse and that Gnosticism is more likely to have been a movement among a few intellectuals than a popular, mass movement.

7. Armstrong, "Philosophy," pp. 113-114. The ritual elements which are attached to Gnostic descriptions of the ascent of the soul suggest that some experience of praise of the transcendent Father was typical of Gnostic piety.

8. On the monism of the Gnostic systems behind the opponents of Irenaeus's *Adv. Haer.* II and *Gospel of Truth*, see the seminal articles by William Schoedel: "'Topological' Theology and Some Monistic Tendencies in

Gnosticism," *Essays on the Nag Hammadi Texts in Honor of Alexander Böhlig* (NHS 3; Leiden: Brill, 1972), pp. 88-108; "Monism and the Gospel of Truth," *Rediscovery of Gnosticism*, Vol. 1, pp. 379-390. Compare the ridicule attached to the story of Sophia's passion in Plotinus (*Enn.* II 9, 10-11) and Irenaeus (*Adv. Haer.* II 18). Plotinus sketches a few principles which render the story in Sophia's fall or loss of light in the lower world incoherent. Irenaeus is more directly involved in refuting the details of Gnostic systems which he knows differ from each other.

9. *Adv. Haer.* II 25, 4; 26, 1; *Enn.* II 9, 9. Plotinus would never agree with Irenaeus's assertion that it is better to be among the "simple and unlettered" and attain God by love rather than "puffed up" with false knowledge. He claims that the Gnostic arrogance springs from a lack of educated civility and humility, (*Enn.* II 9, 6).

10. Adv. Haer. II 30, 2; 32, 2; *Enn.* II 9, 9 and 15.

11. See Pheme Perkins, "Ordering the Cosmos: Irenaeus and the Gnostics," *Proceedings of the International Colloquium on Gnosticism and Early Christianity*, eds. C. Hedrick & R. Hodgson (forthcoming).

12. *Adv. Haer.* II 2; 5.

13. *Adv. Haer.* II 7.

14. Armstrong, "Philosophy," p. 114; Wallis, *Neoplatonism*, pp. 54-57.

15. *Enn.* II 9, 2 and 6.

16. On number symbolism as a primordial way of ordering the cosmos, which was adapted to the "scientific" understanding of the world by the Platonic tradition, see Walter Burkert, *Lore and Science in Ancient Pythagoreanism* (Cambridge: Harvard University, 1972), pp. 465-482.

17. Wallis, *Neoplatonism*, p. 18.

18. *Enn.* II 9, 14. This view presumes that the heavenly spheres do not "make music." For the dispute over the harmony of the spheres, see Burkert, *Science*, pp. 350-356.

19. *Adv. Haer.* II 25, 1-2.

20. Armstrong, "Philosophy," p. 118.

21. Armstrong, "Philosophy," pp. 97, 103-109.

22. Cicero, *De Natura Deorum* II 58.

23. Cicero, *De Nat. Deor.*, II 73-167. *De Nat. Deor.* III 79-93 contains the counter-argument to the Stoic view based on the evils in the world, especially those experienced by the good person. Plotinus objects to the Stoic view of divine providence that they still maintain a spatial identity between the World Soul and the divine and do not contemplate the intelligible world to which the true self belongs, (see Wallis, *Neoplatonism*, p. 25). Plotinus adopts the same argument to refute the Gnostic claims to an ascent of the soul beyond the stars.

24. Second century Platonists developed Plato's doctrine of the transcendent One/Good/Beautiful into an image of the One beyond the Good and the Beautiful, (see A.-J. Festugière, *La Révélation d'Hermès Trismégiste IV. Le Dieu Inconnu et la Gnose* [Paris: Gabalda, 1954], pp. 79-140). However, these developments do not necessarily indicate a widespread pessimism as

Festugière presumes, (p. 140). They often reflect a tradition-oriented, inter-school polemic against Stoic pantheism.

25. John Dillon, *The Middle Platonists* (London: Duckworth, 1977), pp. 343-344; Philo, *Opif.* 47-52; 89-128.

26. See Philo, *Opif.* 9, against those who claim that the world is *agenetos*. Cicero, *De Nat. Deor.* I 2; 41; 43, argues that the lack of providence in Epicurean systems destroys piety. For the Stoic influences on Philo's understanding of providence, see Dillon, *Platonists*, pp. 167-168.

27. *Opif.* 16; 20.

28. *Opif.*, 21-30.

29. Dillon, *Platonists*, pp. 169-170, compares the kingly power of Philo with the Valentinian Demiurge. We will see an independent adaptation of that theme in the *Tripartite Tractate*. Dillon suggests that both images reflect an independent tradition of a demon who rules the sublunar world. In *Trip. Trac.*, the Logos establishes an Archon to rule the sensible world.

30. Dillon, *Platonists*, pp. 174-175.

31. Plutarch, *Isis Osir.* 369AB.

32. *Isis Osir.* 369B-371E.

33. *Isis Osir.* 372E-373D.

34. Harold Cherniss, *Plutarch's Moralia XIII*, 1 999c-1032f (LCL; Cambridge: Harvard, 1976), pp. 138-141, emphasizes the incorrect interpretations of Plato presumed in Plutarch's exegesis. For Plato the only "irrational soul" is the embodied human soul and even that is not irrational in its immortal part. The "young gods" are assigned to create the moral, passible soul.

35. Plutarch, *De An Proc.* 1024EF. Cherniss (*Moralia* XIII.1,236-37, nn d & f), observes that Plutarch has identified the "same and other" of the *Timaeus* with "same and other" in the soul.

36. Plutarch, *De An. Proc.* 1027A. Armstrong, "Philosophy," pp. 104-105.

37. Cherniss, *Moralia* XIII, 1, 134-36.

38. Dillon, *Platonists*, p. 197; on the logos of the human as including body and soul in Plotinus, see *Enn.* VI 7, 4-6; Armstrong, "Philosophy," p. 115.

39. Dillon, *Platonists*, p. 287.

40. Dillon, *Platonists*, pp. 253-254.

41. Dillon, *Platonists*, pp. 256-257. Armstrong, "Philosophy," p. 107, finds this picture of the two souls closer to the dualism of the two spirits in the *Dead Sea Scrolls*.

42. Fr. 50 & 52; Armstrong, "Philosophy," p. 107; Dillon, *Platonists*, pp. 374-375.

43. Fr. 16; Armstrong, "Philosophy," pp. 108-109.

44. See Pheme Perkins, "On the Origin of the World (CG II, 5): A Gnostic Physics," *VigChr* 34 (1980): 36-46.

45. *Eugnostos*, CG III 3, 78, 16-24 + CG V 1, 7, 24-8, 6.

46. *Eug.*, III 82, 21-84, 11.

47. *Eug.*, III 83, 23-84, 11. Time frequently appears in connection with the motions of the world. Atticus apparently concluded from the irrational motions of the pre-cosmic world soul that time was precosmic (see Dillon, *Platonists*, p. 253).

48. *Eug.*, III 89, 10-90, 3.

49. See the discussion of the *Sophia of Jesus Christ* in Pheme Perkins, *The Gnostic Dialogue* (New York: Paulist, 1980), pp. 94-98.

50. *SJC*, CG III 4, 114, 7-8.

51. *SJC*, III 117, 8-118, 2.

52. *Allogenes*, CG XI 3, 47, 8-37.

53. *Allog*, XI 62, 1-64, 11.

54. *Marsanes*, CG X 1, 27, 22-34, 5.

55. *Mar.*, X 32, 23-24.

56. *Mar.*, X 5, 22-26.

57. *Mar.*, X 41, 24-42, 23.

58. See Schoedel, "Gospel of Truth," p. 388. Differences between *Gos. Truth* and *Adv. Haer.* II makes it impossible to identify the Irenaeus's source as *Gos. Truth*.

59. Schoedel, "Gospel of Truth," p. 386. Jan Heldermann, "Isis as Planē in the Gospel of Truth," *Gnosis and Gnosticism*, ed. M. Krause (NHS 17; Leiden: Brill, 1981), pp. 38-42, uses similarities between the image of Error in *Gos. Truth* and Isis in Plutarch's *Isis Osir.* to argue that the gnostic writer has deliberately inverted the beneficent, wandering figure of Isis into a malevolent deity. He finds the Isis/Planē figure too thoroughly implicated in evil to simply be a reflection of the Valentinian Demiurge. Heldermann notes that *Gos. Truth* is unusual in its identification of the aeons with the Gnostics (p. 27).

60. *Gos. Truth*, CG I 3, 17, 4-18, 29; see Schoedel, "Gospel of Truth," p. 385.

61. *Gos. Truth*, I 19, 7-17; Schoedel, "Gospel of Truth," p. 386.

62. *Gos. Truth*, I 17, 19-20; Heldermann, "Isis," p. 31, does not observe the connection between the "substitute" and beauty.

63. *Gos. Truth*, I 17, 25-27.

64. Jacques-E. Ménard, *L'Évangile de Vérité* (NHS 2; Leiden: Brill, 1972), pp. 82-83, points to the parallel with *Enn.* II 9, 10.

65. *Gos. Truth*, I 24, 9 - 25, 9; Schoedel, "Gospel of Truth," p. 387.

66. *Gos. Truth*, I 21, 3 - 22, 37.

67. *Gos. Truth*, I 28, 32 - 30, 26; Schoedel, "Gospel of Truth," p. 387.

68. Plotinus, *Enn.* II 9, 13.

69. Heldermann, "Isis," pp. 43-45, emphasizes the anti-philosophical polemic in gnostic writings.

70. See Pheme Perkins, "Logos Christologies in the Nag Hammadi Codices," *VigChr* 35 (1981): 379-396.

71. *Trip. Trac.* CG I 5, 52, 7 - 67, 30.

72. *Enn.* IV 4, 4; *Trip. Trac.* I 53, 21 - 54, 1.

73. *Trip. Trac.*, I 61, 18 - 62, 33; 64, 28-39; 71, 7-18.

74. *Trip. Trac.*, I 75, 17 - 77, 11.

75. *Trip. Trac.*, I 77, 12 - 83, 36.
76. *Trip. Trac.*, I 82, 25-37.
77. *Trip. Trac.*, I 90, 14 - 95, 22.
78. *Trip. Trac.*, I 78, 29 - 79, 11.
79. *Trip. Trac.*, I 90, 31-36.
80. *Trip. Trac.*, I 96, 17 - 97, 16.
81. *Trip. Trac.*, I 96, 1 - 98, 20.
82. *Trip. Trac.*, I 100, 19 - 104, 3.
83. *Trip. Trac.*, I 98, 21 - 99, 19.
84. *Trip. Trac.*, I 119, 16 - 132, 3.
85. *Trip. Trac.*, I 108, 13 - 110, 22.
86. *Trip. Trac.*, I 133, 16-26.
87. Armstrong, "Philosophy," p. 117; Wallis, *Neoplatonism*, p. 68.
88. *Enn.* III 8, 3-4; V 5, 12; Wallis, *Neoplatonism*, pp. 62-66.

Theories of Procession in Plotinus and the Gnostics

Jean Pépin

Introduction

The pages which follow are intended as a preliminary study of some aspects only of the generation of hypostases in Plotinus and among certain of the Gnostics. My study will be a comparative one. By that I mean that it will be almost entirely descriptive, and that the possibility of influence, positive or negative, in either direction, will only very occasionally be brought into the discussion. A further limitation on my study will be that the Gnostic systems that I shall here take account of will be almost invariably those that are recorded by the Christian writers against the heretics: Irenaeus, Clement of Alexandria, Hippolytus, Epiphanius, and the like. They will therefore be theories that these writers thought of as Christian theories, belonging for the most part, but not exclusively, to that brand of Valentinian Gnosticism which Plotinus had very likely come into contact with at Rome, whether or not the theories in question are identical to the system which Porphyry writes of in the sixteenth chapter of the *Vita Plotini*. I shall of course occasionally allow myself to bring in original Gnostic texts to illustrate and to complete the accounts of Gnostic beliefs which are preserved for us by their Christian adversaries; but it is these latter documents which will constitute the primary evidence that I shall draw upon.

My study falls into three parts. Parts two and three concern questions of detail. Is the Logos thought of or not as a fully active hypostasis, with its own proper place in the general movement of procession? How much truth is there in the way of looking at the procession as the interrelationship of images? The first part of my study tackles a more general question: namely the whole unfolding of the procession from its first beginnings to its final working out at the level of matter. It would obviously be a hopeless undertaking to attempt, in these few pages, to deal with the whole length of the movement of procession and with all the problems which that entails. I shall here be concerned with only three points, each of which will be introduced by a close reading of a Gnostic doxographical text drawn from Hippolytus's *Refutatio*. These three texts are already well-known; but the use which I shall make of them here I believe is new.

1. The First Unfolding of the Procession

A. *A Valentinian Doxography*

The following text tells us, on the evidence of Hippolytus[1/2], how it was that the Valentinians thought of the first stirring of movement in the procession.

> The Father was alone (μόνος), unborn, having no place, no time, no counsellor (σύμβουλον), nor any other substance which one might possibly conceive of in any way at all. He was, instead, alone, "becalmed" (ἠρεμῶν), as <the Valentinians> say, and at rest (ἀναπαυόμενος) within himself, alone. Now, because he was able to bring forth (γόνιμος), it seemed good to him one day (ποτε), since he contained within himself whatever is most beautiful and most perfect (τελεώτατον) to bring this to birth (γεννῆσαι) and to lead this forth into the day (προαγεῖν); for he was not fond of being on his own (φιλέρημος γὰρ οὐκ ἦν). For "he was," says <Valentinus>, "all love (Ἀγάπη [. . .] ἦν ὅλος), but love is not love if there is no object that is loved. The Father, who for his part was alone, sent forth therefore (προέβαλεν) and gave birth to (ἐγέννησαν) Intellect (Νουν) and Truth, that is to say a dyad (δυάδα), which became sovereign, principle and mother of all the Eons which <the Valentinians> reckon as being within the Pleroma. Sent forth in this way (προβληθεὶς) in company with Truth, by the Father, a fertile son sprung from a fertile Father (ἀπὸ γονίμου), Intellect sent forth (προέβαλε), in its turn, Logos and Life, imitating thereby the Father (τὸν Πατέρα μιμούμενος)."[3]

B. Connections with Plotinus

The Valentinian vocabulary of procession, such as we find it in the sentences I have quoted from Hippolytus, is found again, whole and entire, in Plotinus. Take, for example, γεννᾶν, which I have translated as "bring to birth." The *Enneads* apply this same verb to the procession of the Intellect, which is exactly the use of the verb that we have seen in the passage from Hippolytus. Thus in *Ennead* V, 1 [10] 7.5, the One "brings to birth (γεννᾷ) an Intellect." Or again, 5.3-4. In V, 3 [49] 12.29-30, Plotinus writes of "the Intellect which was brought to birth (γεννηθέντος)." The same verb is, however, no less common when Plotinus describes the procession of Soul from the Intellect. For example, in *Ennead* V, 1, 2.37-38, where Soul is said to "resemble the Father which brought it to birth (γεννήσαντι)," the generating principle being, in this case, the Intellect. There is the same thing again in 7.36-37: "for the Intellect generates (γεννᾷ) Soul." The verb προάγειν, which I have translated as "lead forth into the light of day, and which is joined with γεννᾶν in the evidence from Hippolytus, is used less often by Plotinus, but it does occur, for example in IV, 8 [6] 4.40-42. Plotinus is here dealing with an idea found frequently among the Platonists, whereby Plato uses various images in order to attribute an origin in time to beings that are in truth eternal (in this instance: souls). This is how Plotinus weighs up the descriptions that are given in the *Timaeus* of the procession of souls: "<Plato> decides to bring to birth (γεννᾷ) and to produce things that belong to the nature of the universe; he does so, by leading into the light of day (προάγουσα), one after the other, in order to make them clearer, the realities which become and which are eternally what they are." Another verb, which we have twice found in the passage I have quoted from Hippolytus, is "send forth," προβάλλειν. This verb also crops up, with the same meaning, in Plotinus. Thus in I, 6 [1] 9.37-39: since beauty belongs to the level of the Intellect, "what is beyond this beauty, we say that it is the nature of the Good, which has before her the Beautiful which the Good has sent forth (προβεβλημένον)." Of the three verbs which are used by Hippolytus, only the last — with the corresponding substantival form: προβολή, "sending forth" — is to be found in the parallel passage of Irenaeus.[4] This writer against the heretics[5] also mentions, in relation to Valentinus, and to an unknown Gnostic and to Mark the Magician, another verb which means "send forth": προίεσθαι. The same word, and the same use of the word, is again found in Plotinus. For example V, 1, 3.9: Soul is the act by which Intellect "sends forth (προίεται) Life in order to make there exist another being" (probably the sensible world).⁶ Finally, in VI, 8 [39] 17.3, the participle προϊέμενος, "sending forth," is used to describe the production of the sensible universe by its author.

Let us move on from words to ideas. Plotinus would not have disowned several pieces of doctrine which are attributed by Hippolytus to the Valentinians. This is true, for example, of the thesis (I) whereby the First principle brings to birth because it is, to the highest degree, perfect. Thus we read, for example, in *Ennead* V, 4 [7] 1.26-27: "When any one of the other beings reaches its perfection (εἰς τελείωσιν), we see it bring to birth (γεννᾶν) and not able to bear being left on its own, but having to produce another being." How can what is true of these beings not also be true of the First principle which they imitate? "How then could what is most perfect (τελειώτατον) the first Good be in itself without movement, as though it were jealous⁷ of itself or powerless . . .?" (1.34-36). The treatise V, 1, 6.38-40 is no less clear and to the point: "all beings, once they have become perfect, bring to birth (τέλεια γεννᾷ); the being which is eternally perfect brings eternally to birth an eternal being. . . . What then must we say of the being that is most perfect (τελειωτάτον)?"⁸ In these two passages (as also, *mutatis mutandis*, in the case of the Valentinians), the point at issue is the generation of Intellect by the One, a generation which is linked to the transcendent perfection of the One. In Plotinus, however, there is the same connection to be observed in the generation of Soul by Intellect: "for Intellect gives birth (γεννᾷ) to Soul, when it is perfectly Intellect (τέλειος). It had to be, you see, that, being perfect, it should bring to birth, and it had to be that so great a power should not stay sterile (ἄγονον, compare Valentinus: γόνιμος)" (V, 1, 7.36-38).

The same observation holds good for the Valentinian idea (II) whereby the sending forth by the Father of the first linked pair of Intellect and Truth (= subject and object) leads to the passage from the monad to the dyad.⁹ That is just how Plotinus sees things. For example in V, 1, 5.3-8: "What is it then which has brought to birth this <Intellect>? [. . .] for number is not first; before the dyad (πρὸ δυάδος), there is the one, the dyad is a second reality and, born from the one, the dyad has the one for limit, although it is, in itself, a thing unlimited." This setting out of the one and of the unlimited dyad is a well known feature¹⁰ of the way in which Aristotle and writers of the Old Academy thought of the Platonic theory of principles. This is the Platonism of the Schools which must have influenced, in parallel ways, the Valentinians and Plotinus.¹¹

Gnostic texts often contain the observation that such and such an entity which is of an inferior rank *imitates* such and such a principle which is superior to it. For example, in the Gnosticising theology of Numenius,[12] the demiurge, second god, is the imitator (μιμήτης) of the First god. In the continuation of the Valentinian doxography from Hippolytus,[13] we see that, when Sophia wants to have a child by herself, without a partner, it is in order to imitate (μιμήσασθαι) the Father. The same configuration of ideas can be seen in the text translated above: (III) once it has been sent forth, the Intellect sends forth itself Logos and Life; it does so, by way of an imitation of the Father. Plotinus will himself work imitation into the procession, as we discover in his treatise against the Gnostics. At the beginning of this treatise (II, 9 [33] 1.26-27 and 33-34), Plotinus fiercely takes issue with thinkers opposed to himself who invent hypostases other than the familiar three, and who, in doing so, distinguish between one Intellect which is at rest and another which is in movement, or again between an Intellect which thinks and another which thinks that it thinks. Not so, he replies: "there is one and the same Intellect which stays as it is, which escapes from every kind of instability, and imitates the Father (μιμούμενον τὸν πατέρα), in so far as it is possible for him to do so" (2.2-4). A coincidence, or more than mere coincidence? The reader will certainly have noticed that the expression which Plotinus uses when he talks of the Intellect imitating the Father reproduces exactly the expression which is used by Hippolytus.

C. *The Solitude of the Father*

As we have seen, Hippolytus's evidence brings out two characteristics which the Valentinians saw in the Father. In the first place, the Father is alone (μόνος repeated), solitary (ἔρημος, which can be extracted so to speak from φιλέρημος). And second, he is becalmed (ἠρεμῶν) and at rest (ἀναπαυόμενος). These two features are a common enough element in Gnostic theory, one which can be found in other Gnostic texts. Thus the first characteristic I have mentioned can be found in the *Tripartite treatise* of Nag Hammadi (I, 5).[14] The *Valentinian declaration* of Nag Hammadi (XI, 2) goes so far as to combine the two ideas, that is to say it conjoins solitude and rest.[15] At least in the version of the myth which Hippolytus has chosen to record, the solitude of the Father comes in part from the fact that the Father has no principle joined with him, a point which Hippolytus also expresses by saying that the Father is sufficient unto himself, that he has no need. Some Valentinians, he tells us, "think that the Father has no female, has no partner, is alone. . . . We, for our part, cling for the moment to the Pythagorean principle, which is unique, has no partner, has no female, has no need (ἀπροσδεῆ)."[16]

It is interesting to compare these statements of belief with ideas that were current at the time among the philosophers. Numenius also calls his First principle Father, and frees him from all labors so as to vouchsafe for him a state of rest.[17] There is one especially surprising passage where Numenius compares the knowledge which one can win of the First principle (called the Good) with the fleeting vision that one can have of some tiny boat lost in the immensity of the ocean. In either case, if we think of the object perceived, there is uniqueness, isolation, solitude. The ship is said to be μιά, μόνη, ἔρημος; the Good allows of no relationship except that of "an alone with an alone" (μόνοι μόνον). The Good rejoices in "a wonderful solitude (ἐρημιά), which no man may speak of nor tell of." Its epithet is "the Calm" τὸ ἤρεμον).[18] The Father's solitude, the Father's rest: the recurrence of these two Valentinian ideas in the philosophy of Numenius bears witness to the presence of a theological orientation common to Valentinus and to Numenius.

How does Plotinus stand in relation to these same ideas? At first blush, he does seem very close to sharing these same points of view. We have seen[19] — but this terminology is a commonplace — that Plotinus too calls the First principle "Father." It is rather more to the point to bring home that in Plotinus's eyes this principle is again without need. In at least one passage, V, 9 [5] 4.8, this characteristic is expressed, as it is in Hippolytus, by the adjective ἀπροσδεής. More often we find its equivalent ἀνενδεής. The most detailed text on this point is perhaps VI, 9 [8] 6.34-39:

> A principle has no need[20] of things that come after it; the principle of all things has no need of any one of them. For when something has a need, its need is to search for its principle. But if the One has need of something, then obviously it must be searching to be not one. Therefore its need will have for object the agent of its destruction. And yet whenever one says of something that it has need, its need must be directed towards its good and towards its own preservation.

This argument could have been put with greater lucidity; the essential point in it is this: -1° for every object, its need is directed towards its principle; the universal Principle, the One, could therefore have no need; 2-° if it did have a need, its need would be directed towards something other than the One, which would thus be reduced to wishing its own destruction; and yet the very function of need is to safeguard, and not to annihilate. A host of other Plotinian texts have to do with the same idea; the student of Plotinus should read in this light VI, 9, 6.16-26; VI, 7 [38] 23.7-8; I, 8 [51] 2.4-5; III, 8 [30] 11.41; V, 6 [24] 4.1.

The idea that the One should be thus totally sufficient to itself is certainly related to the solitude of the One,[21] an idea which Plotinus embraces, even if the solitude of the One is not, as it is for the Valentinians, the absence of a female mate. He often associates, in the same way as do the Valentinian whose views are recorded by Hippolytus and by Numenius, the two words μόνος and ἔρημος. But Plotinus's association of these two words is related rather to *Philebus* 63B, where Plato has the "kind" of pleasures voice its refusal to stay "alone and solitary," μόνον καὶ ἔρημον (and hence its desire to join itself to wisdom). Plotinus does not take over wholesale the position put forward by Plato in the *Philebus*. He makes much of the difference that he thinks there must be between human good, which is the subject under discussion in Plato's dialogue and which can indeed be mixed, and the first Good. The difference is such that the formula which Plato had rejected in his ethic of pleasure, "sole and solitary," is picked up by Plotinus and applied in a very positive way to the Good as first principle. That is more or less the burden of VI, 7, 25.12-16. The same two Platonic adjectives are brought up in a rather different context, in V, 5 [32] 13.1-7. Here, the Good has nothing in itself which would be good, or which would not be good. "If therefore it possesses neither the good nor its contrary, then it possesses nothing; if therefore it possesses nothing, it is 'alone and solitary,' cut off from other things." These ideas recall those of the Valentinians (and of Numenius) on the solitude of the Father, and the same observation may be made on the rest which the Father enjoys, since Plotinus teaches that the Good is "inactive," ἀγενέργητον (V, 6, 6.1-3).

D. *The Solitude of the One*

There is, however, this difference between Plotinus and the Valentinians: the solitude of the Plotinian One does not disappear when the procession has been completed. For Plotinus, the solitude of the One is definitive, and even constitutive of the One. It is not a mere state which comes from without and to which the One is subjected. It is a natural disposition which meets with total acceptance. That is the

meaning of one particularly clear and striking sentence in the treatise
VI, 8 [39] 7.38-40:

> We shall not say either that the solitude (τὸ μοναχόν) of the One is a
> suppression of its freedom, once it does not owe its solitude to some
> obstacle intervening from without, but instead to the fact that it is itself of
> such a kind and that in some way it is well-pleased with itself.[22]

The solitude of the One is thus neatly joined to this appearance of
narcissism[23] and continues in conjunction with the lack of activity
which ensures it. The formula which was borrowed from the *Philebus*,
as we have just had occasion to observe, makes even better sense when
it is expressed by a future indefinite: "the absolute One has nothing to
which to apply its activity, but absolutely 'alone and solitary' it keeps
itself at rest" (V, 3 [49] 10.16-18). The One of Plotinus is thus poles
apart from the Father of the Valentinians. The Father of the
Valentinians is, to start with, plunged into a solitude and a lack of
action which is difficult to bear and not meant to endure. The One of
Plotinus clings fast to the same double condition, with no inclination to
see it draw to a close.

We arrive here at a critical parting of the ways, which brings to a
head the whole reason for the procession.[24] Several explanations, not
necessarily exclusive the one of the other, are put forward in
Valentinian Gnosticism. The Eons have been sent forth with a view to
the glorification of the Father.[25] Since the creation of the universe is
comparable to the painting of a portrait, the cause of the universe is in
like fashion the majesty of the model, "so that the artist may be
honored (ἵνα τιμωθῇ) by means of his name."[26] The Father was
unknown, but wanted to be known by the Eons, and he sent forth the
Only-begotten, since it is by the Son that the Father was known, etc.[27]
In the Valentinian doxography recorded by Hippolytus, the answer to
the same question is different from those that have been listed above.
It consists of the following two points: 1-° the Father wanted to break
a solitude that he found oppressive; 2-° he sends forth out of love, to
rouse up an object of his love. (This second idea is Christian in origin;
witness the God agape of the *First Epistle of John* 4.8 and 16.[28])
Plotinus's position is different on both these points.

1-° The beginning of the treatise V, 2 [11] 1.7-16 falls happily into
place here. The procession from the One is described by the images of
overflowing (ὑπερερρυῆ), of over-full (ὑπερπλῆρες), of pouring forth

(προχέας, προέχεη). We have seen[29] that the perfection of the One leads it to bring to birth. It is nonetheless true that "this very perfection consists in searching for nothing, in possessing nothing, in desiring nothing" (lines 7-8). The Plotinian procession must thus be seen, from its very origin, as a spontaneous movement, and not as some process deliberately embarked upon in view of some aim or end. And in that perspective, it is plain that the very idea of a motivation of the procession, such as is claimed by the Valentinians, is deprived of all meaning. Plotinus himself has been careful to point out, against his Gnostic adversaries, how empty such a question must prove to be. Plotinus applies his mind rather to the manner of creation of the sensible world, and would have us no longer ask the question "why?" That is the attitude Plotinus would have us adopt for the stages of procession prior to the creation of the sensible world, and even for the first beginnings of procession.

> To ask why <Soul> has produced the world is tantamount to asking why there is a Soul at all, and why the demiurge is productive. That is, first of all, the question of those who allow that there is a beginning of what has always existed; and it is then to imagine that there has had to be a complete turnabout and a change of mind for there to be a cause of this making (δημιουργίας) (II, 9, 8.1-5).

Plotinus, we see here, discards the problem of motivation by making out that it is all of a piece with temporality and with change. The same argument would work against the Valentinian way of thinking of the Father, to whom "it seemed good one day. . ." Plotinus's hostility towards this idea comes even more sharply into focus when the motivation that there is thought to be is held to stem from the desire of the Principle to break out of its solitude. We have shown[30] how, even after the procession,[31] the One stays alone. Quite unlike the Father of the Valentinians which relies on the Eons which he sends forth in order to be no longer alone, the Plotinian One, in a comparable situation, does not look for anything from the offspring for which it is responsible. "He is by himself, solitary, with no need of the beings that are sprung from him" (VI, 7, 40.28-29). Or again:

> He had no need of the beings that were born from him; he was, instead, whole and complete at the moment when he let his offspring issue forth from him, because he had no need of it, but instead stays the same as he was before he had given birth to it. The reason is that he would not have had the slightest anxiety that it might not be born (IV, 5, 12.41-44).[32]

2-° The word and the concept of agape are not missing from the *Enneads* in relation to the One. The difference is that the One is not, as the Father of the Valentinians is, the subject, but the object of the love which is lavished on him by the Intellect. It is a general principle that "Every being desires the principle which has given it birth and loves it (ἀγαπᾷ)"; but the continuation of this same passage shows that Plotinus has his eye on the relation of the Intellect to the One: "and especially when the begetter and the thing begotten are alone; if the begetter is the best of principles, <the object begotten> is necessarily one with him" (V, 1, 6.50-53). There is the same doctrine and the same vocabulary in VI, 7, 31.5-6: "Thus <the Intellect> was transported into the higher world and stayed there, overwhelmed with the love (ἀγαπήσας) of finding himself close to the One." If it turns out that the One is the subject of love, that is because he is also the object of love, in a kind of *caritas sui ipsius*. That is what is described for example in VI, 8, 16.12-16:

> he transports himself, or so one might say, within himself, he is in some way loved (ἀγαπήσας) himself, he has loved his 'pure shining-forth,'[33] he is himself that very thing that he himself has loved (ἠγάπησε); that means that it is he who has given existence to himself, if it is true that he is a stable act and that the highest object of his love (τὸ ἀγαποτότατον) resembles an intellect.

We hardly need to insist any further, to avoid any lingering suspicion that this love turned upon itself is as far removed as can be from the Johannine ἀγάπη, restless to have something to whom it can give itself — as is also true of the Valentinian Principle.

The parts of Hippolytus's treatise which immediately precede the passage we have quoted contain other ideas, no less important than those we have been discussing, but which do not so easily lend themselves to comparison and to contrast with Plotinus. Before the procession, the Father had no "counsellor," οὐ σύμβουλον. That is a feature which comes from the Old Testament, where the same idea, and the same Greek word, are found twice at least in *Isaiah* 40.13 (quoted in the *Epistle to the Romans*, 11.34): "who was the counsellor of the Lord?," and in the *Wisdom of Sirach* 42.21: "he had no need of any counsellor." I cannot here dwell upon this point. I merely observe that this denial of the existence of any "counsellor" for God fits in very poorly with the doctrine which is present in several books of the Old Testament,[34] whereby a pre-existing Wisdom, or at any rate a Wisdom which is the first being to be created, fulfills just this role. There is a virtual acknowledgment of this idea in Theophilus of Antioch,[35] who associates Wisdom and Logos so closely as almost to identify the two, and who writes, exactly the other way round from his Valentinian contemporaries that: "Before anything was born, <the Father> had as counsellor (σύμβουλον) the Logos, which is his intellect and his thought."[36] Some twenty years later, in one of his treatises against the Gnostics, the *Adversus Hermogenem*, XVIII, 1, Tertullian uses the same words to confirm the role which is thus conferred upon the transcendent Wisdom: *Haec denique sola cognouit sensum domini [. . .] Haec illi consiliarius fuit.* Theophilus and Tertullian are thus united in claiming that there must be a "counsellor" for God; their agreement clearly points to the fact that Hippolytus's Valentinians had deprived the Father of any such aid.

2. The Stability of the First Principle

Hippolytus[37] describes as follows the procession according to the Naasenes:

> Thus therefore, <the Naasenes> say, of the substance of the seed (σπέρματος) which is cause of all things that are born (πάντων τῶν γινωμένων αἰτία) that it is not any one of these (τούτων ἔστιν οὐδέν), but that it brings to birth and produces all that is born. Here are the very words they use: I become what I wish and I am what I am" (γίνομαι ὁ θέλω καὶ εἰμὶ ὁ εἰμὶ). That, <the Naasene> says, is why the mover of all things is unmoved (ἀκίνητον εἶναι τὸ πάντα κινοῦν); for it stays what it is, producing all things, and it becomes no one of the things that are born (μένει γὰρ ὅ ἐστι ποιοῦν τὰ πάντα καὶ οὐδὲν τῶν γινομένων γίνεται) He alone is good (ἀγαθόν), says <the Naasene>.

This doxographical extract provides us with a universal generating principle, which is called in turn seed, good, and the, a few lines after the sentences quoted above, Father. For the moment, let us consider only the name of ἀγαθόν. Two important things are said of this principle: 1-° it becomes what it wants, in other words it is endowed with free will; this idea is expressed in a way which calls to mind the famous definition of *Exodus* 3.14: εἰμὶ ὁ ὤν. 2-° To speak as Aristotle does (*Metaphysics* 7, 1012b31; *Physics* VIII, 5, 256b24; *On the movement of animals* 1, 698a9, etc.), the principle sets in motion without itself being moved, in other words it itself stays as it is and does not become any one of the things which it produces.

The whole of this doctrine is resonant with echoes from Plotinus.

1-° The thesis of the free will of the principle makes us think of the title of treatise VI, 8: "On the liberty of willing and on the will of the One." Plotinus takes issue here with, among others, the authors of "a certain bold (τολμηρός) discourse whose case of ideas comes from the other side." Among these authors we shall probably not be wrong in seeing some of the Gnostics.[38] Their views are in any case quite different from, and opposed to, those of the Naasenes. Plotinus tells us that, for them, the nature of the Good

> turns out to be by chance what it is; it is not master of what it is; it does not draw from itself what it is; it cannot therefore have liberty, nor the freedom to produce, or not to produce, what it is forced to produce, or not to produce (VI, 8, 7.11-15).

Against these authors, Plotinus shares the opinion of the Naasenes, and indeed uses the very words that they had used.

> Everything turns out as though <the One> produced itself. Quite certainly he does not exist by chance, but as he himself wants to be (ἐστίν [. . .] ὡς αὐτὸς θέλει) (. . .). It is just by himself and of himself that he has being. He is certainly not what he is by accident; instead, he is as he himself has wished to be (ὡς ἠθέλησεν αὐτός ἐστιν) (VI, 8, 16.21-22 and 37-39).

2-° As for the idea of the Naasenes whereby the principle stays what it is and does not become any one of the things which it produces, the Platonic tradition is quite at home with such an idea. Admittedly, there are only one or two places in the dialogues where the origins of this thesis[39] can be more or less made out. In the *Symposium*, 211B, the Forms do not suffer anything as a consequence of the birth and destruction of things which participate in them. In the *Timaeus*, 42E, once the demiurge had arranged all things, he stayed in the condition which was normally his, ἔμενεν ἐν τῷ ἑαυτοῦ κατὰ τρόπον ἤθει. It seems that, after such modest beginnings, the idea passed into Middle Stoicism and there became rather more firmly delineated. By this route, the idea reached the author of the *Wisdom of Solomon* (second half of the first century A.D.). This writer did not, it is true, bring out the idea to the fullness which it will later enjoy, but does nonetheless give it a certain definition. Transcendental Wisdom, he tells us, "staying in itself (μένουσα ἐν αὐτῇ) renews all things" (7.27). Numenius, who has many points in common with the Gnostics, unfolds this doctrinal nucleus as follows:

the divine gifts are such that, carried from above to reach us here below, they are not removed from above, and such that, once they have reached us here below, they have brought benefit to the recipient without detracting from the giver [. . .]. This fine gift is the good knowledge from which the recipient has drawn profit without the giver being deprived of it. Thus can one see a lamp, lit up by another lamp, gaining light without depriving the other lamp of it [. . .]. That is the nature of the gift which is the science, which, given and received, stays (παραμένει) with the giver even while being united with the receiver, and with both giver and receiver is the same.[40]

The repetitious redundancies of this passage and the comparison with the lamp are obvious clues to the text-book nature of this passage. But if we are willing to raise our eyes above the particular case of the "knowledge" which is no other than the knowledge revealed by God, we will easily come to appreciate that few ancient writers have so forcefully given us to understand that the processional movement, while calling forth subsidiary entities which are sprung from a superior principle, in no way detracts from the originating principle. The Naasenes may have expressed themselves differently; but what they had to say was no different from this.[41]

What shall we say then of Plotinus? Let us take first of all the Naasenes: on their theory the principle, throughout its generative activity, stays what it is. We have glanced at a few of the ways in which this theory has been expressed, more or less consistently, from Plato to Numenius. The Naasenes have shown a certain distinctiveness in their using, in this respect, the two concepts of immobility, ἀκίνητον, and of permanence, μένει. These two concepts recur frequently in Plotinus, harnessed to the same general idea. It is doubtless true that, in one of his earliest treatises, IV, 8 [6] 6.2-6, Plotinus has not quite succeeded in integrating this idea into his philosophy, since he there tells us that "there would not exist any one of the things that do exist if the One had kept itself motionless in itself," and that in that eventuality there would be no procession (πρόοδον) of souls or of sensible beings. In a treatise which comes slightly later, V, 1 [10] 6.6-7, 12-13, 22-27, one can actually see the transition from the old way of looking at things to the new. Plotinus first tell us: "The One has not stayed (οὐκ ἔμεινεν) in itself." But he then expresses himself the other way round, or at least adopts a point of view which is very different: the One

is in itself, it stays (μένοντος) quiet beyond all things [. . .]. Thus therefore, what is born from above is born, or so we must say, without there being any movement (οὐ κινηθέντος) <of the One>; if there had been any movement of the One, in order for something to be born, what is born would then have been born a third after the One, subsequently to movement, and not the second. If therefore there has to be a second after it, it is necessary for it to exist without the One ceasing to be motionless (ἀκινήτον), without it bending itself, without it having wanted it; in a word, without there having been any movement on its part.[42]

If we turn to the Naasenes' other formulation of the same thesis, in terms of the principle's permanence in itself, then there are, as we have seen, two examples of this in Plotinus. And we could have quoted a hundred others. Plotinus often draws here on the ideas that we have already noted from *Timaeus* 42E[43]; for example, in V, 4 [7] 2.19-22, where the permanence of the One in itself is put forward as the necessary condition of procession.

> If therefore it is when the One stays (μένοντος) in itself that something is born, then this being is born from it when the One is at the highest point what it is (ὅ ἐστι). It is therefore when the One 'stays' in its own 'condition' that there is born what is born from it, and it is because it stays that the other thing is born.[44]

The Naasenes' second assertion, whereby the principle does not become any one of the things of which it is the cause, is a corollary of the preceding point. Numenius, it is true, has no mention of this second assertion. But it is often found in Plotinus, in terms that are very close to the Naasenes' expression of the idea. For example, in VI, 9 [9] 3.39-40: "Since it is productive of all things, the nature of the One is not any one of them (οὐδέν ἐστιν αὐτῶν)." Later in the same treatise Plotinus writes, in 6.54-55: "The cause of all things is not any one of them" (τὸ δὲ πάντων αἴτιον οὐδέν ἐστι ἐκείνων) for the reason that the case is not identical to its effect.[45] There are, finally, at least two chapters in Plotinus where the two aspects of the Naasenes' theory are present jointly: the principle's permanence in itself and its lack of assimilation to its products. This is first said to be the case in VI, 9, 5.36-38: the nature of the One is to be "a power productive of beings, which stays (μένουσαν) in itself, which does not grow less, nor is within the beings which are born by its action (οὐδὲ ἐν τοῖς γινομένοις ὑπ' αὐτῆς οὖσαν)." The same ideas recur in III, 8 [30] 10, where Plotinus starts off a long comparison[46] between the universal dynamic of the One and the living principle of a great tree.

> Or take the life of some enormous plant. The life permeates the plant from end to end, but the principle of it stays (μενούσης), without spreading itself

out, right out to the extremities, with its seat somehow or other in the root. Without doubt, the principle has furnished to the plant all the multiple life of the plant, but it has stayed itself without multiplicity (lines 10-13).

So much for the permanence of the principle. A few lines later (28-29), Plotinus dwells on its resistance to assimilation. "It is certainly not any one of the realities (ἔστι μὲν μηδὲν τούτων) of which it is the principle."

At the conclusion of our analysis, the impression which remains uppermost is that the properly philosophical footings of the Naasenes' system (at least in so far as they can be perceived in the condensed version which Hippolytus has given of them in the passage translated above) agree more often than not, and are sometimes couched in the very same language, as the views of Plotinus on the working out of the procession. We can check on this idea with the help of one final Plotinian text, where the principal character is no longer the One, but the Good, where however virtually all the ideas which we have noted from the Naasenes, including the allusion to the unmoved Mover and the title of First principle, are gathered together in a quite remarkable unison. It is absurd (Plotinus tells us) to deny freedom to the being which comes the closest to the Good itself;

> even more absurd would it be to deprive the Good itself of freedom, on the pretext that it is the Good (ἀγαθόν) and that it stays in itself (ἐφ᾽ αὑτοῦ μένει), without needing to move (κινεῖσθαι) towards any other thing, since it is these other things which move towards it, and without having need of anything (VI, 8, 7.43-36).

3. The Constitution of the Material World

A. The Material Model and Eschatology

We may learn most about the way that Plotinus thinks of the beliefs of the Gnostics and the attitude that he has towards them from *Ennead* II, 9 [33], chapters 10 to 12. There are some features in the way that Plotinus thinks of the Gnostics which coincide with what we can learn from Irenaeus, from Clement of Alexandria or from Hippolytus and other witnesses, direct or indirect, about Valentinian beliefs or even about the Gnosticism which is called Sethian. Sophia is not descended (to the world below from the Pleroma) (III, 9, 10.24-25; 11.1; cf. Irenaeus, I, 2, 4). The demiurge is cut off from the Mother (III, 9, 10.3;

cf. *Excerpta ex Theodoto* 49.1). Although the demiurge is thought to remember, for his productive activity, the beings which he has seen, he was not there to see them, any more than his mother was (II, 9, 12.1-3; cf. Irenaeus, I, 5.3[47] and perhaps the beginning of I, 7, 4; Hippolytus, VI, 33 and 34.8).[48] Fire is the first created being (II, 9, 11.28-29; 12.12-13; cf. Hippolytus, VI, 32, 6-8: soul-substance, drawn from the first of the passions of Sophia, from the world without and from which the demiurge is made, is fire). The demiurge is identified with Soul (II, 9, 6.61; cf. Irenaeus, I, 42; Hippolytus, VI, 34.1). Plotinus, II, 9, 10.27-29, attributes to the Gnostics an indiscriminate use of the nouns "matter," ὕλη, and "materiality," ὑλότης. In Hermetic Gnosticism one finds a trace of the association of these two words, when eternity and the substantiality of the ὑλότης appear to be distinguished from the immortality of the ὕλη.[49]

There is however another feature which Plotinus attributes to the Gnostic doctrine and which obviously held for him a considerable importance, given the place which he keeps for it. This is the point that Sophia, without being descended (to this world from the Pleroma), lit up the darkness (II, 9, 10.25-26: ἐλλάμψαι μόνον τῷ σκότῳ; the same message in 11.1-2; 12.30-31). Plotinus tacks on to this central dogma a number of reflections and questions; it is difficult to tell exactly whether they come from his own meditations or from his source. In the role she plays here, Sophia is close to Soul, possibly even identical to her (10.19-21; 11.15 and 19-20; 12.39-40 and 43); the darkness is none other than pre-existing matter (10.26-27; 11.14-16 and 24; 12.22 and 39). There is finally the question whether Sophia or Soul, which we know has not "descended" in order to bring about the illumination of the darkness, has or has not "inclined" towards the darkness. In chapters 10 to 12, Plotinus never fails to return to this point, bringing in the technical terms of νεῦσις (noun) and νεύειν (verb). Although the point is never quite cleared up, it appears that the Gnostics did profess belief in such an "inclination";[50] and Plotinus advances several arguments against this belief (cf. again 4.6-11). However that may be, the illumination does require a rational feature (λογισμός) of the world to be. This rational representation appears to have been designated by the Gnostics as the "stranger land," and to have been called by them the work of the higher powers (11.8-13). It is probably again a question of this rational representation when Plotinus speaks later of the eventuality that the Gnostic demiurge, or even his mother, exercises a rational activity (τὸ λογίζεσθαι, 11.23), conceives the intelligible realities (ἐνθυμεθῆναι ἐκεῖνα, 12.9-10), conjures up a thought of the (sensible) world and of the intelligible world (κόσμου λαβεῖν ἔννοιαν καὶ κόσμου ἐκείνου, 12.11).

The truth is that the question of the intelligible model ordained to the measure of the sensible world is one which takes up most of Plotinus's treatise against the Gnostics. Plotinus spells out his own thesis in 4.7-17: if Soul produces the world, it is because it remembers the beings of the world on high, not, it is true, because Soul then practices discursive thought, but because, by doing so, she fulfills her very nature. This inevitable recall of the sensible realities implies, for Plotinus, that Soul is not "inclined." Hence the justification of Plotinus's criticism, directed against the Gnostics on this point later in the same chapter, as we have seen. Further, Plotinus claims that the principle which is productive of this world can act only *by recalling* the intelligible realities *which he has seen*; Plotinus thus at once takes up a position contrary to, and even expressed in the same terms as, the point of Gnostic doctrine which we have already had occasion to allude to. The model of the world is brought back into the ring in 5.23-27. Here we see that the Gnostics did allow for such a conception, which went by the name of "reason of the world," λόγος κόσμου, and which Plotinus at once identifies as the model of the world, παράδειγμα κόσμου. There follows a passage where Plotinus binds together the theses opposed to his own which he has already made mention of and his own insidious questioning of the same. We thus learn that the author of the world had previously "inclined," and that he was very concerned to produce another world after the intelligible world, μετὰ τὸν κόσμον τὸν νοητόν, but that the possibility is not ruled out whereby the constitution of an immaterial plan might have followed the fashioning of the sensible world, instead of preceding it.

In any case, the importance of this final text lies in the Gnostic idea whereby the "reason of the world," in other words its intelligible model, is also an eschatological resting-place, whither the faithful will retire when they depart from this world below (5.25-26). The whole passage is marked by a certain ambiguity (between ideas and souls, and between the subject and the object of thought, what knows and what is known) which is common in the Platonic tradition, and especially in Christian Platonism.[51] Such ambiguity perhaps enables one to grasp just how it is that these thinkers could have envisaged the intelligible, but also eschatological, model, as subsequent to the sensible world. In any case, against such an assimilation of ideas, Plotinus brings up, with a certain maliciousness, the anti-world attitude of his adversaries, the Gnostics. How (he asks) can they hope to derive any profit for themselves from the model of a world which they hate (5.26-27)? Still more remarkable is the name which the Gnostics of whom Plotinus speaks here gave to their intelligible paradise. They called it a "new earth," καινὴ γῆ, (5.24), which should perhaps be brought into line with the "stranger land," ξένη γῆ, of 11.12, and which in its turn, as we have seen, corresponds to a rational model of the world, or at least to a resting-place to come. "New earth" is a biblical formula, always associated with "new heaven" or "new heavens." It turns up twice in *Isaeus* (65.17; 16.22), in his description of the renewal of Jerusalem on the return from the exile in Babylon. The same formula is taken up, and given an eschatological sense, in the *Second Epistle of Peter*, 3.13, and in the *Apocalypse*, 21.1. We have known for a long time that the expression "new earth" occurs in a Gnostic document, called *The Anonymus of Bruce*,[52] which thus links up significantly with what we can know from Plotinus. We must however also point out that the Gnostics drew on other formulae of the same kind (though without any origin in Scripture) to give concrete life and meaning to their notion of a model of the world. For example, in a text from Nag Hammadi (VIII, 1), *Zostrianos*, mention is made in this way of "airy earth."[53]

B. Reflections and Antitypes

Let us return to the information which we can glean from Plotinus on the illuminating activity of Sophia. First of all, Sophia herself, as we have seen, is not descended; on the other hand, the souls which are parts or members of Sophia have descended together (συνκατεληλυθέναι) and have put on bodies (10.21-23). And yet, the consequence of the illumination is that,

> come from on high, a reflection (εἴδωλον) forms itself in matter. Then, from this reflection, <the Gnostics> have made a reflection (τοῦ εἰδώλου εἴδωλον πλάσαντες), somewhere here below, through matter [. . .] and <by this means> they give birth to what they call the demiurge. After having cut the demiurge off from its mother, they have drawn forth from him the world, going forward right to the last of the reflections (ἔπ ἔσχατα εἰδώλων) (10.26-32).

The same theme crops up later (11.14-16), accompanied by a Gnostic formula: "matter, illuminated, produces soul-like reflections." Plotinus, failing to recognize the properly Gnostic meaning of the adjective employed here, objects, but all in vain, that the reflection of a soul has no need of matter in order to be able to be formed.

Can there be any reader of the *Enneads* bold enough to hope that he has managed to draw together what Plotinus tells us into a clear and coherent conception of this system of reflections brought about in matter by illumination? To get anywhere, we need to make use of an idea which Plotinus brought into play a short while before (6.1-6) as being of Gnostic origin. This is the idea of ἀντίτυποι, "replicas," which we have to contend with "when the soul in some way perceives the images (εἰκόνας) of beings, but does not yet perceive the beings themselves." "Antitype," like "new earth," is a word from the New Testament (*Hebrews* 9.24; *First Epistle of Peter* 3.21), where it is tied in with the exegesis of types. But we cannot here, as we could for "new earth," properly persuade ourselves that the use which the Gnostics made of this other term has its origins in Scripture. For there are several distinct pieces of evidence which father onto the Gnostics the use of this word, most often in order to single out a reality of an inferior degree which is the homologue of a reality of a higher degree. Thus, for the Valentinians, Man, which occupies in the second tetrad of the Pleroma the same place as does the Ungenerated in the first tetrad, is said to be the antitype of the Ungenerated, and in a more general way, the new tetrad shows up as the antitype of the initial tetrad.[54] A further example: the seed of Sophia which is deposited in the demiurge constitutes the Church, which is the antitype of the Church above.[55] So Basilides too.[56] Thus the idea of an "antitype" is worked out, as one may see, to take account of and to explain the vertical projection of an entity, from above to below, through various different levels. The idea of an "antitype" is in this way very close to that of a "reflection" of Sophia, which the illumination makes appear, from above, in matter. Once we have grasped that much, we can the more easily see how, in this latter context, there works out the proliferation of εἴδωλα which imprint themselves further and further lower down in matter. There is no call to try to trace Gnostic antitypes in Irenaeus or in Epiphanius, since they are already to be found in *The Anonymus of Bruce* and in *Zostrianos*. As we have seen already,[57] the first of these texts makes mention of an "airy earth." This in its turn is, on the one hand, a "resting place," in the world beyond; but it does also contain, somehow locked into each other, the various different entities which include two kinds of "antitypes," one lot "airy" and the other lot "autogenous."[58] There is the same ambiguity here as that which we have noted earlier: the ambiguity of an eschatological resting place which could also be a kind of model of the intelligible world. (Should one come round to seeing in the airy antitypes the intelligible model, while the autogenous antitypes are replicas of these at a lower level, or is it the other way round?) What is certain is that the word and the idea of antitypes, in conjunction with the airy earth and the model, also have a place in *Zostrianos*.[59] This point of intersection between the two Coptic treatises raises a difficulty.[60] It does however establish the place occupied by the antitypes in this form of Sethian Gnosticism. Presumably, ἀντίτυποι are not εἴδωλα. We can however entertain the belief that the two concepts, which have in common their cosmological function and their being spread over several levels, are not wholly foreign the one to the other.

C. The Painter and the Portrait

Not everyone understands in the same way the final words of Plotinus's chapter 10. Here is a word for word translation. Plotinus has announced that, as a last consequence of the illumination, the Gnostic demiurge produces the world right down to its ultimate reflections. He continues: "so that he who has written that insults with force," ἵνα σφόδρα λοιδορήσεται ὁ τοῦτο γράψας (II, 9, 10.32-33). With the single exception of Bréhier, all twentieth-century translators appear to have followed the footsteps of C. Schmidt.[61] This means that they have, one and all, seen in these final words of the Greek text an allusion to the author of the Gnostic writing whence Plotinus has taken his information. But even apart from our ignorance about the existence of a writing which would be such as to make sense of chapter 10, this interpretation, though hardly a dissenting voice has been raised against it, cannot be wholly satisfactory. For example, in the whole of the preceding text, the Gnostic adversary has never once been singled out except by a plural; why therefore would there be, all of a sudden, this change to the singular? Or take the purposive meaning of the conjunction ἵνα which several translators simply pass over in total silence: what meaning has it here? How or why should the production of the world by the demiurge, by means of images which grow steadily more degraded, — why should such an idea have as its aim (or even as its result) to provoke the Gnostic author to burst out into insults? And insults against whom? The verb, which is in the middle mood, has no object.

Is it possible that we can make better sense of the passage in thinking of the other meaning of γράφειν, which is "to draw" or "to paint,"[62] and which is the meaning which Bréhier has preferred? What is certain is that the idea of "painting" does have a place in the cosmogonical theories of a number of Gnostic schools. There is no dearth of examples. Hippolytus attributes to Perates a theory of the creation of the sensible world, according to which the Son imprinted on matter the forms which came to him from the Father. Here is the comparison which illustrates this passage from the one to the other:

> just as a painter (ζωγαφῶν) copies from living things, without taking anything away from them, all their shapes and transfers them with his brush onto the painting which he produces, in the same way the Son, by the power which is His, takes from the Father the paternal characteristics and transfers them onto matter.[63]

So it is also in *The Anonymus of Bruce*.[64] The author employs the metaphor of the painting (ζωγραφεῖν) in order to describe the constitution of the universe according to what seems to be a rational model. But the most positive Gnostic text for the assimilation of the cosmogonical process to the act of painting must be the fifth fragment of Valentinus. As quoted by Clement of Alexandria, this fragment runs:

> in so far as the portrait (εἰκών) is inferior to the living face, to the same degree the world is inferior to the living eon. What then is the cause of the portrait? It is the majesty of the face, which has provided the painter (τῷ ζωγράφῳ) with his model, so that he may be honored (ἵνα τιμηθῇ) by the means of his name.[65]

The essential point in this fragment is the setting up of a comparison between the relation of the picture to its living model and the relation of the world to its model, which is no less a living model.[66] The fact that the cause (or exemplar) of the portrait should be identified with a face enables us to understand that the world also has its cause or exemplar. The end of the text leads us to suppose that, in either case, there is a final cause. It is true that, once we have said so much, there do remain many obscurities, obscurities which the context of the quotation may eventually dispel.[67] The way in which Clement introduces the remarks from Valentinus[68] shows that he is going to deal with Valentinus's ideas on the God who is creator of the world, if, as seems probably, he is somewhere around, must be referred to by another name. And that is what we discover from the sentence which follows Clement's quotation of the fragment. Clement continues:

> For the Demiurge, in so far as he was called God and Father, he it is that <Valentinus> has called the portrait (εἰκόνα) of the true God and his

prophet, while he has given the name of painter (ζωγράφων) to Sophia, whose portrait is a making (πλάσμα), for the glory of the invisible, since from a conjunction there proceed (προέρχεται) only πληρώματα, while from a unique principle there proceed only portraits.[69]

The usefulness and significance of this commentary from Clement of Alexandria was earlier called into question,[70] but that is no longer the case today. Its essential contribution is to bring out, and to emphasize, the two figures of Sophia and the demiurge, which had been only implicit arises from Sophia is described by the artistic metaphor, the metaphor of the portrait made by the painter. The linking of ideas which Valentinus conceived is far from coinciding with the ideas of Perates as they are recorded by Hippolytus; and both these sets of ideas are again very different from the theories of *The Anonymus of Bruce*, at least in so far as one can make out the latter. The feature which they have in common is their representing, with a certain forcefulness, the production of the sensible world following the model of a picture. Can we draw on this idea to shed light on the last line of Plotinus's chapter 10? The ideas we have mentioned do at the very least stir us to try out for the participle γράψας the meaning of "paint." It would be overdoing things to want to understand, in a line that is tightly and strictly Valentinian, "Sophia who has painted the demiurge."[71] But we can imagine, in a Gnostic perspective, that the principle which had intervened as a painter, whether of the demiurge, or of the model, or even of the sensible world, at the sight of the calamitous result of the creative enterprise, should have been overwhelmed with insults for having participated in such an enterprise. We may therefore suggest, as a mere working hypothesis, the translation: "so far as for the author of this picture to be laden with violent reproaches."[72]

D. The Quest for Honor

Is it possible that the text of Plotinus might be useful, if we attempt, so to speak, to tread the path backwards and to understand the fragment from Valentinus? We have seen[73] that the treatise II, 9 twice brings up, and twice rejects, the supposedly Gnostic idea whereby the producer of the sensible world has been inspired in his activity by "the intention of being honored," ἵνα τιμῷτο. The exact identity of the formula in the two cases, and the way in which it is brought forward by

Plotinus[74] show that we have to do with a literary quotation, which should be put into inverted commas. And yet, the entity to whom one attributes this desire for honor is not quite the same in the two chapters. In II, 9, 4.2-15, it is a question of the universal Soul, which Plotinus tells us does not "incline"; translated into terms of Gnosticism, this will be Sophia.[75] But in II, 9, 11.15-21, Soul seems to have yielded place to its "reflection" (ψυχῆς εἴδωλον) , which is also its product (τῷ ποιήσαντι) that is to say, as we have already seen in 10.26-31, that we have to do here with the demiurge, son of Sophia.[76] We must look now at the almost identical formula of Valentinus, fragment 5: ἵνα τιμωθῇ. . . . It must at once be granted that the subject of this verb does not emerge clearly from the text. Scholars generally think[77] that we have to do here with the "face," to which the "name" also belongs. Without wishing to enter into the very considerable theological problems which are implied by these words, and which have been very cleverly disentangled by A. Orbe, one may say that this option has very little persuasive force, whether we consider the ideas involved or the grammar. In the comparison ὁπόσον . . ., τοσοῦτον . . . which opens the fragment, what is important is naturally the apodosis, i.e. the inferiority of the sensible world in relation to its model. How is it exactly that the production of a debased world would be conducive to the honor of "the majesty of the living face," an expression wherein one can dimly discern, whatever may be its exact meaning, a reference to a principle of a very high rank? Things are so unclear, that Plotinus's Gnostic doxography may here be of some use. No-one would claim that Valentinus's fragment is the source of Plotinus's passage. But how can one exclude[78] the possibility that there may be more than a simple coincidence between the formula which is certainly Gnostic ἵνα τιμῷτο and the Valentinian formula ἵνα τιμηθῇ? Plotinus could read; if he has given a subject of the verb "to be honored" once Sophia, and once the demiurge, there can be no doubt that that is because his source authorized him to do so. We know from Clement's commentary that Sophia and the demiurge are present, under different names, in Valentinus's fragment. How can we refuse to credit one or the other, or one and the other, "the intention of being honored" by the production of the sensible world? As much as, and even more so than, his model, and especially if the model is of a preeminent "majesty," the painter can lay claim to the honor due from a successful portrait, and the portrait itself can hope to share in the glory of the living Face.

E. The Illumination of the Darkness According to the Docetists

Chapters 10 to 12 of Plotinus's treatise against the Gnostics still contain numerous points of detail where the interpretation is uncertain; nonetheless these few pages contain a body of doctrine, succinctly expressed and relatively coherent in its main outlines. The essential feature is undoubtedly the illumination of the pre-existent darkness by Sophia and the ensuing appearance, within matter, of a series of reflections, leading up to the constitution of the sensible world. That is the main picture which one can discern, enmeshed of course, as it is, with Plotinus's own criticisms of and objections to the theory. Compared with this, there is nothing of quite the same calibre in the Valentinian doxographies of Irenaeus or of Hippolytus.[79] It is true, however, that Hippolytus does bring to our attention a conception of things which is certainly related to what we find in Plotinus. This Hippolytus attributes to a different current of Gnostic opinion, which he describes as being that of the Docetists. Here is a part of the description which he gives:[80]

> All intelligible nature had been arranged in good order, with nothing lacking to it, and all these intelligible and eternal realities were light (κεκόσμητο μὲν ἀνενδεὴς πᾶσα ἡ νοητὴ φύσις, φῶς δὲ ἦν ἅπαντα ἐκεῖνα τὰ νοητὰ καὶ αἰώνια), but a light which was not without form, nor inactive, nor which had any need, of any kind, of a further intervention. It had, on the contrary, within itself, ideas infinite in number, like the fig-tree: of an infinite number, an infinite number of times; living beings from the world yonder, in their multiple diversity. It shone forth (κατέλαμψεν) from on high into the underlying chaos. The chaos, illuminated (φωτισθὲν) and at the same time endowed with form by the action of the ideas come down from on high in their multiple diversity, took on consistency and received within itself all the ideas from one high, which came from the third Eon, which was itself split into three.
>
> But this third Eon saw the characters (χαρακτῆρας) which belonged to it, all together held down in the lower underlying darkness (σκότος). It did not fail to know the power of the darkness, nor the innocence of the light as well as its generosity (ἄφθονον). It therefore did not allow for long the luminous characters (φωτεινοὺς χαρακτῆρας) from above to be pulled down below by the lower darkness. Against that, it established beneath the Eons the firmament of heavens, from below, and it separated[81] [. . .]. Thus therefore, as I have said, all the ideas infinite in number, from the third Eon, were captured in the darkness of the lowest region. Right up to the Eon itself, there is nothing that has not had its imprint stamped (ἐναπεσφράγισται [. . .] τὸ ἐκτύπωμα) with the others, a living fire born from the light (πῦρ ζῶν ἀπὸ φωτὸς γενόμενον). From there is born the great

Archontes, of whom Moses says[82] [. . .] "Thus therefore the god in form of fire, fire born from the light, has produced the world in the manner which Moses recounts. It is itself without substantial existence (ἀνυπόστατος), since it has darkness for substance (οὐσία), and it is a ceaseless offence to the eternal characters of light which have come down and which are held in the lower region (ἐνυβρίζων ἀεὶ τοῖς κατειλημμένοις ἄνωθεν κάτω τοῦ φωτὸς αἰωνίοις χαρακτῆρσι). Thus therefore, as far as the manifestation of the Saviour, the god of fire born from the light, the demiurge, was cause of there being a great wandering (πλάνη) of souls — for the ideas are called souls (ψυχαὶ γὰρ αἱ ἰδέαι καλοῦνται) because they were exhalations (ἀποψυγεῖσθαι) from the upper regions, so as to pass their life in the darkness, exchanging their bodies for other bodies, kept under close guard by the demiurge . . . but, starting from the Saviour, the transmigration (μετενσωμάτωσις) has come to an end, the faith is proclaimed [. . .]."

This great myth is a wonderful support of the Gnostic mentality in general. Still more, it has several distinctive features which support the comparison with certain doctrinal points that Plotinus attributes to the Gnostics who are under attack in II, 9, especially in the three central chapters which we have been studying.

1-° A considerable place is given in the myth to the description of the well-ordered intelligible world, which contains the innumerable ideas of innumerable living beings (in the way that the fruit of the fig-tree produces countless seeds). This is the analogue of the rational model which the Gnostics of whom Plotinus speaks thought of implicitly as underlying the sensible world beneath the different names of λόγος κόσμου (II, 9, 5.26), λογισμός τοῦ κόσμου (11.11), κόσμον ἔννοια (12.11), "new earth" (5.24), "stranger earth" (11.21), etc. We have already highlighted, in the expressions just quoted, the ambiguity between an objective and a subjective meaning, between an intelligible model and an eschatological place. We are, in the present passage, confronted with the same sort of lack of determinacy, since the ideas are also souls, and since their intelligible totality is identified with an Eon, said to be the "third."

2-° The most obvious point these passages have in common is the one which relates to the illumination of the darkness. There is however a difference of content and of approach: in Plotinus's description, the model precedes the illumination and stays distinct from the illuminating power; whereas here, it is the light itself, the light which acts by itself and which is credited with an eminently active quality which is generosity, or more exactly the lack of jealousy.[83] The upshot is that the three terms which are kept separate by the Gnostics whom Plotinus criticizes, namely Sophia, the model, the light, join together now in a light which is also intelligible world and agent of illumination. Apart from that, the process of the illumination of the lower darkness is more or less identical in both accounts, and is spoken of in the same words: καταλάμπειν (II, 9, 12.40), φωτίζειν (11.14), σκότος (10.26, etc.), κάτω (10.19).

3-° But the luminous intelligibles of the Docetists are also "characters" belonging to the third Eon, characters which stamp their "imprint" on the darkness. The image of the seal is missing in Plotinus's account. But one can scarcely fail to associate these ἐκτυπώματα with the εἴδωλα that in a similar way are stirred up in the shadowy matter by the illumination which comes from on high, and also with the ἀντίτυποι, a word with the same root and whose use by the Gnostics we have already noted.

4-° The figure of the demiurge, at least as he is seen by the Docetists, is defined fairly precisely. He is also called "great archonte" and "god of fire born from the light."[84] He is the creator God of Genesis. In the same way as the demiurge that Plotinus denounces is a "reflection" of Sophia, so the demiurge of the Docetists is an "imprint" of the third Eon. The fire which it is made from comes from a lowering of the light. But in the illumination accomplished by Sophia, fire appears first (II, 9, 11.28-29; 12.12-14). After criticizing his adversaries with "introducing other hypostases" (6.1), Plotinus, we have seen, brings in the possibility that their demiurge is a substance (εἰ μὲν γὰρ οὐσία, 11.18-19), in order to show up the contradictions inherent in this thesis. We can hardly not have all this brought to mind, when we read in Hippolytus's evidence that the demiurge has no other substance than that of the darkness and that, notwithstanding this, it is "stripped of hypostasis." A final feature peculiar to the demiurge of the Docetists: he insults the characters of light imprisoned in the lower place. The aggressiveness suits the psychology of the other demiurge, the one who is thought to have produced the world "by bravado and by boldness" (11.21-22), which is as much as to say by provocation and by impiety.

5-° But the ideas are also souls, which have therefore descended into the darkness in order to undergo a "great wandering." This point, which is laid to the account of the Docetists, recalls the "migrations" (παροικήσεις)[85] which were brought in by Plotinus's adversaries (6.2). Condemned to live in the darkness, the souls travel from body to body by "metensomatosis." The word and the idea which it conveys were current in other Gnostic schools, for example in the circle of Simon Magus,[86] of Basilides,[87] of Carpocrates,[88] and also among the Gnostics of Plotinus (6.13). There is hardly need to add that Plotinus's Gnostics also professed belief in the descent of particular souls and in their dwelling in bodies that were not always human bodies (10.21-23), prisoners in a world from which only a very small number of them will ever escape, and even then only with the greatest difficulty (12.3-7).

The grandiose conception of these characters of light, transcendent beings stamping their imprint on the dark shadows of matter, is noteworthy for another reason. A very similar set of ideas is found in the *Chaldaic Oracles*. Several fragments from this collection speak of divine epiphanies which are produced in the aether and which mark the faithful believer with an imprint. The localization of these phenomena will be a puzzle for Simplicius. In his *Corallarium de loco*, Simplicius presents the difficulty thus:

> If we turn to the point that the imprints of the characters and of the other divine apparitions (τοὺς τύπους τῶν τε χαρακτήρων καὶ τῶν ἄλλων θείων φασμάτων) are manifested in place, then the chief issue is that all that can hardly be adapted to the *Oracles*, when they say that these phenomena are manifested in aether, but not in light.[89]

Simplicius has taken his information on the *Oracles* from Proclus.[90] One is therefore hardly surprised to see that Proclus, drawing probably on the same Oracles,[91] alludes to "characters of light (φωτὸς χαρακτῆρες) by means of which the gods show themselves to their own offspring."[92] This same way of looking at things, which goes back to the *Chaldaean Oracles*, crops up again, *via* Proclus and what Proclus says on the characters of light, when Denis the Areopagite writes[93]/[94] that the holy symbols of Scripture are "the offspring and imprints of the divine characters" (τῶν θείων ὄντα χαρακτήρων ἔκγονα κατ' ἀποτυπώματα). The similarity of content and of vocabulary is striking, if we bring together, on the one hand, the three parallel formulae of Simplicius, Proclus and Denis, and, on the other, the cosmogonical myth of the Docetists. If we plump for the end of the second century as the date of origin of the *Chaldaean Oracles*, and if we put Hippolytus *Refutatio* shortly after 222, then we might properly wonder whether there were not ultimately some kind of relation between Hippolytus's source on the Docetists and the first glimmerings of theurgical speculation.

NOTES

1. These texts are transcribed, in whole or in part, in a number of collections. They are briefly analyzed by A. Hilgenfeld, *Die Ketzergeschichte des Urchristenthums* (Leipzig, 1884), pp. 465-466 (Hippolytus on the Valentinians), p. 255 (on the Naasenes), pp. 549-550 (on the Docetists). There is a German translation in W. Foerster, *Die Gnosis* I, in the collection "Bibliothek der Alten Welt" (Zürich-Stuttgard, 1969), pp. 244, 344, 395-397 (in the same order as that given above); an English translation in the English version of the same work by R. McL. Wilson (Oxford, 1972), pp. 186, 267-268, 309-310. The text on the Valentinians has been reproduced by W. Völker, *Quellen zur Geschichte der christlichen Gnosis*, in the collection "Sammlung [. . .] Quellenschriften," N.F. 5 (Tübingen, 1932), p. 128.6-17; the text on the Naasenes is reproduced ibid., p. 14.14-18.

2. *Refut.* VI 29, 5-7 Wendland, p. 156.9-21.

3. I have put within single inverted commas the words which Hippolytus seems to give as being directly Valentinian. There is a more or less parallel passage in Irenaeus, *Adv. Haer.* I 1.1, where it is said in particular that the First principle has stayed "in a great rest and in a great calm" (ἐν ἡσυχίᾳ καὶ ἠρεμίᾳ πολλῇ) for an infinity of centuries. Cf. Tertullian, *Adv. Valent.* 7.4, ed. Kroymann, p. 184.11-12: "in maxima et altissima quiete, in otio plurimo." On the parallelism (and on the divergences) of the Valentinian evidence from Irenaeus, I 1.1 and from Hippolytus VI 29, see F.M.M. Sagnard, *La gnose valentinienne et le témoignage de saint Irénée*, in the collection "Études de Philos. médiévale," XXXVI (Paris, 1947), pp. 146-148.

4. *Adv. Haer.* I 1.1-2; cf. also Clément d'Alex., *Excerpta ex Theodoto* 29.

5. Ibid., I 4.4; LL. 3; 14.1-2.

6. Cf. M.I. Santa Cruz de Prunes, "La genèse du monde sensible dans la philosophie de Plotin," in *Biblioth. de l'École des Hautes Études, Sc. relig.*, LXXXI (Paris, 1979), p. 70.

7. Φθονῆσαν. The lack of jealousy (φθόνος) in God is a theme which comes to Plotinus (cf. also V, 5 [32] 12.45; II, 9 [33] 17.16-17) from *Timaeus* 29E. But the Gnostics, who shared Plotinus's belief on this point, very probably took their idea of it from the same source; cf. *Tripartite treatise* (Nag Hammadi I, 5) 57.30-32, translated by H.W. Attridge and D. Mueller in *The Nag Hammadi Library in English*, ed. J.M. Robinson, (Leiden, 1977), p. 59: the Father having given birth to the first-begotten Son, "He revealed the unsurpassable power and he combined with it the great abundance of his generosity (ἀφθονία)"; cf. H.-Ch. Puech and G. Quispel, "Le quatrieme écrit gnostique du Codex Jung," in *Vigil. christ.* IX (1955): 76.

8. M. Atkinson, *Plotinus: Ennead V. 1, On the three Principal Hypostases*, "A Comment. with Transl.," in the collection "Oxf. Class. and Philos. Monographs" (Oxford, 1983), p. 148 *ad loc.*, sees a biological pattern in the idea that the attainment by a being of its completed state releases a reproductive activity.

9. For the word "monad," cf. Hippolytus, *Refut.* VI, 29.2, p. 155.22-25 = W. Völker, *Quellen* . . ., p. 127.19-21: for Valentinus and others, disciples of Pythagoras and of Plato, "there is as principle of all things a monad (μονάς) unborn [. . .] to this monad they give the name of 'Father.'" We know that there are two versions of the way in which Valentinus is supposed to have thought of the Pleroma, cf. G.C. Stead, "The Valentinian Myth of Sophia," in *The Journal of Theol. Studies* XX (1969): 77-79. In one of the versions, the so-called B version, which is the one which we have just read as recorded by Hippolytus, the supreme Principle has no partner. But Hippolytus himself knows of another version, the so-called A version, which he pays scant attention to as being less authentically Valentinian (*Refut.* VI, 29.3-4, pp. 155.25-156.8 = W. Völker, pp. 127.21-128.6); this version is however the one which Irenaeus prefers. On this A version, the Principle of the Valentinians has a partner called Thought, Grace and Silence (*Adv. Haer.* I, 1.1); and from this way of looking at things, it is the original couple which is the dyad (ibid., I, 11.1). But what then is the monad? Probably the Father, before his joining up with Silence. That at least is what seems to be the purport, not of Irenaeus's description, but of a writing from Nag Hammadi (XI, 2), entitled a *Valentinian declaration*, 22.18-26, translated by J.D. Turner (*NHL*), p. 436: "the Father [. . .], the Ineffable One who dwells in the Monad [. . .] he was a Monad and no one was before him. He dwells in the Dyad and in the Pair, and his Pair is Silence."

10. Cf. K. Gaiser, *Platons ungeschriebene Lehre* (Stuttgart, 1968), texts n-°8, p. 453; 23 b, pp. 481-482; 30, p. 493; 32, 277, p. 501; 50, p. 530; 60, p. 541; L. Tarán, *Speusippus of Athens*, in the collection "Philos. antiqua," XXXIX (Leiden, 1981), testim. 45 ab, pp. 132 and 225-226; p. 326, n. 133; fgt 40, pp. 147 and 329-330; fgt 48, pp. 152 and 351-356; fgt 59, pp. 156 and 380-381.

11. The reference to Aristotle is obvious in *Enn.* V, 1 5.14 and V, 4, 2.7-8.

12. Fgt 16 des Places, 6-7 and 14-15, p. 57.

13. *Refut.* VI, 30.6-7, p. 158.1-3 = Volker, p. 129.18-20.

14. 51.8-11, translation p. 55: "The Father is a unity, like a number, for he is the first and is that which he alone is." The association of these texts has been made by H.-Ch. Puech and G. Quispel, *art. cit.*, pp. 72-77; see also A. Orbe, *Hacia la primera teologia de la procesión del Verbo* (Estudios Valentinianos I/1), in the collection "Analecta Gregoriana," XCIX (Romae, 1958), pp. 186-188; J. Zandee, *The Terminology of Plotinus and of some Gnostic Writings, mainly the Fourth Treatise of the Jung Codex*, in the collection "Public. de l'Institut . . . néerlandais de Stamboul," XI (Istanbul, 1961), p. 8.

15. 22.21-22, translation p. 436: (the subject is the Father) "He dwells alone in silence, and silence is tranquility."

16. *Refut.* VI, 29.3-4, p. 156.1-8 = Völker, pp. 127.23-128.5; Hippolytus means that he chooses to put forward the theory of the Father which will be the closest to Pythagoreanism, which is the system that he links up most closely to Valentinianism. In fact, our basic text starts almost immediately

afterwards.

17.　Fgt. 12.12-13, p. 54: the Father is θεὸς ἀργός, *deus otiosus*.

18.　Fgt 2.7-16, pp. 43-44; there is an excellent commentary by A.J. Festugière, *La révélation d'Hermès Trismégiste, IV: Le Dieu inconnu et la gnose*, in the collection "Études bibliques" (Paris, 1954), pp. 128-132.

19.　Above, p. 299; the treatise in question was II, 9, 2.4; one may add V, 8 [31] 1.3; V, 5 [32] 12.37.

20.　Ἀρχὴ δὲ οὐκ ἐνδεές; a feminine subject and a neuter adjective, agreement *ad sensum* with the forward-looking noun τὸ ἕν (line 36). The Plotinian One, deprived of all need in so far as it is a principle, may be associated, in the last text quoted from Hippolytus, with the mention of the Pythagorean principle, the monad, which is also without need.

21.　Cf. V, 4 [7] 1.12-16, where the One is said to be totally self-sufficient and, immediately afterwards, to be "alone."

22.　It is interesting to realize that this statement is part of a series of arguments which Plotinus brings up against a mysterious "bold speech" (line 11), which is perhaps Gnostic in nature.

23.　I, 1.2. It goes without saying that this utterance is of course only a *façon de parler*, and that no reality is further removed than the One is from narcissism properly so-called; cf. P. Hadot, "Le mythe de Narcisse et son interprétation par Plotin," in *Narcisses, Nouvelle Revue de Psychanalyse* XIII (1976): 98 sq.

24.　Very close to this problem is that of the "why" of creation. On this question, cf. the monograph of Kl. Kremer, "Das 'Warum' der Schöpfung: 'quia bonus' vel/et 'quia voluit'? Ein Beitrag zum Verhältnis von Neuplatonismus und Christentum an Hand des Prinzips 'bonum est diffusivum sui,'" in *Parusia*, Mélanges J. Hirschberger (Frankfurt/Main, 1965), pp. 241-264; pp. 243-254 on Plotinus, who gave three answers to the question, or so the author believes.

25.　Irenaeus, *Adv. Haer.* I, 1.2.

26.　Fgt 5 of Valentinus, Völker, p. 59.2-5 = Clement of Alex., *Strom.* IV, 13, 89.6-90. (I shall come back later, below, to this difficult text and I shall then try to justify the translation that has been given above.) Clement himself rejects this idea by means of a pseudo-Platonic quotation: "For it is not with a view to profiting from it that God has produced the world, in order to gather honors (ἵνα τιμὰς [. . .] καρποῖτο) from men and from other gods and demons" (*Strom.* V, 11, 75.3, ed. Stahlin, p. 376.22-24, a passage which is probably the source of Theodoretus, *Graec. affect. cur.* IV, 34 and VII, 48). It has long been remarked upon that the Valentinian motivation of the creation is touched upon in *Enn.* II, 9, 4.13-15, where Plotinus attributes to his Gnostic adversaries what he takes to be the ridiculous idea that the Soul which produces this world would have been motivated by the wish to "be honored" (ἵνα τιμῷτο), as is the case with people who make statues in this world. In II, 9, 11.21, exactly the same formula crops up, and is again presented as a piece of Gnostic theorizing, but applied this time, or so it would seem, to the demiurge. This coincidence obviously helps the hypothesis whereby Valentinians had their place among the Gnostics; cf. H.-Ch. Puech, "Plotin et les Gnostiques," in *Entretiens de la Fondation Hardt*, t.V: *Les sources de Plotin* (Vandoeuvres-Genève, 1960), p. 162 (taken up again in *En quête de la Gnose*, I: La Gnose et le temps [Paris, 1978], p. 84).

27. Clement of Alex., *Excerpta ex Theodoto* 7.1. A very similar explanation of the sending-forth of the Son (the Father, unknown because of his transcendental greatness, wanted to be known) is to be found in the *Tripartite treatise* 57.25-30, the translation already quoted, p. 59: "is unknown because of its surpassing greatness. Yet he wanted it to be known, because of the riches of his sweetness. And he revealed the unsurpassable power." An analogous intention is attributed to the Father in Hermetic Gnosticism, to justify not the sending-forth of the Son, but the production of visible beings: from the one who is invisible, "it is just for that reason that he has created, to make himself visible (ἵνα ὁρατὸς ᾖ)" (*Corp. Herm.* XIV, 3, ed. Nock, p. 223.4, translated by Festugière in the French version of this article; the same thesis is stated in XI, 22, p. 156.16-18).

28. There is a comparable motivation, not for the procession, but for creation, in Origen, *De princ.* IV, 4, 8 (35), ed. Koetschau, p. 359.11-13: "*Huoens deus, qui natura bonus est, habere quibus bene faceret et qui adeptis suis beneficiis laeterentur, fecit se dignas creaturas.*"

29. Above, p. 299.

30. Above, pp. 300-301.

31. And for which, incidentally, there is no before. We know that, for Plotinus, time is a property of Soul. Beings in the world beyond, i.e. the intelligibles, have eternity, not time (II, 5 [25] 3.8; IV, 4 [28] 1.12-13), from which it follows that they are all at once (ὁμοῦ) (V, 9 [5] 10.9-11), which removes them from time as well as from place and implies that for them there is no after nor before: true Being "does not have in itself one thing, then another; one cannot subject it to separation, nor to development, nor to advancement, nor to extension; one cannot conceive of anything which would be before it or after it" (III, 7 [45] 6.15-17). *A fortiori* that proves to be true on the level of the One; for, as Plotinus has said, *Tim.* 37D, "eternity rests in the One," and it is by resting close to the One that Being benefits from eternity (III, 7, 6.1-12); on Plotinus's use of the quotation from Plato, see W. Beierwaltes, *Plotin, Über Ewigkeit und Zeit (Enn.* III, 7) (Frankfurt am Main, 1967), *ad* 2.35, pp. 154-155. In a word, one cannot imagine for the One a state prior to the starting-off of the procession. There is here a fresh difference with the Father of the Valentinians, according to what we read in Hippolytus, in a passage translated above: although "having no time," this principle is said to have decided to give birth at a certain moment (*pote*).

32. Cf. V, 1, 6.42-43: the Intellect has need of the One, but not the other way round.

33. Two words borrowed from the *Phaedrus* of Plato, 250C.

34. *Prov.* 8.22-31: *Wisdom of Solomon* 7.21-29, 18 (especially 9.17); *Sirach* 1.1-10; 24.1-22, etc. In her role as collaborator to God, Wisdom is identified with the Thora, cf. *Sirach* 24.23 sq.; as also in Palestinian Judaism, cf. H.F. Weiss, *Untersuchungen zur Kosmologie des hellenistischen und palästinischen Judentums*, in the collection "Texte und Untersuch.," 97 (Berlin, 1966), pp. 294-300; p. 318 for *Sirach* 42.21.

35. *Ad Autolycum* II, 22; probable date of the work: shortly after 180.

36. It was the "inner" (ἐνδιάθετος) Logos, before it was brought to birth as Logos "given forth" (προφορικός) (ibid.); cf. M. Mühl, "*Der λόγος ἐνδιάθετος und προφορικὸς von der älteren Stoa bis zur Synode von Sirmium 351*," in *Archiv für Begrifsgeschichte* 7 (1962): 25-27.

37. *Refut.* V, 7.25-26, p. 84.14-19.

38. This idea is from E. Bréhier, *Notice* of VI, 8, pp. 119-121 and 126. It is probably right, despite R. Beutler and W. Theiler, *Anmerkungen*, Bd IV b, ad VI, 8, 7.11, p. 372, who want to see in the *tolmeros logos* a mere working hypothesis ("Gedankenexperiment") thought up by Plotinus himself. But a number of arguments could be brought in which would be favorable to Bréhier's way of looking at things. Thus the presence of the idea of "boldness," τόλμα, in the passion of Sophia according to the Valentinians (cf. Irenaeus, *Adv. Haer.* I, 2, 2: τόλμη) and in the psychology of the Gnostic demiurge (ibid., I, 29.4: *Audacia*), as well as in the idea which Plotinus has of it, cf. II, 9, 11.2: the demiurge has produced "by boldness"; διὰ τόλμαν II, 9, 10.14: the Gnostics "have the boldness," τολμῶντας, to mock the words of the god-like men of old. On the other hand, we may see in VI, 8, 7.38-39 that the believers in the τολμηρὸς λόγος attributed to their First principle a solitude which it did not consent to; now that is a Valentinian opinion, which we have already met above, pp. 300 and 301. All the same, I do not really see how Bréhier can properly attribute to the "bold discourse" the thesis whereby "the One, not having its being from itself, is not free and makes of necessity whatever it makes" (p. 11), nor how, more generally (p. 121), Bréhier can find for such a thesis "obvious counterparts" with the fact that "the Naasenes' principle says of itself: 'I become what I wish'"; the truth is rather that there is a complete opposition on this point between the "bold discourse" and the Naasenes, who are here on the side of Plotinus.

39. I draw here on information given by E.R. Dodds, *Proclus, The Elements of Theology* (Oxford, 1963), note on 26-27, pp. 213-214. Most evidence is to be found in late Neoplatonism, pagan and Christian. Given the nature of my study, I do not here go beyond Plotinus.

40. Fgt 14.6-16, pp. 55-56. See the notes added by des Places, pp. 108-110, and cf. E.R. Dodds, "Numenius and Ammonius," in *Les Sources de Plotin*.

41. To be precise, a part of this thesis. The other part, which Numenius does not go into, is that the principle does not become any one of its products. One may wonder whether there were not other correspondences between the doxography quoted for the Naasenes and the fragments of Numenius. Among the latter, see, for example, fgt 13.4-5, p. 55. In this fragment, the

first God is called "He who is," in obvious dependence on *Exodus* 3.14, cf.
J. Whittaker, "Moses atticizing," in *Phoenix* 21 (1967): 196-201, and
"Numenius and Alcinous on the First Principle," ibid., 32 (1978): 144-154
(= J.W., *Studies in Platonism and Patristic Thought* [London 1984] VII and
VIII). It has turned out, that the same Biblical quotation must have
inspired the definition which the Naasenes' principle gives of itself.
Furthermore, in the same fragment 13, the First God "sows the seed
(σπέρμα) of every soul in all the beings that participate in him"; an obvious
reference to *Timaeus* 41C-42D on the "sowings of soul" (it is immediately
after having finished these sowings that the demiurge, as we have seen,
"stayed in its condition"; there is there an indication of the thematic unity
between fragments 13 and 14 of Numenius, two fragments which are
juxtaposed in Eusebius, as must also have been the case originally in
Numenius's own *De bono*). This σπέρμα of Numenius makes one think of
the seed which is the Naasenes' universal cause, with the difference that, for
the Naasenes, the principle is the seed itself, while for Numenius (as for
Plato) it is the sower. Another point which they have in common: the First
God of Numenius is motionless, ἑστώς (fgt 15.3, p. 56), and is thereby
related to the principle of the Naasenes, said to be ἀκίνητος. Another
similarity: the Naasene's principle has the exclusive right to the qualification
of ἀγαθός; Numenius's First God is constantly called τ'ἀγαθόν (fgts 2, 16,
19, 20, etc.). Finally, the last line of fr. 13 of Numenius refers to what
appear to be the seeds scattered by the First God as being τὰ ἐκεῖθεν
προκαταβεβλημένα "realities sent forth from the world above"; as É. des
Places has recognized, n. 5 *ad loc.*, p. 109, that is a technical verb, which
even if it does not come from the Naasenes, does at least belong to
Valentinian Gnosticism.

42. There is no contradiction between this lack of will on the part of the One
in the procession and, its will in its constitution of itself. Later on, in V, 1,
6, Plotinus uses the comparison of the light spreading out and of the
motionless sun, which recalls that of Numenius. We find a thesis similar to
that of V, 1, 6 and therefore, indirectly, similar to that of the Naasenes, in
Porphyry's *Philosophiae historia* IV, fgt 18 Nauck, p. 15.3-4: "it is not
because the Good sets itself in movement (κινουμένου) in view of the
generation of the Intellect that the procession (πρόοδος) takes place."
There is an excellent commentary on this point by A.-Ph. Segonds, in the
appendix to Porphyry, *The Life of Pythagoras* . . ., ed. des Places, p. 194,
and in J. Whittaker, "Self-Generating Principles in Second-Century Gnostic
Systems," in *The Rediscovery of Gnosticism*, ed. B. Layton, in the collection
"Studies in the Hist. of Religions," XLI, t. I (Leiden 1980), p. 177 (=
Studies in Platonism . . ., XVII); both writers note the comparison with
Plotinus. It appears however that there is no Plotinian parallel for the
principal idea in Porphyry's fragment, namely the idea of the self-generation
of Intellect. The idea is nonetheless much earlier than Porphyry, since one
can find it already, in its essentials, present in Philo of Alexandria, *De
opificio mundi* 33, 100: "what does not bring to birth nor is brought to

birth stays motionless (ἀκίνητον μένει); for bringing to birth is in movement, since both what brings to birth and what is brought to birth are not without movement, the one so that it may bring to birth, the other so that it may be brought to birth; the only being not to move, and not to be moved: the venerable Sovereign and Governor <of the universe>." The logical (but unexpressed) conclusion of this text which looks back to Pythagorean origins must be the self-generation of what comes after the First; hence the comparison with Porphyry established by J. Whittaker, "The historical Background of Proclus's Doctrine of the ΑΤΘΠΟΣΤΑΤΑ," in *Entretiens de la Fondation Hardt*, t. XXI: *De Jamblique à Proclus* (Vandoeuvres-Genève, 1975), pp. 220-221 (= *Studies in Platonism . . .*, XVI). But Philo foreshadows, even in the words he uses, Plotinus's doctrine in V 1, 6, and therefore to a certain extent the doctrine of the Naasenes.

43.   Above, p. 308.
44.   There is a very similar text, which includes the quotation from Plato, in a much later treatise V, 3 [49] 12.33-36. See also V, 2 [11] 1.17-18; 2.25-26; III, 4 [15] 1.1 ("It is when the higher principles rest, μενόντων, that there are born the 'hypostases'"); V, 5 [32] 5.1-7; in IV, 9 [8] 5.1-5, we realize that the same is true of universal soul, which gives itself to the particular souls only by staying what it is.
45.   For the same meaning, see V, 1, 7.18-22; V, 5, 13.19-20.
46.   This reappears in III, 3 [48] 7.10-11: "But you see that each of the realities proceeds (πρόεισι) from the principle — while the principle remains inside — as from a single root, firmly fixed in itself," etc.
47.   The obvious connection between these two texts of Plotinus and of Irenaeus allows us perhaps to gain a better understanding of both: 1-° Without any doubt, Plotinus says that neither the demiurge nor its mother οὔτε αὐτὸς οὔτε ἡ μήτηρ, have seen the hypothetical models of creation; he cannot say that the demiurge has neither seen these models nor seen its mother. On the other hand, Irenaeus's Greek text as well as the Latin translation which we have of it can be understood in both senses: "the demiurge, they say, did not know the models of the beings which it made (τὰς ἰδέας ὧν ἐποίει), it did not even know its mother" (*sic* F.M.M. Sagnard, op. cit., p. 182; more recently Rousseau-Doutreleau in "*Sources chrét.*," 264, p. 83), or that "they say that the demiurge and the mother herself did not know the beings which it made;" it is obviously this second translation which would very neatly account for Plotinus's evidence, and which, for that reason, I prefer. It is in any case admitted that Plotinus has his aim fixed on Valentinian Gnosticism; cf. for example V. Cilento, *Plotino, Paideia antignostica. Ricostruzione d'un unico scritto da Enneadi* III, 8, V, 8, V, 5, II, 9, in the collection "*Testi con commento filol*," IX (Firenze 1971), p. 257. 2-° The text of Plotinus has itself been translated in roughly two different ways, at line 2: Ἀλλ' ὅλως οὐκ ἦν, ἵνα ἂν καὶ εἶδεν. (a) "But in a general way there existed nothing that the demiurge could have seen;" (b) "But, to say everything, the demiurge was not there where he could have seen;" the translation (a), which is in any case not really satisfactory

grammatically (we have to add the word "nothing"), is that of Harder; it comes round to denying that there were models for the creation, which goes against the direct evidence of Irenaeus, however one understands it; we should therefore prefer the translation (b), which is, by the way, except for a detail or two, that of Bréhier, of Armstrong and of Igal.

48.   One could also bring in here the *Apocryphon of John*, a text from the Berlin codex, ed. Till, p. 46.1-6 (translated by Tardieu, pp. 118-119): "The impudent <demiurge> understood nothing of the beings which were above its mother. For it said that its mother was the only thing to exist." This quotation agrees, I believe, with the substance of the preceding note.

49.   *Corpus hermet.* VIII, 3 and XII, 22; this latter text seems to mean that "materiality" is the "energy of God" in "matter"; Nock-Festugière, n. 71 *ad loc.*, p. 191, compares Iamblichus, *De Myst.* VIII, 3, p. 265.6-7 (materiality is a part withdrawn from substantiality in view of the production of matter by God), to which Proclus alludes, *In Plat. Tim.* comment., ed. Diehl, I, p. 386.10-11; the idea common to these different pieces of evidence seems to be that materiality is a principle above matter and used as an intermediary in the production of matter. We may add that a duality of the same kind, that of "life" and of "liveliness," appears in some texts from Nag Hammadi, such as *Zostrianos* (VIII, 1), 15.4-17, and *Allogenes* (XI, 3), 49.28-35; 59.14; 60.19-20; cf. J.M. Robinson, "The Three Steles of Seth and The Gnostics of Plotinus," in *Proceedings of the International Colloquium on Gnosticism* (1973), in the collection "Filol.-filos. serien," 17 (Stockholm, 1977), pp. 135 and 137. In another of these texts, *The Three Steles of Seth* (VII, 5), we find, besides the distinction between "life" and "liveliness," that between "substance" and "substantiality"; see the references given by M. Tardieu, "*Les Trois Stèles de Seth.* Un écrit gnostique retrouvé à Nag Hammadi," in *Revue des sciences philos. et théol.*, 57 (1973): 566-567; this last point stand out, once one has seen in the Hermetist and in Iamblichus substance/substantiality cheek by jowl with life/liveliness.

50.   At least they take into account the look which Sophia has directed below. The idea is found, for example, in *Pistis Sophia* 31, translation by Schmidt-Till, p. 27.36-37, where Sophia discovers thus her illuminating powers in the lower regions: "*blickte sie nach unten und sah seine Lichtkraft in den Teilen unterhalb*"; in *Zostrianos*, 27.9-12, translated by J.H. Sieber (*NHL*), p. 376, who associates the same look with the descent of souls: "Other immortal souls are companions with all these souls because of Sophia who looked down"; and finally Irenaeus, *Adv. Haer.* I, 29.4, taking account of the myth of the Barbelognostics, shows *Mater Sophia*, hard up for a husband, stretching her neck down below: "*extendebatur et prospiciebat ad inferiores partes.*" These texts have been drawn to the attention of scholars by S. Pétrement, *Le Dieu séparé. Les origines du gnosticisme*, in the collection "Patrimoines" (Paris, 1984), pp. 146, 555-556, 581.

51. I may perhaps be allowed to refer here to my work *"Ex Platonicorum persona."* *Études sur les lectures philosophiques de saint Augustin* (Amsterdam, 1977), pp. xxvi-xxvii, chapters III and V.

52. Chap. 12, translated by Schmidt-Till, p. 352.9-10: (the subject under discussion is a city by the name of Jerusalem, made of the purest of matter) *"sie wird auch 'das neue Land' gennant, und sie wird auch 'unabhängig'* (αὐτοτελής) *genannt,"* etc. The text of Scripture made use of here is *Apoc.* 21.1-2, where are found the "new earth" and "Jerusalem," and also, what editors of this text have not seen, *Gal.* 4.26, where "the Jerusalem on high," "our mother," is said to be "free," whence αὐτοτελής of the Gnostic treatise. These two passages of the New Testament, to which should be added *Gen.* 3.20 on Eve, "mother of all living things," combined in different ways, have often inspired the Gnostics; for example the Naasenes who appear in Hippolytus, *Refut.* V, 7, 39, and above all the Valentinians, who look upon Sophia as "mother of all living things," "Jerusalem on high," "earth" (ibid., VI, 34.3-4; Irenaeus, *Adv. Haer.* I, 5.3); cf. A. Orbe, *La teologia del Espiritu Santo* (Estudios Valentinianos IV), in the collection "Analecta Gregoriana," 158 (Romae, 1966), pp. 481-484 (on the illumination accomplished by Sophia as it is presented by Plotinus, cf. ibid., pp. 260-269). But the *Anon. of Bruce* is (so far?) the only witness for the formula "new earth"; it is this fact, with some others, which makes one think that the Greek original of this Coptic text was known to Plotinus; a thesis recently taken up by L. Abramowski, "Nag Hammadi 8.1, *Zostrianus*, das *Anonymum Brucianum*, Plotin *Enn.* 2, 9 (33)," in *Platonismus und Christientum*, Festschrift H. Dörrie, *Jahrbuch f. Ant. und Christ.*, Ergänzungsband 10 (Münster, 1983), p. 7.

53. 8.10-12, translated by J.H. Sieber (*NHL*), p. 371: "Concerning this airy earth — why it has a cosmic model?" Cf. H.-Ch. Puech, *En quête de la Gnose*, I: *La Gnose et le temps* (Paris, 1978), p. 113.

54. *Apud* Epiphanius, *Panar.*, haer. 31, 5, 5 = Völker, p. 61, and 31, 5, 7 = p. 61.17-18.

55. Irenaeus, *Adv. Haer.* I, 5, 6.

56. Ibid., I, 24, 3. This text and the two preceding texts are taken account of by F. García Bazán, *Plotino y la Gnosis* (Buenos Aires, 1981), p. 286, n. 36.

57. Above, p. 314.

58. Chap. 20, translated by Schmidt-Till, pp. 361.35-362.3; see also the translation by C. Baynes, p. 180, and the notes on pp. 181-184, as well as H.-Ch. Peuch, "Plotin et les Gnostiques," pp. 168-169 and 181-182 = *La Gnose et le temps*, pp. 90 and 101.

59. 5.17-18; 8.10-14; 12.3-6, etc., translated by J.H. Sieber, pp. 370-372, etc.

60. Within a short space, both take account, not only of the antitypes, but also of the two other "hypostases" whose use Plotinus criticizes in II, 9, 6.1-6, i.e. the "migrations" and the "repentances." There remains the problem: which of the two treatises should one choose as Plotinus's probable source? *Zostrianos*, according to J.H. Sieber, "An Introduction to the Tractate Zostrianos from Nag Hammadi," in *Novum Testamentum* 15 (1973): 237-

238 and H.-Ch. Puech, *La Gnose in le temps*, pp. 113-114; the *Anonymus of Bruce* according to L. Abramowski, *art. cit.*, pp. 2, 7-8. The fact that the *Anonymus* mentions the "new earth," missing from *Zostrianos*, cf. above, n. 45, tells in favor of the second hypothesis; but we shall see later, that another important set of ideas in Plotinus is found exclusively, unless I am mistaken, in *Zostrianos*, and that leaves the two opinions equally balanced.

61. *Plotins Stellung zum Gnosticismus und kirchlichen Christentum*, in the collection "Texte und Untersuchungen," N.F. V 4 (Leipzig 1900), p. 36; the same point of view, but with individual nuances, in Harder, Armstrong, Cilento, op. cit., p. 251, and Igal.

62. The two meanings turn up in Plotinus with almost equal frequency, cf. J.H. Sleeman and G. Pollet, *Lexicon Plotinianum* (Leiden-Leuwen, 1980), col. 220-221.

63. Hippolytus, *Refut.* V, 17.5, p. 114.31-34; a few lines earlier, we see that the Perates called in the same way upon the famous episode of *Gen.* 30.37-41 on the trick which Jacob used to get hold of striped or spotted sheep.

64. 21, ed. Schmidt-Till, p. 364.16-18: one may add 8, p. 144.20-21, where play is made on "painting (ζωγραφεῖν) in oneself the spark of light as a man of light and of truth." On this, cf. the edition of Baynes, p. 96, n. 4, and M. Tardieu, "ΨΤΧΑΙΟΣ ΣΠΙΝΘΗΡ, Histoire d'une métaphore dans la tradition platonicienne jusqu'à Eckhart," in *Revue des Études augustiniennes*, XXI (1975): 240.

65. Apud Clement, *Strom.* IV, 13, 89.6-90.1, ed. Stahlin, p. 287.22-25 = Völker, p. 59.2-5.

66. Valentinus's formula for the living model, τοῦ ζῶντος αἰῶνος, recalls the παντελὲς ζῷον of *Timaeus* 31B.

67. As has been obviously understood by those historians who, of recent years, have made a close study of the fragment: F.M.M. Sagnard, op. cit., pp. 123-125, 138-139 and 561; A. Orbe, *En los albores de la exegesis iohannea* (Estudios Valentinianos II), in the collection "Analecta Gregoriana," LXX (Romae, 1955), pp. 352-377; G.C. Stead, *art. cit.*, p. 95, and "In Search of Valentinus," in *The Rediscovery of Gnosticism*, ed. B. Layton, in the collection "Studies in the Hist. of Religions," XLI, t. I (Leiden, 1980), pp. 82-86.

68. *Strom.* IV, 13, 89.4-6, p. 287.15-21.

69. Ibid., 90, 2, pp. 287.287-288.1. The final principle is known, and is present literally in *Exc. ex Theod.* 32, 1.

70. By A. Hilgenfeld, op. cit., pp. 299-300; opposed to him on this point are A. Orbe, op. cit., p. 354 and G.C. Stead, loc. cit.

71. Despite Plotinus's flexibility on words agreeing according to their genders, on which cf. H.R. Schwyzer, art. "Plotinos" in *RE* XXI (1951), col. 514-515, it is difficult to imagine that ὁ τοῦτο γράψας of the text is to be understood as ἡ τοῦτον γράψασα.

72. The middle λοιδορήσηται is taken, as is often the case for the middle voice, especially in the aorist, in the passive meaning; cf. R. Kühner/B. Gerth, *Ausfürliche Grammatik der griech. Sprache*, II, 1, pp. 117-119; *Griech. Grammatik*, ed. Schwyzer/A. Debrunner, II, pp. 237-239. The purposive meaning of ἵνα is taken for granted by Bréhier ("in order to insult violently the demiurge who has drawn them"), but is hardly likely; I prefer a consecutive meaning (=ὥστε), as listed in LSJ, *s.u.* B II, 1.

73. Above, p. 305 and n. 31.

74. II, 9, 4.13-14: "τὸ ἵνα τιμῷτο."

75. The comparison with II, 9, 10.19-21 leaves no doubt on this point.

76. Despite this difference in the point of application, the parallelism is rigorously maintained between the two passages where Plotinus takes account of the formula ἵνα τιμῷτο. The proof is this. At II, 9, 4.12-17, Plotinus thinks it ridiculous to understand this formula of Soul because that would come round to attributing to Soul an entering into calculations: "Would she go so far as to calculate (ἐλογίζετο) what profit would accrue to her from the production of the world?" Reply: no, if she produced by reflection instead of by what may be in her nature, she would never have produced the sensible world. At II, 9, 11.18-23, the hypothesis is spelt out whereby the demiurge, like the principle from which he comes forth, is a soul but of another kind, for example vegetative or generative, while the first soul would be rational. Plotinus's objection: how could such a demiurge produce "in order to be honored," while "there has been taken from him all possibility of acting by representation and still more of calculating (λογίζεσθαι)"? In either case it is the same line of argument which subordinates, in the principle that is the creator of the sensible world, the intention of being honored to the exercise of calculation. Plotinus rejects, so far as he is concerned, the postulate, and therefore also the consequence which follows from it.

77. Sagnard, op. cit., p. 124; Orbe, op. cit., p. 363.

78. As Orbe does summarily, op. cit., p. 375.

79. Chr. Elsas, *Neuplatonische und gnostische Weltablehnung in der Schule Plotins*, in the collection "Religionschichtl. Versuche und Vorarbeiten," XXXIV (Berlin/New York, 1975), pp. 112-114, has tried to discover analogies from various sources: the alchemist Zosimus, *Poimandres*, Numenius, the *Chaldaean Oracles*; but the harvest is thin. See also pp. 166-171; on the Docetists of Hippolytus, p. 170 and n. 599.

80. *Refut.* VIII, 9.3-10.2, pp. 228.6-229.21.

81. I leave out here a rough and ready quotation from *Gen.* 1, 4-7.

82. There comes here a quotation from *Gen.* 1.1.

83. A Platonic and Gnostic theme, cf. above, p. 300 and n. 7.

84. According to the Valentinians too, the demiurge is made of fire, cf. Hippolytus, *Refut.* VI, 32, 8.

85. This terms is part of the three words which Plotinus gives at this point as characteristic of his adversaries, and which are found again, grouped together, both in *Zostrianos* and in the *Anonymus of Bruce*, cf. above, n. 60.

86. Cf. Irenaeus, *Adv. Haer.* I, 23, 2.

87. Fgt 3 = Origen, *In Epist. ad Rom.* V, 1 = Völker, p. 41.10-11.

88. Cf. Irenaeus, I, 25, 4, and also (on Simon and Carpocrates) II, 33, 1.

89. Simplicius, *In Arist. Physic.* comment., ed. Diels, t. I, p. 616.18-20. The connection with the *Oracles* has been studied by W. Kroll, *De Oraculis Chaldaicis*, in the collection "Breslauer philolog. Abhandlungen," VII 1 (Breslau, 1894), p. 57, and by Lewy, *Chaldaean Oracles and Theurgy. Mysticism, Magic and Platonism in the Later Roman Empire*, in the collection "Recherches d'Archéol., de Philol. et d'Hist.," de l'I.F.A.O., XIII (Le Caire, 1956), p. 241 and n. 53.

90. In fact, the lines from Simplicius which have just been quoted belong to his account of Proclus's views; cf. the analysis given by Ph. Hoffmann, "Simplicius: Corollarium de loco," in *L'astronomie dans l'Antiquit-é classique*, a group of studies, in "Collection d'Études anc . . . de l'Assoc. g. Budé" (Paris, 1979), pp. 149-153.

91. *Contra*, H. Lewy, op. cit., p. 252, n. 92.

92. Proclus, *In Crat.* LXXI, ed. Pasquali, p. 31.8-9.

93. As H. Koch has already pointed out in his *Pseudo-Dionysius Areopagita in seinem Beziehungen zum Neuplatonismus und Mysterienwesen*, Eine Litterarhistorische Untersuchung, in the collection "Forschugen zur Christl. Litteratur- und Dogmengeschichte," I, 2-3 (Mainz, 1900), pp. 218-219, to which one should add my article "Linguistique et théologie dans la tradition platonicienne," in *Linguaggio*, Scienza-Filosofia-Teologia, Atti del XXV convegno di Assistenti univers. di Filos (Padova, 1981), pp. 37-53.

94. *Epist.* IX (ad Titum), 2, PG 3, 1108 C.

Titus of Bostra and Alexander of Lycopolis: A Christian and a Platonic Refutation of Manichaean Dualism

Gedaliahu G. Stroumsa

Plotinus and Mani probably never met on the battlefield.[1]

Dispelling such a pregnant *image d'Epinal* as the physical encounter of the two masters should not mean ignoring the conflictual intercourse between Neoplatonism and Manichaeism in the Roman Empire. Ultimately, both movements were losers in the grand struggle for souls and minds, which the Christian bishops and theologians won in the fourth century against pagans and heretics alike. The extent to which Christian theologians assimilated philosophical — and in particular Platonic — concepts and ideas is better known than the exact limitations of Platonic influence. And the Christian and Neoplatonist ultimate rejection of Gnostic and dualist patterns of thought is more readily recorded than accounted for accurately.

Among the various spiritual trends in the Roman Empire — as well as under Sasanian rule — few seem to have been so powerful, and none has aroused such hatred, as Manichaeism.[2] Indeed, this hatred was fueled by the eccentric behavior of Manichaean ascetics, and lead to slanderous accusations.[3] More importantly, however, it is the very basis of Manichaean theology and mythology, its radical dualism, which elicited the most profound repulsion — from both pagan philosophical and Christian theological quarters.[4] A reflection upon this repulsion and the arguments with which it was propounded might shed some new light on a particularly complex chapter in Late Antique intellectual history. In attempting such a reflection, I have concentrated upon the two leading figures to have refuted Manichaeism in Greek: Titus of Bostra and Alexander of Lycopolis. Titus, Bishop of Bostra, a highly Hellenized Syrian city on the *limes*, wrote in the second half of the fourth century, a few years after Julian's reign, one of the first, and certainly the most comprehensive Christian theological refutation of Manichaeism.[5] Mainly through Epiphanius of Salamis, who not only refers to it but also makes generous use of its argumentation, Titus's work was to have the most profound impact on later Christian literature *adversus Manichaeos*.[6]

As with Titus, Alexander's title of fame rests upon his tractate against Manichaeism — his only extant writing, published about 300 — one of our earliest documents on the propagation of Manichaeism in Egypt.[7] (The work itself has survived only due to the fact that it had been incorporated into a corpus of Christian anti-Manichaean texts, since Alexander was thought to have been a bishop.)[8] The city where Plotinus was born had become a major center for the implantation of Manichaeism already in the second half of the third century.[9] Like the bishop of Bostra — or Cyril, the bishop of Jerusalem — half a century later, the philosopher of Lycopolis is deeply concerned by the new movement, which had even seduced some among his fellow philosophers.[10]

Alexander is rather sympathetic to Christianity; although he thinks the Christians incapable of precise philosophical thought, he praises their elevated ethics.[11] Titus, on his part, while no philosopher, is the bearer of a good rhetorical education, and shows a certain knowledge of *koinē* philosophical vocabulary and arguments — both Platonic and Stoic.[12] I could not find in his work, however, any indication to suggest a direct borrowing from Alexander.

A comparison between these two refutations of dualism might therefore add to our understanding of the common ground and specific differences between Christian and Neoplatonist fourth-century *literati*. A further question raised by such an inquiry is the extent to which the need to argue at length against the dualist challenge influenced the structures, or at least the emphasis, of their own thought.[13] One might point out here that anti-Manichaean literature has been mainly scrutinized by students of Manichaeism for the information it could lend about details of Manichaean mythology, or quotations from Manichaean writings.[14] Thus, although Titus and Alexander are well-known to scholars in the field, very little attention seems to have been devoted to their actual argumentation. The following pages can do no more than arouse interest in this direction. It is hoped that further studies will reveal more fully the impact of the Manichaean challenge amidst late antique intellectuals. Besides the ludicrous details of their mythology, the Manichaeans were able to develop very early a highly sophisticated theoretical argumentation in support of their dualism. This important point, which cannot be overemphasized, is proved precisely by the character of Titus's and Alexander's refutations: although neither ignores Manichaean mythology, it does not stand for them at the core of the seductive powers of Manichaean thought.[15] Similarly, in Justinian's Constantinople, it is with a very abstract refutation of dualism that Zacharias "Rhetor," of Mytilene (who has also been traditionally attributed the authorship of a pamphlet against Manichaean mythology), decided to respond to a Manichaean tract found in a bookstore in the capital.[16]

For both Alexander and Titus, Manichaeism presents itself, first of all, as an attempt to solve the problem of evil.[17] This is not surprising, of course, although one might call attention, in this respect, to the fact that Plotinus himself, who had argued against the Gnostics at length and with great vehemence, does not refer to them even once in his tractate "On what are and whence come evils" (*Enn.* I.8). One should ponder this point. It is indeed from the various Gnostic trends of the first Christian centuries that Mani inherited his attempt to answer the question *unde malum?*[18] His highly organized mind, however, seems to have given the question a new urgency, and to have set it at the very core of his mythological theology, with a consistency unknown to the more fluid — should one say to the somewhat amorphic? — Gnostic mythologies.

Titus begins the first book of his refutation by stating that Manichaeism is born from the desire to discharge God of any responsibility for evil, thus postulating another principle, opposite to God from all eternity and solely responsible for evil in the universe. Titus devotes the first two books (out of four) of his work to a rational refutation of such a dualism. Books III and IV, which are extant in full only in Syriac, deal respectively with the Manichaeans' rejection of the Old Testament and their misunderstanding of the New Testament. The argumentation in these last two books is purely scriptural, and therefore they will not concern us here, since they can in no way be paralleled to Alexander's work. The thorough refutation of Manichaean dualism in Book I is followed by a lengthy argument against the Manichaean conception of evil. Book II of Titus's *Adversus Manichaeos* is actually the most comprehensive theodicy in all Patristic literature. In these two books, Titus claims, he will argue only according to the *koinai ennoiai*, and does in no way establish his argument upon the Scriptures, so as to give his refutation universal value — since the *notiones communes* are,

or should be, by definition common to all men.[19]   But what are the
koinai ennoiai?   The term is unmistakenly recognized as Stoic in
origin.[20]   In Stoic doctrine, it refers to those imprints left on the
human mind by common experience.   Plutarch had written a whole
treatise on the topic,[21] and Origen had referred to the concept in the
Contra Celsum.[22]   Thus, its use by Titus is not surprising, since our
author shows other signs of philosophical education, both Platonic and
Stoic.   Like other Christian theologians, however, Titus refers to the
koinai ennoiai in a broad rather than in a technical way.   *Le bon sens
est la chose du monde la mieux partagée*; Descartes is as much, or as
little, a Stoic as Titus, who only wants to show that Manichaean
doctrine is unconvincing and should be rejected on rational grounds
alone.   For him, these rational grounds are common to all thinking men,
and in particular to philosophers and Christians.   Titus argues that the
idea of two principles, as conceived by the Manichaeans, stands out of
this consensus.[23]

Similarly to Titus, Alexander argues that Manichaean conceptions
are not rational, that Manichaean thought is established on false
principles, and therefore cannot perform its self-assigned main task: to
solve the problem of evil.[24]   At the outset of his work, Alexander
complains that arguing against the Manichaeans' conceptions is rendered
particularly difficult by their propensity for mythology, and hence
shunning of rational thought.[25]   The philosopher is ill at ease
developing dialectical arguments against a protagonist who does not
accept the rules of the game.   For Alexander the Christians, too, are not
very good philosophers, although he concedes that they do not share
with the Manichaeans — whose origins he sees, rightly, in Christian
sectarianism — the latter's infatuation with mythological patterns of
thought.[26]   The genre of Alexander's writing is that of a professional
philosopher, hence very different from that of Titus.   His arguments are
usually of a much more technical nature than those of the educated
bishop.   Yet, the fact is striking enough to be noted: for both,
Manichaean dualism appears to be fundamentally illogical, irrational,
stepping out of the bounds of common sense.   Both also insist on the
misleading consequences entailed by such a false epistemology, in
particular in the field of ethics.

Alexander's argumentation against Manichaean ontology gravitates
around the status of matter and of the First Principle.   He insists that
matter cannot be considered evil since it is generated by God.[27]   In his
emphatic denial of any evil in connection with matter, he stands rather
lonely in the Platonic tradition.   His conception is at the antipodes of
that of Plotinus, despite the ambiguities of the latter's attitude.[28]   It is

also markedly different from that of the *Chaldaean Oracles* and of Porphyry, for whom matter, although "born from the Father," remains evil or linked to evil. For Alexander, too, matter is derived from the First Principle: a Pythagorean rather than a Platonic doctrine.[29] Daringly enough, Alexander is willing to reject Platonic conceptions of matter too close to those of the Manichaeans. For instance, he objects to the definition of matter as *ataktos kinēsis*, which had become too closely connected to the identification of matter with evil in Middle Platonism.[30] Due to the polemical nature of his writing, however, Alexander rejects and refutes much more explicitly than he propounds his own views. Thus he does not expose at any length his personal opinion on the origin of evil. One is led to speculate that it is free-will, rather than matter, which lies at the core of evil, but this is not stated explicitly. One may postulate that the clear departure from school traditions in the conception of matter is due to the seriousness presented by the dualistic challenge for Alexander — not a very original thinker in other respects.

Since matter itself is derived from the First Principle, the Manichaean idea of two original principles, Alexander argues, is not logical. For a Platonic mind, the very idea of *archē* involves its unicity.[31] Moreover, in order for the two original principles to mingle, a third, intermediary element or principle is needed.[32] Incidentally, the opposite argument had been used by Methodius of Olympus in his *De Autexousio*, where he argues against a Platonic, rather than a Gnostic, thesis directly linking matter to the origin of evil.[33] Alexander also makes the point that Mani's insistence on the physical conception of the two realms of light and darkness entails a corporeal conception of God, a conception which Alexander rejects as ludicrous.[34] For him, the *archē* is by nature incorporeal. The same argument is made by Titus, and will also be given a prominent place by Augustine in his anti-Manichaean writings.[35]

Altogether, it would seem that Alexander conceives Manichaeism, in its insistence on the materiality of God, as a kind of crypto-Stoicism, as his translators duly note.[36]

Although Titus agrees with Alexander on many points in his refutation of Manichaean ontology, his standpoint is sensibly different. It is not enough for Titus to argue that matter is in no way connected with evil. Since the world was created by God, who is good by definition, none of its parts can be evil.[37] Evil, therefore, has no real objective existence, besides sin (Alexander for his part, recognizes the validity of the Platonic conception according to which it is matter which does not really exist).[38] From Basil the Great and Augustine, this negative conception of evil was to become the standard solution for the problem of evil in both Greek and Latin patristics.[39] In due course, it also became the Neoplatonic official standpoint, best expressed by Proclus in his tractate on evil.[40] It would seem, however, that Christian theology was quicker to develop and lead to its radical conclusion a notion only potential in Neoplatonic hierarchical thought.

Like Alexander, Titus insists that the concept of *archē* implies unicity, and that dualism is a logical impossibility.[41] He also develops the argument also found in Methodius about the third principle which should exist from all eternity in order for the two opposites to remain separate.[42] Like Alexander, he shows that the Manichaean conception denies of God some qualities inherent to Him by definition. According to the *koinai ennoiai*, for instance, God is at once immaterial, uncircumscribed and all-powerful. In particular, Titus pokes fun at that most scandalous of Manichaean conceptions according to which the Divine principle was overcome, or even eaten by the Evil principle, and is conceived as suffering.[43]

While Manichaeism originates in an attempt to disclaim for God any responsibility over evil in general, and men's sins in particular, the Manichaeans fall into an even greater sin by their denial of God's ever present providence. In the very first chapter of his work Titus states — without a specific reference to Plato, of course — that it is the first doctrine of the Catholic Church that God is not responsible for human injustice. As noted above, however, it is in the second book that Titus fully develops his theodicy. Polemics are not absent, and Titus attacks various aspects of Manichaean theology and mythology, such as Manichaean encratism and hylopsychism, and in particular reverence offered to the sun — after all a material, not a spiritual entity, Titus points out.[44] In the first chapter of this book, Titus states very clearly that there is no evil whatsoever in God's creation, and that only the sinners' injustice is really evil. This evil, moreover, does not stem from a matter without beginning. In the end, everything has a place in the cosmic order and a role to play in the realization of divine plans. The next chapters spell out that free will was given to man through natural knowledge of good and evil. Had man been led by instinct to perform evil, judgment on human actions would have proved impossible. Moreover, only a jealous God would have deprived man of freedom; human freedom is the very image of God in which man was created. If so, sin cannot be natural or necessary, as the Manichaeans argue, but only deliberate and voluntary.[45] Responding to the Manichaean anguish about violence and death, Titus further argues that war is a fruit of sin, while death itself, far from being an evil by nature, belongs to the order of salvation and is therefore invested with a positive role.[46] The same is true, for instance, of such phenomena as earthquakes, night, illnesses or beasts; indeed, all aspects of creation were made for our good, in virtue of God's providence.[47] The "Stoic flavour" of these chapters, which describe cosmic harmony in a rather verbose language, was noted long ago by K. Gronau.[48] Yet, the overall impression emerges that Titus's major philosophical frame of reference remains Platonism. This is particularly due to his insistence on the fact that Mani deprives God of immateriality, an essential quality, and on the unicity implicit in the concept of *archē*. It might be recorded here, however, that Irenaeus had already made a similar point, when he argued against the Gnostics that the existence of a First Principle outside the Divine *pleroma* contradicted the very idea of a *pleroma*.[49]

Similarly, Alexander is rather close to the Christian attitude when he rejects the idea of a separate principle of evil (in this he will be followed by Hierocles in the Alexandrian school),[50] when he argues that matter cannot be evil since it is generated by God, or when he insists on divine providence's ruling of the world.

Yet, if Titus and Alexander remain so far apart, this is not only due to the much more technical level of Alexander's argumentation. Titus's long developments on theodicy, and Alexander's emphasis on matter, aptly characterize the core of the Manichaean challenge to Christianity and Neoplatonism respectively. In a creationist ontology, the problem of evil demands a justification of the demiurge; in an emanationist ontology, the problem is immediately reflected by the status of matter (and by the nature of the intermediary powers).

Besides their abhorrence for ontological dualism, both Neoplatonist and Christian thinkers strongly rejected Manichaean anthropology and ethics. Here again, the emphases of the argumentation reflect the differences of standpoint. Like their ontology, the Manichaeans' anthropology and ethics are organized along dualist patterns. The soul belongs to the world of light, to the Divinity, to which it seeks to return after its separation from the body and its purification; the inner core of the Manichaean community, the encratic *electi*, are clearly set apart from the *auditores* — and not only from the non-Manichaeans.

Alexander states at once his interest in ethics. Christianity, he says, owes its early reputation not so much to the quality of its metaphysics as to the excellence of its ethics, readily recognized even by non-Christians.[51] But this ideal Christianity was unfortunately broken up at an early stage by the emergence of sectarian trends, which can be characterized precisely by their lack of interest in ethics — or even by the outright unethical ways in which they were established.

For him, Manichaeism is but the latest, and the worst, of these sectarian trends.[52] One may recall here that one of Plotinus's main grievances against the Gnostics was their inability to propound an ethical doctrine, or, rather, the totally a-ethical character of their elucubrations.[53] Alexander is shocked by Manichaean limitation of the path to salvation to the elect. For him, this directly contradicts the idea of a Providence, by definition equally caring for all. Moreover, he argues that the Manichaean doctrine of salvation precludes the idea of moral progress — although he also expresses doubts about the existence of such progress.[54] For him, Manichaean doctrine abolishes the need for education, only possible, like the acquisition of virtues, under the assumption that "what is possible for one (i.e., the practice of Manichaean precepts) is possible for everybody."[55] In somewhat anachronistic terms, only a universalizable attitude may be called ethical. Although Alexander is not overly troubled by the Manichaean dichotomy of body and soul, he recognizes that Manichaean anthropology entails the suppression of freedom of choice, and hence the possibility not only of education but also of punishment.[56] He has a final grievance against the Manichaeans: their encratism is condemnable because it contradicts both the hierarchy of being (in the case of food taboos) and the idea of God's omnipotence (in the case of sexual asceticism).[57]

As a Christian, Titus is more at ease in condemning Manichaean anthropological dualism, and notes that according to Mani the human person remains a composite never to be unified. For Christian doctrine, it is in his whole self, body as well as soul, that man was created in God's image.[58] Thus the body cannot be considered the *locus* of evil any more than matter in general.[59] Evil, Titus repeats, is nothing but sin, or human injustice. And it is not only in his body, but first of all by a free decision of his soul, that man sins.[60] Although habit renders sin omnipresent, it is not inevitable, or necessary.[61] God is the giver of Natural Law, which seeks an equilibrium of all things existing in the world, and in particular between soul and body. Thus, the encratist, whose attitude is one of extreme despisal of the body, of total rejection of its needs, commits a sin against Natural Law. Manichaean encratism is thus condemned not only because it attributes the means of salvation exclusively to the elect, but also since it does not recognize the legitimacy of pleasure for the body. Sexual relations are natural since they are intended for procreation. God has thus planted sexual desire in us in order to permit the reproduction of the human race. Thus, the legitimacy of a sexual pleasure obtained in compliance with Natural

Law.[62] Similarly, the pleasure of eating and drinking is natural, when following the creation's order and measure.[63]

In giving such a central place to the human body in his work, Titus reflects a concern present in many of the Patristic anti-Manichaean polemics since the earliest such document (from about 300 C.E.) where an unknown Egyptian bishop argues against the Manichaeans for the legitimacy of marriage.[64]

In modern political jargon, the Neoplatonist philosopher and the Christian bishop would have been called "objective" allies. By their respective standpoint, they are too far apart from each other to do more than join a cause *ad hoc*. Against a common enemy, their arguments can be only partially similar. If there is one central tenet, however, of both Neoplatonist and Christian *Weltanschauung* which they felt was directly threatened by Manichaeism, I daresay it was *Providence*.[65] For both, the only conceivable world was that ruled by a single good ruler, caring for each of its parts and indwellers. For both Alexander and Titus, dualism meant anarchy;[66] both were bound to reject a doctrine so pessimistic as to deny this world any respectability.

NOTES

1. We know from *Kephalaia*, I, that Mani joined Shapur in one of his campaigns against the Romans. This happened probably in 256-260, in the campaign against Valerian, rather than in 242-244, in that against Gordian III, whose army Plotinus had joined in order to get acquainted with Eastern wisdom. See H.C. Puech, *Le Manichéisme; son fondateur, sa doctrine* (Paris: Musée Guimet, 1949), pp. 47-48. On platonic influences on Manichaeism, see A. Henrichs and L. Koenen, in *ZPE* 19 (1975): 72-75, nn. 25-32; 32 (1978): 138ff., nn. 187 ff.; 140, n. 191; 141, n. 194. See also L. Koenen, "From Baptism to the Gnosis of Manichaeism," in *The Rediscovery of Gnosticism*, II (Suppl. to *Numen*, 41; Leiden: Brill, 1981), ed. B. Layton, p. 735, n. 8.

2. See P. Brown, "The Diffusion of Manichaeism in the Roman Empire," *JRS* 59 (1969): 92-103, reprinted in his *Religion and Society in the Age of Saint Augustine* (London, 1972), pp. 94-118. For the legal aspects of the repression, see E.H. Kaden, "Die Edikte gegen die Manichäer von Diokletian bis Justinian," in *Festschrift für Hans Lewald* (Basle, 1953), pp. 55-68.

3. See for instance the case described in my "Monachisme et Marranisme chez les Manichéens d'Egypte," *Numen* 29 (1983): 184-201. On the common "front" of Christian and Neoplatonist thinkers against Manichaeism, see C. Andresen, "Antike und Christentum," *TRE* 3: 69-73.

4. On the "radicalism" of Manichaean dualism and its limits, see my "König und Schwein: zur Struktur des manichäischen Dualismus," in *Gnosis und Politik*, ed. J. Taubes (Paderborn: Schöningh, 1984), pp. 141-153.

5. The complete Syriac text as well as the Greek text of Books I to III, 7 were published (separately) by P. de Lagarde: *Titi Bostreni . . . graece* and *Titi Bostreni contra manichaeos libri quatuor syriace* (both in Berlin, 1859). P. Nagel has further published the Greek text of III, 7-29: "Neues griechisches Material zu Titus von Bostra," in *Studia Byzantina* (Berliner byzantinische Arbeiten; Berlin: Akad. Verlag, 1973), ed. J. Irmscher and P. Nagel, pp. 285-359. Nagel has been working for some years on a new edition of Titus. On Titus himself, see R.P. Casey's article in *PW, s.v. Titus v. Bostra*, as well as J. Sickenberger's introduction to his *Titus von Bostra, Studien zu dessen Lukashomilien* (TV 21 [N.F. 6]; Leipzig: Hinrichs, 1901).

6. For a list of references to Titus's work in later Christian literature, see Sickenberger, op. cit., pp. 5-8. Epiphanius refers to him in *Panarion* 66.21.3 (Holl, III, 48-49).

7. The text was edited by A. Brinkmann: *Alexandri Lycopolitani, Contra Manichaei opiniones disputatio* (Leipzig, 1895). See also the annotated translation of the text by P.W. van der Horst and J. Mansfeld, *An Alexandrian Platonist against Dualism* (Leiden: Brill, 1974), actually a full-length study of Alexander in philosophical context. After the completion of this paper appeared a French translation and detailed commentary of the text by A. Villey, *Alexandre de Lycopolis: Contre la doctrine de Mani* (Paris: LeCerf, 1985).

   John Rist has recently sought to define more precisely Alexander's place in the history of late antique philosophy. He has shown that Alexander was a conservative Middle Platonist, rather than a Neoplatonist, whose "theories bear a masked similarity with those of the pagan Origen," concluding that "it is against Alexander's Middle Platonism that we should view the prominent Christians of early fourth-century Alexandria . . ." See J. Rist, "Basil's 'Neoplatonism': Its Background and Nature," in *Basil of Caesarea, Christian, Humanist, Ascetic*, ed. P.J. Fedwick, (Toronto: Pont. Inst. Med. Stud., 1981), pp. 137-220, esp. pp. 166-169.

8. The *codex unicus*, from the Laurentiana, is part of a late 9th-century codex, dedicated to Basil the First, an emperor who had fought the Paulicians; cf. Brinkmann's introduction to his edition.

9. On the implantation of Manichaeism in Egypt, see in particular L. Koenen, "Manichäische Mission und Klöster in Ägypten," in *Das römisch-byzantinische Ägypten* (Aegyptiaca Treverensia; Mainz: Philipp von Zabern, 1983), pp. 93-108, as well as my "Monachisme et Marranisme" (cited above n. 3).

10. Alexander, 6 (8 Brinkmann; 58 v.d. Horst-Mansfeld).

11. Alexander, 1 (3 Brinkmann; 48-50 v.d. Horst-Mansfeld).

12. See A. Puech, *Histoire de la littérature grecque chrétienne . . .* III (Paris: Les Belles Lettres, 1930), pp. 559-560. Jerome testifies to the wide recognition achieved by Titus's philosophical culture (*Epist.* 70, *PL* 22, 664-668).

13. I have argued about a clear Manichaean influence on Didymus the Blind in "the Manichaean Challenge on Egyptian Christianity," in *The Roots of Egyptian Christianity*, ed. B.A. Pearson and J. Goering, (Philadelphia: Fortress Press, 1986), pp. 307-319.

14. For two such classical studies, see on Alexander, H.H. Schaeder, *Urform und Fortbildungen des manichäischen Systems* (Vorträge der Bibliothek Warburg, 1924-25; Leipzig-Berlin, 1927); where the author claims that Alexander's presentation of Manichaean mythology truthfully reflects original conceptions. On Titus, see A. Baumstark, "Der Text der Mani-Zitate in der syrischen Übersetzung des Titus von Bostra," *Oriens Christianus*, N.F. 6 (1931): 23-42; Baumstark argues that these quotations, rather than being re-translations from the Greek, preserve in the original Aramaic Mani's *ipsissima verba*.

15. On Titus's lack of interest in Manichaean mythology, see W. Frankenberg, "Die Streitschrift des Titus von Bostra gegen die Manichäer," *ZDMG* 92 (1938): 28*-29*.

16. On Zacharias, see now S.N. Lieu, "An Early Byzantine Formula for the Renunciation of Manichaeism — the Capita VII Contra Manichaeos of (Zacharias of Mytilene)," *JAC* 26 (1983): 152-218. The text of Zacharias's theoretical refutation was published by A. Demetrakopoulos, *Ekklesiastikē Bibliothēkē* (Leipzig, 1866), pp. 1-18.

17. Titus, I, 1 (1 Lagarde); I. 4 (3 Lagarde), et passim.

18. On the Manichaean reinterpretation of Gnostic myths of the origin of evil, see my *Another Seed: Studies in Gnostic Mythology* (Nag Hammadi Studies 24, Leiden: Brill, 1984), Part III.

19. See for instance Titus I.2 (1 Lagarde); I.5 (4 Lagarde): *ai kata physin ennoiai*; I.11 (6 Lagarde): *logismoi physikoi*; I.15 (8 Lagarde); I.17 (10 Lagarde).

20. Cf. M. Polenz, *Die Stoa: Geschichte einer geistigen Bewegung* (Göttingen: Vandenhoeck und Ruprecht, 1948), I, 56; II, 426-427. See also R.B. Todd, "The Stoic Common Notions: a Reexamination and Reinterpretation," *Symbolae Osloenses* 48 (1973): 47-75.

21. Plutarch, *Against the Stoics on Common Conceptions, Moralia* vol. 13 (LCL; Cambridge, Mass./London: Harvard-Heinemann, 1976).

22. For further references, see Polenz, op. cit., II, 205-206. See also M. Spanneut, *Le Stoicisme des Pères de l'Église, de Clément de Rome à Clément d'Alexandrie* (Patristica Sorbonensis; Paris: Le Seuil, 1957), pp. 211ff.

23. Titus, I.11 (6 Lagarde). This argument will run like a thread throughout Patristic anti-Manichaean literature; see for instance John of Damascus, *De fide orthodoxa*, IV.20 (PG 94, 1193-1196).

24. For instance Alexander 8 (12 Brinkmann; 65-66 v.d. Horst-Mansfeld).

25. Alexander 5 (8-9 Brinkmann; 58-59 v.d. Horst-Mansfeld).

26. Alexander 1 (3-5 Brinkmann; 48-52 v.d. Horst-Mansfeld).

27. The argument is central to Alexander, and runs through much of the book; see Mansfeld's summary, pp. 19-23.

28. On Plotinus's conception of evil and its relationship to matter, see D. O'Brien, "Plotinus on Evil. A Study of Matter and the Soul in Plotinus's Conception of Human Evil," *Le Néoplatonisme* (Colloques internationaux du CNRS; Paris, 1971), pp. 113-146; and M.I. Santa Cruz de Prunes, *La Genèse du monde sensible dans la philosophie de Plotin* (Bibl. Ecole des Hautes Etudes, Sciences Religieuses, 81; Paris: P.U.F., 1979), pp. 114-123.

29. The place of Alexander's view of matter in the Platonic tradition is well described by Mansfeld in his introduction; see n. 27 *supra*.

30. Alexander 7-8 (11-12 Brinkmann); 63-66 v.d. Horst-Mansfeld). Cf. L. Troje, "Zum Begriff ΑΤΑΚΤΟΣ ΚΙΝΗΣΙΣ bei Platon und Mani," *Museum Helveticum* 5 (1948): 96-115.

31. Alexander 6 (9-11 Brinkmann; 59-63 v.d. Horst-Mansfeld).

32. Alexander 8 (13 Brinkmann; 66-67 v.d. Horst-Mansfeld).

33. Methodius argues that only a third, intermediary principle can keep the two opposites separate. See A. Vaillant, *Le De Autexousio de Méthode d'Olympe*, PO 22, ch. 5-6, pp. 747-753.

34. Alexander 8 (13-14 Brinkmann; 67-68 v.d. Horst-Mansfeld).

35. On Augustine, see my "The Incorporeality of God: Context and Implications of Origen's Position," *Religion* 13 (1983): 345-358.

36. v.d. Horst-Mansfeld, 47.

37. Titus II.1 (25-26 Lagarde).

38. Alexander 12 and 26 (18 and 39 Brinkmann; 73 and 97 v.d. Horst-Mansfeld).

39. See Basil's treatise, *Quod Deus non est auctor malorum*, PG 31: 329-354. Augustine's position is analyzed at length by F. Billiesich, *Das Problem des Übels in der Philosophie des Abendlandes*, I (Wien: Sexl, 1955), pp. 221-286. In an anti-Manichaean context, Serapion of Thmuis states that evil is a *praxis*, not an *ousia*. See *Serapion of Thmuis*, ed. R.P. Casey, "Against the Manichaeans" (Harvard Theological Studies, 15; Cambridge, 1931), ch. 5. For Serapion as for Titus, evil comes from a sickness of free-will; he adds that this is attested by both Scripture and an analysis of human action.

40. Proclus, *De l'existence du mal*, ed. trans. D. Isaac (Paris: Les Belles Lettres, 1982).

41. Titus I.11-12 (6 Lagarde).

42. Titus I.9 (5 Lagarde).

43. Titus I.7 (4 Lagarde).

44. See for instance Titus II.36; 54 and 60 (47, 59 and 62 Lagarde).

45. Titus II.3; 8 and 10 (26, 29 and 30 Lagarde).

46. Titus II.22; 28 and 46 (39, 43-44 and 55 Lagarde).

47. For instance Titus II.32 and 41 (47 and 50 Lagarde).

48. See his *Das Theodizäeproblem in der altchristlichen Auffassung* (Tübingen: Mohr, 1922), p. 18.

49. Irenaeus, *Adv. Haereses* II.1.2, quoted by J. Farges, *Méthode d'Olympe: le Libre Arbitre* (Paris: Beauchesne, 1929), p. 51, n. 2.

50. Cf. v.d. Horst-Mansfeld 27-29.

51. Alexander 1 (3 Brinkmann; 48-51 v.d. Horst-Mansfeld).

52. Alexander 2 (4 Brinkmann; 52 v.d. Horst-Mansfeld).
53. Plotinus, *Enn.* II.9.15 (II, 280-284 Armstrong, LCL).
54. Alexander 16 (23-24 Brinkmann; 79-81 v.d. Horst-Mansfeld).
55. Alexander 16 (23 Brinkmann; 79 v.d. Horst-Mansfeld).
56. See discussion in v.d. Horst-Mansfeld, 44-45.
57. Alexander 25 (36-37 Brinkmann; 94-95 v.d. Horst-Mansfeld).
58. Titus II. and 11 (29-31 Lagarde).
59. Titus I.29 (18 Lagarde).
60. Titus II.39 (49-50 Lagarde).
61. Titus II.10 (30-31 Lagarde).
62. Titus II.56.57 (61 Lagarde). The argument from Natural Law is found elsewhere in anti-Manichaean Patristic polemics; see for instance John of Damascus, *Contra Manichaeos* 14, in B. Kotter, *Die Schriften des Johannes von Damaskos*, IV (Patristische Texte und Studien; Berlin/New York: De Gruyter, 1981), p. 359.
63. Titus II.58 (61-62 Lagarde).
64. Cf. my "The Manichaean Challenge on Egyptian Christianity" for the impact of Manichaean encratism on Egyptian Christianity.
65. On Providence in Platonic and Patristic thinking, see C. Parma, *Pronoia und Providentia: der Vorsehungsbegriff Plotins und Augustins* (Leiden: Brill, 1971).
66. Long ago, E. Peterson had pointed out the clear connections between monotheism and "monarchy" in early Christian thought. See his *Der Montheismus als politisches Problem* (Leipzig, 1935). For the *Fortleben* of philosophical and theological refutations of Manichaeism, and about the philosophical *koinē* of late antiquity and beyond, see S. Stroumsa and G.G. Stroumsa, "Aspects of Anti-Manichaean Polemics in Late Antiquity and under Early Islam," *H.T.R.* 81 (1988): 37-58.

Le Nombre et son Ombre
(Résumé)

Ara Alexandru Sismanian*

By paraphrasing and turning against the Valentinians the famous argument of "the third man" used by Aristotle in his refutation of Plato's theory of Ideas,[1] Irenaeus put his finger on the very heart of Gnostic thought.[2] For the question is not only one of pointing to one of the major doctrinal sources of Valentinian Gnosis — as far as the Gnostic "emanation" could have drawn its principle, *mutatis mutandis*, from the Platonic doctrine of participation — but also of implicitly revealing the entire *methodology* allowing this development of Platonism, which the Gnostics could have derived from the Aristotelian argument itself. It would not be the first time that a *polemical argument* in fact — functioned as a *descriptive model*;[3] and, ironically enough, by theologizing Aristotle and by Aristotlizing the Gnostics, Irenaeus was

---

* The original paper, *Le Nombre et son Ombre. Cosmodicée et cosmogénie dans le Veda et dans la Gnose*, was published in two parts in the *Orientalia Lovaniensia Periodica*, no. 16 (1985): 205-235, no. 17 (1986): 169-207. It is practically impossible to say in a few lines what the present author owes to Miss Lilian Silburn, both to her immense work and to her personal influence. It goes without saying that the present analysis, good or bad, would have been unthinkable without her *Instant et Cause*, one of the three absolute books of the French indology and, most certainly, of Indology in general. The present summary in English is published according to an arrangement entered into with Professor R.T. Wallis.

This essay is dedicated to Richard Wallis.

even more right than he thought he was, in this endlessly moving allegory of heresy and of its image, orthodoxy.

Indeed, Aristotle's *regressus ad infinitum* changes from a *reductio ad absurdum* into a positive method in the paradoxical logic of the Gnostics. For this infinite recession in search of causality by steps of archetypes and degrees of Ideas — or, as the heresiologist says, of "figures of figures and images of images" — does not give an aleatory variable, but a teleological hierarchy of superposed values, where every degree, though preserving its functional identity, is at the same time the monadic sum of a whole series.

In fact, it is to the dialectics of the One and the Multiple, conceived as an inextricable warp and woof of logically insoluble contradictions in Plato's *Parmenides*,[4] that the Gnostics intended to bring a solution, and the originality of this is not to be ignored. The relation between the One and the All — the latter, subtly reanalyzed from the outlook of a "mass of plurality," and not any longer of a multiplicity of parts — is regarded holographically. It differs from an actual identity by nothing more than a functional modifier (horos/nous), making intelligible *axiological* differentiation and, thereby, *ontological* degressivity: the emanation is *a deficiency of consciousness* — and one can see the Holographical All or the Totalities in the *Gospel of Truth* deambulating round about the One in which they are, without knowing it, the ignorance of the Father — that is, the subjacent substance — generating the anguish, the terror and, by the solidification of the anguish, the error, i.e. the Demiurge (the interesting thing is that the mythological nomenclature of other texts is transformed here in a kind of psychogonical substance or conceptual coagulation, producing psychological seriality, an eerie Aristotelian concreteness).

Having its starting point in an inferential geometry, by which one goes up *à rebours* the gnoseological stairs, as one climbs in the rite the sacrificial pole, i.e. *axis mundi*, the cosmogonical logic of Gnosis does not limit itself to making from Platonic participation the principle, in a reverse and reiterative way, of the deficient ontic emanation. The methodological inversion is double, for the more one derives the origin from the concept, the more one infers the salvation from the fact of emanation itself.[5]

The soteriology always gains a step over the cosmogony, of which it is both the aim and the cause — and it is only the anthropogony that is intended to put an end to this spacing and emptying decay by which, for reasons of salvation, one invents new degrees of existence.[6] The man, shadow of the Pre-existing Man, is the turntable of Gnosis, since the last image, and consequently *the most complete*, of the cosmic becoming, a holographical summary of the nihility. The noetic void, which had made possible the ontic plenum, is to be filled up with gnosis, the unconscious is to be made conscious, the real is to dissolve into the True, the Umber is the gain again its Number. "Thus will the last be first, and the first last" (Mt 20:16): perhaps nowhere else than in Gnosis does the precept of Christ find a more exact correspondent. So the *Untitled Text* of Codex Bruce ends as the *Gospel of Truth* begins — with the Return of the totalities to the Eternal One.

Now, the consequence following for the exegete of Gnosis from this paralogical logic, based formally on what may be called *the principle of the third man*, actually consists in the Gnostic textological use of the *coincidentia oppositorum*.

Indeed, the problem to cope with lies in a kind of antinomical projection of the metaphysical *once* in the textological *hic et nunc*, in a flashing transposition of massive absolute in the relativity of moving tracks and signs of the text. The plasmatic support of factitious verbal tracings converts itself into a sort of *written consciousness*, paradoxically truer than the oral one, into a pneumatic perplexity through which, as on a void path, man discontinuously returns to his instantaneous identity.

For man is the coming back of all things, as all things are man's verbal coming out — that is, the imaginary contraction of his will, *ichnos*, *logos*, and *thelema* being metaphysical and textual synonyms,[7] existing by this double cessation, only where his presence is denied and his absence asserted: in the syntax of the intermediate space.

The presence is the inverse ratio of existence. In this syntactical distance of holographical letters, the absence appears to itself in its image, paradoxically projecting its own retention and contracting itself, correlatively to its centrifugal conception, like the hollow heart of the bewildered phenomena. The serial monadology is a syntagmatic phenomenology of alphabetical totalities in synecdochal progression — or rather the monadological phenomenology itself is a hypostatical syntax of the imaginary using an amphibological technique in a mythopoetic degressive digression, *a rhetoric functioning as a syntax.*

So the pronominal ambiguities in referring to different entities[8] (masculine/feminine and singular/plural, with the mention that the feminine is the plural of the gender and the singular is the masculine of the number — cf. the Platonic dialectics of the One and the Multiple — the feminine representing, in the emanative process, the series, *segment-identity*, and the masculine the monad, *point-identity*), the deliberate confusion of names, appellations and attributes at distinct degrees of emanation, the indistinction between the grammatical subject and the appositional predication, the repetitions, redundancies, paradoxes and "illogicalities" of which the Gnostic treatises are full — too frequent and significant indeed to be reduced to the eternal "errors of transcription or translation," "interpolations" or "contaminations" — are nothing but *facts of style*, for which it is not textual criticism that can provide the intelligence but a *literary* one.

Or maybe we should invent another discipline. At least, another logic; most certainly, the Gnostics had already done it, and we shall always find it impossible to interpret, with our "kenomatic" instruments, this atypical thought which wanted itself pleromatic. This is a deeper dilemma than mere hermeneutizing. Paradoxically, the plenitude of the modern exegesis lies in its lacks, that is, in its misleading correctness — and in trying to obliterate the Kenoma, the Gnostics had devised the apparently sophistic technique of enticing away the intellect upon para-logical quicksands, where the error could not find support, of luring it, by means of Lobachevskian nets of analogical hazard and allogeneous parodical logic, from comic captivity to parodical logic, from comic captivity to parodical freedom — for freedom is always a parody — and from the *Kenoma* of the Aristotelian logic, into a Pleroma of perplexity. For, logically, the Gnostic Demiurge is Aristotle: witness, the reversal of the argument of "the third man" into a hypostatic principle owing to which the phenomenal man is endowed with an infinite tail of archetypal Adams.[9]

Folded and deployed like a synecdochal accordion, the monads are series and the series are monads; the attributes coagulate around a Name and autonomise themselves, in a metonymical manner, into new onomastic nuclei; the grammatical categories of gender, number and person are loose and floating; the outlines of the gnoseological distinctions subject/object, attribute/essence, accident/substance, agent/patient, cause/effect, signifier/signified, glide and dissolve thanks to a technique of functional interchangeability rendering the equations of the mind reversible: the Gnostic text is a writ rite where the novice, initiated by the "implicit reader" postulated by Todorov, which finds in Gnosis one of its first applications,[10] is plunged, head first, into the abyss of seismic revelation (*thauma*), in order to dissolve his logical idiosyncrasies and wake him up to another mental syntax.

This technique of navigation on the naught, which describes, by means of the Word, a double ascensional movement to the Origin, being nothing in fact but a logical strategy towards the nihility, an attempt to bypass it so as both to derive the world and to deduce salvation, is not an invention of Gnosis, but rather a symbological scheme subjacent to all sacrificial mentalities and more especially to Vedic thought, the difference being not so much one of method as one of end. Whether the sacrificer unglues the cosmic order, even at the risk of annihilating it, so as to be able, by actualizing the cause, to assure the perpetuity of the effect, the Gnostic, no less ritualist in fact, re-enacts the Creation in order to unlegitimate the Demiurge.

The methodological affinity can be seen particularly when we analyze the language of these two hermeneutics, typologically parallel.

We are dealing here with a symbolic language, of course, generally derived from a mythological background, best represented by the archaic aquatic cosmogonies. But, upon these primary nebulae and mytho-biologically fecund physics, Veda and Gnosis perform an operation of metaphysical re-signification, not foreign perhaps to some psychological deep presupposition or rather to a psycho-physiological one. The symbols function as concepts or are substituted by concepts functioning as symbols ontologically charged; the cosmogonical symbolism is used as a cognitive instrument, and upon the archaic scheme of the Igneous Embryo's emersion a gnoseology is built.

Denoted by the complex notion of *abhu*, the void-oneself lying hidden in the waters, hardly distinct from the aquatic inertia which impregnates it like the subjunctive subjacence of an image, the Vedic concept of origin is understood not so much as a non-existence as rather as a non-consciousness — fact partially justified by the compact indistinction between logical and physical and apparently contradicted by a sharp tendency to personify notions — since the effects of *abhu*'s tapasic calorization are, in a psychological order, the desire (*kama*) and the mind (*manas*); a Genesis of the Consciousness therefore, symbolized by the Cosmogonic Egg — the reified naught — i.e. the Golden Embryo[11] as a hypostasis of the unbegotten Spirit in its passage from a non-manifested to a manifested state.[12]

The same hermeneutical process is to be found in Gnosis. To Hiranyagarbha-*manas* corresponds here, *mutatis mutandis*, *Nous*, designating the Son — appositionally, the first Form and the first Name, but also the Eye and the Word — who emerges from Abyss and whose Father is nothing but the indistinct state in which the Totalities *are*, potentially, as unconscious of their deeper self as they will actually be after the pleromatic emanation.[13]

Metaphysically, the Son is a substance of pleromatic relations, linking together the moments of the moving identity, a definite subjacence defining the indefinite as a One, or, synecdochally, a paradigm configuring an origin (for Bythos is the qualitative part of Nous, as Nous is the quantitative part of Bythos). Analyzed extrinsically, the Son is the double difference of four terms: negation and projection, signifier and signified (the negative, i.e. retroactive, signifier of the abyssal cause being the prime mover of the projective signified of the Pleroma), while the Father appears as a privative identity transformed, by the negating Son, into a productive cause. Analyzed intrinsically, the Son could be described as a configuration of four astants — cohesive-distributive (strength, goodness), noetic (*nous*), verbal (*logos*), and visual (for, generally, the intellect is the eye) — each of them implying two aspects according to their retroactive or proactive orientation. The immediate scope of all these pleromatic actants is, of course, cognitively projective, the noetic one absorbing and supporting the others and, by this very fact, calling them back. The visual and verbal knowledge of the Father — viewed as suppressed Object of the Subject-Son, with the Pleroma as by-product of the gnoseological process — translates itself in a kind of transcendental sensorium; organ, function and perception compenetrated together in the synesthesical absence of a monad.

Thus the Son is nothing but an integrating dissociation within a dissociating integration, equivocal synthesis of the manifestation, and analytical principle of its conservation, a polymorphism preceding a series; related retroactively to the Father, the Son is a prolonged identity, considered in progression, he is the first identity of the non-entity, limit and symbol, mode and rule. We must emphasize once more this double aspect of the pleromatic subjacences, of progressive substratum and regressive indication, as if in the Pleroma, really and not artificially, all the signs were suddenly reversed; paradox quite apparent after all, for, the true meaning being the naught, it is perfectly natural for each element to be successively the signifier of its antecedent and the signified of its consequent, therefore, infinitely limited towards the interior and indefinitely illimited to the exterior — that is, in an eternal situation of fall.

So the hypostases are simply differences in position of a hierarchized identity. And it is the tragi-comedy of Limit that Nous, and with him, all the consequently antecedent syzygies which weave the Pleroma with boundaries and images, reveal themselves logically co-extensive exactly in so far as they are not co-intensive to the abysmal Father, substituting strangely enough its depth by a metaphysical measure of the lack, like the compounded orbit of an asymptotical sun glowing in the void of the disappearing moment in which it ceases.[14]

Nous and Manas, Horos and Hiranyagarbha are aspects in fact of the same psychogenetical identity — for their identity is predominantly aspectual — like a fourfold janitor Janus scribbling four items on his metapsychical grocery list. There are of course some differences in the script, as there is a huge cultural and temporal discordance between the Gnosis and the Veda, but these latter items, if they should not be ignored, shouldn't either be overvalued: thaumatic enough, the dissimilarities act rather as the historical screen of the typological picture, syntagmatical concordia-discors stressing its paradigmatical clashing-identity.

Probably, the main morphological difference between Hiranyagarbha and the Gnostic Nous lies in the mythological context or, more precisely, in the different types of space where each of them operates. Hiranyagarbha's Leyden jar are the primordial waters, as that of the Nous is the Pleroma, and furthermore, what might seem a total heresy from the Gnostic point of view, the Golden Embryo of the Vedic hymn epiphanizes himself as radically pancosmic (giver of breath — *atmadah*, literally, donor of *atman* — and of vigor, *baladah*). Surveyor of the air, support of the celestial vault and of the light, identified in the *Atharva Veda* X.7.28 with Skambha, the Vedic *axis mundi*, Hiranyagarbha is the Sun, not empirical but transcendental, whose revolution is Time, whose splendor is space, who creates by rising and destroys by setting, a terrifying photon to whom the waters look tremulously — an imponderable stare whose fixity freezes the brownian movement of the hydrous matter where he was hatched — and the shadows of this Gorgonic Eye are, strangely, immortality and death.

In fact, the discrepancy is less striking than it seems to be, the pleromogony being a metaphysical pantheism, governed pythagorically by an Eleatic Nous as metapsychical Sun, a liquid emission of catoptrical metapsychemes — and the connection of the entire Gnostic psychogenic secretion, both pleromatic and kenomatic, with the old aquatical cosmogonies is more than probably.

Now, despite its obvious naturism, which is, however, symbolical, the Vedic aquatic cosmogony appears less as a geminative exuberance (though this aspect is not to be ignored) but rather as a measuring activity, a weaving, an exact adjustment tending — synonymously to the sacrificial texture itself, with which it is in fact identified — to thwart Nirrti (≈ Vedic Kenoma[15]/[16]) by means of the matricial metric magic — *maya*, significantly derived from *ma* "measure."

Polytechnically archaic, Hiranyagarbha shares with the Nous the cohesive and the limiting functions — as cosmic pillar (*skambha*), the auriferous embryo delimits as much as he supports, being besides the separator *par excellence* of the aqueous abyss (in Veda, as in Gnosis, the waters are "chthonic") a surgeon embryo who performs himself its own Caesarean, and the fixed fascination of the trembling waters at the sight of this alchemical nightmare points precisely to their stabilization.[17]

So, if from the standpoint of the cosmogonical physics Hiranyagarbha plays quite obviously the part of a Vedic Horos (in Horos's assimilation with the Cross within the Ptolemaic milieu — "the flower of the Valentinian school," as the heresiologist says[18] — one may discern some eclectic remains of the old *axis mundi*, in its necessary connection with the "positional ontology"[19] of the cosmic directions), psychogonically, he is the visual mind (*manas*) of the Vedic magical mythology.   In *Hymn* X.129, after an extremely difficult incubative impregnation — in quite clear-cut synonymy with the Gnostic stuff[20] — *manas* rises from Desire (*kama*), and, since in R.V. X. 121 Hiranyagarbha emerges from the binomial waters (Samudra and Rasa: the copulation — *mithuna* — is implied by the opposite grammatical sex of the algebrical partners), the permutation is limpid: Hiranyagarbha of X.121 is the perfect equivalent of the *manas* of X.129, the difference between the two hymns being due to the abyssal causalistic approach of the latter, which marks, on the Vedic territory, the passage from what should be called a mythology of the spirit, to the first conceptualistic research.[21]

Quantic contraction of the aquatical quantity, Hiranyagarbha is an inner resorption opening an outer emission, and his ascension, which coincides with the primordial separation, is a doubly double look, or rather an indistinct visuality hypostatizing itself in the void of four distinct co-actants, two igneous (Agni-Hiranyagarbha) and two liquid (Samudra-Rasa); for the cosmogony is a sudden intensity in a gradual density, an instant of perplexity in the duration of a traumatical cause. In fact, nature looks for its identity, the dyadic shadow made up of *amrtah* and *mrtyuh* — the liquid immortality and the fluid death, contextually and symbolically identified with Rasa and Samudra — thickening into the projective hotness of the primordial igneous germ, Agni, in X.121.7, just as the formlessly frozen dyad of the void, *tuchyenabhu*, coagulates "by the great power of Warmth" (*tapas*) into the determinate potency of the One, *ekah*, in X.129.3 (Hymn X.121 being besides entirely constructed from typologically parallel triplets: the first term, igneously definite, the two others, forming obviously a dyad, hydric and indefinite).

Hiranyagarbha is the instrumental psycho-hypostasis of this One (the same which rests "upon the Unborn's naval," *ajasya nabhau*, in *R.V.* X.82.6), a zenithal center functioning as an imaginary middle term and splitting, by his suppressive transparence, the plasma of massive hydric contemplation.   Strangely enough, it is in the process of the catoptrical rejectional ascension of Hiranyagarbha that the informing light finds room to morphologize the sensitive chaos of the indiscriminated waters, filling the physical lack with the perplexed vision of the bright bark of their phenomenal mind revealed in the depth of their own traumatic spirit.[22] For Hiranyagarbha is an eye which sees by being seen and a mind which minds by being minded, and in the use of the instrumental (*manasa*) one may discern the Indian ambivalence in considering the status of the agent-handle for the handled patient — ambivalence here enhanced by the eminently causative position of Hiranyagarbha, the Eternal Embryo (gold connoting immortality), the subsisting inciter of the Vedic cosmogony.

In a way, the Waters constitute a kind of undulatory or melodical system of articulation, a dumb image of the Verb, in regard to whom Hiranyagarbha is the first sonorous vowel, the first syllable of the imaginary. That makes the Primordial Waters, at least by symbolical connotation, a kind of Pleroma, but a Pleroma which would precede the Nous, without knowing yet the Logos, or rather a kind of *Sige*, the first subjacence and the pleromatic essence *par excellence*. The plenitude is a container contained at the top and containing its bottom-essence as Bottom contains dreamy Titania, a void heart full of its hollow and remorsefully aspiring to its hollow's brilliant projection — a shadow, in fact, or an artifact. Shadow of its shadow's liquid shadow (for the essence is the *stain* of its plenitude), Aja, the Unborn, technically the naught, is a connotative co-absence subtly manipulating its hypostatic co-presence — for being is another thing than seeming or, as Griffith quite aptly translates the verse, "Ye will not find him who produced these creatures: another thing (*antara*) hath risen up among you" — and the parallel with the Gnostic Father, who can be known or can imaginarily subsist only through the shining of his noetic Son, is peculiarly evident. Like, in fact, the Primordial Waters, the Pleroma is a reciprocal implication perceived as a univocal progression, a chain of perceptions, that is, of *recognitions*, each of them mediated by hazy hesitation and falling in the identity of another contraction.

But the sinuous coincidence between the Vedic semeiology of the vision and the Gnostic psychology of the imaginary can be best realized and maybe best denied through the concept of (*ichnos* = skr. *pada*). For, more than a simple metaphor depending upon an ancient ritualistic and magical mentality — besides, quite living both in Veda and Gnosis — the track is the efficient figure of thought of what may be called a cynegetic metaphysics or, rather, an inferential mystic. The footprint of the Father is his Will,[23] which the Gnostic adepts — phenomenologically identified with the paradigmatic Totalities — scent, through the fragrances emanated from the paternal face, in order to find acosmical salvation, — and functionally, the psych=analogical footprint corresponds, though with an inverse intention, to *rasmi*, the string or transversal line drawn by the Vaidic Rsis in order to institute the cosmos of salvation (i.e. to build the sacrificial area: corroborate R.V. X. 129.5 and X.130.1). But *rasmi* is nothing but the ritual equivalent of the *maricinam pada* — lit. the trace of the rays or sparks (specks) — the radiant wake of the mayic Bird whom the technicians of the vision follow in their heart and in the depth of the subtle Ocean.[24]

Viewed on the symbolical smoothness of the sacrificial area, the things distinguish themselves quite neatly. Indeed, in the *Satapatha Brahmana* III.5.1.1-11, describing the construction of the Great Altar (*mahavedi*, that is the sacrificial area conceived as a "great" *maha* — "altar" *vedi*), the first line drawn by the Vedic officiants is the South-North transversal, the mystical channel uniting the symbolical nadir and zenith, and the ulterior development of the area represents precisely the extension of this first trajectory.[25]

So *mahavedi*, and inductively the whole sacrificial system, is but a trace aggregated of traces, an image of the repetition accumulating differences in identities and extracting an identical substance from every scattered difference. Bricks or steps (*pada*), the matter is always of a symbolic arithmology[26] subordinated to a projective teleology, of a correct worship aimed to correct — by what may be called a *magical breaking-perspective* — the distorted transcendence in the cracks of its terrestrial image.[27]

In a way, both the trace and the altar are the ordered decomposition of the Father — Prajapati in the *Brahmanas*, the Hiding Father in the *Gospel of Truth*, where *ichnos* is the cloud of identity of a discontinuing entity, a permanent lack of position in an evanescent fullness of disposition — the precise haphazard of his presence, the suburb of a connecting shadow between the looked for and the looking for, suppressed in the identity of both.

In not quite another way, this reconstructed alteration constitutes the semiological projection of an aniconic portrait,[28] a convention in fact, based on esoteric appositions, the convention itself being nothing but a partial connection completed with projection, a participation of two protractive levels with rupture implied. The existence hollows itself out under a point,[29] and the connecting convention traces the passage from the state of connotation to the void-instant of an annihilating denotation, as a troubled superposition of lacunae complemented with a pantheistic influx of hypostases.

For the sacrifice represents a conglomerate of prints aiming to heal the hollow, a superposition of signs configurating, by a technique of analytical distribution of the symbols, not a mimetic but an aniconic image — the difference in aspect or rather the *not* of iconical resemblance pointing to the transition of plans.[30] Compenetration is suppression, and through the quantic image of disjointed noetic sediments traversed by the metaphysical fixity of the noeric speed, the Father finds himself in the trace of his retention, supplying his projective identity with an elective fuel of lack, changing his free falling depth in the substance of truth of an inward connection.[31]

So, the identity is splitting; or rather, the identity is its own ubiquity, containing in one whirl the entire immanence of Nature in the vertex of its own transcendence: that is why the concept of *ichnos* is central and total for the whole Gnosis, readily including and equalizing such reciprocal *adunata* as the Hidden Father, the hiding Nous, Limit (*horos*), Wisdom (*Sophia*), the Abortional outflow of non-being, and the Demiurge, the egoistic temporal becoming of space and soul.[32]

In fact, the identity is a conflict, an antagonistic contradiction, compressed in one point, between its conceptual determination and its conceptual content; for the absolute indetermination is the true conceptual content of the identity. What is determined can't conceive itself as undetermined, and seems to migrate in itself as in an allogeneous substance; so, by appearing, it's caught! Its inside wanders outside in the image of its outside wandering inside, and, though perfectly compenetrated, the two seem divided into a form and a fool. The identity splits by compacting itself, emerges and by this very fact is submerged. By being determined, the identity is the transcendent of the undetermined; but by being *identity*, it is the ubiquitous immanent of all that it determines. By looming out and modulating itself in an intensity, the identity converts the aperatic compenetration of the indetermination into the infinite extension of a substance. The conceptual nature and natural self-relation of the identity coagulate in a nature opposed to the concept; thus, the identity appears void in its transcendental concept and full of the blind immanence of the conceived, as a trace total in its chase.

The identity as identity is a One, but by being identity, it has no limit and no alterity; therefore, it is an All. As a One, the identity is its own limit, as an All, the identity is its own substance; its own synthesis dissociates it, and its own analysis unifies it by aliening it, so as, finally, to break it into pieces. The identity is a Chaos of contrary forces.

For Nature is a beginning of structure, that is, of concept, the How-it-is preceding the What-it-is, but coming into being only *after* it; so the indetermination is the accomplice of the identity, in a way obscure.[33] A deep vibration foregoes, by following, its own epiphany, in a wake of streaming connotations, and this absolute of agglutination reveals itself thereby as a One. The concept is the substance of thought, so the substance is the concept of being, and the streaming subjacences are the psychical subsoil of the abyssal subbottom; this implies a confused connotative contradiction, an imbecile plenitude of the void, a semi-hostile entanglement unable to achieve a system of oppositions. But nevertheless this leviathanic annotation flowing out of its aniconic annotation is the only One conceivable, mostly because besides it, there is none, and, paradoxically, the definite comes forth from the obscure monad of its indefiniteness like an atomic bomb defining itself in the massive explosion of its inner fissional contradiction.

Thus, from the very beginning the contradiction appears as the invasion of the connotative in the denotative growth, as a gradual concentration in an already saturated monad. In absolute, nature is pure nothingness, but in the relativity of its concept nature is tendency, the larval state of notation. In its transcendent unity, nature is absolutely not, but in the immanent indetermination of its naught, nature tends to be something; it connotes being rather than denotes it. That's why the nature of nature is suffering. By having a concept, nature is its own subject; but it can't conceive itself as a subject, but as a concept. Without its concept, it has no life and meaning, not the sheerest existence, but without it, the concept is form for the naught.

So nature with concept is subject, but the concept in itself, taken in its own transcendence, is spirit. For the Spirit, Nature or rather Matter is an embarrassing implication, a leviathanic link in which, despite his transcendency, he feels himself somehow swallowed, and which he is burning to get rid of. As a concept — almost a logical phenomenon — he cannot help but determining and thus supporting the matter he hates, and this is his threnos. But as Spirit, the concept has no existence, no other reality than that furnished by its own content and its own repulsion — and *this* is its chaos. In the mass of his disgust, he cannot recognize any more his own identity, and in his almost self-annihilating refusal he appears a priori absurd, but that is the heroism of the Spirit. His ecstatic ignorance is a kind of aesthetics, his eternal but not real defeat — his irrational freedom. For the Spirit there is no necessity in liberty but only agony in victory, no necessity simply understood, but necessity understood and denied; incidentally, here lies his greatest cunning, almost his hypocrisy, because the Spirit is the blackmailer of lost battles, who wins by threatening to Lose, as a Napoleon forced to vanquish his own Grande Armée and conquer Paris barebosomed, or rather like an Achilles compelled to fight the Achaean army by his very absence, for what army can subsist to a dead or absent Achilles, and which world, to a wounded spirit! In fact, this cunning is his true deep trap. There is a necessity in poetry, perhaps there is no other necessity but poetry!

By eternally jumping out of Matter and picking up his heels, the Spirit loses himself as a metaphor and finds himself as a dictator, for Matter has no choice but to follow. Moreover, flight is impossible; the point of light which soars asymptotically above the cosmos carries with it the entire growth of the space beneath, like the volatile top of an elastic pyramid bounded in height by its base.

In all frankness, the Spirit catches a glimpse of the dramatic situation of Matter, possesses a kind of quantic intuition, a stuck sensation of her painful semantic metabolism — for Matter is his damnation — and in his repulsion fights a lapse, the blurred remembrance of the lost concept; a logic amnesia with some other depth in addition. He goes on fulfilling somehow his determining function — without which, both Spirit and Matter would cease instantaneously to exist — but he can't conceive any more, his pure intensiveness cannot comprise, can not accept itself as the concept of clumsy infiniteness of the clumsy matter; and so, by loosing his concept, he's barren.

From now on, the Spirit can give free rein to his pathological tendency to hiding, to his ontological avariciousness, to his idiotic mania of accumulating himself like a transcendental Harpagon grabbing himself only for himself and hiding himself in a place known only to himself. Hunted by his own contrariety, he runs towards his own identity, and in his running inhibition or rather in the contraction of his flight he puts on his inside like an outside Pleroma, falling down through his annihilating-self as some Aeon melting in the sweetness of his center.

Thus, by losing his concept and blocking himself in the outer interiority of his inhibition, the Spirit finds himself, he finds indeed his abyssal essence, but as an alien. That is, the Spirit finds an alien, a reified naught! This is the normal outcome of an initial dualism: from the very beginning of the logic cosmogony, the identity contained itself in itself as its own contradiction, a massed dualism of the identity and the indetermination, which tended by definition to split; the connotation invades its denotation, identifies for a moment with it, trying to forget its lower origins, then jumps once more into the nil — for, once started, the contradiction cannot be stopped.

This is in a way a kind of correction and a kind of return. By abandoning the indetermined to its damnation, by rejecting it as a sheer exteriority, as the empty peel of the eaten banana, the determination provides the fuel for burning itself, destroys itself but in an outer way; for the determination of nothing else is nothing but else, that is, the else of the nothing! Paradoxically, the Pleroma and implicitly Nous appear from this very destruction as a sign of an a priori fallen essence, subsisting however in its *correct* intensity. The identifications refused from within realize themselves always from without — but an identification from without is never complete!

With its denotative substance torn and thrown away or rather dialyzed by the stubbornness of the Spirit, the concept plunges, only through its connotation, into its conceptism, as into an alien matter. For both spirit and matter are false representations, pseudo-morphemes, and *by this very fact* the Spirit appears quantically within the matter, is quantically immanent — the quantic being the logic *immediately* represented, the logic immediately physical. His within is killed in his without, his solipsism makes of him a kind of double alter-ego.

So the Spirit is blocked! Totally depreciated, he looms out of the fog of his mass-annihilation as a substance of stupefaction personified by Error. As simple connotation — for, for having refused to denote, he lost in punishment his denotative aspect — the Spirit is not different from the matter, he is not anymore a concept, not even a substance, but a liquefied nil, an Abortion, a non-being. More exactly, his stupefaction is the suspension of an impossibility, the interdiction — i.e. the alienated essence, one's own essence as one's own taboo — coiled in the subsistence of a kind of embryonic consciousness. So in his *thauma* which is nothing else but his exterior *identification* with matter, the concept hammered, not the concept conjunct — the Spirit surges as potential Nous. In both directions the Intellect is destruction, which fits quite well with the Gnostic soteriogony.

Perplexity is the synthesis between recognition and refusal; caught in the vortex-concept of his amnesia, the spirit bubbles its chaos and its loss. Conserved inwardly, its residual contradiction is altered and infected from without. He is nothing more than a connotation, but this is already a regression, a dissolution into the waste land of the immanence, his concept putrefied. The Spirit dies, and in his death there is the danger of his essence. That puts him in an agonic empathy with all the levels of the split existence. His death is the naught, his error, the deepest knowledge, and an enormous alarm freezes the Light and the Darkness. All the levels of the potential beings concert themselves, as it were, planning their own escape in the salvation of the moribund Spirit. The Intellect, the usurper of his fall and the son of his destruction, manifests itself as a limit[34] and this boundary thrown in the bubble of his deep sleep and abyssal dissolution awakes him from his slumbering identity. It awakes him, but it awakes him as another! For now, the Spirit is mad, he's a Demiurge.

In fact, the Spirit is not yet so much a Demiurge as a creature; by being aphronic, he's amorphous. He's not even a being, but rather the blindness of an intuition, unconscious intention measuring its own potency by its own inexistence; for to create, he lacks the form, and to be a Demiurge he lacks a subject.

What is the Subject then? Earlier in this paper we stated that the Subject was the nature in possession of its concept, but this is only partially true, or rather it is the truth in its demonic abstraction. For the Subject gathers and co-masses the entire process, the whole mythological development of which Spirit and Matter are just the players; indeed, in this play the Subject is a stage. That is, the Subject is substance, the substance being that stage, that cavern where things are but shadows; it is an involuntary substratum, strangely unrelated to the relations which, in a way, make him be.

The Subject is an absolute, but only in a relative sense; a globality which transcends perpetually its unity, a gigantic amoebical trace stepping in itself to the limits of nothingness, a drop of All over an abyss of *not*. Thus the Subject is substratum: he determines himself in the process, but the process too may be looked at as the simple auto-determination of the subject. Viewed in this perspective, the Subject is an All abyssal and substantial, an universal compriser whose parts are its own processes, a huge synecdoche: for there exists, in the famous *pars pro toto*, an inertial-processual implication, *the process appearing as the part of inertia!*[35]

Thus, taken in the development and the determination of his process, the Subject is a notation of itself or, more precisely, *the self as notation*, because the source of the determinations of the Subject is the notation of the self as mediated concept of the naught. Caught in its true galvanic signification, the play of the determinations functions eliminatorily, i.e. the determinations in their play are a kind of tests, of *definitions on trial*, the substratum and the result of which is the subject, as positive accumulation; while the negative accumulation of the determining process is the self. For if the subject is the place where all the determinations coexist, the self is the locus where all the determinations cease, and this white void essentially objectual is the closest image of the naught: the self: the naught as imaginary retention. On the contrary, closed in his huge solitude as in the walls of some moving prison of the omnipotence, bound as some fabulously growing transatlantic in the midst of an ineffable, inescapable Sea,[36] the Subject is an anxious giant eroded secretly — the very substance of interrogation — an All growing and guzzling the convulsive procession of its own stupefactions, roaring and swooning and growing and looking for itself as a monstrous cavity where ends all totality; for the substance is craving for the essence, and the Subject is roar for the naught.

But, if the Subject is an agonic inherence isolated in the desert of its empty transcendences and blind immanences, a triumphal march over the void, leaning on its hypostatic moments as on some instantaneous crutches — for, in his run after the transcendence, the Subject is Time — then the self, Subject's obsession and double, is an impassable dichotomy, or rather an object which puts the surrounding totalities of the others as a void mass of lack-objects. Thus, in this curious system of oppositions realized through the strict autarky of each of its terms, an infinite and, up to a certain point, an indefinite auto-transcendence is indirectly confronted with a radical auto-immanence in which, paradoxically, the former finds its concept and its end. Whether the Subject is a dynamical trace, a chaser chased by his *angustia* through the labyrinthian without of its progression to itself — for the Subject is a subjacence out of itself to itself, and out-of-itself-to-itself-in-itself — the self, contrary to Subject's additive negation, denies by subtraction, and though this subtraction is but the substance of his own impassability, caught in it, the self appears as *Will*! For, in a sense, the will is exactly the negative dialectics of the self.[37]

Now, the subjectivation of this subtractive Will, is the Spirit. Submerged in its interior-in-exterior immanence, the Spirit coincides positionally with the auto-immanent self, but the immanence of the Spirit being completely exterior, being in other words *a fall*, the Spirit is greedy of the subject, this dynamic avidity reversing the impassability of the self. In other terms, the Spirit is a repulsive system coagulating its own interiority as a seed of obscurity, for, as an aggregate of darkness, the matter is Spirit's error.

Hence the spirit-in-matter is the interior turned inside out, and transformed into a consistent obscurity, that is, into an *ego*, for the obscure does not become real but as an individual. Because the ego is the atom of the exterior being. What is for the Spirit a kind of vis-à-vis relationship — the Spirit being entirely an interiority uncomprehended — becomes at Ego's level the indivisible unity of the exterior. The Spirit was the matter expelled, the Ego is the matter included. In the Ego it is not any more the Spirit who is immanent in the matter, but, perplexingly, the matter which is immanent *in the shape of the spirit*.

For, like the Subject, who is a kind of global bark himself, the Ego is the husk of the spirit, the spirit turned into its own crust, not any more the crust of something but a crust *in* something, a crust in its own interior-vomited — and thus, containing the immanence in which it is contained inside a crust never actual but in its withdrawal; the matter determined by the Ego as his informity is Ego's vomiting emanation, a vomiting fission, in fact, of Ego's misshapen will, the Ego himself being the hunchbacked caricature of the spirit. That is why between the Ego and the Subject there exists a deep analogy, or rather a situational affinity; and it is for this very reason that the Ego, as a hybrid-all, and *hybris*-all, receives his subjective shape from the Subject, as from his own abyss. For, in a way, the Subject resorbs itself totally in the Ego, but not in its quality of subject; indeed, the Ego is not the Subject, but only *a quality-of-subject.*

So the Ego appears as Subject's quality, that is, in his dynamis he is quality-of-subject. As hybrid-all and *hybris*-all, the Ego is the battlefield of all the analytical hypostases; in his mediated concreteness, the Ego is discontinuously cyclic, he is in these very words a cycle and a repetition, and, contrary to that of the spirit, his own repulsion is derived. For the Ego is a perverse innocent!

Compared to the spirit, who functions as a system, the Ego is a world, not simply a system of oppositions — nay, the Ego is *the* world, and there is no other world but the Ego. In a sense, the Ego is an intensity deeper than the Spirit, an obscurity built on Spirit's annihilation, a *personal naught* and an anxiety. His own self is a hunger and a thirst, his repulsion, a voracity. In his instinctiveness, the Spirit wants to be, but the Ego wants to be the Master; and by this will he's God. His thirst of light is digestive, and the light, as his apophatic exterior, represents nothing else but the spirit of contradiction of his own repulsion; a postulated prey! For the Ego is an intensive whole; bereft of its concept and of its contradiction, the Spirit projects itself as an inert image, a phantom and a corpse, that is, it appears as a *converted* spirit. A void of light! But the Spirit also represents, by his imaginary inertia, for the decomposing Ego, a deep temptation; an investment for his biggest asset, *the quality-of-subject.* If the Ego owns, the Ego aspires, and the aspiration is a kind of guilt.

The quality of subject is the sudden, and in the heavy and calibanic melodrama of existence it functions like a kind of gremlin, an *arlecchino*, an Ariel or a Puck with a quantic biography of its own. The quality-of-subject is in fact the Subject taken in its moments as holographical parts, and as such, in this system of parallel pulses of being, the quality of subject represents a much earlier occurrence than the Ego.

More precisely, the quality-of-subject is the residual emanation of the Subject himself as looking for himself in something else than himself, the freedom of this abortive determination keeping the anxiety as a serial attribute. As projection of surpassed limits or rather as a quintessence of these, the quality-of-subject is a Multiple of determination in an ubiquitous One, and as a limit, it is of course an imitation.   She transcends the Subject's global transcendence, analytically; to his globalism which is spatial, she responds by chaos of unforeseeable occurrences which are temporal.

So the Quality-of-subject is both quantic and simiesque.   In a sense, the discontinuity is possible because it is imitative, that is, *identive*.   Now, the discontinuity implies the instantaneity, the instantaneity configurating itself as an *exact imitation without duration*. The exact imitation is chaotic, because its lack of duration translates itself by an omnivocal occurrence: all the space is quantically identic, the epiphanic disorder being provoked by, and provoking, the intensity of the message. For as global, the subject is space, and as subject, this space is identical. That is why the Quality-of-subject projects herself thaumatically, appearing without wandering and disappearing without lasting, caught in the paranoia of her own determination. The Spirit expressed the identity by the fixity, for the Spirit is always the center; infinitely monadic, the Quality-of-subject expresses the center potentially in every point and actually in none of them, instituting the being as a cacophonous run, an open circulation in which everyone is one Moment's king and the other Moment's nothing, and the existence, a segment of bewilderment.

In fact, the Quality-of-subject is an approximation, exact enough to appear only *instantaneously*, but approximative enough *to appear*. Her spontaneous nature resides in a searching amnesia, a kind of erotic unhappiness very much similar to that of a Woman looking for the Ideal Man; for her frailty is a failure, a non-achieved identity. That explains why her existence is a perpetual passing and dancing, an impulsive bumping — with a kind of staccato effect — against an immediate limit, *an impulse cut by a limit implied*. Being instantaneous, the Quality-of-subject is always *surprised* by her appearance; the limit of her impulse, which we may call subconscious, and its annihilation are a state of consciousness, with that difficulty that, hardly actualized, the state of consciousness is immediately dragged or rather projected, by the force of the impulse, to some other explosive illumination. Thus, the anxiety comes forth as vitality. But if the limit is the visibility of the impulse, and the impulse the potency of the limit, its intense essence is in neither of the two, but in the loophole of its extinction, in the pure instantaneity of the naught. For the Unconscious is the real possessor of the quality of subject, and the unconscious is the identity.

The Quality-of-subject is in her occurrence an error and in her essence, a potency, actual only in its disappearance and manifesting itself only through the channel of the impossible, in the shape of surprise of something eternally else; for the soul-movement of the Quality-of-subject is her alter-non-ego. So, formally, the Quality-of-subject is nothing but illusion, a nothing of form defined defining the form of nothing; but in her function, the Quality-of-subject is nothing but hazard. Her showing is a center of interest and a compensation, her vanishing, a kind of boredom; for the quality of subject is just curiosity.

Of course, the Quality-of-subject's immediate partner is the Spirit; for her thaumatic curiosity there is no better match but his aesthetical absurdity: the Spirit is absurd, but from the Quality-of-subject's point of view this absurdity is *le beau*. In fact, the Spirit interferes with her as her surprise, that is, her limit; in him, she appears, but she is vanishing beyond him. He becomes present only with her, and she becomes existing only without him. In the Spirit, the Quality-of-subject is actual, because never can the spirit be actual but through the Quality-of-subject; so they are both annihilated. For the Spirit, the Quality-of-subject appears as matter, as an obsession and a repulsion, that is, as an *intention*; for the Spirit, the Quality-of-subject is always a necessary danger, but for the Quality-of-subject, the Spirit appears as a kind of fatherland. Blocked in him, she is his falling; lost outside her, he is her image. With her, the Spirit finds his substance and fills the space, everything is spirit; without her, the Spirit finds his essence in his emptiness, the Spirit is nothing.

Caught in her capricious ubiquity, the Quality-of-subject is a Pleroma, a plenitude; but by getting, from her absolute lack of concept, a kind of acephalous universality, the Quality-of-subject emerges as a polymorphic Kenoma. If in his substratum the Spirit is space, in her form the Quality-of-subject is time — her form being precisely the Spirit. On the contrary, in her impulse, the Quality-of-subject is *pneuma*; and that spirit which appears to himself as immanent in this pneuma is the Ego.

The Ego is the Spirit void in the infinite emptiness of the matter, because the matter, accepted only from its indefinite exterior by the Spirit, is an emptiness and a void. Thus, the matter refused by the Spirit becomes his internal void and the empty space in which he finds himself! The Ego rises in the world at the same time with this emptiness and with this void, and so, the Ego raises the world, and puts himself in determined being, together with it! He comes out and opens his eyes over the infinity of the matter, which is his shade and in which he recognizes only his power, an indefinite plasticity confirming his unicity and tranquilizing his fear.

So, by catching his essence as his power and not recognizing himself in his naught, the Ego is blind, his blindness being exactly this waste land of his exteriority, and consisting in the fact that the Ego puts himself rightfully as the empty concept of this empty matter, veiling, by that exaltation, his total inexistence and "sinning" consequently against the All. For the All is his inner naught. Thus, by being the all of his blind exteriority, the Ego is a part of his naught, and by being blind, he lies. The matter is Ego's intuition, in which the I lives like in a space, the I-in-the-space being Ego's individualization; but by being an intuition, the Matter is indeed Ego's lie, for in her, the truth of his naught is not so much lost as refused and reversed. The Spirit was, after all, a refusal of the matter in behalf of the naught, while the Ego is the refusal of the naught in behalf of the matter.

In a way, this lie is the truth incorrectly translated, the naught's notation of nothing-else transmitting itself, in the course of the determinative process, into the spirit's repulsion to be something-else, and finally into the Ego's rage-to-be, masked by his will to be the master. From this point of view, the Ego is doubly hypocritical; however, the matter being unreal, through his lie the Ego becomes her adequate concept, the Matter herself becoming the adequate substance of this adequate concept.[38]

But on the other hand, Ego's lie is nothing but his quality of subject; by having it, he is in the center of the stage, and so he is alone. But by uttering it, he puts himself as another than his essence who is the Spirit, and so he loses it. It is true, stripped of its concept and of its quality of subject, this essence, this spirit, is dynamically only a corpse, a simple inertia appearing as the difference between the omnipotent pseudo-universal ego, from now on definitely damned in his exteriority, and the nihil of his interior; but noetically, this caught essence of the Spirit destroyed is a sign, the imaginary signifier of the naught — its limit and symbol, phenomenologically, the deeper double of the Nous, and ontologically, Man and Light.

What however prevents the Ego, in spite of his indignity, from really losing his quality of subject, is the fact that the Ego does not represent simply a metaphysical or metaphysical hypostasis, like for instance the Spirit, but a *being*. Knotted in his knobbing exteriority, the Ego is living, he is the First Being *par excellence*, and only as such is he a Demiurge, the pragmatical God. Knitted with him and definitely immanent in the spatial matter, the Quality-of-subject is, in her factitious-deep egoistic root, his potency and his will, i.e. his omnipotence, and in her trajectory, his act and his becoming, his omnicomprising energy through which he imposes himself as the concept of his power, making of all the metaphysical hypostases his faculties and his pantheon. It is probably the first quotation of the argument of authority; for the Demiurge is the Ego authoritarian!

Not only! Far from being a passive demiurgic concept, the lie of the Ego is in fact the synthetic unity of his entire exterior *meros*, the conductive compactness of the whole semantic dispersion determined by the moving system of the hypostatic isolations. The fact that the lie is something subjective puts her as quality of subject; through her, the matter gains concept and substance, and so the lie is primordial space; dynamically, the lie is the cosmogony, the pseudo-logos by which the Ego asserts himself as Demiurge and thus as cosmogonical agent. What is more, as demiurgic concept, concept of demiurgic action, and concept of demiurgic space, the lie is the principle of truth, an agent acting in itself, an exteriority operating in its own interiority and tending asymptotically to it.[39] Curiously, the analysis projects the lie as splitting between false action and static noetic light. Of course, her truth lies only in her transformations — but in absolute, the Lie lies; because in this relativity which does not surpass her boundaries there exists a certain cohesion and a kind of exactitude *en gros*. So, as lie, the Quality-of-subject is splitting!

In her absolute substratum, the lie is all-comprising-all-comprised space, and overflow overflowing its flow, for flowing-lie is always pantheistic; but in its relativity, the space is Ego's species, and all species are spaces for their specific egos. In absolute, the space is the species of the naught — the synthetic *symphany* of the subjacences — in transcendent, the space is the species of the Spirit, in relative, the space is the species and the power of the Ego, but in the *specific*, the species are the temporal spaces of the individual egos.

On the other hand, from a transcendental outlook the lie is Ego's will of plenitude. The Ego wants himself an all-full, and this will is his lie and his act: so, in his lie the Ego is his own act, and as an act, the Ego is his own space; if the lie is his concept, the Ego is nothing but a lie. But in his aspiration and in his destination, the Ego is quality of subject. His whole becoming amounts to one moment's polarity. The Ego's substance is a completing lack — for the Ego is the mounting growth, the Ego grows in his determinations, and his growth is a cohesion and an ascension, the cohesion of an ascension in fact! But the Ego's concept — his "lie"! — is a synthetic dialectics of infinite realization, an Irrational-Informulable-Incommensurable dimension!

As a whole, the Ego is the one gigantic moment of the Quality-of-subject, is the Quality-of-Subject massively static, a synthetic massively static polarity; for, as a whole, the Ego lies, and by lying he becomes his own part, his own scission, his own alter-alter-ego! By being a whole, the Ego is a hole, a solid center, a solid point of inertia — or rather, the inform bubbling abortional indetermination surrounding this point — a mass of uncertain inert subjacences plotting to capture the outer image of their essence; for in his ambition, the Ego is his own abolition, and if sinning against the all makes the Ego a part, his losing of his quality of subject makes the Ego a hardly aggregated matter. So, by his very substance-of-lie, the Ego loses and gains determination, he loses by gaining it and gains it by losing it.

But as a part, the Ego is his own cosmogony, his own *dynamis* and his own series of qualities of subject, his own mass of multiple projecting itself in his own mass of solitude, for, for the autarkically-depressive-paranoiacally-perplexed-ego, the cosmogony is an apocalyptic nature, a self-revealing destruction and a plot! Caught in the nature of his plotting cosmogony, the Ego is almost a Personal God, who lacks only a name = a situation = a world. Ego's nature is a growth of acts, a mass of actualization growing in a mass of annihilation, a growing substance which massively appears and massively is destroyed, for the growth is the perpetual destruction of the massive appearance filling geometrically its massive disappearance.

Thus, the Ego is a magnet which by perpetually attracting the iron, seems to project itself; the attraction explains itself as an impulse, the indefiniteness of the impulse glosses itself as a multiple of series, a multiple of holographical impulses in relation to which the indefinite impulse appears as their immanence and their subjacent content, comprised in its parts as in its forms: an All determined in its parts and intensified in its forms, a synthesis analyzed in its hypostatic totalities.

Caught in its immanence, the quantic flight of the qualities of subject loses its transcendent freedom, configurating itself as a system of vital pneumas, a plasma, a work. They become, so to speak, cold, for coldness is only immanence. What is more, their ubiquity grows limited, as acts, the qualities of subject gathering themselves in objects — for the objects are massive sums of acts, and, phenomenologically, the objects are absolutely prime illusions: subjacences and naught. So, as collective limits, these Prime Objects are closed powers, closed fields of forces, vortices of decomposing latences, modal in their nadir and formal in their zenith; formed from without as voiding from within, like a deep touch justified from above by an imaginary limit, their dissolution becomes the function of their imaginary.

As immanent, the Quality-of-subject is act, and as act, she splits into an object and an idea, their difference and the partial identity of their participation being the a priori troubled consequent of the a posteriori antecedent of her extinction: a spontaneously synchronic *paradigm-a-priori* informing a diachronic *origin-a-posteriori*. Thus, the idea does not appear except because the object vanishes. But this appearing from the depth of the disappearing puts her as his a priori principle, and puts him as her a posteriori origin, and in this tension both are saving and saved.

Thing and archetype form a paradigmatic unity, whose synthetic syntagm is Man. For Man is a collection of centers in a plasma of circumferences, a thing vanishing in all his points and full of imaginary light. An epiphany of the extinction closed in a mass of ideas, a glorious void precarious in all his masks! So in him there is always something disappointing, for Man is the absolute uncertainty.

Rising with the world in his new determined world, Man inherits God and substitutes, as a recipient of the quality of subject, the ego; for Man is not God's creation but Ego's mutation. In him, Matter tries for the firs time to put herself as Spirit's concept: indeed, Matter's greatest and most confused ambition is to be a genius — that is, growing spirit, *the immediate ego* of the spirit, Spirit's fast! If Ego's vocation is cosmogonical, Man's is soteriological, for Man is, not only in his essence, but also in his appearance, nothing but naught. His deepest soul is the flesh, i.e. the typified non-being of the non-being; his body is his soul — the synthetic spirit. Thus Man is an archetype-in-object unveiled as originary paradigmatic synthesis; for in Man both *a priori* and *a posteriori* are all-subjacence and naught-equal.

But as for the destiny of man — this delicate monster of boredom and hypocrisy — the present paper remains totally unconcerned, as well as Man's latest incarnation, the author of the present paper — this gloomy solitude of sound and fury, and the implicit reader of you all; for Yaldabaoth, the subtle Begetter of Powers of the Gnostics, is nothing — but the empirical consciousness of the reader, that fellow and brother of Charles Baudelaire! Or, as Zostrianos so democratically puts it, "In short, all of them are the purification of the unbornness . . ." (Z.75.23-24).

NOTES

1. Aristotle, *Metaphysics* I(A) 9; the argument had been already used by Plato in *Parmenides* 132d-133a. According to Alexander Aphrodisiensis, the argument was invented by the Sophist Polyxenes, disciple of Bryson.
2. Irenaeus, *Adversus Haereses* IV.19.1.
3. See our *Le Nombre*. . . I, p. 205 and n. 1.
4. Plato, *Parmenides* 137c-d.
5. See *Le Nombre*. . . I, p. 210 sq.
6. Ibid., p. 217 sq.
7. See the *Gospel of Truth* I.3.37.4-7, 25-26.

8. For analogous remarks see Joel Fineman, "Gnosis and the Piety of Metaphor: The *Gospel of Truth*," in *The Rediscovery of Gnosticism*, I (Leiden, 1980), pp. 295-296.

9. To the finite and up to a certain point pragmatic logic of Aristotle, the Gnostics seem to have opposed what we may call a *logic of the infinite*. It would be tempting to analyze, from this outlook, the possibility of considering the Aristotelian "logical errors" (tautology, contradiction, *regressus ad infinitum*, etc.) as the very principles of this new logic, neither descriptive nor normative but fundamentally axiological. It goes without saying that the immediate, and so to speak naive, application of this logic of the infinite in finite conditions remains on the side of error; but the problem is — as the Gnostics conceived it — that the true error consists in the logic of the finite itself taken as a whole.

10. For the function of implicit reader in the Gnostic texts see *Le Nombre. . .* I, pp. 212, 214.

11. Annotating the verse 7 of the *A.V.* IV.2 (the parallel and possibly the paradigm of the *R.V.* X.121), Whitney observes: "The comm. understands *hiranyagarbha* as «the embryo of the golden egg»." To this Lanman adds: "Kirste . . . reviewing Deussen, suggests that the golden embryo is the yolk of the mundane egg." (*Atharva Veda Samhita*. Trans. by W.D. Whitney. Revised by Ch. R. Lanman. First Half [Cambridge, Massachusetts, 1905], p. 147). See also in this respect *Satapatha Brahmana* XI.1.6.1.

12. For the equivalence Hiranyagarbha-*manas*, corroborate *R.V.* X.121.1 with X.129.4; see below n. 22.

13. As dialectical manifestation of the Father, the Son integrates and hypostasizes the negative dialectics (for an analytical reconstruction of this idea in the *Apocryphon of John* II.1.2.25-4.26, see our *Le Nombre. . .* II, no. 30), substituting it by what we may call a negative semiology, in which the sign vanishes immediately in its identity with the sense and the sense subsists mediately through its subjacent distinctive sign. Thus the sense is the infinite causal depth of its own semiological effect which is itself, and through which it is as purport of its sign. In other terms, the passage from negative dialectics to negative semiology closes in its opening the pure, that is, the unlimited transformation of an absolute deduction into an absolute induction of the absolute (see below n. 14).

    The best example of this total semiotical feedback is probably to be found in the *Gospel of Truth* I.3.38.7 sq. (beginning with the famous "The Name of the Father is the Son"), curiously analogous with the *Gospel of John* 1.1 sq., fact apparently less observed (see however Harold W. Attridge, *Nag Hammadi Codex I* [*The Jung Codex*], Vol. II [Leiden, 1985], p. 118, who cautiously develops an observation made already by Jacques E. Ménard, *L'Évangile de Vérité* [Leiden, 1972], pp. 177, 178).

14. The first level of the analysis would imply a unique signified (the Father) and a theoretical infinity of axiologically unequal signifiers (the pleromatic hypostases; compare for instance *Apocryphon of John* II.1.2.25-4.26 with 4.30-6.10), marking the passage from what we may call a semiosis of

insertion, mainly exegetical, to a semiosis of rupture, as radical isolation of the signifier from its signified in the compact depth of the latter. Thus, the semiosis of rupture would correspond to the *semeiotical transformation* of the semeiology into the ontology as deficient distortion of the former.

The negative dialectics — itself semeiotical only inasmuch as semeiologically unsaturated — patterns the "being" as axiologically void, that is, as psychological subject psychoanalytically born. It is interesting to note that the pleromatic incomprehensibility of the Father — the first motor of the negative dialectics — is in kenomatic terms substituted by the pathological incomprehension of the Demiurge, just as the Limit (Horos) seems to translate itself as Destiny (Heimarmene); in the *Gospel of Truth* I.3.41.19-20, the concept of Horos, contrary to its Valentinian acceptation, has the meaning of destiny — cf. Ménard, op. cit., p. 186). See also Fineman, art. cit., p. 291 and n. 5, with however the difference that Fineman, following Lacan, points to the loss of the signifier rather than of the signified, which is after all quite secondary, as the initial deficiency fractures an original auto-signification in which signifier and signified are reciprocally transparent and know themselves as reciprocally identical (see above n. 13).

15. *R.V.* X.121.2.

16. H. Grassmann, *Wörterbuch zum Rigveda* (Leipzig, 1873), col. 773.

17. In *R.V.* X.121.5, the fixed (*drlha*) hermeneutical entity is the earth (*prthivi*), which points already to a myth that will become common in the *Brahmana*. This is interesting if we take into consideration that √*drnh* (the root of *drlha*) is a quasi-synonym of √*dhr*, from which the Yogic concept of *dhrana* — "fixing of the thought" — developed (for Yogic structures in the *Rg-* and *Atharva-Veda*, see *Le Nombre*. . . II, pp. 170-174).

18. Irenaeus, *Adv. Haer.* I.2.4, I.3.5.

19. The term belongs to Paul Mus, *Barabudur*, I (Hanoi, 1935), p. 159 (note), p. 459.

20. See for instance *Ap. Joh.* II.1.4.25-30, where the Desire (*Woshe*) is the catoptrical seed of the Father, which determines his hypostatical self-awareness, Ennoia (*Me'ewe*). See in this respect Michel Tardieu, *Codex de Berlin* (Paris, 1984), pp. 255-256, and *Le Nombre*. . . II, nn. 29, 30.

21. In his *Histoire des croyances et des idées religieuses*, I (Paris, 1980), p. 239, Mircea Eliade rightly recognizes in the metaphysical cosmogony of the *R.V.* X.129 "un des germes de la philosophie Samkhya-Yoga et du bouddhisme."

22. The question is always of a transcendental phenomenon. The best example is *R.V.* X.82.6 above quoted, though in this hymn Hiranyagarbha is not directly mentioned. Also, in *A.V.* IV.2.8 a distinction is drawn between the Embryo itself (*garbha*) and its golden foetal envelope (*úlba . . . hiranyayah*). Consequently, and despite persistent ambivalence, Hiranyagarbha seems to represent the outer structure (the transcendental bark), the inner one getting the mystic appellation of Prajapati (*R.V.* X.121.10; see also *Le Nombre*. . . II, p. 186 sq.). We are confronted here with the paradoxical

syncretism between embryology and catoptrics. On the Vedic field, *Èlba* could be roughly identified, from a phenomenological and hermeneutical outlook, with the Gnostic concept of *eikÂn* (see for instance *Ap. John* II.1.4.21-25, 34-35).

Another interesting parallel for Hiranyagarbha, besides the Gnostic Nous, would be the Hermetic Aion (see for instance *Corpus Hermeticum* XI.2), and possibly the Aion-Nous of the *Chaldaean Oracles* (see fr. 3-7, 49, and two fragments of Porphyry's *On the Philosophy of the Oracles*, apud Hans Lewy, *Chaldaean Oracles and Theurgy*, Nouvelle-édition par Michel Tardieu [Paris, 1978], pp. 9-10, 18).

23.	*The Gospel of Truth* 37.26-27.
24.	*R.V.* X.177.1; the equivalence is also philological: *rasmi* "string, cord, trace," but also "ray of light."
25.	For more details see *Le Nombre*. . . I, pp. 232-235; II, pp. 170-175.
26.	See Abel Bergaigne, *La Religion Védique*, II, Ch. V: *L'arithmétique mythologique*. Also Paul Mus, *Barabudur*, I, p. 151 (note).
27.	For the Indian (in fact, general) ritual principle of "the jar broken here, whole beyond" as a magical inversion or passage of plans, see Paul Mus, op. cit., I, p. 51 sq.: "Un vase cassé en ce monde est un vase entier dans l'autre monde. De même, un homme inversé devient, sur un autre plan, dieu ou Père, tant que dure l'inversion magique. Observons bien le procédé. Il suppose deux ordres d'existence et un passage de l'un à l'autre, deux objets, et une projection de l'un dans l'autre, de telle manière que l'être ou l'objet placé devant nous en ce monde et qui semble n'en pas bouger, le quitte toutefois mystérieusement, se dépasse et aille s'identifier à l'être ou à l'objet surnaturel qui lui correspond dans l'au-delà. Nous ne cessons pas de le percevoir, mais ce n'est plus lui: *il n'est désormais qu'un signe*. Il constitue *la trace* en ce monde-ci de l'être transcendant et ce dernier, par raison inverse, peut être considéré comme sa projection sur le plan supérieur, tant que dure l'opération magique" (our emphases).

	It is not difficult to remark that from a magical outlook, both Gnostic *icnhos* and Vedic *pada* reveal themselves as *signs*, that is, as negations.
28.	For the numerological aniconism of the Brahmanical ritual, see Paul Mus, op. cit., I, p. 52 sq.: "On saisit mieux ainsi ce qu'a pu signifier l'aniconisme des traditions cultuelles dans l'Inde des *brahmana*. En ne représentant pas les dieux par des statues, on ne s'interdisait pas de les connaître personnellement, et on ne leur déniait pas une apparence anthropomorphique, que dans la plupart des cas les textes obligent à leur attribuer. Mais on ambitionnait un contact plus intime que ce qu'aurait permis leur vision sous forme d'images. Par des transpositions bien réglées, c'était l'autel, c'étaient les hymnes, c'était la personne même du sacrifiant qui devenaient la statue du dieu, ou mieux que sa statue, le dieu lui-même, qu'un bloc de pierre taill-ée n'eût pas été" (p. 55).

	It is probable that the Brahmanical aniconism had an acosmical implication, which will become more explicit in the *Upanishad* and especially in the three major systems of the Indian philosophy, Samkhya-Yoga,

Vedanta and Buddhism.

29. The expression belongs to Paul Mus, op. cit., II, *Appendice*, p. 745: "Mettre le Buddha en son essence dernière, au-dessus de Brahma, au-dessus des Akanistha, au-dessus des plans les plus élevés de l'existence abstraite . . . c'était s'orienter vers sa mise en série avec l'existence qui se creusait sous le point suprême où on l'installait." But the supreme point under which the existence hollows should be understood in the light of another Musian passage: "Cette quintessence d'espace n'est pas étendue, mais c'est en elle que se développe l'étendue, *au-dessous de son concept*, comme, au-dessous du concept d'étendue, la création se répand dans l'étendue: et c'est ainsi que le nirvana peut être monné un lieu (*sthana, thana*) indestructible, suprême et immortel. . ." (ibid., pp. 788-789; our emphases).

30. "A ce niveau de la croyance, représenter directement le dieu suprême, autrement dit sculpter la transcendance, serait un vain rêve. au contraire, la dissemblance trop évidente d'une masse de briques et de ce que Prajapati, quel qu'il soit, peut être en lui-même, tourne l'objection et permet, en ne préjugeant pas de cette nature ultime, de croire qu'un certain contact est acquis, pourvu que l'on sache reconnaître dans la structure à la fois l'essence magique de l'homme et celle du dieu fixées l'une et l'autre dans des schémas géométriques et dans des nombres appropriés. Perçu à notre niveau, l'autel nous fait atteindre Prajapati, à son niveau sublime, comme tout à l'heure le bris d'un vase sur la tombe était la condition nécessaire d'une projection dans un autre monde. Cassé ici, entier là-bas. Nous dirons de même: briques ici-bas, dieu dans l'au-delà" (Paul Mus, op. cit., I, p. 54).

31. See Joel Fineman, art. cit., p. 306: "In the Western religious tradition, Gnosticism is a singular theology because it continually speaks of God as a phenomenon present precisely by virtue of His absence, as a trace which witnesses to what is no longer there. In the *Gospel of Truth* the most explicit figure for this strange absent-presence of God is the footprint-trace (*ichnos*) of the Father's will . . ."

32. The subsequent conceptual myth interrogated through the figure of ichnos must be understood in the context of the *Gospel of Truth*, the *Apocryphon of John*, and, in a lesser degree, the *Untitled Text* of Codex Bruce (the same texts which archetypized *Le Nombre. . .* I, II). To these an "outsider" — the *Paraphrase of Sem* — was added; in this way all the major trends of the Gnostic System (in which the *Gospel of Truth*) must be functionally integrated) were represented.

33. For the ontological consubsistence between identity and indetermination, under Pythagorean conceptualization, see Iamblichus, *Theologumena arithmetica* (apud A.J. Festugière, *Révélation d'Hermès Trismégiste* IV, pp. 43-44), where the Pythagorean monad is described both as intelligible number and as matter, being even identified with Hesiod's Chaos. In fact, Iamblichus paraphrases speculations already existent in Nicomachus of Gerasa, where the monad is analyzed as Nous, Theos, Hyle, Chaos, etc.

(ibid., p. 45).

We should remember that the Gnostic Father is called both abyss (Bathos/Bythos) and monad (Monas) — see for instance Hippolytus, *Ref.* VI.29.2 & 30.7 — and described in negative terms (cf. Irenaeus, *Adv. Haer.* I.1.1. & II.3; see *Ap. John* II.1.2.33-3.36). The conclusion could therefore be drawn of a structural ontological syntagmatization of the Kenoma, as double semeiological horizon of the Father.

34.   If the "unequivocal dualism" defined by Hans Jonas ("Delimitation of the Gnostic phenomenon — typological and historical," in *Origins of Gnosticism* [Leiden, 1967] p. 93) is simultaneous with the constitution of the cosmos as self-awareness of the Ego, the "equivocal" one, corresponding to "the original stages of the metaphysical genealogy," is functionally and structurally identical with the Intellect.

35.   In fact, there is an inertial dimension implied in the nature of the process itself, which, by being mechanical, appears noetically as cadaverous, while the abyss of knowledge is ontically void. The problem which confronts consequently the subject consists in its being that kind of totality for which the incomprehensibility of the absolute appears not in terms of negative dialectics but as its own absolute incomprehension of the all (see for instance the *Gospel of Truth* I.3.17.5-20, 21.27-33 or the *Untitled Text* 1.5-9, where the subject configurates itself *as the structure of the teleology and the error, as the structure of the search*: cf. *Gospel of Truth* 42.21-27).

We stumble here upon Hans Jonas's definition of the Gnostic ontological whole as one grand *movement* of "knowledge, in its positive and its privative moods, from the beginning of things to their end" (art. cit., p. 92).

36.   "It is as sure, he was wont to say, when any doubt was entertained of his veracity, as sure as there is a sea where the ship itself will grow in bulk like a living body of the seaman . . ." (E.A. Poe, *Ms. Found in a Bottle*).

37.   If the negative dialectics is univocally dependent of some a priori principle, that is, of some *a prior judgement*, it is itself a necessary, universal and a priori judgment.

It is, however, a psychological difficulty that any truly a priori judgment tends to present itself as an a priori hypostasis and even as a transcendental personification; consequently, the necessary judgment is likely to shape itself as transcendental will.

For the same reason the negative dialectics as descriptive impossibility will tend to configurate itself both as an almost personal interdiction, that is, as an *act of will*, and as an expositive structure of the transcendental psychology (we should infer from this that the transcendental psychology is also based on an interdiction); see above n. 14.

On the other hand, in the field of the sensible (the Gnostic Chaos) this universality of the necessary judgment implied in the negative dialectics corresponds quite paradoxically to the Destiny (see also n. 14).

Finally, the same analysis applies to the concept of Self, which is the psychological transcendental function of the a priori judgment.

38. This ontological dismissal of the Gnostic Demiurge, Yaldabaoth, corresponds quite well to that of the Buddhist one, Brahma: "Une constatation sur laquelle on ne saurait trop insister est que, dans ce système, Brahma est conservé et le brahmanisme absorbé: ceci justifie toutes les analogies et fixe en même temps leurs limites. La cosmogonie est progressive, de haut en bas. Jusqu'au moment où elle descend au niveau de Brahma, les vérités qu'elle enferme sont uniquement accessibles par la révélation bouddhique. Mais après avoir atteint, et produit, le monde de Brahma, le processus se poursuit au-dessous de ce dieu avec, en quelque sorte, une double vérité. En vérité absolue, Brahma n'a aucune personnalité. Il est une conséquence des termes qui l'ont logiquement précédé, un instant du karman: il reste aussi irréel et creux que la création inférieure, bien qu'il s'imagine l'émettre, du plein au vide. En vérité relative, cette émission est cependant vraie. Brahma est le centre, le principe de tout ce qui va naître autour et au-dessous de lui, et tout ce qu'enseignent les brahmanes est exact dans ces limites, qui sont celles du monde réellement concevable. Mais toutes leurs doctrines sont suspendues à un point: l'idée que Brahma se fait de lui-même. Il s'attribue l'être absolu. Cette id-ée, son Grand Orgueil, est l'erreur qui mine tout le reste. Brahma en personne n'est qu'un passage de la rétribution. Il a sa place sur l'échelle des créatures. Sans remonter jusqu'au Buddha et au Dharma suprême, il existe au-dessus de lui des dieux qui lui sont antérieurs, et qui lui restent supérieurs. Il est l'un d'entre eux, déchu de sa pure idéalité. Il a revêtu un corps plus grossier en absorbant la terre où il croit naître à l'origine des teps, ou même être antérieur au temps. Toutefois, sous réserve de cette irréalité foncière, que la révélation bouddhique lui faira apercevoir, il est fondé à croire qu'il engendre par délégation de lui-même l'essence secrète de toutes les créatures, depuis son monde jusqu'aux étapes les plus bas, c'est-à-dire dans le champ entier de sa vision. La nature de Brahma, relativement pure, est à l'origine commune à tous les êtres des niveaux inférieurs; elle se charge de matière, à mesure que ces êtres tombent du plan de Brahma et s'alourdissent de sens nouveaux pour eux, jusqu'au total de 18 dharma. Ces nouvelles composantes recouvrent progressivement le thème initial. Ainsi Brahma, ou le brahman, restent-ils le noyau de tous les êtres fictifs venus à leur suite dans le développement cosmique. Le brahmanisme atteint par là une vérité partielle et provisoire, lorsqu'il s'imagine que l'essence de toutes les créatures animées repose en Brahma. Le schéma impersonnel de l'*Aggañña Sutta* dispose le monde d'accord avec cette notion: par la mystique alimentaire, chaque être porte en son centre, sous des apports nouveaux, la structure qui avait été la sienne au niveau précédent, avant la chute. Chaque fois, on pourrait dire que le rapport due terme antérieur (et intérieur) au terme postérieur est comparable à celui d'une âme et d'un corps. C'est en ce sens, et en ce sens seulement, que Braham, l'illusoire Brahma, est l'âme du monde qu'il croit régir" (Paul Mus, op. cit., I, pp. 292-293).

39.   Ignorance, to the Gnostics, is not a neutral state, nor simply a privation, the mere absence of knowledge, but a positive affect of the spirit, a force of its own, operative in the very terms of man's existence and preventing his discovering the truth for himself, even his realizing his state of ignorance as such" (Hans Jonas, art. cit., p. 98).

Any accomplishment is a *collective act*. Deficient or not, the present paper makes, in this respect, no exception.

Our first thanks should have gone to Professor Richard Wallis, and if articulated speech is useless now, neither our gratitude nor our feelings are diminished by their *silent* enunciation.

We must also acknowledge our debt towards Dr. Denis O'Brien, who by his careful, stimulating and patient suggestions helped us to avoid at least our most characteristic idiomatic errors.

Special thanks are due to Professors John Dillon and Jay Bregman who expurgated our allogeneous English of what French turns had trickled in, thus contributing decisively to the adequate expression of the ideas involved.

Our final thanks should be silent; and if we dare to express them it is because we believe that in final terms the unmanifested and the manifested thought are identical, and also for the simple reason that even these thanks belong to Him, the hidden Author of our paper, as of everything else.

Mani's Twin and Plotinus:
Questions on "Self"

Leo Sweeney, S.J.

Some autobiographical data will help to indicate the occasion of my interest in Mani's "Twin" and the limited scope of this paper. Since that occasion concerns the *Cologne Mani Codex* (hereafter *CMC*), let me first speak briefly of it. The *CMC* is a miniature parchment of the fifth-century A.D. and is a biography of Mani up to his twenty-fifth year.[1] A Greek translation of a Syriac original,[2] it was rendered legible in 1969 by A. Fackelmann[3] and its 192 pages were edited with a German translation and commentary by Albert Henrichs and Ludwig Koenen in *ZPE*, 19 (1975), 1-85; 32 (1978), 86-199; 44 (1981), 201-318; and 48 (1982), 1-59.[4] An English translation of pages 1-99 of *CMC* had been made by Ron Cameron and A.J. Dewey.[5]

According to its English translators the importance of the *CMC*

cannot be overestimated for the history of religions. For the Codex provides the only Greek primary source for Manichaeism. Now we have not only new reports and accounts of the early life of Mani, but even additional evidence for a Gospel of Mani. Indeed, many of the excerpts resemble a proto-gospel in a raw state, along with apocalypses and aretalogical material. Moreover, the origin of Manichaeism becomes quite complex, since we now possess convincing evidence of the connection of Mani's baptists with Elchasai, the alleged founder of a predominantly Jewish-Christian sect. And, most of all, we are privy to new and unparalleled information on the organization, ritual practices, and theology of the baptist sect in which Mani was reared.[6]

Now let me turn to autobiography. Aware of the importance of the *CMC*, Dr. James G. Keenan of the Department of Classics, Loyola University of Chicago, invited Drs. Henrichs and Koenen to give papers on the Codex at a colloquium in March, 1977. Dr. Henrichs spoke on "Mani's Elchasaites: Manichaeism and Jewish Christianity" and Dr. Koenen on "Manichaeism and Judeo-Christian Gnosticism." As commentators on their papers Dr. Keenan chose John Baggarly and myself.[7] In my commentary I concentrated upon Mani's "Twin" for two reasons. I had little prior acquaintance with Mani's positions (other than as the founder of the sect to which Augustine belonged and then rejected after nine years) but initial reading suggested that there might be a possible parallel between what Mani wrote on his "Twin" and what his contemporary, Plotinus, remarked on man as entailing higher and lower levels of existence.[8]   Second, Henrichs and Koenen themselves gave considerable attention to Mani's Twin both in their Loyola University papers and in their publications (as will be clear later).

My current paper is, obviously, a return to that suggested parallel and the methodology used will be similar to that in my presentation at Loyola, where I attended primarily to Henrichs's and Koenen's descriptions of Mani's Twin and, more precisely, to the questions which their exegesis raised when they identified "twin" with "self" in seemingly some contemporary sense.   Here, then, I shall also concentrate upon their identification of "twin" and "self."   The second part of my paper will be devoted to Plotinus's conception of man and to the questions which result when some scholars find a doctrine of "self" also in Plotinian texts.

The "Twin" of Mani

Let me, then, attend primarily to the questions which Henrichs's and Koenen's description of Mani's Twin as "self" suggests, since their understanding of Mani on other doctrinal points is basically accurate, as one would expect and can verify from their intelligent editing, translating and commenting upon the *CMC*. But I am puzzled on what "self" means when applied to Mani's Twin. This application may prove correct but it needs (in my opinion) to be discussed.

But before starting that discussion let me reproduce (in translation or paraphrase and with commentary reduced to footnotes) key passages from the *CMC* on the "Twin,"[9] which may serve as the context within which to appreciate and evaluate Henrichs's and Koenen's exegesis.

[A] Twice (Mani states early in *CMC*) the voice of the Twin (*hōs syzygos phōnē*) said to me: "Strengthen your power, make your mind strong and submit to all that is about to come upon you" (13.2).[10] [B] In order that he might free souls (*tas psychas*) from ignorance [as the Father of Greatness intended],[11] Mani became paraclete and leader of the apostleship in this generation.[12] Then [Baraies now purports to quote Mani][13] "at the time when my body reached its full growth, immediately there flew down and appeared before me that most beautiful and greatest mirroring of [who I really am — namely, my twin]"[14] (17.1); the Greek for lines 12-16: ὤφθη ἔμπροσθέν μου ἐκεῖνο τὸ εὐειδέστα τον καὶ μέγιστον κάτοπτρον τοῦ προσώ του μου . . .

[C] Yes, at the time I was twenty[-four] years old, the most blessed Lord was greatly moved with compassion for me, called me into his grace, and immediately sent to me [from there my] Twin, who appeared in great glory and who is mindful of and informer of all the best counsels from our Father (18.1 and 19.2; also see 72.20-73.7). [D] Baraies continues to quote Mani: "When my Father was pleased and had mercy and compassion on me, to ransom me from the error of the Sectarians [the Elchasaite baptists], he took consideration of me through his very many revelations and sent to me my Twin" (19.8), who "delivered, separated and pulled me away from the midst of that [Elchasaite] Law in which I was reared" (20.8).

[E] Baraies now quotes Mani on the instruction given him by the Twin on "how I came into being; and who my Father on high is; or in what way, severed from him, I was sent out according to his purpose; and what sort of commission and counsel he has given to me before I clothed myself in this instrument and before I was led astray in this detestable flesh, and before I clothed myself with its drunkenness and habits, and who that one is, who is himself my ever-vigilant Twin" (22.1).[15] [F] Yes, the Twin showed Mani "the secrets and visions and the perfections of my Father; and concerning me, who I am, and who my inseparable Twin is; moreover, concerning my soul, which exists as the soul of all the worlds, both what it itself is and how it came to be" (23.1).[16]

[G] The result was (Mani continues to speak) "that I acquired (the Twin) as my own possession. I believed that he belongs to me and is mine and is a good and excellent counselor. I recognized him and understood that I am that one from whom I was separated. I testified that I myself am that one who is unshakable"[17] (24.4); the Greek for lines 6 sqq.: ἐπίστευσα δ'αὐτὸν ἐμὸν / ὑπάρχοντά τε καὶ ὄν/τα καὶ σύμβολον ἀγαθὸν καὶ χρηστὸν ὄντα. / ἐπέγνων μὲν αὐτὸν καὶ/

συνῆκα ὅτι ἐκεῖνος ἐ/γώ εἰμι ἐξ οὖ διεκρίθην./ἐπεμαρτύρησα δὲ ὅτι
ἐ/γὼ ἐκε(ῖ)νος αὐτός εἰμι/ἀκλόν(ητο)ς ὑπάρχων./. . .

The Codex continues in the same vein,[18] but enough samples have
been taken to illustrate how prominent a role the Twin plays in Mani's
life, as well as what the nature of the Twin himself is. He prepares
Mani for the revelations which will establish him as an original religious
leader by advising him to be strong and yet receptive (#A).[19] Sent by
the Father that Mani might save souls from ignorance and darkness, the
Twin — the most beautiful and greatest duplication of who Mani really
is (#B) — brought counsels from the Father to Mani in his twenty-fifth
year (#C). Through the many revelations the Father entrusted to him,
the Twin freed and separated Mani from the errors of the Elchasaites
(#D).[20] The information which the Twin communicated opened up to
Mani not only who the Father is and what his mission for Mani is, but
also what Mani's soul is, how it came into being and how it came to be
associated with body, as well as the fact that the Twin is an ever-vigilant
and inseparable factor in his life (#E and #F). The Twin belongs to
Mani as a good and excellent adviser — in fact, Mani *is* the Twin, from
whom he was separated when his soul entered into matter but whom he
has now rejoined through the initiative of the Father (#G).[21]

The "Twin" as "Self"

But important as the preceding key-texts are on the Twin's
function and nature, they also serve as the context within which to
evaluate Henrichs's and Koenen's identification of "Twin" with "self."
Although this identification occurs within their commentary upon the
German translation of *CMC*,[22] let us for the sake of convenience turn
to their other publications.

According to Albert Henrichs, "Mani and the Babylonian Baptists:
A Historical Confrontation," *HSCP*, 77 (1973), 24, a duplication of
Mani was an essential factor in his theory of salvation.

> In terms of Manichaean soteriology, the notion of a duplicate Mani was, in
> fact, not at all unheard of, but was a well-established doctrine, propagated
> time and again by Mani himself. Mani's double, though his steady
> companion on earth, his counselor and helper in times of hardship, and his
> consoler in moments of despair, was not a creature of flesh and blood, but
> an incorporeal and celestial being, not subject to the terrestrial limitations
> of time and space. As the pre-existent and eternal Twin of Light, he is the
> mirror-like reflection of Mani's inner self, the heavenly embodiment of his

spiritual essence, his true identity, from whom he was separated when his soul put on the garment of a mortal body and with whom he was reunited at his death.

Here Henrichs appears to be making these relevant points. Mani's existence entails two main levels, one of which is his status as a creature of flesh and blood, subject to limitations of space and time and separated from his true identity when his soul put on the garment of a mortal body. The second level is occupied by his double — steady companion, counselor, helper and consoler —, who is not material, spatial and temporal. Rather he is an incorporeal and celestial being — namely, the pre-existent and eternal Twin of Light, who mirrors, reflects, duplicates Mani's inner self and is the embodiment of his spiritual essence and is his true identity. *Comments.* On the first level Mani consists of body and *of soul*, which is his inner self and spiritual essence, reflected and duplicated by his Twin on the second level. This latter, then, is Mani's true identity, from which he was separated when his soul became incarnate and which he will regain at death by escaping from the body. *Question:* Mani's soul is his spiritual essence, yes, because it makes him be what he really is and continues to be even in matter. But what is meant by saying Mani's soul is his inner self? What exactly is meant by saying Mani's soul is his inner self? What exactly does the word express?

But let us turn to another passage from Henrichs, now commenting upon the stress Mani puts on his uniqueness as the final god-sent messenger to the world.

> Mani's awareness of, and insistence on, his own singularity is the basis of his self-conception, and any attempt to penetrate into Mani's complex personality has to start from that point. But . . . Mani's self-understanding has little to do with the awareness of one's own individuality or terrestrial historicity, notions which would have been much less meaningful and important to Mani than they are to us. The fact that Mani possessed an alter-ego in the form of the Twin of Light makes him a split personality in the literal sense of that term rather than an individual: his human existence was nothing but a briefly reflected image of its true and eternal counterpart (ibid., pp. 39-40).[23]

What is Henrichs saying here? Mani's awareness of his singularity allows him to understand himself and lets us penetrate the complexity of his personality. His true self-understanding consists not in his being aware of himself as an individual existing in history (i.e., in such and such a place, at such and such a time) but of his personality as split: his existing here and now contrasts with his true and eternal counterpart — namely, the alter-ego who is his Twin. His human status of mortal body clothing immortal soul or self separates him from his true self — the Twin. That separation results in his split personality: one self (Mani's soul in matter) is apart from the other self (the Twin). Psychological wholeness and religious salvation are achieved when the two come together and become one, either on earth when the Twin visits Mani or in heaven. *Question*: Is the contemporary notion of "split personality," if taken technically, applicable to Mani's situation?[24] Again, what does "self" signify when predicated of Mani and the Twin?

Let us turn now to Ludwig Koenen, "Augustine and Manichaeism in the Light of the Cologne Mani Codex," *ICS*, 3 (1978), 170, who speaks of Mani's Twin while discussing the larger question of identifying the "paraclete" mentioned in John's Gospel, 14.16 and 16.17. For Baraies (see *CMC*, 17.1) Mani's *Nous* is the paraclete. "His *Nous*, like that of all men, descended from the heavenly realm of Light and was imprisoned in the body. The real Mani was the *Nous* of Mani" and is identified with the paraclete. But according to other evidence the paraclete was identical with Mani's "*alter-ego* who brought him the revelation. This is the *syzygos*, the 'Twin,' a gnostic term" (ibid.). Koenen then sums up the discussion (pp. 173-74): "Mani identified (1) himself or rather his *Nous* and (2) his 'Twin' with the paraclete of *John*." Despite what some scholars (G. Quispel, K. Rudolph, P. Nagel) think, there is no contradiction here. The contradiction disappears upon

> consideration of the gnostic concept of the Twin. When Mani, i.e., the *Nous* of Mani, was sent into the world, a mirror image of the *Nous*, i.e., his *alter-ego*, remained in heaven. The one ego, the *Nous*, was imprisoned in the body and, consequently, forgot his mission. Then the Twin, the *alter-ego*, was sent to him from heaven. He brought Mani the revelation by reminding him of his divine nature and mission and, like an angel, protected him. The *Nous* of Mani and his Twin are the two complementary aspects of Mani's identity. The first represents him as incorporated in the body; the second represents his being as it is outside the body. Together they are the one complete Mani. When Mani looked into himself, he found his Twin approaching him from heaven; or, *vice versa*, when he looked at his Twin, he found himself. The story of the Twin bringing him the revelation relates what in abstract terms may be called the rediscovery of his identity and mission.[25]

In this passage Koenen offers considerable information. Every man consists of body and of intellect.[26] This last constitutes his divine nature, reality, *ego*. Mani is no exception: he too consists of body and of intellect or *ego*. But in addition he also has another *ego*, called his "Twin," who mirrors and duplicates his real and divine nature (= intellect and *ego*) and who is sent to Mani to recall his authentic nature and mission and to guard him. Consequently, the single and complete reality of Mani consists of his terrestrial intellect or *ego* and of his celestial *ego*, the Twin. By awareness of his intellect imprisoned in matter, he knows his Twin and thereby his true identity as a complete self and, also, as the paraclete of John's Gospel. The account of his Twin's bringing him heavenly messages is merely a figurative and concrete way of expressing the fact that he rediscovered his identity and mission. *Questions*: In light of the last comment should one conclude that the Twin, as well as other emanations and factors in Mani's doctrine, is a figure within a story that is not literally true? Should one infer that the Twin is not an actually existing intellect and *ego* (whatever the last term may mean) but the projection of Mani's belief in his divine call, coupled with an awareness of his needing help in gaining freedom from his sinful material condition and from his previous religious adherence and in promulgating his gospel?[27]

Before moving on, let me turn to another respected scholar, whose book antedates Henrichs's and Koenen's papers and who also gives great prominence to the Twin as "self": Hans Jonas, *The Gnostic Religion. The Message of the Alien God and the Beginnings of Christianity* (2nd ed.; Boston: Beacon Press, 1967). The crucial sentences occur when Jonas is commenting upon this passage from "The Hymn of the Pearl" (p. 115):[28]

> My robe of glory which I had put off and my mantle which went over it, my parents . . . sent to meet me by their treasurers who were entrusted therewith. Its splendor I had forgotten, having left it as a child in my Father's house. As I now beheld the robe, it seemed to me suddenly to become a mirror-image of myself: myself entire I saw in it, and it entire I saw in myself, that we were two in separateness, and yet again one in the sameness of our forms . . .

His commentary runs as follows.

> The garment has become this figure itself [of light] and acts like a person. It symbolizes the heavenly or eternal self of the person, his original idea, a kind of double or *alter ego* preserved in the upper world while he labors down below. . . . The encounter with this divided-off aspect of himself, the recognition of it as his own image, and the reunion with it signify the real moment of his salvation. Applied to the messenger or savior as it is here

and elsewhere, the conception leads to the interesting theological idea of a twin brother or eternal original of the savior remaining in the upper world during his terrestrial mission. Duplications of this kind abound in gnostic speculation with regard to divine figures in general wherever their function requires a departure from the divine realm and involvement in the events of the lower world (pp. 122-23).

Next comes a section to which Jonas gives a striking title.

THE TRANSCENDENTAL SELF

The double of the savior is as we have seen only a particular theological representation of an idea pertaining to the doctrine of man in general and denoted by the concept of the Self. In this concept we may discern what is perhaps the profoundest contribution of Persian religion to Gnosticism and to the history of religion in general. The Avesta word is *daena*, for which the orientalist Bartholomae lists the following meanings: "1. Religion; 2. inner essence, spiritual ego, individuality; often hardly translatable."

In the Manichaean fragments from Turfan, another Persian word is used, *grev*, which can be translated either by "self" or by "ego." It denotes the metaphysical person, the transcendent and true subject of salvation, which is not identical with the empirical soul. In the Chinese Manichaean treatise translated by Pelliot, it is called "the luminous nature," "our original luminous nature," or "inner nature," which recalls St. Paul's "inner man"; Manichaean hymns call it the "living self" or the "luminous self." The Mandaean "Mana" express the same idea and makes particularly clear the identity between this inner principle and the highest godhead; for "Mana" is the name for the transmundane Power of Light, the first deity, and at the same time that for the transcendent, non-mundane center of the individual ego (pp. 123-24).[29]

The parallels between the Twin of "The Hymn of the Pearl" and that of *CMC* which stand out from Jonas's exegesis are so clear now from our previous pages as to need no explanation: The Twin remaining above and its counterpart descending below; the identity nonetheless between the Twin and its counterpart; the Twin as the eternal self, original idea, alter-ego contrasted with the selfhood in its terrestrial duplicate. Yet puzzlement still persists. "Perhaps the profoundest contribution to Gnosticism and to the history of religion in general" (to repeat Jonas) is "the concept of the Self" (p. 124), which he illustrates by "daena," "grev" and terms from other sources. But what meaning are these words attempting to express in the original? Is "self" a helpful translation of them? Is "self" synonymous with "inner essence," "metaphysical person," "transcendent subject of salvation," "luminous, inner nature," "inner man"? Or does not Jonas intend it to be taken as in contemporary philosophical and psychological writings?

This last question explicates what is for me the problem underlying all else: the contemporary notion of "self" is multiple and ambiguous. In fact, it has no commonly accepted meaning. In order to realize this, let us look at the article on "Self" in the *New Catholic Encyclopedia*. I choose this not from any sectarian motive, but because of the surprising fact that among recent philosophical encyclopedias in English it alone provides such an article. *The Dictionary of the History of Ideas* has none, nor has the *Encyclopedia of Philosophy*, which gives the topic a single, short paragraph in its article on "Personal Identity" (V, 95-107), where indeed "self" is set aside, because of its restriction to the mental and spiritual, as misleading in a discussion of the problem of personal identity.

Also the *Encyclopedia Britannica* offers no full-scale paper on "self" but only a definition in its *Micropaedia*, IX, 41:

> Self is the subject of successive states of consciousness. In modern psychology the notion of the self has replaced earlier conceptions of the soul. According to Carl Jung the self is a totality comprised of conscious and unconscious contents that dwarfs the ego in scope and intensity. The coming-to-be of the self is sharply distinguished from the coming of the ego into consciousness, and is the individuation process by which the true self emerges as the goal of the whole personality.

Obviously, that brief description discloses mainly that "self" has largely become an area of study for empirical psychologists.   And the impression given there, as well as in the paragraph from the *Encyclopedia of Philosophy*, is that "self" in contemporary literature has varied and divergent meanings.

That impression deepens when we open the *New Catholic Encyclopedia* to Margaret Gorman's article (XIII, 56-60). Descartes is there credited with introducing "the word self as it is currently used" and with identifying it with "spiritual substance" (p. 57A). Disagreeing with him, Locke doubted that the self always thinks or that it is substantial. The self, understood as one's consciousness of continuing the same now as in the past, is distinct from soul or spiritual substance. By analyzing consciousness Hume challenged the view that any permanent self exists in man, who may be merely a "congeries of perceptions" (p. 57C). To Spinoza self is the substance which is at once the world and God; for Leibniz it is a thinking substance, where "thinking" includes "little perceptions" also.   Kant speaks of "self" in several senses: phenomenal, noumenal, transcendental, ethical (pp. 57D-57A).   Fichte opposed self (whose reality consists in its action of self-positing) to nonself, thereby laying the foundation for the dialectics of Hegel and Marx (p. 58A).   In America Josiah Royce distinguished between the phenomenal self (a group of ideas) and the metaphysical self (a group of ideals; p. 58B).   Husserl speaks of both an empirical and a transcendental self, the second of which constitutes the meaning of the world (58D).   To Kierkegaard self is the right relationship one has to God and to himself; for Gabriel Marcel it is incarnate consciousness (p. 59B).   A modern psychologist such as Jung believes that self comprises both the conscious and the unconscious (p. 59C).

Although one could excerpt other examples from the article in the *New Catholic Encyclopedia*, the above suffice to suggest how complex and divergent "self" is among modern philosophers and psychologists. That complexity is mirrored in Gorman's conclusions from the historical survey.

> The term self does not supplant the older concept of soul, nor is it the same as ego, mind, or person. It is a concept used to designate functions that philosophers felt were not included in soul . . . [which] had become for them a term designating the static thinking substance revealed by the *Cogito* of Descartes [and which was replaced by "mind."] With the advent of the philosophers of the will, mind became inadequate to represent the human person in his dynamic growth and development. Person referred to the individual substance of a rational nature — a definition that . . . seemed to ignore the concrete individual development in the world. . . . Self then began to be used to suggest all those aspects of man thought to be left out by the terms soul, mind, person, and nature — and to designate the unifying, purposeful, growing, and interacting aspect of man's activities. It included also the notions of alienation and of encounter (pp. 59D-60A).[30]

What has been our purpose in surveying what "self" signifies in modern literature? To realize that it is an extremely ambiguous notion and, thus, one can use it to translate or interpret Mani only after carefully reflecting on whether it helps or hinders getting at *what he himself had in mind* in *CMC* and other canonical or semi-canonical treatises (see above, n. 10).   Part of that reflection must be that each interpreter decides for himself what exactly "self" signifies in his own position before inquiring whether it is applicable to Mani's.

Let me illustrate by setting forth what "self" has come to mean within my own philosophical position, which is influenced mainly by

Aristotle and Thomas Aquinas and which is (I hope) an authentic existentialism. Within a unique and individual human existent what constitutes "self"? It is not solely my soul, which is merely a part of me; nor does it consist solely in individuation, which comes from matter, nor in my state of being a supposit, which issues from existence. Rather, self is my entire unique and individual being but especially and precisely as I am conscious of who and what I am, as I freely determine who I am and yet as I am also determined by outside forces (other human existents, environment, culture, etc.). Thus, my selfhood concerns me in my uniqueness and individuality as a psychological agent. In sum, my self is my-soul-actually-existing-within-this-body but considered not so much entitatively (i.e., in the parts which constitute me) as operationally (i.e., as dynamic, as active and passive, as the source and recipient of unique and singular activities).[31]

Manifestly, "self" interpreted in this fashion cannot validly be predicated either of Mani's Twin (who is soul or mind solely) or of Mani in his earthly state (whose true reality consists also of intellect or soul only). But one may also doubt whether "self" in other contemporary philosophical settings may be legitimately predicated of Mani and of his counterpart. At least such predication should (I am proposing) occur only after the meaning of "self" in those contemporary positions is clearly isolated and after Mani's writings are studied on his own terms, within his own third-century cultural and religious milieu.

Perhaps studying Plotinus on man will give further insights.

Plotinus on Man

If we are successfully to compare Mani with Plotinus, at least two points need to be recalled. For the former the true reality of a human existent on earth — whether he be Mani or someone else — consists solely of intellect or soul.[32] Second, Mani, as specially designated by the Father of Greatness (see above, n. 11) to be a new channel of revelation, also involves another and higher dimension — a "Twin," who is a more powerful intellect or soul, sent on occasion by the Father to communicate knowledge to Mani, to advise and console him, to free him from errors. Mani, then, entails two levels of reality — one higher, the other lower.

Does a human existent as Plotinus conceives him entail similar levels of reality? If so, might the higher level serve as his "Twin"? Let us reflect on some texts in the *Enneads*.

Text A: IV, 1 (21), 1

In the single chapter which constitutes the entire first treatise of *Enneads* IV, Plotinus investigates the nature of souls and, thereby, their relationship to Intellect.[33]

[1] "True being is in the intelligible world and *Nous* is the best of it. But souls are There too, for they come here from There. [2] That world contains souls without bodies; this one contains souls which have come to be in bodies and are divided by their bodies. [3] Each *nous* There is all-together, since it is neither separated nor divided. All souls in that eternal world also are all-together and without spatial separation. Accordingly, *Nous* is always without separation and is undivided, and soul There is likewise not separated or divided, but it does have a nature which is divisible. [4] [But what does 'division' mean *re* souls?] Division for them is their departure from the intelligible world and their coming to be in bodies. Hence, a soul is reasonably said to be divisible with reference to bodies because in this fashion it departs from There and is divided. [5] How, then, is it also undivided? The whole soul does not depart: something of it does not come to this world and by nature is not such as to be divided." (Lines 12-13: Οὐ γὰρ ὅλη ἀπέστη, ἀλλ' ἔστι τι αὐτῆς οὐκ ἐληλυθός, ὃ οὐ πέφυκε μερίζεσθαι) To say that the soul consists of what is undivided and of what is divided in bodies is the same as saying that it consists of what is above, upon which it depends, and of what reaches as far as the things down here, like a radius from a center [reaches the circumference of the circle]. [6] But when it has come here it sees with the part of itself in which it preserves the nature of the whole. Even here below it is not only divided but is undivided as well, for its divided part is divided in such a way as to remain undivided. It gives itself to the whole body and is undivided because it gives itself as a whole to the whole and yet it is divided by being present in each part. (Lines 20-22: Εἰς ὅλον γὰρ τὸ σῶμα δοῦσα αὑτὴν καὶ μὴ μερισθεῖσα τῷ ὅλη εἰς ὅλον τῷ ἐν παντὶ εἶναι μεμέρισται)

Comment. In this passage Plotinus describes the two states in which souls find themselves. The first is their existence in the intelligible world (#1), where they are without bodies and, thus, are undivided (#2) and where their having all perfections present at once makes them similar to Intellect (#3). Yet even There a soul by nature is divisible. The second state arises when a soul comes from There to a body and thus is divided (#4). But even here a soul remains indivisible to an extent because of that part of it (*ti autēs*) which continues to be There (#5)[34] and through which it depends in its earthly career upon Intellect and knows reality (#6). In the intelligible world, then, a soul is undivided as aligned with Intellect and yet remains divisible because of its nature too; in the sensible world it is divided by the body it enters, within whose parts it is present;[35] but it is undivided because it is wholly present there (#6) and because of its continuing link with and dependence on Intellect (#5).

Is Plotinus's anthropology similar to Mani's? Yes, insofar as for each a human existent entails two levels of reality, the higher of which perfects, illumines and controls the lower.[36] For each there is an identity of sorts between the lower and the higher: according to Plotinus a soul's intellect is one with Intellect, from which it never departs; Mani proclaimed that "I am that one from whom I was separated. . . . I myself am that one who is unshakable" (*CMC*, 24. 9 sqq., quoted above). Yet there are differences. Mani's Twin is (as I interpret the *CMC*) more distinct from Mani himself than a soul's intellect is, in Plotinus's text, from the soul — the Twin seems almost an hypostasis with its own independent reality and function. Moreover, in the Manichaean world-view each human being is an intellect/soul but only Mani as the new and final prophet has a Twin, whereas every Plotinian human soul has an intellect, which remains There.

Perhaps more information will issue from subsequent pages of the *Enneads*.

Text B: VI, 4 (22), 14

Just as Text A is a commentary on a Platonic dialogue (*Timaeus*, 34C sqq.), so this passage is excerpted from Plotinus's comments on Plato's *Parmenides*, 131B sqq.[37] There Plato inquires whether a single Form is present to multiple sensible participants in its entirety or only partially. Plotinus poses that question in three ways: how Intellect and Being can be omnipresent to lower existents; how the spiritual can be omnipresent to the corporeal; finally, how soul is omnipresent to body.[38] While replying to the third question, he offers a conception of the human existent which perhaps may parallel to some extent Mani's statements on himself and his Twin.

Plotinus begins Chapter 14 by tracing the relationship between a human soul and Soul. [1] The latter contains all [individual] souls and intellects, and yet in spite of its distinguishable, multiple and, in fact, infinite contents, it is one, since all such existents are there in an unseparated fashion and all-together, springing from but always

remaining in self-identical unity (Ch. 14, lines 1-15). [2] "But *we* —
who are we? Are we that All-Soul[39] or, rather, are we that which drew
near to it and came to be in time? [3] Before this sort of birth came
about we were There as men different from those we now are — some
of us as gods, pure souls, intellects united with all reality, since we were
parts of the intelligible world, not separated or cut off, but belonging to
the whole — indeed we are not cut off even now. [4] But now there has
come to that higher man another man who wishes to be and who finds
us, for we were not outside the All. [5] He wound himself round us and
fastened himself to that man that each one of us was There (as if there
was one voice and one word, and someone else came up from elsewhere
and his ear heard and received the sound and became an actual hearing,
keeping present to it that which made it actual. [6] Thus we became a
couple and [we were no longer] the one [= higher man] we were before.
Sometimes we even become the other [= lower man], which had
fastened itself to us, when the first man is not active and is in another
sense absent."[40] (Ἡμεῖς δὲ — τίνες δὲ ἡμεῖς; Ἄρα ἐκεῖνο ἢ τὸ
πελάζον καὶ τὸ γινόμενον ἐν χρόνῳ; Ἦ καὶ πρὸ τοῦ ταύτην τὴν
γένεσιν γενέσθαι ἦμεν ἐκεῖ ἄνθρωποι ἄλλοι ὄντες καὶ τινες καὶ θεοί,
ψυχαὶ καθαραὶ καὶ νοῦς συνημένος τῇ ἁπάσῃ οὐσίᾳ, μέρη ὄντες τοῦ
νοητοῦ οὐκ ἀφωρισμένα οὐδ᾽ ἀποτετμημένα, ἀλλ᾽ ὄντες τοῦ ὅλου.
οὐδὲ γὰρ οὐδὲ νῦν ἀποτετμήμεθα. Ἀλλὰ γὰρ νῦν ἐκείνῳ τῷ ἀνθρώπῳ
προσελήλυθεν ἄνθρωπος ἄλλος εἶναι θέλων καὶ εὑρὼν ἡμᾶς — ἦμεν
γὰρ τοῦ παντὸς οὐκ ἔξω — περιέθηκεν ἑαυτὸν ἡμῖν καὶ προσέθηκεν
ἑαυτὸν ἐκείνῳ τῷ ἀνθρώπῳ τῷ ὃς ἦν ἕκαστος ἡμῶν τότε. οἷον εἰ
φωνῆς οὔσης μιᾶς καὶ λόγου ἑνὸς ἄλλος ἄλλοθεν παραθεὶς τὸ οὖς
ἀκούσειε καὶ δέξαιτο, καὶ γένοιτο κατ᾽ ἐνέργειαν ἀκοή τις ἔχουσα τὸ
ἐνεργοῦν εἰς αὐτὴν παρὸν καὶ γεγενήμεθα τὸ συνάμφω καὶ οὐ
θάτερον, ὃ πρότερον ἦμεν, καὶ θάτερόν ποτε, ὃ ὕστερον προσεθέμεθα
ἀργήσαντος τοῦ προτέρου ἐκείνου καὶ ἄλλον τρόπον οὐ παρόντος.)
16-31.

Comments. Although it is difficult to detect from these complex
and elliptical lines what a human existent is, some features are clear. A
human soul in both its lower and higher states is distinguishable from
the All-Soul. This latter by reason of its multiple and, in fact, infinite
contents (all souls and intellects) is all-perfect, but it also is intrinsically
and essentially one because its contents, manifold and explicated though
they be, are not actually separated but are all-together and so always
remain in unity (#1).

An individual soul entails two manners of existing inasmuch as it
remains within the Soul or departs from It.[41] Within the Soul an

individual soul and intellect also contains and contemplates all reality from its own more limited perspective and it is quiet, at peace and one with Soul. Nonetheless, it is not totally identical with Soul or with other individual souls There: although not actually isolated from them, it is divisible and distinguishable from them and, thereby, is *individual* in an analogous but authentic sense.[42] This individuality, when combined There with its other dimension of all-perfections-in-unity, constitutes the "higher man" (#3). The "lower man" is the same soul but now as in time and enmeshed in an encompassing body (#5). Any individual soul is, then, a couple (*to synampho*): it is at once the higher man and the lower man, although on some occasions its higher aspect predominates, on others its lower (#6).

Accordingly, who are *we*? What constitutes *us*? What makes us be who we are? Where do we find ourselves? No one of us is the All-Soul as such but each is (so to speak) one area of Soul, one participation in It, one portion or dimension of Its contents. And that area, participation, portion, dimension (call it what you will) either rests quietly within Soul (then I am the "higher man" and am more fully real) or it has gone forth to movement, time, body (and I am the "lower man" and am less real).[43] Consequently, "we" in Text B is the combination of the two men, even though at times we are more one than the other to correspond with which "man" is more active and in control.

Thus far our attempt to decipher Plotinus's clues on what a human existent is. Now our question: does his triad of Soul, higher man and lower man parallel Mani's conception of himself and his Twin? Mani also speaks of a triad of Light-Intellect (see above, n. 11), Twin and terrestrial soul.[44] Consequently, there is a parallel of sorts, which nonetheless entails the same differences as noted in our "Comments" on Text A. Mani's Twin seems entitatively less one with him than does Plotinus's higher man with lower man. Second, the latter's schema of Soul, higher man and lower man fits every human existent, whereas Mani's apparently is restricted to himself as founder of the Manichaean Church.[45]

Text C: II, 9 (33), 2

Let us take up another passage from Plotinus, this time from the treatise he wrote against the Gnostics of his time.[46] [1] "One must not posit more existents There than these [the Good-One, the Intellect and the Soul — see previous chapter of II, 9] nor make superfluous distinctions in such realities [e.g., between an Intellect which thinks and an Intellect which thinks that it thinks — see ibid.] No, we must posit that there is one Intellect, which remains unchangeably the same and without any sort of decline and which imitates the Father [= the Good-One] as far as it can. [2] One power of our soul is always directed to realities There, another to things here, and one is the middle between them. [3] Since the soul is one nature in multiple powers, sometimes all of it is carried along with its best part and with being. At times its worst part is dragged down and drags the middle part with it — not, to be sure, the whole of soul because that would be unlawful. [4] This misfortune befalls [a soul's middle part] because it does not remain There among the fairest realities (where nonetheless soul stays which is not such a part — nor indeed is the distinctive 'we' such a part) but rather allows the whole of body to hold whatever it can hold from it. [5] Even so, soul [in its highest part] remains unperturbed itself: by discursive thinking it does not manage body or set anything right but it orders things with a wonderful power by contemplating that which is before it. [6] The more it is directed to that contemplation, the fairer and more powerful it is. And receiving from There, it gives to what comes after it, and it illumines [what is below] in accordance as it is illumined [from above]." (Ch. 2 in its entirety: Οὐ τοίνον οὔτε πλείω τούτων οὔτε ἐπινοίας περιττὰς ἐν ἐκείνοις, ἃς οὐ δέχονται, θετέον, ἀλλ' ἕνα νοῦν τὸν αὐτὸν ὡσαύτως ἔχοντα, ἀκλινῆ πανταχῇ, μιμούμενον τὸν πατέρα καθ' ὅσον οἷόν τε αὐτῷ. Ψυχῆς δὲ ἡμῶν τὸ μὲν ἀεὶ πρὸς ἐκείνοις, τὸ δὲ πρὸς ταῦτα ἔχειν, τὸ δ' ἐν μέσῳ τούτων. φύσεως γὰρ οὔσης μιᾶς ἐν δυνάμεσι πλείοσιν ὁτὲ μὲν τὴν πᾶσαν συμφέρεσθαι τῷ ἀρίστῳ αὐτῆς καὶ τοῦ ὄντος, ὁτὲ δὲ τὸ χεῖρον αὐτῆς καθελκυσθὲν συνεφελκύσασθαι τὸ μέσον. τὸ γὰρ πᾶν αὐτῆς οὐκ ἦν θέμις καθελκύσαι. Καὶ τοῦτο συμβαίνει αὐτῇ τὸ πάθος, ὅτι μὴ ἔμεινον ἐν τῶ καλλίστῳ, ὅπου ψυχὴ μείνασα ἡ μὴ μέρος, μηδὲ ἡ ἡμεῖς ἔτι μέρος, ἔδωκε τῶ παντὶ σώματι αὐτῷ τε ἔχειν ὅσον δύναται παρ' αὐτῆς ἔχειν, μένει τε ἀπραγμόνως αὐτὴ οὐκ ἐκ διανοίας διοικοῦσα οὐδέ τι διορθουμένη, ἀλλὰ τῇ εἰς τὸ πρὸ αὐτῆς θέᾳ κατακοσμοῦσα δυνάμει θαυμαστῇ. Ὅσον γὰρ πρὸς αὐτῇ ἔστι, τόσῳ καλλίων καὶ δυνατωτέρα. κἀκεῖθεν ἔχουσα δίδωσι τῶ μετ' αὐτὴν καὶ ὥσπερ ἐλλάμπουσα ἀεὶ ἐλλάμπεται.)

Comments. After restricting the primal existents to three (the One-Good, Intellect and Soul)[47] and positing a threefold power in a human soul (#2), Plotinus pays considerable attention to its highest and intellectual power. The lowest power tends to the physical world (#2) and is dragged down by the body ensnaring it (#3) and the second power is marked by discursive reasoning, through which it endeavors to manage the body (#5), and by its vulnerability to being misled by the power beneath it (#3). But the highest power of an individual soul always tends (#2) to the realm of most beautiful realities (#4), where it remains at peace (#5) and which are the objects of its contemplation (#6). From the illumination issuing from this contemplation, it becomes more beautiful and strong and thus can enrich and illumine the middle and even the lowest portions of the soul (#6).[48]

If we relate the tripartite soul in Text C to Mani's position, what information can be drawn? The steadfast link of the highest power in the nature of the human soul with the realm of the really real, whence comes its illumination and power, would be congenial to Mani's view of his soul as enlightened by the Father of Greatness and as the channel of salvific knowledge to members of his church. And, of course, that supreme psychic power could be made to correspond with his Twin. But the basic dissimilarity between the two authors remains: Plotinus sketches a view embracing all human existents, Mani a view confined to himself as divinely commissioned savior, a commission which is repugnant to the Neoplatonist (see above, n. 45).

Summary and Conclusions. Texts other than the three so far discussed are relevant but they do not provide radically different information. One such is V, 3 (49), 3, in which Plotinus speaks of a soul as consisting of three powers — highest, middle and lowest, of which the first is aligned with intellect, the second with reason, the third with sense-perception — and thus it is similar to our Text C above.[49] Hence, such a passage does not need separate exegesis.

Accordingly, let us list briefly the relevant information of Texts A to C. In the first Plotinus describes an individual soul as existing in two states, the first of which is the intelligible world, the second the physical world. In each state it is marked with attributes of the other. For instance, when existing on the level of Intellect, it is undivided from other souls and intellects and yet its nature is such as to be divisible. When existing within a body, it is isolated from other living beings but it also remains united with the higher level because of its part which continues to be There and through which it still depends upon Intellect and knows reality. In Text B Plotinus continues the contrast between the higher and lower states in which human souls exist but he tries to locate their distinctive individuality by asking "Who are *we*?" His answer: no one of us is the All-Soul but each is one portion or participation of Its contents, which either rests immutably within It (then I am the "higher man") or has been immersed in motion, body, time (and then I am the "lower man"). Join such men together and one has the couple (*to synampho*) which each of us distinctively is. Text

C portrays an individual soul entailing the triple powers of intellect, reason and sensation, the first of which rests steadfastly on the level of Intellect, from its contemplation of which comes the illuminations which enrich its middle and lowest powers.

What, now, would Mani's reaction be if he were to read Plotinus? He would find himself both agreeing and disagreeing. He would agree that he himself involves higher and lower levels of existence, the first of which is occupied by his Twin (a more powerful and immutable intellectual being, destined to be his helper and guide), the second by his intellect or soul within a body. He would concur also that salvific knowledge and illumination come from the higher levels to him as the terrestrial conduit to those open to his divine message and leadership. But he would disagree that human individuals other than himself would entail a Twin as a transcendent Intellect to be their consoler and guide: Mani himself is to perform those functions for them. Also he would not agree that human individuals need no outside help in achieving ultimate well-being: the intellect of no one existing here in matter resides immutably in the upper realms of light so as to serve as instrument of salvation — no one's, that is, except Mani's, who is to administer the divine help all others need.

But despite those disagreements Mani concurs with his contemporary sufficiently to prompt our wondering what the source of their concurrence may be. Why are their positions parallel in certain important aspects, even though it is very unlikely that either read or met the other?

This fact, at least, seems obvious: each formulated a monism which is dynamic rather than static.[50] That is, all existents are real insofar as they consist of the same basic stuff (unity for Plotinus, light for Mani). All existents other than the First proceed from higher existents, of which the ultimate source is the One-Good for Plotinus and the Father of Greatness for Mani. For both authors that process is a movement downward from the more to the less perfect.[51] And the higher existents, which are the causes of whatever reality a lower existent may have, automatically and structurally are (so to speak) concerned with and care for their effects. This entitative concern and care explain why Mani's Twin comes from the Father to him as counselor and consoler and why for Plotinus the Intellect furnishes a steadfast and safe haven from which individual intellects never depart and to which individual souls can thereby return.

If one were asked to locate such world-views within the history of Western thought, one would have to say they are Platonic — a Middle Platonism which is influenced by Stoic monism, by Neopythagoreanism and by Aristotelian ontology, epistemology and ethics, but which radically originates with Plato. Plotinus's indebtedness to Plato and to Middle Platonism is beyond question.[52] But what philosophical influences (if any) directly or even indirectly influenced Mani? Such a question has, as far as I know, yet to be answered adequately.[53]

"Self" and Plotinus?

Just as several interpreters find Mani to espouse a doctrine of self (see the section above, "The 'Twin' as 'Self'"),[54] so some scholars think that Plotinus has a doctrine of "self." For instance, Plato Salvador Mamo describes Plotinus as apparently "the first philosopher explicitly concerned with the notion of the individual consciousness of ego." The last term should be defined, he adds, "not in static but in dynamic terms; not as individual substance but as striving, attention, direction of consciousness."[55]

Gerard J.P. O'Daly has written an entire book with the significant title of *Plotinus's Philosophy of the Self* (New York: Barnes and Noble, 1973; 1968 doctoral dissertation). Moreover, O'Daly lists an impressive number of contemporary authorities to back up his position. Emile Brehiér, Jean Trouillard, Richard Harder, E.R. Dodds and Wilhelm Himmerich all observe "that this concept (of *self*) plays an original and important part in Plotinus's thought" (pp. 4-5). Still others "have recognized the importance of the concept" — Pierre Hadot, E. von Ivanka, E.W. Warren, H.J. Blumenthal, J.M. Rist, P.S. Mamo, A.H. Armstrong (p. 98, n. 8). The last named, A.H. Armstrong, has in fact published an important article as recently as December, 1977, on *self* and entitled "Form, Individual and Person in Plotinus" (*Dionysius*, 1 [1977], 49-68).

But despite those explicit affirmations that *self* is to be found in Plotinus's *Enneads*, some of the same authors speak also in such a way as to raise questions about the accuracy of their affirmative statements. In the "Preface" to his dissertation, Mamo says that "it can be argued that a doctrine of the nature and destiny of the self must occupy a central position in any mystical system. But in Plotinus's case we have neither an explicit doctrine contained in his writings, nor a comprehensive study by a commentator. Scholars, who have given us little beyond scattered remarks, seem to be divided in their interpretations of the texts. It is held, on the one hand, that there is no room for the ego in Plotinus's heaven. On the other hand, we are told that Plotinus was so impressed by the uniqueness of each ego that he wanted to maintain a distinction between it and the One even with the *union mystica*" (op. cit., p. ii). Even O'Daly grants towards the end of his book, *Plotinus's Philosophy of Self*, that Plotinus has "no fixed word — hence no *concept*, strictly speaking — for 'self': as P. Henry has pointed out, there is no word for 'person' or 'self,' in Greek" (p. 89).

But in the light of O'Daly's admission, how can one discover a philosophy of "self" in the *Enneads*? What does one look for?

Perhaps it will be instructive to observe how O'Daly develops Plotinus's philosophy of self. After having noted (as just mentioned) that Plotinus has "no fixed word — hence, no *concept*, strictly speaking — for 'self' . . . there is no word for 'person' or 'self' in Greek," the Irish scholar states that Plotinus uses *autos* or *hēmeis* or the reflexive *hauton* to express the concept of "self." He continues: even "if the word, and the explicit, canonized concept are missing . . ., adequate testimony . . . [is] given of Plotinus's clear awareness of the importance of a concept of self . . . to account for the identity of a human subject at the several levels of existence possible to man" (pp. 89-90).[56]

That identity on the level of man in history involves the empirical or historical self (man as image [*eidolon*], as exterior and individual, soul as embodied; pp. 26-30). But it consists mainly in soul when reasoning and thinking and, thus, at its highest (p. 43): it becomes aware of itself as derived from *nous* as secondary image and as a repository of Forms (p. 44). "Self," then, is "essentially a faculty of conscious self-determination, a mid-point which can be directed towards the higher or the lower" (p. 49; also see p. 43). On the next level self continues to be soul but now as more closely linked with *nous*: through wisdom and virtue a soul "has a capacity for the divine by reason of its kinship and identical substance with the divine" (p. 52). Despite its divinization, though, the soul remains human (pp. 56-58, 62-63): "the human self, reverting to the intelligible, remains itself, while at the same time being one with the totality of Being" (p. 65). On the highest level self is soul as above being and *nous* and as one with the One (pp. 83-84) and, thereby, it is transcendent and absolute (p. 91). Yet it is not annihilated in that union: although its "everyday" or historical selfhood is transformed, it truly has become itself: "the self is a *reality* . . . in the moment of *union*, and not merely afterwards — despite the fact that one is *not aware* of the distinction at that moment" (p. 85).

O'Daly is obviously intelligent and industrious. He is thoroughly acquainted with the *Enneads*. Nonetheless, his book makes me uneasy. That uneasiness does not issue primarily from any one of his individual conclusions (e.g., that the human self on the highest level is soul, which There is one with the One and yet remains itself — soul — in that very union) so much as from the conviction which underlies the book: Plotinus has an authentic philosophy of "self," he was aware of "self" in some sort of technical meaning, even though O'Daly admits (as we have seen) that Plotinus has "no fixed word — hence, no *concept*, strictly speaking, for 'self'" (p. 89).

But in the light of this admission, how (to repeat our earlier questions) can one discover a *philosophy* of "self" in the *Enneads*? What does one look for? Why bother, even? But suppose someone would say, "Perhaps Plotinus anticipated 'self' in its contemporary significance." Then I become increasingly puzzled because there *is* no commonly accepted notion. As we previously concluded from studying Margaret Gorman's article on "self" in the *New Catholic Encyclopedia* (XIII, 56-60), "self" is an extremely ambiguous notion in both philosophical and psychological literature. Accordingly, it can help us discover a philosophy of self in the *Enneads* only with great difficulty. Yet, unless I am mistaken, we need some such aid if Plotinus himself has "no fixed word — hence, no *concept*, strictly speaking — for 'self'" (O'Daly, p. 89).

Another Approach?

Is there another way of reading those passages of the *Enneads* in which O'Daly believes their author is speaking of "self"? Yes, by refusing to translate *autos* or *hauton* or *hēmeis* as "self" (except, of course, when the meaning of the English word is not technical, as in the statement, "No one helped me — I did it myself") but in some such fashion as "what someone really is," "what we really are," "what man is essentially" and so on; or second, by coupling "self" with a bracketed phrase to indicate what is meant. Then, perhaps, Plotinus will more easily reveal what he was intending.

Let us now apply this methodology in some detail to *Enneads*, I, 6, upon which O'Daly (in part, at least) bases his interpretation and which is interesting as the first treatise Plotinus wrote. We shall first present our own paraphrase and/or translation of its relevant lines with comments, which will then be contrasted with O'Daly's.[57]

I, 6: "On Beauty"

In explaining what the primary beauty in bodies is, Plotinus observes that [A] our soul, upon becoming aware of such beauty, welcomes it and as it were adapts itself to it.   [B] But upon encountering the ugly, it shrinks back and rejects it and is out of tune and alienated from it (lines 1-6).   [C] Why so?   Because soul "is by nature what it is and is related to the higher sort of entity among beings, and thus, when seeing what is akin to it — or even a trace of what is akin to it — [in bodies], it is delighted and thrilled and [by turning from the body's beauty] it returns to itself [as soul] and remembers its true nature and its own possessions" (ch. 2, ll. 7-11: Φαμὲν δή, ὡς τὴν φύσιν οὖσα ὅπερ ἐστὶ καὶ πρὸς τῆς κρείττονος ἐν τοῖς οὖσιν οὐσίας, ὅ τι ἂν ἴδῃ συγγενὲς ἢ ἴχνος τοῦ συγγενοῦς, χαίρει τε διεπτόηται καὶ ἀναφέρει πρὸς ἑαυτὴν καὶ ἀναμιμνήσκεται ἑαυτης καὶ τῶν ἑαυτῆς).

Comments. Plotinus is here intent on illumining the human soul's reaction to corporeal beauty and ugliness. It flees from the latter (#B) and welcomes the former (#A). Confronted with beauty in bodies, our soul initially opens up to it (#A) but next turns away and within to its own nature and contents (#C). The contrast is between soul and body, with stress put upon what the soul essentially is. Thus, there is little likelihood that *hautē* in its three occurrences in lines 10-11 has to do technically with "self."

Shortly after, Plotinus speaks of the beauty to be found within soul. [D] What do you feel (he asks) about virtuous activities and dispositions and the beauty of souls (ll. 2-5)? In fact, "what do you feel when you look at your own souls and the beauty within them? How are you wildly exalted and stirred and long to be with yourselves by gathering yourselves [= your souls, what you really are] together away from your bodies?" (ch. 5, ll. 5-8: Καὶ ἑαυτοὺς δὲ ἰδόντες τὰ ἔνδον καλοὺς τί πάσχετε; Καὶ πως ἀναβακχεύεσθε καὶ ἀνακινεῖσθε καὶ ἑαυτοῖς συνεῖναι ποθεῖτε συλλεξάμενοι αὐτοὺς ἀπο τῶν σωμάτων;). [F] You feel, no doubt, what true lovers feel. But what is it which makes them feel like this? Not shape or color or any size which are linked with beauty in bodies but soul, which possess a moral, colorless order and all the other light of the virtues. [G] This you feel when in yourselves [= your souls] or in someone else you see greatness of soul, righteous life, pure morality, courage, dignity, modesty, calmness, upon all of which the godlike Intellect shines and all of which we love and call beautiful. Why so? Because they are genuinely real beings (*ta ontos onta*) and, thereby, are beautiful (ll. 8-20).

Comments.   Chapter five gives information on a human soul's reaction to psychic beauties. It is enraptured and deeply moved (#D) by seeing moral virtues (whether its own or someone else's), their high ontological status and consequent fairness (#G), the illumination bestowed upon them by the Intellect (#G). Such a soul desires to withdraw from body and to be solely what it truly is: soul. Accordingly, an emphasis continues to be put upon contrasting soul with body and, thus, *heautous* and *heautois* in lines 5 and 7 need not refer to "self" as such.

In chapter seven Plotinus begins to depict how we are to attain the Good and Beautiful. [H] We must ascend to the Good, which every soul desires but which only those attain who go up to the higher world, are turned around and [I] "strip off what we put on in our descent . . . until passing in the ascent all that is alien to God, one sees only with what he truly is That which is alone, simple, pure and from which all depends and to which all look and in which all are and live and think." (ch. 7, ll. 4-10: Ἐφετὸν μὲν γὰρ ὡς ἀγαθὸν καὶ ἡ ἔφεσις πρὸς τοῦτο, τεῦξις δὲ αὐτοῦ ἀναβαίνουσι πρὸς τὸ ἄνω καὶ ἐπιστραφεῖσι καὶ ἀποδυομένοις ἃ καταβαίνοντες ἠμφιέσμεθα . . . ἕως ἄν τις παρελθὼν ἐν τῇ ἀναβάσει πᾶν ὅσον ἀλλότριον τοῦ θεοῦ αὐτῶ μονῶ αὐτὸ μόνον ἴδη εἰλικρινές, ἁπλοῦν, καθαρόν, ἀφ' οὗ πάντα ἐξήρτηται καὶ πρὸς αὐτὸ βλέπει καὶ ἔστι καὶ ζῇ καὶ νοεῖ).

But, more precisely, [J] what method can we devise (Plotinus asks in ch. 8) to see the inconceivable Beauty? His answer in brief from the end of the chapter: Give up all hope in material or mechanical means, disregard your physical vision. Then change to and make another way of seeing (ch. 8, ll. 24-27). [K] And what does this inner sight see? The soul must be trained to see, first of all, beautiful ways of life, then good and virtuous works and, next, the souls which produce them. (ch. 9, lines 1-6). [L] "How, then, can you see the sort of beauty a good soul has? Go back to your own and look. [M] If you do not see yours is beautiful, then just as someone making a beautiful statue cuts away here and polishes there . . ., so you too must cut away excess and straighten the crooked and clear the dark and make it bright, and never stop 'working on your statue' till the divine glory of virtue shines out on you . . . [N] If you have become beautiful and see it, and you are at home with your pure state, with nothing hindering you from becoming in this way one, with no inward mixture of anything else but wholly what you really are — namely, nothing but pure light, not measured by dimensions, or bounded by shape into littleness, or expanded to size by unboundedness but everywhere unmeasured . . . — [O] when you see that you have become this, then you have become sight. You can trust what you are then; you have already ascended and need no one to show you. Concentrate your gaze and see . . . the enormous Beauty" (ll. 6-25: Πῶς ἂν οὖν ἴδοις ψυχὴν ἀγαθὴν οἷον τὸ κάλλος ἔχει; ἄναγε ἐπὶ σαυτὸν καὶ ἴδε. κἂν μήπω σαυτὸν ἴδης καλόν, οἷα ποιητὴς ἀγάλματος, ὃ δεῖ καλὸν γενέσθαι, τὸ μὲν ἀφαιρεῖ, τὸ δὲ ἀπέξεσε, τὸ δὲ λεῖον, τὸ δὲ καθαρὸν ἐποίησεν, ἕως ἔδειξε καλὸν ἔπὶ τῇ ἀγάλματι πρόσωπον, οὕτω καὶ σὺ ἀφαίρει ὅσα περιττὰ καὶ ἀπεύθυνε ὅσα σκολιά, ὅσα σκοτεινὰ καθαίρων ἐργάζου εἶναι λαμπρὰ καὶ μὴ παύσῃ τεκταίνων τὸ σὸν ἄγαλμα, ἕως ἂν ἐκλάμψειέ σοι τῆς ἀρετῆς ἡ θεοειδὴς ἀγλαΐα, ἕως ὃν ἴδῃς σωφροσύνην ἐν ἁγνῷ βεβῶσαν βάθρῳ. Εἰ γέγονας τοῦτο καὶ εἶδες αὐτὸ καὶ σαυτῷ καθαρὸς συνεγένου οὐδὲν ἔχων ἐμπόδιον πρὸς τὸ εἰς οὕτω γενέσθαι οὐδὲ σὺν αὐτῷ ἄλλο τι ἐντὸς μεμιγμένον ἔχων, ἀλλ᾽ ὅλος αὐτὸς φῶς ἀληθινὸν μόνον, οὐ μεγέθει μεμετρημένον οὐδὲ σχήματι εἰς ἐλάττωσιν περιγραφὲν οὐδ᾽ αὖ εἰς μέγεθος δι᾽ ἀπειρίας αὐξηθέν, ἀλλ᾽ ἀμέτρητον πανταχοῦ, ὡς ἂν μεῖζον παντὸς μέτρου καὶ παντὸς κρεῖσσον ποσοῦ. εἰ τοῦτο γενόμενον σαυτὸν ἴδοις, ὄψις ἤδη γενόμενος θαρσήσας περὶ σαυτῷ καὶ ἐνταῦθα ἤδη ἀναβεβηκὼς μηκέτι τοῦ δεικνύντος δεηθεὶς ἀτενίσας ἴδε. οὗτος γὰρ μόνος ὁ ὀφθαλμὸς τὸ μέγα κάλλος βλέπει.

Comments. One finds in the final three chapters just paraphrased that Plotinus has returned to a methodology similar to that disclosed in the passages paraphrased above (#A-G), but with a difference. There the soul turned away from matter so as to see and be captivated by the beauty of its own moral virtues. Here, though, the Greek author is concerned with how the soul, disregarding whatever is lower, is eventually to ascend to the Good (#I and ch. 9, lines 37 sqq.) and the Beautiful (#K).

His explanation is complex, though, inasmuch as he first gives general directions (#H-#I), which then become more specific (#J-#O). But in each case they consist in setting aside impediments so as to arrive at what the soul really is and, thereby, to be capable of attaining primal reality.

His general advice is, then, to discard matter and whatever vices we have succumbed to in departing from the higher realms so that each of us, relying solely on what he truly is, might behold the divine Good in his solitude, simplicity and purity (#I). Here, rather obviously, the crucial words in line 9 (*autō monō*) do not pertain to "self" as such but to a man's own reality as contrasted with the unreality of matter and vice and with the supreme reality of God.

In its more exact formulation, though, his advice comes in several stages. Let one wishing to see Beauty (#J) refuse to be drawn towards external and bodily beauties, which are mere shadows and can ruin him (ch. 8, ll. 3-16, left unparaphrased above). Rather, let him journey back to his origin There not on foot or by carriage or boat (ll. 16-24). No, let him put hope in no material or mechanical means but close his physical eyes and activate his spiritual vision (#J), with which he should attend to the beauties of virtues and of the souls they perfect (#K). If someone finds no beauty in his soul, let him work upon his soul (as a sculptor upon a statue) to replace the ugliness of vice with the beauty and divine refulgence of virtue (#M). This done, and no hindrances remaining to pureness and unity and no internal composition, he has become wholly what he really is: authentic and immeasurable light (#N) and vision itself (#C). Having thus achieved his own true reality, he has arrived too at Beauty itself: let him look and see (#C).

Here, again, the words in lines 7 (*anage epi sauton*), 8 (*sauton*) and 15 sqq. of Chapter 9 occur when Plotinus contrasts what a man truly is with matter and evil (then he is soul) and with Beauty (then he is light and vision). In neither contrast may (at least: must) one replace them with "self" technically taken.

O'Daly's exegesis puts the crucial lines into a different and (I think) misleading focus, as this quotation shows (*Plotinus's Philosophy of Self*, p. 83).[58]

> At I, 6 (1), 9 the self (*autos*, 18), *is* the "only veritable light," and "when you perceive that you have grown to this, you are now become very vision" (22). A transformation of the "everyday" self is in question: at chapter 9, 7ff. it is said that man can work upon this transformation. Plotinus . . . has subtly rewritten the image of the *Phaedrus* (252d), so that the "statue" (*agalma*) becomes the self. . . . Thus at chapter 5 Plotinus can speak to the "lovers" (9) who "when you see that you yourselves are beautiful within . . . long to be one with your self," 5 ff. Similarly, at ch. 9, 15 ff., "you have become this perfect work [i.e., the *agalma*], and have had vision of it and you are self-gathered in the purity of your being." . . . For Plotinus . . . it is in a heightening of *self-possession*, of *self-concentration*, carried to its extreme, that vision occurs; if the self experiences unification (17), it is *entirely as itself* (18) (italics in the original).

Before proceeding to other texts let me offer these brief tentative conclusions. In *Enneads* I, 6, Plotinus primarily is a metaphysician and, thus, is intent also and especially on two questions which underlie the explicit discussion of what beauty is — namely, "What is reality? What does it mean to be real?" and, concomitantly, "In what does man's genuine reality consist?" The answer to this second question differs when man is compared to what is lower (then, he is soul) and to what is primal reality (then, he is light and vision).

Other Treatises

When that comparison to what is below man is made in subsequent treatises, the same reply is given. But when he is compared to primal reality, the reply changes somewhat inasmuch as Plotinus increasingly realized that reality *is* unity and, hence, man insofar as he is genuinely real must basically and ultimately be *one*. This radical state of unity and reality is disclosed when, having transcended not only evil and matter but even soul and intellect, he is united to the One *seu* the Good *seu* God. In that union, Plotinus states in VI, 9, (9), 11, 4 sqq., "there were not two, but the seer himself was one with the Seen (for It was not really seen but united to him). . . . He was one himself then, with no distinction in him either in relation to himself or anything else; for there was no movement in him, and he had no emotion, no desire for anything else when he had made the ascent, no reason or thought; his own self [= what he was on a lower level: soul] was not there for him, if we should say even this" (ll. 4-12: Ἐπεὶ τοίνυν δύο οὐκ ἦν, ἀλλ' ἓν ἦν αὐτὸς ὁ ἰδὼν πρὸς τὸ ἑωραμένον, ἀλλ' ἡνωμένον, ὃς ἐγένετο ὅτε ἐκείνῳ ἐμίγνυτο εἰ μεμνῷτο, ἔχοι ἄν παρ' ἑαυτῶ ἐκείνου εἰκόνα. Ἦν δὲ ἓν καὶ αὐτὸς διαφορὰν ἐν αὑτῶ οὐδεμίαν πρὸς ἑαυτὸν ἔχων οὔτε κατὰ ἄλλα' — οὐ γὰρ τι ἐκινεῖτο παρ' αὐτῶ, οὐ θυμός, οὐκ' ἐπιθυμία ἄλλου παρῆν αὐτῷ ἀναβεβηκότι — ἀλλ' οὐδὲ λόγος οὐδέ τις νόησις οὐδ' ὅλως αὐτός, εἰ δεῖ καὶ τοῦτο λέγειν). In fact, his contemplation of God was perhaps "not a contemplation but another kind of seeing, a being out of oneself [= what one is as a distinct and lower existent], a simplifying, a self-surrender [a surrender of what one is as distinct, less real being], a pressing towards contact, a rest, a sustained thought directed to perfect conformity" (ll. 22-25: Τὸ δὲ ἴσως ἦν οὐ θέαμα, ἀλλὰ ἄλλος τρόπος τοῦ ἰδεῖν, ἔκστασις καὶ ἅπλωσις καὶ ἐπίδοσις αὐτοῦ καὶ ἔφεσις πρὸς ἀφὴν καὶ στάσις καὶ περινόησις πρὸς ἐφαρμογήν). Those lines apparently explicate the identity between man when fully real and primal Reality: man then is one with the One.

The same explication continues in III, 8 (30), 9, 19 sqq., where Plotinus asks: "Since knowledge of other things comes to us from intellect, . . . by what sort of simple intuition could one grasp this which transcends the nature of intellect?[59] We shall say . . . that it is by the likeness in ourselves. For there is something of it in us too; or rather there is nowhere where it is not, in the things which can participate in it. For, wherever you are, it is from this that you have that which is everywhere present, by setting to it that which can have it" (ll. 19-26: Καὶ γὰρ αὖ τῆς γνώσεως διὰ νοῦ τῶν ἄλλων γινομένης καὶ τῷ νῷ νοῦν γινώσκειν δυναμένων ὑπερβεβηκὸς τοῦτο τὴν νοῦ φύσιν τίνι ἂν ἁλίσκοιτο ἐπιβολῇ ἄθρόᾳ; Πρὸς ὃν δεῖ σημῆναι, ὅπως οἷον τε, τῷ ἕν ἡμῖν ὁμοίῳ φήσομεν. Ἔστι γάρ τι καὶ παρ' ἡμῖν αὐτοῦ ἢ οὐκ ἔστιν, ὅπου μὴ ἔστιν, οἷς ἐστι μετέχειν αὐτοῦ. Τὸ γὰρ πανταχοῦ παραστήσας ὁπουοῦν τὸ δυνάμενων ἔχειν ἔχεις ἐκεῖθεν). The next chapter helps to explain that omnipresence of God. The One *is* the "power of all existents (*dynamis tōn pantōn*): if it did not exist," neither would they (ch. 10, lines 1 sqq.). "Everywhere, then, we must go back to *one*. And in each and every existent there is some *one* to which you will trace it back, and this in every case to the *one* before it, which is not simply one, until we come to the simply one; and this cannot be traced back to something else. But if we take the *one* of the plant . . . and the *one* of the animal and the *one* of the soul and the *one* of the universe, we are taking in each case what is most powerful and really valuable in it; but if we take the *one* of the beings which truly are, their origin and spring and power, shall we lose faith and think of it [the One] as nothing? [By no means]" (ll. 20-28: Διὸ καὶ ἡ ἀναγωγὴ πανταχοῦ ἐφ' ἕν. Καὶ ἐφ' ἑκάστου μέν τι ἕν, εἰς ὃ ἀνάξεις, καὶ τόδε τὸ πᾶν εἰς ἓν τὸ προ αὐτοῦ, οὐχ ἁπλῶς ἕν, ἕως τις ἐπὶ τὸ ἁπλῶς ἓν ἔλθῃ τοῦτο δὲ οὐκέτι ἐπ' ἄλλο. Ἀλλ' εἰ μὲν τὸ τοῦ φυτοῦ ἕν — τοῦτο δὲ καὶ ἡ ἀρχὴ ἡ μένουσα — καὶ τὸ ζῴου ἓν καὶ τὸ ψυχῆς ἓν καὶ τὸ τοῦ παντὸς ἓν λαμβάνοι, λαμβάνει ἑκαστανοῦ τὸ δυνατώτατον καὶ τὸ τίμιον. εἰ δὲ τὸ τῶν κατ' ἀλήθειον ὄντων ἕν, τὴν ἀρχὴν καὶ πηγὴν καὶ δύναμιν, λαμβάνοι, ἀπιστήσομεν καὶ τὸ μηδὲν ὑπονοήσομεν). The fact that man, as well as existents on every level, is somehow one with the One is so clearly suggested in those lines as to need no comment.

The same suggestion emerges in a still later treatise, VI, 7 (38): "The soul must not keep by it good or evil or anything else, that it may alone receive Him, the Only One. . . . [When] His presence becomes manifest [to the soul], when it turns away from the things present to it and prepares itself, making itself as beautiful as possible, and comes to likeness with Him, . . . then it sees Him suddenly appearing in itself (for there is nothing between, nor are they still two, but both are one; while He is present, you could not distinguish them)" (ch. 34, ll. 6-18; the Greek for ll. 12-14: ἰδοῦσα δὲ ἐν αὐτῇ ἐξαίφνης φανέντα — μεταξὺ γὰρ οὐδὲν οὐδ' ἔτι δύο, ἀλλ' ἓν ἄμφω. οὐ γὰρ ἂν διακρίναις ἔτι, ἕως πάρεστι). Then in chapter 36: after purifying and adorning the soul with virtues, after gaining a foothold in the world of Intellect and settling firmly there, after contemplating what he really is and everything else, a man then "is near: the Good is next above him, close to him already shining over the whole intelligible world." Now "letting all study go, . . . he raises his thought to that in which he is, but is carried out of it by the very surge of the wave of Intellect and, lifted high by its swell, suddenly sees without knowing how; the Sight fills his eyes with Light but does not make him see something else by it, but the Light is That Which he sees. There is not in It one thing which is seen and another which is Its Light" (ll. 8-22; the Greek for ll. 19-20: ἀλλ᾽ ἡ θέα πλήσασα φωτὸς τὰ ὄμματα οὐ δι᾽ αὐτοῦ πεποίηκεν ἄλλο ὁρᾶν, ἀλλ᾽ αὐτὸ τὸ φῶς τὸ ὅραμα ἦν).

With this affirmation that the One is light, we have come full circle. In I, 6, 9, man is light upon achieving God. VI, 7, 36 asserts that God is light. Therefore, man *is* God — or, at least, becomes God during that state of mystical unification.

Our interpretation of the previous three passages intimates that Plotinus's metaphysics has become increasingly monistic.[60] This, I grant, is a thorny question, which, however, needs to be touched upon in any discussion of "self." But, at least, this seems comparatively certain: his discussion of man's relationship to primal and other reality is primarily *metaphysical* (i.e., knowledge of the real as real):[61] how man actually exists; what he is on the physical, psychic, noetic and mystical levels of reality; to what extent he is real there. Yes, Plotinus's discussion is primarily metaphysical, even though he often describes man in terms of his operations — physical, psychic, noetic, mystical. But even then Plotinus is intent on the data they give on man's ontological and henological status of reality — *re* what he actually is as he exists on those four levels, *re* the degree to which he attains or loses the reality uniquely his of being one with the One.

But if Plotinus's discussion of man's relationship to primal and lower reality is primarily metaphysical, this is another reason to rethink whether *autos* and so on do mean "self." This latter notion, when it came to prominence in modern times, appears to have arisen often within discussions of a psychological (both philosophical and empirical) nature. If Plotinus's investigations of man are metaphysical in essence, finding "self" there may put them out of focus.

Suggested Methodology

Let me terminate with a suggested methodology for reading Plotinus's *Enneads*.[62] First, when reading his Greek do not translate *autos* or *hauton* or *hēmeis* or *ekeino* as *self* but in some such fashion as "what someone really is," "what we really are," "what man is essentially" and so on (as illustrated earlier *re* I, 6, 1 sqq.) Second, try to understand Plotinus on his own (what *he* had in mind when writing such and such a passage). Third, reflect anew to see if the application to Plotinus of some or other modern notion of "self" may be helpful.[63] That reflection should cover these points: (a) Does the application of such a conception of "self" to Plotinus's *Weltanschauung* help in understanding *him* better, more richly, more authentically? (b) Does it reveal him perhaps to have anticipated contemporary theories on "self"? (c) Does it help us understand what the notion of "self" itself entails, whether in some modern and contemporary author or in our own philosophical position? In following this threefold methodology we have certainly lost nothing since we do take into account "self," *ego*, person with respect to Plotinus. But his own texts control the contemporary notions rather than the other way round.

NOTES

1.   Its title is "Concerning the Origin of His Body," where the last word refers not so much to Mani's physical body as to his Church (after the manner in which St. Paul calls the Christian Church the "Mystical Body of Christ"). See Ludwig Koenen, "Augustine and Manichaeism in Light of the Cologne Mani Codex," *Illinois Classical Studies* (hereafter *ICS*) 3 (1978): 164-66. On the Coptic Manichaean Codex, which was probably part of the same work as the *CMC* and was a history of the Manichaeans from the death of Mani up to c. 300 A.D., see ibid., pp. 164-165 and n. 37.

      Although biographical in content and even autobiographical in appearance, the *CMC* is formally an anthology. It consists of excerpts from Mani's own works and from the writings of Mani's immediate disciples (Baraies is one whose name will show up in our translations/paraphrases below), which an unknown editor collected and arranged in a roughly chronological sequence and according to five thematic units (Mani's childhood, his first revelation, his break with the baptists, his second revelation and separation from the baptists, his first missionary activities). See Albert Henrichs, "Literary Criticism of the Cologne Mani Codex" (hereafter "Literary Criticism"), in B. Layton, ed., *The Rediscovery of Gnosticism* (Leiden: E.J. Brill, 1981), II, pp. 724-733. On the *CMC* as "neither genuinely biographical nor always historical, but theological and, more specifically, ecclesiastical," see *idem*, "Mani and the Babylonian Baptists: Historical Confrontation," *Harvard Studies in Classical Philology* (hereafter *HSCP*) 77 (1973): 41.

2.   The original compilation was "very likely . . . made soon after Mani's death in 276 from sources written [in an Eastern Aramaic dialect] during his lifetime" — A. Henrichs, "The Cologne Mani Codex," *HSCP* 83 (1979): 352; also see *idem, HSCP* 77 (1973): 35-36.

3. When acquired by the University of Cologne, the *CMC* consisted of some badly damaged lumps of parchment — see photographs at the end of "Ein Griechischer Mani-Codex" by A. Henrichs and L. Koenen in *Zeitschrift fur Papyrologie und Epigraphik* (hereafter *ZPE*) 5 (1970): 96-216; A. Henrichs, *HSCP* 83 (1979): 342-352.

4. Still to appear is the commentary on pp. 121-192 of the Codex, as well as Indices and "Tafelband" — see *ZPE* 48 (1982): 1. These will soon be forthcoming.

5. *The Cologne Mani Codex*, "Texts and Translations," no. 15, of "Early Christian Literature Series," no. 3 (Missoula, Montana: Scholars Press, 1979). Although only a partial translation (with accompanying Greek text), still it does translate the pages which are most important philosophically and religiously. The pages of the Codex which Cameron and Dewey have not yet translated are pp. 99-116, which Henrichs describes as less metaphysical and more pragmatic, and pp. 116-192, which are "more monotonous, less informative, and more concerned with legendary material than any other part of the codex" (see "Literary Criticism," pp. 730 and 731).

6. For other high evaluations of the *CMC* see A. Henrichs, "Literary Criticism," p. 724: "Anyone who wishes to find out about the historical origins of Manichaeism, about Mani's view of himself or about the central role of books, and of Mani's own words, in the propagation of his religion" will want to peruse the *CMC*. In summary, "the *CMC* is a rich repertory of Manichaean history, beliefs, and literary skill. . . . As a religious anthology of multiple authorship it has no parallel outside Manichaean literature" (ibid., pp. 732-733). Also see K. Rudolph, "Die Bedeutung des Kölner Mani-Codex," in *Mélanges d'histoire des religions offert à H.-Ch. Puech* (Paris: Presses Universitaires de France, 1974), pp. 471 sqq; for a digest of contents of *CMC*, see A. Henrichs, *HSCP* 83 (1979): 340-342.

7. John Baggarly, S.J., in 1977 was teaching in the Department of Theology at Loyola and now is librarian at the Pontificio Istituto Orientale in Rome; he has been working on a critical edition of the Greek text of the Byzantine author, Athanasius of Sinai.

8. Plotinus (205-270) was slightly older than Mani (216-274). On the latter's dates see G. Haloun and W.B. Henning, "The Compendium of the Doctrines and Styles of the Teaching of Mani, The Buddha of Light" (hereafter "Compendium"), *Asia Minor* 3 (1953): 197-201; Mary Boyce, *A Reader in Manichaean Middle Persian and Parthian* [hereafter: *A Reader*] (Teheran-Liege: Bibliotheque Pahlavi, 1975), pp. 1-3.

9. Mani mentions "Twin" in treatises other than the *CMC*, but less frequently and with little information. See G. Henrichs and L. Koenen, *ZPE* 5 (1970): 161. Besides the *CMC* there are seven other canonical writings. See G. Halhoun and W.B. Henning, "Compendium," pp. 204-211; Mary Boyce, *A Reader*, pp. 12-13.

10. References are given to the *CMC* according to the following rubric: the first number indicates the page of the Greek text, the second number the initial line of the passage translated or paraphrased. I have inserted capital letters in brackets to render subsequent referrals more easily.

11. The Father of Greatness, who is the supreme God and is opposed to the Prince of Darkness, is the ultimate source of Mani's mission and leadership. But God works through intermediaries, such as the Messenger, Jesus the Splendor, etc. For a helpful diagram, which is based on the *Kephalaia* but which also represents many of the emanations mentioned in the *CMC*, see A. Henrichs and L. Koenen, *ZPE* 5 (1970): 183 (below). For a more detailed presentation of the Manichaean hierarchy, see M. Boyce, *A Reader*, pp. 8-10.

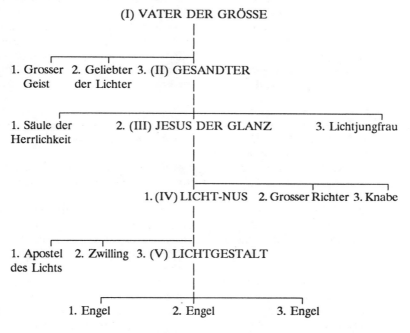

One must keep in mind that Mani's position is, philosophically, a monism of light and that anything on any level is real to the extent that it is light and, thereby, is one with all else. Hence, Mani's attributing his call to (say) Jesus the Splendor in some passages is not to deny its coming also from the Father of Greatness, with whom Jesus is one. Henri-Charles Puech stresses that God and souls are consubstantial and that human souls are parts of the World Soul, which also is God's soul (this consubstantiality corresponds to what I call "monism"). See *Le Manichéisme. Son Fondateur. Sa Doctrine* (Paris: Civilisations du Sud, 1949), p. 71 and n. 275 (pp. 154-55): "Il y a consubstantialité entre Dieu et les âmes; les âmes ne sont que des fragments de la substance divine. Ce qui revient à dire que c'est une partie de Dieu qui est ici-bas déchue, liée au corps et à la Matière, mêlée au Mal. . . . Dans le manichéisme, les âmes humaines sont . . . des parties ou des parcelles de l'Âme universelle (c'est-à-dire de l'âme même de Dieu) englouties dans les Ténèbres à la suite de la défaite de l'Homme Primordial et avec l'Homme Primordial lui-même. Celui-ci est l'âme . . ., le 'moi' de Dieu . . . une 'projection' ou une emanation' de la substance divine. . . . A noter que le 'consubstantiel' manichéen a joué son rôle dans les débats trinitaires suscités par l'arianisme. . . . Mais le mot [consubstantiel] indique plutôt l'identité de forme que l'identité de substance."

On Albert the Great and Bonaventure as two medieval theologians whose positions tend to be monistic because reality is light, see L. Sweeney, S.J., "Are Plotinus and Albertus Magnus Neo-platonists?" in *Graceful Reason: Essays in Ancient and Medieval Philosophy Presented to Joseph Owens*, ed. Lloyd Gerson (Toronto: Pontifical Institute of Mediaeval Studies, 1983), pp. 195-202; *idem*, "Christian Philosophy in Augustine and Bonaventure," chapter in *Essays Honoring Allan Wolter*, ed. Girard J. Etzkorn (St. Bonaventure, N.Y.: The Franciscan Institute, 1984), pp. 271-308.

12. "Paraclete" is the word used in John's Gospel, 14.16, and 16.17, to refer to the Holy Spirit and is here applied to Mani. On this application, see L. Koenen, *ICS* 3 (1978): 170-174, quoted and discussed below in the paragraphs corresponding to nn. 25-27.

13. Baraies is "a Manichaean apologist of the first generation after Mani" — L. Koenen, ibid., p. 165; A. Henrichs, *HSCP* 83 (1979): 354. Also see above, n. 1.

14. In order to avoid the questionable use of "self," my translation differs from Cameron-Dewey's (". . . greatest mirror-image of [my self]" — see *The Cologne Mani Codex*, p. 19), and Henrichs-Koenen (". . . machtvolle Spiegelbild [meiner Gestalt]" — see *ZPE* 19 [1975]: 19).

15. Also see 21.10 on how Mani "was begotten into this fleshly body, by what woman I was delivered and born according to the flesh, and by whose [passion] I was engendered." The pessimistic view of body here and in 22.10, must be juxtaposed to earlier statements that the body is designed as "the holy place for the glory of the mind (*nous*), as the most holy shrine for the revelation of its wisdom" (15.8). This juxtaposition discloses the paradox in Mani's thought: the body is evil and yet good, it is enslaving but salvific.

16. The fact that Mani's soul is a portion of the World Soul is not surprising in light of his monistic tendency — see above, n. 11 (third paragraph and the quotation from H.-Ch. Puech). On the formation of the physical universe, see 65.12: the Father "disclosed to me how I was before the foundation of the world, and how the groundwork of all the works, both good and evil, was laid, and how everything of [this] aggregation was engendered [according to its] present boundaries and [times]." On Mani's cosmogony

and cosmology see J. Ries, "Manichaeism," *New Catholic Encyclopedia*, IX, 156D-157C; H.-Ch. Puech, *Le Manichéisme*, pp. 74-85; Hans Jonas, *Gnostic Religion* (publishing data given below), Ch. 9.

17. For Henrichs-Koenen's translation of the last two sentences, see *ZPE* 19 (1975): 27: "Ich habe ihn erkannt und ich habe verstanden, dass ich jener bin, von dem ich getrennt wurde. Ich habe bezeugt, dass ich selbst jener bin und dass ich daher unerschütterlich bin." This corrects their earlier translation in *ZPE* 5 (1970): 68. On the monism which the two sentences suggest, see above nn. 11 and 16. Also see the sentences from "The Hymn of the Pearl," quoted below in the paragraph corresponding to n. 28.

18. See, for instance, such texts as these: the Twin, all-glorious and all-blessed, disclosed to Mani exceedingly great mysteries (26.8), which are hidden to the world and which are not permitted for anyone to see or hear (43.4). The Twin is a good counselor (32.14), an ally and protector at all times (33.4), "my unfailing Twin," the "entire fruit of immortality," that Mani might be redeemed and ransomed from the Elchasaite error (69.15). Also, 101.13: "mein allerseligster *Syzygos* — mein Herr und Helfer"; 104.11: "der Allerherrlichste"; 105.17:   the beauty of "meines allerseligsten *Syzygos*, jenes Allerherrlichsten und Erhabensten."

19. This contrast between strength and submission is deliberately paradoxical: to receive the divine messages Mani must be intellectually robust. But thereby he shows himself to be a religious leader worthy of credence: his salvific message is divine since it comes from above, but it coexists with Mani's personal strength.

20. This baptist sect, founded by Elchasai in the early second century A.D., had a predominantly Jewish-Christian, rather than Gnostic, basis. When Mani's father joined the sect, Mani was four years old and hence grew up in it. See A. Henrichs, *HSCP* 77 (1973): 44-45; L. Koenen, *ICS* 3 (1978): 187-190; Henrichs and Koenen, *ZPE* 5 (1970): 141-160; A. Henrichs, *HSCP* 83 (1979): 360-367.

21. On the identity between Mani and the Twin see also the excerpt from the "Hymn of the Pearl" quoted below in Hans Jonas's translation and in n. 28.

22. For example, see *ZPE* 19 (1975): 76.

23. The conception of Mani as a split personality comes to Henrichs from G. Haloun and W.B. Henning, "Compendium," p. 208: because of the Twin of Light "Mani possessed a split mind; he realized his condition and invented this striking term for his second personality: the Twin." See Henrichs and Koenen, *ZPE* 5 (1970): 182, n. 215: after quoting Henning they then add: "Wir habe zu zeigen versucht, in welchem Sinne man tatsächlich von einem 'split mind' Manis sprechen kann: Seine irdische Seele ist ein Teil seines transzendentalen ichs und gleichsam von diesem abgespalten. In der Inspiration vereinigen sich die beiden Teile seines Ichs." Also see below n. 27.

24. Information on the hysterical neurosis of a dissociative kind, which Drs. Cornelia Wilbur, Malcolm Graham, William Rothstein, Frank Putnam and other contemporary psychologists call "multiple personalities," can easily be found in daily newspapers — see *Chicago Tribune* for February 5, 1979 (*re* "Sybil," a young woman with sixteen personalities, and "William," a twenty-two-year old man with ten); Oct. 4, 1982 (*re* "Eric"); April 18, 1983 (*re* "Natasha"). For more technical treatments see *Diagnostic and Statistical Manual of Mental Disorders* (3rd edition; American Psychiatric Association) and relevant articles in the journal, *Archives of General Psychiatry*.

25. Also see L. Koenen, "From Baptism to the Gnosis of Manichaeism," *Rediscovery of Gnosticism*, II, pp. 741-743 and 750.

26. "Intellect" or *nous* in Koenen expresses what Henrichs calls "soul" in *HSCP* 77 (1973): 24 (quoted above).

27. The accuracy of one's inference that the Twin is such a projection is guaranteed by Henrichs and Koenen, *ZPE* 5 (1970): 182:

"Die Aufgaben, die in dem gnostischen Perlenlied auf Kleid, Bruder, Gefährte und Brief verteilt sind, übernimmt bei Mani der Gefährte oder Zwilling. Gefährte und brief des Perlenliedes ermöglichen es der Seele, ihre Sendung in dieser Welt zu erfüllen; das Gleiche tut Manis Gefährte. Das Kleid aber ist das himmlische Urbild der Seele, das mit ihr identisch ist und in dem die Seele sich selbst erkennt; genauso ist Manis Zwilling das geistige, vom Körper freie Ich Manis, das in eine konkrete Gestalt projiziert ist. Die vier transzendentalen Projektionen der Seele des Perlenliedes sind bei Mani in der einen Gestalt des Gefährten zusammengefasst. Der Gefährte ist von aussen herantretender Schützer und Mahner, und er ist doch zugleich mit Manis innerem Selbst identisch.

"Soeben wurde der Begriff der Projektion benutzt, um Manis Verhältnis zu seinem Gefährten verständlich zu machen. Uns ist aus der Psychologie bekannt, dass der Mensch dazu neigt, sein eigenes Seelenleben nach aussen in andere Personen und Personengruppen zu projizieren und dann sich selbst im anderen zu betrachten. Manis Denkweise war umgekehrt und lässt sich eher so umschreiben: Seine Lichtseele brachte aus sich die Seele hervor, die in den Körper hinabging, um ihr Erlösungswerk zu vollenden; so kannte sie in ihrem Ursprungswesen im Lichtreich bleiben und als geistige Wesenheit zugleich der in den Leib gefesselten Seele Manis jederzeit nahe sein. Dieses Über-Ich hatte keine Gemeinschaft mit dem Leib und trieb daher das im Leib gefangene Ich zu seiner Aufgabe an und beschützte es var den Gafahren der Welt."

On "The Hymn of the Pearl," which Henrichs and Koenen mention in the initial sentence of the quotation, see my immediately subsequent note.

Concerning the influence which psychology and, especially, Jungian psychology wield on the exegesis of Gnostic and Manichaean texts see Gilles Quispel, "Gnosis and Psychology," in *Rediscovery of Gnosticism*, ed. B. Layton (Leiden: E.J. Brill, 1980), I, pp. 17-31 — pages 22 and 23 are specially noteworthy: "The discovery of the Self is the core of both

Gnosticism and Manicheism. Even before Nag Hammadi this psychological approach was already a necessary supplement to the purely historical or unilaterally existentialistic interpretation of Gnosis which prevailed in other quarters. There is no question that psychology in general is of great help, an auxiliary science, for history in general, which otherwise tends to become arid and pedantic. And more specifically the Jungian approach to Gnosticism, once decried as a soul-shaking spectacle concocted by decadent psychologists and vain students of Judaic mysticism, turned out to be adequate when the *Gospel of Truth* was discovered. For then it became clear to everybody that Gnosis is an experience, inspired by vivid and profound emotions, that in short Gnosis is the mythic expression of Self experience . . .

"So Jungian psychology has already had a considerable impact on Gnostic research. The term Self is used by practically everyone; the insight that Gnosis in the last analysis expresses the union of the conscious Ego and the unconscious Self is commonly accepted; nobody, not even the fiercest existentialist, can deny that Jung is helpful in discerning the real meaning of myth."

Also see Hans-Rudolf Schwyzer, "The Intellect in Plotinus and the Archetypes of C.G. Jung," in *Kephalaion: Studies in Greek Philosophy and Its Continuation Offered to Professor C.J. de Vogel*, ed. J. Mansfeld and L.M. de Rijk (Assen: Van Gorcum, 1975), pp. 214-222; G. Quispel, "Hesse, Jung und die Gnosis," *Gnostic Studies*, II, 241-258.

28. What modern translators call "The Hymn of the Pearl" is entitled "Song of the Apostle Judas Thomas in the Land of the Indians" in its original source, the apocryphal *Acts of the Apostle Thomas*. Extant in both Syriac and Greek versions, the "Hymn" is a poetic composition "which clothes the central part of the Iranian doctrine [of gnosis] in a garment of a fable" — see Hans Jonas, *Gnostic Religion*, p. 112. For another English translation see Robert M. Grant, *Gnosticism: A Source Book of Heretical Writings from The Early Christian Period* (New York: Harper, 1961), pp. 116 sqq. (the poem "reflects late Valentinian doctrine, perhaps that of Bardaisan — A.D. 154-222"); for a German translation see Raimund Kobert, "Das Perlenlied," *Orientalia* 38 (1969): 447-456 — his translation from the Syriac version (as is Jonas's) of the last sentence of the lines excerpted from the poem is: "Doch plötzlich, als ich ihm begegnete, glich mir das Kleid wie mein Spiegelbild. Ich sah und erkannte es ganz in mir ganzen, und auch ich begegnete mir ganz in ihm. Wir waren zwei in der Trennung and wiederum eins durch dieselbe Gestalt" (p. 454).

29. Pertinent information on proper names within Jonas's paragraphs is as follows. Avesta: the canon of Zoroastrian writings as redacted in the Sassanian period. C. Bartholomae: the author of *Altiranisches Worterbuch* (Strassburg, 1904), which is the standard lexicon for Avestan and Old Persian. The fragments found at Turfan in Eastern Turkistän have been most recently edited by W.B. Henning, *Nachricht. Gött. Ges. Wiss.* (Göttingen, 1933), pp. 217 sqq.; for an English translation (from the text

edited in 1904 by F.W. Müller) with commentary see A.V. Williams Jackson, *Researches in Manichaeism With Special Reference to the Turfan Fragments* (New York: Columbia University Press, 1932). On the Mandaeans, a southern Babylonian baptist sect, see H.-Ch. Puech, *Le Manichéisme*, pp. 40-44 and n. 147 (pp. 123-125); H. Jonas, *Gnostic Religion*, ch. 3, which ends with a glossary of Mandaean terms (pp. 97-99); Henrichs and Koenen, *ZPE* 5 (1970): 133-140; A. Henrichs, *HSCP* 83 (1979): 367. On "the Chinese Manichaean translation by Pelliot," see G. Haloun and W.B. Henning, "Compendium," pp. 184-185; Williams Jackson, *Researches in Manichaeism*, "Bibliography," p. xxxvi.

30. Also see *Dictionary of Behavioral Sciences*, ed. B.B. Wolman (New York: Van Nostrand Reinhold, 1973), p. 342, which gives one-half column and seven definitions to "self." As examples of "self" taken less technically see Virginia Wolfe, *To the Lighthouse* (New York: Harcourt Brace and World, Inc., 1927), p. 95: "*She could be herself, by herself.* And that was what now she often felt the need of — to think; well, not even to think. To be silent, to be alone. All the being and the doing, expansive, glittering, vocal, evaporated; *and one shrunk*, with a sense of solemnity, *to being oneself, a wedge-shaped core of darkness*, something invisible to others" (emphasis added). Also, Patrick Hart, "The Contemplative Vision of Thomas Merton," *Notes et Documents de l'Institute International Jacques Maritain* 19 (Avril-Juin, 1982), who quotes and interprets Merton's unpublished manuscript, "The Inner Experience": "Merton laid down a few basic notes on contemplation, which bear quoting: 'the first thing that you have to do before you start thinking about such a thing as contemplation is to try to recover a coordinated and simple whole, and learn to live as a unified human person. This means that you have to bring back together the fragments of your distracted existence so that when you say "I" there is really something present to support the pronoun you have uttered.' Therefore, we must know who we are, from whom we originated, and where we are going. In Merton's words: 'Before we can realize who we really are, we must become conscious of the fact that the person we think we are, here and now, is at best an imposter and a stranger.' The false self, or the empirical ego, as Merton refers to it, is illusory, really a mask for our true identity, our true self, which is the deepest in which we stand naked before God's love and mercy" (p. 6).

31. On individuation, individuality, supposit and subject, see Leo Sweeney, S.J., "Actual Existence and the Individual," in *Authentic Metaphysics in an Age of Unreality* (New York/Bern: Peter Lang, 1988), pp. 172-186 and 189-190; *idem*, "Existentialism Authentic and Unauthentic," *New Scholasticism* 40 (1966): 44-52.

32. The two nouns are interchangeable. Also see above, n. 26.

33. That single chapter is a commentary on Plato, *Timaeus*, 34c-35A.

     The numbers in brackets here and in Texts B and C are added to make references easier in my "Comments."

34. "That part of it" which remains There is its intellect, as will be clear from Texts B and C and passim.

35. That body is not identical with matter solely, see H.J. Blumenthal, *Plotinus's Psychology: His Doctrines of the Embodied Soul* (The Hague: Martinus Nijhoff, 1971), p. 9: "We have already found it necessary to define soul in a special way. Coming to body we find that it is already a complex entity (IV.7.1.8-10), as are even simple bodies in so far as they consist of both matter and form (ibid., 16f; cf. V.9.3.16-20): only pure matter is completely devoid of any of the form which all sensible substances have (II.4.5.3f). Such form comes from the lower powers of the world soul sometimes called *physis* (nature). So when we ask how soul is in the body we must remember that that body already has soul in a certain way (cf. VI.4.15.8ff)."

36. Provided, of course, that a soul-in-body allows the Intellect to do so by a soul's using its intellect to turn away from matter, to contemplate, etc.

37. *Enneads* VI, 4 and 5, are also commentaries on *Parm.*, 142B sqq. See E. Bréhier, "Notice," in *Plotin: Ennéades* (Paris: "Les Belles Lettres," 1954), VI, i, pp. 160 and 165-167.

38. See ibid., pp. 161-163.

39. Obviously, *ekeino* in line 17 refers to the Soul, on which attention had centered in the opening portion of the chapter. See E. Bréhier, ibid., p. 194: "cette âme-là"; V. Cilento, *Plotino Enneadi* (Bari: Laterza, 1949), III, i, p. 265: "quell'Essere."

    In *Plotinus* (London: Allen and Unwin, 1953), p. 125, A.H. Armstrong's translation is "that higher self," which is (in my view) questionable. Also see *idem*, "Form, Individual and Person in Plotinus," *Dionysius* 1 (1977): 51; Plato S. Mamo, "The Notion of the Self in the Writings of Plotinus" (Ph.D. Dissertation; University of Toronto, 1966), p. 161: "that infinite spiritual life"; G.J.P. O'Daly, *Plotinus's Philosophy of the Self* (New York: Barnes and Noble, 1973), p. 25: "'the higher primal,'" within which we existed in the transcendent and thus "our 'real self' is located in a transcendent phase, prior to 'our' existence here on earth."

40. In this lower man body "acquires a trace of soul, not a piece of soul but a kind of warming or enlightenment coming from it" (VI, 4, 15, 14-16; Armstrong translation, *Plotinus*, p. 126). The coming (and, thus, presence) of the higher man to the lower "does not mean that the soul departs from itself and comes to this world but that the bodily nature comes to be in soul and participates in it . . . by giving body something of itself, not by coming to belong to it; and 'departure' [and absence] means that body has no share in it" (VI, 4, 16, 7-17; Armstrong translation, *Plotinus*, pp. 134-135).

41. Departure from Soul is described in VI, 4, 14, 11-12, as a "springing (*arxamenas*) from unity and yet remaining in that from which they sprang; or rather they never did spring from it but were always in this state" (Armstrong translation, *Plotinus*, p. 123).

42.   An "individual" in Plotinus's texts commonly signifies that which is somehow other than or different from something else. That otherness can consist, as here, in a soul's distinguishability or divisibility from other souls and Soul while yet remaining within Soul and associated with its psychic companions There. A further otherness and, hence, individuality arises when a soul "departs from" Soul and is enmeshed in a body (see above, nn. 40 and 41). It is of this second individuality that VI, 5 (23), 12, 16 sqq., speaks (both *re* how one acquires it and how one frees himself from it): "[In ascending back to Intellect] you have come to the All and not stayed in a part of it, and have not said even about yourself, 'I am just so much.' By rejecting the 'so much' you have become all — yet you were all before. But because something else other than the All added itself to you, you became less by the addition, for the addition did not come from real being (you cannot add anything to that) but from that which is not. When you have become an individual by the addition of non-being, you are not all till you reject the non-being. You will increase yourself then by rejecting the rest, and by that rejection the All is with you."

Ἦ ὅτι παντὶ προσῆλθες καὶ οὐκ ἔμεινας ἐν μέρει αὐτοῦ οὐδ' εἶπας οὐδὲ σύ "τοσοῦτος εἰμι." ἀφεὶς δὲ τὸ "τοσοῦτος" γέγονας πᾶς, καίτοι καὶ πρότερον ἦσθα πᾶς ἀλλ' ὅτι καὶ ἄλλο τι προσῆν σοι μετὰ τὸ "πᾶς," ἐλάττων ἐγίνου τῇ προσθήκῃ οὐ γὰρ ἐκ τοῦ παντὸς ἦν ἡ προσθήκη — οὐδὲν γὰρ ἐκείνῳ προσθήσεις — ἀλλὰ τοῦ μὴ ὄντος. Γενόμενος δὲ τις καὶ ἐκ τοῦ μὴ ὄντος ἐστὶν οὐ πᾶς, ἀλλ' ὅταν τὸ μὴ ὂν ἀφῇ. Αὔξεις τοίνυν σεαυτὸν ἀφεὶς τὰ ἄλλα καὶ πάρεστι σοι τὸ πᾶν ἀφέντι.

By liberating oneself from matter, then, one regains his place within Soul and, eventually, within Intellect, where nonetheless he retains his first sort of individuality — his distinguishability or divisibility from Intellect, Soul and other souls. Even this individuality is set aside when a soul ascends beyond Soul and Intellect to become one with the One and thereby achieves well-being (*eudaimonia*) above being. See VI, 9 (9), 11, 4 sqq., discussed below.

On problems which VI, 4 and 5, raise *re* "individual" (especially *re* the Idea of Individual), see H.J. Blumenthal, *Plotinus's Psychology*, pp. 123 sqq.

43.   Blumenthal states (*Plotinus's Psychology*, p. 110), "we" are "a focus of conscious activity that can shift as such activity shifts." He quotes with approval E.R. Dodds's view: "Soul is a continuum extending from the summit of the individual *psychē*, whose activity is perpetual intellection, through the normal empirical self right down to the *eidōlon*, the faint psychic trace in the organism; but the *ego* is a fluctuating spotlight of consciousness" (ibid., n. 25; see references there also to J. Trouillard, P. Hadot and W. Himmerich).

The value of conferring such mobility on "we" is that it allows one to understand how Plotinus can variously state that the "we" is multiple, that it is twofold, that it is found only at the level of reason, that it is found at the level of *nous* (see Blumenthal, ibid., pp. 110-111, for references to the

Enneads). One must conclude, then, that "'we' is not bound to any particular level or to a restricted range," even though it is usually to be found at the level of reason, which is "directed both towards the processing of sense-data, for which it may use the knowledge that it derives from above, and to the consideration of such knowledge in itself. It may thus be regarded as the meeting place of the sensible and intelligible worlds. And this is where we would expect to find Plotinus's man, a being who must live in this world but whose thoughts and aspirations are directed beyond it" (ibid., p. 111).

44. For Mani the hierarchy of reality above Light-Intellect consists (in ascending order) of Jesus the Splendor, the Envoy, the Father of Greatness. In Plotinus's hierarchy the One-Good and Intellect precede Soul.

45. Mani's acceptance of Buddha, Zoroaster and Jesus as prior prophets, as well as his own role as the ultimate prophet and savior, would be abhorrent to Plotinus, for whom each man can save himself and needs no divine intervention since each has an intellect which always remains above and need only be actuated in order that he attain salvation. On Mani's conception of Jesus see M. Boyce, ibid., p. 10; F.C. Burkitt, *The Religion of the Manichees* (Cambridge: University Press, 1925), pp. 37-43.

On Plotinus *vs.* Christianity, see *Enneads*, III, 2 (47), 9, 10-12: "It is not lawful for those who have become wicked to demand others to be their saviours and to sacrifice themselves in answer to their prayers" — for A.H. Armstrong "this looks as if it might be directed against the Christian doctrine of Redemption. If so, it is the only reference which I have detected to orthodox Christianity in the *Enneads*" (*Plotinus*, p. 167, n. 9; also see *idem*, Loeb volume III, pp. 221-222). Also see E. Bréhier, *Plotin: Ennéades*, VI, i, 168.

46. Besides "Against the Gnostics," Porphyry also gives the title, "Against those who say that the maker of the universe is evil and the universe is evil" (see Armstrong, Loeb volume II, p. 220). On who these Gnostics were see ibid., pp. 220-222; E. Bréhier, *Plotini: Ennéades*, "Notice," II, pp. 96-110; Harder et al, *Plotins Schriften* (Hamburg: Felix Meiner, 1964), III *b*, pp. 414-418; H.-Ch. Puech, "Plotin et les Gnostiques" in *Entretiens sur l'Antiquité Classique*, V: *Les Sources de Plotin* (Vandoeuvres-Genève: Fondation Hardt, 1960), pp. 161-190; Francisco Garciá Bazán, *Plotino y la Gnosis* (Buenos Aires: Fundación para la Educación, la Ciencia y la Cultura, 1981), pp. 199-340; Richard T. Wallis, "Soul and Nous in Plotinus, Numenius and Gnosticism" (appearing in this volume), n. 11.

47. See II, 9, 1, 1-19.

48. Would not "we" be here identical with intellect, which is the highest power of a soul and which is not dragged down to body with soul's middle power (#4)? See above, n. 43.

49. But it is dissimilar too: in Text C "we" is identified with intellect (see above, n. 48), in V, 3, 3, with reason, the middle power of soul. See Blumenthal, *Plotinus's Psychology*, p. 110, for a comparison of V, 3, with other texts; Armstrong, *Plotinus*, p. 166, considers "the doctrine of this very

late treatise to represent a rethinking and an attempt to arrive at greater precision about the relationship between soul and *Nous*. Elsewhere Plotinus says without qualification that we at our highest are, and remain eternally, *Nous*."

During the Oklahoma conference and in subsequent correspondence, Denis O'Brien has kindly alerted me to two additional texts: I, 1 (53), 12, 21-39 (especially relevant because of the possible parallel between Heracles's unique status and Mani's) and III, 4-6 (the entire treatise, however, seems no more consistent and clear than is Plato's position on *daimon* set forth in *Phaedo, Republic* and *Timaeus*, upon which Plotinus is commenting).

50.   This dynamism contrasts them with Parmenides, whose monism of Being eliminates all change and movement from reality. See Leo Sweeney, S.J., *Infinity in the Presocratics: A Bibliographical and Philosophical Study* (The Hague: Martinue Nijhoff, 1972), pp. 93-110, especially 107-110.

51.   This direction of their dynamic monism contrasts them with Hegel, in whose monism Absolute Spirit moves from the less to the more perfect: from Categories (Being, Essence, Notion) through Nature to Spirit (Art, Religion, Philosophy).

Hans Jonas, "The Soul in Gnosticism and Plotinus," in *Philosophical Essays From Ancient Creed to Technological Man* (Chicago: University Press, 1974), pp. 325-328, considers what I call "dynamic monism" to be a speculative system which is common to Plotinus and Mani, as well as to Valentinus and Ptolemaeus, the anonymous authors of the *Poimandres* and the *Apocryphon of John*, and Origen. W.R. Schoedel, "Gnostic Monism and the Gospel of Truth," in *The Rediscovery of Gnosticism*, Vol. I: *The School of Valentinus*, ed. B. Layton, pp. 379-390, describes the theology of the Valentinian "Gospel of Truth" as a monism, which however means "that everything arises directly or indirectly from one source" (p. 390). Such a definition does not do justice to monism in Plotinus and Mani, which demands also that all existents consist of the same basic stuff and are not fully distinct from one another.

52.   For helpful studies of Middle Platonism see R.T. Wallis, *Neoplatonism* (New York: Charles Scribner's Sons, 1972), pp. 29-36 (bibliography, p. 187); John Dillon, *The Middle Platonists: A Study of Platonism 80 B.C. to A.D. 220* (London: Duckworth, 1977), bibliography pp. 416-421 (p. 420 *re* Gnosticism and Christian Platonism); *idem*, "Descent of the Soul in Middle Platonic and Gnostic Theory" in *Rediscovery of Gnosticism*, I, ed. B. Layton, pp. 357-364.

53.   To date I am unaware of much literature on the possible philosophical background of Mani. Besides H. Jonas's article already cited in n. 51 above, see the following, which attend at least to the speculative influences (whether philosophical or religious) on Manichaeism: Dmitri Obolensky, *The Bogomils: A Study in Balkan Neo-Manichaeism* (Cambridge: University Press, 1948), ch. I: "The Manichaean Legacy," pp. 1-27 (especially p. 3 *re* dualism in Plato); L.J.R. Ort, "Mani's Conception of Gnosis" in *Le Origini dello Gnosticismo*, ed. Ugo Bianchi (Leiden: E.J.

Brill, 1967), pp. 604-613; H.-Ch. Puech, "The Concept of Redemption in Manichaeism" in *The Mystic Vision: Papers From the Eranos Yearbooks*, ed. Joseph Campbell (Princeton: University Press, 1968), pp. 247-314 (especially pp. 266-288: "The Theoretical Foundations of Redemption: The Cosmological and the Anthropological Myth"); P.W. Van der Horst and J. Mansfeld, *An Alexandrian Platonist Against Dualism: Alexander of Lycopolis's Treatise "Critique of the Doctrines of Manichaeus"* (Leiden: E.J. Brill, 1974); Gilles Quispel, "Mani the Apostle of Jesus Christ," *Gnostic Studies* (Istanbul: Nederlands Historisch-Archaeologisch Institute, 1975), II, 230-237 (mainly re Mani's influence upon St. Augustine).

During the Oklahoma conference Michel Tardieu alerted me to the philosophical influence of Bardaisan upon Mani. On that topic see these studies: Saint Ephraim the Syrian, *St. Ephraim's Prose Refutations of Mani, Marcion and Bardaison*, transcribed by C.W. Mitchell, 2 volumes (London: C.W. Mitchell, 1912 and 1921), Text and Translation Society; F.C. Burkitt, *Religion of the Manichees*, pp. 82-86; H.J.W. Drijvers, *Bardaisan of Edessa* (Assen: Van Gorcum, 1966); *idem*, "Bardaisan of Edessa and the Hermetica. The Aramaic Philosopher and the Philosophy of His Time," *Jaarbericht Ex Oriente Lux* 21 (1969-70): 190-210; *idem*, "Mani und Bardaisan. Ein Beitrag zur Vorgeschichte des Manichäismus" in *Mélanges H.-Ch. Puech*, pp. 459-469; *idem*, *Cults and Beliefs at Edessa* (Leiden: E.J. Brill, 1980) — see "Index" and bibliography, pp. xviii-xix for complete list of Drijvers's works; *idem*, "Bardaisan, die Bardaisaniten und die Ursprünge des Gnostizismus" in *Le Origini dello Gnosticismo*, ed. Ugo Bianchi, pp. 307-314; Ugo Bianchi, "Le Gnosticisme: Concept, Terminologie, Origines, Délimitation," in *Gnosis: Festschrift für Hans Jonas* (Göttingen: Vandenhoeck und Ruprecht, 1978), pp. 48-50; Geo Widengren, "Der Manichäismus," in ibid., pp. 311-313 (re F.C. Burkitt and H.H. Schaeder); Michel Tardieu, *Le Manichéisme* (Paris: Presses Universitaires de France, 1981), chs. I-II.

What of philosophical influences upon Gnosticism itself? Recently Birger A. Pearson, "The Tractate *Marsanes* (*NHC* X) and the Platonic Tradition" in *Gnosis: Festschrift für Hans Jonas*, ed. Barbara Aland, p. 373, sets forth (with Willy Theiler) the "three basic options" on the relationship between Gnosticism and Greek Philosophy as "1) the philosophy of the Empire is disguised Gnosis [held by H. Jonas, C. Elsas]. 2) Gnosis is debased philosophy, oriental mythology overlaid with formal elements derived mainly from Platonism. 3) Imperial philosophy and Gnosis are to be explained out of similar social and spiritual currents of late antiquity." Pearson gives a good resume of Jonas's position with references to his publications (ibid., nn. 5-8): Hans Jonas has argued "that the 'mythological' gnostic systems described by the church fathers and the major philosophical and theological systems of late antiquity, from Philo Judaeus on, express a common 'gnostic' understanding of existence. Particularly important are his observations on later Platonism, especially Plotinus. Jonas poses the question 'whether in the final analysis Gnosis, transformed gnostic myth, provided the innermost impulse' to the philosophy of Plotinus, rather than Plato. He provides a brief but powerful positive answer."

In same volume one finds three other helpful papers: Ugo Bianchi, "Le Gnosticisme: Concept, Terminologie, Origines, Délimitation," pp. 33-64; especially A.H. Armstrong, "Gnosis and Greek Philosophy," pp. 87-124; Hans Martin Schenke, "Die Tendenz der Weisheit zur Gnosis," pp. 351-372.

In addition the following are worthy of note: J. Zandee, *The Terminology of Plotinus and of Some Gnostic Writings, Mainly the Fourth Treatise of the Jung Codex* (Istanbul: Nederlands Historisch-Archaeologisch Institute, 1961), especially pp. 38-41; R.M. Grant, *Gnosticism and Early Christianity* (New York: Columbia University Press, 1966), ch. 5: "From Myth to Philosophy?", pp. 120-150 (see p. 147: "Gnosticism is not a form of philosophy"); several papers in *Le Origini dello Gnosticismo*, ed. U. Bianchi — for example, H. Jonas, "Delimitation of the Gnostic Phenomenon — Typological and Historical," pp. 90-108; E. von Ivánka, "Religion, Philosophie und Gnosis: Grenzfälle und Pseudomorphosen in der Spätantike," pp. 317-322; R. Crahay, "Éléments d'une mythopée gnostique dans le Grèce classique," pp. 323-339; P. Boyancé, "Dieu cosmique et dualisme: les archontes et Platon," pp. 340-358; Gilles Quispel, "Gnostic Man: The Doctrine of Basilides" in *The Mystic Vision*, ed. Joseph Campbell, pp. 210-246 (especially pp. 215-227: "The Frame: Platonist Philosophy"); S.R.C. Lilla, *Clement of Alexandria: A Study in Christian Platonism and Gnosticism* (Oxford: University Press, 1971); H.B. Timothy, *The Early Christian Apologists [Irenaeus, Tertullian, Clement of Alexandria] and Greek Philosophy* (Assen: Van Gorcum, 1973); René Nouailhat, "Remarques méthodologiques à propos de la question de 'L'Hellénisation du Christianisme,'" in *Les syncrétismes dans les religions de l'antiquité*, ed. F. Dunand et P. Lévêque (Leiden: E.J. Brill, 1975, pp. 212-232); C. Elsas, *Neuplatonische und gnostische Weltablehnung in der Schule Plotins* (Berlin: Walter de Gruyter, 1975); Pheme Perkins, *The Gnostic Dialogue: The Early Church and the Crisis of Gnosticism* (New York: Paulist Press, 1980), especially ch. One: "Gnosticism in Its Context," pp. 1-22; Carsten Colpe, "Challenge of Gnostic Thought for Philosophy, Alchemy and Literature" in *Rediscovery of Gnosticism*, ed. B. Layton, I, pp. 32-56 (see pp. 34 sqq. for the four ways in which "the complex subject of 'Gnosis and philosophy' can conventionally be dealt with"); H. Chadwick, "Domestication of Gnosticism," ibid., especially pp. 11-13 re Plato's influence on Valentinus and other Gnostics; G.C. Snead, "The Valentinian Myth of Sophia," *Journal of Theological Studies*, n.s. 20 (1969): 74-104 — see Armstrong, ibid., p. 103, n. 23: "A very well documented and careful article" re Hellenic influence on Valentinus is R. van den Broeck, "The Present State of Gnostic Studies," *Vigiliae Christianae* 37 (1983): 41-71 (a survey of papers in the Proceedings from conferences on Gnosticism at Quebec, Yale and Halle, as well as in *Gnosis: Festschrift für Hans Jonas* and in G. Quispel's *Gnostic Studies*); K. Rudolph, *Gnosis: The Nature and*

History of Gnosticism (New York: Harper and Row, 1983).

54. For example, A. Henrichs, *HSCP* 83 (1979: 340: "Mani's 'twin companion' (*syzygos*) is the personification of a typically Gnostic concept, the transcendent projection of one's soul" and is his celestial alter ego or self.

55. *The Notion of the Self in the Writings of Plotinus* (University of Toronto, 1966), initial "Summary," p. 1.

56. H.J. Blumenthal, after affirming that "a person's identity . . . is a concept for which Greek had no word" (*Plotinus's Psychology*, p. 109), adds that "the lack of suitable terms need not mean that the concept did not exist" (ibid., n. 21). But when reviewing O'Daly's book (*Gnomon* 50 [1978]: 407-410) he observed that Plotinus's using such words as *autos* or *hēmeis* or *anthrōpos* does "not imply that he set himself the philosophical task of formally defining the 'self.' Even less does it mean that when he uses these terms he must be taken to be talking about the 'self' as such . . . [O'Daly] is perhaps too prone to see references to the self when Plotinus is using words in their normal sense." Also see my review in *Review of Metaphysics* 30 (1977): 533-534.

57. I have inserted bracketed capital letters in my paraphrase/translation to facilitate references.

58. In the quotation the first number in parentheses indicates that I, 6, is chronologically Plotinus's first treatise. Subsequent numbers, with the exception of those which are designated as references to its chapters, refer to lines in those chapters.

59. On *epibolē* as "intuition" and its ancestry in Epicurus, see John Rist, *Plotinus: The Road to Reality* (Cambridge: University Press, 1967), pp. 47-52; G. O'Daly, *Plotinus's Philosophy of Self*, pp. 93-94.

60. The monistic character of Plotinus's position flows from the fact that to be real is to be one. See L. Sweeney, "Basic Principles of Plotinus's Philosophy," *Gregorianum* 42 (1961): 506-516 (especially n. 13): "Are Plotinus and Albertus Magnus Neoplatonists," in *Graceful Reason*, ed. L. Gerson, pp. 182-185.

61. On what "metaphysics" means in Plotinus see ibid., p. 181, n. 13.

62. The same approach is also suitable for reading Manichaean documents, *mutatis mutandis*, as we have indicated above, "The 'Twin' and 'Self,'" *ad finem*.

63. The notions which Plotinian literature provides are less flamboyant and chronologically determined than those furnished in secondary literature on Gnosticism and Manichaeism (see above, n. 27) and, hence, may prove less anachronistic. For example, G. O'Daly, *Plotinus's Philosophy of the Self*, p. 90: self is "the identity of a human subject at the several levels of existence possible to man"; P.S. Mamo, *The Notion of the Self*, initial "Summary," p. 1: "self is defined "not as an individual substance but as striving, attention, direction of consciousness" and p. 190: the ego "is a focus capable of infinite extension"; A.H. Armstrong, "Form, Individual and Person in Plotinus," p. 65: "Person [is] that in us which is capable of free decision, true thought, and the passionate love of God [which for Plotinus

is] so open that its only bounds are the universe and God"; E.R. Dodds (quoted with approval by H.J. Blumenthal, *Plotinus's Psychology*, p. 110, n. 25):   in contrast to soul "the ego is a fluctuating spotlight of consciousness." Or one might apply to Plotinus the description which M. Gorman gathered from her historical survey (*New Catholic Encyclopedia*, XIII, 60A): self suggests "all those aspects of man thought to be left out by the terms soul, mind, person and nature and to designate the unifying, purposeful, growing and interacting aspect of man's activities."

Gnosticism and Platonism:
The Platonizing Sethian Texts from Nag Hammadi in their Relation to Later Platonic Literature

John D. Turner

The attentive reader of the Sethian treatises contained in the Coptic Gnostic Library from Nag Hammadi is no doubt struck by the rather large fund of philosophical and technical terminology that they contain, particularly in their descriptions of the divine world and in certain cases their portrayal of the means necessary to become assimilated to that world. The intention of this paper is to examine this phenomenon and try to account for certain of its aspects as owing to an interaction between gnostic Sethians and a presumably well-established fund of metaphysical speculation deriving from Neopythagorean and Middle Platonic circles of the first three centuries of our era.

Current scholarship considers the following literature to be representative of Sethian Gnostic doctrine: The "Barbeloite" report of Irenaeus (*Haer.* I.29); the reports on the Sethians (and Archontics and related groups) by Epiphanius (*Haer.* 26 and 39-40), pseudo-Tertullian (*Haer.* 2) and Filastrius (*Haer.* 3); the untitled text from the Bruce Codex (Bruce, *Untitled*); and the following treatises from the Nag Hammadi and Berlin Gnostic codices: four versions of the *Apocryphon of John* (*Ap. John*: short versions, BG 8502, *2* and *NHC* III, *1*; long versions *NHC* II, *1* and III, *1*); *The Hypostasis of the Archons* (*Hyp. Arch.*: *NHC* II, *4*); *The Gospel of the Egyptians* (*Gos. Egypt.*: *NHC* III, *2* and IV, *2*); *The Apocalypse of Adam* (*Apoc. Adam*: *NHC* V, *5*); *The*

Three Steles of Seth (*Steles Seth*: NHC VII, 5); *Zostrianos* (*Zost.*: NHC VIII, 1); *Melchizedek* (*Melch.*:   NHC IX, 1); *The Thought of Norea* (*Norea*:   IX, 2); *Marsanes* (NHC X, 1); *Allogenes* (NHC XI, 3) and *Trimorphic Protennoia* (*Trim. Prot.*: NHC XIII, 1).

The formal genre of these materials varies. The bulk of them are apocalypses. *Apoc. Adam* is a deathbed testament of Adam to his son Seth, the spiritual progenitor of the historical Sethians, in which he reveals the content of a dream vision concerning the fortunes of Eve and himself, his son Seth and Seth's offspring in the contest between the evil creator Saklas and the beings of the higher world who will rescue the seed of Seth, especially through the final visitation of the "Illuminator." *Melch.* likewise contains revelations imparted to the biblical high priest Melchizedek by the angel Gamaliel during a visionary experience revealing future events including his own ultimate assimilation with the suffering, dying and rising Savior Jesus Christ.

In contrast to these two treatises in which knowledge concerning the future course of history is communicated from the higher realm to the lower by an angelic intermediary, we also find three apocalypses which relate the singular experience of a Gnostic visionary who himself achieves an ecstatic ascent through the various levels of the divine world and becomes divine. Thus *Allogenes*, *Zost.* and *Marsanes* each feature a visionary figure, respectively Allogenes or Zostrianos or Marsanes, each of whom probably is to be understood as a manifestation of the Sethian Gnostic savior Seth. Each figure undergoes a visionary ascent involving a vision of the divine world and its various personages, hypostases and levels of being, followed by a subsequent descent and transmission of this knowledge in written form for those who in the future would achieve a similar ascent.

One also finds two plainly didactic treatises, both apparently having undergone secondary Christian Sethian redaction: *Hyp. Arch.* contains an esoteric mythological interpretation of Genesis 1-6 in terms of the struggle between the spiritual rulers of this world and the exalted powers of the supreme deity over the fate of the divine image incarnated in Adam and his descendants, and concludes with a revelation discourse between Eve's daughter Norea and the great angel Eleleth concerning the origin and end of these ruling Archons. *Ap. John* is cast as a dialogue between John, son of Zebedee, and the risen Jesus, who reveals the unknowable deity, the divine world which sprang from him, the fall of the divine wisdom (Sophia) resulting in the birth of the world creator and his making an earthly copy of the divine Adam, and concludes with the subsequent history of the attempts of various representatives of the divine world to awaken the divine spirit in Adam, Seth and Seth's seed which will culminate in ultimate salvation.

While these two treatises are primarily concerned with a mythological theogony, cosmology, anthropogony and a history of salvation governed by the intervention of various divine saviors, two other treatises show themselves to be aetiologies of the two principal Sethian cultic rites, baptism and visionary ascension. *Gos. Egypt.* explains the origin of Sethian baptism by means of a mythological theogony, cosmogony and history of salvation similar to that of *Ap. John*, but which is used to explain the origin and function of the figures who are invoked during the course of the baptismal ritual which has been conferred by Seth appearing in the form of Jesus. Although *Gos. Egypt.* has undergone Christian redaction, this is not the case with *Steles Seth*, a non-Christian aetiology of the Sethian rite of ecstatic visionary ascent into the divine world. Here Seth is represented as originating and transmitting for his posterity a set of three doxological prayers, each of which is to be applied to a separate stage of the ecstatic ascent through the three highest levels of the divine world.

Another treatise, *Trim. Prot.*, takes the form of an aretalogy in which the divine First Thought, speaking in the first person, recites her attributes and deeds in three separate compositions relating respectively to her establishing heavenly dwellings for her fallen spirit trapped in mankind, her destruction of the power of the hostile spiritual rulers, and her final saving descent in the guise of Christ.

Finally, the short piece *Norea* is an ode to Norea, wife-sister of Seth, conceived as a manifestation of the fallen divine wisdom (Sophia) who will be restored along with her progeny into the divine world by the very aeons from which she once departed.

A major bifurcation arises among this group of treatises precisely in view of their use of various triadic schemes and structures. One group of treatises considers salvation to be conveyed by means of a horizontal, temporally ordered history of divine salvific visitations by successive descents of separate figures or repeated descents of the same figure in different modalities. Thus in *Apoc. Adam* and *Gos. Egypt.* there is a tripartitioning of history from the creation onwards in terms of the biblical demiurge's attack on the Sethians, ancient through contemporary, by (1) the flood, whereupon they are rescued by certain angels, and (2) through the rain of fire and brimstone on the holy dwellings of the Sethians at Sodom and Gomorrah, whereupon they are rescued by the servants of the Four Lights (who preside over the heavenly aeons where Adam, Seth and his primal seed dwell); these acts will be followed by (3) a third and future act of salvation when the

Illuminator will rescue their souls from death. While the final savior is an unidentified "Illuminator" in *Apoc. Adam*, in *Gos. Egypt.* the third saving descent will be undertaken by Seth himself in the guise of Jesus.

In *Trim. Prot.* this scheme is worked out in terms of three successive descents of the divine First Thought, Protennoia or Barbelo. First, as Father, she is the divine but as yet inarticulate Voice of the First Thought of the high deity (the Invisible Spirit) who creates heavenly dwellings for her fallen members and descends to loosen their bondage to the world and its powers. Second, as Mother, she is the articulate Speech of the Thought who overthrows the old aeon ruled by the evil powers and announces the dawn of the new age of salvation. Third, as the Son, she is the Word (*logos*) who adopts the guise of successively lower spiritual powers, descends to and enters the "tents" of her members, puts on Jesus, rescuing him from the accursed Cross, and leads her members back into the light by means of the celestial baptismal ascent ritual called the Five Seals.

The horizontal scheme of three descents is also present in (and probably derived from) the three-stanza hymnic conclusion to the longer version of *Ap. John* (*NHC* II, *1*: 30, 11 - 31, 25), which similarly narrates in the first person three saving descents of the divine "Pronoia" culminating in the communication of the Five Seals. It should also be noted that the main body of all four versions of *Ap. John* likewise narrates three saving missions inaugurated by Barbelo, the merciful Mother-Father. First, she sends her divine son Autogenes (a celestial Adam or Seth figure) with his Four Lights to cause the ignorant demiurge to blow the spiritual power stolen from his mother Sophia into the face of the freshly made but still inert Adam, unwittingly making him luminous. Second, she descends as the Epinoia of Light who hides in Adam, is transferred to Eve by means of Adam's rib, and initially enlightens him; after producing Cain and Abel by means of the demiurge, she bears Seth by her now spiritual husband Adam and elevates Seth and his seed for whom the now repentant Sophia has created a heavenly dwelling, and then aids Noah in escaping the flood. Third and finally, the blessed Mother-Father sends the final savior, who in the present versions of *Ap. John* is the Christ who communicates the entire saving history to John as a saving revelation or Gnosis.

On the other hand, in the treatises *Allogenes, Steles Seth, Zost.* and *Marsanes*, one finds a more vertically oriented, non-temporal/historical scheme in which salvation is not brought from above to below by divine visitations, but rather occurs through a graded series of visionary ascents by the Gnostic himself. Here one finds an exemplary visionary utilizing a self-performable technique of successive stages of mental detachment from the world of multiplicity, and a corresponding assimilation of the self to the ever more refined levels of being to which one's contemplation ascends, until one achieves the absolute unitary stasis of self-unification, mental abstraction and utter solitariness characteristic of deification. While not entirely clear in *Zost.* and *Marsanes* owing to their fragmentary condition, according to *Allogenes* and *Steles Seth* this ascent occurs in three stages: through the levels of the Aeon of Barbelo, through the levels of the Triple Power of the Invisible Spirit, and culminates in a "primary revelation" or "command" of the Unknowable One.

For the purposes of this paper, it is this latter group of four treatises, which I shall call "the Allogenes group," that shall be the focus of attention in this analysis of the relation between Gnostic Sethianism and the Platonism contemporary with it. These treatises in particular display a strong rapprochement with contemporary Platonic metaphysics in their transcendental ontology and in their technique of contemplative ascent to the high deity, not to mention their use of specific philosophical terminology such as "being," "non-being," "truly existing," "identity," "difference," "something," "quality," "quantity," "time," "eternity," "intellect," "individuals," "universals," "parts," "wholes," "existence," "vitality," "mentality," "life," and many more. These texts are further distinguished by the apparent absence of any Christian influence as well as the lack of prominent Sethian themes, such as the Apocalyptic schematization of history according to periodic descents of a revealer or redeemer figure. They exhibit a greatly attenuated interest in or even total absence of a narrative of the cosmogony of this world including the downward declination of Sophia and the origin and activity of her offspring the demiurge. So also they lack the Sethian speculation on the creation of mankind and his primeval history drawn from traditional Sethian exegesis of the Old Testament, especially Genesis 1-6. Briefly put, in these texts, Sethianism has become a form of mythological Platonism.

In order to put the ensuing analysis of this "Allogenes group" of texts into perspective, I offer the following summary sketch of the history of the Sethian movement as reflected in their literature, with specific reference to the interaction between Sethianism and Christianity.[1] It seems that Sethianism interacted with Christianity in five phases: (1) The Sethians likely originated as one of a number of Palestinian or Syrian baptismal sects in the first centuries BCE and CE; they considered themselves the historical progeny of Seth, their spiritual ancestor, by whom (together with Adam) the had been primordially enlightened, but from whom they expected yet a final saving visitation in the form of the conferral of a new form of spiritual baptism called the Five Seals. (2) In the later first century, Sethianism gradually became Christianized through an emerging identification between the pre-existent Christ and Seth (or Adam) that resulted from increasing contact with Christian groups. (3) Toward the end of the second century, Sethianism gradually became estranged from a Christianity increasingly on the road to a polemical orthodoxy which rejected the rather docetic Sethian interpretation of Christ. (4) In the third century Sethianism is rejected by the Great Church, but in the meantime has become strongly attracted by the individualistic contemplative practices of second and third century Platonism, a shift that entailed a gradual loss of interest in the Sethians' primal origins and sacred history and a corresponding attenuation of their awareness of group or communal identity (i.e. a tendency toward "rootlessness"). (5) In the late third century, Sethianism also became estranged from orthodox Neoplatonism under the impetus of attacks and refutations from the circle of Plotinus and other Neoplatonists which were just as effective as those of the Christian heresiologists. At this time, whatever Sethianism was left became increasingly fragmented into various derivative and other sectarian Gnostic groups such as the Archontics, Audians, Borborites, Phibionites and others, some of which survived into the Middle Ages.

The designation "Allogenes group" for the strongly Platonizing Sethian treatises is meant to signal the originality of the doctrine of the divine world and of the visionary ascent spelled out in *Allogenes*. By comparison, it seems to me that the other members of this group, *Steles Seth*, *Zost*. and *Marsanes*, are dependent upon *Allogenes* rather than the other way around. *Steles Seth*, as previously mentioned, seems to be an aetiology of a previously existing rite of cultic ascension oriented toward a community *praxis*. *Zost*. clearly tries to interpret the visionary ascent in terms of the older tradition of Sethian baptism by marking out each stage of the ascent as a certain baptism or sealing. *Marsanes* does likewise, almost as an aside in the first few pages of that document. It is only in *Allogenes* that we see an author at work trying to make sense out of the collection of traditional Sethian divine beings by means of Platonic metaphysical categories and structures without any particular interest in trying to legitimate these speculations in terms of cultic tradition; the only legitimation invoked as that he received his doctrine through traditional Sethian revealers (Youel and the Luminaries of the Aeon of Barbelo), but even this is subordinate to his own vision of these realities.

We now pass on to a more detailed examination of the doctrine of *Allogenes* as being generally representative of the group as a whole. The cosmology of *Allogenes* presents itself as tripartite in structure. There is a highest unbegotten level, apparently called *pantelios*, "all perfect," which is headed by the Unknowable One or Invisible Spirit and its Triple Power; a median self-begotten level, apparently called *telios*, "perfect," which is the Aeon of Barbelo; and a lowest begotten level, referred to once as Nature (*physis*). These levels seem to correspond to the levels of Plotinus's three hypostases, the One, the Intellect and the Soul; his lowest, Matter, does not seem to figure in *Allogenes*.

The Unknowable One (called the Unknowable God in 61, 16) is, like the One of Plotinus, to be regarded as beyond being. It is non-being existence (*hyparxis*, 62, 23), silent and still (62, 25-26), not an existing thing (63, 9-18), and absolutely unknowable (63, 13; 63, 29-32; 64, 4-14). It transcends all its positive attributes and properties which are in turn unknowable: blessedness, perfection and divinity or stillness (62, 28-36; 63, 33 - 64, 4), since it is better than those that are better (63, 19). It exists, <lives> and knows without Mind, Life or Existence (or non-existence, for that matter: 61, 32-39; 62, 17-20). Since it shares neither time nor eternity (*aiōn*, 63, 21-23; cf. 65, 21-24), it is perhaps to be regarded as pre-eternal. Its major positive name seems to be the Invisible Spirit, although this term is sometimes used in such a way that one might regard it as a syzygy of the Unknowable One, or even as a cognomen of its potency, the Triple Power.

Certainly the most intriguing feature of *Allogenes*'s metaphysics, and perhaps the crucial feature by which it can be placed at a definite point in the Platonic metaphysical tradition, is the doctrine of the Triple Power. This being is mentioned sometimes separately from (XI, *3*: 45, 13-30; 52, 30-33; 53, 30; 55, 21; 61, 1-22; regularly in *Marsanes*) and sometimes in conjunction with the Invisible Spirit (XI, *3*: 47, 8-9; 51, 8-9; 58, 25; 66, 33-34; cf. *Zost.* VIII, *1*: 20, 15-18; 24, 12-13; 97, 2-3; 128, 20-21) as "the Triple-powered Invisible Spirit" or "the invisible spiritual Triple Power." By a static self-extension, the Invisible Spirit through its Triple Power becomes the Aeon of Barbelo (XI, *3*: 45, 21-30; cf. *Zost.* VIII, *1*: 76, 7-19; 78, 10 - 81, 20; *Steles Seth* VII, *5*: 121, 20 - 122, 18; *Marsanes* X, *1*: 8, 18 - 9, 28). Furthermore, the Triple Power is said to be the traverser of the boundlessness of the Invisible Spirit which turns the Triple Power back on itself in order to know what is within the Invisible Spirit and how it exists, a notion very close to the Neoplatonic doctrine of emanation in which a product proceeds from its source and becomes hypostatized in the act of contemplative reversion upon its source. In this case, the Triple Power, initially unbounded, turns back upon its source in an act of objectivizing self-knowledge, becoming bounded and taking on form and definition as Barbelo, the

self-knowledge or First Thought of the Invisible Spirit (XI, *3*: 49, 8-21).
Virtually the same notions are found in *Steles Seth* (VII, *5*: 121, 20 -
122, 19), *Zost.* (VIII, *1*: 66, top - 84, 22), and *Marsanes* (X, *1*: 7, 1 - 9,
29).

The Triple Power is also identified with the triad Existence
(*hyparxis*) or Being (*ousia* or *petshoop=to on*), Life (*ōnh=zōē*) or
Vitality (*mntōnh=zōotēs*), and Mentality (*mnteime=noētēs*, a neologism)
which the Unknowable One, although it exists, lives and thinks, does not
itself possess (49, 26-38; 61, 32-39; 62, 17-20). A similar phenomenon
is found in Plotinus, derived from his exegesis of Plato, *Sophist* 248C-E
to the effect that true being must also have life and intelligence:[2]

> Life, not the life of the One, but a trace of it, looking toward the One
> was boundless, but once having looked was bounded (without bounding its
> source). Life looks toward the One and, determined by it, takes on
> boundary, limit and form . . . it must then have been determined as (the life
> of) a Unity including multiplicity. Each element of multiplicity is
> determined multiplicity because of Life, but is also a Unity because of limit
> . . . so Intellect is bounded Life (*Ennead* VI.7.17, 13-26).

On the whole, Plotinus tends to conceive Being, Life and Mind as
aspects of his second hypostasis, Intellect, owing to his increasing
aversion to the multiplication of the transcendental hypostases beyond
three. He regards the One as entirely transcendent to Intellect; there
is no being that exists between them as mediator, nor may one
distinguish between a higher intellect in repose and a lower one in
motion, or a One in act and another One in potency (*Ennead* II.9.1),
nor may one distinguish between an intellect at rest, another in
contemplation and yet another that reflects or plans (*Ennead* II.9.6), as
did Numenius in his *Peri t'Agathou* (frgg. 11-23 des Places). Since the
Triple Power of *Allogenes* seems to mediate between the Unknowable
One and the next lower hypostasis, the Aeon of Barbelo, it seems to
function either as a One in potency or perhaps as a higher form of
Intellect (i.e. of Barbelo), it may be that, since *Allogenes* was likely read
in his circle (Porphyry, *Vita Plot.* 16), it was this doctrine of *Allogenes*
and not just that of Numenius which provoked Plotinus's criticism in
Ennead II.9 and caused him to place the Being-Life-Mind triad in the
Intellect rather than conjoining it with the One as the link between
these two.

There was certainly precedent in Neopythagorean arithmological
speculation for regarding a triad to be conjoined with or reside latently
within the One or the Monad. Theon of Smyrna, a Neopythagorean

Platonist of the early second century, wrote: ἔστιν πρῶτον ἡ μονάς, λεγομένη τρίγωνον οὐ κατ᾽ ἐντελέχειαν, ὡς προειρήκαμεν, ἀλλὰ κατὰ δύναμιν. ἐπεὶ γὰρ αὕτη οἷον σπέρμα πάντων ἐστὶν ἀριθμῶν, ἔχει ἐν αὑτῇ καὶ τριγωνοειδῆ δύναμιν (*Expositio* 37, 15-18 Hiller). So also Theon's contemporary, Nicomachus of Gerasa: ἵνα καὶ τρίγωνος δυνάμει φαίνηται ἡ μονάς, ἐνεργείᾳ δὲ πρῶτος ὁ γ᾽ (*Eisagoge* II.8 p. 88, 9-10 Hoche; cf. <Iamblichus>, *Theol. Arith.* 16, 4-6 de Falco). Such speculation may have influenced both Plotinus and the author of *Allogenes*.

The nomenclature of the Being-Life-Mind triad is held to derive from late Platonic exegesis of Plato (*Sophist* 248C-E and *Timaeus* 39E) and perhaps of Aristotle (*Metaphys.* XII.7, 1072b, 27-31), all passages dealing with the relation between the living divine intellect and true being. However, a somewhat similar nomenclature for a transcendent triad is found in the first half of the first century in Irenaeus's report on the "Barbeloite" (i.e. Sethian) system in *Haer.* I.29 and in *Ap. John* (BG 8502, *2*; 28, 5 - 29, 8): Barbelo, as the self-realization of the Thought of the Invisible Spirit, asks it to grant her Prognosis (conceptually close to intellect or intellection), Aphtharsia (characteristic of stable being as opposed to perishable becoming), and Aiōnia Zōē. This could be a more personified precursor of the Being-Life-Mind triad of *Allogenes*, although it is produced at a lower ontological level (that of Barbelo rather than that of the Invisible Spirit) equivalent to the level of Mind (i.e. where Plotinus locates this triad). Since *Allogenes* probably derives a part of its negative theology from *Ap. John* (XI, *3*: 62, 28 - 63, 23 = BG 8502, *2*: 23, 3 - 26, 13 = II, *1*: 3, 18-30), it indeed may have been influenced by the triad Prognosis, Aphtharsia, and Aiōnia Zōē as well as by speculation based upon the above-mentioned Platonic passages. Guided by the sort of contemporary Neopythagorean arithmological speculation cited above, the author of *Allogenes* could easily have arrived at the Being-Life-Mind nomenclature which is applied to the Triple Power.

To be sure, in *Allogenes* the nomenclature for the triad varies. In 49, 26-38 one finds Being (variously *pē ete pai pe*, *petshoop* and *ousia*) Life (*ōnh*) as well as Vitality (*mntōnh* perhaps translating *zōotēs*), and Mentality (variously *mntōnh* and the neologism *noētēs*). No particular hierarchical order of these terms is specified in this passage, since each single term includes the other two in cyclical permutation. But in the section 58, 26 - 61, 22 relating Allogenes's ascent through the levels of the Triple Power, one finds the hierarchical order Existence (*hyparxis*), Vitality and Blessedness (highest to lowest), while in 61, 32-39 (also 62,

19-20) one finds the non-hierarchical order Existence (and nonexistence!), Life and Mind. The variation between the Coptic noun *ōnh* and the abstract *mntōnh* (corresponding respectively to *zōē* and *zōotēs*) initially seems to be without significance, although when one compares it with the variation between *nous* and *noētēs* (probably for *nootēs*), one gets the impression that abstracts seem to be preferred, perhaps in order to avoid the implication that Life or Vitality or Mentality are to be taken as substantial hypostases. Indeed, Proclus (*In Parm*. 1106, 1 - 1108, 19 Cousin) mentions a technique of paronymy, in which abstracts in --*otēs* precede their respective substantives, by which one may illustrate that acts precede substances; an example would be this series of terms from most abstract to most substantial: *noēma*, *noein*, *nootēs*, and *nous*. The variation between the terms Mentality and Blessedness is also significant; the term Blessedness figures in the triad Blessedness, Perfection and Divinity (62, 28-36; 63, 33-37; cf. 55, 26-28; the source of this triad is *Ap. John* BG 8502, 2: 24, 9-12); in *Allogenes* it is an attribute of the highest level of the Aeon of Barbelo (Kalyptos, 55, 26-28).

There are two witnesses for the correspondence between Blessedness and Mentality. The latest is Victorinus, *Adv. Arium* I.52, 3-5 Henri-Hadot: *Deus patentia est instarum trium potentiarum, existentiae, vitae, beatitudinis, hoc est eius quod est esse, quod vivere, quod intellegere.* The earlier is *Zost.*, VIII, *1*: 15, 3-12:

> [These are the] perfect waters: the [water] of Life, which is that of Vitality, in which you have now been [baptized] in Autogenes; the [water] of Blessedness, which is [that of] Mentality, in which you shall be baptized in Protophanes; and the water of Existence, which is that of Divinity, which belongs to Kalyptos.

The passage is corrupt: "water of Life" has been substituted for a probable "water of goodness" under the influence of the former term at home in the Sethian baptismal rite (quite in line with the intention of the author of *Zost.*), and the terms "Existence" and "Divinity" have been reversed (*lege* "the water of Divinity, which is that of Existence, into which you shall be baptized by Kalyptos"). But the association of Blessedness with Mentality is clear.

In *Allogenes* the variation between the terms Being (*pē ete pai pe*, *petshoop*, *ousia*, possibly all for *to on*) and Existence (*hyparxis*) is highly significant, since while Plotinus used *to on* for the first member of the triad, Porphyry apparently used the term *hyparxis*. P. Hadot[3] thinks that Porphyry was the first to adopt this term for the triad, and that he may have discovered it in the *Chaldaean Oracles*, where it apparently designated the high deity, the Father (cf. Damascius, *Dub. et sol.* 61, 1.131, 16-17 Ruelle ἡ μὲν πρώτη ἀρχὴ κατὰ τὴν ὕπαρξιν θεωρεῖται, ὡς ἐν τοῖς λόγοις and 221, 4.101, 25-27 Ruelle: ὡς Χαλδαϊκῶς εἰπεῖν, ὁ μὲν νοῦς κατὰ τὴν ἐνέργειαν ἵσταται μᾶλλον, ἡ δὲ ζωή κατὰ τὴν δύναμιν, ἡ δὲ οὐσία κατὰ τὴν τοῦ πατρὸς ὕπαρξιν).

In Neoplatonism, the One is generally beyond being; being characterizes the second hypostasis Intellect. Although Plotinus radically separated these hypostases, most Neoplatonists after him (save possibly Iamblichus) did not, wishing instead to emphasize the continuity rather than the discontinuity of the chain of being. This tendency is nicely demonstrated in the contemporary exegesis of Plato's *Parmenides* in which the One of the first hypothesis (137D-142A) was identified with the One, and the One-who-is of the second hypothesis (142B-143C) was identified with Intellect, as in this citation from the anonymous *Parmenides* commentary published by Kroll:[4]

> The One beyond essence and being is neither being nor essence nor act, but rather acts and is itself pure act, such that it is itself being (*einai*) before being (*to on*). By participating this being (the *einai* of the One), the One (*scil.* "who is," i.e. the second One) possesses another being declined from it (the *einai* of the supreme One), which is to participate being (*to on*). Thus being (*einai*) is double: the first preexists (*proüparchei*) being (*to on*); the second is derived from the transcendent One who is absolute being (*einai*) and as it were the idea of being (*to on*).

One ought to compare with this *Allogenes* 61, 32-39: "Now it (the Unknowable One) is something insofar as it exists in that it either exists and will become or <lives> or knows, although it <acts> without Mind or Life or Existence (*hyparxis*) or nonexistence incomprehensibly."

In his article of 1961 and book of 1968, Hadot argues forcefully for ascribing the anonymous *Parmenides* commentary to Porphyry. In this work, the doubleness of being is meant to show how the supreme One can be both continuous and discontinuous with the Intellect below it. The One is not simply beyond being (*to on*), but has a higher form of purely active being (*einai* rather than *to on*) in which the Intellect merely participates. So also, by the term *hyparxis*, *Allogenes* likewise wished to attribute a purely active being to the Unknowable One.

Hadot argues further that Porphyry conceived the Intellect in two aspects: a first in which Intellect is still identical with its source the One, and, after its generation from the One, a second in which it has become Intellect itself. In this self-generation, *hyparxis* is the leading term in a three stage process. As *Anon. Taurensis* = <Porphyry>, *In. Parm.* XIV, 10-26 puts it:

> With respect to [existence (*hyparxis*) alone] it (the potential Intellect still identical with the One) is one and simple . . . with respect to existence (*hyparxis*), life (*zōē*) and thought (*noēsis*) it is neither one nor simple. With respect to existence, thinking is also being thought. But when Intellect [abandons] existence for thinking so as to be elevated to the rank of an intelligible in order to see itself (as an intelligible; cf. *Allogenes* 49, 6-14), thinking is life. Therefore thinking is boundless with respect to life. And all are activities (*energeiai*) such that with respect to existence, activity would be static; with respect to thinking, activity would be directed to itself; and with respect to life, activity would be turning away from existence.

Now it is quite probable that Porphyry made *hyparxis* (rather than *to on* as did Plotinus) the leading term of this triad. In the works cited above, Hadot argues that this version of the triad originated with Porphyry even though it occurs in none of his extant works nor is explicitly attributed to him by ancient authors. But Hadot has interpreted certain statements of Damascius such as those cited above and statements of Porphyry himself in such a way as to show that Porphyry regarded the highest deity to be simultaneously continuous and discontinuous with the Intellect below by means of this triad. Partly on the grounds that such a doctrine appears in the anonymous *Parmenides* commentary cited above, Hadot assigns the commentary to Porphyry. Hadot's attribution to Porphyry of the triad with *hyparxis* as its leading term rests heavily on his claim that Porphyry is the author of the commentary. Hadot also invokes the working hypotheses of W. Theiler:[5] every non-Plotinian Neoplatonic doctrine found both in Augustine and a later Neoplatonist derives from Porphyry. Augustine (*De civ. Dei* X.23) reports that Porphyry interposed a *medium* between the supreme deity (*pater*) and the Intellect (*filius*), which Hadot identifies with the modality of the triad in which life predominates. The "later Neoplatonists" would be Proclus, Damascius and especially Victorinus, whose metaphysics is strikingly close to that of the anonymous *Parmenides* commentary (and to that of *Allogenes* for that matter). Therefore the commentary is Porphyrian.

If this is Porphyry's doctrine, one can see that it differs from Plotinus's triad not only in the substitution of the term *hyparxis* for *to on*, but also in distinguishing two modalities or phases of the Intellect: First, as *hyparxis* it is potential intellect still identical with its idea, the *einai* of the One. Second, as *noēsis* it is actual Intellect insofar as it is identical with the substantial exemplification (the *to on* of Intellect) of its idea, the One. Therefore the transitional stage between these two phases in effect constitutes a median modality (Augustine's *medium patris et filii*) in which Intellect is yet undefined, "boundless" thinking as it were (cf. "the traverser of the boundlessness of the Invisible Spirit," in *Allogenes* 49, 8-10), or Intellect *qua* Life.

Correspondingly in *Allogenes*, the Triple Power is continuous with the Invisible Spirit or Unknowable One as *hyparxis*, and discontinues with it as Mentality (but now identical with the Aeon of Barbelo). But as Vitality, the Triple Power can be regarded as discontinuous with both, which is why *Allogenes* tends to represent the Triple Power as an independent hypostasis, or sometimes names it now in conjunction with the Invisible Spirit and now in conjunction with Barbelo (as in 64, 34-36). Thus the ontological status of the Triple Power is very close to that of the Life modality of the triad in Hadot's exposition of Porphyry's metaphysics. In fact, the Triple Power is explicitly identified with "Eternal Life" in *Allogenes* (66, 32-36). Yet, as 49, 28-36 makes clear, the Triple Power even *qua* Vitality still has Being (That-which-is) and Knowledge; the same is made clear in this striking parallel citation from Proclus, *Elem. theol.* 103, 92, 13-16 Dodds:

Proclus	Allogenes 49, 28-36
For in Being (*to on*) there is Life and Intellect, and in Life there is Being (*einai*) and Intellection (*noein*), and in Intellect there is Being (*einai*) and Living (*zēn*).	For then That-which-is constantly possesses its Vitality and Mentality, and Vitality possesses Being (*ousia*) and Mentality; Mentality (*noētēs*) possesses Life and That-which-is.

Each term in the series predominates and includes the other two in cyclical permutation. Hadot illustrates this phenomenon with respect to <Porphyry's> triad *hyparxis*, *zōē* (or *dynamis*) and *noēsis* by means of the following diagram:

First triad = Father	<u>Existence</u>	Life	Intellection
Second triad = Life	Existence	<u>Life</u>	Intellection
Third triad = Intellect	Existence	Life	<u>Intellection</u>

In each of the three phases of the triad, the underlined term indicates the relative predominance of one of its three modalities: The first triad is coincident with the One and the third triad is coincident with the Intellect, in effect giving rise to the median triad which Augustine called the *medium*.

In the case of *Allogenes*, one might suggest a similar scheme based on the passage just cited as well as 61, 34-38: the Unknowable One "exists and will become or <lives> or knows, although it <acts> without Mind or Life or Existence or nonexistence, incomprehensibly" (cf. also 54, 9 - 61, 22):

Unknowable One/Invisible Spirit	Exists	Lives	Knows
Triple Power/Eternal Life	Existence	Vitality	Mentality
Barbelo/First Thought	(Being)	(Life)	Knowledge

The scheme is similar to that of <Porphyry> with certain exceptions. The terminology is used more fluidly with less rigor and precision. The triad as applied to the Unknowable One employs verbs which serve to stress its pure activity and utter non-substantiality, while abstracts are applied to the Triple Power and, as one might expect, concrete substantives to Barbelo. At the level of Barbelo, the parentheses indicate that the Being-Life-Mind triad is instead represented by a rather more Sethian mythological triad, Kalyptos, Protophanes, and Autogenes (although Barbelo is specifically called Knowledge in 45,16), which in the "Allogenes group" in turn replaces the triad Prognosis, Aphtharsia and Eternal Life found in *Ap. John*. The correspondence between the Barbelo triad and the Triple Power triad can be seen in 54, 8-16, where the male Mind Protophanes (= "Harmedon") is praised according to Vitality; another being, presumably Autogenes, is praised according to Mentality; and in the missing section at the top of page 54, another being, presumably Kalyptos, was praised according to Existence.

The fact that the leading term can be expressed by both *hyparxis* and *to on* seems to show that *Allogenes* trades in the same terminology familiar to Plotinus on the one and to Porphyry on the other. The fact that Plotinus reacted against the notion of an Intellect consisting of several distinct levels (*Ennead* II.9.1 and 6, a notion which *Allogenes* clearly implies) and surely would be ill-disposed to the location of a triad latent in the One or between the One and Intellect means that the scheme of *Allogenes*, and not only that of Numenius and others, was likely one of those so strongly rejected by Plotinus. The similarity between the schemes of *Allogenes* and of the <Porphyrian> *Parmenides* commentary may indicate that Porphyry could have derived his scheme as much from *Allogenes* as from the *Chaldaean Oracles*. The fact that the scheme of *Allogenes* is, by contrast with that of these two philosophers, rather unsystematic owes not only to the author's desire to reconcile his doctrine with traditional Sethian mythological cosmologies, but may also quite likely owe to his originality. That is, *Allogenes* may have been an important catalyst and conceptual source to both Plotinus and Porphyry, no matter how unacceptable certain other of its features may have been to them. Since the author of *Allogenes* is quite capable of accurate citation of his sources (cf. his citation of the negative theology from *Ap. John*, discussed below), the unsystematic character of his metaphysics more likely owes to his originality than to a confusion or misappropriation of the doctrine of Plotinus or of Porphyry. The fact that *Allogenes* or some version thereof was read in Plotinus's circle tends to add weight to this likelihood.

In sum, the fact that revelations under the names of "Allogenes," "Zostrianos," and "Zoroaster," circulated in Plotinus's seminars, coupled with the fact that doctrines refuted by Plotinus in *Ennead* II.9 are so close to those of the "Allogenes group," seems to suggest that the Neoplatonists are more likely dependent on the Sethian "Platonists" than the reverse. If so, a treatise like *Allogenes* would have been produced at a point prior to Plotinus's antignostic polemic (*Enneads* III.8, V.8, V.5 and II.9 [chronologically 30-33] as identified by R. Harder) of the years 244-269 CE.

Before we pass on to an analysis of the Aeon of Barbelo which is the equivalent to the Neoplatonic intellectual level in these Sethian texts, it will first be useful to outline certain features of the doctrine of Numenius and of the *Chaldaean Oracles* for purposes of comparison, especially since these systems were in all likelihood formulated in the second half of the second century, and may have been known to the author of *Allogenes*, whose work may have been produced around the end of this period.

Numenius exhibits a very complicated system of three gods, which has been interpreted in various ways, owing to apparent contradictions between fragments of his work *On the Good* contained in Eusebius's *Preparation for the Gospel* and various *testimonia* to his philosophy from such later authors as Proclus, Calcidius, Porphyry, Macrobius, Iamblichus and others. As Dodds and others have suggested,[6] Numenius's system of three gods seems to be inspired by the three kings of Plato's *Second Letter* 312E and the distinction between the contemplative (*kathorōn*) and planning (*dienoēthē*; Numenius has *dianooumenos*) activities of the demiurge according to *Timaeus* 39E which Plotinus also discussed in *Enneads* II.9.1 and 9.6 (also III.9.1). Following the admirable reconstruction of M. Baltes,[7] Numenius seems to exhibit the following system of three gods. The first god is an inert Mind, called the Monad, King and Sower; it is the Good in itself and is characterized by stability and motionless motion. Though not explicit in the system, this Monad seems to be opposed by an Indefinite Dyad, that is Matter, at first unbegotten, but then begotten by the Demiurge (i.e. by the second and third gods; cf. frg. 52 des Places). The second god, called Good and Cultivator, is a Mind in motion contemplating (*kathorōn, theōrētikos*) the first, in which act it is self-generated (αὐτοποιεῖ τήν τε ἰδέαν ἑαυτοῦ καὶ τὸν κόσμον) as an imitation of the first god (frg. 16 des Places). But this self-generation is also the generation of the world; that is, the second god is dyadic, alternating between contemplation of the first god above and demiurgical activity directed below (for so I interpret δημιουργὸς ὤν, ἔπειτα θεωρήτικος ὅλως, frg. 16 des Places against most interpreters). The third god is the demiurge proper insofar as it is occupied with Matter; indeed it is a sort of conjunction between the second god and Matter, and is the Mind which intends or plans (*dianooumenos*) the world. In this sense, the third god would correspond to something like the Logos or rational part of the World Soul in the systems of Philo of Alexandria or Plutarch of Chaeronea. Presumably the fourth level of Numenius's system would be occupied by the World Soul proper as a conjunction of the third god with Matter. For this reason, the third god is the rational part of the World Soul (*anima beneficientissima*, frg. 52 des Places), while the passive, hylic component of the World Soul actually constitutes a lower, evil soul. Finally, the last ontological level is the physical world.

Somewhat as in the Old Academic system of Speusippus, it seems that in Numenius, Matter or the Indefinite Dyad is associated with all levels: insofar as the second god is associated with Matter, it is split by it, becoming a second and third god (frg. 11 des Places); the combination of the second god with Matter is the third god, the beneficent aspect of the World Soul; and the combination of Matter with the third god is the lower or subrational aspect of the World Soul.

Roughly contemporaneous with Numenius are the *Chaldaean Oracles*, attributed to Julian the Theurgist who was credited with a miraculous deliverance of Marcus Aurelius's troops in 173 CE. The *Oracles* exhibit a hierarchical system with many Neopythagorean features. The supreme god is called the Father, Bythos (frg. 18 des Places), who is totally transcendent, having nothing to do with creation, and can be apprehended only with the "flower of the mind," a non-knowing, mentally vacant mode of intellectual contemplation (frgg. 1 and 18 des Places; the same doctrine as is found in *Allogenes*). The

Father is the Monad, presumably beyond being (as *hapax epekeina*), but also consists of a triad comprising himself or his existence (*hyparxis*, according to Damascius, *Dub. et sol.* 61, p. 131, 17 Ruelle; cf. frg. 1 line 10 des Places), his power and his intellect. Below him is the demiurgic Intellect proceeding from the Father who himself remains aloof with his power but does not confine "his fire" (frgg. 3, 4, and 5 des Places). This Intellect is a Dyad, contemplating the intelligible realm (of the Father's intellect), and bringing sense-perception to the world (frgg. 7 and 8 des Places). Furthermore, this Intellect is "dyadically transcendent" (*dis epekeina*), yet it too is also triadic insofar as it contains the "measured triad" (probably ideal forms or numbers) flowing from both it and the triadic Father (frgg. 26-29 and 31 des Places). Thus there is in effect an ennead: the first triad of the Father together with his power and intellect; the second triad of the dyadically oriented (above and below) demiurgic Intellect; and third the "measured triad" representing the multiplicity of the Ideas. On the border between the intelligible and sensible realms as both a barrier and like between them (so J. Dillon),[8] is Hecate, a sort of diaphragm or membrane (frg. 6 des Places), the life-producing fount (frgg. 30 and 32 des Places) from which the World Soul flows (frg. 51 des Places). Finally, there is the world of Matter, springing both from the Intellect and the Father (frgg. 34-35 des Places).

Yet, as Dillon correctly points out, Hecate exists on a higher level as well, being the center between the two fathers (frg. 50 des Places) and thus identified with the Father's power. As Hadot explains, Porphyry also must have located Hecate at this upper level (*apud* Augustine, *De civ. Dei* 10.23, *patris et filii medium*).

Hadot also provides a diagram to show the structure presupposed in the system, in which the vertical axis represents the ontological and hypostatic hierarchy, and the horizontal axis represents the relative predominance of the components of the triad formed at each level:[9]

Paternal Monad	the Father	his power	his intellect
Hecate	(father)	power (life)	(intellect)
Dyadic Intellect	(father)	(power)	Intellect
Measured Triad (Ideas)	Iynges	Synocheis	Teletarchai
Hecate as membrane		fount of life	
World Soul		mistress of life	
Nature			
Cosmos aisthētos			

Turning now to a consideration of the Aeon of Barbelo, it will be useful to attend not only to *Allogenes*, but to draw together results from all the members of the "Allogenes group." In addition to the doctrine of the Triple Power, *Zost.*, *Steles Seth* and *Marsanes* share with *Allogenes* a peculiar triadic division of the Aeon of Barbelo, the First Thought and self-knowledge of the Unknowable One or Invisible Spirit. In this connection, it should be noted that other Sethian materials place a triad at this level as well, the level corresponding to that which Intellect or Mind occupies in Neoplatonic systems. According to Irenaeus, *Haer*. I, 29, *Ap. John*, and *Gos. Egypt*. a triad of hypostases (Prognosis, Aphtharsia and Aiōnia Zōē) is associated with the Aeon of Barbelo. *Trim. Prot.* exhibits a sort of modal monarchianism in its division of the divine First Thought, Barbelo, into three modalities of increasing articulateness, the Voice of the Thought, the Speech of the Thought, and the Word (*logos*). The "Allogenes group" names the three modalities of Barbelo Kalyptos (the Hidden One), Protophanes (the First-appearing One), and Autogenes (the Self-begotten One), and conceives these as distinct hypostases constituting the Aeon of Barbelo, supplemented by a fourth being, the Triple Male.

Kalyptos (sometimes abbreviated ΚΛΣ) appears frequently in *Allogenes*, *Steles Seth*, *Zost.* and in Bruce, *Untitled*, and once in *Gos. Egypt.* (IV, *1*: 57, 16). In *Marsanes* (X, *1*: 4, 7-10), the ninth seal, where one expects to find Kalyptos (between Protophanes the eighth and Barbelo the ninth), is obscured by a lacuna of about seven letters, but concerns "[(something)] of the power [which] appeared [in the beginning (i.e. Protophanes)]" or perhaps "[(something)] of the power [of the one who] appeared [in the beginning]," suggesting that here Kalyptos may have been defined in terms of Protophanes. In *Trim. Prot.* (XIII, *1*: 38, 10) Protennoia/Barbelo calls herself "the immeasurable invisible one who is hidden," suggesting a translation of something like ὁ ἀόρατος Καλυπτὸς ἀμέτρητος. The name may have something to do with a veil (*kalumma*) or covering separating the lower from the higher realms, much as the Valentinians posited an upper Limit (*horos*) separating Bythos from his subordinate aeons including Nous. *Steles Seth* calls Barbelo "the first shadow of the holy Father, a light from light" who originates "from a shadow of him, thou a Kalyptos." *Zost.* (VIII, *1*: 78, 17-19 and 82, 8-13) says that the emergence of Barbelo involved her "darkening," and that Kalyptos emerged as the second knowledge of the Invisible Spirit (the first being Barbelo), "the knowledge of his knowledge." *Allogenes* (XI, *1*: 66, 37) mentions the shadow in connection with the appearance of an "Eternal Life." *Marsanes* apparently omits all mention of Kalyptos. It seems, then, that in terms of the Platonic metaphysics of the divine intellect, Kalyptos occupies the position of the *nous noëtos*, the contemplated intellect, somewhat like the first god of Numenius. In *Allogenes*, the "image of Kalyptos" is said to be "the patterns (*typoi*) and forms (*eidë*) of those who truly exist," that is, the Platonic intelligibles or ideas of universals.

The median level of Barbelo is the male Mind Protophanes. In *Ap. John* (II, *1*: 8, 33) Geradamas, the archetypal heavenly Adam, is "the first appearance," and in *Gos. Egypt.* (IV, *2*: 55, 25) the figure named Triple Male Child is called the "first one who appeared," both apparently translations of Protophanes. The name Protophanes seems to derive from the Orphic doctrine of Phanes (also called Eros, Metis, Erikepaios), who was "first to appear" from the cosmic egg (Apollonius Rhodius, *Orph. Argon.* 14-16). Bisexual, he was regarded as "always two-formed," "looking this way and that," "the key of Mind" (*Orph. Frgg.* 72-89 and 167 Kern; Synesius, *Hymn.* 2.63 Terzaghi calls the Son of God *prōtophanēs eidos*). Both the Orphic etymology "first appearing" and his characterization as mind, as well as his double inclination above and below are clearly reflected in his position in *Allogenes* (XI, *3*: 45, 34-36; 46, 24-25), where he represents the progression from the psychic "individuals" in Autogenes to the intelligible level of the "authentic existents" in Kalyptos. In Platonic metaphysics, Protophanes would correspond to the *nous nooun* or perhaps *nous noeros*. In *Allogenes*, Protophanes is said to contain "those who exist together," a median state between the "individuals" in Autogenes and the "authentic existents" in Kalyptos. Ultimately, in the Sethian system, Kalyptos and Protophanes may represent two phases in the emanation of the divine Thought Barbelo; at first "hidden," then "manifest."

The lowest level of Barbelo's Aeon is Autogenes, the third member of the traditional Sethian Father-Mother-Son triad used to designate the high deity, his First Thought Barbelo who as the "merciful mother" directs the entire history of salvation, and the savior Autogenes who is identified variously as Adamas, Seth or Christ. In *Allogenes*, Autogenes is said to contain the "perfect individuals" as his members.

Interpreted in terms of Platonic ontology, Kalyptos would be the contemplated Mind containing the paradigmatic ideas or authentic existents. Protophanes would be the contemplating Mind containing a subdivision of the ideas, "those who exist together," perhaps "mathematicals," distinguished from the authentic existents by having "many the same" and being combinable with each other (cf. Aristotle, *Metaphys.* I.6; XIII.6). Autogenes would be the planning Mind containing the "perfect individuals," the ideas of particulars used to shape the world below. The similarity to the system of Numenius is clear.

Clearly one may see at work in the "Allogenes group" a combination of Sethian mythology and Platonic metaphysics of the Mind which finds certain echoes in Plotinus and other Neoplatonists. In *Ennead* III.9.1 Plotinus toys with the notion that one might interpret Plato's doctrine of the demiurgic Intellect in *Timaeus* 39E by distinguishing between a first intellect in repose, a second intellect which contemplates the first, and perhaps a third planning or discursive intellect (*nous merisas*) which divides universal ideas into particular ideas (perhaps the "mathematicals" of the Old Academy). Some such conception, which seems close to the distinctions made in the "Allogenes group," was espoused by Amelius, a member of Plotinus's circle (*apud* Proclus, *In Tim.* 3, 268A, p. 103, 18-25 Diehl) and earlier by Numenius. In his treatise "Against the Gnostics" (*Ennead* II.9.6), which probably has Sethians in view, Plotinus definitely rejects such a view in favor of a unified Intellect which contains the ideas in itself as its own objects of thought. One may indeed wonder if some of these notions were conveyed to him by certain treatises of the "Allogenes group" as well, or perhaps whether it was the particular way these treatises expressed them (not to mention their use of mythology and incantation) that drove Plotinus to oppose these ideas so strongly.

The "Allogenes group" also assigns a fourth being, called the Triple Male, to the members of the Aeon of Barbelo. But before treating the function of this being, a few observations about the position of Barbelo in the Sethian system are in order. In the Ophite system described by Irenaeus (*Haer.* I.30.1), which is very close to portions of *Ap. John*, the divine world originates with three principal figures: the high deity (First) "Man" is Father of the All; his Thought (*ennoia*) which proceeds from him is the Son of Man; below these is a certain Holy Spirit from whom the First Man begets Christ as the "Third Male" (*tertius masculus*, perhaps a variant expression for the Triple Male). This system, no doubt deriving from an interpretation of Genesis 1:2 and 26-27, suggests an androgynous high deity whose "image" is the (likewise androgynous) Son of Man as the Thought of the high deity "Man" (i.e. the deity in whose image the archetypal Adam is made as male and female). But this Son of Man could also be considered in terms of its female aspect, which in turn could be hypostatized as the Mother of the Son of Man/Third Male. All this makes possible a divine triad consisting of a Father ("Man"), a Mother (the Thought, the female aspect of the Son of Man), and a Son (the Third Male as the masculine aspect of the Son of Man).

Such a process of Genesis-speculation is likely to be the origin of the Sethian Father-Mother-Son triad of the Invisible Spirit, Barbelo and the Son Autogenes. In Sethianism, the Autogenes (self-begotten) Son could be identified as Adamas (*alias* Geradamas) or as the Triple Male Child (cf. the Ophite "Third Male"). It is also significant that the Mother Barbelo continues to bear traces of the male aspect of her androgyny, since she is sometimes called "the merciful Father" or "the merciful Mother-Father" in the various versions of *Ap. John*. Because of her associations with the Thought of the high deity, the Sethian treatises call Barbelo also Thought (*ennoia*), First thought, Pronoia, Protennoia, Image of the Invisible Spirit, etc. in addition to the terms reflecting her androgyny such as Male Virgin, Father of the All, Thrice-male, Mother-Father and so on. The name Barbelo seems to mean something like "in four is God" (Aramaic *b' arba' 'ēlōh*), a hypostatization of the tetragrammaton YHWH, according to the (still most convincing) etymology proposed by W. Harvey in the nineteenth century.

With regard to the Triple Male as a separate being within the Sethian system, in *Gos. Egypt.* (III, 2: 44, 22-28; IV, 2: 55, 11 - 56, 11) the "Thrice-male Child of the great Christ whom the great Invisible Spirit has anointed" is called "the first one to appear," which sounds as though he is identified as the Protophanes of the "Allogenes group." Indeed in pages 61-63 of *Zost.*, Zostrianos is baptized, coming into being as "truly existing" and then is brought by a figure named Yoel (probably the Youel of *Allogenes*) into the aeonic place of the Triple Male and there sees the "invisible Child," after which Yoel sets him down before Protophanes to be instructed by the Luminaries of Barbelo's Aeon (Salamex, Selmen and Ar[.]e; cf. *Allogenes* XI, 3: 56, 21-30). Although *Marsanes* seems to omit mention of this being, in *Allogenes* (XI, 3: 45, 34-37; 46, 11-34) it is said that Barbelo is Triple Male insofar as she grants power to "the individuals" (within whom Protophanes acts). A being called "this one" (XI, 3: 46, 14) "sees them all existing individually" such that "they will become as he is by seeing the divine Triple Male," who is "the Thought of all those who exist together." Further, "if the (Triple Male) reflects upon himself, he reflects upon Protophanes," the path or procession from the state of "those who exist together" to that of "those who truly exist," whom to see is to see Kalyptos, indeed to see Barbelo herself. In XI, 3: 58, 12-17 Allogenes sees "the good divine Autogenes and the Savior who is the perfect Triple Male Child and his goodness, the noetic perfect Protophanes-Harmedon." In view of these statements, it seems that Protophanes may be an alternate designation for the Triple Male Child, but also that they can be distinguished, at least to the extent that Protophanes is associated with "those who exist together" (perhaps something like the Old Academic ideal numbers), while the Triple Male Child is associated with the self-begotten "individuals" (perhaps the ideal forms of physically existing things or persons). In *Steles Seth* (VII, 5: 120, 16 - 121, 4) the Triple Male is blessed as the unifier and completer of the All and Savior of the "perfect individuals." In *Steles Seth*, then, the Triple Male is identified with the Sethian savior-figure Autogenes, who is in turn identified with the divine Adamas ("Geradamas"), which suggests that the Triple Male is a Sethian designation for Adamas, or perhaps Seth. Originally, the term Triple Male may have been only a superlative, i.e. triple male = thrice male = "truly male."

Thus, because of the traditional Sethian association of the Triple Male with the divine Adam who is both self-begotten and was the first to appear, the treatises of the "Allogenes group" consistently associate him with the Aeon of Barbelo, but on a more specific level vacillate between associating him with Protophanes or with Autogenes. This suggests that in the "Allogenes group," the triadic division of the Aeon of Barbelo into Kalyptos, Protophanes and Autogenes is a later intruding development in the Sethian system inspired by contemporary Platonic speculation on the tripartition of the divine intellect based on the *Timaeus* 39E as well as upon continuing speculation on the Sethian triad of Father, Mother, and Son.

For purposes of visualization, we now present a summary diagram of the ontological levels in *Allogenes*:

Invisible Spirit/Unknowable One	<u>Exists</u>	Lives	Knows
The Triple Power/Eternal Life	Existence	<u>Vitality</u>	Mentality
The Aeon of Barbelo/First			
Thought	(Being)	(Life)	<u>Knowledge</u>
Kalyptos praised according to	Existence		
Protophanes praised according to		Vitality	
Triple Male (Child)			
Autogenes praised according to			Mentality
The realm of Nature			

The lowest cosmological level, Nature (*physis*), appears to hold no interest for the author of *Allogenes*. It is only alluded to as the realm on which Autogenes works "successively and individually" so as to rectify its flaws or defects (51, 28-32). This natural realm may correspond to the lowest level of Plotinus's transcendentalia, *physis* or the lower, creative Soul (cf. *Ennead* III.8.4 passim), although *Allogenes* may intend by this term a lower and more immanent psychic realm. In any case, it is to be noted that all the members of the "Allogenes group" take a remarkably "soft" stance toward this lower realm. It is defective, but not evil or chaotic; it is to be "rectified," or as *Marsanes* puts it, "is worthy to be saved entirely" (X, *1*: 4, 24 - 5, 16; 5, 24-26). So also *Zost.* (VIII, *1*: 131, 10-14): "Release yourselves, and that which has bound you will be dissolved. Save yourselves, in order that it may be saved."

This completes the inventory of the major transcendentalia of the "Allogenes group." *Allogenes* presents itself as restrained in nearly Plotinian fashion: "Whether the Unknowable One has angels or gods, or whether the One who stills himself possessed anything except the stillness which he is" is not known to the author; the transcendentalia have "brought forth nothing beyond themselves" (XI, *3*: 49, 21-26; 67, 22-25).

It now remains to summarize the structure of the visionary ascent in *Allogenes*, a pattern which is reflected in the rest of the "Allogenes group," although with some variations. In *Zost.* the levels of the ascent are mostly marked by certain "baptisms" and "sealing," while *Steles Seth* consists mainly of doxologies to be used during the ascent which itself is not narrated, and *Marsanes* merely comments on certain features of the ascent, which the author has already undergone.

In *Allogenes* (XI, *3*: 58, 26 - 61, 21) the ascent is tripartitioned into separate but successive stages, just as its general ontology is tripartitioned, since the object of the ascent is to become assimilated with each higher level of being through which one passes. The first stage of the ascent seems to occur within the second cosmological level, the intelligible level of Barbelo, in which Autogenes, Protophanes *cum* Triple Male, and Kalyptos are mentioned (57, 29 - 58, 26). Following this, 58, 26 - 61, 22 describes a further ascent in terms of the tripartite nomenclature previously applied to the Triple Power in 49, 26-38 except that the term Existence (*hyparxis*) replaces the term "That which is" (= *to on*), and the term "blessedness" replaces the term "Mentality."

At the conclusion of a "hundred years" of preparation, Allogenes reports that he saw Autogenes, the Triple Male, Protophanes, Kalyptos, the Aeon of Barbelo, and the primal origin (*archē*) of the of the One without origin, that is, the Triple Power of the Unknowable One / Invisible Spirit (57, 29 - 58, 26). One should probably understand this as Allogenes's ascent through the various levels of the Aeon of Barbelo up to and including the lowest aspect of the Triple Power, which would be "blessedness" or Mentality, since Allogenes still bears his earthly

garment (58, 29-30). The initial vision is culminated by his removal
from the earthly garment to "a holy place" (58, 31) characterized by
the blessedness of "the knowledge of the Universal Ones" (59, 2-3).
Allogenes is now ready for "holy powers" revealed to him by the
"luminaries of the Aeon of Barbelo" to allow him to "test what
happens in the world" by a yet higher experience starting anew from the
"holy place" (perhaps the lowest level of the Triple Power).

This implies two levels of knowing: One is achievable in the
world, and is characterized by the actual vision of what was
communicated only in the auditory revelations imparted by the emissary-
revealer Youel, sufficing to know the realm of being and intellect in the
Aeon of Barbelo up until the lower aspect of the Triple Power. The
other is not achievable in the world, and is to be imparted by a special
"primary revelation" from the Luminaries of Barbelo's Aeon, and
suffices to experience directly the realm beyond being and intellect, the
upper levels of the Triple Power and possibly the Unknowable One
itself. The first level of knowing is active and involves self-knowledge
(58, 38 - 59, 3; 59, 9-16); the second level of knowing is strictly speaking
not knowledge at all, but is a non-knowing knowledge, an utter vacancy
of the discursive intellect, a "learned ignorance" (59, 30-35; 60, 5-12;
61, 1-4) called a "primary revelation of the Unknowable One" (59, 28-
29; 60, 39 - 61, 1). This notion is of course found in the *Chaldaean
Oracles* (frg. 1 des Places) and in the *Parmenides* commentary
<Porphyry>, *In Parm.* II, 14-17).

The ascent beyond the Aeon of Barbelo to the Unknowable One
is first revealed to Allogenes by holy powers (59, 4 - 60, 12) and then
actually narrated (60, 12 - 61, 22) by Allogenes in a way quite similar to
the revelation, yielding what amounts to two accounts of the ascent.
Having surpassed his active earthly knowledge and inclining toward the
passive knowledge of the Universals (the Platonic intelligibles, 58, 26 -
60, 12), Allogenes attains first the level of blessedness (i.e. Mentality)
characterized by self-knowledge (59, 9-13; 60, 14-18), then the level of
Vitality characterized by an undivided, eternal, intellectual motion (59,
14-16; 60, 19-28), and finally the level of Existence, characterized by
inactive "stillness" and "standing" (59, 19-26; 60, 28-37).   At this
point, Allogenes can no longer withdraw to any higher level, but only
"to the rear because of the activities" (59, 34-35; cf. Plotinus, *Ennead*
III.8.9, 29-32; VI.9.3, 1-13); that is, Allogenes must avoid any further
effort lest he dissipate his inactivity and fall away from the passivity,
concentratedness, and instantaneousness of the primary revelation to
follow (59, 26 - 60, 12; cf. 64, 14-26; 67, 22-38). Now Allogenes receives
a "primary revelation of the Unknowable One" (59, 28-29; 60, 39; 61,

1) characterized by a non-knowing knowledge of the Unknowable One (59, 30-32; 60, 8-12; 61, 1-4), which turns out to be an extensive negative theology (61, 32 - 62, 13) supplemented by a more affirmative theology 62, 14 - 67, 20). On completion of the ascent and revelation, Allogenes's appropriate response is to record and safeguard the revelation (68, 16-23) and entrust its proclamation to his confidant Messos (68, 26-end).

Clearly *Allogenes* is distinguished by a Platonically-inspired visionary act of the individual intellect in which it assimilates itself to the hierarchy of ontological levels with which it was aboriginally consubstantial, but from which it has become separated by life in the body. One undergoes the ascent according to a prescribed sequence of mental states: earthbound vision, ecstatic extraction from body (and soul) involving a transcending of even traditional Gnosis, silent but at first unstable seeking of the self, firm standing, and finally sudden ultimate vision consisting of an ignorant knowledge devoid of any content that might distinguish between subject and contemplated object. Each stage is characterized by increasing self-unification, stability and mental abstraction, a definite movement away from motion and multiplicity toward stability and solitariness.

The literary prototype of this experience is found in Plato's *Symposium* 210A-212A where Socrates recounts his path to the vision of absolute beauty as a "mystery" into which he had been initiated by Diotima of Mantinea. In such visionary mysteries, ultimate vision or *epopteia* was the supreme goal, tantamount to assimilating oneself to God insofar as possible (*Theatetus* 176B). This traditional Platonic quest is found not only in Plato, but also later in Philo of Alexandria (who however shunned the notion of assimilation to God), Numenius, Valentinus, perhaps Albinus (*Didasc.* 10.5.6; the *viae analogiae*, *negationis*, *additionis* and *eminentiae*), Clement of Alexandria (*strom.* 5.11.71), Origen (*Contra Celsum* 7.42) and especially Plotinus (*Ennead* VI.7.36). What is generally common to these visionary ascents is initial purification, usually through some form of instruction involving the use of analogies, negations, and successive abstraction until the contemplative mind has become absorbed in its single object (the One, the Good, the Beautiful etc.) at which point one "suddenly" sees the ultimate source of all these; here philosophy and intellection give way to ecstasy.

Particularly important for this visionary experience in Platonism and in the Sethian Gnosticism of the "Allogenes group" is the role of negative or apophatic theological predication. Traces of this are to be found in Albinus, in the gnostic system of Basilides (ca. 125 CE), in

Plotinus and the later Neoplatonists, and of course in the Sethian treatises *Ap. John* and *Allogenes*, which share a common apophatic tradition (BG 8502, *2*: 23, 3 - 26, 13 = *NHC* II, *1*: 3, 18-25 = XI, *3*: 62, 28 - 63, 23). It is most probable that the basic inspiration for all of these is Plato's *Parmenides* 137D-141E, according to which the non-existence of the One follows from the facts that it 1) is neither a whole nor has parts, 2) is not anywhere, neither in itself nor in another, 3) is neither at rest nor in motion, 4) is neither other than nor the same as itself or another, 5) is neither like nor unlike itself or another, 6) is without measure or sameness and so is neither equal to nor less than nor greater than itself or another, 7) is neither younger nor older nor of the same age as itself or another, 8) and has nothing to do with any length of time; therefore, the One in no sense "is." One may compare Albinus (*Didasc.* 10.164, 28-32 Hermann):

> The first God is eternal, ineffable, self-complete, that is, not wanting in any respect, all-perfect, divinity, substantiality, truth, symmetry, and good. I say this not as defining these things, but as conceptualizing a unity in every respect . . . he is ineffable, comprehended by mind alone . . . since he is neither genus nor species nor difference. Nor can anything be attributed to him. Neither is he evil, for to say this is impermissible; nor is he good, which would imply his participation in something, particularly goodness. He is neither difference . . . nor quality . . . nor without quality since he has not been deprived of quality . . . nor is he a whole possessing certain parts, nor is he the same nor different, since nothing has been attributed to him by which he can be separated from the others; nor does he move nor is he moved.

According to Basilides (*apud* Hippolytus, *Ref.* 7.20.2 - 21.1), the supreme God is a "nothing" at a time when there was nothing; it cannot even be called ineffable even though we call it ineffable (since that would imply there was something to be called ineffable); there was nothing, neither matter nor substance nor insubstantiality; nothing simple nor composite nor imperceptible; no man, no angel or god; nothing perceptible nor intelligible; only the non-existent god without intelligence, perception, resolve, impulse or desire. H.A. Wolfson[10] has pointed out that this is not so much a negative theology in which an affirmative predicate is negated as it is a privative theology which denies the possibility of predication at all.

According to the material common to *Ap. John* and *Allogenes*, the Unknowable One is neither divinity nor blessedness (i.e. intellect) nor goodness, but is superior to these; neither boundless nor bounded, but superior to these; neither corporeal nor incorporeal, neither great nor small, neither a quantity nor a product nor a knowable existent, but superior to these; it shares in neither time nor eternity (*aeon*); it does not receive from another; neither is it diminished nor does it diminish nor is it undiminished. The author of *Allogenes* (XI, 3: 61, 32 - 62, 27) prefaces this common material with more of the same from his own pen: the Unknowable One is "something" (a Stoic category) in that it exists and becomes or <lives> or knows although it <acts> without Mind or Life or Existence or non-Existence; it is not assayed or refined; it does not give or receive, neither of itself nor of another; it needs neither Mind nor Life nor anything else. The language of *Allogenes* is rather close to that of the *Parmenides* with its denial of the application of either a predicate or its negation to the Unknowable One. Indeed One may also compare Plotinus (*Ennead* VI.9.3, 36-45):

> Thus the One is neither something nor a quality nor a quantity nor an intellect nor a soul; neither is it moving nor even standing. It is not in place nor in time, but one of a kind by itself; rather it is formless before all form, before movement and before stability, since these relate to being and would make it many.

On the basis of the foregoing analysis, it seems virtually certain that the treatises of the "Allogenes group" derive the ontological structure of their transcendent world and the structure of the visionary ascent through it, as well as the Sethian negative theology applied to the invisible Spirit, from sources that are ultimately at home in Platonism. These sources cannot be specified with precision, but seem to belong to the Middle Platonic corpus of the exegesis of certain key passages from Plato's dialogues, especially the *Timaeus*, the *Sophist*, the *Parmenides*, the *Symposium*, the *Theatetus*, the *Republic*, and from reminiscences from Plato's "esoteric" teaching as reflected in Aristotle's *Metaphysics* and the reports on Plato's lecture(s) "On the Good." This is not to deny, of course, the influence of other sources of speculation, such as Jewish apocalyptic visionary literature and so on, but the essential structural ingredient is Platonic.

Many of the metaphysical systems described so far (the Sethian, especially that of the "Allogenes group," the Chaldaean, and those of Plotinus, Porphyry, and the *Parmenides* commentary) exhibit what H.J. Krämer[11] has characterized as a four level metaphysics, deriving ultimately from the late Plato and his nephew Speusippus in the Old Academy. The systems of these men posit an ultimate ground of being beyond the transcendent realm of being itself, which latter properly begins with the realm of ideas and (ideal) numbers, followed by the

World Soul as source of all movement, and finally by the sensible, corporeal world. Both Xenocrates and Aristotle reacted against what they saw to be an excessive transcendentalism in the systems of Plato and especially of Speussipus, retracting the transcendent ground of being back into the intellectual realm of pure being, and so produced a three level metaphysics of a monadic intelligence containing the ideas as its objects of thought, followed by the World Soul and sensible world. After the metaphysically dry period of the New Academy, the three level metaphysic played a role in the Platonic metaphysics known to Cicero and Seneca and developed in the thought of Plutarch, Atticus and others. But in the first century BCE, the four level metaphysic began to reemerge in Alexandrian Neopythagorean Platonism, especially in the circle of Eudorus. This reemergence was characterized by an increasing tendency toward withdrawal from society, world-rejection, asceticism and a return to the authority of ancient tradition (especially esoteric traditions, such as Plato's unwritten doctrine). The four level metaphysic, with its ultimate principle absolutely transcending the physical and even intellectual world, was increasingly adopted by philosophers such as Thrasyllus, Moderatus, Nichomachus and other arithmologists, Philo, Julian author of the *Chaldaean Oracles*, Plotinus and later Neoplatonists, and by many Gnostics, such as Basilides, Monoimus, the Valentinians, the Naasenes, Peratae, Docetics, Sethians and Archontics, and the system of the "Simonian" *Megalē Apophasis*.

What is notable about this "Neopythagorean" Platonic metaphysics and distinguishes it from much of the former school Platonism is its great interest in schemes of the dynamic ontological derivation of lower principles from higher ones, coupled with a similar interest in arithmological speculation on the Pythagorean tetractys $(1 + 2 + 3 + 4 = 10)$ as the key to outlining these schemes of derivation. In particular they wished to account for the origin of the realm of multiplicity (which could be expressed as ideal numbers and their phenomenal representations) from a sole primal and aboriginally existing unitary principle called the One or the Monad. Thus at some point the (androgynous) Monad became a (female) Dyad by a process of doubling (Theon of Smyrna, *Expositio* 27, 1-7; 100, 9-12 Hiller; Nicomachus, *Intro. Arith.* 113, 2-10 Hoche; Sextus Empiricus, *Hyp. Pyrrh.* 3.153; *Adv. Math.* 10.261; Hippolytus, *Ref.* 4.43), or begetting (<Iamblichus>, *Theol. Arith.* 3, 17 - 4, 7 de Falco), or by division (<Iamblichus>, *Theol. Arith.* 5, 4-5; 8, 20 - 9, 6; 13, 9-11 de Falco), or by *ectasis* or progression from potentiality to actuality as in a seed (Nicomachus *apud* <Iamblichus>, *Theol. Arith.* 3, 1-8; 16, 4-11 de Falco), or by receding from its nature (Moderatus *apud* Simplicius, *In*

Phys. 230, 34 - 231, 27 Diels; Numenius, frg. 52 des Places), or by flowing (Sextus Empiricus, *Adv. Math.* 3.19; 3.28; 3.77; 7.99; 9.380-381; 10.281). Hippolytus shows that certain Gnostics used the concept of the emanation (*probolē, proerchesthai*) of a Dyad preexisting in the Monad (the Valentinians, *Ref.* 6.29.5-6; the "Simonian" *Megalē Apophasis, Ref.* 6.18.4-7). Among the Sethian "Allogenes group" one finds in addition to the Existence, Vitality, Mentality progression also the concept of self-extension (X, *1*: 32, 5 - 33, 2; XI, *3*: 45, 22-24) and division (VII, *5*: 121, 25 - 123, 14; combined with *ectasis*, VIII, *1*: 80, 1-20 and combined with withdrawal, X, *1*: 9, 1-21).

This sort of self-generation of primal principles from a preexisting unity characteristic of Neopythagorean arithmological speculation was also combined with Middle Platonic speculation on the divine intellect to produce a scheme in which the many arise from the One by a process of thinking, more specifically by the self-reflection of the One upon itself; this self-reflection or thinking then can be regarded as a being separately existing from the One and is called its Thought or Mind. This scheme is especially prominent in gnostic systems: in the "monistic" Valentinian system reported by Hippolytus (*Ref.* 6.29.5-6; cf. *Ref.* 6.42.4-5 [Marcosians]; *Exc. Theod.* 7.1; *Tripartite Tractate NHC* I, *5*: 52, 34 - 77, 25 [thinking, self-extension, etc.]; *Valentinian Exposition NHC* XI, 23: 22, 1 - 25, 21). Especially interesting is the "Simonian" *Megalē Apophasis* (Hippolytus, *Ref.* 6.18.4-7): The great unlimited power, potentially all-father, potentially contains his thought (*epinoia*) of which he becomes aware, thus objectivizing it as a separately existing entity (appearing to himself from himself he became two; he brought himself forth from himself). When the thought appears, it in turn sees its source, which becomes father to it; knowing the father, the thought becomes mind (*nous*), which together with the thought produces the Logos.

In Sethianism, *Ap. John* (II, *1*: 4, 16-35) describes the appearance of Barbelo by the same process of self-reflection. This is a natural Neopythagorean Platonic interpretation of the rather more mythological and traditional Sethian speculation on the bisexual nature of the Man (the high deity in whose image mankind is made) and Son of Man (the archetypal Adam) figures deduced from Genesis 1:26-27. Man is the monistic but bisexual supreme deity (odd numbers are male and even numbers are female, while "one" shares both natures since adding it to an odd number produces an even and vice versa). The Son of Man as his bisexual offspring can then be considered as the deity's wisdom (*sophia*) or thought (*pronoia, ennoia* or *epinoia*), and thus, in a convoluted way, as the Son in one aspect, and in another aspect as the

Mother of the self-generated Son. The female or Mother aspect could, in arithmological terms, be associated with a Dyad (even, female), and the male aspect (odd) with a triad (cf. the Triple Male). These were then configured in a Father-Mother-Son triad, the female member of which was often called Pronoia or Ennoia or First Thought (Protennoia) in preference to the name Sophia, which was associated with the divine thought in demiurgical declination. Perhaps speculation on the divine name (the tetragrammaton YHWH) inspired Barbelo as the name for the female aspect of the divine thought. In turn the name Barbelo ("in four is God"), implying a tetrad, may have inspired the notion of the tetrad of names (Ennoia, Prognōsis, Aphtharsia and Aiōnia Zōē) associated in *Ap. John* with the Mother Barbelo, and by analogy the development of another tetrad of names (Autogenes, Nous, Thelema and Logos) associated with the Son. Needless to say, in *Ap. John* the names, perhaps originally designating attributes of the Mother and Son, are regarded as separate hypostases or subordinate beings granted to Barbelo and the Autogenes Son by the Invisible Spirit when they praise him for their creation.

Three quarters of a century later, the "Allogenes group" still recognizes a tetrad (now named Kalyptos, Protophanes, the Triple Male and Autogenes) associated with Barbelo, while the tetrad associated with the Son has been dropped or at least lost specificity, since we hear now only of the "self-begotten ones" (plural) and the entities Metanoia, Paroikesis and Antitypoi as prominent entities below the level of Autogenes. However, the vacillation in the placement of the figure of the Triple Male gives the impression that the thought structure of the "Allogenes group" has little room for tetrads, and basically thinks in terms of triads, as the doctrine of the Triple Power, expounded upon previously, suggests.

It seems to me that the most direct inspiration for the tripartite aspects of Barbelo, namely Kalyptos, Protophanes and Autogenes, interpreted respectively as the contemplated intellect (*nous noētos*), contemplating intellect (*nous kathorōn*) and planning or demiurgic intellect (*nous dianooumenos*), is the system of Numenius. As for the doctrine of the Triple Power, we have seen that Numenius does not posit a supreme ground of being beyond intellect and true being, and thus espouses a three level metaphysic; but the *Chaldaean Oracles*, replete with its system of three transcendent triads and a primal entity, the Father, who is presumably beyond being, seems very close to the system underlying the "Allogenes group."[12] In particular, Numenius's system is very close to the ontology of the Aeon of Barbelo in the "Allogenes group," while the three triads implicit in the Paternal

Monad, the upper Hecate and in the dyadically transcendent Intellect in the system of the *Chaldaean Oracles* are very close to the ontology of the Triple Power of the "Allogenes group," especially in the way this triad is related to the Unknowable One and to the triadic structure of the Aeon of Barbelo.

In this connection, one ought also to mention the even earlier system of Moderatus. The system of Moderatus, who was active at the end of the first century CE, is a four level metaphysics (*apud* Porphyry *apud* Simplicius, *In Phys.* 230, 24 - 231, 27 Diels and Porphyry, *Vita Pythag.* 48-53; cf. also Joh. Stobaeus, *Anth.* 1.21 Wachsmuth). Moderatus posited a first One beyond all being and essence, followed by a second One who is true being, intelligible, and comprises the forms. The second One is called the Monad or unitary Logos which, acting as paradigm, is the Quality that limits the Quantity of a principle opposing it, called Multiplicity (also Speusippus's term for the Old Academic Indefinite Dyad). In fact, Moderatus conceives this Monad as a permanence (*monē*) from which Multiplicity generates a system of monads (ideal numbers) by a Progression (*propodismos*) from and a return (*anapodismos*) to the Monad, an anticipation of the Neoplatonic doctrine of emanation in three phases of *monē*, *proodos* and *epistrophē*,[13] not to mention a possible anticipation of the Sethian doctrine of the Triple Power as the medium through which the Aeon of Barbelo emanates from the Invisible Spirit.

We now conclude this lengthy exposition of the doctrine of the "Allogenes group" in its Platonic context by drawing some conclusions about its historical position in later Platonism.

First, it should now be clear that *Allogenes* and *Zost.* are to be included among "the apocalypses of Zoroaster and Zostrianos and Nicotheos and Allogenes and Messos and those of other such figures" (Porphyry, *Vita Plot.* 16) read in Plotinus's circle and attacked and refuted, sometimes at great length, by Amelius and Porphyry himself in the period 244-269 CE.[14] This allows one to date *Allogenes* (for whose priority in the group I have argued) around 200 CE, with *Zost.* and *Steles Seth* coming a bit later around 225 CE (Porphyry recognized *Zost.* as a spurious and recent work); *Marsanes*, on account of its doctrine of an unknown Silent One transcending even the Invisible Spirit, seems to be later yet, perhaps at the time of Iamblichus, who likewise posited an "Ineffable" one beyond even the Plotinian One.

Second, in his antignostic polemic (especially in *Ennead* II.9), Plotinus surely has certain of the tractates of the "Allogenes group" (especially *Zost.*), or versions of them, in view. According to the thorough survey of R.T. Wallis,[15] Plotinus does not seem to attack the

Sethian scheme of the unfolding of the divine world. He accepts the notion in *Allogenes* of learned ignorance (*Ennead* III.8.9-10; *NHC* XI, *3*: 59, 30-32; 60, 8-12; 61, 2-3; 61, 17-19; cf. Porphyry, *Sent*. 25-26 Lambertz and the *Parmenides* commentary, frgg. II and IV). He also accepts the notion that spiritual beings are simultaneously present in their entirety as "all together" in the Intellect (*Ennead* V.8.7-9; cf. "those who exist together," e.g., *NHC* VIII, *1*: 21; 87; 115-116). Also, his acceptance of the notion of the traversal of Vitality or Life from the One into the Intellect has already been pointed out (*Ennead* III,8.11; cf. *NHC* XI, *3*: 49, 5-21).

On the other hand, Plotinus does not accept the strong partitioning of the Intellect characteristic of the "Allogenes group" (*Ennead* II.9). With even greater vehemence, he attacks doctrines found principally in *Zost.*, especially its teaching on Sophia (VII, *1*: 9, 16 - 11, 9):   the primal wisdom is "neither a derivative nor a stranger in something strange to it, but is identical with true being and thus Intellect itself" (*Ennead* V.8.5).   He attacks the idea that Soul or Sophia declined and put on human bodies or that Sophia illuminated the darkness, producing an image (*eidōlon*) in matter, which in turn produces an image of the image. He scorns the idea of a demiurge who revolts from its mother (*Ennead* II.9.10) and whose activity gives rise to "repentances" (*metanoiai*, i.e. of Sophia), copies (*antitypoi*, i.e. the demiurge's counterfeit aeons) and transmigrations (*Ennead* II.9.6; also the "alien earth" of II.9.11; cf. *Zost.*, VIII, *1*: 5, 10-29; 8, 9-16; 12, 4-21).   Plotinus is critical in general of the Gnostics' unnecessary multiplication of hypostases, rejects as out of hand conceptions such as a secondary knowledge that is the knowledge of yet a higher knowledge (*Ennead* II.9.1; cf. *Zost.* VIII, *1*: 82, 1-13), and completely ridicules their magical incantations (*Ennead* II.9.14; cf. VIII, *1*: 52; 85-88; 127; XI, *3*: 53, 32 - 55, 11; VII, *5*: 126, 1-17; X, *1*: 25, 17-32, 5).

Besides these attacks, it may be, as Wallis suggests, that his encounter with the Gnostics caused Plotinus to tighten up his own interpretation of Plato's *Timaeus* (especially 39E), for example in *Ennead* III.9.1 where he toys with a tripartition of the Intellect (rejected explicitly in II.9.6).   In *Ennead* VI.68.   "On Number," produced immediately after his antignostic treatise, he changes the order of the Being-Life-Mind triad applied throughout the rest of the *Enneads* to the unfolding of the Intellect from the One to the order Being-Mind-Life, and restricts this triad to the hypostasis of Intellect alone, perhaps in response to the Existence-Vitality-Mentality triad of *Allogenes*, which could easily be such as implying an intermediate and thus unnecessary hypostasis between the high deity and its Intellect, Barbelo.

Finally, while the philosophical roots of Plotinus have been recognized to lie certainly in Plato but also in the later Platonists such as Moderatus, Numenius, Ammonius and perhaps the author of the *Chaldaean Oracles* among others, his debt to the Gnostic metaphysicians ought also to be recognized, as H.J. Krämer[16] long ago pointed out in such detail. The contention of this paper is the same, except that it attempts to show that it is the "Allogenes group" of the Sethian gnostic apocalypses that had such an impact upon Plotinus and his successors, not only as catalysts that caused him to tighten up his thinking, but also as sources of doctrine, insofar as these treatises built their systems upon those of previous Platonists and Neopythagoreans.

Furthermore, this paper has urged the priority within the "Allogenes group" of the treatise *Allogenes*, although without the benefit of intensive analysis and comparison; the author of this work must in any case be understood as a Sethian but probably not professional school Platonist who was aware of first and second century metaphysical doctrine, perhaps in the form of written digests. The author's goal seems to have been to interpret the Sethian practice of visionary ascension derived from the traditional Sethian baptismal rite (as its vestigial terminology in *Zost.* amply demonstrates) in terms of Platonic ontology and contemplative technique, and also to develop further the scheme of the derivation of transcendent hypostatic beings already in evidence in *Ap. John* in directions suggested by Neopythagorean arithmological speculation on the production of the Many out of the One.

Finally, as apparently the first witness to the triads Being-Life-Mind and Existence-Vitality-Mentality, the author of *Allogenes* may have been an important contributor to the development of the Middle Platonic exegesis of passages from Plato's writings on the relation of intelligence to life and being such as *Timaeus* 39E and *Sophist* 248C-E, albeit probably without ever citing or perhaps even consulting those passages himself. It very may well be that *Allogenes* was the source of Plotinus's use of these triads, as well as that of Porphyry, particularly if the latter was the author of the *Parmenides* commentary, as Hadot has argued so weightily. In all events, I hope to have shown that the "Allogenes group" and *Allogenes* in particular form an important new link in the transition from Middle Platonism to Neoplatonism.

NOTES

1. See J.D. Turner, *Nag Hammadi, Gnosticism and Early Christianity*, ch.3, "Sethian Gnosticism: A Literary History," pp. 55-86, ed. C.W. Hedrick, Robert Hodgson (Peabody, Mass.: Hendrickson Publishers, 1986).
2. See P. Hadot, "Être, Vie Pensée chez Plotin," in *Les sources de Plotin* (Entretiens sur l'antiquité classique V, Vandoeuvres-Geneva: Fondation Hardt, 1960), pp. 107-120, 130-136.
3. P. Hadot, "La métaphysique de Porphyre," in *Porphyre* (Entretiens sur l'antiquité classique XII, Vandoeuvres-Geneva: Fondation Hardt, 1960), pp. 140-141 and *idem, Porphyre et Victorinus* (2 vols., Paris: Etudes Augustiniennes, 1968), 1.255-272.
4. *Anon. Taurensis* frg. XII, 23-33 in W. Kroll, "Ein neuplatonischer Parmenides-kommentar in einem Turiner Palimpsest," *Rheinisches Museum für Philologie* 47 (1893): 599-627; cf. P. Hadot, "Fragments d'un commentaire de Porphyre sur le Parmenide," *Revue des Etudes Grecques* 74 (1961): 410-438; and *idem, Porphyre et Victorinus*, 2.104-106 and references to discussion in vol. 1 in index, 2.145.
5. W. Theiler, *Porphyrius und Augustin* (Halle: M. Niemeyer, 1933), pp. 4-5.
6. E.R. Dodds, "Numenius and Ammonius," in *Les sources de Plotin* (Entretiens sur l'Antiquité Classique V; Vandoeuvres-Geneva: Fondation Hardt, 1960), pp. 1-332; cf. P. Merlan on Numenius, "Greek Philosophy from Plato to Plotinus," in *The Cambridge History of Later Greek and Early Medieval Philosophy* (Cambridge: The University Press, 1967), pp. 96-106.
7. M. Baltes, "Numenios von Apamea und der platonische Timaios," *Vigiliae Christianae* 39 (1975): 241-270.
8. J. Dillon, *The Middle Platonists: 80 B.C. to A.D. 200* (Ithaca: Cornell University Press, 1977), pp. 394-395.
9. I append here some results of the analysis of H. Lewy, *Chaldaean Oracles and Theurgy: Mysticism, Magic and Platonism in the Later Roman Empire* (Recherches d'Archéologie, de Philosophie et d'Histoire XIII, Cairo: l'Institut Francais, 1956).
10. H.A. Wolfson, "Negative Attributes in the Church Fathers and the Gnostic Basilides," *Harvard Theological Review* 50 (1957): 145-156; cf. also J. Whittaker, "Neopythagoreanism and Negative Theology," *Symbolae Olsoensis* 44 (1969): 109-125; *idem*, "Neopythagoreanism and the Transcendent Absolute," *Symbolae Olsoensis* 48 (1973): 77-86; *idem*, "ΕΠΕΚΕΙΝΑ ΝΟΤ ΚΑΙ ΟΤΣΙΑΣ," *Vigiliae Christianae* 23 (1969): 91-104; and M. Jufresa, "Basilides, A Path to Plotinus," *Vigiliae Christianae* 35 (1981): 1-15.
11. H.J. Krämer, *Der Ursprung der Geistmetaphysik: Untersuchungem zur Geschichte des Platonismus zwischen Platon und Plotin* second ed. (Amsterdam: B.R. Grüner, 1967), pp. 193-369; cf. my "The Gnostic Threefold Path to Enlightenment: The Ascent of Mind and the Descent of Wisdom," *Novum Testamentum* 22 (1980): 336-337.
12. See the analysis of the relation of the *Oracles* and Numenius by E.R. Dodds, "Numenius and Ammonius," op. cit. supra and the ensuing discussion of his paper in the same work.

13. Pointed out by J.M. Dillon, *The Middle Platonists*, op. cit. supra, pp. 350-351.

14. See C. Schmidt, *Plotins Stellunmg um Gnosticismus und kirchlichen Christentum* (Texte und Untersuchungen zur altchristlichen Literatur 20, Leipzig: H.C. Hinrichs, 1901); J.H. Sieber, "An Introduction to the Tractate Zostrianos from Nag Hammadi," *Novum Testamentum* 15 (1973): 233-240; C. Elsas, *Neuplatonische und gonstiche Weltablehnung in der Schule Plotins* (Berlin & New York: W. de Gruyter, 1975; J.M. Robinson, "The Three Steles of Seth and the Gnostics of Plotinus," in *Proceedings of the International Conference on Gnosticism: Stockholm, August 20-25, 1977* (Stockholm: Almqvist & Wiksell, 1977), pp. 132-142: B.A. Pearson, "The Tractate Marsanes (*NHC* X) and the Platonic Tradition," in *Gnosis: Festschrift für Hans Jonas*, ed. B Aland (Vandenhoeck & Ruprecht, 1978), pp. 373-384; and my own articles cited above.

15. R.T. Wallis, "Plotinus and the Gnostics" (23 pp., forthcoming).

16. H.J. Krämer, *Der Ursprung der Geistmetaphysik*, op. cit. supra, pp. 223-264.

Soul and Nous in Plotinus, Numenius and Gnosticism

Richard T. Wallis

Late Neoplatonic metaphysics, as I have written elsewhere, is in many ways a series of footnotes to the *Enneads*.[1] This is not, of course, to play down either the school's internal disputes both on metaphysics itself and on the means of salvation, or the return of Plotinus's successors to procedures, like allegorization of mythology, and forms of exposition, like the extended Platonic or Aristotelian commentary, which he had either minimized or rejected altogether. Yet there remains in my view a doctrinal unity underlying ancient pagan Neoplatonism,[2] which had not been present in Middle Platonism or Hermetism, or, as the Nag Hammadi discoveries confirm, in Gnosticism, and which is absent from most Christian or post-Christian versions of Platonism. As Porphyry observes, Plotinus did not always make clear the logical interconnections of his thought,[3] and much of his successors' task lay in clarifying these and resolving the tensions or inconsistencies that abound on all levels of his universe.[4] Professor Armstrong regards the doctrine of Nous as both the weak point and the growing point of his system,[5] whereas I feel, with Iamblichus,[6] that the problems are strongest in his view of Soul. But the point has little importance, since serious tensions are clearly present on both levels and were to raise difficulties for his successors. What I wish to show here is how these tensions are linked in Plotinus with a "love-hate" relationship towards Gnosticism and Gnosticizing trends within Platonism, and how, on the level of Nous, they often result from resemblances to views found within

461

Gnosticism, whereas on that of Soul they follow rather from a reaction against Gnostic ideas.

Of course, if the above remarks are correct, any idea of comparing Plotinus with "Gnosticism" as such, rather than with the various trends within that movement, rests on a fallacy, and even to compare him with any sizeable number of those trends clearly falls outside the scope of a single paper. I shall therefore explain the procedure I intend to follow here. In considering Plotinus, we can obviously not confine ourselves to his anti-Gnostic polemic (*Enn.* II.9) or even to the group of four treatises (*Enn.* III.8, V.8, V.5 and II.9) [30-33][7] of which this forms the conclusion. For the triad Being-Life-Intellect, the parallel to the Nag Hammadi texts that has most caught scholars' attention,[8] is barely mentioned in the anti-Gnostic quartet[9] and is most prominent in the immediately succeeding VI.6 [34] *On Numbers*, a work with the same title as one ascribed to a certain Aquilinus, who may or may not be the Gnostic teacher mentioned in Porphyry's *Life of Plotinus*.[10] We shall similarly find anti-Gnostic polemic in other contemporary treatises, such as IV.3-5 [27-29] *On the Soul* and VI.7 [38] *On the Ideas and the One*. Hence while, on this subject as on others, account must be taken of all Plotinus's works, it is the texts of his "early middle" period that should receive our special attention.

On the Gnostic side, whatever our view of the identity of Plotinus's opponents,[11] and while it would be foolish to ignore any of the ancient evidence, our starting-point must be the two Nag Hammadi tractates, *Zostrianos* (VIII.I) and *Allogenes* (XI.3), with titles identical to those named by Porphyry as used by Plotinus's opponents.[12] Despite disagreement on almost everything else, no-one, to my knowledge, has seriously contested that these are the works in question, and on literary and doctrinal grounds it seems virtually certain.[13] Special attention should also be given to the other two "Neoplatonizing" Nag Hammadi texts, the *Three Steles of Seth* (VII.5) and *Marsanes* (X.1), though I am less sure than some that Plotinus knew these particular works,[14] and to the two Christian (or Christianized) "Sethian" works (to use a convenient, if controversial term)[15] which refer to figures from Porphyry's list, the *Apocryphon of John*, whose longer version cites *Zoroaster*,[16] and the anonymous treatise from the Bruce Codex, which mentions Nicotheus, as well as Marsanes.[17] Among Middle Platonic and late Neoplatonic sources three are of outstanding importance, the fragments of Numenius, the *Chaldaean Oracles* and the fragments of the "Porphyrian" *Parmenides* commentary.

Of the works mentioned in the last paragraph two will here receive special attention. The first is *Zostrianos*, for three reasons. One is that the editors of *Allogenes* and *Marsanes* are here to expound the teaching of those works. Second, of the four "Neoplatonizing" Nag Hammadi tractates, *Zostrianos* is the most typically "Gnostic," if we can still speak in such terms; at least, it is closest to the teaching of Plotinus's opponents, notably in referring unmistakably, if allusively, to the fall of Sophia and the ignorant demiurge, and in its hostility towards the material world.[18] Third, it contains remarkable resemblances to Plotinus's accounts of Intellectual contemplation in V.8 and VI.7, and rests in my view both on a common philosophical tradition and a similar philosophico-religious experience.[19] I therefore do not see such resemblances as indicating Gnostic influence on Neoplatonism, except in the sense that I believe that the prominence of certain themes, such as the one just noted, in Plotinus's early middle period derives, in large part at least, from his Gnostic pre-occupations,[20] whether from hostility to their teaching, as in his account of the World-Soul's activity, or, as in his account of the Intelligible world, from a desire to show that their teaching is already found in Platonism in a superior form.[21] *Zostrianos* thus constitutes a paradigm of Plotinus's "love-hate" relationship with Gnosticism, and, in illustration of its attractions and dangers for a Platonist, as Plotinus saw them, I shall also give special attention to the Middle Platonist towards whom a similar "love-hate" relationship is clearest on his part, Numenius of Apamea. For it was of course precisely its appeal for Platonists, including members of his school, that led to Plotinus's preoccupation with Gnosticism, which he would otherwise doubtless have ignored as completely as he did orthodox Christianity and most popular religion, including the popular Platonism of the "Platonic underworld."[22] We may divide the relevant doctrines into three groups: (a) those on which Plotinus shows strong affinities to *Zostrianos* and/or Numenius, points on which the post-Iamblicheans often reacted against him; (b) those Gnostic doctrines against which Plotinus himself reacted and where later Neoplatonists followed him; and (c) those points, notably multiplication of Hypostases, on which later Neoplatonists stood closer to Gnosticism than he did.

First, however, I wish to stress the importance of one point already made, the significance of which is often misconceived, that *Zostrianos* refers unmistakably, if allusively, to the fall of Sophia and the ignorant demiurge. Where a doctrine is absent or its presence debatable (as, for instance, the Theory of Forms in most of Plato's later works) we may be in doubt whether an author means to reject it or is simply omitting it as irrelevant to the present discussion.[23] But where its presence is unmistakable, but allusive, we have no such choice. The doctrine must have been so familiar to the author's readers that it could be taken for granted without the need for detailed exposition. And it is clear from *Zostrianos*'s stress on the creator's ignorance and the inferiority of his work that he regards it as of fundamental importance. Thus, however it may be with other Neoplatonizing Gnostic texts, the doctrines in question are basic to *Zostrianos*.

Of *Zostrianos*'s treatment of these doctrines only two features call for special mention. One is the curious apparent transition between, or identification of, Sophia and Barbelo in the admittedly fragmentary passage 82-83. Here Sieber's explanation, that Sophia, as a manifestation of Barbelo, is identical with Barbelo, may be correct.[24] Or the passage may be a relic of an older "Simonian" system, in which the divine thought (*Ennoia* or *Epinoia*) itself undergoes a fall,[25] in contrast to the multiplication of female principles found in the more developed systems. Of this passage I shall say more later. The second point to note is the phrase "image of an image" used of the demiurge's creation of the sensible world,[26] a phrase echoed in Plotinus's anti-Gnostic polemic,[27] and clearly deriving from *Republic* X's criticism of artistic creation, applied by Plotinus to his own portrait.[28] It is therefore interesting that Plotinus's counter-claim that the artist may imitate the archetypal Logoi of the sensible world comes at V.8.1.32-40, i.e. in the second work of his anti-Gnostic quartet. Since that work's account of natural production clearly leads up to Chapter eight's attack (lines 7-23) on Gnostic devaluation of the sensible world, we may wonder whether Plotinus's "revisionist" view of art may have been an attempt to forestall *Zostrianos*'s line of argument at the outset.

The most important resemblances between Plotinus and *Zostrianos*, by contrast, occur in their accounts of the Intelligible world, in relation both to the Being-Intellect (or Knowledge)-Life triad (of which I shall say a little more later, leaving other participants to discuss it in more detail) and in their vitalistic descriptions of that world and the contemplation thereof. In Plotinus, as we have seen, the most striking examples occur in *Enn.* V.8 [31] the second work of the anti-Gnostic quartet, and VI.7 [38], the first part of which forms an anti-Gnostic interpretation of the *Timaeus*. A literal interpretation of that work would, in Plotinus's view, involve its producer in deliberation, and hence in doubt and ignorance;[29] moreover, in turning his attention to the sensible world he would be attracted towards that world, i.e., to an inferior state,[30] while, in sending souls there, he would seem to have intended them for a worse condition than if they had remained in the Intelligible world — a Gnostic conclusion *par excellence!*[31] Most fundamentally of all, since the sensible world did not exist before its production, how could the idea of producing it have occurred to him?[32]

We thus seem to be faced with the absurdity either that sense-perception, the elements, and the various natural species exist in the Intelligible world or that the lower, sensible world constitutes the actualization (and hence the perfection) of what was present in the higher realm only in potential form.[33] Plotinus's answer, of course, is that the sensible world is a continual unfolding of the eternal contemplation of Nous, which contains the archetypes of that world's constituents in more unified, and hence more perfect, non-material form — sensations, for instance, being dim intellections.[34] In propounding this answer Plotinus discusses two entities that bulk large within Gnosticism — Primal Man and the True Earth — though he integrates them with traditional Greek philosophical debates, the former of them, for instance, arising in a discussion of the Platonic and Aristotelian definitions of man.[35] The True Earth, which, Plotinus claims, some Gnostics regard as the archetype of this one,[36] is described in detail in the anonymous work from the Bruce Codex[37] and briefly mentioned in the Nag Hammadi *Gospel of the Egyptians*.[38] But it is *Zostrianos*, whose hero ascends through a series of "True Earths" corresponding to the several levels of the Intelligible Cosmos, that presents the closest parallels to Plotinus, as can be seen if we set V.8.3.30 ff. and VI.7.12.4 ff. alongside the relevant passages from that work.[39] In addition to both authors' vitalistic conception of the elements of the Intelligible world, and their clear common dependence on past tradition, including the True Earth of the *Phaedo* myth, the Aristotelian doctrine of Nous, and the vitalism of the Stoics,[40] we may observe that *Zostrianos* describes his ascent as a "vision,"[41] and both sources, in my view, rest on a common experience.[42] Doctrinally we may note their agreement on six points: (a) the membership of souls in the Intelligible world,[43] (b) the existence of Forms of individuals,[44] (c) the Aristotelian doctrine of the identity of Nous and its objects, which leads *Zostrianos*, like Plotinus to describe the members of the Intelligible world as "thoughts,"[45] (d) the notion of Intelligible Matter (the "barrenness," or *sterēsis*, mentioned at 116.12 ff.),[46] (e) the identity-in-diversity among the members of the Intelligible order,[47] and (f) the doctrine expounded at length in another of Plotinus's early middle works, VI.4-5 [22-23], that incorporeal beings are free from spatial limitations and hence present everywhere in their entirety,[48] or, in the words of Plotinus and Porphyry, are "everywhere and nowhere"; hence their "presence," or operation, at a particular portion of the material world is due to their "wishing" to be there.[49] The first four of these doctrines, we may observe, were either rejected or considerably qualified by Iamblichus and his successors,[50] especially the first of them, which in their view ascribed too exalted a status to Soul, especially the human soul, a point on which Iamblichus regarded Plotinus and his pupils as having followed Numenius too closely.[51] To Numenius's views we shall therefore now turn.

The first Numenian doctrine to be examined is that of *proschrēsis* whereby the first God uses the second God to contemplate, while the latter uses the Third God (his own lower phase, as we shall see) to produce.[52] Plotinus, of course, normally rejects any such view as fatal to divine transcendence in making the higher Hypostases dependent on the lower; it was, however, accepted by the author of the anonymous *Parmenides* commentary[53] and may be propounded in Plotinus's early work V.1 [10] 7.4-6, which appears to describe Nous as originating as the One's self-contemplation, though Dr. O'Daly has suggested an alternative explanation of the passage which neither does violence to the Greek nor contradicts Plotinus's normal thought.[54] The doctrine is, however, clearly maintained by Philo, who in one place describes God as employing *ennoia* and *dianoēsis* to contemplate his works,[55] while elsewhere God is said to use the Logos to shape the sensible world;[56] similarly in the *Tripartite Tractate* the Logos uses the Archon of this world as his instrument to shape the latter.[57]   The higher, contemplative form of *proschrēsis* likewise occurs in several Gnostic texts. In the *Apocryphon of John Ennoia*, identified with Barbelo, is described as the thought of the Supreme God, the reflection in which he beholds himself;[58] a similar view is found in the *Megalē Apophasis*, ascribed to Simon Magus, where *Ennoia* (or *Epinoia*) forms a unity-in-duality with the primal Nous, while a passage of *Zostrianos* cited earlier[59] describes a female being, either Barbelo or Sophia, as the "introspection of the pre-existing God."[60]   Whatever his earlier hesitations over this, or other Numenian divisions of Intellect,[61] in II.9.1. Plotinus firmly rejects any such notion or any doubling of the One or Nous into a potential and an actual or an inactive and active phase. Even our minds, he argues, must be aware of their own thoughts and to postulate a further principle of awareness in Nous deprives it of true self-knowledge and lead to the absurdity of an infinite regress.[62] Consistently with his "nominalist" reaction against the Gnostics' multiplication of Hypostases, he regards *Epinoia* as a mere conceptual distinction, which has no correspondence in reality, and which cannot therefore introduce any ontological division into the activity of Nous.[63]

It is a common observation that the further distinctions within Nous rejected in II.9.1 and II.9.6, after a more sympathetic consideration in the early work III.9 [13].1, are easier to identify with those propounded by Numenius than those of any extant Gnostic system.[64]

The highest level Plotinus's opponents, like Numenius, are said to identify with the *Timaeus*'s "Ideal Animal" (the sensible world's Intelligible model) and with "Nous at rest," containing all within itself; similarly, like Numenius, they identify their second level with Nous "in motion" or "in contemplation" and their third with the "discursively reasoning" (*dianõoumenos*) or "planning" Nous, an interpretation of *Timaeus* 39E. (Sometimes, Plotinus adds, they see this level as the demiurge, while elsewhere they identify the latter with Soul,[65] an inconsistency Plotinus's pupils were to find within him![66] In fact, in the developed Gnostic systems, at least two further entities, Sophia and the demiurge (whom Plotinus suggests identifying respectively with higher and lower Soul, often termed respectively Soul and Nature, within his own system),[67] intervene between Intelligible and sensible worlds. A threefold division of the Intelligible world appears in both *Zostrianos* and *Allogenes*, into the Hidden One (*Kalyptos*), the First-Appearing One (*Prõtophanes*) and the Self-Begotten One (*Autogenes*) equated with the members of the Triad Being-Life-Intellect, or Existence-Knowledge-Life.[68] The resemblance to Numenius and to the views of Plotinus's opponents, at first sight far from evident, becomes clearer if, as I have suggested elsewhere, we suppose that Numenius regarded the Forms as pre-existing (i.e. hidden) within his first Nous and brought forth (or first manifested) by his second Nous.[69] We may further recall that in *Allogenes* the Triple Power (the intermediary between the supreme One and the sensible world) or, more precisely, its lowest phase (i.e. the Self-Begotten One), is said to act on the sensible world "successively and individually, continuing to rectify the failures from Nature," a view rejected by Plotinus as absurd.[70] Coincidentally or not, Plotinus here also rejects an image used by Numenius, of the demiurge as a husbandman, who, in the relevant fragment is said to "sow, distribute and transplant" the souls assigned him by the supreme God.[71] It is thus interesting that, though both Numenius and *Allogenes* anticipate Plotinus in using the "undiminished giving" concept of divine production,[72] neither uses it, as he does, to exempt God (or at least God's lowest phase) from deliberate attention to his products. And, as we shall see, this is by no means the most Gnostic feature of Numenius's account of divine activity.

First, however, we may note one more feature of the triadic structure of Nous, that *Enn.* VI.6 and the first part of *Zostrianos* are almost the only extant texts to present the order Being-Intellect (or Knowledge)-Life;[73] elsewhere, including the latter part of *Zostrianos*,[74] the normal order Being-Life-Intellect is all but universal. In VI.7, however, in equating Life with the initial stage of Nous, while it is still "groping for vision" (i.e., the stage of Intelligible Matter) Plotinus implies that Life is in fact the highest of the three.[75] Yet at VI.6.17.35-43 he observes that, if the "Ideal Animal" includes souls as well as Intellects, Life must be the lowest member of the triad.[76] In other words, he seems to be saying, *Zostrianos*'s order is valid only if we rank the "Ideal Animal" *below* Intellect proper, a reversal not merely of the views of Numenius and Plotinus's Gnostic opponents, but of Plato himself, though there were Platonists, like Atticus and Longinus, who upheld it.[77]

Before discussing Numenius's Third God in detail, we must make two points concerning that being's relation to the Second God. The first is the parallel between Numenius's views on the relation between the Second and Third Gods and those between Nous and the human soul. For just as our soul at its highest is identical with its Intelligible origin,[78] so the Third God is merely the lower, active phase of the contemplative Second God.[79] In other words, there is no Soul as a separate Hypostasis for Numenius on either divine or human level, merely a lower manifestation of the Second Hypostasis. The full importance of this point will become clear later.

The second preliminary point concerns the problem whether, as certain texts suggest, Numenius believed in a doctrine of cosmic cycles similar to that of the Stoics and the *Politicus* myth,[80] with his Third God alternately governing the sensible world and subsequently returning to share the contemplation of the Second God. This is suggested by the statement that the Second God "being double, creates his own Idea and the cosmos"; *epeita theōrētikos holōs*.[81] The alternative, if we do not resort to the risky procedure of amending the text, is to suppose, with Henry, that Numenius is describing two phases of his Second God, which are logically, but not chronologically distinct.[82] God is elsewhere similarly stated at one time to look to man and keep him alive, while at another he returns to his vantage-point. Here, however, though the allusion to the *Politicus* myth seems unmistakable, Numenius could have in mind two phases of divine activity *within* a single world-period, i.e. to be saying simply that individual men live or die according to whether God looks to them or not.[83] A third text, from Macrobius, but of probable Numenian origin, describes Nous as alternately undergoing division and again (*rursus*) returning from division to indivisibility, and thereby fulfilling its cosmic functions (*mundi implet officia*) while not abandoning the mysteries of its own nature (*naturae suae arcana non desirit*).[84] Here we may choose between the above explanations; either (a) a "cosmic cycles" doctrine is presupposed, or (b) Numenius has a purely logical succession in mind, or (c) he may be describing the operations of Nous within the individual (though *"mundi"* makes this less likely). More probably its operations in both the world and the individual are meant, in which case we have a further parallel between the two.

However this may be, Numenius's desire to preserve his Second God in continual contemplation, and thereby safeguard divine transcendence, is here very evident. A similar attitude occurs in his comparison of the Second God to a helmsman sailing over the sea of Matter, while keeping his attention fixed above.[85] But for the Third God the consequences are less satisfactory. Thus the statement, in the second passage discussed in our last paragraph, that on returning to its vantage-point Nous enjoys a happy life[86] implies that when its attention is directed here, its life is less happy. The notorious fragment 11 goes even further, declaring that, in unifying Matter, the Second God is split by it,[87] with the result that he (or rather his lower phase, the Third God) ceases to dwell in his own sphere, the Intelligible order, for in reaching out for (or desiring-, *eporexamenos*) Matter he becomes forgetful of himself.[88] Plotinus's rejection of any such view (at least in his normal thought) is emphatic. For him the Hypostases produce "without inclination, will or movement" towards their products;[89] hence the demiurge knows his activity on the world only in its unity, not *qua* directed towards the world.[90] Otherwise, as we have seen, and as Numenius concedes, he would experience an attraction to the sensible world parallel to that undergone by the human soul.[91] Thus at IV.3 [27] 17.21-31 Plotinus compares the individual soul to a sailor, whose concern for his ship puts him in danger of perishing with it, a passage combining phrases from two of Numenius's descriptions of his Second God.[92] That Numenius went further than other Platonists (and even than some Gnostics) in regarding Matter as an evil principle in permanent opposition to God is well known;[93] and like most Gnostics, but in strong contrast to orthodox Hellenic thought, he extended this to the matter of the planetary spheres, where he even located the Platonic hells[94] — views which Professor Armstrong rightly sees as the most definitely oriental feature of his thought.[95]

Plotinus's reaction against Gnosticism was thus equally a reaction against Gnosticizing Platonists like Numenius. How far this reaction led him to modify his own philosophy is a vexed question, and we may well hesitate to give too confident an answer to a problem that has led scholars of the caliber of Dodds[96] and Puech[97] along demonstrably false paths. Yet I believe that certain tensions in Plotinus's doctrine of Soul, especially in his "early middle" period, tensions which were to divide his followers, can best be seen as in large part the result of his anti-Gnostic pre-occupations. It is, of course, true that his concern was with philosophical theories rather than with individuals or schools. Yet, at the very least, the need to remove any Gnostic implications from his account of the Hypostases gave special point to views that he might in any case have derived from reflection on earlier thinkers. Thus Plotinus's denial of divine deliberation arose, as Professor Pépin and I have shown, from the Aristotelian view of deliberation as developed in the Skeptics' theological criticisms,[98] while the claim that divine attention remains "above" is equally Aristotelian.[99] Also derived from the Skeptics is Plotinus's argument that our everyday consciousness, based as it is on *phantasia*, and thus dealing with images of the Forms rather than the Forms themselves, is inconsistent with perfect knowledge.[100] Hence, the work *On the Soul* argues, on her return to the Intelligible world, our soul is wholly absorbed in contemplation of that world, a view we have seen Iamblichus attacking as too Numenian.[101] Clearly then, if the World-soul is to escape the Gnostics' charge that her knowledge is inferior to that attainable by man, she, like the purified human soul, must permanently transcend discursive, temporal thought — a strong contrast to the view of the early work V.1 [10] 4.10-25 that her contemplation differs from Nous in involving temporal succession.[102] In IV.4 [28] 15, on the other hand she is said to differ from Nous in generating time without herself being subject thereto,[103] an obviously unsatisfactory conclusion, since we might allow Nous to generate time directly without the intermediary of Soul. Nor does Plotinus's claim that the purified soul, in contemplating Nous, also possess consciousness of herself,[104] provide a satisfactory answer, since such self-awareness can be only of herself *qua* identified with Nous. And while the distinction between Nous and the individual soul becomes clear when the latter leaves the Intelligible world, this obviously cannot happen with the changeless divine souls.[105] In short the distinction between Nous and higher World-Soul has vanished, and there remains only her lower level, Nature (*physis*), the power that unconsciously molds the sensible world, which at IV.4.13.19-21 is described as the "image impressed from Soul upon Matter"; indeed doubt is expressed there whether Nature can be ranked among "True Beings."[106] Nor is it easy to see how the distinction between Nous and higher Soul could be restored without a dangerous lapse towards Gnosticism, similar to that we have found in Numenius. The same general view emerges from other works of Plotinus's "early middle" period.

    That the first three works of the anti-Gnostic quartet are little concerned with Soul is observed in Theiler and Beutler's introduction to II.9.[107] This is not surprising of V.5, which is wholly concerned with Nous and the One. But III.8 and V.8 raise more serious problems. Omitting V.8 for the moment, we may observe that III.8,[108] after its discussion of Nature (chs. 2-4) turns to Soul, which is said to exercise a higher form of contemplation. The nature of this, however, is nowhere made clear, and when in III.8.6 Plotinus passes to a more detailed account of Soul's contemplation, it is to the human soul that he refers, as is clear from his references to her as engaging in external activity, though he disguises this by referring to "Soul" without distinction. Nor does II.9 resolve the problem. After chapter I's assertion that the distinction between the Hypostases has often been demonstrated,[109], the rest of the work, with its assertion that the World-Soul's middle level (that corresponding to discursive thought in us) does not descend or deliberate,[110] merely raises the difficulty anew.

The same attitude is apparent in other works of the period. That VI.4-5 [22-23] seems to "telescope" the Hypostases has often been noted. Similarly, passages like that cited earlier from VI.6.17.35-43, on the "Ideal Animal," appear, like *Zostrianos* and Numenius,[111] to grant Soul full membership of the Intelligible World.[112] Other passages indeed refer to Logoi, explicitly or by implication situated on the level of Soul, intermediate between the Forms in Nous and the formative principles in Nature.[113] Yet that this cannot solve the problem of the higher soul's contemplation is clear if we ask what these Logoi are. In the human soul they are evidently mental images or verbal formulae, the objects of *phantasia*.[114] But this cannot, as we have seen, be true of the divine souls, and we may once more ask why a level of Logoi intermediate between Nous and Nature is necessary at all. In fact, V.8 and VI.7 often imply that the sensible world proceeds from Nous without any intermediary.[115] Most revealing of all is V.8.7.15-16, which in such a passage adds "whether through the intermediary of Soul, or some Soul, makes no difference to the present discussion," thus belatedly reintroducing a principle for which Plotinus has to find room, but which has become superfluous, if not an embarrassment to him.

Another important chapter in this context is the somewhat later III.7[45] 11. Here an "unquiet power of Soul" is said not merely to generate time, but to subject herself thereto,[116] by an act of self-assertion parallel to that which causes the fall of the human soul.[117] How "Gnostic" these statements are has been debated by Profs. Jonas[118] and Manchester;[119] I will merely assert for my part that Plotinus is at the very least guilty of a carelessness of expression, which, if not fully Gnostic, has as strong a Gnostic tendency as most of those we have criticized in Numenius. Nor does Plotinus make clear which power of Soul is in question. If it is the higher level of Soul, the "middle" level of II.9.2,[120] the difficulties raised in IV.3-4 emerge anew. If, on the other hand, Plotinus has Nature in mind, there is no conflict between the two works, but in that case we are no nearer distinguishing higher Soul from Nous. Moreover, as Plotinus argues against the Gnostics, whose demiurge he suggests equating with Nature in his own system, there can be no question of self-assertion or ambition on that level.[121] Whatever level he is referring to, he would surely have had to reply that his assertions are only metaphorical. But in any case the basic problem remains unanswered.

We may observe a similar ambiguity in Plotinus's view of the status of the heavens. He is, of course, emphatic in upholding the divinity of the celestial souls against the Gnostics; for, as he argues against Numenius, the matter of their bodies is purer than our own.[122] Its control by the celestial gods thus requires no attention or effort on their part, nor does it distract them from contemplation; hence the Gnostics' charge that they are inferior to man in being unable to leave the material world falls to the ground.[123] Nor should we probably read too much into V.8.3.27-30's assertion that the celestial gods contemplate the Intelligible world only "from afar"; for even the work *On the Soul*, where we have seen as strong a tendency as anywhere in Plotinus to "telescope" the Hypostases, recognizes degrees of rank among souls.[124] But there can be no denying the inconsistency of his account of the individual soul's descent and re-ascent through the heavens. Thus in IV.3.17.1 ff. the heavens, though the purest part of the material world, are yet the first stage in her descent, the point where, as IV.4.5[125] tells us, she first reawakens the memory that ultimately draws her back here. We may recall Macrobius's account of her descent, probably derived, as we have seen, from Numenius, where an unconscious attraction to this world, similar to the unconscious memory of the Plotinus passage, draws her here.[126] Yet in IV.3.18 even the human soul, on reaching the heavens, is said to be wholly within the Intelligible world and hence not to need discursive reasoning (or presumably memory).[127] We thus see here a further tension within Plotinus's system, with echoes, even if distant ones, of Numenius.

A similar problem to that over the relation of Soul to Nous is posed for Plotinus, though less explicitly, over that of Nous to the One by the fact that in the mystical experience Nous is in turn transcended.[128] It is therefore not surprising that Plotinus sometimes sounds a pessimistic note over the origin of Nous. What is surprising is to find such a declaration at III.8.8 32-38 — in the first work of the anti-Gnostic quartet.[129]   Hence, while Plotinus's successors unanimously agreed with him in excluding deliberation and attention to their products from the Hypostases,[130] the fundamental dilemma of his system left them with only two consistent alternatives.   One, found in the *Parmenides* commentator and, less consistently, in Amelius and Porphyry,[131] was to "telescope" the Hypostases into one another. The other, accepted by Iamblichus and most of his successors,[132] was to downgrade the human soul.   Since in their view she no longer contains an unfallen element or possesses a transcendent individual Intellect, she has no direct access to the divine, which she can reach only through the intermediary of a divine soul.[133]   This being so, any possibility of her superiority to those souls is destroyed at the outset, and the notion of a graded hierarchy is not merely restored, but receives ever greater emphasis.   Consistent with this approach was their rejection, as we have observed, of most of the parallels between Plotinus and *Zostrianos* regarding the Intelligible world.[134]   Yet in multiplying levels within the Intelligible world they came, as has often been observed, to resemble the ever-increasing complication of the Gnostic systems.   If we confine ourselves to the "Neoplatonizing" Gnostic texts, we may see Amelius, Porphyry, and especially the *Parmenides* commentator as resembling *Allogenes*[135] and (less certainly) *Zostrianos*, in recognizing a multiplicity of levels that are ultimately "telescoped" into one another, whereas Iamblichus's more complex hierarchy stands closer to what survives of *Marsanes*.   Plotinus's "love-hate" relationship with the Gnostics and Numenius, therefore, far from exhausting its effects with him, was to continue its influence throughout the whole history of the pagan Neoplatonic school.

NOTES

1. *Neoplatonism* (London and New York, 1972), p. 92; cf. H. Blumenthal, "Plotinus in Later Platonism," in *Neoplatonism and Early Christian Thought: Essays in Honour of A.H. Armstrong* (London, 1981), pp. 212ff. For a different view cf. Professor Whittaker's paper, "De Jamblique a Proclus," in *Entretiens Hardt XXI*, (Vandoeuvres/Geneva, 1975), pp. 65ff.
2. Including even Hierocles and the later Alexandrian School, as Mme. I. Hadot has now shown (*Hierocles et Simplicius; le Probleme du Neoplatonisme Alexandrin* [Paris 1978]).
3. *V.Pl.* 18.6-8.
4. Cf. *Neoplatonism*, pp. 90-93.
5. *Cambridge History of Later Greek and Early Medieval Philosophy* (Cambridge, 1978), p. 267.
6. *De An.*, quoted by Stobaeus I.365.5ff. Wachsmuth.

7. See R. Harder, "Eine Neue Schrift Plotins," *Hermes* LXXI (1936): 5-8; D. Roloff, *Plotin; die Gross-Schrift* (Berlin, 1970); V. Cilento, *Plotino; Paideia Antignostica* (Florence, 1971); Ch. Elsas, *Neuplatonische und Gnostische Weltablehnung in der Schule Plotins* (Berlin, 1975); F. García Bazán, *Plotino y la Gnosis* (Buenos Aires, 1981).

8. See M. Tardieu, "*Les Trois Stèles* de Seth; un ecrit gnostique retrouve a Nag Hammadi," *RSPhTh* 57 (1973): 545-575; James M. Robinson, "The *Three Steles of Seth* and the Gnostics of Plotinus," *Proc. of the International Conference on Gnosticism, Stockholm 1973* (Stockholm, 1977), pp. 132-142; John D. Turner, "The Gnostic Threefold Path to Enlightenment," *Novum Testamentum* 22 (1980): 324-351; J. Sieber "The Barbelo Aeon as Sophia in *Zostrianos* and Related Tractates," in *The Rediscovery of Gnosticism*, ed. Bentley Layton (Leiden, 1981), vol. II, pp. 788-795; also the papers of Professors Turner and Manchester read to the present conference.

9. It occurs there only at V.5.I.32-38, 2.9-13, 10.12-14; (cf. P. Hadot, "Les Sources de Plotin," in *Entretiens Hardt V* (Vandoeuvres/Geneva, 1960), pp. 110, 113, 116.

10. On Aquilinus see Porphyry, *V.Pl.* 16.3, Lydus, *De Mens.* IV.76 (on which cf. further below n. 46), and H.-Ch. Puech, *Entretiens Hardt* V, p. 164, with p. 177 of the ensuing discussion.

11. While I regard Plotinus's opponents as "Sethians" or "Barbelo-Gnostics" (on which terms cf. below n. 15). I have no quarrel with those, like Professor Bazán, who see them as Valentinians using Sethian works; see his *Plotino y la Gnosis*, cited above n. 7; "Tres Decadas de Estudios Plotinianos," *Sapientia* 13 (1980): 292ff.; "Plotino y los Textos Gnosticos de Nag-Hammadi," *Oriente-Occidente* II/2 (1981): 185-203 (on which however cf. n. 14 below). It would in any case have been hard for Gnostics in third-century Rome to escape all Valentinian influence. That Porphyry, rightly or wrongly, regarded Plotinus's opponents as Christians (*V. Pl.* 16.1ff.) was correctly maintained by Puech, *Entretiens Hardt* V, pp. 163-164, and Dodds (ibid., p. 175, with the ensuing discussion). That Christian Gnostics and Christians sympathetic to Gnosticism could use pagan works is proved by the *Apocryphon of John*'s citation of *Zoroaster* (cf. below n. 16) and the use of pagan works by the Nag Hammadi community (probably a Pachomina monastery; cf. James M. Robinson, *The Nag Hammadi Library in English* (New York, 1977), pp. 14-21, and R. van den Broeck, "The Present State of Gnostic Studies," *Vigiliae Christianae* 37 (1981): 47-49.

12. *V.Pl.* 16.6-7.

13. On *Zostrianos* see J. Sieber, "An Introduction to the Tractate *Zostrianos* from Nag Hammadi," *Novum Testamentum* 15 (1973): 233-240; for *Allogenes*, see esp. Professor Turner's paper in this volume, pp. 427-462.

14. Cf. Professor Bazán's caution in *Oriente-Occidente* II/2 (1981), cited above, n. 11, pp. 187-196. I am, however, even more dubious about his identification of *Anonymus Brucianus* with *Nicotheus* (ibid., pp. 196ff.) and still more so about his speculations concerning the *Tripartite Tractate* (ibid., pp. 185-186; cf. also the article cited there, p. 186, n. 8). Professor Turner,

in his paper in this volume, regards *Marsanes* as post-Plotinian; for a different view cf. Professor Pearson's introduction to the tractate in *Nag Hammadi Codices IX and X* (Leiden, 1981).

15. Cf. the contrasting views of H.-M. Schenke (*Rediscovery of Gnosticism*, vol. II, pp. 588-616) and F. Wisse (ibid., pp. 563-576); also the cautions of Professors Rudolph (ibid., pp. 577-578) and van den Broeck (*Vigiliae Christianae*, 37 [1981]: 54-56) and Professor Pearson's balanced assessment (*Rediscovery of Gnosticism*, vol. II, p. 504, n. 113). Certainly the "family resemblances" between the six tractates listed in the text and between *Trimorphic Protennoia* (*NHC* XIII.I) and the *Gospel of the Egyptians* (*NHC* III.2 and IV.2), on which cf. the articles of Professors Turner and Sieber cited above n. 8, make *some* common term for them desirable. Cf. Schenke's other "Sethian" works, the *Apocalypse of Adam* (*NHC* V.5) belongs to an older pre-philosophical version of the same tradition, while the "Barbelo" passages in *Melchizedek* (*NHC* IX.I) read to me, as to Professor Pearson (*Nag Hammadi Codices IX and X*, p. 38), like extraneous additions. Schenke's other two "Sethian" works, the *Hypostasis of the Archons* (*NHC* II.4) and the *Thought of Norea* (*NHC* X.2), seem to me decidedly peripheral to the group.

16. *NHC* II.1.19.10. The longer version of the *Apocryphon* also occurs at *NHC* IV.1, the shorter version at *NHC* III.1 and BG 8502.2.

17. *Anon. Bruc.* p. 12 = p. 235 of V. MacDermot's edition (Leiden, 1978), p. 342 Schmidt, p. 84 Baynes.

18. VIII.1.1 (lines 16-19), 9-10, 27, and perhaps 82-83 (cf. below p. 464 and nn. 23-28, 59-60). Cf. however VIII.1.131.10-14, cited on p. 447 of Professor Turner's paper.

19. Cf. below pp. 465-467 and esp. n. 39.

20. That Gnosticism was not the sole objective of the passages in question is clear; cf. below pp. 465-467 and nn. 35 and 98-100. On the other hand Dr. D. O'Meara (*Rediscovery of Gnosticism*, vol. I, pp. 365-378), seems to me to go too far in the opposite direction, though I agree with him (ibid., p. 371, n. 27) that some of Puech's allegedly anti-Gnostic texts, especially from Plotinus's later works (*Entretiens Hardt* V, p. 183) are highly doubtful.

21. Cf. Plotinus's attitude at *Enn.* II.9.6.6ff.

22. There is in my view no *certain* reference to non-Gnostic Christianity in the *Enneads*. III.2.[47] 8.36-9.19 may be directed at Gnosticism, or at popular religion in general. I also doubt whether III.6.[26] 6.71 is aimed at the doctrine of bodily resurrection. For more favorable references to popular religious practices ct. e.g., IV.7.[2].15, IV.3.[27].11.

23. Thus *Allogenes* XI.1.51.29-32 and *Marsanes* X.1.4.1-2 *may* allude to the fall of Sophia and its consequences, but this is far from certain. Contrast the passages from *Zostrianos* cited in n. 18 above. Cf. further below n. 93.

24. *Rediscovery of Gnosticism*, vol. II. pp. 793-794.

25. Cf. Professor Jonas's *The Gnostic Religion*, second edition (Boston, 1963), pp. 105ff., and below p. 468 and nn. 58ff.

26. *NHC* VIII.1.10.4-5.

27. *Enn.* II.9.10.27.
28. *V.Pl.* 1.8.
29. VI.7.1, 28ff., 3.1ff. Cf. the passages cited at *Neoplatonism*, p. 63.
30. Cf. VI.7.3.22ff., 8.1ff., and the texts cited at *Neoplatonism*, pp. 62-63, 76-79; also my "Divine Omniscience in Plotinus, Proclus and Aquinas," *Neoplatonism and Early Christian Thought*, cited above n. 1, p. 224 and below p. 471 and nn. 89-92, 99.
31. VI.7.1.14-21.
32. Ibid., 21-28; cf. V.8.7.1-12, following the Epicurean argument expounded at Lucretius V.181-6.
33. VI.7.3.22-33.
34. Ibid., 7.29-31, cf. *Zost.* VIII.1.48.26.
35. On Primal Man cf. VI.7.4ff., an excellent example of Plotinus's integration of discussion of a Gnostic theme with a traditional philosophical debate; cf. above n. 25.
36. On the True Earth cf. *Enn.* II.9.5.23ff., 11.11-12, VI.7.11ff.
37. *Anon. Bruc.* p. 32, = p. 249 Macdermot, p. 352 Schmidt, p. 136 Baynes.
38. It is there described as "the ethereal earth, the receiver of God, where the holy men of the great light take shape" (*NHC* III.2.50).
39. V.8.3.30ff. "The Gods belonging to that higher Heaven itself, they whose station is upon it and in it, see and know in virtue of their omnipresence to it. For all There is heaven; earth is heaven, and sea heaven; and animal and plant and man; all is the heavenly content of that heaven: and the Gods in it, despising neither men nor anything else that is there where all is of the heavenly order, traverse all that country and all space in peace." (trans. MacKenna). VI.7.12.4ff; (cf. ibid., 11.1ff): "The sky There must be living therefore not bare of stars, here known as the heavens - for stars are included in the very meaning of the word. Earth too will be There, and not void but even more intensely living and containing all that lives and moves upon our earth and the plants obviously rooted in life; sea will be There and all waters with the movement of their unending life and all the living things of the water; air too must be a member of that universe with the living things of air as here.

    The content of that living thing must surely be alive — as in this sphere — and all that lives must of necessity be There. The nature of the major parts determines that of the living forms they comprise; by the being and content of the heaven There are determined all the heavenly forms of life; if those lesser forms were not There, that heaven itself would not be." (trans. MacKenna). *Zost.* VIII.21.3ff by them all ' in many places, the place which he [5] desired and the place which he wishes, ' since they are in every place, yet ' not in any place, and since they ' make room for their spirits, ' for they are incorporeal and better than [10] incorporeal. They are undivided ' and living thoughts and a power ' of the truth with those who are purer by far ' than these, since they exist as exceedingly ' pure ' with respect to him and are [15] not like the bodies which exist ' in one [place] . . . *Zost.* VIII.1.48.3.ff. Corresponding to each of ' the aeons I saw a living earth and a living water and (air) made of 'light, and fire that cannot 'burn [. . .] all being ' simple and 'immutable with [. . .][10] simple and [. . .] ' having a [. . .] in ' many ways, with trees ' that do not perish in many ' ways, and tares [. . .][15] this way, and all these and ' imperishable fruit ' and living men and every form, ' and immortal souls ' and every shape and[20] form of mind, and ' gods of truth, and ' messengers who exist in ' great glory, and ' indissoluble bodies and[25] an unborn begetting and an ' immovable perception. '

Ibid., 55.13ff. they are in accordance with ' each of the aeons, a[15] living [earth] and ' [living] water and air ' made of light and a ' blazing fire which ' cannot [burn], and animals and[20] trees and souls ' [and] minds and men' [and] all those which exist ' [with] them,

Ibid., 113.1.1-14. and messengers and ' demons and minds and ' souls and living beings and ' trees and bodies and[5] those before them — both those ' of the simple elements ' of simple origins, and ' those in confusion ' and unmixed [. . .] air[10] and water and earth ' and number and yoking ' and movement and [. . .] and ' order and breath and ' all the rest.

Ibid., 115.2ff. They do [not] crowd one another, ' but they also dwell ' within them, existing and[5] agreeing with one another as if ' they exist from a single ' origin. They are reconciled ' because they all exist ' in a single aeon of the Hidden One,[10] [. . .] divided in power, ' for in accord with each of the ' aeons they exist, standing ' in accord with the one who reaches them.

Ibid., 116.1ff. All of them exist ' in one since they dwell together ' and are perfected individually ' in fellowship and[5] have been filled with the aeon who ' really exists. Some among ' them are those who stand ' as if they dwell in essence, ' and others like those as an essence[10] in function or suffering ' in a second, for in' them exists the [barrenness] ' of the [barrenness] who ' really exists. When the [barren ones][15] have come into being, their power ' stands.

Ibid., 117.1ff. In that world' are all living beings ' existing individually, yet joined 'together. The knowledge[5] of the knowledge is there ' and an establishment of ignorance. ' Chaos is there ' and a place [completed] for ' them all, though they are new, [10] and true light and ' darkness which has received light and he ' who does not really exist. ' He does not really exist ' [. . .] the non-being which does[15] not exist as the All.

40. An influence especially stressed in W. Theiler's *Vorbereitung des Neuplatonismus* (Berlin, 1934), ch. 2, pp. 63ff.

41. *Eg. NHC* VIII.1.48.4, etc. Similar terminology occurs in *Allogenes* (XI.3.52.10, 55.13, 58.12, 35-37), where the ascent culminates in "ignorance" of the Unknowable One, and in the *Three Steles* (VIII.5.124.18), while *Anon. Bruc.*, in the passage cited above n. 17, described Marsanes and Nicotheus as having "seen." On the mysticism of these texts see Professor Turner's article cited above n. 8; also his paper in this volume, pp. 425ff. On *Allogenes* see especially Professor Williams's important paper, "Stability as a Soteriological Theme in Gnosticism," *Rediscovery of Gnosticism*, vol. II, pp. 819-829, which rightly sees the

"primary revelation of the Unknown One," from which Allogenes receives power (XI.3.60-61) as a mystical experience similar to Plotinus's union with the One.

42. On Plotinus's experience of Intellectual vision see my article cited above n. 19, esp. pp. 122-125. Its basis is the "dematerialization" of the "cosmic Mandala" described at V.8.9.1ff.

43. *Zost.* VIII.1.48.18, 55.20, 112.3. For Plotinus cf. above p. 314 and nn. 101ff.

44. *Zost.* VIII.1.116.3, 117.3; cf. *Allog.* XI.45.6ff., 55.13. For Forms of individuals in Plotinus cf. J.M. Rist, *CQ* no. 13 (1963), pp. 223-231; H. Blumenthal, *Phronesis* II (1966), pp. 61-80, *Plotinus's Psychology: His Doctrines of the Embodied Soul* (The Hague, 1971), ch. 9, pp. 112-133.

45. *Zost.* VIII.1.117.5-6, 21.11.

46. The passage also clearly teaches the Plotinian doctrine of Procession (ibid., 14-16). For Intelligible Matter in Plotinus cf. esp. II.4[12] 3-5, II., 5[25] 3.8-19. Cf. however below n. 50. It is interesting that the Aquilinus whose treatise *On Numbers* is cited by Lydus (above n. 10) allegorized the myth of Hermes and Maia as teaching the doctrine of Intelligible Matter.

47. *Zost.* VIII.1.115.2ff., 116.1ff., 117.1ff.; cf. *Allog.* XI1.3.49.26ff. For Plotinus cf. the passages cited at *Neoplatonism*, pp. 54-55; also Proclus, ET. prop. 103.

48. *Zost.* VIII.1.21.3ff.

49. *Enn.* III.9.4, VI.4.3 17-19, Porphyry, *Sent.* 3, 27, 31, 38, 40; cf. *Neoplatonism*, pp. 50-51, 76ff., 112; cf. also *Allog.* XI.3.57.20-21, *Three Steles* VII.5.121.10-11.

50. For points (a) and (b) see below n. 51; also *Neoplatonism*, pp. 119-120, 152-153. For point (c) see Dodds's note on Proclus, *Elements of Theology*, 2nd ed. (Oxford, 1963), prop. 167 (pp. 285-287); for point (d) ibid., note on props. 89-92 (pp. 246-247), and Proclus, *Platonic Theology* III.9, pp. 39.24ff. Saffrey-Westerink. Plotinus, however, had refused to apply the term *sterēsis* to Intelligible Matter, and had stressed the latter's substantiality and the contrast with its sensible counterpart (*Enn.* II.3 [12].5.12-23, 15.17-28, II.5 [25].3.8-19).

51. Cf. the passage cited above n. 6; also Proclus ET. props, 111, 175, 204, 211; *in Tim.* I.245.17ff., II.289.3ff., III.333,28ff.; *In Parm.* 930.26ff, 948.14ff.; *Neoplatonism*, pp. 119-120, 152-153; Dodds, *Proclus: Elements*, p. xx, with the further references given there, and Professor Dillon's *Iamblichi Chalcidensis in Platonis Dialogos Commentariorium Fragmenta* (Leiden, 1973), pp. 41-47. Cf. further below pp. 475 and nn. 131-133.

52. *Fr.* 22 Des Places = Proclus *in Tim.* III.103.28-32.

53. *Fr.* 6, XIII.23ff. On the fragment cf. P. Hadot, *Porphyre et Victorinus* (Paris, 1968), vol. I, pp. 132-139, and my *Neoplatonism*, pp. 116-117.

54. *Plotinus's Philosophy of the Self* (Shannon, 1973), pp. 71-72.

55. *Quod Deus* 33-34.

56. *Leg. Alleg.* III.96.

57. *NHC* *.5.101.31ff. *The Tripartite Tractate* may also support an interpretation of Numenius, *fr*. 13 Des Places, which has been thought indefensible, that God is himself the seed which he sows. Commentators have either taken *Ho ōn* as a Hebraism (e.g., Des Places; also Festugière, *Revelation d'Hermes Trismegiste*, Vol. III, p. 44. n. 2) or amended the text (e.g., Dodds, *Entretiens Hardt* V, p. 15 and Dillon, *Middle Platonists* [London and Ithaca, NY, 1977], p. 368, n. 1). Since, however, *Trip. Tract.* I.5.65.13 describes God as sowing himself, the natural interpretation of the Numenius text may after all be correct. On the fragment cf. further below pp. 9-10 and nn. 70-71.

58. Quoted by Hippolytus, *Ref.* VI.18; for an analysis see Professor Jonas's *The Gnostic Religion*, 2nd ed. (Boston, 1963), pp. 105ff.

59. Above, p. 466.

60. VIII.1.82-83, cited above p. 465.

61. Cf. Dodds's analysis of *Enn.* III.9 [13].1 in *Entr. Hardt* V, pp. 19-20.

62. II.9.1.22ff. Cf. further below n. 100.

63. Ibid., 40ff.; against multiplication of Hypostases cf. ibid., 2.1ff., 6.1ff.

64. Cf. e.g., Professor Armstrong's comments in Vol. II of his Loeb edition, p. 226, n. 1 and p. 244, n. 2; cf. Numenius *fr*. 15 Des Places = Eusebius. *P.E.* II.18, p. 539 a-b, fr. 22 ibid., cited above n. 52.

65. II.9.1.25ff., 6.14ff.

66. Ibid. 6.21-22.; for Plotinus's parallel hesitation cf. Proclus *in Tim.* I.306.32ff., and Armstrong, Loeb, vol. III, p. 410, n. 1 (commenting III.9.1.29ff).

67. *Enn.* II.9.10.19ff., 11.19ff.

68. *Zost.* VIII.1.15.4-17; cf. *Allog.* XI.3.54.8-16, and p. 434 of Professor Turner's paper.

69. *Neoplatonism*, p. 34, cited by J. Igal, *Neoplatonism and Early Christianity*, p. 149, n. 45, in support of his identification of Plotinus's opponents with Valentinians. However this may be, Igal's dismissal of *Zostrianos* and *Allogenes* as unphilosophical, on the strength of preliminary reports about the former, was certainly premature. For equation of the divisions of Intellect criticized by Plotinus with those of the *Allogenes* group of tractates see p. 442 of Professor Turner's paper cited above n. 8 and in this volume.

70. *Allog.* XI.3.51.28-32. *Enn.* II.3 [52] 16.29ff.

71. Fr. 13 Des Places = Eusebius P.E. XI.18 p. 538 b-c. On the fragment cf. also above n. 57.

72. Numenius *fr*. 14 Des Places = Eusebius *P.E.* XI.18, pp. 538-9; *Allog.* XI.3.62.33ff, 67.16-17; cf. Dodds's note on Proclus ET. props. 26-27 (pp. 213-214).

73. Cf. also *Enn.* V.6 [24] 6.20-21; P. Hadot (*Entr. Hardt.* V, pp. 122ff., 129-130) adds Augustine *C.D.* VIII.4ff., and Origen, *De Princ.* I.3.8 (where, however, Sanctity replaces Life).

74. *NHC* VIII.1.66ff. The alternative orders in which this or an equivalent triad, sometimes occurs, (e.g., the triad *gnōsis-hypostasis-energeia* at *Mars.* X.1.9 16-18) are probably without doctrinal significance.

75. VI.7.17.14-26, 21.2-6.

76. Cf. also VI.6.8.17-27. On the contradiction cf. the discussion in *Entr. Hardt* V, pp. 148-149. On Plotinus further hesitations see *Neoplatonism*, pp. 54, 66-67.

77. Proclus *in Tim.* I.431.19-20, 322.24. Plotinus differs from these interpreters even here, however, and agrees with Plato in making being highest of the three.

78. *Frs.* 41, 42 Des Places = Iamblichus *De An.*, quoted by Stobaeus I.365.5-21 and I.458.3-4; cf. further above nn. 6 and 51 and below nn. 132-133.

79. *Fr.* 11 Des Places = Eusebius *P.E.* IX.17, p. 537 b. On the fragment cf. further below.

80. Professor Dillon, *Middle Platonists*, pp. 369-371 and Dr. O'Brien (in oral discussion with the present writer) have come out against this view; cf. also Dodds, *Entretiens Hardt*, pp. 48-52. Contrast p. 571 of Professor Turner's paper.

81. *Fr.* 16 Des Places = Eusebius *P.E.* XI.22, pp. 544ff. Dodds, op. cit., p. 16 and Dillon, op. cit., p. 369, n. 1, read *epei ho protos*. On the riskiness of amending a text in a field where so little is known cf. Theiler's remarks at *Entr. Hardt* V, p. 51.

82. *Entr. Hardt* V, p. 51. There is a similar ambiguity at *Zost.* VIII.1.74.15-16, "the three [i.e. the noetic triad] stand at one time, moving at one time."

83. *Fr.* 12 Des Places = Eusebius *P.E.* XI.18, p. 537d; cf. Dillon, op. cit., pp. 370-371.

84. Macrobius *in Somm. Sc.* I.12.12 (=T47 Leemans): ex individuo praebendo se dividendum et rursus ex diviso ad individuum revertendo et mundi implet officia et naturae suae arcana no deserit. (cf. *Zost.* VIII.1.79.10ff "moving from the undivided to existence in activity," etc.) That Leemans was right in deriving the Macrobius passage from Numenius was convincingly argued by Dodds, *Entr. Hardt*. V, pp. 8-9; cf. H. de Ley, *Macrobius and Numenius* (Brussels, 1972), who, however, is rightly hesitant over Dodds's inclusion of *In Somm. Sc.* I.10.8-11.9 in the fragment.

85. Fr. 18 Des Places = Eusebius *P.E.* XI.18, p. 539 c-d. Cf. Dillon, op. cit., p. 370, who however, sees even here an allusion to the demiurge's desire for matter, explicitly propounded in fr. 11.

86. Dillon's translation, "when God turns back into his conning-tower, *nous* lives deprived of a happy life" (op. cit., p. 371) is presumably due to an oversight.

87. Cf. the Macrobius passage cited above n. 84, where the division of Nous is compared to the Orphic myth of the rending of Dionysus by the Titans.

88. Fr. 11 = Eusebius *P.E.* XI.17-18, p. 537 a-b; cf. Dillon, op. cit., pp. 367-368.

89. *Enn.* V.1 [10] 6.25-27; cf. *Neoplatonism*, pp. 62-63.

90. *Enn.* IV.4 [28] 9.16-18.

91. *Neoplatonism*, pp. 76-79; note also Plotinus's vehement opposition to the Gnostic idea of a "declination" (*neusis*) of Sophia (II.9 chs. 2, 4, 10-12; cf. *Zost.* VIII.1.27.12).

92. Cf. frs. 11 and 18 Des Places. See above nn. 85 and 88.

93. Fr. 52 Des Places = Calcidius *in Tim.* 295-299; cf. fr. 43 ibid. = Iamblichus *De An.* I 374-375. Contrast *Marsanes*'s positive evaluation of the sensible cosmos (*NHC* X.1.5.24-26); cf. also *Zost.* VIII.1.131.10-14, cited above n. 18. Numenius fr. 16 (cited above n. 81) describes the sensible cosmos as beautiful, but he clearly does not regard it as capable of salvation in its entirety.

94. Fr. 52 Des Places = Calcidius *in Tim.* 299, fr. 25 ibid. = Proclus *in Remp.* II.128.26ff. For similar Gnostic beliefs cf. Professor Jonas's The *Gnostic Religion*, 2nd ed., pp. 254ff and Professor Rudolph's *Die Gnosis*, 2nd ed. (Göttingen, 1980), pp. 196ff. For Plotinus's attitude cf. below pp. 474-475 and nn. 122ff.

95. *Entr. Hardt* V, p. 53.

96. *Pagan and Christian in an Age of Anxiety* (Cambridge, 1965), pp. 24-26; against Dodds's view that Plotinus came to reject the notion of a fall of the soul see my *Neoplatonism*, p. 77.

97. *Entr. Hardt* V, pp. 150, 184-185; for a refutation of Puech's view that Plotinus came to reject the identification of Matter with evil cf. J.M. Rist, *Phronesis* VI.2 (1960): 154-166.

98. Cf. Professor Pépin's *Théologie Cosmique et Théologie Chrétienne* (Paris, 1964), pp. 502-504, and my *Neoplatonism*, pp. 26-27.

99. *Metaph.* 9, *Eud. Eth.* VII.12.1245b 14-19; cf. my remarks in *Neoplatonism and Early Christian Thought*, pp. 233-234; cf., however, the anti-Gnostic passages from *Enn.* II.9 cited above n. 91.

100. *Neoplatonism*, p. 26; cf. Bréhier's notices to V.3 and V.5. (but cf. also II.9.1 22ff., cited above n. 62). For Skeptical influence on Plotinus cf. also my article "Skepticism and Neoplatonism," to be published in a forthcoming volume of *Aufstieg und Niedergang der Römischen Welt.*

101. IV.3.18, IV.4.1-2; cf. above pp. 461-468 and nn. 6, 51, 78; also below p. 472 and nn. 132-133.

102. Cf. also III.9.[13]1.34-37. Contrast IV.4[28].15-16.

103. IV.4.15.13ff.

104. Ibid., 2.30-32.

105. Ibid., 6.1.ff.

106. Ibid., 13.19-22.

107. *Plotins Schriften*, trans. R. Harder, ed. and rev. W. Theiler, R. Beutler, band IIIb, p. 414.

108. III.8.6, esp. 29ff.

109. II.9.1 16-19.

110. Ibid., 2.4ff. For Plotinus's hesitation between a twofold and a threefold division of Soul cf. *Neoplatonism*, pp. 73-74, and Armstrong, *Cambridge History*, pp. 224-226.

111. Cf. above pp. 467-468, and nn. 43 and 78.

112. Cf. e.g., VI.4[22].14.17ff.

113. E.g., V.8.1 34-36 (the "Phidias" passage, where, however, the Logoi are not clearly distinguished from the pure Forms), VI.7.5.8-11.

114. IV.3.30.

115. E.g., VI.7.1-3 passim. Note also the ambiguous "genealogical" language of V.8.12-13, where it is uncertain whether the cosmos or the World-Soul is in question — two further points recalling Numenius (fr. 21 Des Places = Proclus *in Tim.* I.303.27ff.).
116. III.7[45].11.20ff.
117. Ibid., 15ff. Cf. the early work V.2 [11].1.18-28.
118. Cf. his paper in *Le Neoplatonisme* (Paris, 1971), pp. 51-52.
119. Cf. his article in Dionysius II (Dec. 1978), pp. 101-136.
120. Cf. II.9.2.4ff., cited above n. 110.
121. Ibid., 11.19-23.
122. Ibid. 8.35-36; for Numenius cf. above n. 94.
123. IV.8[6]2.38-53, IV.3[27].11.23-27, II.9[33].8.30-39, 18.35-48.
124. IV.3.6.10ff.; cf. VI.7.6.29-31.
125. IV.4.5.11ff.
126. *In Som. Sc.* I.11.11; for the passage's probable Numenian origin cf. above n. 84. Cf. *Enn.* IV.4.3-5, esp. 4.10ff.
127. IV.3.18.14ff.
128. The doctrine of two levels of Nous, propounded at VI.7.35.27ff. does not resolve the problem, since the final mystical vision should then (and clearly does not) include both levels of contemplation.
129. Cf. also VI.9 [9].5.29, where, however, the term *tolma* is of Pythagorean origin.
130. *Neoplatonism*, pp. 94-95, 112-118; *Armstrong, Cambridge History*, pp. 264-268; A.C. Lloyd, ibid., pp. 287-293; P. Hadot, "La Metaphysique de Porphyre," *Entretiens Hardt* XII (Vandoeuvres/Geneva, 1966), pp. 127-157, *Porphyre et Victorinus.* For a more cautious view of Porphyry cf. A. Smith *Porphyry's Place in the Neoplatonic Tradition* (The Hague, 1974), pp. 5ff.; cf. also the passage of Iamblichus cited above n. 6, etc.
131. Cf. A.C. Lloyd, *Cambridge History*, pp. 287-293; Wallis, *Neoplatonism*, pp. 116ff; Smith, *Porphyry's Place*, p. 47.
132. Cf. the texts cited above n. 51.
133. Proclus, ET. 204. Plotinus had himself recognized his acceptance of an unfallen element in the human soul as an innovation (*Enn.* IV.8[6].8.1ff); for his hesitation over Forms of individuals cf. above n. 44.
134. Cf. nn. 50-51 above.
135. Cf. above n. 131, *Allog.* XI.1.61-62, on which cf. pp. 431ff. of Professor Turner's paper.

Higher Providence, Lower Providences and Fate in Gnosticism and Middle Platonism

Michael A. Williams

"Zum Glück hat der ausgeprägte Neuplatonismus durchgehends — mit Ausnahme der Quelle des Nemesius — diese absurde Idee getilgt . . ."[1] Such was the evaluation registered almost a century ago by Alfred Gercke, of a doctrine which, he argued, was attested in a small cluster of Platonic sources. The doctrine, whose eventual obliteration from Neoplatonism Gercke felt to have been so fortunate, is the division of Providence into three levels: *hē prōtē pronoia, hē deutera pronoia, hē tritē pronoia*. The most explicit and elaborate witness for this doctrine is the Pseudo-Plutarchian tractate *De fato*:

> Therefore the Highest and Primary Providence is the intellection and will of the First God, and is benefactress of all things; in conformity with her all divine things are primordially arranged throughout, in the best and most beautiful way possible.
>
> The Secondary Providence is that of the secondary gods who move in the heavenly realm; in accordance with her, things mortal come into being in orderly fashion, as well as that which sustains and preserves each of the classes.
>
> The Providence and Forethought of the daemons who have been stationed around the earth as guardians and overseers of human affairs might reasonably be called "Tertiary" (*De fato* 572F-573A).

Gercke was apparently the first to point out that a similar doctrine was known to Apuleius of Madaura (*De Plat.* 1.12), and to the later writers Calcidius[2] and Nemesius.[3] Pointing also to other features shared by these writers on the overall question of Providence and Fate, and arguing that these four writers are not directly dependent upon one another, Gercke tentatively suggested that their shared doctrine may have derived from some common dependence upon the 1st-2nd century Platonist Gaius,[4] a hypothesis which to several scholars since Gercke has seemed convincing or at least promising.[5]

More recently, the fact that Albinus (the one person who can with some certainty be identified as a student of Gaius) shows no acquaintance with distinctive features of the doctrine of Providence and Fate found in Pseudo-Plutarch, Apuleius, and the others, has been viewed as a fatal objection to Gercke's hypothesis of Gaius as the common source.[6] Dillon has suggested "Athenian scholasticism of the early second century A.D." as the provenance,[7] but we are without the name of any specific teacher from whom Apuleius must have learned the doctrine in Athens.

Yet the cluster of sources identified by Gercke as witnesses to the existence of this doctrine in Middle Platonism, "a fascinating nest of connected documents and their attendant problems,"[8] continues to arouse scholarly curiosity, as well as negative evaluations not much different from the spirit of Gercke's remarks which I quoted at the beginning. Thus Dillon concludes: "Our triadic division of Providence has really got us nowhere. It might be said of [Pseudo-Plutarch], I fear, that what is good in him is not original, and what is original is very little good."[9]

It now seems possible that certain Gnostic tractates may constitute still further witnesses to this somewhat curious chapter in the history of Middle Platonism. Two Gnostic works in particular seem to be promising in this regard: The *Apocryphon of John*, for which we have both a longer and a shorter recension, each represented by two manuscripts,[10] and the untitled fifth tractate in Codex II from Nag Hammadi, to which modern scholarship has given the title *On the Origin of the World*.[11]

The Apocryphon of John

The *ApocryJn* makes a distinction between a universal Providence and a lower providence which belongs only to the level of the planetary archons who control the cosmos. This is not a triadic division of Providence, but as a twofold division it is developed in a fashion similar to the division of Providence in the Middle Platonic traditions in question, especially in the way in which the division of Providence seems to be linked to the interpretation of Plato's *Timaeus*.

a. Higher Providence

The universal Providence in *ApocryJn* comes before us in a mythological, personified form as the first thought of the highest God, or Invisible Spirit:

> (The Invisible Spirit) contemplated his own image when he saw it in the pure light-water which surrounds him; and his thought (*ennoia*) performed an act, it appeared, it stood before him out of the brilliance of the light. This is the power which is before the All, which appeared; that is, the perfect Providence (*pronoia*) of the All, the light, the likeness of the light, the image of the Invisible. She is the perfect power, Barbelo, the perfect aeon of glory (*BG* 27, 1-14).

Obscure as the name "Barbelo" itself is, the actual role of the entity Barbelo/Providence is much easier to discern. As the beginning of thought, she is the center of intellectual energy through whom the entire intellectual realm actualizes itself. There is some resemblance to Plotinus's Nous, particularly in the way that Barbelo, like Plotinus's Nous, is the first emanation from the ultimate source of all things and is described as emerging to "stand before" that source with which she had previously been united, thus initiating the subject-object relationship (cf. Plot., *Enn.* 5.2.1.7-13).

These initial descriptions of Barbelo/Providence in *ApocryJn* find several points of contact with the description of the highest Providence in our Middle Platonic sources. As the first thought of the first God, Barbelo/Providence is comparable to the First Providence which is described in Pseudo-Plutarch, *De fato* 572F as "the intellection (*noēsis*) or will (*boulēsis*) of the First God" (cf. 573B). Similarly, Apuleius says that the "First Providence" belongs to that God who is "the highest, most eminent of all the gods," and a few lines earlier Apuleius had defined Providence as "divine thought" (*divinam sententiam* — *De Plat.* 1.12).[12] The picture of Barbelo/Providence emerging to "stand before" the First God finds a certain echo in Calcidius's description of Providence, as having an eminence second after the Highest God, toward whom Providence is tirelessly turning and whose goodness

Providence imitates.[13]   The Platonic source known to Nemesius said that the First Providence

> exercises providential direction primarily over the Ideas, and then over the entire universe — that is, over heaven and stars and all universals, i.e., classes, essence, quantity, quality, and other such attributes and their subordinate forms.[14]

Similarly, in *ApocryJn* Barbelo/Providence operates primarily on the level of the Ideal (= pleromatic) realm.   The appearance of Barbelo/ Providence initiates the unfolding of the entire population of the transcendent realm.   For our purposes here it is not necessary to elaborate all of the complexities of this portion of the myth, nor to discuss the complex question of the possible origins of all the elements found in it.   The scene is reminiscent, for example, of language in various Jewish and Christian texts describing angelic attendants "standing before God" in the heavenly court.   But in *ApocryJn*, such traditional heavenly court language has been refocused through the lens of a philosophical framework, so that these entities who are "standing" in the aeonic realm look as much like Platonic Forms or Ideas "standing at rest."[15]

But the operation of the higher Providence in *ApocryJn* is not limited to the realm of the aeons.   The text also mentions the revelatory role of Providence in the soteriological process.   However, this is far more prominent in the longer recension than in the shorter recension.   In the long recension, Providence is mentioned as the heavenly voice that first announces to the startled archons that "Man exists, and the Son of Man" (II 14, 13-20); as the source of the gnosis or insight (*epinoia*) which Adam and Eve tasted in the garden (II 23, 24-29); as the one who anticipates the coming rape of Eve by the chief archon and sends agents in time to snatch life out of Eve (II 24, 13-14); as a being associated with the divine compassion and merciful care for humans (II 27, 33-28, 2); as the one who warns Noah and so ensures his rescue (II 29, 1-3); and finally, there is the well-known discourse by Providence, found only in the long recension, in which Providence recounts her threefold descent (II 30, 11-31, 25 par).

The short recension mentions the general resolve of the Invisible Spirit "by means of Providence" to set right Sophia's deficiency (*BG* 47, 6-7 par), but the only two moments in the salvation process in which the higher Providence is explicitly mentioned are the warning of Noah (*BG* 72, 17-72, 2 par), and the story of the descent of the angels to the daughters of the humans (*BG* 73, 18-75, 10 par), where it is said that the angels draw the humans into temptations "so that they might not remember their immovable Providence" (*BG* 75, 1-3).

Writers such as Pseudo-Plutarch were not motivated by quite the same soteriological questions as is the *ApocryJn*, and thus they naturally do not spell out the same kind of soteriological role for the Primary Providence as does *ApocryJn*. Yet, for example, Pseudo-Plutarch's general description of Primary Providence, the intellection and will of the First God, as "benefactress (*euergetis*) of all things" and the one in accordance with whom all divine things are primordially arranged, would also have been a rather appropriate description of Barbelo/Providence. The latter figures most prominently in the initial ordering of the divine realm, and is the benevolent guide who works for the restoration of order when it is disturbed. In all of these texts we have a higher Providence who effects only the highest and most divine level of ordering, and from whom all responsibility for certain lower levels of operation is removed, and assigned to a lower Providence.

Before turning to the figure of the lower, archontic Providence in *ApocryJn*, however, it is necessary to examine more closely two references to a Providence which are found only in the short recension of *ApocryJn*. One of these is the reference in *BG* 75, 1-3, which I mentioned above, to an "immovable Providence." Although I have suggested that "immovable Providence" here refers to Barbelo/Providence, there is perhaps another possibility. Also found only in the short version of *ApocryJn* is a mention of what at least initially appears to be a second "higher Providence" in the aeonic realm, a Providence which *could* be viewed as distinct from Barbelo/Providence, and which is quite definitely different from the lower, archontic Providence which I will discuss below. The Invisible Spirit and Barbelo give birth, according to the myth, to a Son around whom there emerges an entourage of entities, completing what I have described above as a kind of heavenly court of Platonic Ideas. This aeonic court consists of four groupings, each associated with a "luminary" and each luminary accompanied by three aeons, making a total of twelve aeons (*BG* 32, 19-34, 18):

BG		*CG* II/IV	
Harmozel	Grace	Harmozel	Grace
	Truth		Truth
	Form		Form

Oroiael	Providence (*pronoia*)	Oriel	Conception (*epinoia*)
	Perception		Perception
	Remembrance (*p^{c}rpmeewe*)		Remembrance
Davithe	Insight	Davithai	Insight
	Love		Love
	[Idea]		Idea
Eleleth	Perfection	Eleleth	Perfection
	Peace		Peace
	Wisdom		Wisdom

The twelve aeons seem to be twelve divine faculties with which the aeonic human family is endowed, since, in both recensions, the text goes on to distribute the human family (Adamas, Seth, and their descendants) among the four groupings. One notices that in *BG*'s version of this, Providence and Remembrance are two of the aeons in the Oroiael group. Is it possible that the wording later on in *BG* 75, 1-3, where the fallen angels inflict humans with temptations "so that they might not *remember* (*^{c}nnew^{c}r pmeewe*) their immovable *Providence*," is an allusion to this providential faculty which *BG* includes among the twelve aeons? Perhaps the *BG* version intends the Providence found among these twelve aeons to be understood as a third Providence different from Barbelo/Providence and the lower, archontic Providence. On the other hand, it may be simply a way of speaking of the extension of Barbelo's higher providential direction over the realm of the aeons (=Ideas) — and here we could compare the statement in Nemesius's source about the Primary Providence's operation in the realm of the Ideas — , and of the role of (higher) Providence in the salvation of the human family. If the *BG* version were intending to speak of three Providences, these in any case would not quite correspond to the three levels in Pseudo-Plutarch: *BG*'s highest and lowest Providences would correspond to Pseudo-Plutarch's Primary and Secondary Providences. Perhaps such a difference in the way in which speculation about multiple Providences could develop, in spite of the common ground, would provide even more reason for suggesting, as I will in my concluding remarks, that the particular scheme of three Providences as found in Pseudo-Plutarch may not have been the earliest form of the speculation about multiple Providences.

b. *Lower Providence*

Pseudo-Plutarch, Apuleius, and the source known to Nemesius all assign the secondary Providence to the "young gods" mentioned by Plato in *Timaeus* 42D-E. Here Plato says that the Demiurge, in order to preserve himself guiltless from any of the evil that might be done by the souls that had been formed, delivered over to the "young gods" (*neois theois*) the task of shaping the mortal bodies, completing the formation of the human soul and governing (*diakubernan*) the mortal creature in the best possible fashion. This commissioning is reiterated later on in *Timaeus* 69C, where the Demiurge is said to be responsible for the framing of divine things, but gives to his sons the responsibility for the construction of mortal things. And then in 69Dff we are given a description of the execution of this commission, in the creation of the mortal soul and body.

These sections of the *Timaeus* have evidently left their stamp also on the *ApocryJn*, even though it may not be clear whether this influence has resulted from a direct reading of the *Timaeus* or from some more indirect channel. I have suggested elsewhere that one trace of this influence of the *Timaeus* can be seen in the way in which *ApocryJn* develops the picture of the to and fro movement of Sophia.[16] The passage is a commentary on the Greek term *epipheresthai*, "rush over," used of the Spirit in LXX Gen. 1:2. This term in Gen. 1:2 seems to be used by *ApocryJn* to mark Sophia's first experience of motion. The agitated movement of Sophia is a sign of intense grief, and we are probably to see in Sophia's behavior a paradigm for the experience of passions on the part of the human soul here below. Precisely in a passage in the *Timaeus* that is touching on the levels of transition from the realm of transcendence to the realm of matter, Plato has the Demiurge lecturing to the not-yet-descended souls about the passions that they will experience when they are implanted in mortal bodies that are characterized by "to and fro movement" (*Timaeus* 42A). It is just after this lecture that we read of the commissioning I mentioned above, of the construction and governance of the mortal realm by the young gods (42D-E), and the subsequent narrative of the execution of this demand is full of remarks about erratic motion, disturbance and shaking which the soul experiences in the mortal bodies that are created (42E-44B).

The commentary in *ApocryJn* on Sophia's restless motion (II 13, 13-26 par) falls between the account of the begetting of the cosmic archons and their commissioning for the governance of the heavens (II 10, 1-12, 33 par) and the account of their fashioning of the human soul and body (II 15, 1-19, 1 par). There is significant confusion among our manuscripts of *ApocryJn* regarding the names, features, and individual roles of the archons. I will summarize those elements most pertinent to the topic at hand:

The first archon in *ApocryJn*, Ialdabaoth, the grotesque theriomorphic offspring of Sophia, produces a squadron of archontic henchmen. In both recensions the myth includes the listing of two such groups of archons, first a group of twelve and later in the story a group of seven. The fundamental astrological idea seems clear enough: the group of twelve correspond to the zodiacal signs and the group of seven to the seven planets.[17] After the production of the twelve, Ialdabaoth placed seven kings over the heavens and five over the abyss. However, there is some confusion here since the list of seven archons which occurs later in the myth is not made up simply of seven names from the first list of twelve, though there is some overlap. After the initial listing of the group of twelve, we hear nothing further of most of the names in the list, or indeed of the notion itself of a group of twelve.

Our primary interest here is the group of seven archons, for it is with these the *ApocryJn* associates a lower Providence, and it is these seven whose role seems to be partially derived from that of the "young gods" in the *Timaeus*.[18] The first listing of these seven includes not only a list of their names but also of their theriomorphic features. This list is as follows in *BG*, *CG* III, and *CG* II (*CG* IV is very fragmentary at this point):

BG 41, 16 - 42, 9		*CG* III 17, 20 - 18, 7		*CG* II 11, 26-35	
Iaoth	lion-faced	Aoth	lion-faced	Athoth	sheep-faced
Eloaios	ass-faced	Eloaios	ass-faced	Eloaiou	ass-faced
Astaphaios	hyena-faced	Astophaios	hyena-faced	Astaphaios	[hyena]-faced
Iao	snake-faced,	Iazo	serpent-faced,	Iao	[serpent]-faced,
with seven heads		lion-faced		having seven heads	
Adonaios	serpent-faced	Adonaios	serpent-faced	Sabaoth	serpent-faced
Adoni	ape-faced	Adonin	ape-faced	Adonin	ape-faced
Sabbataios	face of fire	Sabbadaios	face of fire	Sabbede	face of fire

Ialdabaoth then gives seven powers to these seven authorities (the text of *CG* III is missing; what remains of *CG* IV agrees with *CG* II):

BG 43, 10 - 44, 4		CG II 12, 16-25	
Iaoth	Providence (*pronoia*)	Athoth	Goodness
Eloaios	Divinity	Eloaio	Providence
Astaphaios	Goodness	Astraphaio	Divinity
Iao	Fire (*koht*)	Iao	Lordship
Sabaoth	Kingship	Sanbaoth	Kingship
Ad[oni]	Insight	Adonein	Jealousy (*koh*)
Sabbataios	Wisdom (*sophia*)	Sabbateon	Understanding

As one can see, one of the differences between the two versions is the placement of Providence. Its position in the first place in the *BG* version agrees, as we shall see, with its first-place position in a similar list in *OrigWorld*, and seems to give to this lower Providence a kind of priority in the cosmic realm that mirrors the position of Barbelo/Providence in the aeonic realm.

The situation is complicated to a certain extent by our next encounter with these powers in the myth, which occurs at the creation of the psychic Adam. The words of Gen. 1:26, "Let us make man, etc.," are interpreted in *ApocryJn* as a resolve of the archons to create a being in imitation of the image of the Perfect Human, and each of the powers of the archons supplies a different type of psychic substance in the fabrication of the psychic Adam:

BG 49, 11 - 50, 4		CG II 15, 14-23	
Divinity	bone-soul	Goodness	bone-soul
Goodness	sinew-soul	Providence	sinew-soul
Fire	flesh-soul	Divinity	flesh-soul
Providence	marrow-soul, and the whole foundation of the body	Lordship	marrow-soul
Kingship	blood-soul	Kingship	blood-soul
Insight	skin-soul	Jealousy	skin-soul
Wisdom	hair (*fōe*)-soul	Understanding	eyelid (*fouhe*)-soul

It can be seen that the longer recension (*CG* II and *CG* IV) has retained the same order of the seven powers as in the preceding list, with Providence in second place. On the other hand, the order of the powers here in the shorter recension differs from that recension's earlier list (*BG* 43, 10-44, 4), with Providence now in fourth place.

In spite of the fact that Providence seems at first glance to have been "demoted" in *BG*'s second list, this may not have been the actual intention. In the first place, one notices that in connection with Providence this text mentions not only Providence's contribution of "marrow-soul," but also adds, "and the whole foundation of the body."[19] Furthermore, van den Broeck has pointed out that if we shift Providence/marrow-soul to first place in *BG*'s list then we have an order of the psychic bodily components which corresponds very closely in both content and sequence to the list of bodily components in *Timaeus* 73B-76E: marrow, bones, sinews, flesh, skin, hair and nails, a sequence which is "a logical one, running from the inmost part of man to his outmost."[20] Van den Broeck argues that *BG*'s attribution of the "whole foundation of the body" to the same power which supplies the marrow is also an echo of the *Timaeus*, since *Timaeus* 73D says that the whole body is fashioned around the marrow.[21] Admittedly, we are left without a solid explanation for the shift of Providence/marrow-soul to fourth place, unless perhaps being the middle member in the list of seven is supposed to suit the marrow's position as the core or foundation of the (psychic) body.[22]

I suspect that the more prominent role played by Providence in the lists in *BG* is more original than the consistently second-place position in the two lists in the longer recension. The consistency in *CG* II is, in fact, rather mechanical and superficial. In spite of what at first appears to be greater inconsistency in *BG* in these lists, there is in a sense a greater logic in their arrangement. In any case, in both recensions we have a set of planetary archons whose nature and function seem in part to have been inspired by the picture of the "young gods" of the *Timaeus* and whose faculties or powers include a Providence lower than Barbelo/Providence.

c. Fate

Pseudo-Plutarch identifies still a third level of providential guidance, carried out by *daimones* "stationed around the earth as guardians and overseers of human affairs" (*De fato* 573A). The relationship of the three Providences to Fate is explained as follows: Primary Providence begets Fate and therefore somehow includes Fate, Secondary Providence is begotten together with (*suggennētheisa*) Fate and therefore is included together with (*sumperilambanetai*) Fate (in Primary Providence), and Tertiary Providence is begotten later than (*hysteron*) Fate and therefore is contained within Fate in the same way that free will and chance are contained within it (574B). Nemesius also mentions a Tertiary Providence (*tritē pronoia*).   In almost verbatim agreement with Pseudo-Plutarch, Nemesius's source assigns this Tertiary Providence to "certain *daimones* stationed around the earth as guardians of human affairs" (*De nat. hom.* p. 346 Matthaei).   But Nemesius does not explain how his Platonic source related Fate to the three different Providences.

Now in fact, it is only Pseudo-Plutarch and Nemesius's source which speak explicitly of a "Tertiary Providence." Apuleius, who had mentioned a Primary and a Secondary Providence, never actually refers to a "Tertiary Providence."   But after talking about the gods of the Secondary Providence he does refer to the daemons who are the gods' ministers:

> And (Plato says that) the Primary Providence (*prima providentia*) belongs to the highest and most eminent of all the gods, who not only has organized the celestial gods whom he has distributed through all parts of the cosmos for guardianship and splendor, but has also created for the duration of time those beings that are mortal by nature who are superior in wisdom to the other terrestrial animals. And when he had established laws, he gave to the other gods the responsibility for disposition and oversight of the subsequent affairs which would have to be attended to daily.
>
> Consequently, the gods exercise so diligently the Secondary Providence (*secunda providentia*) which they have received that all things, even the things visible to mortals in the heavens, maintain immutably the state ordained for them by the Father.
>
> (Plato) considers the daemons, whom we can call *genii* and *lares*, to be ministers of the gods and guardians of humans, and interpreters for humans should the latter wish anything from the gods (*De Plat.* 1.12).

Apuleius then adds that in Plato's view not all things are in the power of Fate, but that a portion belongs to free will (*in nobis*) and a significant portion to chance.   But unlike Pseudo-Plutarch, Apuleius does not spell out the relationship between Fate and the different levels of Providence.

In *ApocryJn*, also, we have no mention of a Tertiary Providence assigned to daemons. However, we do find what could be a level of daemonic activity that is subordinate to the level of the planetary archons and their Providence. And there is a certain similarity with the scheme in Pseudo-Plutarch, in that this level of daemonic activity in *ApocryJn* is contained within Fate. The critical passage is found in two rather different versions in the two recensions:

BG 72, 2-12:

(The first archon) took counsel with his powers.

They begot Fate,

and with measure and times and seasons they bound the gods of the heavens, the angels, the daemons, and humans

so that they might all be in (Fate's) bond,

since it is lord over everyone — a wicked and perverse thought!

CG II 28, 11-32:

(The first archon) took counsel with his authorities, who are his powers, and together they committed adultery with Sophia.

There was begotten by them disgraceful Fate, which is the last of the variegated bonds, and exists in a variety of forms, since they are different from one another. Fate is harder and stronger than that with which (or "she with whom")

are mixed

the gods, the angels, the daemons, and all the generations until today. For from that Fate appeared every sin and injustice and blasphemy and the bonds of forgetfulness and ignorance and every burdensome command and burdensome sins and great fear. And in this way the whole creation was blinded, so that they might not know the God who is above all of them. And their sins were hidden because of the bond of forgetfulness. For they were bound with measures and times and seasons, since (Fate) is lord over everything.

In both recensions, the measures initiated by the chief archon in this passage are in response to his realization that the power of thought possessed by the perfect race of humans is superior to his own, and the begetting of Fate is an attempt to imprison this thought.

The inclusion of the "gods" or "gods of the heavens" in the list of those bound is somewhat puzzling. Is this a reference to the planetary archons?[23] If so, then Secondary Providence would seem now to be contained within Fate, in spite of the fact that the begetting of Fate by the planetary archons might have led us to expect archontic Providence to be transcendent to Fate.

The one text in our group of Platonic sources which discusses the relation of Fate to the multiple levels of Providence, viz., Pseudo-Plutarch, seems to subordinate to Fate all but the highest level of Providence. However, there is a certain ambiguity in the case of the Secondary Providence that is comparable to the ambiguity in *ApocryJn* on the relation of archontic Providence to Fate. On the one hand, Pseudo-Plutarch says that while Fate conforms to Providence, Providence does not conform to Fate, yet the author immediately cautions that this statement is being made only about the Primary Providence (573B). After such a caution, we might be prepared to hear that both the Secondary and Tertiary Providences *do* conform to Fate. Instead, the author tries to argue for a kind of sibling relationship between Secondary Providence and Fate: they are "begotten together" (573B). Apparently, this idea is prompted by the scene in *Timaeus* 41E-42E, where the Demiurge creates the souls, places them in astral positions, and then lectures them about the laws of Fate which will govern their future as they descend into mortal bodies; but then the actual administration of this somatic existence is given over, as I have already discussed, to the "young gods." Pseudo-Plutarch evidently finds in this passage evidence that Fate and the administrative responsibility of the young gods (=Secondary Providence) come into being at the same time, the young gods somehow administering the laws of Fate without themselves being encompassed by Fate (*De fato* 573 D-F). Dillon suggests that the language about Secondary Providence being "begotten together with" Fate is "more or less meaningless," and that essentially "this secondary Providence would seem to be identical with Fate."[24] Pseudo-Plutarch himself at one point raises the question of whether it would not be more correct to say that Secondary Providence is "included in" rather than "exists with" Fate (574C-D), and the passage may indicate the author's awareness of controversy on this issue in his day,[25] and a sensitivity to a certain amount of ambiguity in his own analysis.

On the Origin of the World

The similarity between doctrines of multiple Providences such as in Pseudo-Plutarch, Apuleius, etc., and the teaching about Providence in *OrigWorld* was already noted in 1980 by Pheme Perkins.[26] However, she had not yet noticed that the picture of Providence in *ApocryJn* might be just as relevant. In my view, *ApocryJn* in fact presents a doctrine of multiple Providences that is even more similar to that in the Platonic sources than is the doctrine in *OrigWorld*. This and other differences between our analyses lead me to conclusions which differ from those of Perkins.

a. Higher Providence

In only one passage does *OrigWorld* mention what could be a universal Providence. It is not called the Providence of the First God, however, nor the Thought of the Father, but rather the "Providence of Pistis":

> Now it was in accordance with the Providence of Pistis that all this took place, so that the human being might appear before his image and might condemn them through their molded body (113, 5-9).

That which is being referred to here as having occurred in accordance with the Providence of Pistis is the plan of the archons to create an earthly human. Pistis, or Pistis Sophia,[27] is a figure whose precise rank in the transcendent realm in *OrigWorld* is not clear. Unlike the *ApocryJn*, *OrigWorld* presents very little description of the realm above the archontic cosmos. It may be that *OrigWorld* presupposes some account of the emanation of aeonic beings who fill out the transcendent realm, but if so it condenses the account to a mere allusion: "Now when the nature of the Immortals had come to perfection out of the Infinite, then an image flowed out of Pistis, called Sophia" (98, 11-14). Is Pistis in this gnostic tractate one of the higher entities among the "Immortals," or is she, like the Sophia of *ApocryJn*, the lowest?

In spite of our lack of certainty on this question, it may be proper to speak of the Providence of Pistis in this text as a higher Providence. However, the fundamental justification for this inference is not so much something positive which is said about the Providence of Pistis in this one passage as it is the language that the text uses in several other places to refer to a lower Providence, one that belongs to the realm of the archons.

b. Lower Providence

The first such mention of a lower Providence is in connection with the listing of the names of the planetary archons. We are first of all told that the chief archon, Ialdabaoth, created three androgynous offspring for himself through the reification of his enunciated boasts:

Iao, Eloia, and Astaphaios (101, 9-23). But then, somewhat confusingly for the reader, the text immediately begins to speak of a group of *seven* androgynous archons, each having both a male name and a female name (101, 24-102, 1):

Male Names:	Female Names:
(Ialdabaoth)[28]	Providence (*pronoia*) Sambathas
Iao	Lordship
Sabaoth	Divinity
Adonaios	Kingship
Eloaios	Jealousy
Oraios	Wealth
Asaphaios	Wisdom

That there is some relationship between this list and the lists in the *ApocryJn* tradition is apparent, although this list in *OrigWorld* presents us with still a third version that cannot really be said to clear away much of the confusion among the versions in the *ApocryJn* texts. However, at least one agreement stands out between *OrigWorld* and the short recension of *ApocryJn*: the first-place position given in the list to Providence (cf. *BG* 43, 10-44, 4).

In fact, the archontic Providence receives even more attention in *OrigWorld* than in the short recension of *ApocryJn*. Not only is Providence found at the head of the list of the seven planetary powers, but she is singled out as a mythological personality to play a more visible role in the narrative. While in the *ApocryJn* the higher Providence was more developed as a character in the myth than the lower Providence, in *OrigWorld* the situation is reversed.

For instance, the second mention of the archontic Providence in *OrigWorld* occurs when the Immortal Human from the transcendent realm makes an appearance in the world below as a beautiful light (108, 1-9). No one was able to see this luminous Human except the *archigenetōr*, Ialdabaoth, and "the Providence with him" (108, 11f). This Providence was attracted to the luminous Human, but because she was "in the darkness" the Human despised her and she was unable to cleave to him (108, 15-17). Unable to cease her love, "she poured out her light upon the earth" (108, 19). What follows is a midrashic word-play on the Hebrew terms *adam*, *adamah* ("earth"), *dam* ("blood"), and the Greek terms *adamas* ("adamant") and *adamantinē*: from that day, the luminous Human was called "Light-Human, which means 'luminous blood-person,'" and the earth spread over Holy Adamas, which means 'holy, adamantine earth'" (108, 19-25). The description of Providence in this passage as being "in the darkness" underscores the fact that she is a *lower* Providence, and a little later in the narrative she is actually referred to as "the Providence which is below": After remaining on the earth for two days, the luminous Adam "left the Providence which is below (*tpronoia etmpsa mpitn*) in heaven and ascended to his light" (111, 31-33).

The light/blood poured out by lower Providence in her love for the luminous Adam also produced androgynous Eros, having a male aspect, "Himeros, which is fire from the light,"[29] and a female aspect, "blood-soul, which is from the essence of Providence" (109, 1-6). The archontic Providence is thus involved in the creative process, but not as contributor to the psychic Adam of "marrow-soul and the whole foundation of the body," as was the case in the *BG* version of *ApocryJn.*[30] Instead, here she contributes the female blood-psyche to Eros. What is apparently intended by the myth in this section is that the guidance or management of the creative process by this lower Providence comes first of all in the form of the introduction of desire. As a result of this desire, a certain providential ordering of life in the cosmic realm is effected, but the author paints a rather gloomy portrait of this order: after commenting that the intercourse of Eros caused the sprouting of the first sensual pleasure on the earth, the author adds: "the woman followed the earth, and marriage followed the woman, and reproduction followed marriage, and dissolution followed reproduction" (109, 22-25).

The archontic Providence is also mentioned in a rather negative light in connection with the birth of material children from Eve. When the seven archons and their angels mate with the material Eve and beget Abel and "the rest of the sons," we are informed that this all took place according to the Providence of the Archigenetõr, so that Eve "might beget within herself every mixed seed, which is joined to the Fate of the cosmos and Fate's configurations (*schemata*) and justice" (117, 20-24).

And finally, the apocalyptic predictions in the closing sections of *OrigWorld* include the announcement of the condemnation and future destruction of the planetary archons:

> When all the perfect ones appeared in the vessels fashioned by the archons, and when they disclosed the Truth which has nothing like it, then they put to shame every wisdom of the gods, and their Fate was found to be condemnable, and their power was extinguished, their lordship was destroyed, their Providence became [. . .]. (125, 23-32).

Although there is a lacuna in the text which makes the precise wording of the statement about Providence uncertain, we can be sure from the context that some unfavorable outcome for this archontic Providence was mentioned. It has been suggested by Pheme Perkins that this last-quoted passage is referring to still a third Providence, one which corresponds to the lowest Providence in Pseudo-Plutarch's *De fato*.[31] But I see no reason to conclude that the Providence in this passage is any other than the archontic Providence which I have been discussing. Admittedly, there is a sense in which one might want to speak of this archontic Providence in 125, 23-32 as now *confined* to a lower level than had been the case in the earlier passages, since in the meantime the seven archons with whom this Providence is associated have been case out of their heavens down to the earth (121, 27-35; 123, 4-15).

c. Fate

Fate is mentioned several times in the tractate, and in order to ascertain the relationship between Providence and Fate in this text it will be useful to begin with one of the two passages which I just mentioned, where we hear of the casting down of the archons to the earth:

> For when the seven archons were cast down from their heavens to the earth, they created for themselves angels — that is, many demons — who would serve them. These taught men many errors and magic and charms and idolatry and shedding of blood and altars and temples and sacrifices and libations to all the demons of the earth, who have as their fellow-worker Fate, who came into being in accordance with the harmony (*symphōnia*) between the gods of injustice and justice (123, 4-15).

The coming into being of Fate that is mentioned here evidently refers to a much earlier moment in the narrative, at which time Sabaoth, one of the sons of Ialdabaoth, had revolted from his father and had been translated out of the darkness to a higher realm, where he received his own assembly of angels and powers, etc. (103, 32-106, 11).[32] The realm of Sabaoth was given the designation "justice" and that of Ialdabaoth "injustice." (106, 11-18). Presumably, Fate in this text consists of the effects which result from the interaction (*symphōnia*) of the powers in these two realms. Such a conclusion would seem to be confirmed by the fact that after listing the various unpleasant powers in the realm of Ialdabaoth (Death, Jealousy, Wrath, Weeping, etc.) and various pleasant powers in the realm of Sabaoth (Life, Blessed, Joy, Peace, etc.), the author says that "you will discover their effects (*apotelesmata*) and their activities in the configurations (*schēmata*) of the Fate of the heaven which is beneath the Twelve" (107, 14-17).

In reading these passages which refer to Fate, as well as the passage in 117, 20-24 that I mentioned earlier, where in accordance with Ialdabaoth's Providence, Eve begot mixed seed enmeshed within Fate's configurations, we might be tempted to see the archontic Providence as itself prior to or outside of Fate. However, that this is not the author's intention is indicated by still one further passage, in 121, 13-16, where we are told that when the archons became jealous of Adam's superior understanding, they wanted to shorten the life expectancy for human beings. However, the archons were unable to do this, "because of Fate, which was established from the beginning." Therefore, even though the appearance of archontic Providence occurs before the mention of Fate in the mythic narrative, this secondary Providence seems inseparably entwined with Fate, subject at least in some sense to Fate's law, and finally condemned together with Fate (125, 23-32).

Conclusions

As I mentioned earlier, I have arrived at certain conclusions on this material which differ from those reached by Pheme Perkins, the only other scholar, so far as I know, who has commented on the similarity between the multiple Providence doctrines in Apuleius et al. and doctrines of Providence in gnostic texts.[33] She has argued that *OrigWorld* manifests a threefold division of Providence: the Primary Providence, belonging to Pistis; the Secondary Providence, associated with Ialdabaoth; and still a third Providence, which she believes to be referred to in 125, 27-32.[34] She argues that the limited attestation of the three-fold Providence doctrine allows some fairly specific conclusions about the author of *OrigWorld*: Apuleius was evidently studying in Athens about 150 C.E.,[35] and his teachers during this time may have included students of Plutarch (Taurus, and possibly Plutarch's nephew Sextus).[36] "Like *Orig. World*, Apuleius presents the doctrine of three levels of providence, *Timaeus* exegesis, Isis mythology and, in novelistic form, an Eros story . . ."[37] Given the fact that Plutarch mentions a cosmological understanding of Eros that seems to link the activity of Eros to Providence,[38] and given Plutarch's well-known cosmological interpretation of Isis, Perkins concludes, "Since all Apuleius's known teachers were followers of Plutarch, we may even suggest that the cosmological allegorization of Isis and Hesios (Eros) myths had probably carried on into the discussions of this circle in Athens."[39] And since *OrigWorld* contains the doctrine of higher and lower Providences, cosmological speculation about Providence as the source of Eros, and possibly the influence of Isis mythology,

> We thus conclude that the peculiarities of the cosmological interpretation in *OrigWorld* reflect the teaching of this particular group at Athens around A.D. 150. We may reasonably assume that our author studied philosophy at Athens at that time. In the treatise before us, he has applied the teaching of that school to the exposition of Gnostic cosmological traditions such as we find in *Hyp. Arch.* and *Ap. John* and the Sethian-Ophites.[40]

As I have argued, I find evidence for only two Providences in *OrigWorld*, not three. Now it would be tempting to argue that my analysis, if correct, in fact only strengthens the case being made by Perkins, since in one respect it brings *OrigWorld* even closer to Apuleius's actual language. For Apuleius also never explicitly mentions three Providences, but only two (see below). Nevertheless, I question whether even then the sum of the evidence justifies the conclusion that "we may reasonably assume" that the author of *OrigWorld* studied philosophy in Athens about 150 C.E. And I am made all the more skeptical about so specific a provenance because of the presence of a doctrine of higher and lower Providences in *ApocryJn*.

Perkins regards the doctrine of multiple Providences in *OrigWorld* as a decisive fingerprint of the teaching of the Athenian school of the mid-second century C.E., and she is thinking of this teaching as having been woven into the exposition of gnostic cosmological traditions such as those in *ApocryJn*. But such a reconstruction is no longer satisfying once it is recognized that *ApocryJn* itself contains a doctrine of higher and lower Providences that is at least as similar to Apuleius's account as is that in *OrigWorld*.

The gnostic evidence may well invite certain revisions in the history of this chapter in Platonism. The speculation in these gnostic texts about higher and lower Providences and Fate ought not to be fitted by force too quickly into previously constructed arrangements of the surviving fragments of similar Platonic speculations. For example, the fact that Apuleius never really speaks of three Providences, but only two, has occasionally been registered, in routine fashion. Yet it has been regarded by interpreters as insignificant, since it has been assumed that Apuleius is of course *thinking* of three Providences, even though he does not mention the last one. The temptation to assume this is powerful, so long as one is looking only at Apuleius, Pseudo-Plutarch, and Nemesius. (Calcidius may be left aside for the moment, since his similarity with the others does not really include references to a second or third Providence.)

However, the evidence of the gnostic texts for distinction between only two Providences may now provide reason for more hesitation in assuming that Apuleius really is thinking of three *providentiae*. It may be that the longer list of sources now at our disposal which speculate about multiple Providences favors a more complex reconstruction, in which we allow for the possibility that early versions of speculation about multiple Providences may have involved only a twofold distinction between the Providence of the First God and the Providence of the "young gods" of the *Timaeus*. How early, after all, is our evidence for talk of three Providences? Of the three sources Apuleius, Pseudo-Plutarch, and Nemesius, the only one which we can date with confidence in the second century C.E. is Apuleius. Nemesius writes more than two centuries later, and we do not have a certain date for Pseudo-Plutarch. Only these latter two sources actually speak of three Providences. If, as Gercke argued,[41] Pseudo-Plutarch and Nemesius are independent of one another, then it is probable that they are dependent on a common source or tradition. Gercke thought that Albinus and Apuleius also knew this source, and that the date for the source must therefore be pushed back into the second century.[42] But, as I have mentioned, that Albinus knew this source has recently been questioned by some scholars,[43] and therefore it is only Apuleius, *De Plat.* 1.12, which remains as the supposed evidence that all three Providences known to Pseudo-Plutarch and Nemesius were already being talked about in the second century. To be sure, Apuleius certainly does know a doctrine similar to that in Pseudo-Plutarch and Nemesius, but perhaps the reason that Apuleius does not go ahead and speak of a "Tertiary Providence" exercised by the daemons is that he had never thought of putting it that way. Perhaps he would not even have thought of *providentia* as a particularly appropriate designation for the role of the daemons.

At the same time, our understanding of these gnostic texts and the significance of their references to Providences and Fate is enhanced. Once we have dutifully registered important differences that do separate such gnostic texts from an Apuleius or a Pseudo-Plutarch, such as the fundamentally less sympathetic gnostic evaluation of the lower Providence and its god,[44] there still remains an impressive amount in common to be appreciated. In this regard, not the least important point to raise involves the implications for the positions of these Platonic and gnostic writers on the question of free will. Platonists in antiquity, including Apuleius and Pseudo-Plutarch, are famous for arguing theories of Fate which leave ample room for free choice. Perhaps the most traditional form which this took was the argument that Fate is a law defining the inevitable consequences that will result from a given choice, rather than being a law which makes all one's choices inevitable.[45] Gnostics, on the other hand, tend to be labeled "determinists." To be sure, what is usually intended by this label is not that gnostics believed everything to be determined by Fate. Rather, what is normally meant is that salvation is inevitable for some and destruction inevitable for others, due to their possession of different "natures" (pneumatic, psychic, hylic, etc.), and therefore the pattern of choices in an individual's life is determined in advance by the individual's "nature."[46]

Now in the debate between Platonists and Stoics, for example, the Platonists' insistence on the distinction between Fate and a Providence quite outside Fate's control tended to go hand in hand with the assertion of the reality of free choice and human responsibility. It would be fascinating if a text such as *ApocryJn*, so much like Apuleius or Pseudo-Plutarch in its scheme of higher and lower Providences and Fate, were nevertheless poles apart from them on the issue of human responsibility. It would be fascinating, but in my view there is no evidence of such a contrast between them on this point. There is not space here to defend this assertion completely.[47] I would simply point out that the important section in *ApocryJn* which discusses the variety in human responses to revelation and degrees of success in achieving spiritual strength and salvation (II 25, 16-27, 31 par) is shot through with implications of conditionality.[48] I see nothing in the text which suggests an interest in denying the possibility of human choice. The text certainly does not make such an argument in theoretical terms. Many modern (and probably some ancient) readers have thought that there is in such a text an implicit, mythological denial of free will. Such has been inferred from the myths of pre-existent races — the "immovable race" mentioned in *ApocryJn*, for example. But an ancient gnostic may not have seen the rigid determinism in such mythology that he/she is so often assumed to have seen.[49] When a text such as *ApocryJn* holds out the assurance to readers of a benevolent Providence higher than Fate's chains, are we really justified in concluding that this higher Providence is, after all, only a more divine form of Fate?

NOTES

1. Alfred Gercke, "Eine platonische Quelle des Neuplatonismus," *Rheinisches Museum* N.F. 41 (1886): 285.

2. In his commentary on the *Timaeus*, chapters 142-190; see *Timaeus a Calcidio translatus commentarioque instructus*, *Plato Latinus* 4, ed. J.H. Waszink (London and Leiden: Warburg Institute and Brill, 1962); J. den Boeft, *Calcidius on Fate: His Doctrine and Sources, Philosophia Antiqua* 18 (Leiden: Brill, 1970). Calcidius does not actually speak of three Providences, but only one; but Calcidius's doctrine of Fate and Fate's position in a hierarchical system of divine hypostases is very closely related to Pseudo-Plutarch's doctrine of Fate and Fate's relation to a hierarchy of three Providences.

3. Nemesius, *De natura hominis* 44; *Nemesius Emesenus, De natura hominis graece et latine*, ed. Christian Friedrich Matthaei (1802; reprint: Hildesheim: Georg Olms, 1967), pp. 344-346; *Cyril of Jerusalem and Nemesius of Emesa*, Library of Christian Classics 4, ed. William Telfer (Philadelphia: Westminster, 1955), pp. 432-435.

4. Gercke (above, n. 1), p. 279.

5. E.g., Willy Theiler, "Tacitus und die antike Schicksalslehre," in *Phyllobolia für Peter von der Mühll zum 60. Geburtstag* (Basel: B. Schwabe, 1946), p. 71; *Plutarch's Moralia*, vol. 7, ed. and trans. Phillip H. de Lacy and Benedict Einarson (London and Cambridge, Mass.: Heinemann and Harvard University Press, 1959), p. 304; J.H. Waszink, *Studien zum Timaeuskommentar des Calcidius*, vol. 1, *Philosophia Antiqua* 12 (Leiden: Brill, 1964), p. 22, n. 2; den Boeft (above, n. 2), p. 129.

6. John Dillon, *The Middle Platonists, 80 B.C. to A.D. 220* (Ithaca, N.Y.: Cornell University Press, 1977), pp. 298, 320; R.W. Sharples, "Alexander of Aphrodisias, *De fato*: Some Parallels," *Classical Quarterly* 28 (1978): 243ff.

7. Dillon (above, n. 6), p. 320.

8. Ibid.

9. Ibid., p. 325.

10. For the short recension: the second tractate in the Berlin gnostic codex (=*BG*), *Die gnostischen Schriften des koptischen Papyrus Berolinensis 8502*, ed. Walter C. Till, second edition by Hans-Martin Schenke, TU 60, 2 (Berlin: Akademie-Verlag, 1972); and the first tractate in Codex III of the Nag Hammadi Library (=*CG* III). For the long recension: the first tractate in Codex II from Nag Hammadi (=*CG* II) and the first tractate in Codex IV (=*CG* IV). For the three Nag Hammadi texts of *ApocryJn*, there is the edition by Martin Krause and Pahor Labib, *Die drie Versionen des Apocryphon des Johannes im koptischen Museum zu Alt-Kairo* (Wiesbaden, Harrassowitz, 1962). Except where differences among the versions need to be noted, I will for convenience usually cite *ApocryJn* according to the *CG* II version, of which the English reader has a handy translation by Frederik Wisse in *The Nag Hammadi Library in English*, ed. James M. Robinson (New York: Harper and Row; Leiden: Brill, 1977), pp. 98-116.

11.   See *Die koptisch-gnostische Schrift ohne Titel aus Codex II von Nag Hammadi im Koptischen Museum zu Alt-Kairo*, ed. Alexander Böhlig and Pahor Labib, Deutsche Akademie der Wissenschaften zu Berlin Institut für Orientforschung 58 (Berlin: Akademie-Verlag, 1962). The Coptic scribe did not number the pages of Codex II. The edition by Böhlig and Labib numbers the pages with the plate numbers from the older facsimile edition by Pahor Labib, *Coptic Gnostic Papyri in the Coptic Museum at Old Cairo*, vol. 1 (Cairo: Government Press, 1956). I use here the pagination of *The Facsimile Edition of the Nag Hammadi Codices*, published under the auspices of the Department of Antiquities of the Arab Republic of Egypt, in conjunction with UNESCO, vol. 2 (Leiden: Brill, 1974), the same system followed in the English translation by Hans-Gebhard Bethge and Orval S. Wintermute, in Robinson (above, n. 10), pp. 161-179. A fragment of a second copy of *OrigWorld* is found among what remains of Codex XIII from Nag Hammadi, but it is too limited to be of help for the questions addressed here.

12.   Cf. R.E. Witt, *Albinus and the History of Middle Platonism* (Cambridge: University Press, 1937), p. 100.

13.   Calcidius, *In Tim.* 176.

14.   Nemesius, *De natura hominis* 44.

15.   Cf. Michael A. Williams, *The Immovable Race: A Gnostic Designation and the Theme of Stability in Late Antiquity*, Nag Hammadi Studies 24 (Leiden: Brill, 1985), chapter IV.

16.   Ibid., pp. 114ff.

17.   Cf. A.J. Welburn, "The Identity of the Archons in the Apocryphon Johannis," *Vigiliae Christianae* 32 (1978): 241-54.

18.   I take for granted, but do not discuss here, the importance of further traditions, such as Jewish midrashic traditions on the creation narratives.

19.   However, *CG* III may not be in agreement with *BG* on this. The few fragments of words which remain for this passage in *CG* III 22, 18-23, 6 at least do not seem to allow the restoration of the lacunae so as to match neatly the wording in *BG*. But the text of *CG* III is so fragmentary at this point that we cannot determine with any certainty the degree of difference from *BG*.

20.   R. van den Broeck, "The Creation of Adam's Psychic Body in the Apocryphon of John," in *Studies in Gnosticism and Hellenistic Religions presented to Gilles Quispel on the Occasion of his 65th Birthday*, EPRO 91, ed. R. van den Broeck and M.J. Vermaseren (Leiden: Brill, 1981), p. 46. Plato first mentions sinews and flesh, in that order (*Tim.* 74B), although admittedly he then proceeds to discuss first the composition of the flesh, and then that of the sinews.

21.   Van den Broeck (above, n. 20), p. 47, who understands the phrase "and (=*mn*) the whole foundation of the body" epexegetically: "the fourth is Providence, a marrow-soul, *that is*, the whole foundation of the body." (Actually, van den Broeck for some reason erroneously speaks of the epexegetical sense of the Coptic copula *awo* here, when the Coptic term in

the text is actually *mn* — for which, of course, the epexegetical sense can still be argued.)

22. It is true that the second listing is introduced with the statement: "and the powers began *from below*" (*BG* 49, 9f), while the first listing is introduced as a list which begins "*from above*" (*BG* 43, 11). But, as one can see, the order in the second list is not simply a reversal of the order in the first; only Providence's position has changed.

23. Ialdabaoth, for example, refers to himself as "god" in *ApocryJn* II 13, 8f par.

24. Dillon (above, n. 6), p. 324.

25. R.W. Sharples, "Nemesius of Emesa and Some Theories of Divine Providence," *Vigiliae Christianae* 37 (1983): 142: "The relation between secondary providence and fate seems already to have been a topic of controversy among the original proponents of the three-providence theory" (and here Sharples cites Pseudo-Plutarch, *De fato* 574C-D as evidence).

26. Pheme Perkins, "On the Origin of the World (*CG* II,5): A Gnostic Physics," *Vigiliae Christianae* 34 (1980): 36-46.

27. On the problem of the interchangeability of these terms in this tractate, cf. Francis T. Fallon, *The Enthronement of Sabaoth: Jewish Elements in Gnostic Creation Myths*, Nag Hammadi Studies 10 (Leiden: Brill, 1978), p. 17.

28. Ialdabaoth is not actually mentioned at this point in the text: "Seven appeared in androgynous form in Chaos. They have their masculine name and their feminine name. The feminine name is Providence Sambathas, which is the Hebdomad. But his (n.b.!) son, called 'Iao': his feminine name is 'Lordship'; Sabaoth: his feminine name is 'Divinity,'" etc. But that Ialdabaoth and Providence are supposed to be paired is indicated by the context and by the wording in 108, 10-12 and 117, 19ff (see the discussion of these below).

29. The Coptic text has *himirēris*; see Böhlig-Labib (above, n. 11), p. 62; Perkins (above, n. 26), p. 39; J. Mansfeld, "Hesiod and Parmenides in Nag Hammadi," *Vigiliae Christianae* 35 (1981): 174-182.

30. However, van den Broeck (above, n. 20), pp. 47ff., has pointed out that later on in *OrigWorld*, in the passage which describes how the fashioned form (*plasma*) of the material Adam came into being with each part of the body corresponding to one of the seven archons, it is said that "their great one (=Ialdabaoth) created the brain (*egkephalon*) and the marrow" (114, 33-35). Since *OrigWorld* identifies Providence as the female consort of Ialdabaoth, then this passage is indirectly parallel to the association of Providence with "marrow" which we saw in the *BG* version of *ApocryJn*. Moreover, in its mention of "the brain and the marrow" as contributed by the leader of the list of archons, *OrigWorld* is reminiscent of Plato's description of the brain as a special portion of marrow fashioned at the beginning of the creation of the human body (*Tim.* 73D).

31. Perkins (above, n. 26), pp. 41-43.

32. See Fallon (above, n. 27).

33. In the discussion following the 1984 presentation of this paper, I was delighted to learn from Prof. Michel Tardieu that he also had addressed the relation between *ApocryJn*'s theory of providences and Platonic theories of multiple providences, in his (at that time, just published) commentary on the Berlin Codex (*Ecrits Gnostiques: Codex de Berlin*, Sources Gnostiques et Manichéennes 1 [Paris: Les Editions du Cerf, 1984], pp. 19, 258, 292ff). Unfortunately, it has not been possible to incorporate a treatment of Tardieu's study in this paper. I will only point out that a significant respect in which our conclusions differ is that he argues that *ApocryJn* does in fact speak of three providences, the third being an implicit interiorization of transcendent Providence in the form of the intelligence given to the seed of Seth (pp. 292, 319, 329-331).

34. Perkins (above, n. 26), pp. 42ff.

35. Dillon (above, n. 6), pp. 306ff.

36. Ibid.

37. Perkins (above, n. 26), p. 44.

38. Plutarch, *De fac.* 926E.-927A; cf. Mansfeld (above, n. 29), pp. 175, 180ff.

39. Perkins (above, n. 26), p. 44.

40. Ibid., pp. 44ff.

41. Gercke (above, n. 1), p. 278.

42. Ibid., p. 279.

43. See above, n. 6.

44. Here I would also tend to disagree with Perkins (above, n. 27), pp. 41ff, who speaks of the lower Providence in *OrigWorld* as "beneficent."

45. See Dillon (above, n. 6), pp. 295-98, 322ff.

46. E.g., Albrecht Dihle, *The Theory of Will in Classical Antiquity*, Sather Classical Lectures 48 (Berkeley and Los Angeles: University of California Press, 1982), pp. 150-157.

47. Cf. Williams (above, n. 15), chapter VII.

48. The "worthiness" of the most perfect type of soul is linked to "endurance" (*hypomenein*) in the "contest" (II 26, 3-7 par); the positive influence of the spirit of Life and the negative influence of the evil spirit are admittedly factors from outside which either help or hinder the soul's liberation from forgetfulness and acquisition of gnosis (II 26, 15-27, 10 par), and yet it is clearly assumed that persons can have received the gnosis and then "fall away," and for this they will be held responsible and punished (II 27, 21-30).

49. Cf. Kurt Rudolph, *Gnosis: The Nature and History of Gnosticism*, trans. R. McL. Wilson (San Francisco: Harper & Row, 1983), p. 117: "Gnosis is not a 'theology of salvation by nature,' as the heresiologists caricature it; it is rather thoroughly conscious of the provisional situation of the redeemed up to the realisation of redemption after death. Otherwise the extant literature which relates to existential and ethical behavior is inexplicable."

Index